Egyptology
at the
Dawn
of the
Twenty-first
Century

Egyptology at the Dawn of the Twenty-first Century

Proceedings of the
Eighth International Congress of Egyptologists
Cairo, 2000

Volume 1
Archaeology

Edited by
Zahi Hawass

In collaboration with
Lyla Pinch Brock

The American University in Cairo Press
Cairo New York

Dar el Kutub No. 7147/01
ISBN 977 424 674 8

Designed by the AUC Press Design Center
Printed in Egypt

Contents

Contents

Preface

Zahi Hawass

The Eighth International Congress of Egyptologists, held in Cairo in March 2000, marked the opening of the new millennium as an opportunity to evaluate and redefine the focus and goals of Egyptology in the twenty-first century. Through the Millennium Debates and the papers of other participants published here, we are made aware that now more than ever, Egyptology is facing a period of change and challenge and we must meet these challenges if our field is to remain relevant to the modern world. The Congress was attended by some 1,400 scholars, and of the 400 papers delivered, 248 were selected by our scientific review committee to be published in these volumes. It is notable that this Congress included a higher number of Egyptian Egyptologists than we have seen in many years. In fact, some 500 Egyptian Egyptologists attended the conference. Their inclusion with the more well-known names in Egyptology is an indication of one of the frequently mentioned themes in the Congress: the need for education and training of more Egyptian scholars and excavators to study and maintain their country's monuments as part of the world's heritage.

The enormous quantity of submissions to the Proceedings led to the decision to publish them in three volumes. Volume One contains all the archaeology papers; Volume Two, those dealing with history and religion; and Volume Three covers the topics of language, literature, museology, and conservation. Each volume of these Proceedings opens with the text of the corresponding Millennium Debates and their respondents, and the papers of the specific subjects follow in alphabetical order by the contributor's name.

The Millennium Debates formed a special focus for this Congress. Chaired and responded to by eminent experts in the field, the Debates covered archaeology, art, history, language, literature, museology, religion, site management, and conservation. In his paper (opening the Debates in Volume One) on "Egyptology in the Twenty-first Century," David O'Connor provides a cogent summary of the trends in field work in Egyptology in the last forty years and discusses three points crucial to the future of Egyptian archaeology: the changing attitudes of Egyptians toward their archaeology, the need for comprehensive mapping (rather than excavation) of the national archaeological landscape, and theoretical issues and their impact on archaeology, epigraphy, and other scholarly disciplines.

Volume Two continues with keynote speakers addressing the Millennium Debate issues of history, art history, and religion. In his paper, "Writing the History of Ancient Egypt," Donald B. Redford challenges the appropriateness of new approaches to historiography such as retrospective economic theory, Egyptology as anthropology, deconstruction, and 'history from below,' as he characterizes the tendency to use anecdotal evidence to draw far-reaching conclusions about the 'common people' in Egyptian history. Edna R. Russmann, in her contribution to the Millennium Debate on the study of the art of ancient Egypt laments the failure of Egyptian art scholarship to coalesce into a recognized subdiscipline with an academic tradition of acknowledged interests and methods of its own. She goes on to give a summary of the most urgent needs facing the study of Egyptian art as well as possible solutions. In the last Millennium Debate paper in Volume Two, Herman te Velde writes on "The History of the Study of Ancient Egyptian Religion and its Future," which he considers one of the most urgent topics in Egyptology today, since the core of ancient Egyptian culture is its religion. He speculates that although Egyptologists with various special interests will contribute to the study of religion, the most progress should be expected from those willing to focus their research specifically on religion and its accompanying issues, such as polytheism versus monotheism, pharaonism versus local religions, and religion in life as well as death.

Perhaps the most challenging of Millennium Debate papers come in Volume Three. John Baines' comprehensive examination of the current and future possibilities for research on Egyptian literature is complemented by Antonio Loprieno's notes on the problems and priorities in Egyptian linguistics. Baines provides extensive analysis and definition of the Egyptian literary corpus, its relation to the wider stream of tradition and range of written forms, and the social and ideological situation and status of what was written. Loprieno concentrates on the achievements of Egyptian linguistics over the last fifteen years and considers the impact of recent developments in linguistic research on Egyptian phonology and lexicography. Regine Schulz's paper, "Museums and Marketing: A Contradiction" is a timely examination of the pressures facing museums around the world to provide "blockbuster entertainment" while maintaining their five basic mandates of collecting, preservation, research, presentation, and mediation. Finally, my own contribution to the Millennium Debates, "Site Management and Conservation," addresses some of the principal problems and threats to the conservation of Egyptian heritage sites and makes recommendations, some perhaps controversial, for improving site management methods and protection as well as giving suggestions for salvage and excavation over the next ten years.

In addition to being a forum for debate and report, the Congress honored several prominent Egyptologists for their outstanding contributions to the field, including Abdel-Aziz Saleh and Sayed Tawfik from Egypt; Harry Smith of England; William K. Simpson from the United States; Rainer Stadelmann from Germany; Jean Leclant of France; Sergio Donadoni from Italy; Kazimierz Michalowski of Poland; and the late Gamal Mokhtar, former Chairman of the Antiquities Organization of Egypt and Member of the Supreme Council of Culture.

I took great pride in the many complimentary comments I received regarding the organization and success of the Eighth International Congress of Egyptologists, but credit for this must be shared with the many people whose efforts made that success possible. I would like to thank the members of the different committees who planned and executed the many aspects involved in holding such a large conference. The Congress was held at the Mena House Oberoi Hotel in the shadow of the Giza Pyramids and thanks to its General Manager, Rajiv Kaul, everything ran smoothly in the day-to-day operations. The Congress would also not have been possible without the financial support of many Egyptian business corporations. Another important contributor was the American University in Cairo Press. Its director, Mark Linz, and the Press's editorial staff were of great help in completing the Congress's mission by publishing the Abstracts, edited by Angela Jones, and of course these final three volumes of Proceedings edited in collaboration with Lyla Brock.

In conclusion, I would urge the International Association of Egyptologists to review and expand its activities in the future, with the aim of making itself better known to the general public and potential sponsors. This would enable it to raise the funds to undertake and complete valuable projects, many of which are discussed in these volumes. I would also urge that scientific studies and research programs should be geared less to the personal interests of the researcher, but should follow an overall action plan targeting those areas where monuments are especially endangered, such as the Delta and the great deserts of Egypt. I believe that all who participated in the Eighth International Congress of Egyptologists and all those who read these volumes of Proceedings will take wise and positive action in regard to these concerns.

Abbreviations

ARCE/EAP	American Research Center in Egypt/ Egyptian Antiquities Project
CNRS	Centre National de la Recherche Scientifiques
DAI	Deutches Archäologisches Institut, Cairo
EAO	Egyptian Antiquities Organization
EEF	Egypt Exploration Fund
EES	Egypt Exploration Society
IFAO	Institut Français d'Archéologie Orientale
SCA	Supreme Council of Antiquities
USAID	United States Agency for International Development

Publications

AA	American Anthropologist
AcOr	Acta Orientalia
ADAIK/AVDAIK	Archäologische Veröffentlichungen, Deutsches Archäologisches Institut, Abteilung Kairo
Aegyptus	Aegyptus: Rivista Italiana di Egittologia e di Papirologia
AEB	Annual Egyptian Bibliography
Afr. Archaeol. Rev.	African Archaeological Review
AJA	American Journal of Archaeology
AJPA	American Journal of Physical Anthropology
Amer. J. Roent	American Journal of Roentology
AR	Ancient Records of Egypt (James Henry Breasted, Chicago, 1906)
ASAE	Annales du Service des Antiquités de l'Égypte
ÄA	Ägyptologische Abhandlungen
ÄgForsch./ÄF	Ägyptologische Forschungen

ÄL	Ägypten und Levante
BÄBÄ/BeiträgeBf	Beitrage zur Ägyptischen Bauforschung und Altertumskunde
BACE	Bulletin of the Australian Center for Egyptology
BASOR	Bulletin of the American Schools of Oriental Research
BdE	Bibliotheque d'Étude, Institut Français d'Archéologie Orientale
BES	Bulletin of the Egyptological Seminar
BIE	Bulletin de l'Institut Égyptien
BIFAO	Bulletin de l'Institut Francais d'Archéologie Orientale
BiOr	Bibliotheca Orientalis
BMMA	Bulletin of the Metropolitan Museum of Art
BSAA	Bulletin de la Société Archéologique d'Alexandrie
BSEG	Bulletin de la Société d'Égyptologie de Genève
BSFE	Bulletin de la Société Français d'Égyptologie
CAH	Cambridge Ancient History
Cah. de Karnak	Cahiers de Karnak
CdE	Chronique d'Égypte
CG/CGC	Catalogue Général des Antiquités égyptiennes du Musée du Caire
CRIPEL	Cahier de Recherches de l'Institut de Papyrologie et d'Égyptologie de Lille
DE	Discussions in Egyptology
DFIFAO	Documents de Fouilles de l'Institut Français d'Archéologie Orientale du Caire
EA	Egyptian Archaeology
FIFAO	Fouilles de l'Institut Français d'Archéologie Orientale du Caire
GM	Göttinger Miszellen
HÄB	Hildesheimer Ägyptologische Beiträge
HPBM	Hieratic Papyri in the British Museum
IEJ	Israel Exploration Journal
JARCE	Journal of the American Research Center in Egypt
JdS	Journal des Savants
JEA	Journal of Egyptian Archaeology
JEOL	Jaarbericht "Ex Oriente Lux"
JESHOH	Journal of the Economic and Social History of the Orient
JNES	Journal of Near Eastern Studies
JSSEA	Journal of the Society for the Study of Egyptian Antiquities
KRI	Ramesside Inscriptions (K. A. Kitchen, Oxford, 1968)
LAAA	Liverpool Annals of Archaeology and Anthropology
LÄ	Lexikon der Ägyptologie
MÄS	Münchner Ägyptologische Studien
MDAIK	Mitteilungen des Archäeologischen Instuts Abteilung Kairo
MEEF	Memoirs of the Egypt Exploration Fund
MIFAO	Memoires publies par les Membres de l'Institut Français d'Archéologie Orientale
OBO	Orbis biblicus et orientalis
OIP	Oriental Institute Publications
OLA	Orientalia Lovaniensia Analecta

OMRO	Oudheidkundige Mededelingen uit het Rijksmuseum van Oudheden te Leiden
Or	Orientalia
PAM	Polish Archaeological Mission reports
PGM	Papyri Graecae Magicae
PM	Topographical Bibliography of Ancient Egyptian Hieroglyphic Texts, Reliefs, and Paintings (Bertha Porter and Rosalind Moss, Oxford, 1960)
PN	Die Ägyptischen Personennamen (Hermann Ranke, Glückstadt, 1935–1952)
PSBA	Proceedings of the Society of Biblical Archaeology
Quart. Sci. Rev.	Quarterly Scientific Review
RdE	Revue d'Égyptologie
RecTrav	Receuil de Travaux
RevArch	Revista Archaeologia
RSO	Revista degli Studi Orientali
SAGA	Studien zur Archäologie und Geschichte Altägyptens
SAK	Studien zur Altägyptischen Kultur
SAOC	Studies in Ancient Oriental Civilization (University of Chicago)
SPAW	Sitzungsberichte der Preussischen Akademie der Wissenschaften
VA	Varia Aegyptiaca
Vic.Or.	Vicino Oriente
Wb	Wörterbuch der Aegyptischen Sprache (Adolf Erman, Berlin, 1982)
WdO	Die Welt des Orients
WZKM	Wiener Zeitschrift für die Kunde des Morgenlandes
YES	Yale Egyptological Studies
ZÄS	Zeitschrift für Ägyptische Sprache un Altertumskunde

Egyptian Archaeology
in the Twentieth Century

David O'Connor

Institute of Fine Arts, New York University

Looking forward only gains meaning by looking back, specifically at the successes, failures, and omissions of Egyptian archaeology, as practiced by Egyptians and foreigners over the last 40 years (the Nubian Salvage Campaign providing both a useful and significant starting point). In assessing the present and future status of Egyptian archaeology, I will to some extent be reiterating points already familiar from earlier discussions by Manfred Bietak, Harry Smith, and others. However, even the familiar can benefit from repetition, and I think in some ways my presentation has a somewhat different focus from theirs. Of course, as a participant in those 40 years, the speaker must speak as an involved party, his own work representative of what has been good, and what insufficient about the last 40 years, and how each relates to the future of Egyptian archaeology.

Looking forward, prospects are exciting but extremely challenging, and the greatest challenge is human, and it is two-fold: the changing attitudes of Egyptians towards their archaeology, and the changing attitudes of Egyptologists towards the aims and methods of archaeology as a humanistic and scientific mode of research.

Initially, the achievements and record of the last 40 years needs to be quickly reviewed. These include the Nubian Salvage Campaign, valuable in itself but even more so as a model that is still insufficiently applied to Egypt and its archaeology as a whole. Other aspects include the expanding efforts of Egyptian authorities to encourage exploration, yet also manage an increasingly difficult situation as regards the conservation and recording of monuments, and the protection and management of sites. We also need to note the increasing numbers, and widening geographical spread of archaeological projects; the continuity of the traditional aims of those projects, as well as the development of new trends in research; and the productive foundation of these projects and related developments in the academic and museological worlds of Egypt, Europe, the US, and elsewhere, offer for the future development of archaeology in Egypt.

Lets now look in a little more detail at these achievements of the last 40 years in Egyptian archaeology. The Nubian Salvage Campaign, extending mostly through the early 1960s, was I think, a spectacular success even if, like any ambitious endeavor, it had its imperfections. There are two aspects of it I would particularly like to highlight:

First, the collaborative effort of the Egyptian and Sudanese governments, UNESCO, and a host of non-Egyptian institutions and scholars made the campaign of great intrinsic benefit. Much new excavation was undertaken. Some rounded out what we already knew, some was startlingly new. To cite but two examples from opposite ends of the time scale I would note the discovery of the A-Group royal cemetery of Qustul in Egypt, important for our understanding of early Egypt, as well as early Nubia, and the wonderful frescoes of the Christian period decorating the walls of the great cathedral of Faras, in Sudanese Nubia.

In addition, as we all know, a whole series of large, sometimes gigantic monuments—such as the Abu Simbel temples—were removed from their threatened sites, and reconstructed elsewhere—surely one of the greatest achievements of salvage archaeology any where in the world.

The Nubian Salvage Campaign has a second aspect, still important to us today: It showed how, even in terms of a complex collaborative effort, the archaeology of a whole region of the Nile Valley could be mapped, documented, and to a degree, selectively excavated, even without some of the more sophisticated technologies we could apply to this task today. The results were not perfect, and some still remain unpublished, but nevertheless it was a most considerable achievement, and provides a model that could be applied to the entire Egyptian Nile Valley, a point to which I shall return.

What archaeologically has happened in the Egyptian Nile Valley since the Nubian Salvage Campaign? Thanks to the generosity of the Egyptian government and its agencies, archaeology—involving both Egyptians and non-Egyptians on a large scale—was able to flourish on a scale perhaps never seen before, at least insofar as truly scientific archaeology was concerned. And here I must make it clear that by archaeology I include the complementary fields of epigraphy and art history, insofar as they involve field activity. And I should also like to emphasize that Egyptian archaeology is a seamless whole, covering prehistoric, ancient, medieval, and recent remains—even if circumstances, and the context of this congress, will lead me to speak mainly about the archaeology of ancient Egypt.

However, even as we acknowledge the liveliness and scope of archaeological research in Egypt today, we need to look carefully at some of the details to appreciate what is going on, what is not receiving sufficient attention and what might be done in Egyptian archaeology in the future. For these purposes, I'm going to briefly compare two slices of field archaeology, and indeed epigraphy, the one covering 1967–1968, right after the Nubian Salvage Campaign; the other, 1996–1997, some 30 years later. My source is Leclant's invaluable annual reviews, published in *Orientalia*, and my data and suggestions are necessarily broad, approximate, and tentative.

Throughout those 30 years, and up to today, there have been efforts on the part of Egyptian government agencies, especially the Supreme Council of Antiquities, as well as research institutions to promote work in areas considered to be archaeologically poorly-represented, such as the Delta; or the excavation of types of sites not generally well represented in the Egyptian archaeological record to date—e.g. the excavations of substantial urban remains which have occurred at, to name some of the sites, at Tell al-Dab'a, al-Amarna, Abydos, and Elephantine.

Nevertheless, to a large extent excavation has been structured by the particular research interests of institutions and individuals, individual dynamics which I think are most important for the vitality of archaeology in Egypt. And alongside this, the Supreme Council of Antiquities, as well as sponsoring (like some Egyptian universities) substantial excavations of its own, has struggled valiantly—as we all know—with a rising flood of salvage archaeology. All over Egypt, develop-

mental needs for agricultural land, or factory sites, or the like have required areas known or sus-
pected to contain archaeological remains to be excavated, And sometimes new sites have been
discovered by accident, such as the great monuments of Ramesses II and his family at Girgeh.

Let us now turn to the comparison of 1967–1968 with 1996–1997, starting at the simplest
level: how many sites (some involving several contemporaneous projects, many only one) were
involved in archaeological or epigraphic activity during those two spans of time?

In 1967–1968 there were about thirty, in 1996–1997 about 66 (note for my purposes here I
count Thebes as a *single* site, despite the many subsites of which it is composed). This is a good
index to the great expansion (almost 70 percent) in the amount of archaeology carried on, and
to the increasing investment of both human and financial resources in that archaeology.

When, however, we turn to the regional picture, a more complex situation emerges. On the
one hand, there were, over that thirty-year period, significant increases in regional coverage. In
1967–1968 the regions involved could be defined as the northwest desert and the Delta as one
entity; the Cairo region (Giza, Saqqara, etc.); the Fayoum; Middle Egypt (for my purposes, Dahshur
to Thebes); Thebes; and southern Egypt (Thebes to Aswan). All these regions of course were still
being explored from 1996–1997, but additional regions could now be added: Sinai; the western
oases, such as Siwa, Bahariya, Kharga, and Dakhla; and the Eastern Desert and Red Sea coast.

On the more negative side, although there had been an overall quantitative increase in the
number of sites affected by archaeological or epigraphic work, within that context the *proportional* investment in terms of scholarly effort and financial resources has stayed the same, or even
declined, in terms of specific regions. For example, of the total sites involved in the 1967–1968,
and 1996–1997 phases respectively, about 39 were in the northwest desert, the Delta, and Sinai
in *both* periods, so the proportional effort dedicated to the Delta and contiguous regions has
remained pretty much the same.

Moreover, in Middle and Southern Egypt there has actually been a drop in the relevant sta-
tistics. In 1967–1968 Middle Egypt represented 26.7 percent of the total sites.

It is, however, noteworthy that insofar as sites other than Thebes and the Cairo area are concerned, there has been an impressive number of projects which have undertaken long-term,
indeed, sometimes virtually indefinite research commitments. In 1967–1968 such long-term projects had already gotten underway at sites such as Tell al-Dab'a, Herakleopolis, Abydos, and
Hierakonpolis, and are all still quite active today. By 1996–1997 other long-term commitments
had been added to the list, such as Buto, Qantir, Tanis (where Montet's pioneering work has been
resumed), Tell Basta, Tell al-Amarna, and Elephantine. This is not a complete listing (which could
also include some largely epigraphic projects, as well as some Coptic sites), but it reveals an
important trend.

This brief overview provides a context for the rest of my discussion. Let me now move to three
points that I believe are very important in the future of Egyptian archaeology. These are first, its
Egyptian dimension; second, the comprehensive mapping and documentation, rather than excavation, of the national archaeological landscape; and third, theoretical issues and their impact on
archaeology, epigraphy, and the various scholarly disciplines as a whole.

The Egyptian Dimension

The most important aspect of Egyptian archaeology in the twenty-first century is the Egyptian
dimension itself. Archaeology here must be understood in a broad sense. It involves all the material remains of ancient (and medieval and later) Egyptian town sites, and monuments such as
temples, churches, and mosques; mortuary sites, whether of ancient decorated tombs, or the "City

of the Dead" near Cairo; and the entire archaeological landscape, which includes the larger impact of human activity and interpretation upon the natural landscapes of floodplain, low desert and high desert.

The Egyptian dimension has multiple aspects, but two interrelated ones are foremost. These are first, the extraordinary generosity Egypt has shown over the twentieth century to foreign institutions desiring to excavate or carry out epigraphic documentation in Egypt; and second, the future reality that the long term stability of Egyptian archaeology as a material reality (the sites and related landscapes) and as a discipline with a comprehensive approach to the exploration and study of that reality will depend primarily on the Egyptians themselves.

I believe cordial and productive relationships between Egypt and foreign archaeologists will continue to be a major factor through the twenty-first century, to their mutual benefit. For its part, Egypt itself has a most distinguished cadre of professional scholars focused upon the ancient, medieval, and more recent cultures and their histories, literatures, art, and archaeology, as well as a substantial administrative entity, the Supreme Council of Antiquities, charged with the protection and management of Egypt's cultural and archaeological resources. These too are essential foundations in future development.

But I think two points are most important. First, Egyptian archaeology, in terms of its excavation, documentation, and conservation requires a comprehensive approach that foreign institutions can never provide, however productive and important their roles may be in other ways. This comprehensive approach can only be brought into play by Egyptian institutions such as the Supreme Council, the universities, and others.

Second, on a broader scale, the whole future of Egyptian archaeology, both in terms of future research and in terms of its future existence, i.e. its literal survival as a material entity, depends upon the Egyptian population at large, and its attitudes toward that archaeology. I would say that while Egyptians, increasingly well educated at every social level, are conscious and proud of their country's extraordinary cultural heritage, they are often less clear about the role of archaeology in both preserving and expanding knowledge of that heritage, and about the importance of preserving the material reality of as much of that archaeology as possible—especially at a time when societal and economic needs are so pressing. This is an important issue that needs to be addressed. Throughout the world, I would say, what brings ultimate stability to any country's archaeology, to its study and conservation, is a strong level of interest and support that is both national and popular.

Nevertheless, these two points I believe are crucial for the future of Egyptian archaeology. The professional cadre in Egypt needs support and collaboration in developing resources that will further enhance its outstanding professionalism, and enable that professionalism to be more widely applied. And the larger, public dimension is also important, in two ways. First, it is from the younger generation at large that future Egyptian archaeologists will be recruited, and hence the more focused and stimulating the public's understanding of Egyptian archaeology is, the better. Second, the initiatives of the professional Egyptian scholars and archaeologists, and their ability to develop, protect, and preserve Egyptian archaeology depends very much on public interest in and knowledge of the subject, at many levels—ministerial action, legislation, and education all the way down to the attitudes of specific regional and local government officials, and the population at large.

Several other points need to be brought into play here. So far as foreign institutions are concerned, the issue is not collaborative projects in a formal sense; these are difficult for all involved parties to manage, and in any case there are an extraordinary number of sites and other initiatives such as surveys needing attention. Rather, the relevant roles of foreign institutions are to provide opportunities and resources enabling the scholarly and official cadre in Egypt to further enhance the training and knowledge of its younger echelons; and to collaborate with their Egyptian peers in the further development of the interest in and understanding of the broader Egyptian public in Egyptian archaeology.

Let me be a little more specific about some aspects of the points I have just made. A concrete example of the ways in which non-Egyptian institutions can enhance existing resources for additional training and experience for the younger generations of the Egyptian professional cadre is the archaeological field school run for several years by the American Research Center in Egypt, in close collaboration with the Supreme Council of Antiquities. This was but one of several such opportunities available to such Egyptians, who might also receive field training through various Egyptian universities, or by such active programs as that directed by Zahi Hawass at Giza, for example.

Still, in present circumstances, every resource counts, and the ARCE field school provided an important opportunity for Supreme Council of Antiquities archaeologists specializing in both ancient and medieval archaeology. It is much to be regretted that the grant funding the ACRE field school has ended, and I would hope it could be revived in some form, and that other non-Egyptian institutes might take up similar initiatives.

Again, I emphasize the purpose is to enhance the experiences of established Egyptian professionals, typically inspectors employed by the Supreme Council of Antiquities, and of course that all such initiatives require the approval and collaboration of the relevant Egyptian authorities.

As to the broader issue of public education about archaeology and its significance, building on an already significant level of interest and support from elementary school level upwards, I admittedly speak from ignorance, and would welcome additional information. Just how widely is the archaeology of Egypt, as distinct from its history and culture, taught, with regard to elementary, and high school children, and at the undergraduate level? I know, of course, that considerable attention is paid in all these venues, but does it include addressing the specific values and current and future needs of archaeology in Egypt?

As to the public in general, I am again ignorant as to the degree Egyptian archaeology (again, as distinct from current or medieval Egyptian culture and history) is covered in the media and what the particular emphases are of that coverage. Surely leading Egyptian scholars who are also often members of the Supreme Council of Antiquities, give interviews, and discuss their work or aspects of current and medieval Egyptian archaeology, and of course the Council itself issues a steady stream of well-reported stories about recent discoveries and developments.

All this is important, and coverage may be even wider, and more in-depth than I have discussed here. But are there Egyptian television series dedicated to Egyptian archaeology; are programs about Egyptian archaeology for foreign television and radio also shown or broadcast in Egypt; what is the Supreme Council's policy or that of the Ministry of Culture about public education as regards Egyptian archaeology, and how does it mesh with those of other ministries, such as that for education?

Egyptologists and those specializing in the archaeology of medieval and recent Egypt, themselves need to be much better-informed as to what is going on in these areas for, I repeat, the basic strategy of Egyptian archaeology in the future is going to depend not only on government policy, which has long been applied, but by the informed and even enthusiastic support of the Egyptian public.

Obviously, insomuch as that involves the future of Egyptian archaeology, the issue of education is primarily one for Egyptian leadership and development, as it has been in the past. But we non-Egyptians involved in Egyptian archaeology need to be better-informed about what is happening, and to be ready to provide whatever collaboration might be requested, whether talking at a high school near one's site, or participating in a television program. It may also be that the Supreme Council might find a task force on public education about Egyptian archaeology a useful device, in which they could include non-Egyptian colleagues with the appropriate experience and enthusiasm. However things may develop, I believe the issue of public education, and to impact upon future generations of Egyptians who will develop careers in Egyptian archaeology, is a crucial one, perhaps the most crucial for the twenty-first century.

The Archaeological Landscape

I should now like to focus on the Egyptian archaeological landscape itself. The issue here is simple, but urgent. Because of the highly-confined nature of Egyptian archaeological remains, crowded within the narrow zones of floodplain and low desert, and not scattered or dispersed over a wide area; and because of the inevitable and legitimate developmental needs of modern Egypt and its population, the archaeology of Egypt—in its broadest sense—is under extraordinary pressure, as all interested parties are very well aware.

Here three issues are especially important, involving both the Egyptian professional cadre and foreign institutions. First, there is the issue of site management, involving the protection, stability, and accessibility to scholars and interested public alike of archaeological sites in general, but especially of certain major sites, much visited by the Egyptian public and tourists, specifically. This topic, however, is being treated by another speaker at this Congress.

A second major issue is salvage archaeology, already underway to some degree, but a process that would be much enhanced by the national mapping and survey described above. Salvage archaeology functions at several levels; as particular parts of existing concessions, as new or unexplored sites required for agricultural or other development, and, more generally, as a national phenomenon requiring some prioritization.

However, how would we prioritize both salvage archaeology, and for that matter individual and institutional research? Here I come to my third point, which is I think the most important aspect of the archaeological landscape; namely, that we have no idea what it is. We know bits and pieces of that landscape—famous sites such as Giza and Thebes; sites that have attracted interest for obvious reasons, such as cemeteries clustered around decorated tombs at places like Beni Hassan, Hawawish, or Aswan; and others which have been encountered either accidentally, or by purposeful yet—in the larger sense of things—random surveys.

But there *are* only bits and pieces, and I believe one of the most important tasks that should be undertaken in the twenty-first century is the complete exploration and documentation of Egypt's entire surviving archaeology, i.e. a Nubian Salvage Campaign on a grand scale, with the emphasis, however, on survey and mapping, rather than selective excavation and salvaging of monuments.

Obviously, this will not be a complete map, but it would cover all surviving archaeology insofar as this is recoverable via surface remains, which will be mapped and surface collected, and perhaps cored so as to obtain a clearer picture of their time span and stratigraphy. And it should cover also subsurface archaeological remains when these are accessible to ground-penetrating devices. Evidently, not all archaeology will be thus located, and the floodplain will be an especial challenge—here, intensive coring on a systematic basis may be a better procedure to follow than relying on surface indications, although the latter should not be overlooked, as they may be more common than we suppose, e.g. in the form of disturbed but still significant shard scatters.

However, even an incomplete national map, constructed in this way, would be a tremendous advance; and enable us to next focus more specifically on the as yet missing archaeology, and on techniques and strategies that would enable us to recover it as well. Such a map has great intrinsic value, for it would provide a much richer, and more secure frame of reference for discussions and analyses of general trends in ancient or medieval times, e.g. in population sizes and distributions, and changes in them over time; or of regional archaeologies and their historical and cultural significance.

The map would also have other, more pragmatic benefits. Clearly, it would provide much better guidance than what we have now to researchers—whether focused on archaeological or epigraphic data—interested in following up specific issues, such as locating and excavating village sites of any period (almost a complete gap in our archaeological knowledge save for the few famous, but extraordinarily rare exceptions); or exploring socioeconomic structure as revealed by cemetery remains; or simply more fully-documenting important archaeological and epigraphic materials pinpointed on the map.

However, the most important pragmatic result of such a map would be to help stabilize the archaeology, in the sense that the relevant Egyptian authorities would have a much better overall idea of what archaeological sites existed, where they were, and some approximate idea of their extent or density. This would make the defining and protecting of archaeological remains a much better articulated and comprehensive process, albeit one that is *always* going to be difficult in the context of a rapidly developing country with very limited living space. But I believe nevertheless such a map, which could be continually added to, would be a tremendous resource to the Supreme Council of Antiquities and other agencies involved in the protection of archaeological sites.

The proposed map is unquestionably a tremendous undertaking, which would take in the best of circumstances many years—10, 20, *30?*—to complete, and even then be incomplete! But insofar as any concerted pooling of knowledge, energy, and resources is concerned, the map seems to me a much more productive process than to simply keep expanding the coverage of individual excavations and surveys so as to cover more and more of the archaeology. What the latter *have* achieved is invaluable and such individual or institutional initiatives should continue (though surveys should be integrated into the larger mapping project) for these individual initiatives are the life-blood of a dynamic Egyptian archaeology. Nevertheless, neither the Egyptian cadre, nor the non-Egyptian, will ever have the resources to cover the whole, or even the majority of Egyptian archaeology in this way. I think my earlier survey of the last 40 years of archaeology in Egypt made this point—increasing numbers of sites excavated alongside unchanged, and even diminished, investment in important regions. Hence, the importance of a national map, making use of all available technologies and resources, including much ground survey, as well as resource to satellite photography, computerized survey techniques, and other relevant procedures. How such an initiative might be structured, the kind of collaboration involved between Egyptian and non-Egyptian cadres and institutions, and the sources of guaranteed and long-term funding are issues that need to be dealt with in future discussion. But here above all is, I think, the best case for sustained collaborative effort, and a pooling of resources.

The Priorities of Egyptian Archaeology

Finally, I turn to the priorities of Egyptian archaeology in the twenty-first century in a more specifically scholarly sense, and relevant both to the Egyptian and the foreign scholarly cadres mentioned earlier. Here several points are relevant. The exploration of low desert sites (primarily mortuary and temple, but with some significant urban or settlement components) is relatively well developed, and should continue to develop. Alongside it, however, the location, mapping, and excavation of floodplain sites—while more extensive than it used to be—needs to be much further developed, despite the serious difficulties involved. Egyptian archaeology has an equal role to play in the future reconstruction of Egyptian society and culture alongside that of philological and documentary study: Essentially, the two fields are complementary, each compensating for the omissions or absences in the other—but Egyptian archaeology cannot properly perform its role without having a more comprehensive map of floodplain archaeology (surface and insofar as possible, subsurface) and following this up with prioritized, yet selective excavations. Here, the distinction often made between the archaeological needs of the Delta, as compared to those of the "better-explored" remainder of Egypt are, I think, irrelevant: the approach to the issues discussed here should be fully national, not particularized into regional concerns.

Low desert and floodplain archaeology are not two distinct entities: rather, at several levels— individual sites, regions, nationally—they interact with and complement each other, since each is a product of the other to a large extent. Thus, I argue here not for a diminishing of the more traditional foci of Egyptian archaeology, but instead a widening or expansion of these foci, so as to include—at all the levels specified—floodplain archaeology on a much more substantial scale.

Finally, there are two further, related issues. First, we need to continue to develop (as is already happening) appropriately trained and oriented younger cadres, both Egyptian and foreign, in order that the scholarly aims outlined here can be pursued and, to the degree practically possible, achieved. This point raises important questions about the status and roles of archaeological evidence, and its recovery, in the broader field of Egyptology, with its traditional academic emphasis on philological and textual evidence (especially in universities) and art (especially in museological contexts).

The second issue is a more theoretical one, really underlying the whole of the Egyptological endeavor (including archaeology), but it is one requiring concerted attention. This is the issue of model building, testing, discarding, and reformulating: this is fundamental in Egyptological (as in all) research, yet Egyptology often professes to be pragmatic and data-focused, the evidence as it were, "speaking for itself." In archaeology and other fields we need to be more self-critical of implicit and explicit model building, and at the same time become engaged in organized discussion of this issue. So far as models and theory are concerned, such discussions always have the potential to become arid and self-referential, but I think if the realities of the Egyptian evidence (archaeological and other) and of the process of recording and stabilizing that evidence are kept in play, the process can be productive, and indeed essential for the future of Egyptian archaeology in the twenty-first century.

Let me give an example of how surprisingly far apart archaeologists can be on theoretical issues, a circumstance which can impact strongly upon the interpretation of archaeological remains, and the transmission of those interpretations into more general Egyptological discussion.

Recently Manfred Bietak and I independently published interpretations of the famous "elite house type" of Middle Kingdom Kahun—those very large and complex houses that are a minority at the site and housed the elite officials of the town, their families, and their households. Each house can fairly easily be divided up into different formal elements that are repeated in identical or similar form from one house to another. Such elements include relatively obvious entities such as large and regularly planned granaries and a central residential suite (identified most obviously by the presence of a bedroom with its typical bed-recess). Many other of the recurrent components, however, are much less easy to identify in terms of function, as repeated debates over the years have illustrated.

What is revealing about my discussion and Bietak's is, that starting from the same, formally identifiable components we each reach very different conclusions. In particular, for reasons

8

derived from a general study of ancient Egyptian house styles and articulated very clearly in his essay Bietak identifies about seven separate residential units within the larger complex. The suggestions are tentative, but he identifies:

- one as the suite occupied by the head of household, his wife, and family
- one as a suite occupied by the eldest son and his family
- one occupied by the steward of the household and his family, several occupied by groups of servants, to some degree specialized in function, and even hierarchical in organization.

Taking these very same components, I identify:
- one as the suite of the head of household
- one as the suite of his wife, the senior woman of the family (as has been done by others). In both cases, servants may have "lived in."
- one occupied by the male children and their attendants.
- one occupied by the female children and their attendants
- other components Bietak identified as residential, I identified as "office space" or as unknown in function.

The point is not who is correct and who incorrect: who can tell? We lack any *in situ* artifactual or other data that might help to resolve some of the differences. The real point is that the two interpretations are based upon two very different theories as to how Middle Kingdom elite society was structured and functioned, based upon each scholar's understanding of the same set of source materials—biographies, other texts, art-historical data, etc.

This is but one example of theoretical issues and their impact on archaeology that could be repeated many times over, for all periods, both ancient and later. What it points to is that we do need to debate, refine, and adjust the general theories according to which we archaeologists strategize our excavations and interpret the results.

To conclude with reference to a grander issue, I would note that David Warburton has recently subjected Egyptological theories about ancient Egyptian economies to a searching critique, and come up with his own tentative model as to how major aspects, at least of the Egyptian economy, were structured. Again, whether he is right or wrong will be a matter of debate, but it is worth pointing out that archaeology can contribute in broad but significant ways to our understanding of changing economies and their impact on societal structure—and this is particularly important in Egypt where the textual data will never be sufficient to do more than indicate questions about the economy which need to be explored, to the extent possible, via archaeology.

But of course, the selection of sites, the excavation methodology, and the subsequent interpretation involved are all strongly influenced—consciously or unconsciously—by the theories entertained by the excavator, and hence I return to my original point: we need to debate the theoretical constructs that both archaeologists and others entertain more frequently and more critically, not so much to settle which one is "theirs," but rather to keep open legitimately different options, and explore them through archaeological and other means.

9

Response to D. O'Connor

Karol Myśliwiec

Polish Academy of Sciences / Warsaw University, Poland

"To excavate or not to excavate"—this is the first question that an archaeologist has to answer before undertaking any research in Egypt. On the face of it, the answer is not as easy as it may seem. At previous Congresses it has been proposed that all excavations in Egypt should be stopped for many years in order to concentrate on research on museums and collection reserves. Other scholars have suggested assigning absolute priority to rescue excavations in the Delta area in order to save the scarce archaeological remains from the ravages of a humid climate and hasty urbanization. Thus, the question remains whether, where, when, how, and by whom should excavation in Egypt be carried out.

It is my deep conviction that systematic and professional excavations all over the country, not only in the Delta, should be encouraged by all possible authorities. There are at least two beneficiaries: Egypt in particular and the world of science in general. Competent excavators reduce the eventuality of accidental or clandestine discoveries, thus protecting ancient objects against robbery and destruction, and the site itself against environmental disasters. Of equal importance is the role of systematic excavation on a scientific level: nothing can replace the experienced eye of a scholar in observing and recording the archaeological context of particular discoveries, without which a proper interpretation is hardly possible. Context has been lost in so many important cases during the past two centuries that we can no longer afford to tolerate rash discoveries and explorations.

Ever since hieroglyphs were deciphered, Egyptology has taken over from the ancient Greeks the responsibility for studying and reconstructing the history and civilization of pharaonic Egypt. Although tremendous progress has already been made in this field—with contributions from so many countries all over the world—there remain considerable lacunae concerning long periods of time and vast geographic areas. We will never be able to understand the historical processes occurring in "well-known" periods unless we discover the missing links, and to do so we need new sources. The value of new evidence is complete only if the context of its discovery is known and the only way to obtain such new data is through scholarly excavation. Stressing the role of archaeology for our knowledge of ancient history and for the integrity of the monuments themselves, I would like to conclude at this point that the bigger the number of aware and competent excavators working in Egypt, the better for this country and for science in general.

When I speak of excavators being "aware," I mean that they should bring, or better still, "invest" in Egypt not only their knowledge, but also their sensitivity. Every archaeological mission without exception should be judged by its exploration methods, publications, and perhaps foremost, the care extended over the excavated area. Careful exploration of all strata and proper conservation of the discoveries during and after the excavations should be the condition *sine qua non* in considering granting concessions. If I dare repeat this truism, it is with the hope that practice will follow theory.

Surveying and mapping is no doubt extremely important. How often, however, do the executors of such projects realize they have come too late! What they see are the disintegrating remains of an excavation started but left unfinished, never published nor even mentioned anywhere, and of course, showing no sign of any conservation measures whatsoever. The results of such exploration are irrevocably lost. That is why I believe that excavations as such deserve particular attention.

My own field experience shows that good cooperation with Egyptian colleagues is essential to the successful outcome of a project. It is particularly important to share responsibilities in all important matters, including the scientific ones. Supreme Council of Antiquities representatives, commonly referred to as inspectors, should in fact be colleagues entrusted with specific aspects of the research. One aspect in particular need of a spirit of common responsibility is conservation. In this respect, archaeological missions should serve as international "training centers" helping to teach students how to practically protect Egyptian antiquities.

From an archaeological point of view, Egypt must be considered as a unity. It would be nonsense to divide it into parts of greater and smaller importance. However, there are important differences in methods of excavating in Upper and Lower Egypt, differences that are obvious to anyone who has had the experience of both. Geological, climatic, and particularly hydrological conditions of the Delta imply the use of different methods, often more complicated and expensive than those used in the drier parts of Upper Egypt, and the results there are usually not as rewarding as in the south. Given the importance of Lower Egypt in history on one hand, and the scarcity of archaeological remains on the other, as well as the various factors accelerating their disintegration in this part of the country, let me express my support for the scholars who have been promoting and supporting field research in the Delta, while not forgetting about Upper Egypt, where the progressive destruction of the "well-preserved" monuments is becoming alarming.

While a special panel discussion on museology is anticipated at the present Congress, it would not do to refrain from mentioning here the importance of museums for archaeology. Archaeologists are particularly interested in the balance between the two functions of Egyptological collections: the display of masterpieces and the storage of excavated material in readiness for further study and conservation. Our gratitude to the Egyptian authorities for the enormous effort of building so many modern museums all over the country can never be great enough. Some of them are already operating as archaeological workshops as well. They will be one of the most important factors in the development of Egyptian archaeology in the twenty-first century. Hearing that even Benha is thinking of building an archaeological museum, I will be forgiven for being an optimist and hoping that the number of these museums will continue to grow. Let us hope that the coming century will bring a lasting solution to the problems of the Egyptian Museum in Cairo as well. The Museum and interested scholars both need extensive storage space where all the objects would be readily accessible. Although projects of this kind have already been formulated and accepted for many years, their execution has met with unending obstacles. It would be a milestone in the development of Egyptian archaeology if joint efforts of the International Organization of Egyptologists and the Supreme Council of Egyptian Antiquities could bring about the erection of a modern Egyptian Museum in Cairo within our lifetime.

Response to D. O'Connor

Rainer Stadelmann
Director Emeritus of the German Archaeological Institute, Cairo

A s a retired director of a foreign institute with many missions working in Egypt, I would like first of all to express my appreciation and my warmest thanks to the Egyptian authorities and to all my colleagues and friends for allowing us to undertake excavations and research without any restrictions, and for working together with us in a spirit of friendly cooperation.

David O'Connor has referred to the Egyptian dimension as an important factor for future archaeological prospects: During the last ten years or more we have noticed more and more pupils being guided through monuments and museums. As a result, these young people are being acquainted with their own history and cultural heritage. From time to time there are also excellent television broadcasts with Egyptian colleagues discussing the riddles and mysteries of their civilization with these students. This is without any doubt a very positive development. On the other hand, I have the impression that the *intelligentsia* and the business community, except people like Shadi Abd es-Sallam and some very open-minded journalists, are standing aside. I think it is urgent and necessary to attract the wealthy and educated sector and make them aware of, and care more for, their monuments. One could think of an association or group calling itself, "Friends of Egyptian Monuments" or "Friends of Islamic Monuments," or something similar. One must not even avoid using slogans, such as, "The Association for Cultural Heritage."

There is little to add to the subject of the "Archaeological Landscape." I would propose that every mission make an effort to prepare an archaeological map of the area where they are working. I can only speak for the German Institute, which has been mapping sites at Elephantine, Thebes, Abydos, and Dahshur. Other missions have already done the same thing. It would certainly be very useful to coordinate this work as soon as possible and to prepare an archaeological map as proposed by Fathi Saleh and Nicholas Grimal.

Mapping the archaeological sites is an important undertaking. However, this is not the first priority for the twenty-first century. The priority is the conservation and salvage of the endangered monuments. No difference should be made between the importance of those in the Delta or those in Middle and Upper Egypt. Nearly all archaeological sites and most of the monuments are in immediate danger. The main problems are: rising water tables, not only as a result of the Aswan High Dam, but also due to irrigation, rainfall, and land reclamation; and urban development due to the demand for housing as a result of the increasing population. In Thebes, for example, not only statues and decorated walls, but almost all the temples, columns, and column bases are whitened by the salt absorbed by the stone; this is destroying thick layers of the surface. The enormous task of salvage and conservation cannot be achieved by the Egyptian authorities alone; it is an international challenge.

Appropriate scholarly education is a major issue that concerns universities in Egypt and abroad. There, more and more, Egyptology is emphasizing the purely academic traditions such as philosophy and religion. Art and archaeology are regarded as disciplines that can be acquired incidentally. For example, chairs of art or archaeology no longer exist in German universities. This also applies to other countries. On the other hand, Classical archaeology or art history is taught at all universities, and Egyptian art attracts more people than all other art subjects. We should be aware of this fact and arrange the curriculum accordingly, rather than risk the growth of a large gap between the expectations of the public and a scholarly elite unable to satisfy the intellectual desire of an intelligent public. If these expectations are not realized, then we have a fertile ground for a subculture of charlatans and the perversion of history and values.

Response to D. O'Connor

Miroslav Verner
Czech Institute of Egyptology, Charles University, Prague

The paper prepared by Dr. David O'Connor concerning his vision of Egyptian archaeological priorities for the new century is well-balanced and includes a number of inspiring ideas. Let me first briefly discuss some of the more important ones:

According to O'Connor, one of the especially important and urgent issues in Egyptian archaeology today is the complete exploration and documentation of the entire remaining archaeological corpus of ancient Egypt. In principle, this idea is admirable. We archaeologists know very well that regardless of all our efforts made so far, the documentation and recording of Egyptian monuments done to date has been insufficient. There are still a great number of monuments which remain unrecorded. O'Connor is right when he says that the issue is gaining urgency. All of us field archaeologists who have been working in Egypt for many years know very well how swiftly Egypt's face changes before our eyes. The changes, for example, in population, housing, and industrial and agricultural development, are many-faceted, deep, and various. The rapid economic development that modern Egypt is experiencing has introduced a number of new projects which, in the majority of cases, are being launched in an extremely restricted area confined by the desert and the Nile where both the population and the cultural heritage of Egypt have been struggling to coexist for some time. We do not need to emphasize that this economic boom brings with it a potential—and often a real risk—that some monuments will never have the chance to be examined, recorded, or even located. Moreover, in Egypt as elsewhere in the world, these intense economic activities bring with them unwelcome side effects that sometimes impact irreversibly on the environment. Of course, these affect all monuments whether they are unrecorded or not. As a result, much of the cultural heritage of Egypt is at risk. And here, in my opinion, is the crux of the problem.

Other issues pinpointed by O'Connor, such as salvage archaeology, the exploration of low desert sites, the location and excavation of floodplain sites, or site management are of course very important, but they represent, in my opinion, only the secondary or consequent aspects of the problem. I presume that at the core of the problem are not only the aforementioned issues, but also the meshing of these practical aspects of archaeology with the primary political and global decisions closely linked with the economic and social planning of the country. Archaeology and its very real demands, here in Egypt or elsewhere in the world, are only a small part of the entire social, political, and economic whole of the country. We who are archaeologists can only understand a small fraction of the demands made by the overall management of the society that the Egyptian government has to handle. Nevertheless, we should not refrain from putting forth the needs of archaeology, for we see this as an integral element within the strategic planning of the state. This highlighting of archaeological needs, as far as I can see, has been the long-standing policy of the Supreme Council of Antiquities in Egypt.

These extremely complex and demanding problems are not specifically Egyptian. We in the Czech Republic have to cope with problems that are in principle similar, though with regard to the quantity and importance of monuments our problems are of a lesser magnitude than those faced by Egypt.

The second issue that I should like to mention briefly in this context is David O'Connor's reminiscence concerning the Nubian campaign, which he considers to be valuable not only in itself, but even more so as a model that is still insufficiently applied to Egypt and Egyptian archaeology.

I absolutely agree with David O'Connor that the Nubian salvage campaign was a milestone—not only in terms of Egyptian, but also in world archaeology. It is needless to try and remind this informed audience of all the enormous achievements and the unique atmosphere of friendship and collaboration that marked that Nubian salvage campaign. However, regardless of all the positive aspects, I remain hesitant to use this particular campaign as a model to apply to Egyptian archaeology. Times have changed, and with their passing, so has the nature of Egypt's archaeological problems.

The Nubian campaign was a response to a unique situation; the time factor was critical and it was necessary for the Egyptian government to call for broad, UNESCO-sponsored assistance to save the cultural heritage of the vast land of Nubia. At the time, Nubia was about to be flooded due to the building of the Aswan High Dam. Though very complex and in some aspects quite serious, the present problems within Egyptian archaeology are not of the same critical nature as those in Nubia at the end of the 1950s. Of course, I do not want to say that large-scale projects and broad international cooperation in Egyptology would not be useful or welcome—on the contrary. However, in my opinion the response to the present problems we face in Egyptian archaeology should not be envisaged as one mammoth project, but as a series of smaller, more realizable projects that have been systematically planned as a series of stages within an overall scheme. Planning, as I see it, is the indispensable key to the success of such a scheme. What we can see here in Egypt in more recent years is the general movement in this direction already undertaken by the Supreme Council of Antiquities.

Finally, let me touch on one other issue raised by David O'Connor: the appropriate training and orientation of young scholars. Again, I must concur with him on both the importance and the urgency of this issue. Certainly, future problems will need well-trained experts who are capable of an interdisciplinary approach to Egyptology and its future challenges and tasks. This problem concerns not only young Egyptian scholars, but also young foreign scholars who need to obtain specialized training in Egyptian archaeology in Egypt itself. Obviously, with regard to the various methods and approaches to training that are now in use in various countries, the optimum stage in this training should be at the postgraduate level. Not only is it necessary for young Egyptians to go abroad to learn different methodologies and practices to apply to archaeological methods and the protection of their cultural heritage, but it is also necessary for foreign students to experience the full range of expertise that Egyptian scholars have to offer. The quotas available for such training schemes will vary from one country to another according to their means, but we should all endeavor to facilitate such fruitful exchange schemes for the young scholars who will come to take our place over the coming years.

The time available to me is very short and I cannot present the full range of ideas that I have had on this subject. These are just a few of my reflections on the stimulating paper David O'Connor prepared for our discussion. As you can see, I have agreed in principle with the majority of ideas he offered, though perhaps my thoughts have at times taken a different track. No doubt my colleagues here will have further contributions to offer along other lines, and I certainly look forward to hearing their ideas as well.

The Mallawy Papyrus No. 602/1-602/5:
A Comprehensive Study of the Document
and the Professional and Administrative Titles

Soad Abd el-Aal[1]
Cairo University

The Mallawy Museum is in possession of Demotic Papyrus 602/1–602/5.[2] It is located in vitrine 36 on the ground floor. This papyrus was acquired in 1976 from the Sharunah excavations, about 5 km north of al Kom al-Ahmar, in Minia Governorate.

Description of the Papyrus

The papyrus is an incomplete legal document with one or more sheets missing. The remaining five must have originally constituted a document written on a single papyrus. These sheets are consecutively numbered from one to five, but the sequence is 602/1, 602/4, 602/2, 602/5, and 602/3.[3] The roll measures more than 3 m long and is 28 cm wide.

The general condition of the papyrus is good. It is reddish-brown in color and there are many vertical joints about 15 cm apart. Many lacunae are present, especially on the first and the third sheets. The text is written on the recto. It consists of nineteen lines of Demotic and a line of signatures of people mentioned throughout the text. There is also a Greek endorsement at the end of page two.[4]

The handwriting is clear, varying from small accurate strokes in the first three lines, to the fourth line where there are more ligatures. The document shows the hands of different members of one family of scribes, as the eighteenth line proves.

Dating of the Text

The text is dated to day 29 of Phamenoth in Year Two of Ptolemy XII, Neos Dionysos, and Queen Cleopatra V called Trephania (who ruled together from 81/80 to 69/68).[5] This date corresponds to 7 April 79 BCE.[6]

The main subject is a deed of apportionment among the embalmers of the necropolis. Also mentioned are the duties and administration of the embalmers' organization.[7] The deed was concluded between eleven God's Sealers and another God's Sealer called *p3 ḥtr*. It was drawn up for

18

the latter as a lector priest after his parents' death, as it appears from the context that both were lector priests. The document determines all places and parts of the Stipendiary Foundation[8] and all related benefits such as income, revenues, and endowments attached to the priestly function. Furthermore, fourteen shares or portions of emoluments were to be divided among the first and the second party. Every embalmer had a fixed share which varied from one to the other, because, as mentioned throughout the text, every one could increase his own share or property by participating in what was called, ꜥiš-n-pr ꜥ3, or official auction.[9]

In the following paragraph, collections or offices possessed by every lector priest are mentioned. Each unit of these collections consists of a number of bodies which form the greater part of this very long text. Each of the deceased was the responsibility of one of the community of embalmers. A number of accounts assigned to every embalmer is mentioned in the following paragraph, but unfortunately only seven accounts are cited. Next, a list of remuneration or payment is specified, in addition to the provisions possessed by only two of the embalmers. They were entitled to enjoy these provisions throughout their lifetime only.

At the end of the contract, the first party confirmed the share which the second party (p3 ḥtr) would obtain. In the eighteenth line, the scribe states that the writing of the text was his own responsibility along with his sons, and no one else. From this information, it is possible to conclude that:

1. Although we have no conception of the roles of the necropolis attendants to which our document belonged, we may deduce that twelve funerary priests bore the title ḫtmw-ntr, apparently an honorary title rather than a professional one, but their actual function was ḥri ḥb.[10]

2. The Stipendiary Foundation or ꜥwi-šty, represented burial places or funerary possessions in the necropolis where the embalmers were confined to perform their work. These places were owned and divided among the embalmers of the necropolis and granted them revenues in return for mummifying and burying deceased persons in addition to the care given to the tombs and to their inhabitants.[11]

   In our document, the embalmers distributed every place and all parts of this foundation, which granted them payment (isw) acquired as a result of selling or buying properties, regular revenues (šty), and irregular payment (ini) given to them on special occasions, which together formed the endowment or sꜥnḫ.

3. The document, which concerns a necropolis in Middle Egypt, describes in detail the actual function of the embalmers in the necropolis and their position in the funerary service. It explains the duties of the lector priest and the work performed, according to an oath he was obliged to swear.

   It is interesting to note the order of these duties, which helps us to understand the funerary procedures. First, the deceased is prepared with spells, then he or she is taken to the funerary workshop for mummification, and finally buried with other deceased members of the population.

4. According to what was called ḥp n ḥri ḥb, "the law of the lector priest," that is, the rules that bound the community of the embalmers together and were adopted by them all. These rules and regulations were enforced by embalmers chosen from their ranks.[12] This law stated that every lector priest was authorized to perform his own work in the area alloted to him according to an oath that he had to swear, and that he must not intrude on another embalmer's work. He had no authority to collect his payment individually. Collection was the responsibility of those embalmers who carried out the law in the necropolis.

5. The lector priest had the right to share in what was called ꜥiš-n-pr-ꜥ3, official auction, and ꜥiš n sḫt, the local auction of the town or village to which he belonged.

6. Women were also practitioners (*ẖri-ḥb*). As we see after his parents' death, *P3-ḥtr* inherited from his father and mother who had a fixed share in the necropolis. This ownership had reached his mother's hand as a lector priestess, as mentioned in 602/5 line 1: *mtw=k wb3 t3y =w wpt ẖri - ḥb*. It seems these priestesses were responsible for mummifying and burying deceased women, but unfortunately none of them are mentioned.

7. The present document is characterized by an enormous list of proper names representing the deceased buried in the tombs of the necropolis. From their titles, they appear to be families of laborers or simply employees attached to an institution or employed individually. They

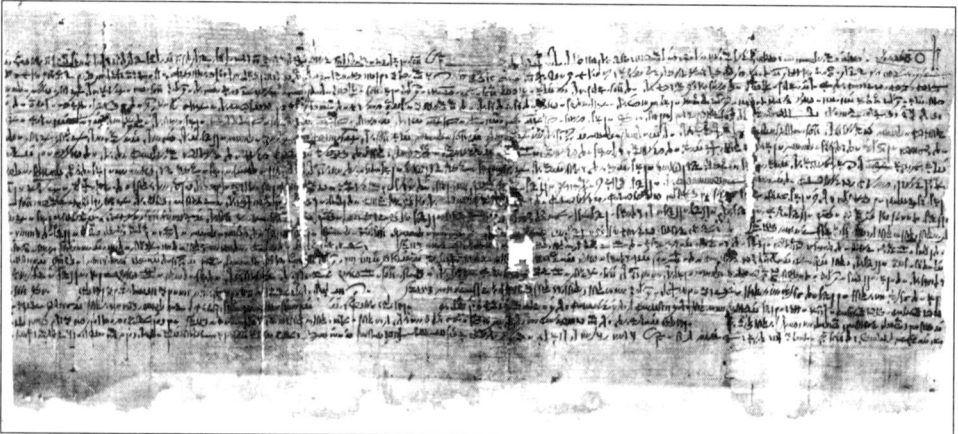

Fig. 1: Pap. 602/1

Fig. 2: Pap. 602/4

were buried in collective tombs for people of low rank. These were Egyptians and foreigners working in or living near the village called *ḥr-wḏ3*, about which we have no further information but, as cited in the text, the place called *ḥr-ti* was its necropolis.

Fig. 3: Pap. 602/2

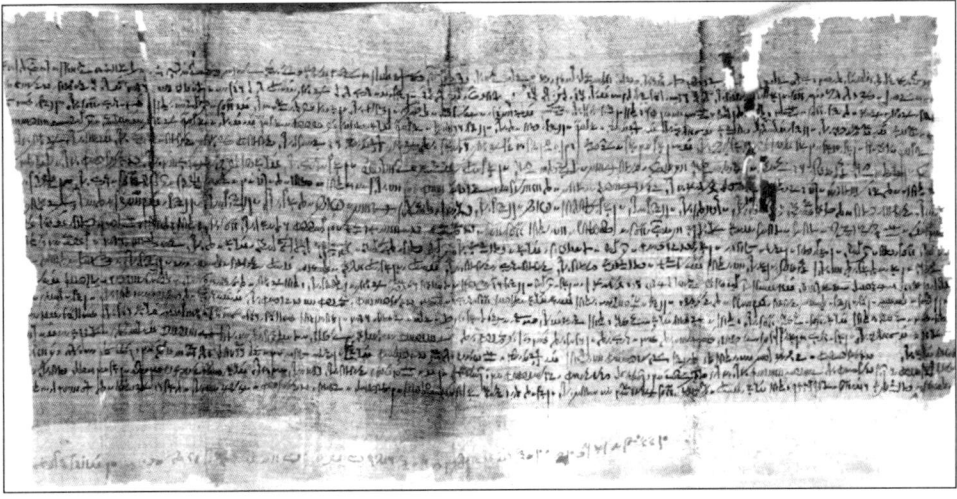

Fig. 4: Pap. 602/5

Notes:

1 This paper is a summary of a Ph.D. thesis which I submitted some years ago to Cairo University, forthcoming.

2 This Papyrus was mentioned by S. Zaghloul in "Fruhdemotische Urkunden aus Hermopolis," *Bulletin of the Center of Papyrological Studies* ll, (1985), 11.

3 See Pl. 1–5.

4 Pl. 4, sheet 602 / 4.

5 W. Pestman, *Chronologie Egyptienne d'apres les texts Demotiques (332 BC–453 AD), P. L. Bat. 15,* (Leiden 1967), 76.

6 Th. C. Skeat, *The Reigns of Ptolemies, Munchener Beitrge zur Papyrusforschung und antiken Rechtsgeschichte 39,* (Munchen, 1954), 8ff.

7 E.A.E. Reymond, *Catalogue of Demotic Papyri in the Ashmolean Museum, 1, the Embalmers Archive from Hawara* , (Oxford, 1973), 23; see also P. W. Pestman, *The Archive of Theban Choachytes (second century B.C.),* (Studia Demotica ll; Leuven 1993).

8 Reymond, *Hawara*, 31ff.

9 Th. K. Zauzich, "ʿiš n pr ʿ3," *Enchoria* 1 (1971), 79ff.

10 P.W.L. Pestman, *Archivio di Amenothes figlio di Horos,* (Milano 1981), 5ff ; H. Kees, " Der Sogenannte Oberste Vorlesepriester," *ZAS* 87, 119ff; Reymond, *Hawara* 24; *LA* 1, col. 940ff.

11 Reymond, *Hawara*, 24.

12 Reymond, *Hawara*, 25.

Tutankhamun's Embalming Cache Reconsidered

Susan J. Allen

The Metropolitan Museum of Art

In 1909 the Metropolitan Museum of Art in New York received as a gift from Theodore M. Davis, the wealthy and very successful American excavator in the Valley of the Kings, a group of objects that have come to be known as Tutankhamun's Embalming Cache. They represent a single deposit which was found by Edward Ayrton, who was in charge of Davis' excavations, in an unfinished tomb shaft (KV 54), in the hill above the Tomb of Ramesses X in December of 1907.[1] Herbert Winlock of the Metropolitan had visited Ayrton in January, 1908 and seen the deposit, which was made up of perhaps seven large whitewashed storage jars, assembled in front of Davis' excavation house. When he returned late on the afternoon of January 17, 1908, however, he found the deposit in disarray. Davis had unpacked the jars to impress a lunch guest, but had been bitterly disappointed to find that they contained only broken pottery, bags of natron, animal bones, bits of linen, remains of floral collars, and one small gilt mummy mask. The scattered contents were gathered up and stowed in a magazine until Winlock returned two years later to pack them up and ship them New York.[2] No photos exist of the jars *in situ* in KV 54, none before they were unpacked, and no notes were made when the jars were emptied.

No one knows how many jars existed originally. Winlock stated that the KV 54 pit could comfortably contain about a dozen, which he recalls being the number mentioned at the time. Ayrton only collected the intact jars.[3] In the end six complete jars and their contents were transferred to the Metropolitan Museum. Winlock carefully packed up all the contents—linen, floral collars, broken pottery, bones, burnt sticks, and perhaps half of the bags of natron and chaff . By the 1920s the pottery was mended and on display in the Egyptian galleries, but it was not until 1941, after he had retired as Director of the Museum, that Winlock sat down to write an account of the discovery of the cache and a study of its contents. In his *Materials Used at the Embalming of King Tutankhamun,* he meticulously cataloged, illustrated, and described all of the objects in the cache. The animal bones were sent to a zoologist for study and a botanist consulted about the floral collars. By this time, of course, Carter had discovered the tomb of Tutankhamun (KV 62) in 1922 and had died in 1939. Carter had also been present in Thebes when the cache was found and was familiar with its findspot and contents.[4]

One of Winlock's great gifts was his ability to breathe life and history into archaeological remains. As he says in at the beginning of his account, "It is the story of how Theodore M. Davis once upon a time found the things which had been used at the funeral of King Tutankhamun in 1306 B.C."[5] In his publication of the cache he made certain assumptions: That the cache contained the remains of the embalming materials and final funerary banquet of Tutankhamun, and that it had been deposited in the pit some distance from the tomb of Tutankhamun because it was too impure to be placed in the tomb itself. He based this latter assumption on many smaller caches of embalming materials that the Metropolitan expeditions had found in Thebes, which were located outside of tombs, such as that found next to the tomb of Ipi of the early Twelfth Dynasty.[6]

In doing so, Winlock ignored evidence of two other caches of embalming materials deposited inside tombs in the Valley of the Kings during the second half of the Eighteenth Dynasty—that found in Maiherperi (KV 36), which was discovered by Loret in 1899,[7] and that from the tomb of Yuya and Tuya (KV 46), which was found by Davis in 1905.[8] Four of the jars from the Yuya and Tuya cache, in fact, had been in the Metropolitan's collections since 1911.[9] In Maiherperi's tomb, 13 large jars were found leaning against the back wall of the burial chamber. In the tomb of Yuya and Tuya, 52 jars were found in a pit at the far end of the burial chamber with the chariot, bed, and wig basket piled on top. All were sealed with the official necropolis seal of the jackal over the nine bows.

These deposits show that embalming materials could be placed in a tomb. In a tomb as small and heavily furnished as Tutankhamun's, the entrance corridor would be the only area left for this deposit. Carter, in his unpublished notes on the object cards for the staircase and entrance corridor of the tomb, also realized the connection between the cache and what he found in there, including fragments of large white *zirs* containing rubbish from the burial, fragments of linen, broken mud trays, and fragments of clay seals.[10] It was not until 1990, however, that Nicholas Reeves, in his study *Valley of the Kings*, proposed that the cache had been deposited secondarily in KV 54 and that it had originally been placed in the entrance corridor of KV 62.[11] It had been removed by necropolis officials after the first robbery of the tomb so that the corridor might be completely filled with rubble to deter further robberies. The first tomb robbers must have known what the jars contained, since most were apparently found sealed—as were the jars in Yuya and Tuya and Maiherperi. The necropolis officials obviously considered them important enough to go to the trouble of removing 12 large, heavy jars through the partially-blocked first doorway of the tomb and carrying them some 200 meters up the valley to where they could use the unfinished pit of KV 54 to rebury them.

They did not, however, clean out the corridor before refilling it, as Carter's notes show. Near the entrance he found a number of small "red cups of foundation deposit type," clearly small offering cups. At the far end of the corridor he found a decorated spouted pottery jar with lid—a *nemset* vessel—and the famous wooden head of Tutankhamun as a child emerging from a lotus.[12]

Figures 1 and 2 show a plan and isometric reconstruction of the corridor as the priests prepared to seal the final doorway after the funeral ceremonies had been completed. The jars, cups, and head have been returned to their original positions.[13] Lining most of one wall for the full length of the corridor were twelve or more large white jars some 50 cm in diameter and 70 cm high. The small offering cups had been placed on the floor near the first door. At the far end of the corridor in front of the inner doorway, the head of the king as a child being reborn from the lotus flower and the *nemset* jar were deposited.

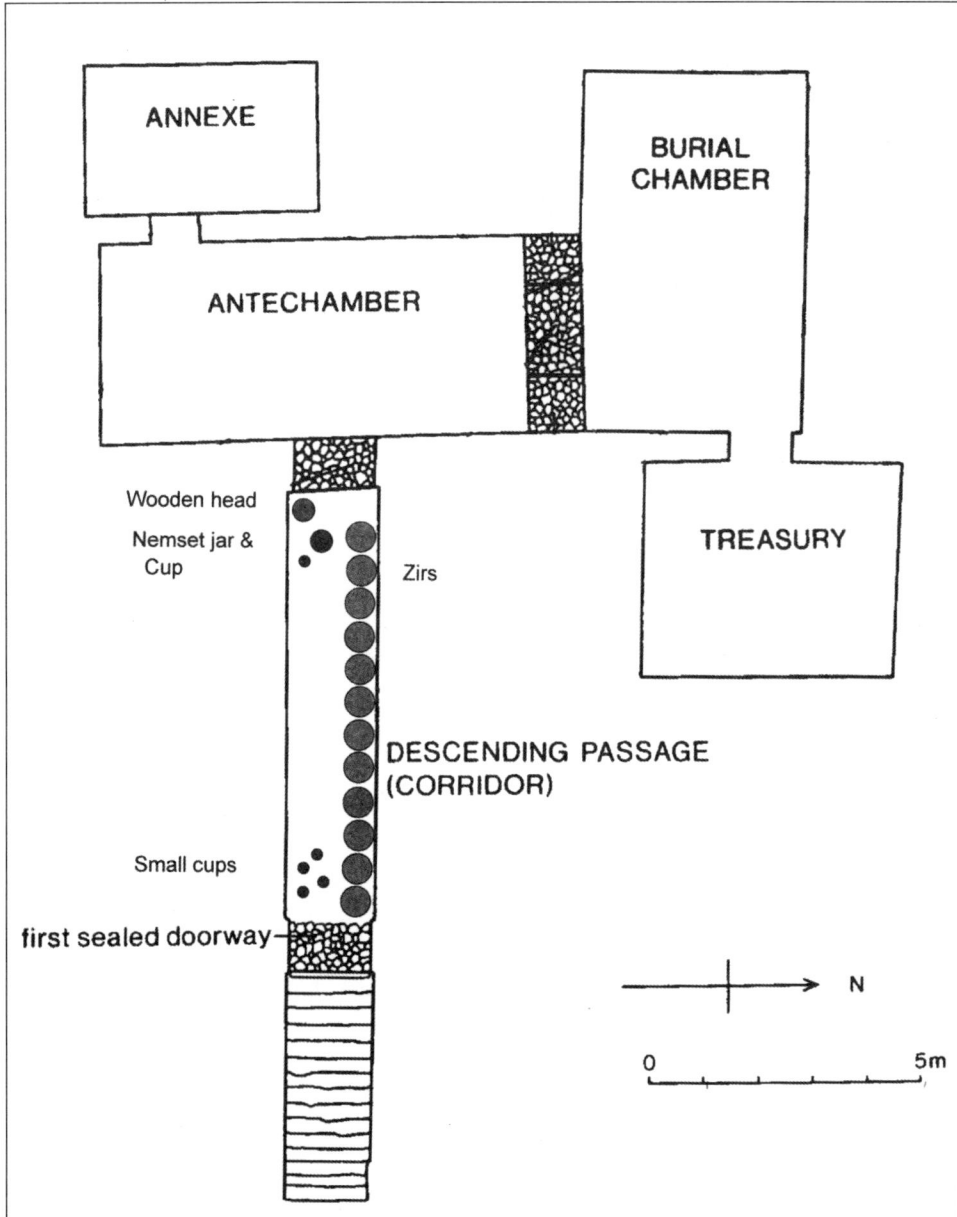

Fig. 1: Ground Plan – KV 62 Tutankhamun.

Some scholars have said that this head was dropped there by robbers, and even the excavators seem to have set it aside in their wonder at the overwhelming contents of the tomb which lay beyond that doorway. The first tomb robbers, however, were after valuable items that could be easily and discretely disposed of: perfumes and ointments, linen, metals and jewelry. They would have no use for a painted wood head which was clearly recognizable as the deceased king and which was also the potent symbol of the sun god being reborn from the lotus flower. More likely this head was placed intentionally before the entrance to the burial at the end of the funeral ceremonies to ensure the rebirth of the king as he left the tomb each day.[14] The spouted *nemset* jar placed with it may have been for ritual purification and another red cup was found in the rubble nearby. The necropolis officials deliberately left the head where it was when they filled the corridor so that it could continue to perform its religious and magical function for eternity. They reburied it in place. Reconstructing the deposit in the entrance corridor of the tomb allows us to restore the burial to its original state and adds significantly to our knowledge of these caches in the Eighteenth Dynasty.

The mixed contents of the jars, however, remain problematical. The following is an inventory of what the cache contained.

185 pottery vessels
19 lids of papyrus
3 fiber jar stoppers
bones of ducks, geese, cow, and sheep/goat
3+ floral collars (plus many fragments)
2 fiber brooms
3 linen wig covers
3 linen sheets with inscriptions
180 lengths of linen bandages
24 lengths of cloth ripped from sheets
4 pink-dyed linen pieces ripped for bandages
26 wide linen pieces (including one from a shirt)
50 pieces of specially-woven linen tape or bandage
61 linen bundles/packets of natron, salt, chaff
about 20 sticks, reed, papyrus, and wood, some burnt
4 small blocks of limestone, fairly well-polished

We do not know if all the categories of finds were distributed randomly throughout the jars or segregated by type. Winlock only says that they were packed in clean chaff and sealed. The mixture of embalming materials—bags of natron and chaff, sharpened sticks, scraps of linen and bandages, and the four limestone blocks—with broken pottery, floral collars, and disarticulated bones of meat and fowl seems strange. Added to this were the sealing fragments and the mud trays, which were similar to others found in the tomb proper, where they were associated with wood emblems. And then there was the small gilt mask. Reeves has also demonstrated that this mask was originally intended for one of the fetal mummies buried inside the tomb, but was not put on the mummy because it was too small.[15] This mask did not come with the 1909 group from Davis, and after Davis died, another mask from his private collection which he also left to the museum, was confused with it and published by Winlock as coming from the cache.[16] The little gilt mask from the cache is today on display in the Cairo Museum in Room P12, and a good case could be made for moving it to join its sibling in the Tutankhamun Collection.

The cache then seems to be a mixture of embalming materials, a ritual meal, and a sort of tidying up of loose ends and items. As far as we know from the other caches in the Valley of the

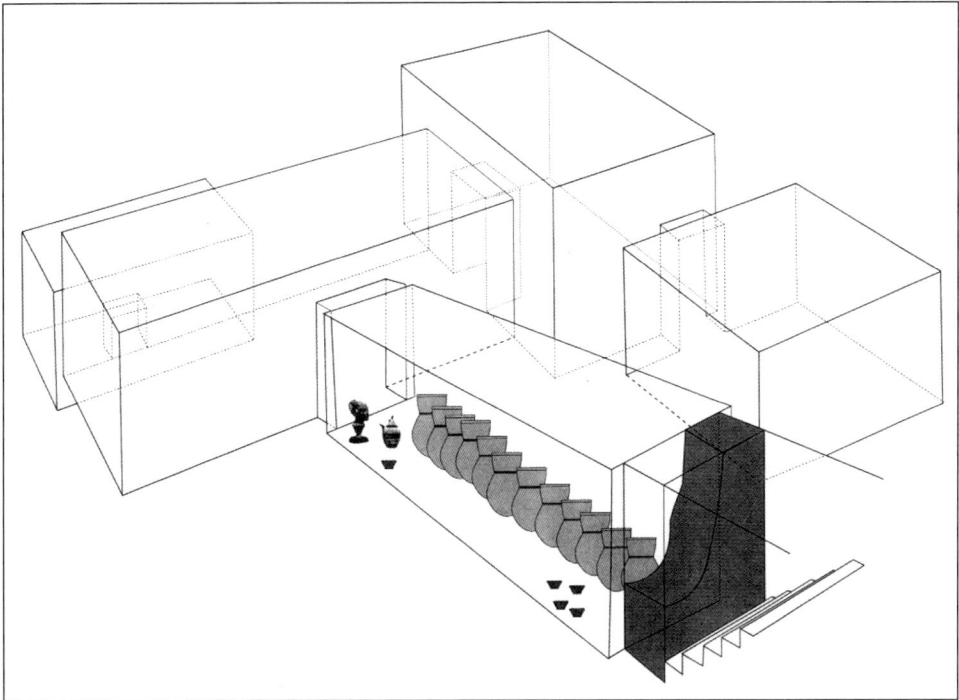

Fig. 2: Isometric Reconstruction – KV 62 Tutankhamun.

Kings, only bags of natron were packed into the jars. Recently one of the sealed jars from Yuya and Tuya in the Metropolitan was CAT-scanned, but proved too dense to allow its contents to be distinguished. So the Tutankhamun cache would seem to be the only one we know of containing pottery from the funerary meal and perhaps other rituals, deliberately or ceremonially broken. Recently, however, Daniel Polz has found an interesting deposit in a private tomb of the time of Thutmose I in Dra Abu al-Naga.[17] Two large storage jars had been placed in the entranceway of a tomb chamber. Inside the jars were six plates mixed with burnt organic material and two stones which had apparently been used to smash them.

The pottery in the Tutankhamun cache falls into four general groups. To the first belong the large jars in which the deposit was packed. Second are the four large storage vessels found broken within. Third are serving pieces: wide-mouth funnel-necked jars, the two-handled jar, large and medium-sized plates, elegant bottles, miscellaneous jars, lids, and lamps. Lastly are what could be called dinnerware: small jars, beakers, smaller plates, saucers, and perhaps cups. The large number of small cups and those with hieratic dockets indicating their contents are perhaps to be associated with part of the funerary ritual rather than an actual banquet. They may be token offerings left by mourners who were not part of the official party.

Nearly all the pottery appears to be made of Nile silt clay. All the big jars and storage jars are whitewashed. Most of the rest of the pottery, except for the small cups and some small plates, is coated with a thick red slip, which is sometimes polished. Only the white, burnished two-handled jar is identified by Winlock as being made of "Qulleh" ware, that is, marl clay. A few of the pieces bear the blue-painted floral decoration for which the late New Kingdom is known. These include one group of six funnel-necked jars which have floral collars around their shoulders, the elegant flask with papyrus umbel rim, a cream-slipped ovoid beaker with bands of floral decoration, and a deep bowl. Clearly, decorated pottery was not a priority, as these same shapes are included in plain or polished forms.

None of the pottery is similar to that found inside the tomb except for the simple cups and plates and the beaker with bands of floral decoration. In the tomb were many amphorae and long-necked flasks. Nearly all the vessels from the tomb proper were sealed. The shapes of the *zirs*, funnel-necked jars, beakers, lamps, and two-handled jar are all drawn from the corpus of every-day pottery in the latter part of the Eighteenth Dynasty. The elegant flasks with their burnished red surfaces, however, are copied from contemporary metal prototypes.[18] They probably contained water used for purification.

The bones of nine ducks, four geese, cow, and sheep or goat included in the jars would seem to support the idea that the dishes were from a ritual meal. The tomb itself was amply provisioned with victual mummies in special containers and sealed wine amphorae, so it would not seem necessary to have provided additional food offerings in this cache. All the other components of the funerary meal—liquids, breads, fruits—were probably completely consumed and any uneaten portions removed by the attendants, leaving only the disarticulated bones from the meats. Winlock did, however, note silty residues on the interior of some of the jars, which he took to indicate that they had contained water.

Winlock concluded that there were probably eight guests at the banquet.[19] There are eight drinking beakers and many other forms come in groups of four or multiples. There are a great many plates in the group. Those used as serving pieces can be separated from those used a dinnerware by diameter. Pieces below 20 cm in diameter were probably used as dinnerware. In all likelihood, many of the plates were used in pairs, one acting as a cover: as the ancient Egyptians said "one on its fellow."

It has also been suggested that the broken pottery may have been part of the ceremony of the breaking of the red pots.[20] I think this is unlikely because of the variety of pottery forms represented, and the presence of the floral collars and food bones. However, it may be that the Dra Abu al-Naga find represents this ceremony. It is also possible that the pottery in the Tutankhamun cache represents a symbolic banquet presented to the dead king, rather than a meal eaten by the principal mourners, as vessels also occur in multiples of four in the funerary meal. But someone does appear to have eaten all the food and carefully collected all the bones for the cache.

The study of this material arose from the recent reinstallation of the Metropolitan's Amarna galleries. It has provided an opportunity to look again at what has heretofore been considered a well-known and published group of objects. New labels were prepared reflecting the new research and the little mask was relocated correctly to the main Eighteenth Dynasty gallery. However, many more caches remain to be evaluated, some of which have only been recently discovered and await publication. It is also possible that similar caches existed in the side chambers of other royal burials in the Valley of the Kings. Careful examination of the debris from these usually severely disturbed burials may indicate that the types of objects and materials found in this cache are also present there.

Notes:

1 T. M. Davis *et al.*, *The Tomb of Queen Tiyi*, (London, 1910) 4; T. M. Davis *et al.*, *The Tombs of Harmhabi and Touatânkhamanou.* (London, 1912) 3, 112, 135, and fig 15.

2 H. E. Winlock, *Materials used at the embalming of King Tut-ankh-amun*, (The Metropolitan Museum of Art Papers No. 10; New York, 1941) 5-7. All references to the contents of this deposit are taken from this publication.

3 This pit was recently re-excavated by a Swiss team working in the Valley of the Kings. A report of their excavations was presented at the Congress. See E. Grothe, B. Luscher and T. Schneider, "Recent Work in the Royal Tombs of Ramesses X and Siptah in the Valley of the Kings," *Abstract of Papers, Eighth International Congress of Egyptologists, Cairo, March 28–April 3, 2000, 77.*

4 Winlock. *Materials*, 7, n 6. Carter also corresponded with Winlock in 1915 about the contents of the cache in a letter dated June 25, 1915 from Winlock to Carter now in the archives of the Department of Egyptian Art of the Metropolitan Museum of Art.

5 Winlock, *Materials*, 5.

6 H. E. Winlock. "The Egyptian Expedition 1921–1922: Excavations at Thebes," *Bulletin of the Metropolitan Museum of Art* 17, II (December, 1922), 33-34.

7 G. Daressy, *Fouilles de la Vallée des Rois 1898-1899*, (Cairo, 1902) 1ff; Appendix A, site 5.

8 J. E. Quibell, *The Tomb of Yuaa and Thuiu*, (Catalogue Général des Antiquités Égyptiennes du Musée du Caire No. 51001-51191; Cairo,1908), vi.

9 MMA 11.155, 6, 7, 8, 9; W. C. Hayes, *The Scepter of Egypt II, The Hyksos Period and the New Kingdom (1675-1080 B.C.)*, (Cambridge, 1959), 261-262.

10 H. Murray and M. Nuttall, *A Handlist to Howard Carter's Catalogue of Objects in Tut'ankhamun's Tomb*, (Oxford, 1963) 1, items 1m, 2, 3, 5c, 5d; H. Carter, *The Tomb of Tut-ankh-amen I*, (London, 1923), 77. Copies of unpublished tomb cards are in the archives of the Dept. of Egyptian Art, MMA. These materials are presently being placed on line on the web site of the Griffith Institute, Oxford University.

11 C. N. Reeves. *Valley of the Kings: The Decline of a Royal Necropolis*, (London, 1990), 67, 69.

12 Murray, *Handlist*, 1, items 5b (pottery cups), 8 (head of king), 9 (*nemset* jar), 12s (pottery cup).

13 This plan and isometric have been redrawn after those published by C. N. Reeves in *The Complete Tutankhamun*, (New York, 1990), 71, 96.

14 For an illustration of the deceased being reborn from a lotus, see Chapter 81A of the Book of the Dead.

15 C. N. Reeves, "On the Miniature Mask from the Tutankhamun Embalming Cache." *Bulletin de la Société d'Égyptologie Genève* 8 (1983), 81-93.

16 MMA 30.8.231 Winlock, *Materials*, 12, pl. II.B.

17 D. Polz, "Bericht über die 2. und 3. Grabungskampagne in der Nekropole von Dra' Abu el-Naga/Theben-West," *MDAIK* 49 (1993), 237; pl. 44b.

18 A. Radwan, *Die Kupfer- und Bronzegefässe Ägypten*, (Munich, 1983), 139-144, pl. 70.

19 Winlock, *Materials*, 14.

20 J. van Dijk, "Zerbrechen des roten Töpfe," *LÄ* VI, (1986), 1389-1396.

Excavations at Ezbet al-Tel, Kufur-Nigm: The Third and Fourth Seasons(1988 & 1990)

Mohamed I. Bakr
Zagazig University

Ezbet al-Tel, also called Tel Kufur Nigm, is situated approximately five kilometers southwest of Kafr-Saqr in the Ibrahimia Province, Sharqiya, near the west bank of the Tanite branch of the Nile (now Moas Canal), and about three kilometers north of al-Khudariya and Kufur-Nigm.[1] Several other archaeological sites can be found in its near vicinity, e.g. Tel Beni Amer, al-Iswid, Ibrahim Awad, al-Dab'a, Hurbeit, Tel al-Fauziya,[2] Abu Yasin, and Tukh al-Qaramus. This area is rich in history and ancient activities and is therefore a focus-point for archaeological research.

Excavations by Zagazig University

Since Zagazig University started excavating in 1984, the entire site was divided into squares of 100 x 100 meters. The horizontal axis of this grid was given alphabetical capitals, the vertical axis Roman numerals. Each square was then divided into 10 x 10 meter squares, using lower case letters for the horizontal axis and Arabic numerals for the vertical axis. While digging, a baulk half a meter wide was left standing at each side of each square, thus enabling us, by means of these sections, to study layers, approximate duration of periods, physiographic changes, and at the same time facilitating easy access to the separate squares and making it possible to avoid stepping on walls just uncovered. A zero point for measuring the levels of the excavation areas was designed.

Zagazig University's third excavation season on this site was from March 21 to April 9, 1988. During this time it was possible to excavate three squares of 10 x 10 meters (nos. CIV b3, c3, BIV. i3–though of the square no. BIV. i3 only 550 x 300 centimeters was accessible as the rest of the square extends under the agricultural land). Seventeen tombs were uncovered (no. 95 and nos. 99–114), two of which are Pithoi child burials in jars nos. (101 and 108). The tombs contain offerings for the deceased, needed to resume life in the hereafter, such as vessels for storing food and drink, jewelry and bracelets, schist palettes, stones, and copper and pottery vessels. The majority of these pots bear marks identifying their contents.

Inside the coffins, the deceased lies on his left side in a contracted position, head to the north, face to the southeast, many are in very bad condition because of the high level of the ground water. Five skeletons were found on the first level (nos. 93, 94, 95, 97, and 98), in square no. CIV, c3. All these skeletons are on their back, heads to the west. North of skeleton no. 93, the remains of three pots were found.

Zagazig University's fourth excavation season was from February 20 to March 16, 1990. During this time it was possible to excavate the following squares: nos. CIV. b2, CIV. a6, CIV. c2, and also Square no. BIV. J6 (470 x 340 centimeters only), no. BIV. J7 (440 x 80 centimeters only), and no. CIV. a7 (10 x 3.30 meters only). The balance of these latter squares is under agricultural fields. In squares nos. CIV. b2, CIV. c2, excavations were started, although there was not enough time to finish the work.

Fig. 1: Members of the 1990 excavation standing by Tomb 125.

Seven skeletons were found (nos. 115–121) in squares nos. CIV. b2 and CIV. c2 in the first level, on their back, heads to the west, faces to the southeast and arms at their sides.

Only one bronze anklet was found with skeleton no. 119, on the right leg (reg. no. 1629). No other gifts were found. Three copper vessels in very poor condition were discovered in tomb 127.

Thirteen tombs were found (nos. 122–134) containing offerings for the deceased, two of which are Pithoi child burials in jars (nos. 133–134). Inside the coffins, the deceased lies on his left side in a contracted position, the head to the north, the face to the east south, in very bad preservation because of the high level of the ground water. All the objects and pottery coffins found by the expedition from Zagazig University are in Zagazig University Museum.

The tombs nos. 104, 106, 111 were chosen for example from the third season in 1988, and nos. 123, 125, 127 from the fourth season in 1990. These are quick descriptions of some examples of the types of tombs and their offerings.

31

Tomb no. 104
Date 5-4-88.
Square CIV. C3.
Meas. of the coffin: 117 x 60 - 90 x 2 - 5 cm.

- Pottery coffin with a covering consisting of two parts and between them, two layers of small pottery pieces to fill the space between.
- Remains of three pots were found outside the coffin in the south side.

Tomb no. 106
Date 6-4-88
Square B1V0–13
Meas. of the coffin: 84–86 x 46–48 cm.
Meas. of the whole burial: 110x127 cm
Thickness of the bricks: 10 cm

- Pottery coffin with a covering consisting of two parts, surrounded by a layer of mud bricks.
- Seven pots were found outside the coffin in the south side as well as a piece of alabaster in the southeast corner and another piece in the northeast corner. Inside the coffin, four alabaster pots were found: two in the east side and another two in the west side. Three of these pots are in very bad condition.

Tomb no. 111
Date 7-4-88
Square: Civ-C3
Meas. of the whole burial: 131–147 x 91–92 cm

- Pottery coffin with a covering consisting of two parts, surrounded by a layer, of mud bricks.
- Five pots were found outside the coffin in the east side as well as a pot inside the coffin towards the northwest side.

Tomb no. 123
Date 1-3-90
Square: CIV-a7
Meas. of the burial: 167 x 87 cm.

- Rectangular pit surrounded by mud bricks.
- Twenty-seven objects were found around the remains of the skeleton, including pottery, alabaster, schist, and a group of beads. These objects are under nos. 1613–1644, 1722, 1726, 1727, 1728 in the Zagazig University Museum. The other objects are broken and in a bad condition.

Tomb no. 125
Date 4-3-90
Squares. BIV-j6, j7, CIV.a6, a7.
Meas. of the burnt bricks: 37 x 23 x 2 cm.

Fig. 2: Tomb 125.

Meas. of the tomb: 240–245 x 180–205 x 64 cm.
Meas. of the storeroom: 165 x 26 cm

- Large rectangular pit surrounded by burnt bricks on all sides, even the ground; the roof was also covered with burnt bricks. There is a storeroom in the south side surrounded by mud bricks. The whole tomb was covered with burnt bricks. No holes are in the upper layer of the burnt bricks to carry the roof, so it was probably carried by pieces of wood put on the burnt bricks lining the inside of the tomb.

- Forty-one pots were found inside the tomb and in the storeroom, most of these objects are broken and the rest are under nos. 1648–1654, 1729–1730, and 1752 at the Zagazig University Museum.

Tomb no. 127
Date: 8-3-90
Square: CIV-a7
Meas. of the burnt bricks:
32–37 x 17–25 x 3 cm

Fig. 3: Tomb 127.

33

Meas. of the whole tomb:
335–380 x 200–260 x 70 cm.

- Large rectangular pit, surrounded by mud bricks, but the ground was also covered with burnt bricks. The roof of the tomb was probably carried by pieces of wood as in tomb no. 125.
- Sixty-five objects were found inside the tomb from all sides around the deceased, mostly broken and in very bad condition, three of them are copper pots in very bad state of preservation, (not registered).
- Outside the tomb, the remains of five pots and an animal's bone were found 70 cm away from the east side of the tomb. In addition, the remains of a pot with an animal's bone were found in the south side.
- The objects under nos. 1667–1676, 1678–1693, 1741–1750 in the Zagazig University Museum.

Conclusion

The site apparently had been first used as a settlement during the late Predynastic Period and continued to be thickly populated during the Archaic Period. Mud-brick walls, traces of fireplaces, workshop containers apparently for pressing grapes to produce wine and the like are good evidence for this. According to these findings we are expecting that future excavations will reveal more data and will yield more information about daily life and culture in the Archaic Period in the Eastern Delta.

Fig. 4: Large container from sector CIV. a2.

REG.NO.	POSITION	DESCRIPTION	MATERIAL	MEASURE	REMARK
1631	CIV. a7, tomb 123 beside the head of the burial	A cylindrical cup, big mouth, round base	Alabaster	Diam. of the mouth: 11.4 cm. Diam. of the base: 8.9 cm. H. 22.4 cm.	1.3. 1990
1632	CIV. a7, tomb 123 northwest of head of the burial	A plate, round base	Alabaster	Diam. of the mouth: 16 cm. Diam. of base: 4.4 cm. H. 3.4 cm.	1.3. 1990
1633	CIV. a7, tomb 123 northwest of the head of the burial	A cylindrical cup, big mouth, round base	Alabaster	Diam. of the mouth: 6.3 cm. Diam. of the base 5.2 cm. H. 14 cm.	1.3. 1990 missing a part of the mouth
1634	CIV. a7, tomb 123 east of burial's chest	A plate, round base	Alabaster	Diam. of the mouth 16 cm. Diam. of the base 5 cm. H. 4.8 cm.	1.3. 1990
1635	CIV. a7, tomb 123, east of the burial's chest	A small cup, round base	alabaster	Diameter of the mouth: 9.4 cm. Diameter of the base: 3.5 cm. H. 6.4 cm.	1.3. 1990
1636	CIV. a7, tomb 123, east of the burial's chest	A small cup, round base	alabaster	Diameter of the mouth: 7.2 cm. Diameter of the base: 5.6 cm. H. 13 cm.	1.3. 1990
1637	CIV. a7, tomb 123, east of the burial's chest	A small cup, round base, black color	red pottery	Diameter of the mouth: 3.5 cm. Diameter of the base: 4 cm. H. 7 cm.	1.3. 1990
1638	CIV. a7, tomb 123, west of the burial's chest	A small cup, big mouth	alabaster	Diameter of the mouth: 8 cm. Diameter of the base: 5.9 cm. H. 15 cm.	1.3. 1990
1639	CIV. a7, tomb 123, west of burial's chest	A rectangular palette	schist	1. 10.3 cm. w. 7 cm. thickness .1 cm.	1.3. 1990
1640	CIV. a7, tomb 123, west of the burial's chest	A rectangular palette	schist	1. 9.7 cm. w. 4 cm. thickness .3 cm.	1.3. 1990
1641	CIV. a7, tomb 123, storeroom	A big pot, unround base	pottery	Diameter of the mouth: 10 cm. H. 36.5 cm.	1.3. 1990 broken mouth restored

35

REG.NO.	POSITION	DESCRIPTION	MATERIAL	MEASURE	REMARK
1642	CIV. a7, tomb 123, storeroom	A big pot, unround base	pottery	Diameter of the mouth: 9.4 cm. H. 37.5 cm.	1.3. 1990 broken mouth restored
1643	CIV. a7, tomb 123, storeroom	A big pot, unround base	pottery	H. 34.5 cm.	1.3. 1990 broken mouth restored
1644	CIV.a7, tomb 123, east of the burial's chest	A rectangular palette	schist	1.12cm. w. 7.7 cm. thickness .3 cm.	1.3. 1990
1722	CIV. a7, around neck of the burial no. 123	group of beads, had 4 ammulets: 1. amulet in animal's head form 2. amulet in ephemera form 3. amulet in caterpillar form 4. amulet of God Dhuty in bird form	gold, stone, carnelian, faience	L. 42 cm.	1.3. 1990 newly arranged
1726	CIV. a7, tomb 123 around the hand	3 rings A,B,C.	schist	A: 5.3 cm. B: 6 cm. C: 5.2 cm.	1.3. 1990
1727	CIV. a7, tomb 123 around the hand	2 rings 1,2	flint	1: 6 cm. 2: 5.5 cm.	1.3. 1990 broken, restored.
1728	CIV. a7, tomb 123	A small pot, round base	schist	Diameter of the mouth: 11 cm. Diameter of the base: 3.6 cm.	1.3. 1990 missing a

REG.NO.	POSITION	DESCRIPTION	MATERIAL	MEASURE	REMARK
				H. 6 cm.	part of the mouth, broken, restored
1648	CIV. a6,7 BIV. J6,7 tomb 125 from inside	A small pot, round	alabaster	Diameter of the mouth: 5.7 cm. Diameter of the base: 4 cm. H. 12 cm.	4.3. 1990
1649	CIV. a6,7 BIV. J6,7 tomb 125 from inside	A small pot, round base bearing remains of black color	alabaster	Diameter of the base: 2.1 cm. H. 7.3 cm.	missing most of the mouth
1650	CIV. a6,7 BIV. J6,7 tomb 125 from inside	A rectangular palette	schist	1. 25.7 cm. w. 18.9 cm. H. 20.7 cm.	on it remains of colors, missing some parts of all sides
1651	CIV.a6,7 BIV.J6,7 tomb 125 from inside	An offering standard	red pottery	Diameter of the mouth: 24.5 cm. H. 45 cm.	4.3.90 broken, missing some parts, restored
1652	Tomb 125, storeroom	A big pot, have a pot mark round base	red pottery	Diameter of the mouth: 10.8 cm. Diameter of the base: 5.5 cm. H. 72 cm.	4.3.90
1653	Tomb 125, store-room	A big pot, have a pot mark	pottery	Diameter of the mouth: 11.6 cm. Diameter of the base: 4.5 cm. H. 74.6 cm.	4.3.90 missing part from

REG.NO.	POSITION	DESCRIPTION	MATERIAL	MEASURE	REMARK
		round base			lower, broken, restored
1654	Tomb 125, storeroom	A big pot, have a pot mark, round base	pottery schist	Diameter of the mouth: 13.5 cm. Diameter of the base: 5.7 cm. H. 67 cm.	4.3.90
1729	Tomb 125, inside	A big plate, round base		Diameter of the mouth: 36.5 cm. base 9 cm. H. 7 cm.	4.3.90 missing some parts, broken, restored
1730	Tomb 125, inside	A big plate, round base	alabaster	mouth 30.5 cm. base 8 cm. H. 5 cm.	4.3.90 broken, missing parts, restored
1752	Tomb 125, inside	A big plate, round base	schist	mouth 30 cm. base 7.50 cm. H. 5 cm.	4.3.90
1667	CIV, a7 tomb 127	A cylindrical cup, big mouth Unrectangular	alabaster	mouth 8.2 cm. base 6.9 cm. H. 18 cm.	missing parts of the mouth
1668	CIV.a7 tomb 127	palette An oval pot,	schist	1. 17.9 cm. w. 11.5 cm.	8.3.90
1669	CIV. a7 tomb 127	round base, big mouth A big pot,	alabaster	mouth 10.9 cm. base 12.2 cm. H. 19 cm.	8.3.90 bad condition
1670	CIV.a7 tomb 127	round base, have a pot mark	pottery	mouth 10.8 cm. base 4.5 cm. H. 72 cm.	8.3.90 broken, missing parts, restored

REG.NO.	POSITION	DESCRIPTION	MATERIAL	MEASURE	REMARK
1671	Tomb 127	A cylindrical cup, big mouth, with a hole in its base and a covering	alabaster	mouth 15.8 cm. base 14.3 cm. H. 36 cm. base's covering 4.2 cm.	8.3.90 missing parts
1672	Tomb 127	A cylindrical cup, big mouth, round base	alabaster	mouth 11.8 cm. base 10.2 cm. H. 21.5 cm.	8.3.90 8.3.90 broken, restored
1673	Tomb 127	A cylindrical cup, big mouth, round base	alabaster	mouth 17.7 cm. base 14.7 cm. H. 22 cm.	8.3.90 8.3.90 broken, restored
1674	Tomb 127	A big pot, round base	pottery	mouth 12.5 cm. base 4.5 cm. H. 64 cm.	8.3.90 missing parts of the mouth
1675	Tomb 127	A big cylindri-cal pot, unflat base from its middle, big mouth	alabaster	mouth 31.9 cm base 32.5 cm. H. 57.5 cm.	missing parts of the mouth, broken, restored
1676	Tomb 127	A small cup, round base	schist	mouth 8.5 cm. base 3.6 cm H. 4.2 cm.	8.3.90 broken into two parts, restored
1678	Tomb 127	A big pot, round base, bearing a pot mark	red pottery	base 5.2 cm H. 69 cm.	8.3.90 missing the mouth, broken, restored

39

REG.NO.	POSITION	DESCRIPTION	MATERIAL	MEASURE	REMARK
1679	Tomb 127	A cylindrical cup, big mouth	alabaster	mouth 18 cm. base 14.5 cm. H. 26.5 cm.	8.3.90 bad condition
1680	Tomb 127	A cylindrical cup, big mouth	red pottery	mouth 7.9 cm. base 5.4 cm. H. 12.8 cm.	8.3.90
1681	Tomb 127	A big pot, pointed base	pottery	H. 34.7cm.	missing, the mouth, and a part of the body
1682	Tomb 127	A big pot bearing a pot mark	red pottery	mouth 11 cm. base 4 cm. H. 63 cm.	broken, missing parts, restored
1683	Tomb 127	a cylindrical cup, big mouth	alabaster	mouth 9.7cm. base 7.3 cm. H. 20.8cm.	8.3.90
1684	Tomb 127	An oval pot, round base, big mouth	alabaster alabaster	mouth 8.8 cm base 11.3 cm. H. 12.5 cm.	8.3.90 the mouth is broken, restored
1685	Tomb 127	A cylindrical cup	alabaster	mouth 17.1 cm base 17.5 cm li. 41.5 cm	8.3.90
1686	Tomb 127	A cylindrical cup	alabaster	mouth 11.7 cm. base 9.2 cm. H. 22. cm.	missing a part of the mouth
1687	Tomb 127	A cylindrical cup	alabaster	mouth 7.5 cm. base 5.4 cm. H. 15.5 cm.	8.3.90
1688	Tomb 127	A cylindrical cup	alabaster	mouth 15.3 cm. base 12.8 cm.	bad condition

REG.NO.	POSITION	DESCRIPTION	MATERIAL	MEASURE	REMARK
				H. 19.4 cm.	
1689	Tomb 127	A cylindrical cup	red pottery	mouth 9 cm. base 6.6 cm. H. 15.8 cm.	broken, missing parts restored
1690	Tomb 127	A big pot with a pot mark, base round	red pottery	Mouth 11 cm. base 4 cm. H. 72.3 cm.	broken, missing parts, restored
1691	Tomb 127	A big pot with a pot mark, round base	red pottery	mouth 11 cm. base 5.5 cm. li. 67.5 cm.	Missing parts, broken, restored
1692	Tomb 127	A cylindrical cup	red pottery	mouth 8.7 cm. base 7.3 cm. H. 13.2 cm.	missing parts, broken, bearing remains of black colour, restored
1693	Tomb 127	A cylindrical pot, open from the bottom	pottery	mouth 14.9 cm. base 15.5 cm. H. 21.5 cm.	bad condition, broken, missing parts, restored
1741	Tomb 127	A plate, round base	schist	mouth 23 cm. base 6.5 cm. H. 3.5 cm.	broken, missing parts of the mouth, restored
1742	Tomb 127	A big pot,	alabaster	mouth 25.5 cm.	broken,

REG.NO.	POSITION	DESCRIPTION	MATERIAL	MEASURE	REMARK
		round base		base 7.8 cm. H. 13.6 cm.	missing parts, restored
1743	Tomb 127	A big pot, round base	schist	mouth 24.5 cm. base 8.5 cm. H. 11 cm.	broken, missing parts, restored
1744	Tomb 127	A plate, round base	schist	mouth 26.4 cm. base 8 cm. H. 7.5 cm.	broken, missing parts, restored
1745	Tomb 127	A cylindrical cup	alabaster	mouth 9.5 cm. base 6.8 cm. H. 30.5 cm.	broken, missing parts, restored
1746	Tomb 127	A plate, round base	schist	mouth 29.5 cm. base 9 cm. H. 4.5 cm.	broken, missing parts, restored
1747	Tomb 127	A plate, round base	alabaster	mouth 29 cm. base 9.2 cm. H. 7 cm.	broken, missing parts, restored
1748	Tomb 127	A plate, round base	schist	mouth 29.cm. base 9 cm. H.4.5 cm.	broken, missing parts, restored
1749	Tomp 127	A plate, round base	schist	mouth 38.8 cm. base 9.5 cm. H. 5.9 cm.	broken, missing parts, restored
1750	Tomb 127	A pot, round base	schist	mouth 21.5 cm. base 7 cm. H. 7.5 cm.	broken, missing parts, restored

Notes:

1 Survey of Egypt (SOE) topographical maps, series 1:25000, sheet nos. 89-660 (Kafr-Saqr), co-ordinates 894-672.

2 Tell al-Fauziya has been recently leveled and the area is now under cultivation. Soundings were made there on behalf of the E.A.0. in 1980 and 1981 and are now in the Scientific Archive of the EAO; see also M. Ramsy, *The Geographical Dictionary of Egyptian Cities and Villages, Part I* (in Arabic) (Cairo, 1964), 129.

3 For previous excavations of the author in the same site of Kufur Nigm see: "The New Excavations at Ezbet el-Tell, Kufur Nigm, the first Season, 1984," *Archaeology of the Nile Delta*, 49-62; "Excavations of Kufur Nigm," in *Hommages à J. Leclant* (*BdE* 106/4, 1993), 9-17; *Orientalia* 54 (1985), 344, 345; *Orientalia* 55 (1986), 244, figs 4-8.

The Shaft Tomb
of Iufaa at Abusir

Ladislav Bareš

The Czech Institute of Egyptology, Charles University, Prague

The tomb of Iufaa is the second structure in a group of huge Late Period shaft tombs, on the southwestern outskirts of the Czech archaeological concession at Abusir, to have been examined archaeologically. Only the nearby tomb of the famous Udjahorresnet has been fully excavated.[1] Since the last Congress in Cambridge, where the first report on the tomb of Iufaa was presented,[2] much more work has been completed.[3] At the beginning of 1996, the main shaft of the tomb was completely cleared. At the bottom, at a depth of about 22 m, an intact burial chamber came to light. It was the first tomb of its kind in Egypt in 55 years to be found intact.

The burial chamber, constructed of rather uneven and roughly-worked blocks of local limestone, is orientated east-west. In shape it imitates a giant sarcophagus with raised ends and a vaulted ceiling. The outer face of the stone blocks was left rough, except for the northern portion of the western wall where smoothing had begun. Somewhat surprisingly, there is no aperture in the roof of the chamber to facilitate filling it with sand after the burial ceremonies took place.

Rather unexpectedly, the entrance to the burial chamber is situated in its western wall, just opposite the corridor leading from the western subsidiary shaft. The western wall of the burial chamber was not connected with the western wall of the main shaft, the free space between both walls being about 1.7 m wide. The remains of one pair of vertical wooden posts measuring about 10 cm in diameter were found lying adjacent to the sides of the entrances to both the corridor and the burial chamber. Between the posts, tiny remnants of disintegrated reed mats were discovered, certainly not strong enough to protect the passage once the main shaft had been filled with sand. These lateral walls therefore represent only symbolic boundaries of the passage to the burial chamber. Without any doubt, the passage and indeed the whole main shaft as well, would have been left open until the moment of the burial.

The burial chamber, measuring 4.9 by 3.3 m inside, is dominated by a huge rectangular sarcophagus cut out of two white limestone blocks. The sarcophagus is surrounded on all four sides by a corridor about 0.5 m wide, uncommon in this type of tomb. This corridor was found half-filled with a thick layer of sand, covered from above with partly crushed mud brick and here and there, a number of very rough limestone blocks. Most probably, those blocks helped to keep the lid of the outer sarcophagus raised to the moment of the burial. There were no traces of the device for lowering of the lid of the outer sarcophagus: This normally consisted of two pairs of vertical shafts with wooden props. In the corridor, atop a layer of sand and mud brick, pieces of the original burial equipment were found. North of the entrance a damaged wooden chest with a cavetto cornice had been placed. Under the broken bottom of this chest were heaped the remains of its contents: ten faience vases with lids, six small faience cups and ten pottery vases. All contained the remains of ointment. The names of the respective sacred oils were written on the outside of the vases in black ink. In addition to those vases, a small bronze vessel, two bronze models of offering tables, four miniature alabaster blocks, two small schist amulets (a double ostrich feather and an Upper Egyptian crown), two miniature models of offerings made of wood and ivory respectively, a magic brick of silt faintly inscribed with the usual Chapter 151A of the Book of the Dead, the remains of a papyrus roll completely destroyed by humidity, and unidentified copper, iron, and faience fragments were found.

Along both the northern and southern sides of the sarcophagus, one flat open box was discovered full of blue-glazed *shabtis* (203 in the north and 205 in the south, 408 together), as well as one taller chest, resembling a *naos* in shape and crowned on its lid with a small figure of a jackal. Each chest contained two canopic jars. Due to the very high level of humidity caused by the water table, all those chests, made of wood and originally embellished with texts and representations painted in ochre on a thick layer of black varnish, were almost completely destroyed. All four canopic jars, made of alabaster and about 30 cm high, were closed by conical lids carved with a representation of a human face. Each jar bore incised inscriptions mentioning one of the four sons of Horus as well as his image. In addition, a name of one of the four protective goddesses (Isis, Nephthys, Selqet, and Neith) was written in black on the lid. All the jars were almost completely full of a resinous matter, now carbonized.

Adjacent to the eastern wall of the burial chamber, two stone vessels were discovered, a small one made of alabaster and a larger (46 cm high), of pink limestone inscribed with an Anubis formula and an incised representation of that god. This vessel, similar to a canopic jar in shape and full of a resinous matter, most probably served to store the materials left after the mummification.

Tiny remnants of another papyrus roll, again completely disintegrated, were found in the northwestern corner of the chamber. In the sand west of the sarcophagus were three more magical bricks made of Nile silt and bearing Chapter 151A of the Book of the Dead, and a few other amulets, among them a fine *djed* pillar of green faience.

Because of the poor quality of the shale (*tafla*) into which the main shaft had been dug, it was necessary to strengthen the walls before continuing work. A huge cover in the shape of a gabled roof of reinforced concrete was installed at the bottom of the main shaft. This structure, measuring 11.5 m square and about 9 m high, covers the whole of the lowermost portion of the main shaft.

Only after this time and labor-consuming task had been completed was it possible to continue copying the scenes on the walls of the burial chamber and the limestone sarcophagus. The texts are purely religious in nature, made up of long excerpts from the Pyramid Texts, the Book of the Dead, and other compositions. Interestingly, some of the texts appear more than once in the tomb, e.g. Chapters 26 through 30B and 72 of the Book of the Dead are inscribed on both the exterior of the outer sarcophagus and on the lid of the inner sarcophagus. Together, the texts take up more than 80 square m of space. Only after the difficult task of tracing the relief decoration had been done could the huge limestone outer sarcophagus be opened.

The box of the inner sarcophagus stands on a platform raised about 35 cm above the floor that is made of rather small local limestone blocks. The sarcophagus is about 3.8 m long, 2.3 m wide, and its box is 1.4 m high. The lid, originally cemented to the chest by means of a thick layer of a coarse whitish or greyish lime mortar, is about one meter thick. To open the sarcophagus, it was necessary to raise the lid, weighing about 24 tons, by more than one meter and lay it aside. Before this operation, all necessary measures were taken to protect the reliefs.

A cavity of roughly anthropoid shape was hollowed out in the box. The vertical inner sides are completely covered with inscriptions and representations of deities (among them Re-Horakhty, Sekhmet, Bastet, Wadjet, Shesemtet, and the less known god Tutu) and religious symbols, finely carved in incised relief. Inside, the hieroglyphic signs, register lines, and images were colored black, red, blue, brown, green, and yellow.

The lid of the inner sarcophagus was mostly covered by an irregular layer of gypsum mortar and on top of this was a layer of crushed mud brick. The mud-brick layer has not yet been satisfactorily explained. Since mud brick is a very strong desiccant, it might have been intended to diminish the very high level of natural humidity inside the sarcophagus, or perhaps was the remains of a structure used during the manoeuvring of the lid. Finally, a possible association with Osirian funeral rites has been put forward.

The layer of gypsum mortar filled almost all the space remaining around the inner sarcophagus, thus sealing the lid. Patches of molten resin were found inside here and there. Partly inside this layer and over it, were scattered shards of red ware storage jars. A possible connection with the ritual of "breaking the red vessels" cannot be excluded, but perhaps the vessels may have simply been to transport the mortar.

The anthropoid inner sarcophagus, made of basalt or possibly schist, filled the above-mentioned cavity almost completely. This sarcophagus, orientated with its head to the east, is 2.20 m long, and its maximum width is 90 cm. Except for the face framed by long lappets of a tripartite wig and the convex upper surface of the feet, the exterior is again completely covered with incised hieroglyphic texts. On the chest, under the curved beard identifying the deceased as Osiris, is a large, finely carved scarab beetle. Very probably, the lower part of the inner sarcophagus is decorated on its outer side as well but it is still firmly embedded in mortar. Thus, only a small piece of its exterior (just behind the head) has been cleared, revealing incised inscriptions. The interior of the lid and chest of the inner sarcophagus are also inscribed.

Under the lid of the inner sarcophagus, the remains of a wooden anthropoid coffin were revealed. Unfortunately its lid had split lengthwise and was almost completely destroyed by moisture. The coffin was 1.84 m long and 48 cm at its widest (across the shoulders). Originally, the exterior was covered with a thick layer of ochre-colored stucco. Remains of black-painted decoration were partly preserved on the lid, among them three columns of roughly-rendered hieroglyphs. The text on the left side was the best-preserved, although only remains of the title *ḥrp ḥwwt* "Administrator of the palaces" and the name of the deceased could be imperfectly read.

Under the broken lid was a damaged fine bead net composed of larger tubular and smaller globular faience beads. It had originally covered the mummy of the deceased almost completely, except for the head. There were faint traces of gilding here and the eyes were painted black. Basically, the net consisted of light blue tubular beads arranged into rhomboids in a fashion typical of the time. At a number of places, however, there was a more complex decoration of much smaller disc-beads. There was a *wsḫ*-collar under the chin and representations of the goddess Nut and the four sons of Horus on the chest, and Isis and Nephthys around the calves. Between the thighs, a yellow oval was visible, outlined with black and with a single column of black hieroglyphic signs mentioning the title and name of the deceased and the name of his mother. The text is identical with that on the *shabti* figures.

Inside the mummy wrappings, a number of artifacts were uncovered. All the finger and toe tips were encased in sheaths made of pure gold with the nails represented. Another thin metal plate made of gilded copper covered the penis. On the body of the deceased and inside the wrappings were a number of amulets: six *udjat*-eyes, three scarabs (including a heart scarab, unfortunately uninscribed), three hearts, two Isis knots, one headrest, one small tablet, one *dd*-column, one *w3d*-column, and one snake's head. Four barrel beads were also found on the mummy.[4]

The floor of the inner sarcophagus was also decorated with texts and representations of deities and religious symbols and scenes in incised relief. Among them, and perhaps most interesting, are the images of the enthroned Atum and a syncretised figure of Tatenen depicted as a scarab with the head of a hare and one human hand.

According to the inscriptions found mainly in the burial chamber, the tomb belonged to a dignitary named Iufaa, born to a lady Ankhtes; the name of the father is here so far unattested. Interestingly enough, even the name of Iufaa's mother is mentioned only on *shabtis* and on the bead net protecting the mummy. Only on those places does his title *ḥrp ḥwwt*, "Administrator of the palaces" appear. No other title in the tomb can be indisputably be connected with him.

The rather common title of the deceased seems to be in sharp contrast to his huge funerary monument, relatively well-decorated and equipped. Moreover, according to the preliminary anthropological examination done by Eugen Strouhal, Iufaa died at the young age of 25 to 30 years (35 maximum).

A number of unique features are attested in his burial complex when compared to other Late Period shaft tombs of the same type:
- an extensive use of mud brick
- the paneled outer face of the enclosure
- the existence of two smaller lateral shafts giving access to the bottom of the main pit an interrupted corridor to the burial chamber
- the position of the outer sarcophagus surrounded by a corridor inside the burial chamber
- the absence of the device for lowering of the lid of the outer sarcophagus
- the position of the deceased with his head to the east
- the type and enormous amount of the decoration inside the burial chamber and especially on both the outer and inner sarcophagi

The dating of the tomb is still far from certain. Judging from its location, especially its proximity to the more firmly-dated tomb of Udjahorresnet and the numerous finds of imported eastern Greek and Aegean pottery, dated by Smoláriková to the last quarter of the sixth century BCE, the tomb could be tentatively dated to the beginning of the Twenty-seventh Dynasty (around 500 BCE). On the other hand, some features quoted above might point to a somewhat later date, perhaps even the beginning of the fourth century BCE. In addition to these, the shape of the *shabtis* are closest to Schneider's class XIA5–Thirtieth Dynasty and early Ptolemaic period.

Only future archaeological work will bring answers to those and other questions connected with Iufaa and his tomb. At the same time, restoration is in progress and the consolidation of the relief decoration will be continued. After all the necessary work is finished, the tomb should be opened to the public and become, we hope, one of the most interesting places in not only the Abusir necropolis, but the whole Pyramid Zone as well.

Notes:

1 L. Bareš, *The Shaft Tomb of Udjahorresnet at Abusir*, (Prague, 1999).

2 See L. Bareš, "Saite-Persian Cemetery at Abusir," (Report for January 1995), *GM* 151 (1996), 7–17.

3 The following preliminary reports have been published; L. Bareš - K. Smoláriková, "The Shaft Tomb of Iufaa at Abusir," (Preliminary report for 1995/1996), *GM* 156 (1997), 9–26; L. Bareš - E. Strouhal, "The Shaft-Tomb of Iufaa, Season of 1997/98," *ZÄS* 127 (2000). See also C. M. Sheikholeslami (ed.), *The Egyptian Museum at the Millennium, A Special Exhibition in honor of the VIIIth International Congress of Egyptologists, 28 March–3 April 2000, Cairo, Egypt*, (Cairo, 2000), 42–43 and pls. 33–35.

4 At present, the amulets are being prepared for final publication by Vivienne Gae Callender.

Zur antiken Ideenähnlichkeit: Personifikationen im Pyramidentext-Spruch 205 und der Elemente des Empedokles

Hans-Georg Bartel

Humboldt-Universität zu Berlin

Es ist das Anliegen dieses Beitrags, der Feststellung von Siegfried Morenz: *„Leider liegt die Forschung bei der Wiedergewinnung altägyptischer Naturlehren noch im argen. Das Wenige zeigt aber deutlich genug, daß es sie gegeben hat und daß sie schon damals in religiöse Nutzung versteckt gewesen sind.“*[1] in dem Sinne Rechnung zu tragen, daß Personifikationen, die im Spruch 205 der Pyramidentexte (PT 123 a–e)[2] Erwähnung finden, als ein frühes Pendant zu den vier Elementen des Empedokles (ca. 495–435 v.Chr.) gedeutet werden. Da auch dieser vorsokratische Philosoph in seinem Werk περὶ φύσεως die von ihm 'Wurzelkräfte' (ῥιζώματα) genannten Elementarprinzipien als göttliche Personifikationen einführt, kann hier von einem Beispiel von Ideenähnlichkeit in der frühen ägyptischen und der griechischen Antike gesprochen werden. Die nachfolgenden Ausführungen sind nur als ein erster Überblick dazu zu werten, der in nachfolgenden Arbeiten detailliert ausgeführt wird.

Zum Text von PT 123a–e

Abbildung 1 zeigt den hieroglyphischen Text, wie er in der Unas-Pyramide angeordnet ist.[3] Seine Umschrift in der sonst üblichen Gliederung lautet:

(123a) *iw nk.n Wnis Mw.t iw sn.n Wnis šw-s.t*

(123b) *iw dmd n Wnis m N(i)-ḥ.wt*

(123c) *iw nk.n Wnis Nfr.t-nr(w)=f šw tbtb šsšs*

(123d) *in ḥm Nfr.t-nr(w) n Wnis rdi=s t n Wnis*

(123e) *ir=s n=f nfr.t m hrw pn.*

Sie berücksichtigt bereits die unten zu diskutierenden Lesungen der Personifikationen.

Zum Zwecke des Vergleichs seien drei Übersetzungen genannt:

(a) *„W. beschläft die mwy-t[.] W. küßt die šw-st[.] W. vereinigt sich mit der nḫb-wt[.] W. beschläft seine Buhlerin šw(-t) tbtb šsšs. Die Buhlerin des W. ist es aber, die ihm Brot giebt und die ihm Gutes thut heute.“* [4]

(b) *„123a. N. has copulated with Mw.t; N. has kissed šw-s.t; 123b. N. has united with Nḥbw.t. 123c.*

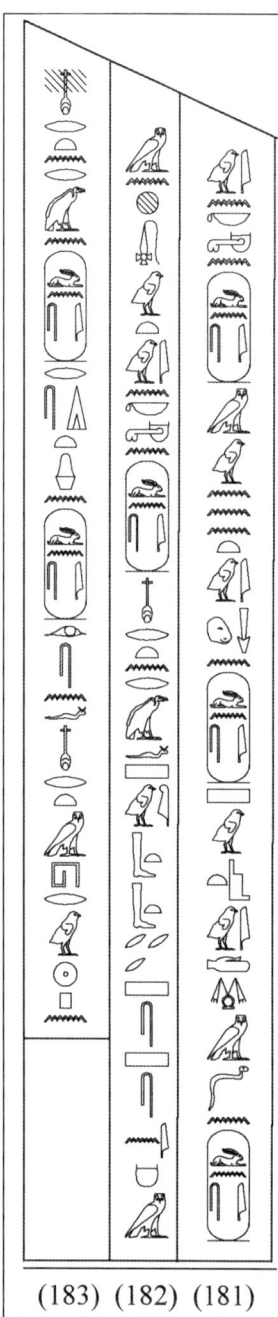

(183) (182) (181)

Abb. 1: Anordnung von PT 123a–e in der Sargkammer der Unas-Pyramide.

N. has copulated with his beloved, deprived of *tbtb* (grain?, seed?) and of *ššśs. 123d. But as to the beloved of N., she gives bread to N.; 123e. she did well by him in that day.*" [5]

(c) „*§ 123 The King has copulated with Mowet (Semen personified as a goddess?), the King has kissed Shuset (Meaning unknown.), the King has joined with Nekhebut (Fruitfulness personified? Cf. nhbt as an epithet of Nût in § 4a.), the King has copulated with the Beauteous One, for his dread is the lack of food and drink(?). Assuredly it is the Beauteous One who cares for the King, she gives bread to the King and she treats him well today.*" [6]

Dem Pyramidentext können eine Variante des MR {Grabstein des *wr-mḏ-šmˁw Nḥy* (Abydos, mittlere Nekropole)[7]} und des NR {Hatschepsut-Tempel (Deir el-Bahari, südliche Opferhalle, Südwand)[8]} gegenübergestellt werden (Abbildung 2).

Im Kontext des PT-Spruchs 205, der zu den „*Zaubersprüchen gegen Hunger und Durst*" gehört,[9] geht der tote König in PT 123a–d mit diesem Ziel engste Beziehungen mit vier wegen dieser Nähe als göttlich zu bezeichnenden Prinzipien ein,[10] die ohne Zweifel als Personifikationen zu bezeichnen sind.[11]

Die die Wechselwirkung des Königs mit den vier Gottheiten beschreibenden Verben sind *nk, sn, dmḏ* und wiederum *nk*. Dabei steht der erotische Charakter von *nk* gemäß Wb II 345,3 („*den Beischlaf vollziehen*") außer Frage. Ihm darf als rituelle Handlung keinerlei negative Bedeutung unterstellt werden.[12] Bei *sn* ist kaum an „*eine Frau küssen (als Liebesbezeigung)*" (Wb IV 153,11) zu denken, sondern an das Berühren der Nasen von König und Gottheit zur „*Belebung des Königs ..., wobei der Atem des Gottes die göttl. Kraft auf den König überträgt.*" [13]

Auch *dmḏ m* ... meint keine geschlechtliche Vereinigung „*mit einer Frau*" (Wb V 458,11)[14]. Es ist anzunehmen, daß eine Prozeßdurchführung beschrieben wird, deren Resultat eine Einheit wie der ![Hieroglyphen] *dmḏi* ('Vereinigte')[15] der Sonnenlitanei darstellt. Eine entsprechende Bedeutung hat das Verbum in PT 941c[P] und PT 942a[P], die somit als 'zur Einheit werden mit ...' wiedergegeben werden darf.

Die Bedeutung von *šw* schließt an Wb IV 426, 16 („*von Personen. ohne etw. sein, eine Sache nicht besitzen*")[16] oder Wb IV 427,14 („*fehlen, nicht vorhanden sein*") an. Es liegt dann ein Partizip (*masc. sg.*)[17] oder eine Relativform vor.

Anders als in der Übersetzung von Faulkner soll *nr* hier in keinem Fall als Verbum aufgefaßt werden.[18]

Nicht eindeutig ist die Zuordnung der maskulinen Form von *šw* in PT 123c zu Unas (wie es Mercer betont)[19] oder zu *Nfr.t-nr*. Die letztere wird hier vorgeschlagen, angeregt durch die Übersetzung (a) sowie die jüngeren Textvarianten, welche die

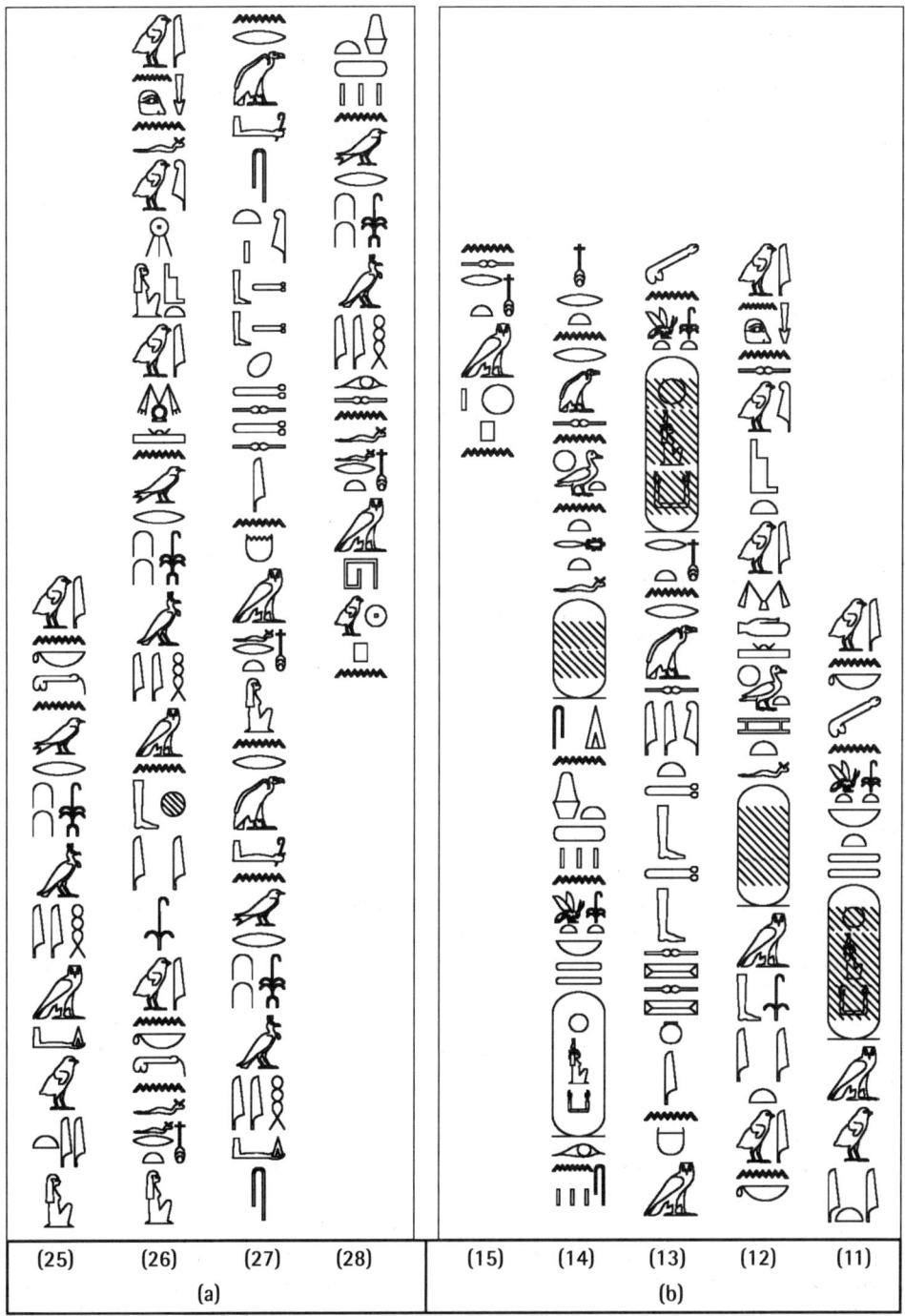

(25)	(26)	(27)	(28)	(15)	(14)	(13)	(12)	(11)
	(a)					(b)		

Abb. 2: Varianten zu PT 123a–e (a) Grabstein des Nehy (MR), (b) Tempel der Hatschepsut in Deir el-Bahari.

51

Lesungen *nr=s šw.t/šw.yt ṯbṯb ṯzṯz/zšzš* und die Übersetzung „*Sie [Nfr.t] ist schrecklich, (indem) sie ṯbṯb und ṯzṯz/zšzš nicht besitzt.*" erlauben.[20] Somit soll angenommen werden, daß die PT-Version die Aussage des Zugleichs von Schönheit/Vollendetheit (*nfr.t*) und Schrecklichem (*nrw*) in der zweikomponentig-androgynen Personifikation *Nfr.t-nr* zusammenfaßt, während sie zumindest bei Nehy sinnerhaltend in zwei Anteile aufgeteilt wurde. *šw* bezieht sich dann auf die zweite Komponente der *Nfr.t-nr*, diese begründend.[21]

Statt einer weiteren Übersetzung möge eine freie Inhaltsangabe von PT 123a–e gegeben werden: Unas geht durch Kopulation eine enge Beziehung zur *Mw.t* ein, um seine Zeugungskraft zu garantieren. Wiederbelebende Kraft gewinnt er durch den (Nasen)kuß mit *šw-s.t* und wird zur Einheit mit *N(i)-ḥ.wt*. Als eine solche begattet er ein viertes Prinzip, das als *Nfr.t-nr* Schönheit/Vollkommenheit als auch Schrecklichkeit besitzt. Deren Zustand wird durch einen (vorläufigen) Mangel an *tbtb* und *ššš* angezeigt,[22] er kann auch als Jungfräulichkeit verstanden werden. Als Resultat der ehelichen Vereinigung des Unas/*Ni-ḥ.wt* mit *Nfr.t-nr* bringt diese ihm zu seinem Nutzen die Frucht der Erde zur Welt.

Interessanterweise finden sich inhaltlich ähnliche Aussagen im „*600. Kapitel*" des Amunshymnus pLeiden I 350:[23] *ḥ.t=f Nnw ỉmỉ st ḥꜥpỉ ḥr ms nt.t nb.t sꜥnḫ wnn.t ḥḥ=f ṯꜢw r šr.t nb.t šꜢ.yt Rnn.t ḫr=f n bw-nb ḥm.t=f JꜢḫ.t stỉ=f r=s mtw.t=f ḫt n ꜥnḫ rḏw=f npr*, wobei zu beachten ist, daß Amun-Re (*=f*) *a priori* als vereinheitlichte Gottheit vorausgesetzt wird.

Personifizierte Elemente

Personifikationen sind in den Pyramidentexten keine Seltenheit. Erik Hornung bezeichnet ihr Entstehen als einen Prozeß, „*der zu der Gestaltwerdung von Göttern vielfache Verbindungen hat.*"[24] So ist es nicht auszuschließen, daß die vier Personifikationen in PT 123a–d zumindest teilweise Gottheiten wurden, die wie Schu und Tefnut nach W. Barta „*kosmische Elemente*" repräsentieren.[25]

Daß die Ägypter solche für ihre welttheoretischen Betrachtungen formuliert hatten, zeigt beispielsweise CT VI 280s–u, 281a–c:

In der Entstehungsreihenfolge der Neunheit wird entsprechend der ersten Position mit den getrennten *p.t tꜢ*[26] ihr trennendes Prinzip Schu und gemäß der zweiten mit *mw* und *nnw* „*die als Tefnut Gestalt gewordene Feuchte ..., das Urelement des Wassers*"[25] impliziert. CT VI 280s–u nennt somit die Elemente 'Himmel', 'Erde', 'Luft' und 'Wasser', wobei die beiden ersteren ebenfalls mit Geb und Nut Erwähnung finden.[27]

Auch Empedokles führt in περὶ φύσεως die Vierzahl seiner Elemente nicht - wie für einen Griechen zu erwarten - als Begriffe ein, sondern bild- und gleichnishaft als göttliche Personifikationen:[28]

τέσσαρα γὰρ πάντων ῥιζώματα πρῶτον ἄκονε-
Ζεὺς ἀργὴς Ἥρη τε φερέσβιος ἠδὲ Ἀιδωνεύς
Νῆστίς θ᾽, ἣ δακρύοις κρούνωμα βρότειον.[29]

Dabei besteht hinsichtlich der Gleichsetzung des Zeus mit dem 'Feuer' und der sizilischen Göttin Nestis mit dem 'Wasser' bei allen antiken und modernen Kommentatoren Übereinstimmung.[30] Anders verhält es sich bei der Zuordnung von Hera und dem mit Hades identischen Aidoneus zu 'Erde' und 'Luft'. Ohne auf Einzelheiten einzugehen, die einer in Vorbereitung befindlichen gesonderten Publikation vorbehalten sind, sei hier nur erwähnt, daß Platon, Cicero, Philodelmos, Menandros, Eusebios, Macrobius und Aëtios Hera mit der Luft, dagegen Probus, Pseudo-Herakleitos, Athenagoras, Diogenes Laërtios, Hyppolytos und Stobaios mit der Erde in Verbindung brachten, wobei in den meisten Fällen eine Zuweisung des jeweils komplementären Elements an Hades erfolgte.

Wechselseitige Zuordnung der Gottheiten des Pyramiden- und Empedokles-Texts

Bei der Annahme, daß die vier Gottheiten in PT 123a–d Element-Personifikationen sind, die mit denen des Empedokles vergleichbar sind, darf man im ägyptischen Text dieselbe Gleichverteilung des Geschlechts (2:2) erwarten, wie sie im griechischen vorgefunden wird.

Offensichtlich bereitet die wechselseitige Abbildung der weiblichen Gottheiten *Mw.t* und Nestis wie ihre Zuordnung zu 'Wasser', 'Sperma' oder allgemein 'Feuchtheit' kein Problem.

Übersetzt man *šw-s.t* in Analogie zu Wb IV 4,16–19; 5,1–8 (*wsḫ-s.t, wʿb-s.t, Nfr(.t)-s.t, ḫntí -s.t, št3-s.t, ḏsr-s.t*) 'Einer, dessen Platz/Raum leer ist', so ist eventuell an eine ausführliche Namensvariante für Schu zu denken, der sich *„als die Personifikation des trockenen, leeren Luftraums verstehen"* läßt.[31] *šw-s.t* ist somit gleich Schu der Leerraum zwischen Himmel und Erde (vgl. CT VI 280s), erfüllt mit Luft, deren Einatmen lebenswichtig ist und durch die Handlung *sn* mit einem Gott belebend wirkt.

Obwohl immer wieder diskutiert, bleibt es doch wahrscheinlich, daß dem Namen Ἄιδης bzw. Ἀϊδωνεύς die Bedeutung 'unsichtbar', 'nicht anzusehen' mit der Wurzel *ἀ-Ϝιδ zugrunde liegt. Diese Ähnlichkeit zu der nicht sichtbaren Leere, die Tatsache, daß Schu und Hades „theoretische" Götter ohne Kultstätte sind und einige weitere, an anderer Stelle ausführlicher zu behandelnde Argumente im Zusammenhang mit dem griechischen Gott, sprechen dafür, daß diese beiden männlichen Gottheiten das Element 'Luft' personifizieren.

Es kann vermutet werden, daß die späteren Schreibungen *Nḫby.t/Nḫbw.t* für ⬚𓏺𓆼 darauf zurückzuführen sind, daß man bei der Wiederverwendung des PT-Spruches die ursprüngliche Bedeutung des Wortes nicht mehr kannte und deshalb eine Substitution mit dem vertrauteren und dem Kontext gemäßen Namen *Nḫb.t* einer Personifikation der Fruchtbarkeit (Wb II 309,1) vornahm.

Obwohl mit der Nisbe *n(i)* bzw. *n.t* gebildete Götternamen mit der Bedeutung 'Der/die zu ...gehört' sehr selten sind, wird für ⬚𓏺𓆼 eine solche Bildung mit der Lesung *Ni-ḫ.wt* 'Der zu den Feuern/dem Feurigen gehört' vorgeschlagen.[32] Als Parallelbeispiel sei auf die Gottheit Nr. 867 in der 12. Stunde des Amduat 𓏴𓏴 hingewiesen,[33] die Hornung *Ni-skmw* liest und *„Der zu den grauen (Haaren) gehört"* übersetzt.[34]

Die Personifikation *Ni-ḫ.wt* des Feuerelements ist demnach maskulin wie ihr Pendant Zeus, den die Griechen mit Amun bzw. in seinem Aspekt als Sonnengottheit mit Amun-Re gleichstellten, wie sie es andererseits mit Hera und Mut taten.[35]

Die drei dem Feuer bzw. der Sonne in Verbindung stehenden Gottheiten *Ni-ḫ.wt*, Zeus und Amun-Re haben jeweils eheliche Beziehungen zu *Nfr.t-nr*,[36] Hera bzw. Mut, von denen wiederum mit einigen Argumenten wahrscheinlich gemacht werden kann, daß sie der Erde bzw. dem Erdelement nahe stehen. In der nachfolgenden Übersicht sind in einer jeweiligen Auswahl von Hinweisen die Erdbezogenheit und weitere vergleichbare Eigenschaften dieser drei Göttinnen belegt:

53

GÖTTIN	ERDBEZOGENHEIT	SCHÖNHEIT	SCHRECKLICHKEIT
Nfr.t-nr	Nach Begattung mit dem durch 'Wasser' und 'Luft' zeugungs- und lebensfähigen feurigen, sonnig-warmem Prinzip Hervorbringen von Brot (= pflanzliche Nahrungsmittel), Analogie zu Empedokles' Element +Ηρη[37]	*nfr.t*	*nr(w)*
Hera	„Berührungspunkte" mit „chtonischen Gottheiten" veranlaßt „Gleichstellung von H. mit der Erde", „ursprüngliche chtonische Göttin"[38]	Wettstreit um den goldenen Apfel, Homerische Hymnen	Schrecklich in Eifersucht und Rache, einer „zornigen Erdengöttin, einer Demeter Erinys oder Graia, ähnlich"[39], parthenogenetische Zeugung des Typhon (= Seth)
Mut[40]	Beifügungen: *wtt w3ḫ.y(t)* ('welche die Kornfülle gebiert', IX,4), *srwḏ rnpw.t nb(.t)* ('die alle Ackerpflanzen/-früchte gedeihen läßt', IX,7), *dgs=s nb.t w3ḏ,* ('alles, was du betrittst, grünt', XI,5)		Anrufung als Sachmet (*Sḫm.t <m> bḏš r=n*, XIX, 3-4, u.ä.)

GÖTTIN	ZYKLISCHE JUNGFRÄULICHKEIT	ANDROGYNE GOTTHEIT[41]	EHEGÖTTIN
Nfr.t-nr	Leersein an *tbtb* und *šsšs*, gedanklicher (jahres)zeitlich-zyklischer Durchlauf in PT 123a-e für ewige Versorgung des Unas	Name	–
Hera	jährliches Bad in der Quelle Kanathos bei Nauplia[42]	Ἥρη δ' Ἥφαιστον κλυτὸν οὐ ὑλότητι μιγεῖσα (Hesiod, *Theogonie* 927)	Schützerin der Ehe
Mut		Darstellung bei Lanzone[43]	Muttergöttin

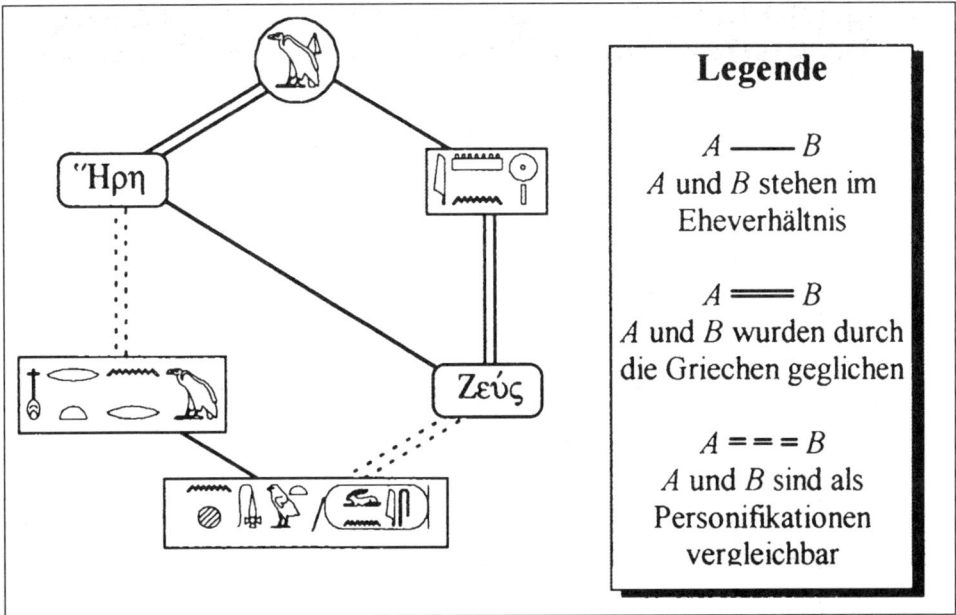

Abb. 3: Relationen zwischen den Göttern Zeus, Amun-Re und *Ni-ḫ.wt* sowie Hera, Mut und *Nfr.t-nr*.

Bezeichnet man die Relation des Eheverhältnisses mit einer einfachen Linie (————) und die der Gleichung mit einer doppelten (⹀), so ergibt sich das Diagramm der Abbildung 3, das nunmehr auf Grund der zusammengestellten Ähnlichkeiten sowie dem Vergleich der Personifikationen in PT 123a–d und im Empedokles-Fragment durch eine zusätzliche Vergleichbarkeitsrelation (Kennzeichnung: = = =) ergänzt werden kann.

Das durch den Vergleich des ägyptischen und griechischen Textes gewonnene Ergebnis zeigt Abbildung 4. Ohne sie zu kommentieren, werden die Interpretationen der ägyptischen Bezeichnungen wiedergegeben, welche zwei Wörterbücher darbieten. An den aufgeführten griechischen Begriffen, die Empedokles neben denen der Personifikationen für seine Elemente benutzte,[44] läßt sich deren Zuordnung zu den ägyptischen und griechischen Gottheiten ablesen. Abschließend sei darauf hingewiesen, daß diese durch die Herstellung von Relationen zwischen den theoretischen Vorstellungen zweier Kulturen möglich wurde, die äußerlich recht unterschiedlich erscheinen, deren innere Übereinstimmung auf Grund der universellen Gleichheit menschlichen Denkens und dessen zeitlich und räumlich kaum variierenden Basis vorausgesetzt werden darf.

Unas	Nehy	Hatschepsut	Wh[a]	Empedokles	Handwb[b]
Mw.t	?		II 53,11 *mw.t* Bez. einer Göttin (Personifikation des Samens ?)	Νῆστις θάλασσα ὄμβρος πόντος ὕδωρ	S. 1208 *Mmt f* Memet, "Hervorquellendes Wasser" (e. *Personifikation*)
šw-s.t			IV 423,9 Ob *Sws.t* ? neben anderen Personifikationen wie *mwt*, *nḥbw.t*	Ἀϊδωνεύς ἀήρ αἰθήρ αὐγή (εἶδος) οὐρανός	S. 1242 *šw-sti* Shusti
Ni-ḫ.wt			II 308,15 *nḥbw.t* eine Göttin vgl. *nḥb.t* Personifikation der Fruchtbarkeit	Ζεύς ἠέλιος ἠλέκτωρ ἥλιος Ἥφαιστος πῦρ φλόξ	S. 1217 *Nḥby* *Nechbi* *Nḥbt f* "Knospung" (e. *Personifikation*)
Nfr.t-nr			II 278,11 *nfr.t nr* die Geliebte jemds. (mit folg. männl. Genitivexponenten)	Ἥρη αἶα γαῖα γῆ χθών	–

Abb. 4: Gegenüberstellung der ägyptischen und griechischen Bezeichnungen.

[a] Zur vorgeschlagenen Lesung und deren Übersetzung s. Text.

[b] Den Angaben des Wb liegen nur der PT und die MR-Variante zugrunde.

[c] R. Hanning *Großes Handwörterbuch Ägyptisch*. Mainz 1995.

Abkürzungen

Die Abkürzungen folgen der von S. Grunert und J.S. Karig herausgegebenen „*Liste der Abkürzungen und Kurztitel in ägyptologischen Publikationen*" (International Association of Egyptologists, *egyptology* 2, Berlin 1964) mit der Ausnahme, daß statt 'Pyr' 'PT' verwendet wurde.

Dank

Für hilfreiche Unterstützung und Beratung bei der Anfertigung der Arbeit bin ich dem Leiter, Herrn Priv.-Doz. Dr. S. Seidlmayer, und allen Mitarbeitern des Akademie-Vorhabens „Altägyptisches Wörterbuch" der Berlin-Brandenburgischen Akademie der Wissenschaften zu Dank verpflichtet.

Anmerkungen:

1 S. Morenz, Die Begegnung Europas mit Ägypten, *SSAW* 113(5) (1968), 128.

2 Dieser PT-Spruch ist nur in der Sargkammer der Unas-Pyramide (Ostwand) belegt.

3 Die Darstellung folgt den Blättern 3A, 3B, 4A und 4B (Zeilen 181–183) aus dem Abklatscharchiv der Berlin-Brandenburgischen Akademie der Wissenschaften, Inv.-Nr. 1298 (*Pyramidentexte VII*, Kasten Nr. 591).

4 Wb, Belegst. *Pyramidentexte Kap. 3 nach W. 181–183 <123>*

5 S.A.B. Mercer, *The Pyramid Texts, Vol. I*, New York-London-Toronto 1952, 56.

6 R.O. Faulkner, *The Ancient Egyptian Pyramid Texts,* Oxford 1969, 38. In Klammern gesetzte Einfügungen sind im Original Fußnoten. Das angesprochene Epitheton der Nut in PT 4a^T ⌒◡ stimmt hinsichtlich der Schreibung nicht unmittelbar mit derjenigen der Personifikation in PT 123b^W überein.

7 CG 20520, H.O. Lange/H. Schäfer, *CGC 20001–20780, Grab- und Gedenksteine des Mittleren Reichs, Theil II*, Berlin 1908, 119; *Theil IV*, Berlin 1902, Tf. 36.

8 Nach E. Naville, The Temple of Deir el-Bahari, Part IV, *EEF* 19 (1901), pl. 110.

9 Zu dieser Bezeichnung für die Sprüche 204–212 vgl. J. Spiegel, Das Auferstehungsritual der Unas-Pyramide, *ÄA* 23 (1971), Abb. 3.

10 Es wird relativiert werden, daß dieses Verhältnis ausschließlich erotischer Natur ist, wie es S.A.B. Mercer, *The Pyramid Texts, Vol. II*, New York/London/Toronto 1952, 65 darstellt.

11 Vgl. S.A.B. Mercer, *The Pyramid Texts, Vol. IV*, New York/London/Toronto 1952, 56–57.

12 Sie findet sich in neuägyptischen Texten wie *smi r p3 nk i-ir=f ʿnḫ(.t) n nw.t* ... (pTurin 1887, rt. 1,5; RAD 74,11, „*Klage über die Unzucht, die er mit der Bürgerin ... betrieb.*") oder *mk ḥrw nk=k mw.t=f 3s.t*, den Wb, Belegst. *Pap. Mag. Harris VII 9–10 <57>* mit „*siehe Horus*[,] *er hat seine Mutter Isis vergewaltigt*" übersetzt. Selbst in PT 239b^W ist nk positiv zu werten, da es die immerwährende Macht des Königs verdeutlicht. Ähnliche Grundbedeutung findet sich in PT 510b^W, 1321a^P.

13 R. Schlichting, s.v. Kuß, küssen, *LÄ* III (1980), 901. Als Illustration s. den Nasenkuß von Sesostris I. und Ptah auf dem Pfeiler JE 36809 (M. Saleh-H. Sourouzian, *Die Hauptwerke im Ägyptischen Museum Kairo*, Mainz 1986, Nr. 86). Sie verdeutlicht, daß beide Partner durchaus maskulin sein können.

14 Hier und Wb IV 153,11 läßt die Gleichsetzung von „*Frau*" mit einer weiblichen Gottheit die Aussage unverändert.

15 E. Hornung, Das Buch der Anbetung des Re im Westen (Sonnenlitanei), Teil I, *AH* 2 (1975), 1.122.179.180.239; Teil II, *AH* 3 (1976), 61.77.84.92. Hornung, Sonnenlitanei II, 99 kommentiert: „*Offenbar ist dmḏ(i) eine spezielle Bezeichnung für die Verbindung von Re und Osiris zu einer Gestalt*".

16 Es liegt eine auch anderweitig belegte Weglassung der Präposition *m* vor. Beispiele (mit *m*): PT 1455c[P] (*n šw p.t m Ppy pn, n šw t3 pn m Ppy pn d.t: Der Himmel wird nicht ohne diesen Pepi sein, diese Erde wird nicht ohne diesen Pepi sein ewiglich.*) und ähnlich PT 363c[P] sowie Urk. V 19,11 (= Tb. Kap. 17, Abschn. 9: *ir.ti=fi pw šw.ti m tp=f. Es sind seine Augen, die an seinem Kopfe nicht vorhanden sind.*).

17 Da in den Pyramidentexten „*das fem. sg. ... ganz regelmäßig mit der Femininendung ⌒t versehen*" ist (C.E. Sander-Hansen, *Studien zur Grammatik der Pyramidentexte*, Kopenhagen 1956, 52), ließe sich eine defektive Schreibung diskutieren (vgl. Übersetzung (a)), welche die Varianten des MR und NR nahe legen, die aber nicht wahrscheinlich ist.

18 Faulkner, *Pyramid Texts*, 38 stellt das erste *nr(i)/nr(w)* als auf den König bezogenen 'Schrecken' (Wb II 277,4.11) dem zweiten *nr(i)* 'sich sorgen, (be)hüten' (Wb II 278,15) der *Nfr.t* als Wortspiel gegenüber. Gegen den direkten Bezug von *Nfr.t* und *nr* in PT 123d, den die Übersetzung (c) voraussetzt, spricht das Fehlen der Femininendung (s.o.). Wahrscheinlich hat sich Faulkner an der Version von Deir el-Bahari orientiert (vgl. seine Deutung von *šsšs* als Getränk [?] wegen des Determinativs ⊃ in [13]), in der [13-14] gelesen werden kann: *in hm Nfr.t nr=s n z3.t* etc. („*Es ist aber Nfr.t, sie sorgt sich für die Tochter ...*"), was seiner Auffassung entgegenkommt, aber der grammatischen Form in PT 123d entgegensteht.

19 Mercer, *Pyramid Texts II*, 65. Offensichtlich ist auch Faulkner dieser Meinung.

20 Im Falle der Deir el-Bahari-Variante kann sich das Personalsuffix *=s* auch auf die Königin in folgerichtiger Abwandlung des maskulinen *=f* in PT 123c beziehen.

21 Eventuell ist *šw tbtb šsšs* ein eigener Satz: „*tbtb und šsšs fehlen (ihr)*". Die jüngeren Versionen hätten dann die Form, nicht aber den Sinn abgewandelt.

22 Eine Diskussion dieser Begriffe erfolgt in einer gesonderten Darlegung, in der vorgeschlagen wird, daß diese Aufzählung das Leersein an allem Lebensnotwendigen, das der Boden enthalten kann, ausgedrückt.

23 A. H. Gardiner, Hymns to Amon from a Leiden Papyrus, *ZÄS* 42 (1905), 38–39; A. Erman, *Die Literatur der Ägypter*, Leipzig 1923, 372.

24 Hornung, Sonnenlitanei II, 33.

25 W. Barta, Untersuchungen zum Götterkreis der Neunheit, *MÄS* 28 (1973), 91.

26 Die originale Anordnung ist ⌐⌐ ⊤ ⌐⌐ .

27 Das ägyptische Element *p.t* oder *Nw.t* ist wegen der dort glänzenden Sonne und Sterne dem griechischen Feuer (πῦρ, auch ἥλιος, Ζεύς ἀργής) zu vergleichen. Während oᵃranøq bei Empedokles einmal die Luft vertritt, benutzt es Hesiod (*Theogonie* 737) als Feuer. Andererseits wird der von Empedokles nur als Luftelement verwendete αἰθήρ von Cicero, Pseudo-Herakleitos, Aëtios und Stobaios dem 'Feuer' zugeordnet.

28 Von den vier genannten wird nur Nestis in einem zweiten Fragment erwähnt. In zwei Belegstellen fungiert Hephaistos bei Empedokles als Feuer-Personifikation.

29 Fragment B6 mit der Übersetzung „*Denn die vier Wurzelkräfte aller Dinge höre zuerst: Zeus der schimmernde und Here die lebenspendende sowie Aidoneus und Nestis, die durch ihre Tränen irdisches Quellwasser fließen läßt.*" aus H. Diels, *Die Fragmente der Vorsokratiker*, 1. Band., Berlin [7]1954, 311–312.

30 Der Name wird gewöhnlich von νάω ('fließen') abgeleitet (K. Preisendanz, s.v. Nēstis, *PW* 33 (1936), 108). Als sizilische Göttin nennen sie Eustathius (καὶ Σικελικὴ δέ τις, φασί, θεὸς Νῆστις ἐλέγετο. *Eustathii Archiepiscopi Thessalonicensis commentarii ad Homeri Iliadem, Tomus IV*, Leipzig 1830, 122) und Photius (Νῆστις: Σικελικὴ θεός· Ἄλεξις. R. Porson, *Photii Lexicon, Pars prior*, Leipzig 1823, 257). Mit Νῆστις δὲ καὶ κρούνωμα βρότειον ο·ονεὶ τὸ σπέρμα καὶ τὸ ὕδωρ ordnen Aëtios (H. Diels, *Doxographi graeci.*, Berlin [3]1958, 287) und Stabaios (K. Wachsmuth, *Ioannis Stobaei anthologii libri duo priores qui inscribi solent Eclogea physicae et ethicae, Vol. I.*, Berlin 1884, 121) Nestis dem Wasser und dem Samen (Sperma) zu. Da auch *mw* für 'Samen' gebraucht wird (Wb II 52,11), ist die Interpretation der *Mw.t* als „*Personifikation des Samens ?*" (Wb II 53,11) in den Übersetzungen nicht ohne griechische Parallele. Νῆστις δὲ τὸ ὕδωρ· findet sich bei Diogenes Laërtios (R. D. Hicks, *Diogenes Laertius: Lives of Eminent*

58

Philosophers, Vol. II., London-Cambridge/Mass. 1958, 390) und Hippolytos (P. Wendland, *Hippolytus Werke, 3. Band,* Leipzig 1916, 211). Es gibt allerdings einige wenige Andeutungen, daß Nestis auch für die Luft stehen kann, auf die aber erst in einer gesonderten Publikation eingegangen wird.

31 Barta, Neunheit, 86.

32 Die Diskussion weiterer Schwierigkeiten wie der sonst nicht belegte Plural von *ḥ.t* ('Feuer', Wb III 217, 10-20; 218, 1-13) und die in den Pyramidentexten erwähnte Gottheit ⬡ 𓍯𓏏𓊖 (*Nḥb.t*, Wb II 308,14) wird in einer späteren Arbeit erfolgen.

33 E. Hornung, Texte zum Amduat, Teil III, *AH* 15 (1994), 826.

34 E. Hornung, Das Amduat, die Schrift des Verborgenen Raumes, Teil II, *ÄA* 7 (1963), 189.

35 Für Herodot vgl. G. Strasburger, *Lexikon zur frühgriechischen Geschichte,* Zürich-München 1984, 154 [s.v. Götter], für Diodor s. Th. Hopfner, Plutarch über Isis und Osiris, I. Teil, *ArchivOr* 9 (1940), 18 mit der bei Herodot nicht nachweisbaren Gleichsetzung von Hera und Mut.

36 Für *Ni-ḥ.wt* ausgedrückt durch seine Einswerdung mit Unas (s.o.) und dessen Kopulation mit *Nfr.t-nr*.

37 Bei Anerkennung der Zuordnungen *Mw.t* → Nestis, *šw-s.t* → Aidoneus und *Ni-ḥ.wt* → Zeus kann schließlich *Nfr.t-nr* → Hera gefolgert werden.

38 S. Eitrem, s.v. Hera VIII, *PW* 15 (1912), 398-399.

39 Eitrem, Hera, 399.

40 Die Angaben beziehen sich auf den „*Hymnus an Mut"* (pBerlin 3053).

41 Urelemente können möglicherweise aus demselben Grunde wie Urgötter androgyn sein (s. W. Westendorf, s.v. Götter, androgyne, *LÄ* II (1977), 633-635). Der Name *Nfr.t-nr* (und auch *šw-s.t*) ergänzt die nicht lange Liste zweigeschlechtiger Gottheitsbezeichnungen wie *Ni.t-šr* (= Neith-Osiris = Nr. 803 bei Hornung, *Amduat III,* 779; Hornung, *Amduat II,* 180).

42 ἐντα θα τὴν Ἥραν φασὶν Ἀργεῖοι κατὰ ἔτος λουμένην παρθένον γίννσθαι. (Pausanias, Buch II 38,2. F. Spiro, *Pausaniae Graeciae Descriptio, Vol. I,* Stuttgart 1959, 229-230).

43 R. V. Lanzone, *Dizionario di mitologia egizia,* Torino 1886, tav. 136. *«La dia è rappresentata fallofera e pterofera»* (Lanzone, *Dizionario* (1881), 335).

44 Hierfür wurde M. R. Wright, *Empedocles: The Extant Fragments,* New Haven-London 1981 benutzt. Soweit zu erkennen ist, ergibt sich durch A. Martin-O. Primavesi, *L'Empédocle de Strasbourg,* Berlin/New York 1999 keine Veränderung.

Consolidation and Restoration of Monuments and Sites: Tomb No. 1703, Anch-Ib, Western Cemetery, Giza Plateau

Samiha J. Basta
Research & Conservation Center, The Supreme Council for Antiquities (S.C.A.)

The aim of the work was to discover suitable techniques and materials for the consolidation and restoration of a mud-brick monument (Tomb of Anch-Ib, Western Cemetery). The experimental materials used were Befix (acid mineralic hardener for natural silicates) and Namex (complex of an organic polymer with silicate chemical-reactive groups in aqueous solution). Two methods were tried, namely surface coating and surface brushing. These gave good results for restoration and consolidation. The results showed no change in the physical and chemical properties of the treated materials.

Introduction

Consolidation is the physical addition or application of adhesive or supportive materials into the actual fabric of the monument in order to ensure its continued durability or structural integrity. Restoration is intended to revive the original concept or legibility of the object. Damage and destruction to the tomb caused by humidity, chemical agents, and all types of pests and microorganisms must be stopped in order to preserve the object or the structure. The consolidating materials that used were Namex and Befix. Namex was used in one of the most damaged parts of the tomb as consolidating material to complete the missing parts. The missing parts must integrate harmoniously with the whole but at the same time must be distinguishable from the original, so that restoration does not falsify the artistic or historic evidence. Befix has also been used for the consolidation of other parts of the tomb. Two methods have been used, namely surface coating and surface brushing. The efficiency of any material depends mainly upon the properties of the monuments and its stage of deterioration, as well as the properties and chemical composition of the consolidating materials. The consolidating materials chosen for their preservation should not change the physical and chemical properties of the treated materials.

The Experiment

Two techniques were used for the consolidation and stabilization of mud brick (adobe) namely, brushing with Befix and coating with Namex. Part of the mud brick of the tomb was brushed with diluted Befix starting with 1:5, 1:3, 1:2, and finally a 1:1 solution of Befix to limewater. The first treatment must always be preceded by thorough mechanical cleaning and drying of the surface. A mixture of Namex cement and sand was used to coat most surfaces of the tomb. The Namex mixture was prepared by thoroughly mixing sand, cement, and Namex in the proportion of (1:1:0.3) and water. The mixing of Namex with cement resulted in a new silicate material of high-quality performance.[1]

The analyses carried out before and after treatment were:
1) Percentage of porosity was determined using Porosimeter 2000
2) Calculation of percentage of water absorption
3) Determination of pH values
4) Mineralogical and elemental analyses were determined using X-ray diffraction,[2] and the scanning electron-microscope (SEM) [3]

Results and Discussion

Description of the tomb

The tomb is rectangular in plan. Its dimensions are 36 x 15 x 12 m. It is built of mud brick and has two shafts. The eastern wall of the tomb has three false doors. The first one has a small depression 26 cm wide. On the upper part of the false door there are two limestone steps. The upper step carries the name of the wife (Khentytes). The lower step is in the shape of a half-circle and carries the name of the owner (Anch-Ib). The upper part of the false door was destroyed. The third false door (south) has a step from limestone. There is an inscription indicating the name of the owner (Anch-Ib) who was an Overseer of Workmen. The tomb dates to the early Fifth Dynasty.[4]

Physical characteristics

1) The total porosity, measured by Porosimeter 2000, reached 37 percent before treatment and decreased to 22 percent after treatment with Befix and seven percent after treatment with Namex.
2) The percentage of water absorption reached 7.6 before treatment and 7.4 after treatment with Namex.

Chemical and Mineralogical Analyses

1) pH Value Analysis:

The pH value reached 12.6 before treatment and 12.7 after treatment with Namex, while in the case of Befix, there was no change in pH value.

2) X-ray Diffraction Analysis:

a. The X-ray diffraction pattern of the treated mud brick sample from the tomb of Anch-Ib is presented in figure 1a. It indicates that free quartz SiO_2 is the predominant mineral, followed by mainly calcium carbonate, traces of dolomite, and a minor amount of clay mineral, namely montmorillonite, albile, kaolinite, and illite in decreasing order.

b. This mineralogical composition did not change with treatment as detected from the X-ray diffraction pattern (fig. 1b).

3) Scanning Electron Microscope (SEM) Analysis:

The scanning electron microscope (SEM) plategraphs and analyses were carried out on samples of mudbrick before and after treatment. Different spots were tested and showed the following results:

a. Plate 1 shows the fabric of treated material before treatment. Notice the wide interconnected chambers between the unsorted subangular grains. Some pores are filled with fine material, i.e. clay. Rounded quartz grains are embedded in the clay matrix.

b. Platemicrograph of the sample after treatment with Befix in Plate 2, shows a network on the edge of the sample. The same plate shows the penetration of the treated material (Befix) through pores, binding the different grains and the blocks of the mud brick samples, leaving open passages for air and moisture. It can be noted that Befix produced a natural solid binding material without making any morphological changes in the treated materials.

c. Plate 3 is a platemicrograph of the sample after treatment with Namex showing the coating materials (Namex), consolidating and binding the grains of the mud brick sample.

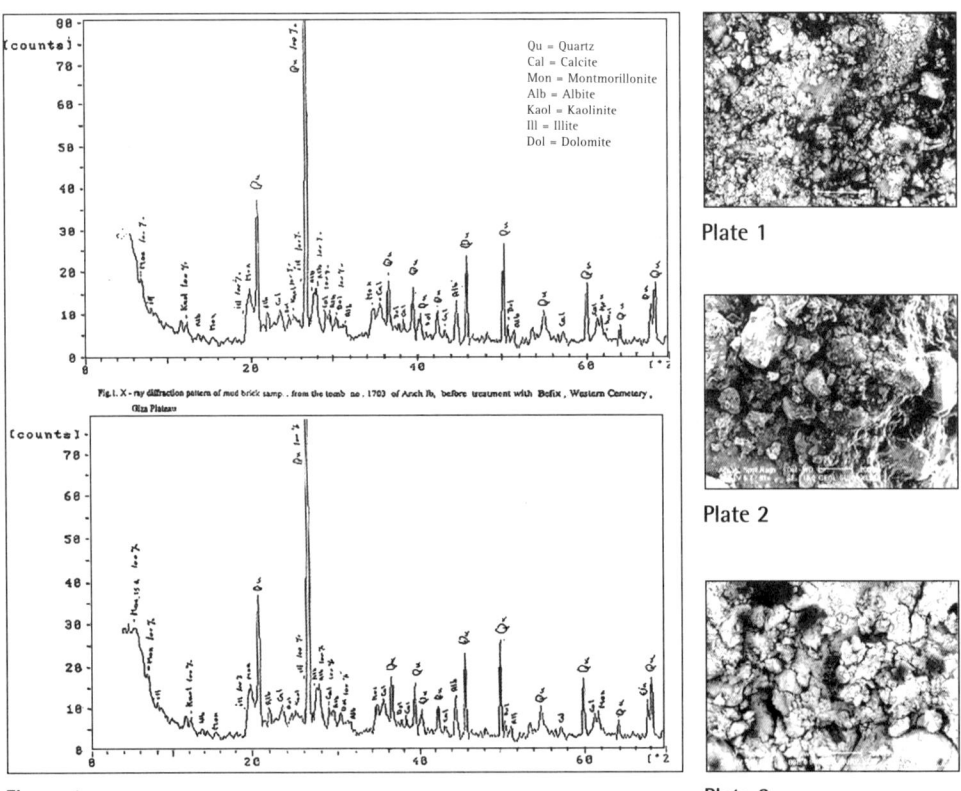

Qu = Quartz
Cal = Calcite
Mon = Montmorillonite
Alb = Albite
Kaol = Kaolinite
Ill = Illite
Dol = Dolomite

Fig.1. X - ray diffraction pattern of mud brick samp. . from the tomb no . 1703 of Anch Ib, before treatment with Befix , Western Cemetery , Giza Plateau

Plate 1

Plate 2

Plate 3

Figure 1

Conclusions

The consolidating materials selected to preserve the deteriorated mud brick of tomb no.1703, Anch-Ib, Western Cemetery, Giza Plateau, are Befix and Namex. Befix is the commercial name for an acid mineralic hardener for natural silicates, i.e. a siliceous solidifying agent, and Namex is the commercial name of a complex of organic polymer with silicate chemical-reactive groups in aqueous solutions.

The choice of these materials for consolidation in this work was mainly based on the percentage of clay minerals, especially montmorillonite. The results obtained show that Befix is a suitable consolidating material when the composition of mud brick contains lesser amounts of montmorillonite, and vice versa in the case of Namex.

Befix creates a silicate bond with the treated materials in the presence of limewater, leading to a new stable silicate compound. At the same time the surface becomes hydrophobic (water repellent). Its action can be demonstrated theoretically in the following steps:

1) Solubility reaction

$$Ca_2SiO_4 + 4H_3O^+ \xrightarrow{\text{acid effect}} 2\,Ca^{2+} + 4H_2O + H_4SiO_4$$

2) Crystallization reaction

$$2\,Ca^{2+} + 4H_2O + H_4SiO_4 \xrightarrow{\text{catalyst effect}} Ca_2SiO_4 + 4H_3O^+$$

An additional application of Namex mortar on the treated surface produced the desired stabilization and consolidation of the surface.

In this work, we have used cement instead of lime (used in the Roman Period), which reacts with the corrosion products in the presence of water, yielding an aqueous cement.

1) $2(3CaO.SiO_2) + 6\,H_2O \Rightarrow 3CaO.2SiO_2 \cdot 3\,H_2O + 3Ca(OH)_2$

2) $3Ca(OH)_2 + 2SiO_2 \Rightarrow 3CaO.2SiO_2$ (Aqueous Cement) $\cdot 3\,H_2O$

After the addition of the suitable silicate material (Namex) to the resultant aqueous cement, it will have poor capillary absorption, a high water vapor diffusion and a slightly higher elasticity than the treated materials, as well as an excellent adhesion to the treated surface. These applications have been tested specially on the severely deteriorated bricks, and gave excellent results.

It may be concluded that the existence of a unique preservation material or process is doubtful because many factors, such as the properties of the mud brick, causes and degree of deterioration, vary to a great extent from one structure to the other. The consolidation and restoration of each mud-brick structure should therefore be considered as an individual problem.

Notes:

1 Personal communications, Prof. Dr. Hugo Hubacek, Head of the Institute for Silicate Technology, Vienna, Austria.

2 ASTM (1968) Index (Inorganic) to the Powder Diffraction File, American Society for Testing and Materials.

3 SEM Model Philips XL 30 Attached with EDX Unit. Personal Communication, Egyptian Geological Survey and Mining Authority. Laboratories Sector, Cairo, Egypt.

4 Personal Communication, Dr. Zahi Hawass, Director General of the Giza Plateau, Supreme Council of Antiquities, Cairo, Egypt.

Geoarchaeological Evidence of the Relationships between the Terminal Drought in North Africa and the Rise of Ancient Egypt

Farouk El-Baz

Center for Remote Sensing, Boston University

Introduction

Like other scientific endeavors, geoarchaeology greatly benefited from advancements in space technology. During the last three decades, as space platforms began to photograph Earth, the value of the unique perspective from orbit became clear. When photographs taken at different times were compared, it was realized that they were ideal for understanding the changes to the environment in space and time.

Nowhere was this as important as in the understanding of the origin and evaluation of the arid landforms of Earth.[1] The desert remained the least geologically-known of all the features of Earth for three reasons:

1. Earth sciences began in Europe, which is the only continent on Earth that does not have a desert. Therefore, the fathers of geology did not write about arid landforms, and those who came after them followed suit. To this day, some textbooks about Earth lack a single chapter on desert features.

2. Arid lands are vast and harsh; therefore, few researchers venture into them because of the immensity of scale and the dangers of desert travel.

3. In the course of fieldwork, geologists seek solid rock *in situ*, to sample for later study. Most desert surfaces, however, are covered by transported mixtures of rock fragments, soil, and sand. Therefore, there is little for the conventional geologist to do in a desert.

During the last three decades, space photography presented us with a new tool to study the deserts, because: a) arid regions are usually free of clouds and are easy to photograph from above; b) space photographs cover large areas and allow the recognition of regional patterns; c) due to the lack or scarcity of vegetation cover, a space photograph can be considered a map of the chemical composition of the exposed rocks, soils, and sands; and d) radar waves are able to penetrate the sand cover and reveal the buried topography, illuminating environmental conditions of the past.

Photographs of the Western Desert of Egypt were utilized during the past 25 years to better

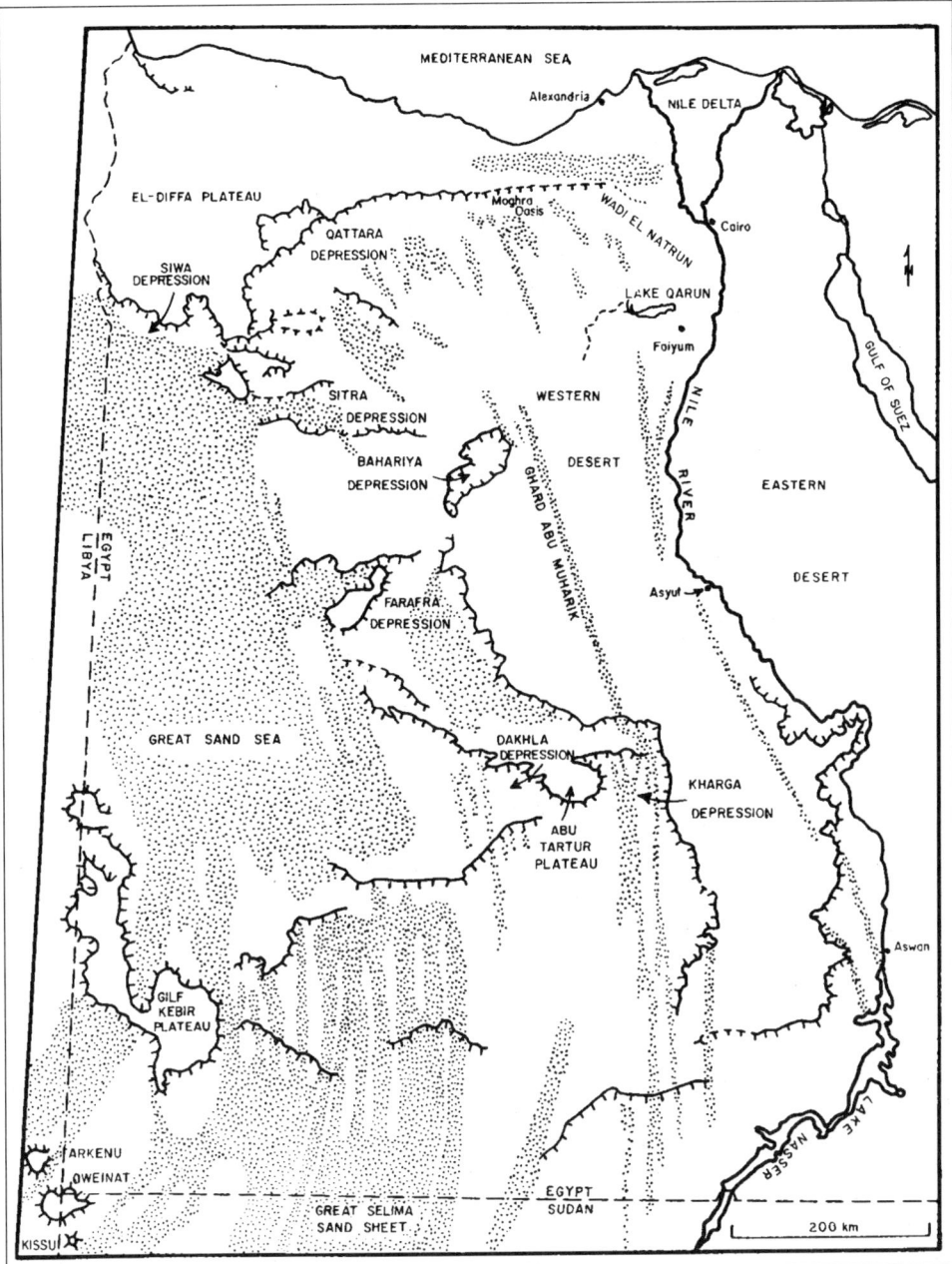

Fig. 1: Map of the oases depressions and sand dune fields in the Western Desert of Egypt. (after Gifford et al., 1979, 225)

65

understand the evolution of its landforms and the origin of its sand deposits.[2] The results have a direct bearing on the geoarchaeology of Egypt, particularly at the initiation of ancient Egyptian civilization.

Sand and Wind

The Great Sahara of North Africa includes some of the driest regions on Earth. Particularly in the Western Desert of Egypt, the received solar radiation is capable of evaporating over 200 times the amount of rainfall.[3] In this desert, precipitation is extremely variable and unpredictable; in some regions it rains only once in 20 to 50 years.

Regional views of the Great Sahara indicate that surface winds trend in an arcuate pattern that emanates from the coast of the Mediterranean Sea.[4] This regional pattern was first suggested for the eastern Sahara based on field mapping by Bagnold.[5] It was also displayed in the rest of the Sahara by satellite image data.[6] Wind-produced erosional scars throughout the desert suggest that this regime was effective during much of the Pleistocene. Sand dune chains in the Western Desert of Egypt (fig. 1) proved the consistency of this regime at least during the past 5,000 years.[7]

Throughout the Sahara, and especially in the Western Desert of Egypt, sand accumulations occur within topographic depressions.[8] This must be explained in any theory regarding the origin of the sand and the evolution of the dune forms in space and time. Also, the dune sand is composed mostly of well-rounded quartz grains.[9] The exposed rock to the north of the sand seas is mostly limestone, which could not have been the source of the vast amounts of quartz sand.

These two facts cannot support the conventional view of the origin of the sand by wind erosion and its transportation from the north. The majority of the sand appears to have formed by fluvial erosion of Nubian sandstone rocks exposed in the southern part of the eastern Sahara. Because areas presently covered by dune sand are topographically low, they must have formed inland basins that received sediments from northward flowing stream channels in the geological past. When the conditions of climate changed to dry, the wind from the north sculpted these sand deposits into various dune forms and sand sheets.

Dry Water Channels

Radar images from space unveiled the locations of numerous channels of former rivers and streams in the eastern Sahara.[10] The sand cover of these channels inhibited their observation in other types of satellite images. Vast drainage features were revealed in the southwestern part of Egypt's Western Desert. Many of these channels (fig. 2; upper left group of lines) emanate from the Gilf Kebir plateau, a prominent topographic high in southwestern Egypt. The plateau is bordered by numerous dry valleys (*wadis*) indicating that its edges were shaped by surface water erosion. The *wadis*

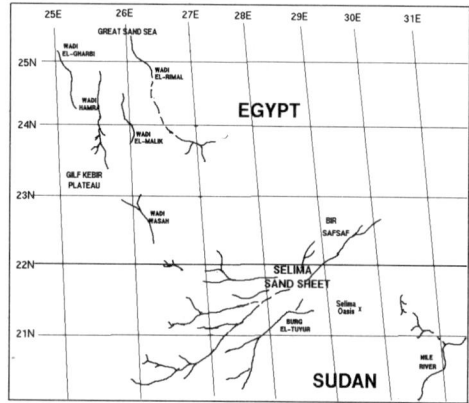

Fig. 2: Tracings of former river channels in the southwestern part of the Western Desert of Egypt. These sand-buried channels were revealed by radar images from space. (after El-Baz, 2000, 781)

66

are truncated at the top, which suggests that an upper surface layer of softer sediments had been eroded by both water and wind processes.

Many drainage lines in the vicinity of the Great Selima Sand Sheet were also revealed by radar images[11] with four major lines leading directly to it from the southwest (fig. 2; lower group of lines). The northernmost drainage system trends due east and measures 150 kilometers in length. The longest *wadi* system is also very broad and is aligned in a NE-SW direction. Such broad channels usually develop under sheet flood conditions with plentiful surface water. Several of these broad channels display small braided streams in their floors. Braiding usually develops by smaller amounts of surface water, indicating several episodes of water flow.[12]

Archaeological Evidence

The vast arid belt of the Great Sahara of North Africa experienced earlier periods of greater effective moisture. In addition to the unveiling of dry courses of ancient rivers, this is evident from archaeological sites associated with remnants of playa or lake deposits.

An early Holocene pluvial cycle is well documented by geoarchaeological investigations at Neolithic playa sites in Egypt.[13] Late Pleistocene lake deposits with associated early and middle Paleolithic archaeological sites are exposed in the Bir Tarfawi region of southwestern Egypt.[14] Similar associations occur in northwestern Sudan.[15]

This undisputed archaeological evidence of previous human habitation, in addition to remains of fauna and flora, confirm the presence of surface water in the past. Calcium carbonate deposits associated with some of these buried river channels are believed to have precipitated in the upper portions of the zone of saturation during pluvial episodes, when water tables were higher that they are today.

The uranium-series technique was used to date lacustrine carbonates from Bir Tarfawi, Bir Sahara East, Wadi Hussein, Oyo Depression, and the Great Selima Sand Sheet localities.[16] Results indicate that five paleolake-forming episodes occurred at about 320–250, 240–190, 155–120, 90–65 and 10–5 *ka*. Four of these five pluvial episodes may be correlated with major interglacial stages 9,7,5e, and one, the 90–65 *ka* episode, may be correlated with the interglacial substage 5c or 5a.[17] Furthermore, radiocarbon dating confirmed that the eastern Sahara experienced a period of greater effective moisture during the early and middle Holocene, from 11,000 to 5,000 years ago.

Rise of Egyptian Civilization

From the above discussions, the following concepts are established beyond a doubt: (1) the prevailing wind direction in Egypt is from north to south; (2) the sands of the Western Desert originated from rocks exposed in the southern part of the desert; (3) the sand was carried northward by river courses during humid phases in the past; and (4) the last humid phase persisted from 11,000 to 5,000 years ago.

Archaeological evidence shows that the industrious builders of the Egyptian civilization came at least 2,000 years after sedentary farmers had populated the banks of the Nile River. For twenty centuries these early inhabitants tilled the rich soil of the Nile Valley and Delta, but they did not initiate a civilization.

As the land west of the Nile began to dry up 5,000 years ago, civilization began to flourish along the banks of the Nile. The two events must have been inextricably related. Climate change gradually brought extreme aridity to northeastern Africa, prompting a mass migration of its inhabitants to the only dependable source of water, the Nile. The banks of the river, however, were already teeming with a sedentary population. The dynamic convergence of these two peoples may have planted the seeds of ancient Egypt, and signaled the beginning of history.

During the 2,000 years before the rise of ancient Egypt, the agrarian people living along the banks of the Nile had developed an advanced "river technology." They lived in harmony with the ebb and flow of the river. They measured the strength of annual floods and ingeniously lifted water from the river and channeled it to their fields. They directed their thoughts downward toward the earth, which they tilled with great expertise.

Those who migrated from the west had "desert wisdom." They learned how to live with erratic rainfall and where to seek greener pastures. To escape the scorching heat of the sun, they traveled at night and were adept at astronomy. These nomadic people kept their sights turned upward toward the sky, contemplating man's place in the universe—a philosophical orientation that permeated Egypt's recorded history.

The arrival of the desert people on the banks of the Nile doubled the population, requiring better social organization to produce enough food—a prerequisite for civilization. The cultural interaction of the two groups, and the mixing of river technology with desert wisdom, created a vigorous new society. It may have been the cross-fertilization of these two distinctly different cultures that ignited the spark of civilization in ancient Egypt.

One of the most fascinating aspects of the birth of Egyptian civilization is the unique acceleration of change in the few centuries just before and just after the recorded history of the first Dynastic Era. Never again was there as much growth. During the 3,000 years that followed, there was reasonable continuity and progression, with a few setbacks, until the Roman Era. Therefore, there must have been a powerful reason for the unparalleled growth just before the appearance of writing and the establishment of the Egyptian State.

The influx of people from the drought-stricken western land to join those tied to the banks of the Nile provides a plausible explanation. The social organization, division of labor, and increased land productivity to feed the population would have resulted in a fertile ground for a highly-organized society. The mixing of the two cultures, each with its own knowledge base, would have planted the seeds of civilization.

Oldest Stone Monuments
The Pyramids

King Menes or Narmer ruled over Upper Egypt at the time of the drought in the land west of the Nile 5,000 years ago. With a well-trained army he took control of Lower Egypt as well and became "King of the Two Lands." From about 3100 BCE forward, Egypt was ruled by one strong state whose borders were little changed to this day.

Only 440 years passed from the time of unifying Egypt by Menes to the building of the first pyramid-type structure, the step pyramid of Saqqara, by Imhotep the architect of King Djoser, around 2660 BCE. What is more amazing is that only 125 years later the three majestic pyramids of Giza were completed. The energy and growth of the Early Dynastic Period and the first part of the Old Kingdom (3100–2500 BCE) have no parallel in human history. The pace of development, the meticulous organization, and the artistic elegance of that period dwarf the technological advancements of recent times.

None of these achievements would have been accomplished if it were a time of "business as usual." There must have been a drastic reason to organize the population, such as the need to feed huge numbers of immigrants from drought-stricken North Africa. There must have also been a positive influence from the wisdom of those migrants from the deserted land. Furthermore, there must have been visionary leaders who were able to motivate the people in accomplishing the improbable, and to leave behind tangible evidence of their greatness.

The greatest achievement of that era was the erection of the Great Pyramid of Giza. Even today, with our intelligent machines, powered by the internal combustion of petroleum products, the building of the Great Pyramid would be a technological and managerial nightmare. For it to have been built during the twenty–three-year reign of its builder, King Khufu, tens of thousands of people must have been employed. If it were being built everyday during those years, some 300 giant blocks, each weighing an average of two and a half tons, would have had to be quarried, shaped, moved to the site, and set in their proper locations each day.

In Khufu's time, all the work must have been effected by human force—and ingenuity—aided only by animals. Devices like the pulley and the wheel had not yet been invented. The workforce of the rock cutters and sculptors must have had an equivalent number who constructed ramps along which the blocks were dragged, maintained all the tools, and provided food and drink.

Khufu must have been a visionary leader who thought of a public works project that would bring together the people of Egypt's north and south who had remained apart since the symbolic unification by Menes. Working together, they would learn from each other, befriend one another and intermarry to become one nation.

Fig. 3: Three natural cone-shaped structures resulting from wind erosion west of the Kharga Oases. Note that the largest two are faceted, giving them pyramidal shapes.

If "Egypt is the gift of the Nile," as Herodotus said, then the pyramids are a gift of the desert! It must have been the numerous, imposing pyramidal hills in the dry land west of the Nile that inspired the design, which mimicked the natural landforms (fig. 3). This notion would have been relayed by those who migrated from the Sahara to the dwellers on the Nile banks.

It is reasonable to assume that the original idea of building the monumental structures in a pyramidal form would have come from ancient knowledge of the endurance of this particular

69

shape. No wonder that the hieroglyph denoting desert hills depicted a mound-like form—a concept most likely brought into the Nile Valley by the immigrants from the domain of the sands.

The ancient Egyptians left much evidence that they knew where things were in the desert. They must have also realized that the shapes that they encountered there were no accident. The conical or pyramidal shapes evaded destruction by leading the wind upslope to surround a smaller volume as it glides upward. This way, the erosive power of the wind would be funneled to the apex where its energy dissipates.

Today, the pyramids of Giza exist in near perfect harmony with their environment. They predate the other Seven Wonders of the World by approximately 2,000 years, yet only they remain standing. Had the ancients built these majestic rock monuments in the shape of a cube, a rectangle, or even a stadium, they would have been erased by the ravages of wind erosion long ago.

The Sphinx

The origin of the Sphinx may be just as intriguing. Some scholars contend that the bulk from which it was formed had been left by the quarrying of rock to build the Great Pyramid. However, there is a more plausible and natural explanation (fig. 4).

Fig. 4: A wind-sculpted yardang in the shape of a reclining animal in layered carbonate rock south of Farafra Oasis.

Desert environments usually display wind-carved ridges called *yardangs*, from the Turkic word *yar* meaning steep bank. These often occur as protrusions of ridges arranged in parallel rows with gullies in between. Many such yardangs exist in the Western Desert of Egypt. One of the largest fields in the world may be that north and east of the Kharga Oasis, where the wind-carved ridges extend for hundreds of miles. These look like inverted boat hulls with prows pointing into the wind.[18]

The reclining lion body of the Sphinx could have originally been designed after shapes that were naturally carved by the wind. A yardang of tough limestone rock may have protruded above its surrounding area on the eastern edge of the Giza plateau. The ancient engineers may have elected to reshape its head in the image of King Khafre wearing a headdress, giving the Sphinx its original name of *šsp ʿnḫ*, or "living image." They also gave it a convincingly lion-like body. To do so, they had to dig a moat around the natural protrusion. The farther into the surrounding rock, the deeper they had to dig into the Giza plateau.[19] When the moat was completed, they added the legs of the seated lion's body to give the Great Sphinx its characteristic shape.

Conclusion

In the land west of the Nile River, wet climates alternated with dry episodes during the past 300,000 years. The last rainy period persisted from 11,000 to 5,000 years ago. The terminal drought that formed the Great Sahara of North Africa coincided with the rise of ancient Egyptian civilization about 3,000 BCE. Nomadic populations of the deserted land must have immigrated to the Nile Valley to save their lives and what was left of their animals. The interaction between the two different cultures, and the organization that was required for food production, played key roles in the rise of ancient Egypt. The desert inhabitants imported knowledge of natural land-forms and their resistance to wind erosion at the start of Egyptian civilization. This included the endurance of conical and pyramidal rock structures in the windy environment. In addition, the Sphinx mimicked wind-carved yardangs that naturally occurred throughout the Western Desert of Egypt.

Notes:

1 F. El-Baz, "Origin and evolution of the desert," *Interdisciplinary Science Reviews* 13 (1988), 331–347.

2 A. W. Gifford, D. M. Warner, and F. El-Baz, "Orbital observations of sand distribution in the Western Desert of Egypt," *Apollo-Soyuz Test Project Summary Science Report* II, (1979), Earth Observations and Photography, NASA SP-412, 219–236; F. El-Baz, "Satellite observations of the interplay between wind and water processes in the Great Sahara," *Photogrammetric Engineering and Remote Sensing* 66 (2000), 6, 777–782.

3 D. Henning and H. Flohn, "Climate Aridity Index Map," *U.N. Conference on Desertification,* (UNEP; Nairobi, 1977).

4 F. El-Baz and R. W. Wolfe, "Wind patterns in the Western Desert," in F. El-Baz, and T. A. Maxwell, (eds.), *Desert landforms of southeast Egypt: A basis for comparison with Mars,* NASA CR-3611, (1982), 119–139.

5 R. A. Bagnold, *The Physics of Blown Sand and Desert Dunes,* (London, 1941), 265.

6 M. M. Mainguet, *L'homme et la Secheresse*, (Mason Collection Geographie; Paris, 1995), 335.

7 El-Baz, "Satellite," 778.

8 El-Baz, "Satellite," 777.

9 F. El-Baz, M. H. Slezak, and T. A. Maxwell, "Preliminary analysis of color variations of sand deposits in the Western Desert of Egypt," *Apollo-Soyuz Test Project Summary Science Report II: Earth Observations and Photography*, NASA SP-412, (1979), 237–262.

10 J. F. McCauley, G. G. Schaber, C. S. Breed, M. J. Grolier, C. V. Haynes Jr., B. Issawi, C. Elachi, and R. Blom, "Subsurface valleys and geoarchaeology of the Eastern Sahara revealed by Shuttle radar," *Science* 218 (1982), 1004–1020; C. Robinson, F. El-Baz, M. Ozdogan, M. Ledwith, D. Blanco, S. Oakley, and J. Inzana, "Use of radar data to delineate palaeodrainage flow directions in the Selima Sand Sheet, eastern Sahara," *Photogrammetric Engineering and Remote Sensing* 66 (2000) 6, 745–753.

11 C. A. Robinson, F. El-Baz, and V. Singhroy, "Subsurface imaging by Radarsat: Comparison with Landsat TM data and implications for ground water in the Selima area, northwestern Sudan," *Geological Association of Canada* (1998) (*in press*).

12 Robinson, "Use of radar data," 745.

13 F. Wendorf, and R. Schild, *Prehistory of the Eastern Sahara*, (New York, 1980), 414; H. J. Pachur and G. Braun,"The paleoclimate of the central Sahara, Libya, and the Libyan Desert," in M. Sarentheim, E. Siebold, and P. Rognon, (eds.), *Paleoeco. Afr.* 12 (1980), 351–363; B. Gabriel and S. Kropelin, "Holocene lake deposits in northwest Sudan," in J. A. Coetzee, and E. M. van Zinderen-Bakker, (eds,) *Paleoecology of Africa and the Surrounding Islands*, (Rotterdam,1989); C. V. Haynes Jr., C. H. Eyles, L. A. Pavlish, J. C. Rotchie, and M. Rybak, "Holocene paleoecology of the Eastern Sahara: Selima Oasis," *Quat. Sci. Rev.* 8 (1989), 109–136.

14 F. Wendorf, A. E. Close, and R. Schild, "Recent work on the Middle Paleolithic of the Eastern Sahara," *Afr. Archaeol. Rev.* 5 (1987), 49–63.

15 C. V. Haynes Jr., "Quaternary studies, Western Desert, Egypt and Sudan-1979–1983 field seasons," *National Geographic Research Reports* 16 (1985), 269–341; Haynes *et al.* "Holocene paleoecology," 109.

16 B. J. Szabo, C. V. Haynes, Jr., and T. A. Maxwell, "Ages of Quaternary pluvial episodes determined by uranium-series and radiocarbon dating of lacustrine deposits of Eastern Sahara," *Paleogeography, Paleoclimatology, Paleoecology* 113 (1995), 227–242.

17 Szabo *et al.*, "Ages of Quaternary pluvial," 227.

18 F. El-Baz, "Desert builders knew a good thing when they saw it," *The Smithsonian* 12 (1981) 1, 116–122.

19 El-Baz, "Desert builders," 120.

TT 320 and the History of the Royal Cache during the Twenty-first Dynasty

Galina A. Belova
Russian Academy of Sciences

To the northwest of Hatshepsut's temple at Deir al-Bahari, on a small rocky outcrop hidden by stone ledges, is an unfinished tomb designated TT 320. During the Twenty-first Dynasty, TT 320 was used to cache the mummies of some of the most powerful pharaohs of New Kingdom Egypt, among them, Thutmose III, Sety I, and Ramesses II.

The importance of this find by the Abd al-Rassul family in the latter part of the nineteenth century is belied by the very high degree of uncertainty that surrounded the circumstances of its discovery. The family reputedly plundered its most valuable pieces for about a decade before Brugsch descended its shaft in July of 1881. Brugsch, who in the absence of Maspero was acting head of the Antiquities Service, was singularly impressed by the large number of coffins he found there as well as by the rich collection of funerary equipment in the tomb. Brugsch was a professional photographer and had worked for the Antiquities Service for many years. Consequently, it is difficult to understand why, although he hurriedly removed some 6,000 objects from the tomb, he failed to take a single photograph or make a sketch. Neither are there any detailed records describing the finds nor a description of the arrangement of the objects. Some months later Maspero and Wilson, an American photographer, descended into the tomb for an additional survey and made some notes concerning the disposition of the items within the cache from memory.[1] In all probability Maspero and Wilson would have asked Brugsch to report on his actions, however, his response seems not to have provided much clarification.

In 1898 Breasted described the condition of the tomb and the large amount of fallen stone inside. In 1919 an expedition of the Metropolitan Museum of Art noted that it was dangerous to carry out work in the tomb because of the condition of the rock.[2] A year later, Lansing of the Metropolitan Museum of Art entered the tomb, which was by then blocked by fallen stone.[3] In 1938, at the request of Černy, the French Institute in Cairo provided money to clear the shaft so that he could record the graffiti near the tomb's entrance.[4] Then, in November 1975, Dewachter "quickly surveyed the shaft,"[5] but by March of 1976, when Romer visited, he found it nearly filled up with sand.[6]

It is thus questionable whether studies made before 1998 can in any meaningful way be considered true archaeological investigations. Indeed, Romer felt justified in complaining that the reports on the secret burial and its contents are so poor that one would not be surprised to find that facts about the cache and its robbery were concealed by Maspero and the authorities.[7]

Some scholars have attempted to reconstruct the history of the cache from the inscriptions and what is known about the relative positions of the coffins (see below). However, in the absence of reliable notes one must seriously doubt the validity of such studies. Moreover, the Abd al-Rassuls had ample opportunity to rearrange the mummies and their sarcophagi while searching for valuables before Brugsch ever arrived. Additionally, long before the Abd al-Rassul family found the cache its contents had been tampered with in the course of the "restorations" which took place in the Twenty-first Dynasty.

The main questions which need to be answered in order to adequately understand the royal cache have been outlined succinctly by Niwiński: When was the tomb built? To whom did it belong? And what is the history of the cache in the Twenty-first and Twenty-second Dynasties?[8]

Although the construction date for TT 320 is uncertain, a number of scholars have followed Brugsch in his belief that the tomb was quarried in the Eighteenth Dynasty. Lansing subsequently commented that TT 320 was originally a small tomb which was later extended. Although this view has become generally accepted,[9] Reeves has questioned whether there would be sufficient reason to increase the size of a small tomb in the late New Kingdom or Third Intermediate Period.

Romer seems to have been the first to note that the adz marks preserved in the upper part of the northeast corner of the shaft could provide a basis of dating the tomb.[10] Niwiński believes that TT 320 had been finished by the time of Pinedjem II's burial, i.e. by the Year Ten of Siamen's reign. This dating is based on the similar layouts of TT 320 and a more securely dated tomb in Bab al-Gasus.[11]

The first owner of the tomb cannot be determined because of the great number of mummies present and the absence of any record of their archaeological context. However, Winlock's hypothesis that the original burial belonged to Queen Inhapi, wife of the Seventeenth Dynasty king Sekenenre–Tao II, has been widely subscribed to.[12] The Queen's mummy was found here and a number of dockets written on the coffins of Ramesses I, Sety I, and Ramesses II mention her name. However, among the alternative points of view are those of Breasted who believed that the royal cache was the burial of Amenhotep I.[13] Schmitz came to the same conclusion.[14] Others have thought that the tomb was originally the family burial place of the High Priest Pinedjem II.[15] This is supported by the fact that the coffins of Pinedjem II's family were discovered at the far end of the burial chamber and were relatively intact in comparison with those that were found in the passages and by the sides of the burial chamber. The disposition of coffins implies that Pinedjem II's family were interred before the cached coffins were brought here. Likewise, the somewhat poorer condition of the other coffins is consistent with their having been moved further or more often than those of the high priest's family. Reeves has also pointed out that the mummy of Inhapi lay close to the entrance, in front of the bodies of Sety I, Ramesses II, and not inside the burial chamber, thus calling her ownership of the tomb into question. The personal stamps of members of Pinedjem's family appear on the shrouds of Ramesses IX and others. This indicates that these people were either involved in or responsible for the care of the mummies in the cache. A graffito made near the tomb's entrance by the officials who buried the high priest's family indicates that Nesikhons and Pinedjem were originally buried in this tomb and, in Niwiński's opinion, it must have been their intention that TT 320 serve both as a final resting place for themselves as well as a cache for royal mummies.[16]

In November and December, 1998, a joint Russian–German expedition conducted the most thorough investigation of TT 320 thus far. In light of the information gathered on that occasion and recent surveys of neighboring tombs it has been possible to piece together some of the cache's history

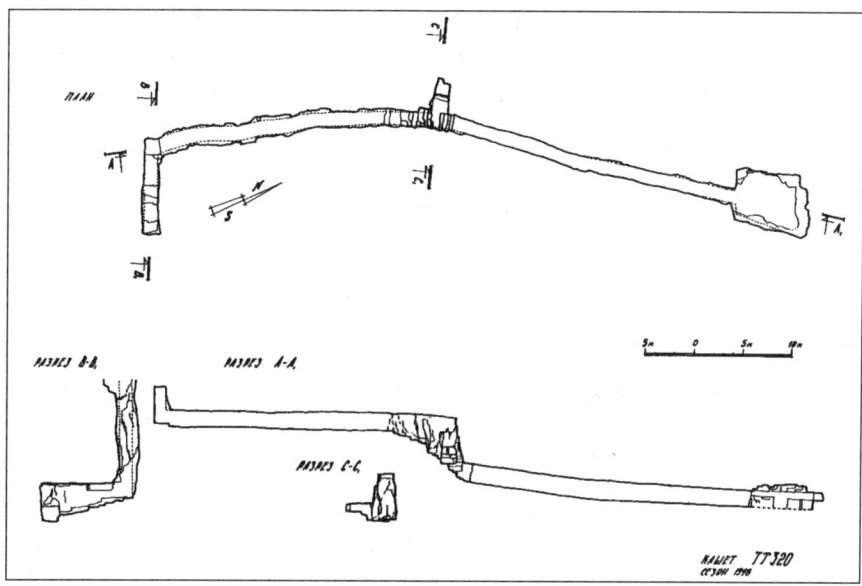

Fig. 1: The layout of the Royal Cache TT 320. Architect N. A. Reshetnikova.

During his two-hour visit to the tomb Brugsch outlined the tomb's layout in the most cursory fashion. The corrections made by Maspero during his subsequent visit to the tomb did not substantially improve Brugsch's brief plan. By contrast the plans made by the 1998 expedition's architect, N. Rechetnikova, show the true dimensions of the tomb (fig. 1).

The new plans mean that some of the errors that resulted from reliance on the older plan can now be corrected. For example those who believed that Inhapi was the original owner of TT 320 have hypothesized that the "upper burial chamber E" was "the height" (k3y) of Inhapi mentioned on some of the mummy dockets. Indeed, Thomas assumed that no less than twenty-four coffins, including the gigantic Ahmose-Nefertari coffin, were found in E. However, this is physically impossible because E is only 3.15 meters long and between 1.40 and 1.75 meters wide by 1.70 meters high. (Others have suggested that the k3y of Inhapi, could have been the chamber where the body of Amenhotep I was placed.[17])

About 700 m southwest of TT 320 and further up the mountainside at a height of 750 m, is a tomb surveyed by Robichon in 1931 (WN A). At that time he concluded that although this tomb was probably built for an individual it was later reused as a cache.[18] The tomb appears to have had royal status during the Eighteenth Dynasty and Reeves has suggested that this elevated burial was none other than the k3y of Queen Inhapi. Indeed, local inhabitants refer to this as the "hanging tomb." Recently, however, French Egyptologists have surveyed the "hanging tomb" and have concluded that it should be dated to a period later than the assumed death of Inhapi. Their conclusion is based on the quarrying marks which remain on its walls. These indicate that the tool used to cut the tomb resembled an adz or *gaddoum*, which has an horizontal blade, rather than the simple pick which was used in tombs which date to around the same time as Queen Inhapi (e.g. the tomb of Ahmes-Nefertari at Dra Abu al-Naga).[19]

Inscriptions indicate that the mummies were moved and cached because of the threat of desecration. Papyrus Mayer indicates that as early as the first year of Ramesses IX the people who had desecrated the tombs of Ramesses II and Sety I were brought to trial.[20] Papyrus Abbot indicates that in Year 16 of Ramesses IX an inspection team sent to evaluate the state of the tomb of Amenhotep I found it untouched.[21] The tomb of Seqenenre Tao II was also found untouched.[22] Some time later, in the sixth year of his reign, Herihor had to "renew the burial places" of Ramesses I, Sety I and Ramesses II. According to dockets on the coffins of Sety I and Ramesses II he reburied them (*whm krs*) at this time.[23] Hence, the mummies had remained in their own tombs until that day (i.e. Seti I in KV17 and Ramesses II in KV7).

From Year 1 to Year 19 of Smendes and Pinedjem I the authorities were active in renewing burial places and restoring mummies. In Year 10 Seti I's wrappings were renewed because the state of his mummy was a cause for concern and in Year 15 Ramesses II was taken to the Tomb of Sety I as a part of his own renewal. During this period there is evidence for establishing a restoration workshop in the tomb of Sety I and it is thought that the mummy of Herihor's wife, Nodjmet, may have been re-wrapped there as early as the Year 1 of Smendes and Pinedjem I. If this is correct then the tomb of Seti I would have served in this capacity for around 15 years.

According to one of the dockets on his coffin, Amenhotep I was reburied in Year 6 of Pinedjem I. Ten years later Amenhotep was again reburied. It seems likely that this burial would have been in the *k3y* of Inhapi and that its designation as the "royal place where Amenhotep lay" dates from this period.[24] That Amenhotep's mummy spent at least a few years here is attested by a graffito found near the tomb entrance, "so and so is here forever, before Amenhotep." This graffito clearly implies an expectation that Amenhotep would rest here permanently. Indeed, it is possible that the proximity of this tomb to his mortuary temple may have influenced the decision to move the king's body to this particular location.[25] About a month later Thutmose II was similarly reburied (once again judging from the date given on his docket), but there is no evidence as to where this may have taken place, in the *k3y* or in the tomb of Sety I.

Special attention was also paid to the mummy of Ramesses III during the reigns of Smendes and Pinedjem I. It was twice re-wrapped in Years 9 and 10 of their reigns. The name of Ramesses III's own mortuary temple at Medinet Habu has been found written on his mummy wrappings.[26] Since this temple is known to have been used as a place in which to restore mummies it seems very probable that Ramesses III's own restoration took place here.[27] In Year 13 the mummy of Ramesses III was again restored. At some stage the body of Ramesses III was consolidated with those of the other kings. This last act of restoration provides an ideal opportunity for this to have occurred, perhaps in the tomb of Sety, which was where the other mummies had been restored.

In Year 6 of Psusennes I (Year 37 of Pinedjem I) by order of Menkhepererre, the wrappings of Seti I were again renewed and the next year he was re-buried after the restoration in his own tomb (*krs*). A few months later in the same year the mummy of the king's daughter and the great king's wife Iahmes-Sitkames was restored and in Year 8 the mummies of Iahmes I and King Siamen were, likewise, renewed.

All of this prompts us to ask where the vast majority of the royal mummies were stored at this time. Amenhotep I and Sety I seem to have been afforded tombs of their own, but it seems unlikely that either one of these tombs would also have contained the mummies of others.

In Year 5 of Pinedjem II, Nesikhons, his wife, was buried in "in the house of eternity where

Amenhotep I is too." Fifteen days later Pinedjem II was also laid to rest.[28] Thereafter the bodies of Sety I and Ramesses II were transferred to the tomb of Inhapi.[29]

There are two possibilities here. The first is that Nesikhons and then Pinedjem II were laid in TT 320, and that they were soon followed (if Reeves is correct) by Ramesses II, Sety I, and (presumably) the other royal mummies. If this is correct then the "hanging tomb" can have only served as a cache for three days.[30] However, if this is the case then the reference to Nesikhons being buried in the place where "Amenhotep is too" would imply that Amenhotep had already been moved to TT 320. This does not present a problem in itself, and it must be said that the Nesikhons' reference to the "house of eternity" accords well with a graffito within TT 320 which uses this same term to refer to the tomb.

This raises a question as to when Amenhotep was moved to TT 320. If Amenhotep had not shared the *k3y* with others who were deposited there after him, his removal would in all likelihood have taken place before Nesikhons burial. Had this been necessary and had there been a distinct intention on the part of Nesikhons and Pinedjem to benefit not only from the prestige or *mana* of the great kings of the past but also from the sanctity of the holy king, then it seems likely that others would not also have accompanied Amenhotep to TT 320 at this time. However, were this done, then one of the few more-or-less reliable facts which we can take from Brugsch is cast into doubt, namely, that if the body of Amenhotep was put in "E" then the family of the high priest was found at the far end of the burial chamber.

Also, given the prestige of Ramesses II (nine kings followed him with the same name) it is conceivable that his coffin would have been sent off to the *k3y* and buried with him. Also, the policy of mass burial, which seems to have evolved in the direction of ever-greater concentrations of royal remains, and the safety presumed to have accompanied them, militate against the idea that Pinedjem would have wanted to be buried with a small group.

On the other hand, it is possible that Nesikhons and Pinedjem II were buried in TT 320 and that they were soon followed by Ramesses II and Thutmose II. In Year 7 of Sheshonq I and Iuput, when notes on the shrouds of Ramesses IX mention "the expedition to the temple (*hwt*)," that there was activity in the TT 320 at this time is supported by the term *hwt* which appears on seal impressions found in the tomb. Were this the case, then the Nesikhons text mentioning "where Amenhotep I is too" would have referred to the place with which his presence had been associated for almost a century. Similarly, the otherwise problematic movements of Ramesses II and Seti I into the *k3y* for a mere three days evaporate. Similarly, this sort of last-in-first-out effect fits well with the position of Pinedjem II at the far end of the chamber and of Inhapi near the entrance.

In the process of clearing the shaft during 1998 season it became obvious that the integrity of the limestone fabric of the tomb is in an advanced state of decomposition. When the shaft had been cleared to a depth of nine meters, the danger of landslide became so obvious that the local workmen would no longer enter the shaft. At this time two members of the expedition, Erhart Graefe and Alexej Krol, continued this work at the risk of their lives. It was necessary to separate threatening rocks from the interior surfaces of the shaft using spades while suspended from a cable. The excavation showed that the rocky *massif* with its monuments is in critical condition and the immediate task of the Supreme Council of Antiquities should be a thorough geological survey of the area.

The finds made in the course of the 1998 excavation of the cache are of interest. One inscription concerning the burial of Pinedjem II was found but the text is partly destroyed as a result of weathering. The Supreme Council of Antiquities have decided to conserve this inscription (fig. 2).

Fig. 2: One of the inscriptions about the burial of Pinedjem II.

The finds of numerous fragments of clay and clay seals indicate that the tomb was sealed time and again. We found a seal made of unbaked Nile clay in the shape of a cartouche with the inscription "Amen-Ra" (fig. 3) as well as ten impressions of cartouches, but the inscriptions are practically unreadable.

Fig. 3: A seal of unbaked Nile clay in the shape of a cartouche.

In the tomb were two ostraca. One had an image of a human face with a branch (or hand?); the other carried a possible representation of the tomb layout. In the course of work fragments of *ushabtis* including those of Henuttawy and Pinedjem II were found. The inscription on Pinedjem's *ushebti* was completely preserved (fig. 4).

Some fragments of wooden furniture, which formed part of the funeral equipment, were found as were fragments of inlay, parts of coffins including a pharaoh's beard, and many fragments of coffin decoration, some of them inscribed with dates. Other finds include wooden objects such as an elegant hair pin the upper part of which is a cobra's head, some fragments of decoration from queen Isiemkheb's canopic chest which were made of good quality leather in pastel greenish and pinkish tones. Pieces of fabric of different quality, often in small rolls, were perhaps thrown away by robbers after tearing them off the mummies. Some fragments of mats were found during the 1998 tomb clearance, as were some pieces of canvas coated with a thin layer of mortar.

Fig. 4: Ushabti of Pinedjem II.

The excavations of the Royal Cache have thrown some light on the enigmatic history of the Twenty-first Dynasty but many difficult questions still remain, which cannot be completely answered at this time.

Notes:

1 G. Maspero, "Les Momies Royales de Deir Al-Bahari," *MMAFI* 4 (1889), 521.

2 J. Romer, *Valley of the Kings*, (London, 1981), 141.

3 A. Lansing, *BMMA* 2 (15 Dec., 1920), 12.

4 J. Černy, "Studies in the Chronology of the Twenty-first Dynasty," *JEA* 32 (1946), 25.

5 M. Dewachter, "Contribution à L'Histoire de la Cachette Royale de Deir Al-Bahari," *BSFE* 74 (1975), 32.

6 Cf. E. Thomas, "The *k3y* of Queen Inhapi," *JARCE* 16 (1979), 91.

7 Romer, *Valley*, 145.

8 A. Niwiński, "The Bab Al-Gusus Tombs and the Royal Cache in Deir Al-Bahari," *JEA* 70 (1984), 73.

9 Romer, *Valley* 141; Thomas, 85, 91.

10 Romer, *Valley* 141; C. N. Reeves, *Valley of the Kings. The Decline of a Royal Necropolis*, (London, 1990), 187.

11 Niwiński, "Royal Cache," 77.

12 H. E. Winlock, "The Tomb of Queen Inhapi. An Open Letter to the Editor," *JEA* 17 (1931), 108–110.

13 J. H. Breasted, *Ancient Records of Egypt*, IV (New York, 1906–1907), 690.

14 F. J. Schmitz, *Amenophis I*, (Hildesheim, 1978), 205.

15 Reeves, *Valley*, 188.

16 Niwiński, "Royal Cache," 77. At the same time, as S. Tasker mentioned to me in private correspondence, the aspirations to royalty which the High Priests of Amun had at this time would seem to consider burial with pharaohs as appropriate.

17 See Niwiński, "Royal Cache," 79.

18 C. N. Reeves and R. H. Wilkinson, *The Complete Valley of the Kings*, (London, 1996), 197.

19 L. Gabolde, A. Hassan Ibrahim, P. Ballet, M. Chauveau, "Le 'Tombeau Supendu' de la "Vallée de l'Áigle," *BIFAO* 94 (1994), 228.

20 Breasted, *Records*, 545–553.

21 Breasted, *Records*, 513.

22 Breasted, *Records*, 518.

23 See Reeves, *Valley*, 229, 234; Breasted, 593 - 594.

24 Breasted, *Records*, 665–667; Reeves, *Valley*, 231.

25 Gabolde *et al.*, "Supendu," 229.

26 Reeves, *Valley*, 208.

27 Romer, *Kings*, 143.

28 See Reeves' table 10, 43, 44.

29 See Reeves as above 40, 41.

30 Gabolde *et al.*, "Supendu, 228.

The Qurnet Murai Necropolis (Thebes West)

Francesca Berenguer

Archaeological Clos Foundation, Aula Aegyptiaca

This paper presents the preliminary findings of the Qurnet Murai Research Project based in the Theban Necropolis of Qurnet Murai. After a period of gestation, the research was begun in 1999. Its aim was, and still is, to study the state of the art of this necropolis, that is, the present condition of its tombs. But its ultimate aim, however, is to "rescue" and "rediscover" some paradigmatic tombs forgotten and to try, as much as possible, to prevent their disappearance. This is why, at present and in order to accumulate data, the Qurnet Murai Research Project is building up a photographic register of all of these tombs. This will be published together with some other information about the necropolis itself. We are also considering the possibility, in the near future, of carrying out archaeological intervention—including the drawing of a new topographic map—as well as the restoration and conservation of some of these tombs. So far, we are still working on the very first step of this research.

The area of interest is located in Thebes West—Southwest of the Ramesseum and just behind the Funerary Temple of Amenhotep III and the Memmon Colossi—and embraces a vast area of the Theban necropolis. It might be the least known and the least documented area of all Thebes West. Officially, as reported in Porter and Moss, it contains 17 private tombs—plus a new one (number unknown) recently restored (discovered in 1997) by the Supreme Council of Antiquities, belonging to the New Kingdom. From the Ptolemaic Period there are also three "lost tombs" of the 51 documented ones: TT D1, TT D2, and TT D3. The SCA has blocked the entrance of most of them with iron doors to help preserve them. The access to some is already difficult.

These tombs are quite small; all are decorated with painted plaster and all have the usual T-shaped plan. In spite of their deterioration, their decoration and iconography is striking. They are historically very valuable due to the fact that they belong to some of the highest dignitaries within the pharaonic administration. For example, such important people as Merymose, (TT 383) whose tomb was discovered in 1989 by Inspector Mohamed el-Bialy, was Viceroy of Kush during the reign of Amenhotep III; Amenhotep, also called Huy (TT 40), who was successor to the latter as Viceroy of Kush during the reign of Tutankhamun; and another Viceroy of Kush, called Nehi (TT D1), of the Thutmose III period.

Concerning decoration and iconography, the Ramesside tomb TT 277 belonging to Amenemonet, stands out. Its iconography is quite unique within the different topics covered in the Theban tombs: the procession of the huge statues of Amenhotep III and Tiye, both deified, to the holy lake of their funerary temple. Another scene in this tomb shows the deceased offering libations to Nebhepetre Montuhotep (IV) and to the queen Neferu, also deified, as well as four other people carrying a mummy. Also worth mentioning is tomb TT 276 belonging to Amenemopet (*temp.* Thutmose IV) which contains scenes of Nubian tribute, his the funeral procession with Anubis together with the mummy, and the peculiar scene of the deceased in his chariot, hunting gazelles, hare, hyenas, and oryx with his bow in the desert.

Fig. 1: TT 276. Q. M. Inner room, left wall. Funerary procession.

However, it has to be pointed out that very little documentation has been done in these tombs and hence, little information is available. Only 10 of the 17 tombs with an official number still preserve their original mural decoration; some are partially-published or remain unpublished. There are almost no photographs or drawings of the decoration and three of their ground plans are still to be drawn. Even today, it is difficult to confirm the exact location of some of these tombs. To put it succinctly, a monograph or a deep and systematic study of this necropolis does not exist, hence our knowledge is partial and poor.

The importance of the Qurnet Murai necropolis rests not only in the tomb owners and the iconography which is often quite unique, but also in other historical aspects perhaps less obvious, but also interesting. For example, of 30 "Viceroys of Kush" documented, three were buried in Qurnet Murai. Considering the fact that only five tombs of these very respectable dignitaries

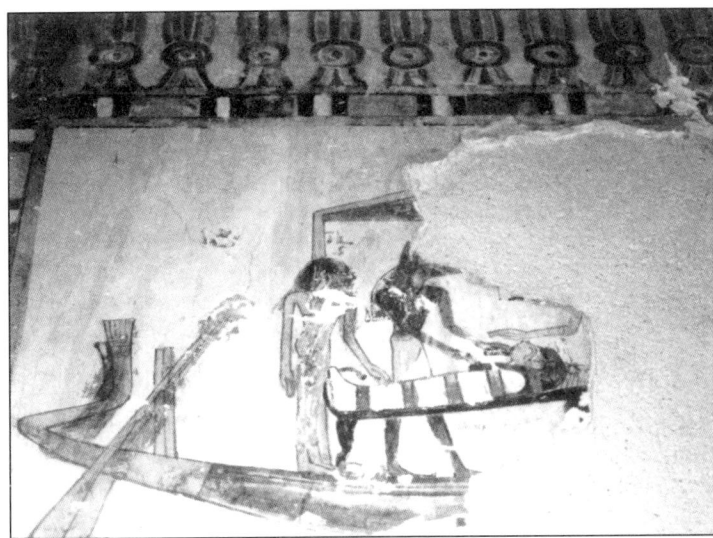

Fig. 2: TT 276. Q. M. Tomb of Amenemopet. Inner room. Funeral procession, including boat with Annubis tending mummy.

have been found, the relevance and fame of this necropolis is quite clear. We are referring to the three Viceroys already mentioned (from the Eighteenth Dynasty) and another two whose tombs are in Dra Abu al-Naga belonging to the Ramesside Period—TT 289 belonging to Setau and TT 300 belonging to Anhotep. This means that the first Viceroys of Kush were buried in Qurnet Murai, but later they were buried in Dra Abu al-Naga.

Once the importance of this necropolis was confirmed, our next step was to build a photographic register of all the documented tombs in Qurnet Murai in order to safeguard what is left of them. Thanks to the SCA, this task was carried out in the following: TT 40, TT 271, TT 272, TT 273, and TT 276. We hope to document the rest in the near future. At the same time a ground plan of each tomb was drawn-up. They often demonstrated a lack of similarity with the published ones. There are some mistakes, such as the north direction in TT 235. We also hope to enter the burial chambers in the near future, if only to register and document them.

On the other hand, the fact that there are only 18 documented tombs in Qurnet Murai, out of 415 tombs belonging to all of the Theban nobility, is also surprising since it is an unbalanced proportion. To mention some of the others, there are 85 in Dra Abu al-Naga, 148 in Sheikh Abd al-Qurna, 59 in Khokha, and 54 in Deir al-Medina. This difference in numbers aroused our curiosity and led us to research why there are so few tombs in such a privileged site as Qurnet Murai. As was expected, the findings were not only positive but also astonishing: There are more tombs than the ones documented and officially numbered in Qurnet Murai. These have been used as dwellings or stables by *Gurnawi* families for some generations. This is one of the reasons why some tombs have lain unnoticed, and to make things worse, some of the tomb-dwellers, apprehensive about curious visitors, have always kept and still keep access to these tombs very restricted. We do not mean that they are completely unknown, as the SCA might have registered them; nevertheless, we have ignored how much information has been collected about them—how many there are, their official number, and so on. In short, all these tombs are not published or documented—not even by Porter and Moss—a fact that, from my point of view, makes them nonexistent in the field of Egyptology.

The second main objective of the Qurnet Murai Project was to carry out soundings in order to confirm and verify whether more tombs exist than those published, including the "lost tombs." Although the exact location of D3 is not certain, we know it is very close to TT 382. These surveys were centered on the southwest of Qurnet Murai hill; the area surrounding tombs TT 271 and TT 382 and west of D3–which may be the lost tomb belonging to Mahu, Eighteenth Dynasty–as cited by Bruyère in a brief paper in 1931; and except X4a and X4b, very near TT 235 and TT 270 further north. When this research began, the Qurnet Murai necropolis, measuring 622 meters in length and in width 444 meters, was provisionally divided into sections. This was to facilitate its study and to help locate the tombs. Sections A, B, C, D, E, F, G, and H: Each section is 220 meters long and 155 meters wide and is subdivided into smaller sections: A1, A2, A3, A4 and so on, measuring 111 meters x 78 meters (see maps). Due to a lack of information, the seven tombs which have been located thus far have been registered provisionally with the letter "X" plus a number showing the order in which they were found: X1, X2, X3, X4a, X4b, X5, and X6. This has been possible thanks to the kindness of the Gurnawi families who let us into their homes. But not only are "X" tombs used as dwellings or stables, some documented ones are also used as such, for example, TT 235, TT 381, and TT 382. It is impossible to prepare plans of some of them due to the modifications carried out by their inhabitants: They have built news walls, blocked doors and wells, and even, as has been documented, have divided one tomb into two different houses.

All these tombs are huge; they are the biggest in all Thebes after the royal tombs. To mention some proportions; the hall in tomb X5 is 24 x 9 meters and contains 16 pillars; the one in tomb X2 is 28 x10 meters with 16 pillars that are completely destroyed—its floor shows the common T-shaped ground plan, with pillars, offerings halls, niches, and very deep, long burial chambers. They are well-deteriorated yet no decoration or text is left; therefore, although they belong to someone from the New Kingdom period, we do not know who. All of them had initially been covered with a coat of red sandstone which was later painted and decorated. Access to the burial chambers has not yet been possible, though we expect to have it sometime in the future, so we cannot tell whether there are any sarcophagi, decoration, texts, or any other information about the owners. Despite all these difficulties, we have managed to register photographically all of the "X" tombs and to draw the plans of the following: X2, X4a, X4b, X5, and X6.

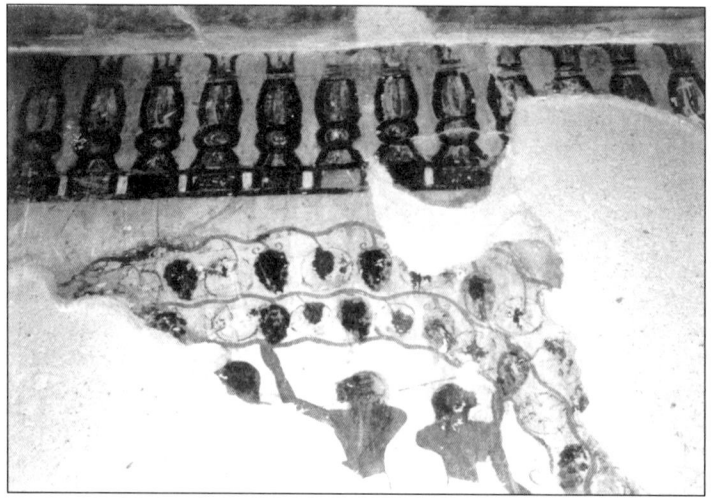

Fig. 3: TT 276. Q. M. Tomb of Amenemopet. Tem. Tutmosis IV. Hall. Men picking grapes.

In summary, the rediscovery of these tombs in Qurnet Murai brings about a new perspective to the importance of the necropolis. The fact that they are huge tombs, with the floors laid out as an inverted T and their location—in a strategic and privileged site—leads us to believe that they belong to the highest dignitaries of the Eighteenth Dynasty. When we compare them to the rest of the tombs found in the necropolis we wonder who their owners were, since the tombs have such enormous proportions. It is true that the Viceroys of Kush were buried in this site, but it is also true that their tombs were quite modest—as were their neighbors from Sheikh Abd al-Qurna, including the viziers .

As a final comment, we want to emphasize the preliminary nature of this investigation. It responds to the need to explain the progression and findings of the research carried out in 1999 in the Qurnet Murai necropolis. As has already been stated, most of the documented tombs have been registered photographically and some of their plans have been drawn; therefore, both their architectonic and decorative state have been examined. The rediscovery of tombs numbered "X" has also been possible, together with their subsequent photographic documentation, plans, and drawings and location on the map. Nevertheless, it is still very early to draw any conclusions. So far, we can only confirm the well-established historical relevance of the Qurnet Murai necropolis which promises to be reinforced as a result of the continuation of this interesting investigation.

Fig. 4: TT 40. Viceroy of Kush. Amenhotep called Huy. King Tutankhamon and Huy.

An Alternative Strategy
for the Transportation of Quarried
Hard Stone from Lower Nubia
to Giza during the Old Kingdom[1]

Elizabeth Bloxam
The Institute of Archaeology, University College London

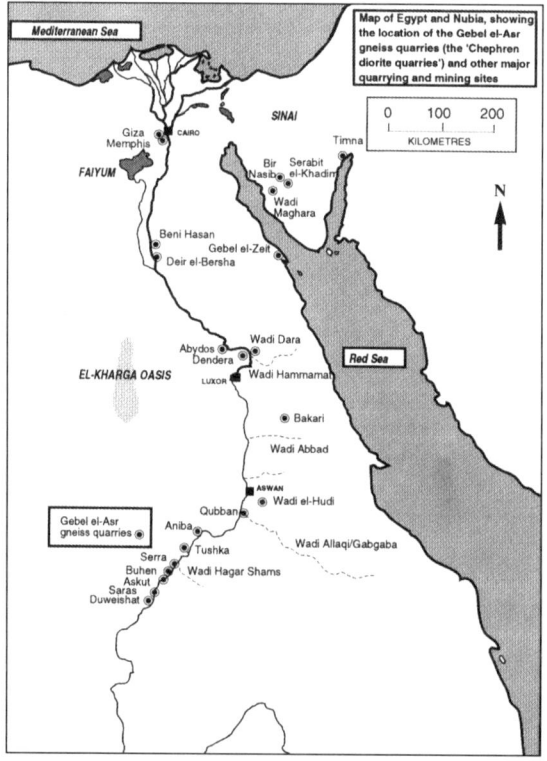

Map of Egypt and Nubia, showing the location of the Gebel el-Asr gneiss quarries (the 'Chephren diorite quarries') and other major quarrying and mining sites

"Chephren's Quarry" in the Western Desert of Egypt, 65 km northwest of Abu Simbel in Lower Nubia (fig. 1), was the source of blue iridescent banded gabbro-gneiss of which the Fourth Dynasty seated statue of Khafra is an example. The Egyptian state-run monopoly of exotic raw material acquisition and transportation from remote locations formed a major component of economic and ideological practices during the Old Kingdom.

Stone-built ramp structures dating to the Old Kingdom (2686–2181 BCE) are unique features of the quarry site, rising to approximately 1.5 m at their face. The first systematic excavation of the loading ramps and settlement at Chephren's Quarry was conducted in April 1999 by the Institute of Archaeology, University College, London, under the directorship

Fig. 1: Pharaonic quarrying and mining sites in Egypt and Nubia (after Shaw 1999).

86

of Ian Shaw. Archaeological evidence from the excavation suggests that alternative strategies for the transportation of stone to Lower Egypt were used to overcome the geographical, geomorphologic, and environmental difficulties that the site presents.

Interpretation of the fresh archaeological evidence and a comparative analysis of other contemporary quarry sites suggests the *kelek* or buoyed raft was an alternative method to transport stone from the quarry. This concept incorporates the utilization of the depression of the Wadi Tushka as a closer source of water to the quarry than the Nile to minimize haulage overland.

There have been many attempts to reconstruct how heavy weights of quarried stone were transported over long distances in antiquity. Some well-known examples include the bluestones of Stonehenge transported from West Wales to Wiltshire in south-west England, the Moai of Easter Island, and the obelisks from Aswan. These examples cover a time span of over 3,000 years. Common to all of them is the fact that the archaeological record has provided no evidence to reconstruct the practice. Experimental archaeologists have tried to do this with varying degrees of success. Most have concluded that a sledge on rollers in conjunction with some kind of prepared track seemed the most feasible explanation of how the stone was transported from its source.

Engelbach and Murray[2] were the first archaeologists to visit Chephren's Quarry in Lower Nubia in the 1930s. Their reports highlighted the enigmatic nature of two stone-built loading ramps located in the south of the quarry close to the Khufu Stele platform. They partly excavated one of the ramps and discovered two deep parallel tracks emanating from the ramp's face. The depth of the tracks and the extreme height of the ramps were features which perplexed Engelbach and Murray. This was because the evidence suggested that a vehicle other than a simple sledge must have been employed to remove the stone from the quarry.

Sixty years later, in April of 1999, a team of archaeologists from the Institute of Archaeology at University College London, under the directorship of Ian Shaw, returned to Chephren's Quarry to commence a season of survey and excavation. The main objectives were to excavate the workmen's settlement at Quartz Ridge and as part of the author's PhD research, to excavate the two stone-built loading ramps found by Engelbach and Murray at "Khufu Stele Quarry" in the south.

The exposed loading ramps show an exterior of large chipped blocks of gabbro-gneiss with an interior of loose spoil fill. Loading Ramp 1 (LR1) is located where the quarry workings are completely obscured and possibly worked out. Loading Ramp 2 (LR2) is located two kilometers to the north-west within the still visible quarry workings at Khufu Stele Quarry. It seems probable that the logistical construction of the ramps within the quarry workings was the focal point for the collection and transportation of stone away from the quarry.

The 1999 excavation of the loading ramps involved the removal of up to half a meter of wind-blown sand to expose the face of each ramp down to the original ground surface. During removal of the aeolian sand, pottery shards dating to the Old Kingdom were revealed. No pottery dating to later periods was found in any part of Khufu Stele Quarry whereas in areas of the quarry to the north, the pottery shards indicated both Old and Middle Kingdom activity.

When the original ground surface was reached, two parallel tracks (figs. 2 and 3) approximately 75 cm wide by 33 cm deep were revealed. The dimensions of excavated LR1 at its face are:

Width	4.70 m.
Height of actual stone exterior	1.22 m.
Height from base of tracks	1.63 m.
Angle of slope	10 degrees.

Fig. 2: Parallel tracks leading from Loading Ramp 1 at "Khufu Stele Quarry," "Chephren's Quarry." (photograph: E. Bloxam, 1999).

Fig. 3: View of parallel tracks from Loading Ramp 2 "Khufu Stele Quarry," "Chephren's Quarry." (photograph: E. Bloxam, 1999).

The dimensions of excavated LR2 at its face are:

Width	5.50 m.
Height of actual stone exterior	1.00 m.
Height from base of tracks	1.32 m.
Angle of slope of ramp	10 degrees.

Once excavation to the base of each track was completed, the surface of the parallel tracks appeared harder than the surrounding original ground surface. It should be noted that the Old Kingdom ground surface would not resemble the deflated ground surface seen today, with its considerable deposition of wind-blown sand. Analysis of soil samples taken from the base of the track at LR2 revealed an abundance of quartz and carbonate minerals in what was originally a *playa* mud or siltstone. On exposure and desiccation this produced a hard stable surface crust, or "duricrust." Moving loads across this surface would not have required the use of rollers.[3]

The size of vehicle that could be accommodated can be estimated from the width of the tracks which are around 70 cm. The distance between the tracks is about 1.7 m, while the height of the vehicle must have been that of the ramp, about 1.5 m. The width could not be greater than that of the ramp (5 m) but its length is more uncertain. However, since the deepest parts of the track lie within 5 m from the ramp, this may be an indication of length. Hence, the vehicle was approximately 5 m x 5 m x 1.5 m (l x w x h). It should be noted that each runner was quite wide (75 cm) distributing the weight over a large surface area and reducing the tendency to dig into the ground. If the width of the vehicle was a function of the distance between tracks (runners) then its size is reduced to 5 m x 1.7 m x 1.5 m (l x w x h).

An interesting and unexpected feature of the parallel tracks at both loading ramps, which Engelbach and Murray had previously overlooked, was that they had been artificially cut rather than worn by constant traffic, because there were no signs of abrasion along their sides. It seems feasible to suggest that the tracks were cut to accommodate the vehicle's runners and to bring the top of the vehicle or platform flush with the top of the ramp.

At both loading ramps the tracks disappear at approximately 9 m from the faces of the ramps further indicating that the tracks are artificially dug. This can be deduced from the fact that once the vehicle was drawn up onto the original ground surface, which is only covered by a thin deposit of wind-blown sand, the tracks would easily have weathered away.

The interpretation of this evidence produces an argument for a vehicle other than the conventional sledge being used to transport stone away from the quarry. This argument is based on two important pieces of evidence; first is the excessive height of each loading ramp, and second, the reason for the artificially cut tracks. As indicated at the beginning of this paper, the archaeological record supplies little evidence for determining how technology was applied to the han-

Fig. 4: Line drawing of Assyrians transporting stone on a buoyed raft: relief from the Palace of Sennacherib (after Casson, L. 1994. *Ships and Seafaring in Ancient Times.* London, BMP).

dling and transportation of stone in antiquity. In ancient Egyptian iconography, sources from only funerary contexts provide an indication of how heavy loads were conveyed overland and these can be unreliable. Scenes depicting the transportation of stone from quarries almost exclusively show the sledge being used in conjunction with rollers and pulled by large numbers of workers. The most notable depiction is that in the Twelfth Dynasty tomb of Djutihotep at el-Bersheh, which shows his statue being hauled on a sledge from the travertine quarries at Hatnub by 172 men. Old Kingdom portrayals of sledges functioning purely as haulage vehicles in non-funerary contexts are so far unknown. The only known representation (in a non-funerary context) of the use of any vehicle other than a sledge, is an Assyrian relief dating to the first millennium BCE from the palace of Sennacherib (fig. 4).

The vehicle is constructed from a light wood frame, laced together with withies, cords, or thongs over which animal hides are stretched. Rafts of this type, known as *keleks*, are still used to navigate the Tigris River and are said to be ideally suited to shallow tributaries and rocky rapids. A similar raft-like vehicle on runners, may have been used to transport stone from Chephren's Quarry. It would have been constructed from a variety of locally-available materials such as acacia and tamarisk wood, with an emphasis on constructing a vehicle that was as light as possible. It is interesting to note that in the Assyrian example, inflated animal hides are used to provide buoyancy. Animal hides identical to those portrayed are still used in the northern Sudan for transporting water from wells: such devices could also have been used to transport water from wells at the quarry.

A block of gabbro-gneiss used for the Khafre statue would weigh approximately four tons. Conveying it via water would be far less arduous and require less human resources than transporting it overland. It had previously been assumed that the Nile at Tushka was the destination for the quarried stone blocks, but this would have necessitated travelling over 80 km of undulating terrain. However, if the destination was the nearby Wadi Tushka tributary, then the overland journey would only be 13 km.

An ancient road connects Chephren's Quarry to the Nile at Tushka (now under Lake Nasser), and at 80 km, it is the longest surviving quarry road. Englebach and Murray discovered the road, and in their survey reports suggested it was an animel-worn track probably used for the conveyance of food and fuel supplies during The Middle Kingdom exploitation of the quarry.[4]

Ball and Haynes have both speculated that the Wadi Tushka, a prominent depression northeast of Chephren's Quarry, was once a tributary draining inland *playa* lakes.[5] If the Wadi Tushka was active in the Old Kingdom due to wetter conditions and higher Nile floods, then it would appear more practical for the stone to be taken north-east from the quarry to there, as it would have been the closest source of water and access to the Nile. This raises the possibility that the geomorphology at the time of the Old Kingdom gave closer access to water for transportation of materials than was previously thought. As Harrell and Bown have observed, the siting of ancient quarries is related to access to permanent water sources.[6]

The overland journey north to the Wadi Tushka from the quarry is approximately 13 km and follows the course of another smaller system that once fed into it. This would have provided an ideal predetermined route of gradual declination relatively free of obstruction. The alternative 80 km route south to Tushka is geomophologically opposite, with undulating terrain and numerous obstructions in the form of sandstone outcrops. Once the vehicle reached the Wadi Tushka it would be floated off on the annual high flood waters then steered independently to the Nile. On its longer journey it could continue being independently steered or towed. As previously mentioned, the *kelek* type vehicle is particularly suited not only to the shallow water of the wadi but also to negotiating the first cataract at Aswan. On arrival at Giza the block would be transferred onto a jetty at the pyramid construction site for final manufacture. The raft would be either dismantled for reuse or sent back.

Discussion on how stone was conveyed from quarries in antiquity has in most cases relied upon iconographic sources due the scarcity of material archaeological remains. This is nowhere more apparent than in Egyptian archaeology. The theory of an amphibious vehicle is proposed because the evidence from Chephren's Quarry requires a reappraisal of stone transportation from remote sources in purely practical terms. The time and effort put into constructing the stone loading ramps means they were purpose-built to accommodate a vehicle other than a conventional sledge. This is borne out by their excessive height and the deep and wide artificially cut tracks.

As previously suggested, it is unlikely that the ancient track located by Engelbach and Murray in 1938 was anything other than a Middle Kingdom supply route. It is clear from the geomorphology of the surrounding terrain that the transportation of blocks of stone weighing several tons along this particular route would have been a considerable undertaking in terms of both time and human resources.

Finally, it is interesting to note that the designation and organization of quarry labor gangs is often attributed to a ship's crew. As Andreu remarks: "...expedition troops had been assimilated to a naval battalion, with a port crew and starboard crew, the rowers having been replaced by the quarrymen."[7]

Notes:

1 The author's work at Chephren's Quarry was funded by the Institute of Archaeology, University College, London, and present research is being funded by the Arts and Humanities Research Board. I would like to acknowledge the hard work and support of all the 1999 excavation team members, in particular Richard Lee, Judith Bunbury, and Debbie Darnell, whose input regarding the findings from the excavation have been central to the interpretation of this site. Special thanks to Ian Shaw, Director of the Gebel el-Asr project, who made this project possible. The success of the 1999 excavation is also attributed to the generous sponsorship by Colin Rogers, Director of el-Alsson School in Cairo, for providing us with essential equipment, supplies, and storage facilities at the school.

2 R. Engelbach, "The quarries of the Western Nubian desert and the Ancient road to Tushka," *ASAE* 38 (1938), 369–90. G.W. Murray, "The road to Chephren's Quarries," *The Geographical Journal* 4 (2) (1939), 97–114.

3 American Geological Institute *Dictionary of Geological Terms*, (New York, 1962), 150.

4 Engelbach, "Quarries," 369–90; Murray, "Road," 97–114.

5 J. Ball, "Problems of the Libyan desert," *Geographical Journal* 70 (1927) 21–83; 105–128; 209–224; 512. C. V. Haynes, "Geochronology of Wadi Tushka - lost tributary of the Nile," *Science* 210: (1980) 68–71.

6 J. A. Harrell and T. M. Bown, "An Old Kingdom basalt quarry at Widan el-Faras and the quarry road to Lake Moeris in the Faiyum," *JARCE* 32 (1995), 71–91.

7 G. Andreu, *Egypt in the Age of the Pyramids*, (London, 1997).

The Hellenistic–Roman Necropolises of Alexandria

Nicola Bonacasa
Università degli Studi di Palermo

Alexandria owns the greatest concentration of Hellenistic-Roman necropolises in the Mediterranean region, and the subject of the Alexandrian necropolises constitutes one of the more debated and complex issues of Greco-Roman archaeology in Egypt.[1]

As we all know, in Egypt the roots of Italian scientific culture reach down into the nineteeth century, especially in Alexandria. However, when the amazing new discoveries from the Egypt of the pharaohs began to be known, the antiquities of Greco-Roman Egypt scarcely circulated at all, and their eventual acceptance by the world of scholarship was due to the indefatigable and disinterested commitment of just a handful of men, all Italians, the most prestigious of whom were indubitably Giuseppe Botti, Evaristo Breccia, and Achille Adriani.

In 1892 Giuseppe Botti created the Greco-Roman Museum in Alexandria; in 1893 the Société d'Archéologie d'Alexandrie was founded; in 1904 Evaristo Breccia succeeded Botti as curator of the museum and Director of Excavations in Alexandria; in the late summer of 1932, following Breccia's return to Italy, Achille Adriani arrived in Alexandria. We can therefore say that in 1982, the year of Adriani's death, Alexandrian archaeology and Greco-Roman archaeology in Egypt in general had been in Italian hands for almost a century. I am proud to have resumed the old tradition established by Adriani in the field of Alexandrian archaeology, to which I endeavor to do full honor both to Italy and to Egypt.

Alexandria was certainly, both politically and culturally, if not the principal center, then one of the centers of the Hellenistic world. In any case, that prominence allowed it to withstand the Roman political expansion for longer than it might have otherwise. Alexandria remained, at the same time, an autonomous artistic-cultural entity. But this particular status of the capital of the Lagides was not the general condition of Ptolemaic Egypt, a country of mixed Greco-Egyptian culture. It is important to mention here that, especially in the field of private funerary architecture, the production of the religious and decorative sculpture, the portrait of mixed style, and also in the sector of artistic craftsmanship, Greco-Egyptian workers could express themselves with unusual freedom, sometimes reaching levels of unexpected quality.

In my view there are two basic matters of current significance, among the many still to be resolved in the field of Alexandrian archaeology: First, the topography of the ancient city and of the history of its town planning and location of its monuments,[2] a subject already considered by a number of distinguished scholars including Mahmoud Bey al-Falaki, Noack, Thiersch, Pagenstecher, Breccia, Adriani, Grimm, Pfrommer, and colleagues of the Polish Mission and the Greco-Roman Museum. Second is the methodological reformulation of the problem of Alexandrian art in an extensive and profound re-examination of the vast phenomenon of the transplantation of Greek art into a country like Egypt. For millennia Egypt had expressed its own art forms that were the antithesis of Greek art, a situation which persisted throughout the Hellenistic-Roman age.

It is within this highly engaging milieu of data collection, scientific research and pondered critical revisions that the *Repertorio d'arte dell' Egitto greco-romano* has always operated and intends to operate in the future. This great international enterprise was founded in Palermo by Achille Adriani, and we of the Institute of Archaeology in Palermo University continue to be interested in it.

With regard to the necropolis at Alexandria, we cannot forget the general work by Rudolf Pagenstecher.[3] This was immediately outdated by the extraordinary discoveries of Breccia and Adriani. But we must also point out that Adriani returned many times to the great themes of the city's topography and layout, and to the history of Alexandrian funeral architecture. Each time he did this with great success, an effort which culminated in the presentation of the two extreme-ly well-received volumes of the *Repertorio*, Series C, I–II.[4] Therein we find a collection of exhaus-tive and updated notes, detailed points of information on individual problems, and above all an irreplaceable documentation. He had collocated and arranged this for the study of one of the aspects of the archaeology of Greco-Roman Egypt, with a view to reconstructing the past appear-ance of Alexandria.

This said, it is scarcely necessary to stress the importance of the Hellenistic funerary archi-tecture of Alexandria,[5] Shatbi, Sidi Gaber, Mustafa Pasha, and Anfushi, and of the later funerary architecture, also monumental, of Gabbari, Mex, and the catacombs of Kom al-Shuqafa. This is not only because it is an imitation of the civic architecture of the city, not a trace of which has survived in Alexandria, but also because it transmits to us a faint echo of Alexandrian wall dec-oration, known to us almost exclusively from the decoration of the hypogea during the Hellenistic and Roman ages.

After this rapid outline of the historico-critical situation, wherein we have considered the "past" of the Alexandrian necropolises, let us now speak of the interventions we believe are absolutely necessary if we hope to save them. We thus enter the field of the "future" of Greco-Roman archaeology in Egypt.

Beginning in 1987, with the authoritative patronage of the Embassy of Italy in Cairo, we began and have renewed through the Italian State Department, our joint mission of the Institute of Archaeology in Palermo and the Central Institute for Restoration in Rome. The project was intended to provide an early programmed intervention for the conservative restoration from the most important and much more degraded complex of the western necropolis onwards; the Greco-Egyptians hypogea of Anfushi (the painted walls have now suffered irreparable damage). This began in September of 1987, a mission in which our friend Umberto Baldini played a part, and the results of the joint Baldini-Bonacasa report were submitted in May, 1988 to our State

Department at Rome, the Italian Embassy in Cairo, the Director of the Italian Institute of Culture, The Supreme Council of Antiquities in Cairo, as well as to the General Director of the Greco-Roman Museum in Alexandria.

The necessary technical work will be long, difficult, and expensive. Even a quick look at the precarious conditions of four of the most important Alexandrian archaeological complexes—two in the western necropolis, Anfushi, and Kom al-Shuqafa, and two in the eastern necropolis, Shatbi and Mustafa Pasha—will immediately show how urgently restoration work is required to save these exceptional finds from complete destruction, finds that are due above all to the intelligent and valuable work of Italian archaeologists, and are part of the heritage not just of Egypt but of the whole world.

Anfushi

This important Greco-Egyptian funerary complex on Pharos Island in the western necropolis,[6] whose exemplary architectural regularity married with the most refined relief and pictorial decoration of mixed style has been devastated by rising sea water, especially in Tombs 3, 4, and 5.

While it is necessary on the one hand to set up a series of permanent drainage pumps all around the complex to be used whenever "high water" occurs, on the other hand we are faced with the need to consolidate and conserve the painted walls. At the same time we must begin to deal with the salt efflorescence on the walls. We are still without a suitable chemical analysis and also need to eliminate former interventions applied in cement or with unsuitable mortars.

The real and definitive recovery of the more at-risk sector of the necropolis of Anfushi (Tombs 3, 4, 5) in the periods of absence of water is tied to the detachment of the original floor of each hypogeum. This involves draining the water and installing a drain with a slope toward the exterior below the floor and also collection canals to let out the waters upon their seasonal return. Subsequently, only the floor can be replaced *in situ*, having had an impermeable resin support surface installed to protect and to preserve it.

In the months of June and July in 1994 and 1995, exclusively in the necropolis of Anfushi, Tombs 1 and 2—the only ones of the complex of the five hypogea uninjured by the above-described—the Institute of Archaeology in Palermo started the first and second campaign of restoration, intended to be a sample campaign of conservative restoration.[7] The necessary funds had been appropriated by the Office of Foreign Affairs. We take this opportunity to thank the following for their collaboration and hospitality: the Supreme Council of Antiquities in Cairo, Chairman Dr. Abd al-Halim Nur al-Din, and the Director of the Greco-Roman Museum in Alexandria, Mrs. Dorreya Said.

All the surfaces of the masonry (local sandstone with poor cohesion), of Tombs 1 and 2 of Anfushi, when distanced from sources of damp, and after accurate cleaning, were submitted to treatment with the consolidant RC/70 (ethyl silicate). The first result of the treatment, repeated over time, seems positive, but some months are needed to ensure that the final result is guaranteed. The whole surface of the painted walls has been checked often, and when necessary we have proceeded with a calibrated fungicide treatment based on Neo-Desogen.

All the painted walls in room 1 of Tomb 1 and the entrance staircase and of room 2 of Tomb 2 have been degreased with volatile substances and cleaned of salt efflorescence by repeated applications of paper pulp and by using the scalpel in some stubborn cases.

After this we are ready to start another experience in Anfushi, in collaboration with our colleagues and technicians in Alexandria.

Kom al-Shuqafa

The present state of conservation of the great catacomb of Kom al-Shuqafa, the best-known and most highly-prized testimony to Alexandrian funerary architecture and culture,[8] is now at the utmost limit of its degradation.

Pending the protection of the whole hypogeum within its own area by appropriate hydraulic engineering installations and the courageous use of drainage pumps, I suggest that it is necessary to dig a wide trench to isolate the monument once and for all from the surrounding subsoil and its abundant groundwater. In addition, a study of the influences and the modifications recently made to the immediately adjacent hydrographic system (water-channels, pipes, etc.), of the penetration of irrigation and rainwater, and of the drainage system are needed.

But that will not be enough. It is also imperative to carry out accurate and on-going tests in the interior of the hypogeum, where a great deal of work is now in progress, in order to study the formation of mineral salts and the masonry's loss of cohesion; thermohydrographic recorders will have to be placed at different levels in order to register the range of the microclimate and thus enable us to calculate its variation in the presence of visitors. The number of visitors will certainly have to be reduced, especially in the peak seasons of summer and winter, and all the present sources of illumination replaced with a special cold light system.

Shatbi

The first steps to rescue the most ancient and glorious Hellenistic necropolis on the east side of Alexandria,[9] the architectural features of which are now almost entirely destroyed, is the creation of a barrier against the wind which is eroding the structures and destroying the plaster, and against the marine and saline erosion from subsoil infiltration which has transformed Shatbi into an accumulation of unhealthy debris.

Two measures are pressing: the raising of the northern boundary wall in accordance with appropriate architectural criteria to afford protection from the continuous attacks of the winds blowing off the sea; and the creation of a covering for the main complex—hypogeum A of the third century BCE—which should be planned so that it has its own museological identity. It will then be possible to proceed to the realization of a system of water channeling and drainage for the definitive recovery of the complex, and to the extremely difficult work of reconstruction, consolidation, and restoration of the structures.

Mustafa Pasha

Here we have an indication of the majestic, luxurious burial customs that existed in Alexandria between the third and second century BCE. This was an articulated complex of seven monumental family hypogea, richly structured, and decorated with pictures and stucco relief.[10] Once the pride of Greco-Roman archaeology in Egypt, this is now in an extreme state of disrepair.

The whole complex, because of the gravity and the diversity of the problems it presents, requires a carefully prepared restoration plan as soon as specialists in the various chemical, physical, structural and technico-practical disciplines have presented their findings. In the meantime Tomb 1, for example, needs some simple microbiological analyses in order to combat the fungus attacking it. Tomb 2 awaits repairs to its protective covering and drainage system, and the walls that are raised or otherwise unsafe also need appropriate coating.

When these and other obvious emergencies have been resolved, we can begin the long and expensive recovery of the structures, the consolidation of the plasterwork, the protection of the paintings and numerous wall decorations, a functional covering of the more exposed hypogea, and a new arrangement of the access and internal routes.

This work is our duty, as scholars and friends of Egypt. In this way my report is sounding an alarm.

Alexandria, the moral capital of the Mediterranean, with the New Alexandrian Library intends to present in modern terms the theme of universal culture. As such it cannot remain insensitive to the progressive deterioration and the certain loss of its monumental necropolises.

Notes:

1 N. Bonacasa, "Repertorio d'Arte dell'Egitto Greco-Romano," in *Missioni Archeologiche Italiane. La ricerca archeologica, antropologica, etnologica.* Ministero Affari Esteri, (Roma, 1997), 23–26.

2 W. A. Daszewski, "Notes on topography of Ptolemaic Alexandria," in *Alessandria e il mondo ellenistico-romano, Studi in onore di Achille Adriani,* I (Roma, 1983), 54–69; M. Rodziewicz, A. Abd El Fattah, "Recent discoveries in the Royal Quarters of Alexandria"; M. Rodziewicz, Daoud Abdo Daoud, "Investigation of a trench near the Via Canonica," in *Bulletin de la Société d' Archéologie d' Alexandrie,* 44 (1991), 131–150, 151–168, including various articles about the excavations after 1960; B. Tkaczow, *Topography of ancient Alexandria,* (Varsovie, 1993), 164–165, passim.

3 R. Pagenstecher, *Nekropolis* (Lipsia, 1919), passim.

4 A. Adriani, *Repertorio d'arte dell'Egitto Greco-Romano.* Serie C, I–II (Palermo, 1963–1966), passim, with the former Bibliography; B. Tkaczow, *Topography of ancient Alexandria,* passim

5 N. Bonacasa, "Un inedito di Achille Adriani sulla tomba di Alessandro," in *Giornate di studio in onore di Achille Adriani,* (settembre 1984), *Studi Miscellanei,* 28, 1984–85 (1991), 3–19; A. Adriani (†), N. Bonacasa, P. Minà, *La Tomba di Alessandro. Realtà, ipotesi e fantasie,* (Roma, 2000).

6 A. Adriani, "Nécropoles de l'Ile de Pharos," in *Annuaire du Musée Gréco-Romain, 1940–50,* (Alexandrie, 1952), 47–128.

7 N. Bonacasa, "The Hellenistic-Roman Necropolis of Alexandria," in *Geosciences and Archaeology in the Mediterranean Countries. Geological Survey of Egypt,* (Cairo, 1995), 303–310; N. Bonacasa, "Le necropoli ellenistico-romane di Alessandria d'Egitto. Anfushi - Rapporto preliminare sulla prima campagna di restauro," in *Science and Technology for the safeguard of cultural heritage in the Mediterranean basin, 1° International Congress,* (Catania-Siracusa, 1995), I (Palermo, 1998), 29–31.

8 Th. Schreiber, *Die Nekropole von Kom, esch-Schukafa, Expedition Ernest von Sieglin,* I (Lipsia, 1908), passim.

9 E. Breccia, *La necropoli di Sciatbi,* (Le Caire, 1912), passim.

10 A. Adriani, "La nécropole de Moustafa Pacha," in *Annuaire du Musée Gréco-Romain, 1933–34/1934–35,* (Alexandrie, 1936), passim; A. Adriani, *Repertorio,* passim, with the former bibliography.

The Sarcophagus Lid of Queen Takhat

Edwin C. Brock
Co-director, Amenmeses Project

In comparison with the burial equipment for kings, hard stone sarcophagi for royal women are not found very often in the New Kingdom before the Nineteenth Dynasty. At present, we know only of one for Hatshepsut as queen, perhaps one for Meryet-ra Hatshepsut, the wife of Thutmose III found in KV42, and at least two Amarna examples, belonging to Queen Tiy and princess Meketaten, respectively the mother and daughter of Akhenaten. This apparent paucity of material may be a factor of the accident of discovery, since many the tombs of royal family members of the Eighteenth Dynasty are still unidentified.

During the reign of Rameses II, several royal women were provided with sarcophagi made of granite, including those for his chief queen Nefertari,[1] and his daughters Meryetamen,[2] Henutmire,[3] and Bintanta[4] that are currently known. Most likely his other chief queen, Isitnefret, mother of Khaemwaset and Merenptah and others, would have had a stone sarcophagus as well, but her tomb yet remains to be found. Royal family members in the Twentieth Dynasty both queens and princes, also had stone sarcophagi, almost exclusively mummiform in appearance. In some cases these appear to have been re-used items, as in the case of the sarcophagus of a prince Amenherkhepeshef/Pares found in the clearance of KV 13 by the mission of Hamburg University, directed by Hartwig Altenmüller.[5] This sarcophagus, or at least the lid, was originally made for Queen Tausert, last ruler of the Nineteenth Dynasty, but altered to reflect the change in status and gender of the second owner, although the name and titles of Tausert remain on the head end of the lid.

In the 1995 excavation season of the Amenmeses Project, an inscribed fragment of red granite was found in the lower strata of debris near the southeast corner of Room E. It bore remains of three incised columns of hieroglyphs and part of the arm and body of a figure near the left edge. The cartouche bore the name of Takhat, inscribed on a surface lower than the surrounding area. When viewed in section, the fragment shows three worked surfaces: the inscribed vertical surface (exterior), a roughly finished but uninscribed surface with a concave curve (interior), and

97

a lower edge with a projecting inner lip. Such a profile suggests that this is a fragment of a lid for a sarcophagus. Evidence for the re-use of this tomb for the burial of a queen named Takhat had been found in previous seasons (unpublished) but the existence of a hard stone sarcophagus increased the likelihood of such an activity.

During the 1998 season, while removing the lower strata on the west and east sides of Corridor G, many more inscribed granite fragments were discovered, some bearing the name of Takhat, while others had figures in sunk relief. Over 200 fragments with a worked surface, the majority bearing remains of texts and figures, were discovered, scattered about in Corridor G, although only a few were on the floor itself. Few fragments were contiguous in relation to each other as found

Only a few fragments were located in Room H, although one did join the first fragment found in Room E discovered four years earlier.

Although the lid is incomplete, with at least 30 percent still missing, enough can be joined to show its overall appearance and dimensions. The lid is rectangular in plan with vertical sides and ends, the lower edge had an inner projecting lip that would have engaged the upper edge of the box with a corresponding outer projecting lip. A concave curve at the top of the inner vertical face marks the transition to the horizontal "ceiling" of the lid on sides and ends. The estimated overall dimensions are a length of approximately 2.5 meters, a width of 1.1 meters and height of 40 cm.

By assembling the lid for the purposes of recording, it has been possible to identify the orientation of the decoration, as well as the sources for the imagery involved. Examination of the orientation of the texts and figures of the upper surface permits the designation of head and foot ends and left and right sides in relation to the occupant of the sarcophagus. Thus the head end is at the top of the panel with the large winged figure worshipped by the two human-headed birds representing the *ba* of the queen. Unfortunately, the head of the winged figure is not preserved, making it uncertain if this represents a falcon or the ram-headed *ba* of Re. The latter image appears in the burial chambers of Merenptah, Tausert, and Rameses III and is encountered, for example, on the effigy on the lid of Sety II. Below this panel is a grid of text bands setting off areas bearing human-headed mummiform figures representing the Four Sons of Horus, Anubis, and probably two others, as yet undiscovered. Along the horizontal edge surfaces are two undulating cobras oriented toward the head end.

On the remains of the head-end panel, part of a winged goddess kneeling on the gold symbol is identified by the texts as Nephthys. She is flanked by two standing goddesses with serpents emerging from their shoulders. This latter pair of figures derives from the upper register of the twelfth hour of the Imydwat. Between Nephthys and the text columns, a cobra is shown supported by two symbols for cloth. This unlabelled figure could be taken from the lower register of either the eighth or ninth hours of the Imydwat. The kneeling winged figure of Isis on the center of the foot end is flanked by two standing goddesses wearing the white and red crowns. As these figures have no identifying labels, it cannot be determined from which hour of the Imydwat they come. Such figures occur in the first, second, fourth, tenth and eleventh hours of this composition.

The long sides of the lid also are decorated with extracts from the Imydwat. On the partially preserved left side, figures from the lower register of the seventh hour of the Imydwat are shown, with the seated falcon-headed figure labeled Horus Hekenu, instead of the expected Horus of the Underworld. Several male figures with stars on their heads, representing hours, walk away from Horus toward the head end. The opposite side has figures taken from the upper registers of the tenth and eleventh hours of the Imydwat. Near the foot end, five figures—a standing male, a scarab beetle, and two seated goddesses representing the Lower and Upper Egyptian crowns—flank a pair of serpents and a sun disk, all from the tenth division. The remainder of the decoration on this side is an abbreviated version of the upper register of the eleventh hour, omitting some of the figures before the quartet of goddesses seated on cobras.

On the upper surface, below the head end panel, it is possible to see two stages of cutting for the texts and figures. To the occupant's left of center the figures and texts are more lightly incised, while to the proper right, the figures have been rendered in sunk relief and the texts are more deeply cut. It is also possible in the more lightly-cut area to find better preserved, and in some cases, unaltered versions of the name of the original owner, Anuket-em-heb. Alterations of the queen's title can be seen on the long horizontal speech of Nut on this side, with "king's daughter" changed to "king's wife" and "mistress of the palace" changed to "great king's wife."

The *ḳrst*-form sarcophagus, associated with the *pr-nw* (Gardiner Sign List O 20), is characterized by a lid with a barrel vault and two vertical end panels projecting above the vaulted surface. It is of great antiquity, and was prevalent in the Old and Middle Kingdoms, in both royal and non-royal burials. It was used in hieroglyphs (Gardiner Sign List Q 6) and representations as the exemplar for this essential item of burial equipment well into the New Kingdom, although other forms had already come into use. None of the surviving stone sarcophagi for royal women of the Eighteenth Dynasty take this form, and it is only in the Nineteenth Dynasty that it recurs specifically in the sarcophagus lids of Nefertari, Meryetamen, and the outer lid of Merenptah. A modified form is also found in the third lid of Merenptah, re-used in the burial of Psusennes I in the royal necropolis at Tanis, and in the fragmentary lid of Sety II. In both of the latter examples, a mummiform effigy of the deceased is sculpted on the upper surface. The Nefertari and Meryetamen lids in particular are similar in both appearance and dimensions. The upper surface curves inwards towards the flattened central area from horizontal platforms inset from the edges along the sides. Even on the outer lid of Merenptah, although of greater dimensions, the same form is used.

The general decorative program of the lids of Nefertari and Meryetamen are very similar, although differing in detail. In general terms, the Takhat lid bears some resemblance to these two, particularly in the division of the upper surface into "cells" by means of lateral and longitudinal text bands. The decoration of the sides with a row of figures, and the placement of protective figures, either Isis and Nephthys, or Anubis jackals, on the end panels is also an iconographic link, although the subject matter is different. These features are shared in a general way by the Takhat lid.

The utilization of extracts from the Imydwat is also found on royal sarcophagi of the Nineteenth and Twentieth Dynasties; for example on the calcite sarcophagus of Rameses II, the granite and calcite sarcophagi of Merenptah, the calcite sarcophagus of Siptah, and the granite sarcophagus of Rameses III. The use of selections from the last four hours of the Imydwat is also a feature of Twenty-first Dynasty papyri such as those from the caches of the priests of Amen.[6]

As noted, the inscriptions in the cartouches appear to be re-carved, and traces of the name of the original owner can be discerned, particularly on the upper surface of the lid. It can be demonstrated that the original owner's name was *ʿnḳt-m-ḥb*, Anuket-em-heb ("Anukis is in festival"). This name is rare and appears only once in this form in Ranke's *Personnennamen*[7] and in Valbelle's study of Anukis.[8] Given that the overall shape, the decorative program, and the paleography suggest a date for the original owner in the Nineteenth Dynasty, specifically during the reign of Rameses II and his immediate successor, it may be useful to search this period for royal women bearing this name. Unfortunately, such an investigation, using lists of royal family members, does not yield positive results. However, in the procession of royal women of Rameses II on the west wall of the first court of Luxor temple, traces of a possible candidate can be found.[9] The name of one the last princesses in the procession, although damaged in the upper part, does bear traces of "... *m-ḥb*" at the bottom of the text column, written in a format similar to the traces on the Takhat lid. Might Anuket-em-heb, the original owner of the sarcophagus, have been a daughter of Rameses II?

None of the recovered granite fragments belong to the box of the sarcophagus. It seems possible that at some point the box was removed for reuse. It may be that at that time, the lid was broken up, perhaps to make room for the removal of the box from the narrow confines of the lower corridor. Subsequent flooding or other activities scattered the fragments in the rear half of Corridor G over a layer of debris already deposited on the floor. The missing parts of the lid remain to be found, and perhaps may yet be located in the stairwell of the pillared hall that is yet to be cleared.[10]

Fig. 1: The ends of Takhat's sarcophagus lid (head end: upper figure, foot end: lower figure).

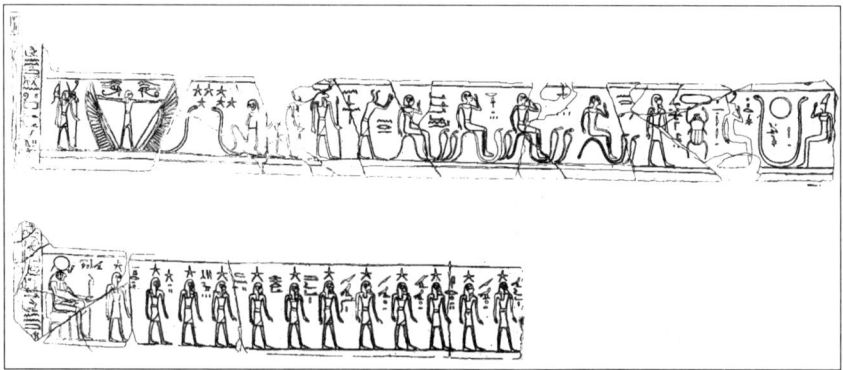

Fig. 2: The sides of Queen Takhat's sarcohagus lid (right side - upper; left side - lower).

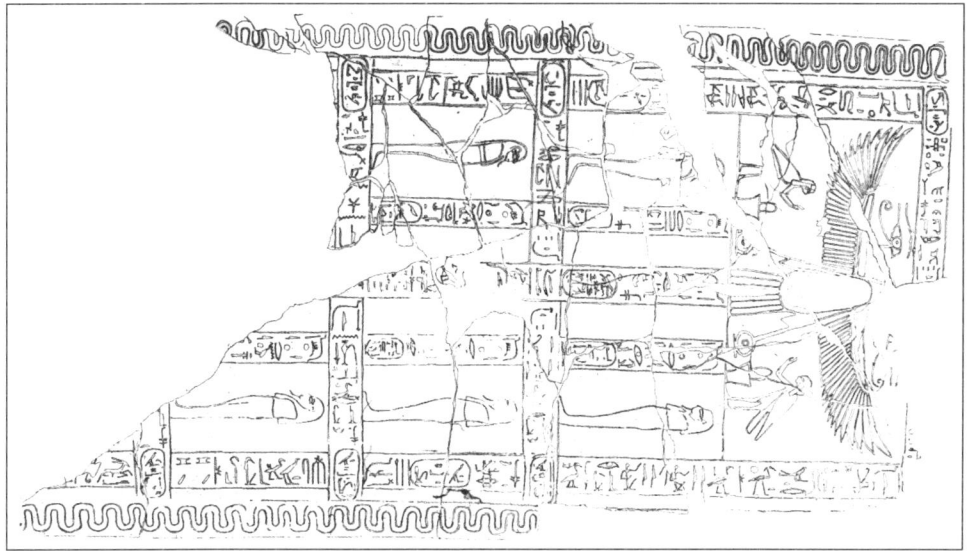

Fig. 3: Queen Takhat's sarcophagus lid, upper surface.

Fig. 4: Detail of head end (upper surface) showing erased cartouches reinscribed for Takhat (courtesy of Hans Otto Schader).

101

Notes:

1 L. Habachi, "Lids of the Outer Sarcophagi of Merytamen and Nefertari, Wives of Ramesses II," *Festschrift zum 150 jährigen Bestehen des Berliner Ägyptologischen Museums, Staatliche Museen zu Berlin* (*Mitteilung aus der Ägyptische Sammlungen VII* [Berlin, 1974]), 105–112, tables 10–12.

2 Habachi, "Lids..."

3 Cairo JE 60137; cf. H. Sourouzian, "Henout-mi-Rê, fille de Ramsès II et grande-épouse du roi," *ASAE* 69 (1983), p. 369; Ch. Leblanc, "L'Indentification de al tombe de Henout-mi-Rê, fille de Ramsès II et grande-èpouse royale," *BIFAO* 88 (1988), 132–133.

4 W. Groff, "La fille de Pharaon." Lettre à Monsieur Gravillot sur une sarcophage ayant appartenu a le Monsieur le Duc d' Aumont et de Villequier, BIE 3e Série, 6 1895 (1896), 313–323; n 7 1896 (1897), 60–87.

5 H. Altenmüller, "Dritter Vorbericht über die Arbeiten des Archäeologischen Instituts der Universität Hamburg am Grab des Bay (KV 13) im Tal der Könige von Theben," *SAK* 21 (1994) 4–7, table I.

6 My thanks to Dr. Thomas Bacs for this observation. For the Third Intermediate Period Imy-dwat papyri see A. el-Aziz Fahmy Sadek, *Contribution à l'étude de l'Amdouat* (OBO 65; Freiburg, 1985).

7 H. Ranke, *Die Ägyptische Personnamen* I (Hamburg, 1935), 62 2.

8 D. Valbelle, *Satis et Anoukis* (Mainz am Rhein, 1981), 185.

9 PM II, (1972), p. 308 (28).

10 K. Kitchen, *Ramesside Inscriptions* 2 (Oxford, 1979), 920 (2).

Mastaba de Khentika:
Gouverneur de l'oasis à la fin de l'Ancien Empire

Georges Castel
IFAO

La ville antique d'"Ayn Asil[1], résidence des gouverneurs de l'oasis à la fin de l'Ancien Empire, se situe près du village actuel de Balat à l'entrée de l'oasis de Dakhla en venant de la Vallée du Nil. À 1 km à l'ouest de la ville s'étend sa nécropole de Qila el-Dabba où apparaissent encore à la surface du désert sept grands tombeaux de gouverneurs dont celui de Khentika[2] (mastaba III[3]), objet de la présente communication.

Découvert en 1972 par l'égyptologue égyptien Ahmed Fakhry, ce tombeau a été fouillé par l'Ifao de 1983 à 1993. Sa superstructure était en partie conservée, bien qu'elle se soit enfoncée de 1 m à 2,50 m dans le sol après l'effondrement des caveaux ; ces derniers étaient inviolés. Ces conditions exceptionnelles ont permis de reconstituer les différents états du monument, d'étudier les techniques de construction en usage à cette époque, et enfin, de mieux comprendre les coutumes funéraires pratiquées dans l'oasis à la fin de l'Ancien Empire.

Le tombeau, orienté est-ouest, est construit au sommet d'un tertre, de formation argileuse, dont la hauteur est de 1,60 m au-dessus de la plaine. Sa superstructure comprend une chapelle, une cour et des salles secondaires, le tout entouré d'un mur d'enceinte (fig. 1a). L'infrastructure se compose de quatre caveaux : un, principal, occupé par Khentika, et trois secondaires, occupés: l'un par son fils Déchérou, qui lui succéda comme gouverneur, et les deux autres, probablement par leurs épouses respectives (fig. 1b). Des puits ouvrant dans la cour permettaient d'accéder aux caveaux.

La construction est en brique crue à l'exception de la chapelle et du caveau principal qui sont en pierre : calcaire pour les sols et les murs et grès pour les plafonds.

Les caveaux sont construits au fond d'une large et profonde fosse de plan carré mesurant 20 m de côté par 9,50 m de profondeur (fig. 2); celle-ci a le fond dallé et les parois doublées d'un épais mur de brique. Une descenderie, à l'est de la fosse, a permis d'évacuer les déblais pendant son creusement et de descendre les matériaux pour la construction des caveaux. Puis, la fosse a été remblayée jusqu'au niveau de la surface, et la superstructure du tombeau, élevée sur le remblai.

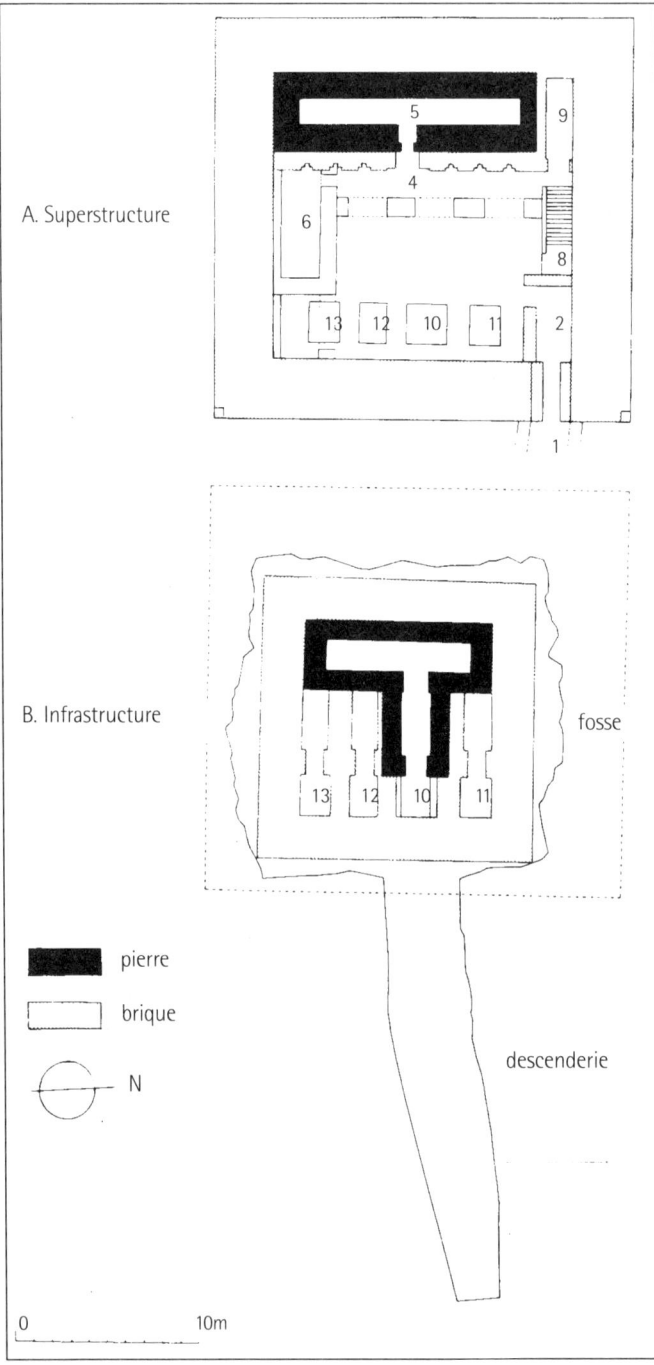

A. Superstructure

B. Infrastructure

fosse

descenderie

pierre

brique

N

0   10m

Fig. 1: Plans de la superstructure et de l'infrastructure du mastaba.

La superstructure

La superstructure comprend quatre phases de construction ; nous décrirons, ici, la troisième, qui est postérieure à l'occupation des caveaux.

Le mur d'enceinte, de plan carré (22 m de côté, ép. 3,20 m, H. initiale 2,75 m), était renforcé dans ses angles nord-est et sud-est par deux stèles de calcaire représentant Khentika. Sa porte d'entrée, située dans l'angle nord-est de l'enceinte, était précédée d'une chaussée (1) montante. Passée cette porte, fermée par un vantail de bois, on pénétrait dans un vestibule (2) rectangulaire, ouvert au sud sur la cour (3). Cette dernière, de plan carré, était limitée, à l'ouest, par un couloir transversal (4) adossé à la façade de la chapelle (5), au sud, par deux salles (6 et 7) appuyées au mur d'enceinte, à l'est, par le mur d'enceinte lui-même, et, au nord, par le vestibule d'entrée auquel était accolé un escalier (8) ; ce dernier desservait une salle située au-dessus de l'annexe (9) de la chapelle.

Le couloir transversal (4) s'ouvrait sur la cour par trois arcades identiques de 2,30 m de large et 1,20 m de haut. À l'intérieur du couloir, quelques terrines à libations, en terre cuite, étaient retournées sur le sol.

La chapelle (5), allongée et étroite, avait sa façade en brique décorée de six niches à redans ; son sol était dallé ; ses murs étaient en pierre sur quatre assises et en brique au-dessus. Sa porte d'entrée, basse et étroite (H. : 1,45 m ; l. : 0,60 m) était fermée par un vantail de bois. À l'intérieur de la chapelle, au milieu de la paroi ouest, se trouvait une stèle au nom de Khentika.

La partie conservée, en pierre, de la chapelle se composait de 450 blocs de calcaire pesant de 200 à 600 kg chacun. Les assises des murs étaient constituées de deux parements de blocs appareillés et d'une fourrure de pierres et de briques. Un mortier de plâtre servait à lier les blocs. 50 blocs sur les 450 possédaient encore sur leurs faces cachées des marques de couleur rouge : repères de construction, anthroponymes et toponymes dont celui de _dsds_ quatre fois mentionné. Si les deux premiers types de marques étaient directement liés à l'organisation du chantier, la présence du dernier—les toponymes—en revanche, reste encore inexpliquée.

La salle annexe (9) située dans le prolongement de l'escalier était fermée par une porte en bois à deux vantaux. Mitoyenne de la chapelle, elle servait vraisemblablement de magasin pour les grandes jarres, à une époque où les salles 6 et 7 n'existaient pas.

La salle 6, voûtée, est adossée au mur à redans de la chapelle. Sa porte, basse et étroite (H. : 1,46 m ; l. 0,60 m) était fermée par un vantail de bois. Deux sols d'occupation en terre battue, d'une dizaine de centimètres d'épaisseur chacun, contenaient le long de la paroi sud, huit empreintes de grandes jarres ; les traces d'un foyer circulaire, par ailleurs, et quelques céramiques utilisées pour les offrandes (supports de vases, coupelles et terrines) étaient conservés au centre de la pièce.

La salle 7, située dans le prolongement de la salle précédente, s'ouvrait sur la cour par une large arcade (l. : 1,96 m ; H. : 1,70 m) ; elle était également voûtée. Cette arcade, par la suite, fut en partie murée et la salle fut renforcée intérieurement avec des murs qui réduisirent sa largeur initiale. Cette salle contenait un lot de céramiques : supports de vases, aiguière à bec verseur, fragments de bassins et terrines.

L'infrastructure

Le caveau principal (10) de Khentika, dont le plan est en forme de T, comprend une antichambre (barre verticale du T) et le caveau proprement dit (barre horizontale du T). Les trois autres caveaux, de plan rectangulaire, sont identiques et parallèles à l'antichambre, celui (11) de Déchérou étant au nord, et les deux autres (12 et 13) au sud. Quatre puits funéraires les reliaient à la superstructure.

Les puits funéraires

Les puits étaient remplis d'un matériel abondant, notamment de vases d'offrandes alimentaires. Bien que ces derniers fussent pour la plupart brisés, leur type a pu être identifié et leur nombre comptabilisé ; une étude stratigraphique du remplissage des puits, enfin, a permis d'en étudier le mode de rangement.

Le puits du caveau (11), par exemple, contenait : 39 petits vases coniques, 5 terrines, 2 plats circulaires « dokkas », 13 moules à pain, 470 jarres, 2 braseros, 5 supports de vases, 15 céramiques fines (coupes, jarres, aiguière et son bassin, vases globulaires), 600 bouchons en terre crue et 109 fragments de scellements en terre sigillaire répartis sur presque toute la hauteur du puits.

La régularité des couches stratigraphiques, tant dans leur épaisseur que dans leur contenu, et l'emplacement du matériel, intact et groupé, permettent de comprendre le processus de comblement des puits. L'absence de sable éolien accumulé entre les couches suggère un processus assez rapide après la fermeture des caveaux.

Après le blocage de la porte du caveau par un mur de brique, une offrande alimentaire était déposée devant la porte : tête(s) de bovidés tournée(s) vers le caveau et quelques vases de

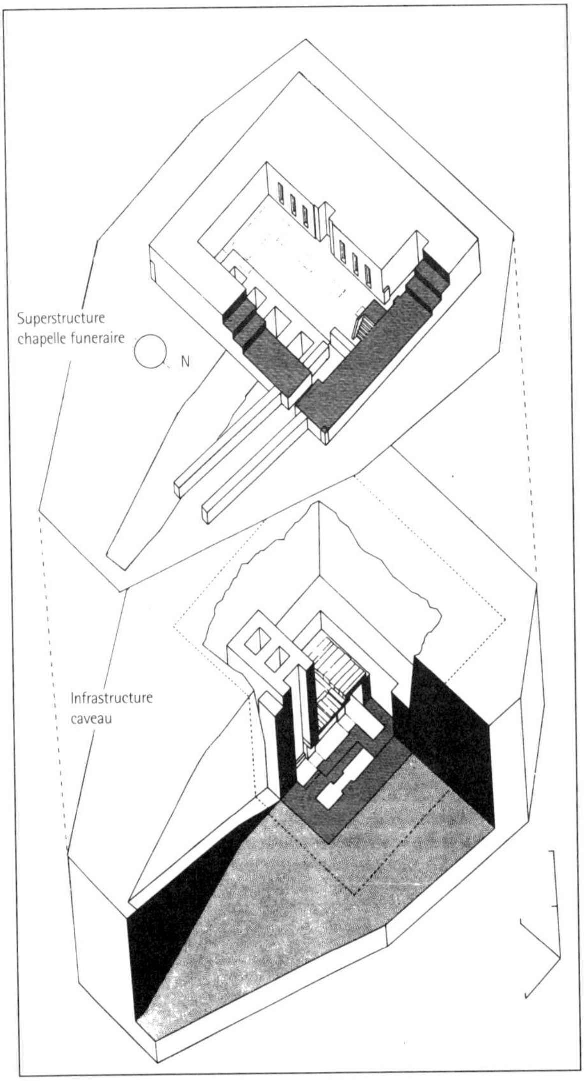

Fig. 2: Axonométrie de la superstructure et de l'infrastructure du mastaba.

céramique grossière. Le puits était bloqué avec de l'argile sur une hauteur de 1,50 m à 3 m. Au-dessus de ce niveau commençait le rangement systématique du matériel, sans doute jusqu'au niveau de l'ouverture du puits. Les coupes stratigraphiques laissent supposer un rangement par niveau : un homme qui se tenait au fond du puits recevait des lots de vases qu'il empilait le long des parois en les calant avec de l'argile. Progressivement, il exhaussait le niveau de travail en faisant monter le niveau de l'argile sous ses pieds, constituant une petite plate-forme qui lui permettait de manœuvrer sans casser les vases. Peu à peu, les couches de céramique montaient jusqu'à l'orifice du puits.

Ainsi est mise en lumière la double fonction du puits, qui servait d'abord d'accès, ensuite de magasin.

Le caveau principal de Khentika

L'antichambre et le caveau proprement dit sont dallés ; leurs murs et leurs plafonds sont en pierre. Les parois, bien qu'altérées par l'humidité, conservent encore des restes de peintures, les mieux conservées étant situées dans la moitié nord du caveau (fig. 3).

Sur la paroi nord, Khentika et son épouse sont assis face à face de part et d'autre d'une table d'offrandes. En haut de la paroi ouest apparaît une frise de *khekherou* et une inscription similaire à celle de la stèle « Offrande que donne le roi, offrande que donne Anubis qui préside au pavillon divin, *imiout* ; offrande que donne Osiris, maître de Bousiris, maître d'Abydos ... ». En dessous, de droite à gauche : Khentika, debout, vêtu d'un pagne à devanteau triangulaire tient le sceptre *sekhem* et le bâton *medou* ; il porte une perruque longue, une courte barbe et une étole. Devant lui, deux personnages présentent des offrandes. Plus loin, une procession de personnages aux bras levés est suivie d'une pancarte d'offrandes. Sur la paroi sud sont représentés des scènes nautiques et des travaux agricoles (labour, moisson, silos à céréales) et sur la paroi est, une scène de chasse à l'hippopotame. Au-dessus de la

Fig. 3: Caveau 10, paroi ouest : Khentika recevant des offrandes. Photo J.-F. Gout, Ifao.

porte d'entrée, un bateau à rames avec une cabine transporte un personnage assis devant une table d'offrandes. Au nord de la porte est représentée une scène de banquet funéraire. Sur deux registres superposés, quatre hommes et huit femmes sont assis devant des guéridons, les uns à la suite des autres, respirant une fleur de lotus.

Ces scènes du caveau étaient, à cette époque, généralement réservées à la chapelle de la tombe. Le décès subit de Khentika et l'inachèvement de la chapelle au moment de sa mort sont, sans doute, la raison de cette anomalie.

Au moment de la fouille, l'antichambre et le caveau étaient presque entièrement remplis d'argile. Une épaisse couche de boue due aux eaux d'infiltration recouvrait le dallage. Seuls étaient conservés les objets en pierre, en métal cuivreux et en terre cuite et les empreintes que certains d'entre eux avaient laissées dans l'argile avant de se décomposer. L'ensemble de ces données a permis de reconstituer le contenu du caveau et de son antichambre.

Au centre du caveau, un sarcophage en bois stuqué était placé sur un plancher de bois porté par trois supports de calcaire. Il contenait les restes d'un homme de 25–30 ans, allongé sur le dos, tête au nord et pieds au sud. Des offrandes alimentaires avaient été déposées sur le sarcophage (tête et antérieurs de bovidé), ainsi qu'un coffret contenant cinq vases précieux (gobelets et vases à onguent et à fard vert et noir) et un chevet funéraire en calcaire ou appui-tête sur lequel était inscrit : « Mille pains, mille bières, pour le chef des équipages, gouverneur de l'oasis, Khentika ». Au nord du sarcophage ont été retrouvés : deux grandes jarres, deux moules à pain et trois coupes renversées ayant contenu des offrandes carnées ; au sud : des objets en métal cuivreux (deux lames de rasoir, deux miroirs, une dague et deux supports de vase) et des récipients en calcite (aiguière et son bassin) et en terre cuite (quatre jarres carénées à fond plat).

Quant à l'antichambre, deux lots de jarres étaient appuyés contre ses parois nord et sud.

Quatre-vingt-huit objets, au total, étaient contenus dans l'antichambre et le caveau de Khentika, chiffre relativement modeste comparé aux deux cents objets (dont certains en or) du caveau inviolé du gouverneur Medou-Nefer (mastaba V[4]). À l'évidence, bien qu'aucune trace de pillage n'ait été constatée dans le caveau de Khentika, une grande partie du « trésor » qu'il contenait a été prélevée après l'enterrement. D'après les données archéologiques, ce prélèvement aurait été effectué avant à la construction de la salle 7.

Les caveaux secondaires (12 à 14) sont en brique crue. Ils ont un plan rectangulaire, sont voûtés et leur sol est dallé. Ils mesurent 2,80 m de long par 1,20 m de large et 1,20 m de hauteur sous clé de voûte. Bien que les murs et les portes aient été entièrement détruits par des infiltrations d'eau, leur emplacement a pu être restitué d'après la position des objets ou de leurs empreintes.

Fig. 4: Caveau 12 : flacon à parfum, composite
Matière : panse constituée d'un oeuf d'autruche, goulot et support en calcite, bouchon en *grauwacke*.
Représentation incisée : faucon (dieu Horus) les ailes déployées. H. (oeuf avec son goulot) : 17 cm. Photo J.-F. Gout, Ifao.

À titre d'exemple, le caveau 11 contenait le long de sa paroi nord un sarcophage en bois stuqué avec, à l'intérieur, les restes d'un jeune homme âgé de 17–18 ans. Ce dernier était allongé sur le côté gauche, tête à l'ouest, pieds à l'est, bras le long du corps, et il portait un bracelet de perles au poignet. Le couvercle du sarcophage, également disparu, a laissé dans l'argile l'empreinte en relief d'une inscription en creux mentionnant les quatre premiers signes de la titulature des gouverneurs : « Chef... (des équipages, gouverneur de l'oasis etc.) », preuve de la présence du gouverneur Déchérou dans ce caveau ; ceci est confirmé, d'ailleurs, par les deux stèles à son nom, retrouvées par Ahmed Fakhry à proximité de son puits[5]. Normalement, en tant que gouverneur, il aurait dû posséder son propre tombeau (mastaba). Le fait qu'il soit avec son père n'a pas encore été expliqué.

Trois coffrets, dont les empreintes étaient conservées dans l'argile, se trouvaient sur le couvercle du sarcophage. Ils contenaient deux chevets de pierre et un de bois, des vases précieux (un vase de calcite fermé par un disque de *grauwacke*, quatre vases de calcite, une coupelle à bec verseur), un miroir et une lame d'herminette en métal cuivreux, collés par la corrosion, et quatre vases de calcite. Deux assiettes et une coupe contenant une offrande carnée étaient posées sur les coffrets.

Dix-sept jarres et une vingtaine de céramiques étaient rangées entre le sarcophage et la paroi sud du caveau. Les céramiques comprenaient : cinq moules à pain, une coupe contenant de la viande de bovidé, quatre grandes jarres, trois petites jarres ovoïdes et leurs coupes, une aiguière et son bassin. Une patte de bovidé, enfin, occupait l'angle nord-est du caveau.

Les deux autres caveaux (12 et 13) contenaient chacun un sarcophage en bois stuqué et un matériel similaire à celui du caveau de Déchérou. Le caveau 12, mitoyen de celui de Khentika, renfermait les restes d'une femme âgée de 40-50 ans et l'autre (caveau 13), ceux d'une jeune femme de 25-30 ans. Étant donné la richesse du mobilier du premier et son emplacement (fig. 3), il est vraisemblable qu'il s'agissait de l'épouse de Khentika qui lui aurait survécu longtemps[6].

Histoire du tombeau

La fouille du tombeau a permis de reconstituer ses différentes phases de construction. Lors de la phase 1, les quatre caveaux sont construits en pierre et en brique crue, au fond d'une large et profonde fosse. Celle-ci ensuite est remblayée avec de l'argile compactée, puis le dallage de la chapelle est directement posé sur le remblai. Les murs en pierre de la chapelle sont à leur tour posés sur le dallage, puis le mur d'enceinte est construit au bord de la fosse, au nord et à l'ouest, et à cheval sur la fosse, à l'est et au sud.

Lorsque Khentika décède subitement à l'âge de 25-30 ans, sa tombe est inachevée. Les murs en pierre de la chapelle n'ont que quatre assises de hauteur et les autres parties de la construction sont inexistantes. Déchérou termine en brique la chapelle de son père et les autres parties du monument : mur à redans de la chapelle, vestibule d'entrée (2), annexe (9) de la chapelle, escalier (8) desservant le second niveau de l'annexe et la rampe d'accès (1).

Dans l'angle nord-ouest de la chapelle, un dépôt constitué de trois céramiques et de soixante-sept bouchons d'argile était caché dans l'épaisseur du mur en pierre, au niveau de sa dernière assise. Ce dépôt rituel correspond certainement à la reprise des travaux dans la chapelle après le décès de Khentika.

Par la suite, seront adossés à la chapelle : à la phase 2, deux magasins voûtés, l'un pour les jarres et l'autre pour le matériel de culte, puis, à la phase 3, un couloir transversal à arcades qui masquera le mur à redans.

Le remblai de la fosse s'étant tassé, les magasins s'effondrent. Leur entrée est condamnée et un enclos de remplacement (phase 4) est alors construit pour abriter les jarres à eau.

L'effondrement des caveaux ayant accentué le tassement du remblai, les salles s'enfoncent davantage, tandis que les murs d'enceinte (nord et ouest) construits en dehors de la fosse restent suspendus à leur place initiale. Les autres murs basculent (mur est) ou se cisaillent (mur sud). Tel était l'état du tombeau en 1984 au début des travaux.

Durée des travaux : essai de reconstitution

Ce calcul couvre la période qui va du début des travaux jusqu'à l'arrêt de la construction en pierre de la chapelle, arrêt momentané qui correspond vraisemblablement au décès de Khentika. Il repose sur une série d'expériences réalisées dans des conditions similaires à celles de l'époque de Khentika. Tous les matériaux étaient locaux. L'argile utilisée dans la fabrication des briques provenait du chantier même. Les architraves en grès étaient extraites d'une carrière située à proximité d'ʿAyn Asil. Les blocs de calcaire, enfin, étaient ramenés de l'escarpement de l'oasis, où ils se trouvaient à l'état délité. La distance de l'escarpement à la nécropole est d'environ 8 km. Les blocs étaient déplacés sur des rondins et les briques étaient transportées dans des couffins. Tous les travaux ont été exécutés manuellement avec des outils traditionnels : pic, pioche et herminette. Les résultats de cette étude devront, toutefois, être pris avec réserve, étant donné le grand nombre d'inconnues qui subsistent, notamment : les effectifs engagés, les horaires de travail[7] et, enfin, le nombre annuel de jours consacrés aux travaux.

NATURE DES TRAVAUX	QUANTITÉ	DURÉE	EFFECTIFS
Fabrication des briques crues	134 000 briques	128 jours	25 ouvriers
Transport des blocs, préparation et ajustement	2353 blocs	235 jours	30 ouvriers
Creusement de la descenderie et de la fosse		30 jours	30 ouvriers
Construction du mur de renforcement de la fosse	349 m^3 de briques	103 jours	40 ouvriers
Dallage de la fosse, murs et plafond du caveau principal	1740 blocs	205 jours	30 ouvriers
Murs et voûtes des caveaux secondaires	8 m^3 de briques	8 jours	40 ouvriers
Puits	441 m^3 de briques	131 jours	40 ouvriers
Remblaiement de la fosse et de la descenderie		15 jours	30 ouvriers
Construction du mur d'enceinte sur hauteur de 1,40 m	357 m^3 de briques	105 jours	40 ouvriers

La durée totale de la construction avec sa part d'inconnues, représente 30 550 journées d'ouvrier. Par ailleurs, l'expérience du chantier nous a montré qu'une quarantaine d'ouvriers était un effectif maximum pouvant travailler sans se gêner. Avec un tel effectif, le travail aurait duré 763 jours, soit un peu plus de deux ans. Il est vraisemblable, en fait, que l'effectif ait varié dans le temps en fonction des travaux agricoles et des priorités de la ville. Si les travaux de construction, par exemple, étaient réalisés durant la période où les travaux agricoles étaient au repos, comme dans la Vallée, un chantier de 3 mois par an avec 40 ouvriers aurait duré près de 8 ans.

Conclusion

Le tombeau de Khentika est le plus remarquable de la nécropole par son architecture, ses matériaux et les ressources économiques et humaines mises en oeuvre. Sa qualité correspond à une période d'apogée dans l'occupation du site urbain : le palais du gouverneur en cours de fouille à 'Ayn Asil a été probablement fondé par Khentika. Bien qu'il soit mort jeune, ce personnage a eu le temps de faire planifier et exécuter deux grands projets (le palais et sa tombe). La prospérité de Balat au moment où il a exercé son pouvoir, de même que le relatif déclin observable sous ses successeurs, reflètent l'évolution de l'ensemble de l'Égypte sous le règne de Pépi II.

Les nombreuses maladresses observées, par ailleurs, dans la construction du tombeau (surépaisseur du mur d'enceinte, fondation de la superstructure sur un remblai, surcharge des dalles de pierre du caveau, épaisseur insuffisante de certaines d'entre elles), ses mauvaises proportions (façade écrasée de la chapelle) et la naïveté de sa décoration le classent de façon caractéristique comme une oeuvre provinciale et montrent, une fois de plus, l'écart existant entre la province et la capitale.

Notes:

1 G. Soukiassian, « A Governors' Palace at 'Ayn Asil, Dakhla Oasis », *EgArch* 11 (1997), 15–17. G. Soukiassian, M. Wuttmann, L. Pantalacci, P. Ballet, M. Picon, *Balat II. Les ateliers de potiers d''Ayn Asil*, FIFAO 34, (Le Caire, 1990).

2 G. Castel, L. Pantalacci, N. Cherpion, *Balat V. Le mastaba de Khentika*, FIFAO 39/1–2, (Le Caire, 2000).

3 Numérotation de l'Ifao.

4 M. Valloggia, *Balat I. Le mastaba de Medou-nefer*, FIFAO 31/1–2, (Le Caire, 1986).

5 J. Osing, M. Moursi, D. Arnold, O. Neugebauer, R.A. Parker, D. Pingree, M. A. Nur el-Din, *Denkmäler des Oase Dachla. Aus dem Nachlass von Ahmed Fakhry*, ArchVer 28 (Mayence, 1982).

6 Dans la scène du banquet (*supra*), elle est assise en face de Khentika.

7 Nos calculs sont basés sur des journées de 8 heures avec une heure d'arrêt pour se restaurer.

The Predynastic Cemeteries at Matmar, Mostagedda, and Badari

Juan José Castillos

Instituto Uruguayo de Egiptología, Montevideo, Uruguay

A more detailed study of published Egyptian Predynastic cemeteries can yield valuable new information overlooked by the authors of earlier reports on those sites. The general characteristics of the Predynastic cemeteries at Matmar, Badari, and Mostagedda are discussed in this paper as well as the size and contents of notable graves possibly belonging to prominent members of local communities. The evolution of the funerary practices in this region differs to some extent from that detected at contemporary cemeteries and might indicate variations in social or political conditions. This paper summarizes such conclusions which in some aspects agree with the results obtained by other scholars using different approaches to the subject. A comparative study of these cemeteries is included below in order to determine the general lines of social evolution in this area of northern Upper Egypt. The recently published study on the Predynastic cemeteries at Mostagedda[1] is part of a larger project which includes the contemporary cemeteries at Matmar[2] and Badari[3] and the published data on other Predynastic sites in Egypt. I will confine my discussion to the three areas mentioned north of Badari itself.

First of all, I would like to explain some of the variables considered in my study. The G (Gini), T (Theil), and V (coefficient of variation, another way to present the standard deviation of the sample) indices that appear in Tables 1, 2, and 3 below, are measurements of inequality used in sociology[4] recently applied on occasion to study inequality in Predynastic Egypt.[5] In my view, these indices represent measurements of what I called the internal inequality in a given group. They were conceived to compare peoples' incomes in modern times and were therefore not designed to express the absolute values of the variables considered. This is understandable if we bear in mind that some of the data could be expressed in Hong Kong dollars or Deutschmarks or United States dollars without the different values of such currencies distorting the general picture. But when we apply these measurements to archaeological data, we want to be aware of such absolute values in order to include the level of inequality and avoid comparing apples and oranges. We would be doing this if we considered as similar the inequality of two groups of tombs or two groups of say, floor areas of houses in a village, that have an identical internal ratio but that differ substantially in actual numbers. For the purpose, we conceived a fourth variable, AD (average difference). This expresses the difference between the averages of the upper and lower (richer and poorer) groups within a community as demonstrated, for example, by tomb size or wealth or the size of their houses. The G, T, and V values in each case are valid, but if we attempt to compare the inequality of a group with another, we should bear the AD figures in mind as well.

As archaeology and Egyptology become more multidisciplinarian, with all the advantages such an approach implies, it would be unwise to ignore the advances in modern sociological research in order to refine our perception of the social structure and the degree of inequality in early Egyptian communities. Very limited attempts in this direction have been made, although I have applied this methodology to a large data base of over 8,000 Egyptian Predynastic and Early Dynastic tombs, using the variables that involved aspects of these funerary practices yielding enough information to make the results significant.

The measurements obtained can be summarized as shown in the following tables. The figures that appear to the right of Size and Wealth Inequality represent the number of tombs in each case.

MATMAR

Size, Wealth, and Inequality Tables					
Period		Badarian	Amratian	Gerzean	Protodynastic
Average size (m^3)		0.76	0.86	1.29	1.39
Average wealth (objects)		1.5	8.0	6.9	6.3
Size most tombs within		0.3–0.6	0.5–0.8	0.5–1.4	0.8–2.0
Size inequality index		55	21	106	66
	G	0.47	0.30	0.46	0.39
	V	1.04	0.61	1.28	0.85
	T	0.39	0.15	0.45	0.28
	AD	1.37	0.79	2.54	1.49
Wealth inequality index		122	24	134	76
	G	0.45	0.44	0.36	0.30
	V	1.00	0.85	0.81	0.54
	T	0.42	0.33	0.23	0.14
	AD	2.64	9.98	6.66	5.61

Table 1

MOSTAGEDDA

Size, Wealth, and Inequality Tables				
Period	Badarian	Amratian	Gerzean	Protodynastic
Average size (m^3)	0.82	0.81	1.32	2.61
Average wealth (objects)	1.7	3.8	5.8	7.2
Size most tombs within	0.1–2.0	0.2–1.3	0.4–2.1	0.8–4.5
Size inequality index	199	41	56	30
G	0.39	0.38	0.32	0.46
V	0.75	0.81	0.72	1.17
T	0.25	0.25	0.19	0.43
AD	0.96	0.91	1.37	5.74
Wealth inequality index	317	49	71	35
G	0.58	0.41	0.26	0.42
V	1.30	0.85	0.48	1.30
T	0.66	0.29	0.11	0.41
AD	3.06	4.54	4.35	10.60

Table 2

BADARI

Size, Wealth, and Inequality Tables				
Period	Badarian	Amratian	Gerzean	Protodynastic
Average size (m^3)	1.25	0.68	1.03	1.62
Average wealth (objects)	2.5	4.4	3.2	3.6
Size most tombs within	0.2–3.0	0.1–1.5	0.2–2.5	0.3–4.0
Size inequality index	223	22	86	53
G	0.44	0.41	0.38	0.43
V	0.87	1.00	0.79	0.86
T	0.31	0.34	0.25	0.30
AD	1.87	0.84	1.18	2.33
Wealth inequality index	267	26	103	63
G	0.54	0.42	0.32	0.30
V	1.32	0.95	0.62	0.59
T	0.57	0.32	0.17	0.15
AD	4.70	6.49	5.20	3.23

Table 3

114

I confined this method to appraise inequality from funerary data due to the scarcity of comparable published information concerning the settlements associated with these cemeteries. It can and hopefully will be expanded to achieve more reliable results from the realm of the living as well as from the dead.

Based on the evolution of funerary practices, Mostagedda exhibits in all respects what we could call normal development from the Badarian to the Protodynastic. In neighboring areas of northern Upper Egypt, to the north and south, Mostagedda was affected by other conditions that altered the expected trend. For instance, the stagnation and regression exhibited by the Protodynastic cemeteries at Matmar is not present at Mostagedda. There this period marks the highest point of cultural development when we compare its funerary goods with those at Matmar or Badari.

I have already suggested[6] that the probable center of the Badarian culture was at Badari itself. This idea seems natural in view of the number of tombs excavated by Brunton and the extent of its area compared to northern counterparts. Although convincing in themselves, these characteristics might not be considered sufficient evidence of special status during the Badarian in the Badari area, and in sites in the immediate neighborhood such as Qau and Hemamieh. However, the average size of the Badarian tombs at Badari is well above that of Mostagedda or Matmar. In addition, the average wealth of the tombs measured as the number of objects found in them,[7] also largely exceeds the figures for Mostagedda and Matmar. In both respects they appear to be very similar.

Besides this evidence, the internal evolution of each area as reflected in the cemetery data, shows that at Badari the cultures that followed had a more limited expression at Badari than at the other two areas farther north. This is the expected result for the center of a culture where resistance to the penetration of outside influences would be higher, and which was increasingly becoming a provincial outpost of later cultures.

At Badari both the internal inequality for size and wealth and the level of such inequality reveal relatively little change from the Badarian to the Protodynastic. The more noteworthy trend is actually a drop in the internal wealth inequality in the tombs as we move forward in time, as expressed in all G, T, and V indices.

At Mostagedda, the situation differs from Badari in the sense that the average size and wealth of the tombs increase steadily over time. The internal inequality for both size and wealth, as at Badari, also decrease until the Protodynastic, where it climbs to the Badarian level or higher. The level of such inequality differs from Badari in the sense that it increases steadily from the Badarian and all through the following periods.

At the Matmar cemeteries furthest from Badari, the averages for both size and wealth of the tombs exhibit higher figures after the Badarian, and the size inequality peaked during the Gerzean (Naqada II) in both its internal and level expressions. In what concerns the extant wealth of the tombs, there was a decrease in the internal inequality through time but the level of such inequality reached in the following periods has considerably higher values than during the Badarian. The unexpected drop during the Protodynastic could be due, as I suggested, to the even more considerable distance of Matmar from the cultural center at a time which perhaps turned its settlements into a sort of backwater with reduced political and economic status.

The fairly consistent picture revealed by these studies may encourage others to use this approach to the archaeological data in order to gain new insights into the social conditions and development through time of Predynastic communities in Egypt.

Notes:

1 J. J. Castillos, "The Predynastic cemeteries at Mostagedda," *GM* 175 (2000), 23–28.

2 J. J. Castillos, "Social development in Predynastic Egypt: Matmar, a case study," *Proceedings of the 1997 Poznan Symposium on the Stone Age of Northeastern Africa* (in press).

3 J. J. Castillos, "The Predynastic cemeteries at Badari," *RdE* 51 (2000), 253–56.

4 J. J. Castillos, "Inequality in Egyptian Predynastic cemeteries," *RdE* 49 (1998), 25–36.

5 W. Griswold, "Measuring social inequality at Armant" in R. Friedman and B. Adams (eds.), *The Followers of Horus*, (Oxford, 1992), 196.

6 J. J. Castillos, "New data on Egyptian Predynastic cemeteries," *RdE* 48 (1997), 251–252.

7 J. J. Castillos, "Wealth evaluation of Predynastic tombs," *GM* 163 (1998), 27–33.

Stratigraphy and Chronology of the Central Tell in Tell al-Farkha

Marek Chlodnicki

Poznan Archaeological Museum, Poland

The site of Tell al-Farkha was identified by the Italian Archaeological Mission in the Eastern Nile Delta in 1987. From 1988–1990, the Mission, directed by Rodolfo Fattovich, carried out a number of excavations at the site. Most of the fieldwork concentrated on the central, biggest mound on the site.

Three trenches were located on the southern slope of the mound and a fourth, the largest, on the summit. Excavations started with the enlargement and cleaning of a section close to the houses of the modern village already exposed by the farmers. Using trenches appeared to be the best way to investigate the lower layers of the site. These were dug to a depth of only three meters, as the water table was reached at this point. At least three main strata became evident.

Deposits were more carefully investigated in the adjacent trench, where six levels had been revealed by the time a depth of 1.7 meters was reached. The two lowest levels yielded evidence of a local Predynastic culture, while the other contained Nagada culture material.

Based on the data collected during previous excavations, it was decided to open a third eight meter by eight meter trench in order to access earlier layers without destroying the Old Kingdom and Early Dynastic architectural structures encountered on the top of the mounds. In this trench, at a depth of 1.7 meters below the surface, evidence of a cultural change marked by a stratigraphic hiatus was recognized. This comprised a thin, salty layer, literally covered with shards and aeolian sand. This was indicative of a period of very strong and continuous wind action. This level marks a distinct change in the site's ceramic assemblages as well as settlement patterns. Layers higher up in the stratigraphic sequence were characterized by the occurrence of mud-brick buildings, while examining downward, only light clay installations, hearths, and pits occur. The lowermost levels of the stratigraphic sequence, situated on the sands of the *gezira*, yielded a very distinctive pottery characterized by zigzag decoration.[1]

The first exploratory activity phase of the Italian Mission's work, which aimed at acquiring knowledge of the general sequence of Tell al-Farkha, was completed with the 1989 campaign. The

1990 campaign marked the start of a new working phase–extensive exploration of the central mound. At the top of the central mound, a 20 meter by 20 meter pit was excavated. The surface deposit brought to light some fire installations, very late pits, and first evidence of architectonic remains. Below, several layers with different mud-brick structures were recorded. All of these buildings dated to the Old Kingdom, only the two lowermost structures were from the Early Dynastic. Unfortunately, these excavations were stopped at the depth of about 1.2 meters without reaching earlier occupational layers.

The Italian Mission discontinued their excavations in 1990 without solving many problems. The work carried out by this mission identified several occupation phases at this site going back to the Predynastic Period, contemporary with earliest phases of Tell Iswid and Buto, and the later ones, dated by them respectively to the Protodynastic Period and Early Old Kingdom.

In 1998 the Polish Archaeological Mission began a new phase of exploration at the site. The aim of the first campaign was to carry out geological, stratigraphic, and geophysical reconnaissance work and to attain as much data as possible for the better planning of the next and much more comprehensive campaign. Three methods of research were used: excavation, geophysical survey, and deep drilling. During the following season's work in 1999, extensive excavations were conducted on the western tell.[2] The results of these excavations are presented in a separate paper by Krzysztof Cialowicz. On the central tell we continued test excavations, geophysical survey, and drilling.

Geophysical survey

Geophysical surveying, carried out by Tomasz Herbich, encompassed the whole surface of the central mound. Distinct traces of buildings dating from the youngest settlement phases nearest the site surface, were identified. These features were particularly prominent in the southern and central part of the *kom*. The surveying equipment registered mud-brick walls clearly enough for their orientation to be established. Evidence of buildings trails off toward the north of the site.[3] This may be due to the increased build-up of deposits overlying structural remains in this area. Survey results also suggest that the older settlement features probably continue further south, underlying the modern village of Ghazala. The features recorded on the top of the mound (at least from the level of seven meters) are most probably of Old Kingdom date. Test pits located on the southern slope confirmed that at least part of the structures located below the level of six meters are of Early Dynastic or Late Predynastic date.

Drillings

Two drilling lines were made cutting across the site. The first line stretched south to north, cutting across the boundary of the western tell, running between it and the central tell. Ten bore-holes 4.5–5 meters deep were situated every 20 meters, starting with the boundary of the village and ending in the fields north of Tell al-Farkha. Drilling enabled us to define the level of sand–the original surface of the *gezira*–and the thickness of the overlying cultural layers. An important discovery was the recognizing of three layers with pottery fragments beyond the extent of the tells. They were separated by thick layers of clean silt.

A second line of bore-hole samples were taken from the site along a west-east axis, passing over the summits of the three *kom*. Bores were drilled to a depth of five to six meters at 20 meter intervals. Two types of Nilotic deposits were identified in the resulting samples. The lower sections of the samples were composed of very fine and fine unsorted sand, with occasional gravel inclusions. The sample profile showed no significant height differences in the surface of this sand.

This could indicate that this sandy island was raised only slightly higher above the surrounding terrain during the earliest phases of its settlement. However, the bore-hole samples taken on the south-north axis show that the elevation at the northern end of the site was more pronounced. Three principal silt deposits lie above the sand. They differ in color and sand inclusions. Numerous artifacts were observed in these silt layers. Distinct concentrations were visible in the bottom half of the lowermost layer of silt. The results of this sampling confirm that three *kom* came into being at this site as a result of intensive human occupation and the seasonal activity of the Nile.

Test Excavations
Trench W 97
This five meter by five meter trench was situated on the northern slope of the western *kom*, at the point where it meets the central *kom*. Excavations were carried out to a depth of two meters. Five archaeological levels were identified during this exploration. The first of these was a layer of brown silt containing a small amount of modern ceramic material interspersed with Old Kingdom pottery shards. A modest quantity of diverse finds was also present in layer two, composed of dark silt. Both strata one and two are backfill layers that came into being as a result of erosion and site leveling in recent times.

The original occupation level of this site is denoted by the third archaeological level, the top of which was recorded approximately 2.8 to 2.9 meters above surface level. This layer consists of very sandy silt, with fine inclusions of gravel (white and grayish-white) in some places and a large concentration of artifacts (pottery, grindstone fragments, and flint flakes). It lies immediately above layer four (2.60–2.50 meters), made up of blue sand with a substantial admixture of loam. A limited amount of small finds were found in the uppermost section of this stratum (pottery vessels among them). Two insubstantial features were registered at the bottom of layer three. Both of these were hollows of blue clay measuring about 20 centimeters in diameter and approximately ten centimeters deep. One of them contained ceramic material that may be linked to the material culture of Lower Egypt. Yellow *gezira* sand was revealed at the bottom of this trench (at a depth of 2.45 m). This sand did not contain any archaeological material. It would seem that layers three and four were created at the edge of the *gezira*, which was seasonally flooded.

The lowest settlement level (four) can be associated with the culture of Lower Egypt. In contrast, level three contains both Lower Egyptian artifacts and pottery dating from the Nagada period and the Old Kingdom. It appears that this level constitutes a rubbish deposit which came into being in the flood plains beyond the contemporary settlement areas of the Nagada-Old Kingdom period. As no Old Kingdom materials were recovered from *kom* W, artifacts of this date found here must have come from the neighboring *kom* C.

Trench C 126
This sondage measured six by two meters and was located on the northern slope of the central *kom*. The uppermost stratum (3.5 meters at the south end and 2.5 meters at the north end) comprised debris containing numerous fragments of pottery, bone, and flint tools. The top part of this level dates to the Old Kingdom. The only architectural feature discovered in this trench was a type of wall-cum-staircase made partly of mud brick and partly of solid silt. This appears to be the remains of a waterfront revetment. Beneath this reinforcing layer lie successive archaeological strata devoid of any features, with the exception of a backfill containing large amounts

of pottery and bone, which can be dated tentatively to the Nagada II-Nagada III period. A sunken feature set in sand was unearthed beneath these layers of backfill, clearly separated from them by a thin layer of blue silt. This structure lay at a level of 2.45 meters and is attributable to Lower Egyptian culture. A clay bead or amulet was found inside it along with pottery shards and a perforated clay object that may have served as a seal that would have been impressed with a fingerprint.

It seems that the sondage in question was situated in an area that, from the Nagada II period onwards, would have been within the immediate vicinity of the shoreline. No domestic buildings were raised here. The only feature present was a rubbish dump, which, as it grew, protected the settlement perimeter from flooding, whilst at the same time gradually raising this area above the flood plain.

Trench C 49

This five by five meter sondage was situated on the south-east slope of the central tell, where magnetic resistance surveying had indicated the existence of a set of linear features and a round structure with strong magnetic properties. Trench C 49 was designed to verify the results of this survey. Excavation confirmed the presence of 50 centimeter-wide mud-brick walls running just below the surface (the top of the walls recorded at a level of 5.50 m), the round feature proving to be a hearth containing a dense layer of ash.

Eleven archaeological levels were identified in this trench. The top three (with which the uppermost wall is associated) can be dated to the Nagada III Period. The lowest level containing mud-brick constructions (at a depth of 4.90 m) dates to the Nagada II d Period. Occupation levels linked to the Nagada culture occur up to a depth of 4.40 meters (level nine). No mud-brick walls were noted in the lowermost levels associated with this settlement phase. Noteworthy, however, was a layer of rubble, up to 20 centimeters thick, consisting of fired "bricks" (plane-convex in section), which extended over part of the excavated area (like the feature recorded in the western tell).

The bottom two levels, which produced the remains of a round shelter, can be linked to Lower Egyptian culture. The shelter had a diameter of about 3.5 meters and was dug in to a depth of approximately 40–50 centimeters. Inside the shelter was a hearth of approximately 70 centimeters in diameter. A number of smaller archaeological features were also found in this level. Features associated with Lower Egyptian culture generally occurred in two stratigraphic contexts. The tops of features in the upper context were recorded at a level of approximately 4.40 meters, while the tops of those in the lower context reached a level of around 3.90 meters. The base of the deepest feature was registered at a level of approximately three meters.

Large ceramic assemblages (including whole vessels) were discovered in this trench, as well as considerable amounts of flint tools. Sickle blades are the most common, with knives occurring in smaller quantities.

Trench C 16

This trench (measuring six by eight meters) was situated on the southern slope of the central *kom*. It was located in an area where part of the site's topmost strata had been damaged by *sebakhin* and farmers extracting sand. The difference between the levels of the trench's surface in the northwest corner (the best preserved part) and southeast corner was two meters. Seventeen cultural layers were identified. The upper ten levels (1–10) are dated to Early Dynastic times. Levels 11–14 are connected with Nagada IIc-d culture. In the levels dating from the Nagada II Period the only evidence of structural features coming in the shape of relict hearths. Between many potsherds and flints also a small stone amulet was found.

The best-preserved level associated with Lower Egyptian settlement yielded the remains of several pits and post-holes. Also recorded were a series of furrows, approximately 20 centimeters wide, forming rectangular ground plans. This level contained a relatively large amount of badly damaged ceramic material—mostly fragments of little, irregularly shaped bowls or small vessels decorated with a zigzag pattern. Apart from pottery shards the pits contained three complete vessels. Part of a clay seal, similar to that recovered from trench C 126, was also found here.

Conclusions

Work carried out by the Polish Mission provided general confirmation of the stratigraphic sequences and major occupation phases of this site as distinguished by Italian archaeologists. The earliest settlement emerged along with the Predynastic culture of Lower Egypt. At this point, the tell had not yet achieved its pronounced topographical form. It was instead a fairly shallow, sandy mound with only the northern end situated much higher than its surroundings. The occupational traces left behind by the inhabitants of this oldest (and probably most extensive) settlement consist of sunken roundhouses and shelters, storage pits and rectangular structures, probably built entirely above ground. This phase can be dated to the Nagada IIc Period, perhaps slightly earlier, possible evidence for this older date coming from two fragments of ripple ware recovered from the lower strata of trenches C 16 and C 49.

The next settlement phase is clearly linked to the Nagada culture, probably starting from phase IId (*ca.* 3,300–3,200 BCE) and continuing through phase III of this culture.

The only archaeological evidence for continued occupation in the Old Kingdom comes from the northernmost part of the site and from the top of the central and eastern mounds.

The role played by this settlement during the formation of the Egyptian state remains unknown. Nevertheless, it seems to have been one of the centers of trade and culture in the Eastern Delta. This is suggested by finds of both pottery imported from Upper Egypt and Palestine and of primitive seals. Further broad-plan excavations on the top of the central mound (continuing the Italian excavations) will no doubt bring us closer to the answers to these questions.

Notes:

1 M. Chlodnicki, R. Fattovich, and S. Salvatori, "Italian excavations in the Nile Delta and new hypotheses on the 4th millennium cultural development of Egyptian Prehistory," *Rivista di Archeologia* 15 (1991), 5–33; M. Chlodnicki, R. Fattovich and S. Salvatori, "The Nile Delta in Transition: A View from Tell al-Farkha," in E.C.M. van den Brink (ed.) *The Nile Delta in Transition: 4th-3rd Millennium B.C.* (Tel Aviv, 1992), 171–190.

2 M. Chlodnicki and K. M. Cialowicz, "Tell al-Farkha, Explorations 1998," *Polish Archaeology in the Mediterranean* 10 (1999), 63–70.

3 M. Chlodnicki and T. Herbich, "The Magnetic Survey at Tell al-Farkha, Egypt," in J.W.E. Fassbinder and W. E. Irlinger (eds.), *Archaeological Prospection, Third International Conference on Archaeological Prospection Munich, 9–11 Sept. 1999* (Arbeitshefte des bayerishen Landesamt für Denkmalpflege 108: Munich, 1999), 19–20.

Trois saisons de fouilles dans la vaste Nécropole de Kôm Firin (terrain de Silvago) dans le gouvernorat de Béheira

Sabri Ali Choucri

Introduction

Avant d'exposer ce que nous avons découvert dans la vaste nécropole de Kôm Firin, je voudrais esquisser les traits de cette région située à l'ouest du Delta et qui appartient au 3e nome de la Basse-Égypte à l'époque pharaonique. En réalité, cette région renferme plusieurs sites archéologiques dont certains représentent des villes antiques, comme Naucratis, Kôm Firin, Kôm el-Hisn, et Kôm Abquaein. Chacune de ces villes était fortifiée par un énorme mur d'enceinte et par une forteresse, car toutes se trouvaient à la limite du désert occidental duquel venaient, de temps en temps, les tribus de Libou et de Mechouaches, menaçant l'Égypte. Les ruines de ces bâtiments de nature défensive étaient en grande partie visibles de surface jusqu'à la fin du XIXe Siècle, et décrites par certains célèbres archéologues comme W. F. Petrie, F. L. Griffith, M.C.C. Edgar et A. Bernand.

Malheureusement, à la fin du XIXe siècle, des activités illégales comme les fouilles clandestines ou la recherche de *sebakh* et le projet de chemin de fer dans le Delta ont rasé, sans pitié, beaucoup de ces ruines.

Le site de Kôm Firin occupe, à présent, une superficie de 49,57 hectares.

Petrie, qui prospecta le site en 1880, étudiant les pierres sur lesquelles étaient gravés les titres et les noms des rois Ahmosis Ier et Ramsès II, estima que la première occupation devait remonter au Nouvel Empire.

En 1981, une découverte accidentelle d'un montant de portail de temple, portant des inscriptions mentionnant aussi les titres et les noms de Ramsès II, est venue confirmer la thèse de Petrie.

Il est certain qu'il y avait une relation entre Kôm Firin et les sites archéologiques qui l'entourent.

Certains archéologues considèrent Kôm el-Hisn comme une désignation de la capitale du 3e nome *im3w*, surnommée « Gynaecopolis » à l'époque gréco-romaine, puisqu'on peut lire le nom *im3w* sur les bases de deux statues de Ramsès II. D'autres voient dans le toponyme *im3w* une allusion directe à Kôm Firin, d'après les inscriptions d'une stèle provenant de cette ville et offerte par Petrie au musée de Londres, qui mentionnent le nom de la capitale dans le contexte suivant : « Sekhmet, maîtresse d'*im3w* ». Peut-être une fouille systématique et exhaustive soit à Kôm el Hisn, soit à Kôm Firin, nous permettrait-elle de décider en faveur de telle ou telle identification. Comme preuves archéologiques, nous avons des tessons de céramiques grecques importées à Kôm Firin, quelques pièces artistiques helléniques provenant de Kôm Firin et conservées au musée gréco-romain, ainsi que des trouvailles provenant des fouilles que j'ai menées dans le cimetière de Kôm Firin : des lécythes, lécythes aribalisques, alabastrons, masques de Méduse et masques de certains cercueils en terre cuite dont les traits appartiennent aux peuples de la mer. Tout cela prouve, à la fois, que Kôm Firin avait des contacts avec le monde hellénique depuis le VIIᵉ siècle av. J.C. et avant l'apparition de la céramique grecque à Naucratis, et que cette dernière ville n'était pas la seule à autoriser l'implantation d'une communauté grecque.

Quant au site dit « Silvago » situé à 1 km au sud-ouest de Kôm Firin et qui représente un vaste cimetière, il a été découvert par hasard pendant les travaux de réforme agraire en 1966. Malheureusement, une grande partie de cette zone a été défrichée au début des années soixante avant d'être connue par les archéologues, ce qui a posé le problème de la définition exacte des limites originelles de la nécropole.

Une fouille a eu lieu en 1967 ; elle a révélé la seule tombe, jusqu'à présent, qui porte des inscriptions[1]. Celles-ci concernent un prêtre dont le nom est Bas. Il portait deux titres religieux : protecteur de l'œil *oudjat* (*hpt-wd3t*) et directeur des temples (*hrp hwwt*). Ce dernier titre appartient à la déesse Neith dont la ville de Sa el-Hagar n'est éloignée que d'une trentaine de kilomètres au sud-est de Kôm Firin.

Les fouilles

De 1992 à 1994, j'ai mené trois campagnescampagnes de fouilles ; l'équipe se composait de Mohamed Abdel Rahman, assistant, Adel Nached, architecte, Latif Wahba, dessinateur. L'archéologue, Ahmed el-Nachar, a participé à la saison de fouilles de 1992[2].

Quatre emplacements (A, B, C, D) ont été l'objet de nos recherches. La multitude des sépultures était concentrée dans les secteurs A et B (fig. 1) où elle a atteint le chiffre de 363, tandis qu'à deux autres emplacements n'ont été découvertes que 14 inhumations.

On a distingué trois niveaux de sépultures superposés sur trois mètres de profondeur environ, qu'on peut dater de l'époque saïte à l'époque romaine. Ces sépultures étaient de types différents qu'on peut classifier de la manière suivante :

1er type

Des morts, enterrés dans de simples fosses creusées dans le sable sans aucune protection, ont été trouvés avec très peu d'objets funéraires : un ou deux vases, des perles de collier, des bracelets, des boucles d'oreilles. Certaines de ces inhumations étaient accompagnées d'enterrements d'animaux tels que béliers, taureaux ou chacals. Sur la fig. 2 apparaît le squelette d'un âne dont la présence était vraiment inattendue puisque, à ma connaissance, les anciens Égyptiens n'ont jamais enterré d'âne dans des cimetières humains ; cette stupéfaction a décru quand on a remarqué la fraîcheur du squelette, puis s'est complètement dissipée quand le propriétaire de l'âne nous a appris que celui-ci était mort en 1988, c'est-à-dire quatre ans avant le commencement de notre fouille !

Cet animal n'était apprécié qu'à la période des Hyksos durant laquelle il fut considéré comme une manifestation du dieu Seth-Baal.

On trouve ainsi dans certains cimetières de Hyksos près de Gaza et Beit Beleid en Palestine quatre ânes enterrés au-dessous de sépultures humaines[3].

Figure 1

Figure 2

125

2e type

La dépouille, ici, devait reposer dans un cercueil de bois, vu les traces de ce matériau près du squelette et la présence de deux clous et trois masques de Méduse en terre cuite qui devaient être appliqués sur ce genre de cercueil. Cette sépulture remonte à la période ptolémaïque.

3e type

D'après l'examen de ce type concernant des dépouilles sommairement momifiées, on peut dire qu'elles étaient du même genre que celles qui furent trouvées dans les cimetières d'époque tardive et d'époque ptolémaïque. Durant ces périodes, on utilisait une substance noir foncé apparentée à du bitume qui, tout en rendant les cadavres très solides, n'était pas très efficace pour la préservation des tissus.

4e type

Il s'agit du cartonnage, dont la méthode consistait ici à entourer le corps avec des bandelettes de lin imbibées soit de résine, soit de liquide bitumineux, le tout renforcé avec du stuc peint qui s'adaptait à la forme de la momie. Ce genre de procédé était largement utilisé aux époques tardives et à l'époque ptolémaïque, au lieu de cercueils en bois dont le coût était élevé.

5e type

Nous avons, ici, un autre genre de tombes, construites en brique crue et se composant d'une seule chambre voûtée avec un ou deux défunts. On en a dégagé la plupart des objets funéraires trouvés dans cette nécropole : des vases, des amulettes (Isis, Thouéris, *ḏt*, *wȝḏ*, *wḏȝt*, scarabées), des perles de collier, des *ouchebtis*, trois pièces en faïence du jeu pharaonique appelé *zenet*, ainsi qu'un vase contenant des œufs de cane dont les coquilles étaient encore intactes[4].

Figure 3

6e type

La nouveauté, dans ce genre de sépultures, réside dans l'utilisation de cercueils anthropoïdes, en terre cuite, dont la première apparition dans la région du Delta remonte aux XXIe et XXIIe dynasties. Ces cercueils étaient intégrés dans une construction en brique crue en forme de sarcophage voûté. De plus, on a observé qu'un grand nombre de masques de cercueils avaient les traits des peuples de la mer, à l'exception de celui qui représente le visage de Bès. En dépit de l'apparence intacte des constructions protégeant ces cercueils, on a découvert ces derniers troués, saccagés et pillés. Malgré cela, un important mobilier funéraire a été mis au jour. Les cercueils de couleur blanchâtre portent des traces de décorations en ocre rouge imitant les bandelettes de la momie entre lesquelles des divinités étaient représentées.

7e type

Des dépouilles reposaient dans des cercueils ovoïdes en terre cuite occupant les couches les plus proches de la surface. La plupart de ces tombes ont été trouvées sens dessus dessous et vidées de leurs dépouilles.

On peut considérer ce genre comme le prototype des cercueils nommés « slipper coffins » et dont l'apparition date de l'époque romaine tardive.

8e type

Deux grands pots semi-coniques emboîtés l'un dans l'autre et utilisés comme un cercueil caractérisent ces inhumations concentrées dans le secteur méridional de la nécropole. Ce type était fréquent dans les cimetières romains.

9e type

Ce type représente un sarcophage en calcaire couplé à un coffre de la même matière supposé contenir les vases canopes. Ce mode de sépultures remonte aux époques tardives et à l'époque ptolémaïque.

10e type

C'était une tombe voûtée en brique, en forme de quadrilatère. On en a dégagé une très belle urne intacte, en albâtre, avec deux anses en forme de tête de canard, renfermant les cendres et les ossements du défunt. Cette inhumation affirme, sans aucun doute, que ce cimetière était utilisé, à une certaine époque, à la fois pour les indigènes et pour des gens appartenant aux peuples de la mer.

11e type

Des amphores et des pots étaient utilisés comme cercueils de bébés. L'étude de ces récipients permet de dater approximativement ces sépultures.

Comme nous l'avons déjà mentionné, aucune des tombes n'a malheureusement été trouvée intacte. Elles avaient toutes été non seulement pillées, à une date ancienne, mais aussi saccagées et en partie démolies. Pourtant, certaines d'entre elles ont été plus chanceuses puisqu'elles n'ont pas été vidées complètement de leur mobilier funéraire.

Nous espérons pouvoir très prochainement étudier minutieusement tout ce matériel trouvé dans cette nécropole et le comparer à celui de l'ancienne ville de Kôm Firin, afin de comprendre si ces deux sites ont été contemporains tout au long de leur histoire respective.

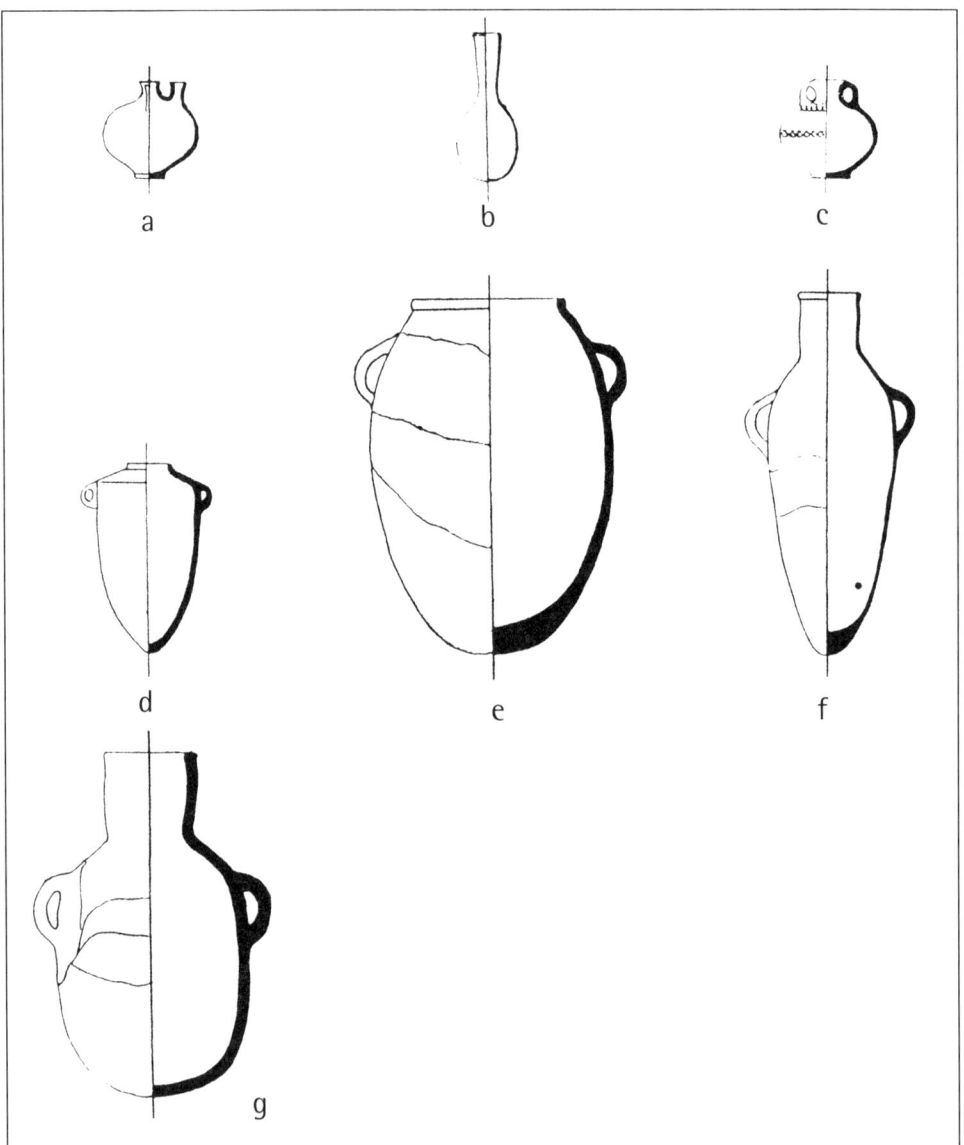

Figure 4

Fig. 4a : Vase à étrier. Pâte rougeâtre. Décor : deux lignes rouges tout autour de la panse (inv. 3873-3874).

Fig. 4b : *Unguentarium* fusiforme. Pâte calcaire rougeâtre.

Fig. 4c : Vase à étrier. Décor noir. Faïence (inv. 3875).

Fig. 4d : Amphore *torpedo jar*.

Fig. 4e, f, g : Amphores d'origine palestinienne. Pâte calcaire beige clair.

Notes:

1 Voir M. Basta, « Excavations West of Kôm Firin », *CdE* LIV/108 (1979), 183-196.

2 Je tiens à remercier, au nom de toute l'équipe, Monsieur Ahmed Abdel Fatah, directeur du département des antiquités de l'ouest du Delta pour la confiance qu'il nous a accordée.

3 O.A.E., A. Badawi, *Vies et Travaux* IV, 68.

4 Voir l'appendice.

Tell al-Farkha:
Excavations at the Western Kom (1998–1999)

Krzysztof M. Ciałowicz

Institute of Archaeology, Jagiellonian University Cracow

The archaeological work at Tell al-Farkha was begun by an Italian mission,[1] and from 1998 has been conducted by a Polish team directed by M. Chłodnicki and the author.[2] The site is composed of three *koms*: eastern, central, and western, covering altogether about four hectares. In the first season our work on the western *kom* was concentrated in the southeast, on the very destroyed edge of the *kom*. In the second season work focused around its center. An area of 150 m^2 was designated for excavation (N-S axis 10 m; E-W axis 15 m). Large quantities of artifacts, numerous settlement features and a complex stratigraphic record measuring over 4 m in depth, resulted in work being completed in the eastern section only during 1999. The western half of the trench was excavated to a depth of 220 cm, and we left it for the next season.[3]

After primarily analysis, five chronological phases of settlement on the west *kom* begin to emerge quite clearly.

Phase One

Phase One is associated exclusively with the culture of Lower Egypt. The occupation probably covered the later stage of Lower Egyptian culture, which is contemporary with Naqada (IIb?) IIc–d1 according to Kaiser[4] or IIC–IID1 according to Hendrickx.[5] This is demonstrated not only by pottery finds but also by the settlement features characteristic of that period. The situation is similar to other sites in Eastern Delta.[6] Already present in the lowermost strata are numerous round and oval pits (measuring 1.20–2.20 m in diameter), often intersecting each other and containing a black fill with a modest amount of small pot sherds. These are probably the remnants of storage pits. Bigger pits, sometimes lined with silt, may have served as dwellings. A series of furrows (10–20 cm wide) with rectangular ground plans were recorded next to the pits. These most probably represent the remains of structures built of organic materials. Very characteristic are concentrations of small, round, or oval pits (20–30 cm in diameter) lined with silt, occasionally fired red. Most of these smaller pits did not contain any artifacts, with only isolated fragments of pottery occurring sporadically in some. Very similar settlement features were found during the excavations of other Lower Egyptian sites, especially in Buto.[7]

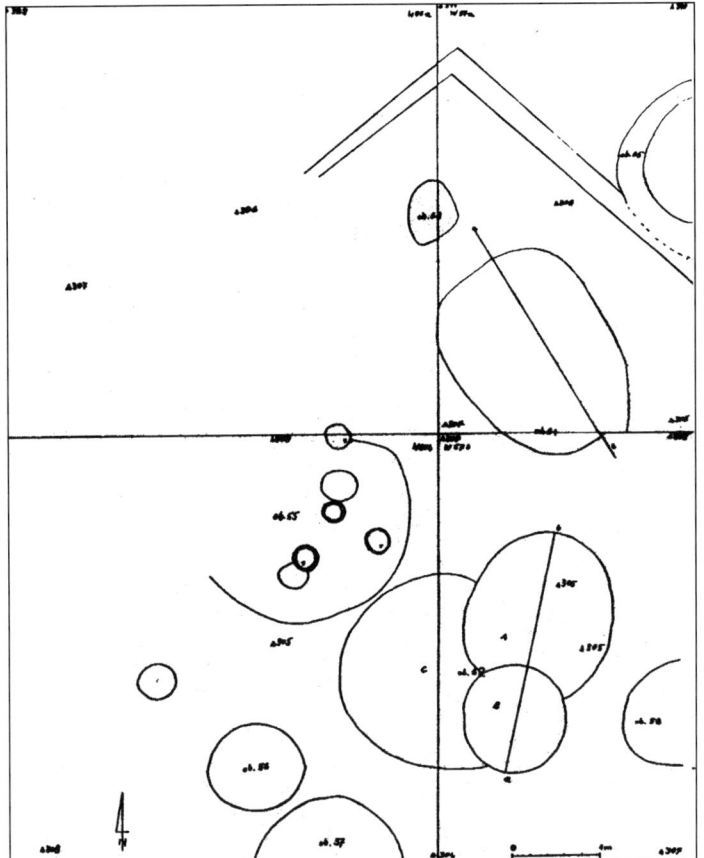

Figure 1

Higher up in the stratigraphic sequence, in layers still dating to phase one, storage pits become virtually non-existent, although furrows and small mud-lined pits are still present. A thin layer succeeds these strata, measuring between 10 and 20 cm, which still contains Lower Egyptian pottery sherds but has no settlement features. This could indicate that the site was temporarily abandoned, though this may not necessarily have been the case. Until the question has been resolved we shall assume the existence of a brief settlement hiatus.

Phase Two

Phase two is dated to a period contemporary with Naqada IId2 (beginning of IID2). Lower Egyptian pottery is still abundant, though Naqada ware also begins to occur in the archaeological record. Very little evidence of buildings survives from this phase. The most commonly encountered traces consist of successive layers of flooring with barely-visible outlines of walls. The best-preserved wall was discovered in one of the oldest strata (50 cm thick) belonging to Phase 2.

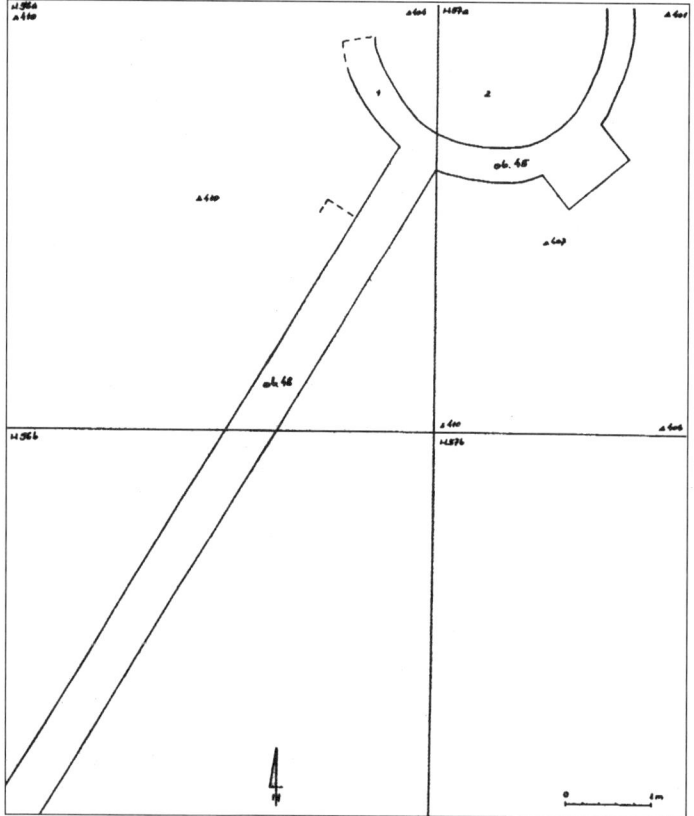

Figure 2

This 9.5 m-long wall was built of mudbrick on a NE-SW axis. Its northern extent links up with a semicircular construction bordered by a broad band (30–40 cm) of compacted silt. Inside the structure several layers of compacted silt floor containing small fragments of pottery were recorded.

Another, entirely independent, construction was revealed immediately beyond the southern end of the wall. As a large proportion of this structure (probably half) lies in that part of the site where excavations were not completed in 1999, the lower sections of it were also left for exploration during the 2000 season. Nevertheless, an initial description of the construction can be given: In plan it is either oval or rectangular with rounded corners. It measures 4 m in length, its width (in the area uncovered) amounting to 2 m. Three post-holes were recorded outside its perimeter—one situated to its south, the other two, located next to each other, to the east of it. Probably the roof of the construction was post-supported.

Fairly regularly laid bricks, measuring approximately 20 cm in length and 10 cm in width, bound the entire building. These bricks, however, differ in shape from those used most commonly, as they are roughly D-shaped in cross-section. Similar bricks, known for instance from Abydos and Hierakonpolis,[8] were usually called *fire dogs*. In Abydos and at Loc. 29 at Hierakonpolis they served as supports for large vessels; at Loc. 11 they were used for the construction of a pottery kiln. In construction from Tell al-Farkha no pottery sherds were found in the 1999 season.

132

In our case bricks were also found inside the structure, arranged in irregular groupings and in various positions: vertical, horizontal, or diagonal. It would appear that what we found was probably a layer of rubble rather than a floor surface. A considerable number of them were fired red or even black, but part of them still has the color of pure silt. The fill of this structure provides clear evidence of a fire; red-fired silt intermixed with large quantities of charcoal and ash. It is worth emphasizing that no other traces of fire were discovered in any other part of this layer. But if it is a kiln, or place where beer was made, or a burnt dwelling, until now is impossible to say.[9]

Phase Three

Phase three is characterized by the occurrence of homogeneous Naqada pottery, mostly IId2/IIIaI–IIIa2(?) or the end of IID2–beginning of IIIA1(?), indicating that traditions from the southern part of the country had been adopted at Tell al-Farkha. The oldest surviving architectural feature is the remains of a large rectangular room measuring 2.75 m in width and at least 6 m in length. The longer walls are built of mudbrick with generous sand inclusions (brick size is approx. 30 x 15 cm) and stand on a NE-SW axis. Their thickness amounts to almost 70 cm, while the shorter walls are nearly 90 cm thick. The construction in question is

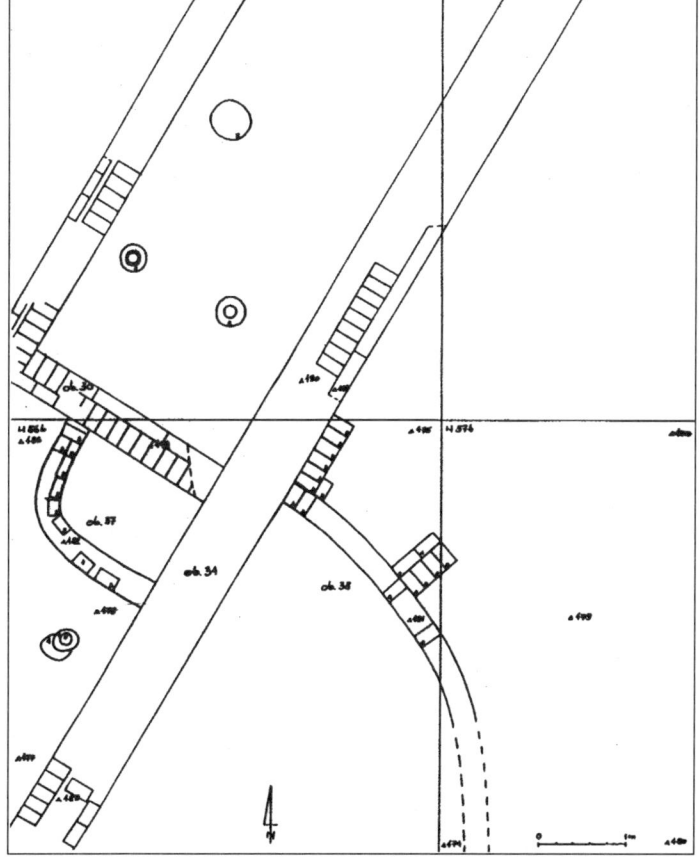

Figure 3

133

very poorly preserved, barely surviving to a height of a few centimeters. This is hardly surprising, since the most fully developed of all the buildings excavated to date was raised not much later on the same spot. This later building lays *ca.* 40 cm above the aforementioned fire dogs and post-built structure. An 80 cm-thick wall, built of bricks similar to those described earlier and measuring 11.70 m in length, runs along a NE-SW axis. Abutting the northwest section of this wall is a rectangular room, at least 5.50 m long, and flanked to the west and south by 50 cm-thick walls. Successive floor surfaces were made of silt and probably thinly coated with a type of lime mortar.

Concentrations of artifacts were found inside this room, particularly at its southern end. These finds included large numbers of pottery sherds and two large storage vessels with pointed bases. These were found intact, each standing *in situ* in a pit lined with a thick layer of silt. Fragments of a third vessel were also recovered, as were six small pots placed on the floor (two of them containing fish bones), a flint knife, and the broad, flat rim of a large stone vessel. The south end of this room adjoins a structure with a rounded corner (1.20 x 1.50 m), encircled by a low brick wall of the same thickness as the length of one brick (*ca.* 30 cm). A similar wall surrounds a semicircular area of *ca.* 4.60 x 4 m next to the southeast section of the main wall. To the north of this lie several groups of bricks oriented in various directions: These may be the remnants of a floor surface. The walls of the complex described above survive to a height of 40–50 cm. They consist of brick courses (in some instances clearly discernible) bonded with a type of lime mortar and raised on what is clearly a destruction layer.

Phase Four

Phase four is distinguished by changes in the ceramic assemblage, with typical Naqada IIIa2–IIIb or IIIA1–IIIB pottery becoming prevalent. Several settlement features belonging to this phase deserve particular attention. Most of them have very close parallels in Buto, layers IIId–IIIf.[10]

A nine meter-long wall runs along the NE-SW axis. It is about 90 cm thick and is constructed of bricks measuring about 30 x 15 cm. On the west is a room measuring about 12 m^2 (3 x 4 m). On the east is a smaller one measuring 3 x 2.5 m with badly preserved traces of a semicircular construction, and a larger room (3 x 5+ m). A semicircular pit (*ca.* 1.0 m in diameter) adjoins the south chamber's southeast section. A narrow wall (10–15 cm) one brick thick encircles the pit.

This building was probably very quickly rebuilt. Now it has two rooms, at least 5 m long on the west. Two hearths were recorded in the north chamber and in the northwest corner of the south chamber. Two round, silt-lined pits (*ca.* 20 cm in diameter) were situated near the latter. Several small, and unfortunately non-diagnostic, pieces of pottery were recovered from one of these pits. Two large ovens were discovered to the west of the thick exterior wall, on the same level as the north chamber. The biggest of these was virtually square. In both of them were four standing vessels. None of the vessels set up in the ovens had bases—each one stood on a platform of pure silt. They are all of the same type, known from Tell Ibrahim Awad, though at that site they were dated earlier, to local Phase 7, contemporary with Naqada IId.[11] The height to which these vessels are preserved ranges between just under 20 cm to 40 cm: This suggests that they were used on numerous occasions and the bases broken with each successive usage. This way it was probably easier to empty the vessel of its contents (dried grain?) without removing it from the oven. This hypothesis is confirmed by the presence of several intermixed layers of charcoal, ash, burnt silt, and pure silt inside the ovens.

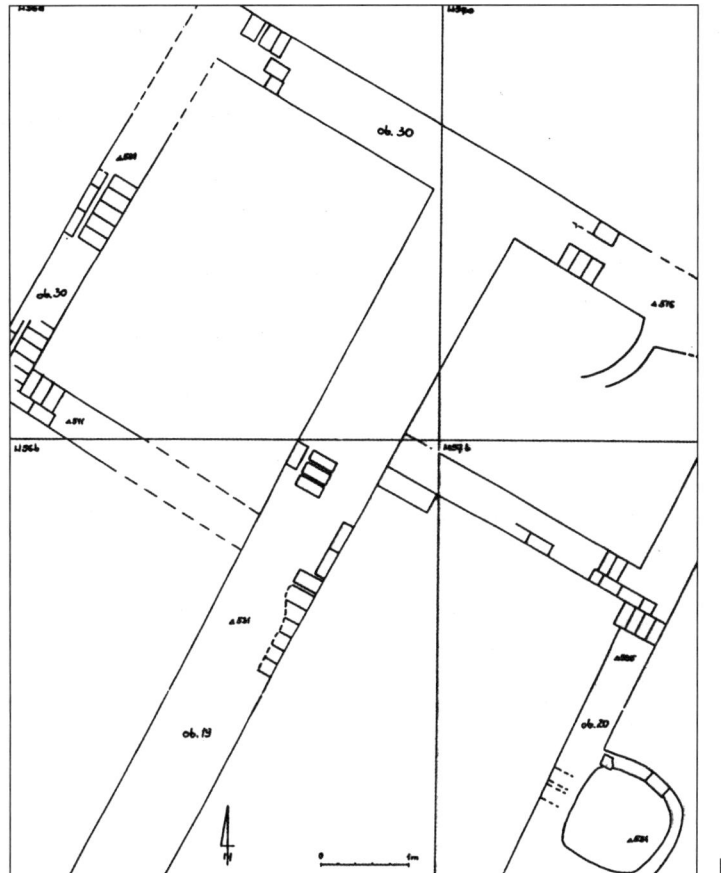

Figure 4

The features detailed above form one of the best-preserved complexes belonging to Phase 4. The walls of these rooms survive to a height of several dozen centimeters, while the stoves and hearths were found undisturbed.

A number of other relict walls and silt floor surfaces, in a much poorer state of preservation, were also found. These belong to rectangular houses, the precise dimensions of which are difficult to assess.

Beneath the corner one of the earliest houses connected with the Phase Four, three cylindrical jars were found. One with a net decoration could be dated precisely to Naqada IIIa2.

Phase Five

Phase Five comprises the site's uppermost strata. Here the archaeological record is characterized by material typical of the transition period Naqada IIIb/IIIc1 or the end of IIIB to IIIC1 (the start of the First Dynasty). As surface finds constituted the only pottery later than that discovered in the excavated section of the *kom*, we can tentatively assume that the west *kom* was abandoned at the beginning of the First Dynasty. Evidence for this phase is extremely scant. There is no distinct gap between this phase and the previous one, although some indications (a thin brown stratum occurring above some earlier structures and containing whole pottery vessels and grinders) may point to the existence of a brief settlement hiatus. The remnants of mudbrick walls were revealed.

The first of these comprised ill-preserved remains visible just beneath the surface.[12] Within their confines, fragments of a silt floor could be discerned, as well as poorly-preserved ovens. Among the best-preserved walls that survive are those that constitute a house with at least two rooms laid out in *en suite*. Each room is about 2.5 m wide and at least 5 m long. The longer walls, running in different directions than before—NW-SE, are three bricks thick (45 cm). The thickness of the transverse wall is approximately 50 cm. The long north wall had a pit (*ca.* 40 cm in diameter) positioned next to it. This was lined with a thick layer of silt and contained part of a grinder stained yellow. The uppermost strata yielded not only rectangular structural features but also round ones (*ca.* 2.50 m in diameter) in the form of a silt floor surface surrounded by a thin layer of compacted mud (*ca.* 10 cm). Beneath the floor, a reddish-black fill was revealed which bore clear traces of burning. Burnt material was also recorded outside this feature, while inside it a small amount of pottery and a large quern stone were recovered. A distinct concentration of sherds was noted in the northern part of the structure.

Apart from the large ceramic assemblages (including several dozen whole vessels) discovered in all of the phases discussed, there were also a number of other categories of artifacts that deserve particular mention. The most notable of these is the relatively large amount of flint tools which are especially numerous in the later phases of the site. Sickle blades are the most common, with knives occurring in smaller quantities. In earlier phases flint tools appear only sporadically. Naqada contexts yielded examples of quern stones and grinders or mortars, fragments of stone vessels, palettes, parts of games, part of a male clay figurine (torso only) and the only metal find recovered to date: a fragment of a copper pin.

Notes:

1 M. Chłodnicki, R. Fattovich, and S. Salvatori, "Italian excavations in the Nile Delta and new hypotheses on the 4th millennium cultural development of Egyptian Prehistory," *Rivista di Archeologia* 15 (1991), 5–33; M. Chłodnicki, R. Fattovich, and S. Salvatori, "The Nile Delta in Transition: A View from Tell el-Farkha," in E.C.M. van den Brink (ed.), *The Nile Delta in Transition: 4th–3rd Millennium B.C.* (Tel Aviv, 1992), 171–190.

2 M. Chłodnicki and K. M. Ciałowicz, "Tell el-Farkha. Explorations 1998," *Polish Archaeology in the Mediterranean* 10 (1999), 63–70; "Tell el-Farkha. Explorations 1999," *Polish Archaeology in the Mediterranean* 11 (2000) (in press).

3 That half of the trench was completely excavated during May–June, 2000.

4 W. Kaiser, "Zur Inneren Chronologie des Naqadakultur," *Archeologia Geographica* 6 (1957), 69–77.

5 S. Hendrickx, "The relative chronology of the Naqada culture: problems and possibilities," in J. Spencer (ed.), *Aspects of Early Egypt* (London, 1996), 39–69.

6 For example, Tell Ibrahim al-Awad or Tell Iswid (South); E.C.M. van den Brink, "A Transitional late Predynastic: early dynastic settlement site in the Northeastern Nile Delta, Egypt," *MDAIK* 45 (1989), 55–108; E.C.M. van den Brink, "Preliminary report on the Excavations at Tell Ibrahim Awad, Season 1988–1990," van den Brink *Transition*, 43–68.

7 T. von der Way, *Tell el-Fara^cin. Buto* I (Mainz, 1997), 66ff.

8 T. E. Peet, *The Cemeteries of Abydos* II (London, 1914), 7–8; M. A. Hoffman, *The Predynastic of Hierakonpolis – An Interim Report, Giza* (Macomb, Illinois, 1982), 14ff; the same type of brick is also known from Buto, but from later layers (compare von der Way, *Tell el-Fara^cin,* 120 ff.)

9 The second half of the construction was discovered during the 2000 season. A substantial amount of evidence suggested that it is the oldest brewery in the Nile Delta: Comp. J. Geller, "From prehistory to history: beer in Egypt," in R. Friedman and B. Adams (eds.), *The Followers of Horus. Studies dedicated to M. A. Hoffman* (Oxbow Monograph 20; Oxford, 1992, 19–26).

10 von der Way, *Tell el- Fara^cin,* 116 ff.

11 van den Brink, "Preliminary report," 54.

12 Most of them are similar to structures found in Buto layer IV (von der Way, *Tell el- Fara^cin,* 126 ff.)

Le sanctuaire de Chentayt à Karnak

Laurent Coulon

Institut français d'archéologie orientale, Le Caire.

Forme spécifique d'Isis, la déesse Chentayt[1]– la « Veuve » – est traditionnellement la figure emblématique des mystères osiriens de Khoïak, au point de donner son nom aux édifices qui abritent leur déroulement. Le « sanctuaire de Chentayt » (*pr šnt3yt*) est ainsi l'un des noms des chapelles osiriennes situées sur le toit du temple de Dendara[2] et désigne le cadre des rituels osiriens décrits sur la « cuve de Coptos »[3]. De tels sanctuaires sont attestés dans de nombreux centres osiriens d'Égypte4. Les textes qui les concernent laissent inférer une équivalence ou tout au moins une proximité d'usage entre la dénomination *pr šnt3yt* et d'autres appellations telles que le « château-de-l'Or » (*hwt-nwb*)[5], le « sanctuaire du Vivant-de-Formes » (*pr ʿnḫ-irw*)[6], la « chambre secrète » (*ʿt imnt*)[7] ou le « château de la Revigoreuse » (*hwt-msnḫt*)[8]. L'édifice doit comprendre au moins une « salle large » (*wsḫt*), ainsi qu'un « local clos » (*ḫnw*)[9]. C'est dans cet espace que sont confectionnées annuellement les figurines osiriennes, objet du « travail de Chentayt », figurines qui sont placées ensuite dans la cuve-jardin (*ḥspt*) ou dans des coffres appropriés. La déesse y est associée très fréquemment à sa parèdre Merkhetes, forme de Nephthys, qui, dans les temples ptolémaïques, n'apparaît jamais indépendamment de sa compagne.[10]

À Karnak, l'existence d'un « sanctuaire de Chentayt » était connue à travers une mention sur la célèbre statue d'Ahmès fils de Smendès (Caire JE 37075), mention qui avait pu être mise en rapport avec les trouvailles de H. Chevrier dans la zone nord-est de Karnak.[11] L'exploration archéologique de ce secteur menée depuis 1993 dans le cadre du CFEETK[12] a permis de mieux évaluer l'importance dévolue aux rites osiriens dans le domaine thébain d'Amon et certaines particularités des cérémonies d'inhumation des figurines divines. En utilisant à la fois les données fournies par les vestiges découverts *in situ* et certaines inscriptions relatives au clergé thébain d'Osiris, nous nous proposons de corroborer la localisation du sanctuaire de Chentayt au sein de la nécropole osirienne au nord-est de Karnak et d'évoquer quelques exemples de prêtres chargés des rites qui s'y déroulaient.

I. Chentayt et ses acolytes dans le complexe osirien de la « grande place »

Il est maintenant bien établi que la nécropole osirienne située au nord-est du temple d'Amon à Karnak, désignée par l'expression *st ⸢ꜣt*, la « Grande Place », était liée spécifiquement à la forme coptite d'Osiris[13]. Deux types d'installations s'y laissent discerner. D'une part, le lieu de sépulture proprement dit qui a connu un développement sur plus d'un millénaire et d'autre part une chapelle dédiée à Osiris coptite,[14] située au nord-est du cimetière et qui était adossée à la « butte » d'Osiris.

Dans son état actuel, ce petit temple se compose d'une salle principale dans laquelle s'ouvrent deux pièces plus petites. La décoration, fortement dégradée, est au nom du pharaon Ptolémée XII et de Tibère, mais la chapelle est construite à partir de nombreux blocs de remplois qui attestent de la présence probable à cet endroit d'une chapelle éthiopienne[15] antérieurement aux réaménagements ptolémaïques.

Fig. 1 : Le temple d'Osiris coptite.

De prime abord, ce petit temple d'Osiris coptite semble un candidat sérieux à l'identification du « sanctuaire de Chentayt ». De fait, la déesse y est représentée, tout comme sa parèdre Merkhetes. La présence de Chentayt, qui n'est plus décelable dans l'état actuel du monument, peut être inférée à partir des notes prises *in situ* par J.-Fr. Champollion au XIXe siècle. Parmi les divinités qu'il identifie sur la « porte A » s'ouvrant au nord de la salle la plus large, se trouvent « Harsiési » et une « déesse en mère » dont il ne peut transcrire le nom : ⬚[16]. La lecture Chentayt s'impose[17]. Quant à Merkhetes, la scène dans laquelle elle est représentée peut être reconstituée à partir de blocs épars et s'intègre à la même porte « A » où Champollion avait repéré la présence de sa parèdre.[18] La déesse dont seule la fin du nom est conservée est représentée assise en train de recevoir deux bouquets des mains du pharaon.

Il est à noter que cette « porte A » semble s'ouvrir sur une niche aménagée à l'arrière de la salle la plus vaste de la chapelle : cette niche était peut-être le lieu où était déposée pendant une année la figurine d'Osiris fabriquée pendant les fêtes de Khoïak avant d'être enterrée définitivement dans la nécropole voisine. Seule l'étude de l'édifice dans sa totalité permettra de vérifier la validité de cette hypothèse.

Le fait que le « sanctuaire de Chentayt » puisse être identifié avec la chapelle d'Osiris coptite se trouve corroboré par les correspondances existant dans la décoration des catacombes osiriennes de Karnak[19] qui accueillent en dernier lieu le « travail de Chentayt » dans son lieu de repos définitif. Ce bâtiment, formé de trois galeries parallèles dans lesquelles s'ouvrent des rangées de niches destinées à recevoir les simulacres osiriens, a reçu sous Ptolémée IV une décoration fort soignée et à l'iconographie extrêmement riche. Le long travail de reconstitution de ce décor à partir des milliers de fragments retrouvés est toujours en cours mais a déjà permis d'avoir une idée précise de sa structure. Pour l'optique particulière qui est la nôtre ici, nous nous limiterons à signaler la présence de Chentayt « la vénérable », dont la légende a pu être reconstituée tout récemment sur la paroi sud de la voûte qui surmonte la galerie sud, et celle de Merkhetes associée à Nephthys sur la paroi nord.

Elles prennent part au cortège de divinités qui se présentent devant Osiris coptite assis sur son trône suivi de cinq divinités momiformes : les quatre fils d'Horus et un personnage dont la tête est surmontée d'un scarabée et qui se nomme le « scarabée vénérable » (ḥprr šps). Il s'agit dans cette représentation d'une transposition iconographique de la composition « réelle » des simulacres osiriens : l'effigie osirienne, les quatre « canopes » qui encadrent la figurine et le scarabée qui est placé au niveau de sa tête[20]. On peut noter également que parmi les divinités se présentant devant Osiris coptite, un grand nombre d'entre elles se retrouvent dans le « sanctuaire de Chentayt » de Dendara[21], par exemple les Pleureuses (ḥȝyty), la

Fig. 2 : Merkhetes et Nephthys dans les catacombes osiriennes de Karnak. Cliché A. Chéné/CFEETK.

Nourrice (*Rnn*)[22] ou les dieux-gardiens de Pharbaïthos. Le décor des catacombes, lieu d'enterrement définitif des simulacres fabriqués lors des fêtes de Khoïak, met ainsi en scène certains acteurs du « travail de Chentayt », dans un contexte où ils jouent avant tout le rôle de protecteur du dieu défunt.

Par la présence de Chentayt et de ses acolytes se confirme la complémentarité entre la nécropole osirienne et le temple d'Osiris coptite immédiatement voisin. Ce dernier est probablement aussi à identifier au « temple d'Osiris » qu'évoque le rituel des cérémonies effectuées en l'honneur d'Osiris au mois de Khoïak contenu dans le papyrus du Louvre N 3176 (S), datable du début de l'époque romaine, en l'associant à la Grande Place et à la « tombe du dieu » (*tpḥt*)[23]. Le fait que la chapelle d'Osiris coptite a connu une restauration sous Tibère corrobore encore cette identification[24], d'autant plus que le temple d'Opet, autre lieu stratégique dans l'organisation des rites décrits par le papyrus, a lui aussi bénéficié de dotations du même empereur[25].

II. Les prêtres associés aux mystères osiriens à karnak

La connaissance que nous avons du clergé d'Osiris à Karnak est très fragmentaire[26], ce qui nous a incité à entreprendre le recensement des différentes prêtrises liés à ce dieu à travers la documentation thébaine, dont une grande partie, surtout pour les périodes les plus récentes, est encore inédite. En prélude à une étude d'ensemble, nous présentons ici, à travers un choix d'exemples[27], un aperçu de la manière dont on peut rattacher certaines données des documents privés au contexte général de l'étude de la nécropole osirienne.

Les mentions du « sanctuaire de Chentayt » sont rares dans les inscriptions de particuliers issues de Karnak, mais deux cas permettent néanmoins de conforter les analyses précédentes. Le premier est fourni par une statue du IVe siècle av. J.-C., issue de la Cachette de Karnak et appartenant à un prêtre nommé Ousirour fils de Hersenef et de Disyimenet (Caire JE 37134)[28]. Il s'agit d'une statue-cube devant laquelle se détache en ronde-bosse une statuette d'Osiris. Entre autres fonctions, Ousirour porte les titres *mr-k3t idnw n pr-šnt3yt*, « chef du travail et serviteur du sanctuaire de Chentayt »[29]. Ces fonctions mettent en lumière le caractère institutionnel de l'édifice, qui dispose d'un clergé spécifique.

La seconde source issue de la documentation privée est fournie par la célèbre statue d'Ahmès fils de Smendès (Caire JE 37075)[30]. Le « pyramidion » du pilier dorsal montre deux scènes symétriques dans lesquelles le prêtre est en adoration, à droite devant la forme primordiale d'Amon, à gauche devant Osiris Ounnefer roi des dieux. La légende de cette dernière scène se lit : *šms Wsir m pr-šnt3yt* « servir Osiris dans le sanctuaire de Chentayt ».

Fig. 3 : Statue d'Ousirour (Caire JE 37134). Cliché J.-Fr. Gout/IFAO.

141

Fig. 4 : Détail du pyramidion de la statue Caire JE 37075 (d'après *JEA* 20, pl. I).

À cette bipartition du pyramidion entre Amon et Osiris Ounnefer associé au « sanctuaire de Chentayt » répond la dualité des proscynèmes sur le rebord du pilier, l'un dédié à Amon-Rê primordial, l'autre à Amon-Rê roi des dieux et à Osiris coptite à la tête du château-de-l'Or[31]. Dans l'inscription qui détaille les différentes fonctions qu'il a occupées, Ahmès rend compte plus précisément de sa participation aux mystères osiriens en tant que prophète de Sokar-Osiris :

iw.i m ḥry-sšt3 m pr ʿnḫ-irw

sʿnḫ Wsir m ḥwt-nwb

« J'étais supérieur-des-secrets dans le "sanctuaire du Vivant-de-Formes",

faisant revivre Osiris dans le château-de-l'Or. »[32]

L'ensemble des données de cette inscription montre l'implication d'un personnage de très haut rang dans la fabrication de figurines osiriennes dans les lieux spécifiques qui y sont consacrés. Par ailleurs, cet Ahmès mentionne explicitement le fait qu'il a « inscrit » l'avant porte du temple de Khonsou à Karnak, ce qui correspondrait à la porte de Ptolémée III (porte d'Évergète).[33] Or, la construction et la décoration des catacombes osiriennes datent du règne de son successeur Ptolémée IV et il n'est dès lors pas inconcevable que ce même personnage ait présidé personnellement à l'aménagement de la nécropole. La mise en exergue du sanctuaire de Chentayt et de la dévotion envers Osiris coptite sur cette statue, ainsi que certains parallèles qui existent entre des textes « originaux » de la porte d'Évergète, comme « l'éloge de Thèbes », et ceux des catacombes pourraient étayer cette hypothèse.

En dehors de ces évocations explicites du « sanctuaire de Chentayt », d'autres allusions aux mystères osiriens peuvent être décelées à travers les inscriptions privées. C'est le cas de celle qu'a laissée Khnemibrêmen fils de Nesmin sur la statue Caire JE 36918[34], d'époque ptolémaïque. La généalogie fournie par les données du texte qu'elle porte[35] peut être complétée par celles d'une autre statue (Caire JE 47277)[36], provenant de la cour du Xe pylône à Karnak et qui appartient de toute évidence à son père Nesmin[37]. L'autobiographie de Khnemibrêmen contient des indications qui ne laissent aucun doute sur la participation effective de ce prêtre aux mystères osiriens. Ainsi, dans le texte inscrit sur le côté droit de la statue, qui débute par un proscynème à Ptah-Sokar-Osiris associé à l'ensemble des dieux de Thèbes, le personnage se présente de la manière suivante[38] :

it-nṯr ꜥk bw ḏsr
sm n ẖnty ḥwt-nwb
rḫ sšt3 m k3t n rḫ
wṯs skr r ḥnw.f

« (...) le père divin qui pénètre dans le lieu sacré,
le prêtre-*sem* de celui qui préside au château-de-l'Or,
qui connaît le secret du travail que l'on ne connaît pas[39],
qui élève Sokaris jusqu'à sa barque-*ḥnw*. »

Dans cette évocation des charges de ce prêtre auprès du dieu « qui préside au château-de-l'Or », épithète privilégiée d'Osiris coptite, et de Sokaris, l'expression « qui connaît le secret du travail que l'on ne connaît pas » est particulièrement notable car elle renvoie précisément aux rituels de confection des figurines osiriennes. Dans les titres des différents traités compilés dans l'inscription des « mystères d'Osiris au mois de Khoïak » de Dendara, le même type d'expression est utilisé :

rḫ sšt3w nw k3t ḥspt nw ẖnty-Jmntt n pr-šnt3yt[40]

« Connaître les secrets du travail de la cuve-jardin du Khenti-Imentet dans le sanctuaire de Chentayt. »

rḫ sšt3 n trḥt ir(w) m bty n skr m k3t n rḫ s(y) m ꜥt-imnt ḥr sp3wt wn <k3t> im.sn[41]

« Connaître le secret du *tereh* fait avec le moule de Sokaris en travail secret dans la salle cachée, ainsi que les nomes dans lesquels <le travail> a lieu. »

De même, dans la chambre de Sokaris de Dendara, qui évoque le rituel de fabrication d'une figurine osirienne au Nouvel An, le roi offrant le récipient de dattes à Osiris est présenté ainsi :

wꜥb-nṯr rḫ m k3t n rḫ [...]

« le prêtre pur expert dans le travail que l'on ne connaît pas »[42]

L'expression « travail que l'on ne connaît pas » désigne sans ambiguïté la fabrication de la figurine osirienne, comme l'attestent encore les prescriptions du papyrus Salt 825[43]. L'analogie des expressions employées laisse entrevoir, même si c'est de manière très allusive, l'activité d'un prêtre dans la confection des figurines. On comparera enfin également aux expressions de Khnemibrêmen le passage suivant de la version thébaine du *Livre de parcourir l'éternité* (pLeyde T32, III, 26-27) :

ꜥḳ.k ḥnꜥ ꜥḳw pr.k ḥnꜥ prw
m ḏsr wr sp sn m ḥwt-nṯr.f
dg3.n.k k3t nn rḫ s(y) m sšt3.s in ḥry-sšt3
nn m33 nn sḏm

« Tu entres avec ceux qui entrent et sors avec ceux qui sortent
en très grande sainteté dans son temple ;
tu regardes le travail que l'on ne connaît pas en son mystère, (fait) par le chef du mystère,
que l'on ne voit ni n'entend. »[44]

L'impératif de silence et de secret qui préside aux mystères osiriens joue probablement un grand rôle dans le caractère rare et peu explicite de leur évocation dans ce type d'inscriptions privées. L'emploi d'expressions spécifiques révèle néanmoins de manière indubitable la participation de prêtres comme Khnemibrêmen dans le déroulement de ces cérémonies et sa connaissance de rituels qu'il paraphrase dans son inscription.

Conclusion

Si nous ne possédons pas pour Thèbes de descriptions des rites de Khoïak aussi détaillées que celles que peuvent nous présenter les compilations tentyrites, divers documents fournissent en définitive, en regard des trouvailles archéologiques, des témoignages épigraphiques de l'existence d'un « sanctuaire de Chentayt » dans la « Grande Place » de Karnak, lieu dédié à la confection de figurines osiriennes, dont l'importance se reflète à travers certaines inscriptions de prêtres thébains. Les sources lient indissociablement cette institution à la forme coptite d'Osiris et aux lieux de culte qui lui ont été consacrés au nord-est du temple d'Amon, alors que d'autres édifices osiriens de Thèbes, comme le temple d'Opet, ne font aucune mention de Chentayt. Ce lien étroit entre la déesse et Osiris de Coptos laisse présager que les rituels de Khoïak pratiqués à Karnak devaient s'apparenter fortement à ceux que nous décrit, à l'époque libyenne, la « cuve de Coptos ».

Notes:

1 Pour la personnalité de cette déesse, on se reportera aux études de J. Yoyotte, *AnnEPHE V*[e] sect. 88 (1979–1980), 195–196, et de S. Cauville, « Chentayt et Merkhetes, des avatars d'Isis et Nephthys », *BIFAO* 81 (1981), 21–40 ; voir aussi G. Nachtergael, « La chevelure d'Isis », *L'Antiquité classique* 50 (1981), 592–594.

2 S. Cauville, Le *temple de Dendara. Les chapelles osiriennes. Commentaire*, BdE 118, (Le Caire, 1997), 209–276, e.g. 216–217.

3 Yoyotte, *AnnEPHE V*[e] sect. 86 (1977–1978), 164.

4 Cf. Yoyotte, *AnnEPHE V*[e] sect. 88 (1979–1980), 196 ; Cauville, « Chentayt et Merkhetes », 25, n. 2. Ajouter, pour Behbeit el-Hagar, Chr. Favard-Meeks, in R. Gundlach, M. Rochholz (éd.), 4. *Ägyptologische Tempeltagung. Feste im Tempel*, ÄAT 33.2, (Wiesbaden, 1998), 129–132 ; pour Hibis, J. *Osing, in Hommages Daumas* II, (Montpellier, 1986), 513 ; pour Busiris, A. D. de Rodrigo, *CdE LXXIV/148* (1999), 241 et 247, n. (5).

5 Cf. Fr.-R. Herbin, Le livre de parcourir l'éternité, *OLA* 58, (Louvain, 1994), 127 (avec références).

6 Cf. S. Cauville, *RdE* 32 (1980), 57, n. 71 ; Herbin, *LPE*, 114–117.

7 Sur la ʿt *imnt* en rapport avec les mystères osiriens, voir É. Chassinat, Le *mystère d'Osiris au mois de Khoïak* II, (Le Caire, 1966-1968), 769 ; J.-Cl. Goyon, *Les dieux-gardiens et la genèse des temples*, BdE 93/1, (Le Caire, 1985), 274, n. (2) ; 427, n. (2). Le prêtre memphite Harimouthes (PP IX, 5460b) est alternativement *ḥri-sšt3 pr-šnt3yt m tnnt* (sur la stèle BM 147, l.21) ou *ḥri-sšt3 m ʿ(t) imn(t) m tnnt* (sur la stèle BM 886, l. 14 et le socle de statue (?) WAG 48.1381). Cf. J. Quaegebeur, *AncSoc 3* (1972), 95 ; *id., in Studies on Ptolemaic Memphis*, (Louvain, 1980), 51-53, n. 2.

8 Cf. Herbin, *LPE*, 123.

9 La salle-*wsḫt* est mentionnée notamment dans les textes de la Cuve de Coptos (Yoyotte, *AnnEPHE* Vᵉ sect. 90 (1981-1982), 189), dans le *Livre de parcourir l'éternité* (pLeyde T32, I, 29-30 et var. = Herbin, *LPE*, 114-115) ou dans le papyrus MMA 35.9.21 (J.-Cl. Goyon, *Le papyrus d'Imouthès fils de Psintaês*, (New York, 1999), 22). Le local-*ḥnw* apparaît dans cette dernière source.

10 Cauville, « Chentayt et Merkhetes », 23.

11 Yoyotte, *AnnEPHE* Vᵉ sect. 86 (1977-1978), 168 et voir infra fig. 4.

12 Voir la communication de Fr. Leclère dans les actes de ce colloque, où l'on trouvera la bibliographie antérieure.

13 P. Barguet, *Le papyrus N. 3176 (S) du Musée du Louvre*, BdE 37, (Le Caire, 1962), 31-34 ; Fr. Leclère, L. Coulon, « La nécropole osirienne de la "Grande Place" à Karnak », *Proceedings of the Seventh International Congress of Egyptologists*, OLA 82 (1998), 656-658.

4 PM II2, 207.

5 J. Leclant, *Recherches sur les monuments thébains de la XXVe dynastie dite éthiopienne*, BdE 36 (Le Caire, 1965), § 13, 54-56.

6 J.-Fr. Champollion, *Notices descriptives* II, (Paris, 1889), 260.

7 Notons que cette graphie, que l'on retrouve sur la statue Caire JE 37075 (*voir infra*), joue sur une analogie graphique avec le mot *šn-t3* « végétation » (cf. Wb IV, 501, 6-11).

8 Nous remercions le professeur Cl. Traunecker, qui est en charge de la publication de la chapelle, de nous avoir autorisé à utiliser cette partie inédite du monument dans notre communication. L'assemblage des blocs figure dans son étude inédite déposée au CFEETK.

19 Sur cet édifice, voir L. Coulon, Fr. Leclère, S. Marchand, *Karnak* X (1995), 205-238, pl. I–XIII ; Fr. Leclère, L. Coulon, *op. cit.*, 653-658.

20 Sur la structure des figurines retrouvées à proximité des catacombes, voir la communication de Fr. Leclère. Cette disposition des fils d'Horus et du scarabée est probablement évoquée également en *Dendara* X, 426, 10-13. Cf. M. A. Stadler, *ZÄS* 128 (2001), 75-76.

21 Voir par exemple la liste de *Dendara* X, 32, 2-8.

22 Sur cette déesse, voir Chassinat, *Khoïak* I, 338-339.

23 Barguet, *Le papyrus du Louvre N 3176 (S)*, 31-34. Le fait que ce temple soit appelé aussi « temple d'Isis » dans le papyrus évoquerait peut-être le rôle central de Chentayt, forme d'Isis, dans ce lieu. Pour la datation, voir J. Osing, *Hieratische Papyri aus Tebtynis* I, (Copenhague, 1998), 29, n. 71 ; J. Fr. Quack, *RdE* 49 (1998), 255.

24 Pour une autre identification possible avec la chapelle d'Osiris *wp-išd*, voir D. B. Redford, « New Light on Temple J at Karnak », *Orientalia* 55 (1986), 1-15.

25 Cf. H. De Meulenaere, *OLP* 9 (1978), 72-73.

26 Voir néanmoins J. Leclant, *Enquêtes sur les sacerdoces et les sanctuaires égyptiens à l'époque dite « éthiopienne »*, BdE 17, (Le Caire, 1954).

27 Nous ne présenterons pas ici la documentation relative aux prêtres d'Osiris coptite qui dépasserait le cadre de ce bref exposé. On notera néanmoins l'inscription très intéressante qui se trouve sur le siège de prêtre d'Imhotep (Caire RT 2/2/21/5 = G. Daressy, *BIFAO* 11 (1914), 235-236) dont le propriétaire possède de très

nombreux titres en rapport avec les cérémonies osiriennes. Nous préparons une nouvelle édition de ce texte important à partir d'un estampage inédit.

28 Cf. L. Coulon, « Un serviteur du sanctuaire de Chentayt à Karnak », *BIFAO* 101 (2001), 137–152.

29 Coulon, *BIFAO* 101,139, n. (b) et (c).

30 H. W. Fairman, « A statue from the Karnak Cache », *JEA* 20 (1934), 1–4, pl. I–II.

31 Fairman, *JEA* 20, 3, C et pl. II, 1.

32 Fairman, *JEA* 20, 2, B5 et pl. I, 1 (col. 5).

33 J. Quaegebeur, « The Egyptian Clergy and the Cult of the Ptolemaic Dynasty », *AncSoc* 20 (1989), 111 et n. 122 ; id., « À la recherche du haut clergé thébain à l'époque gréco-romaine », *in* S. P. Vleeming (éd.), *Hundred-Gated Thebes. Acts of a colloquium on Thebes and the Theban area in the Graeco-roman period (P. L. Bat. 27), 9–11 september 1992*, (Leyde, New-York, Cologne, 1995), 149. Voir aussi Cl. Traunecker, *Coptos*, OLA 43, (Louvain, 1992), 366–367, § 334–335 ; Ph. Derchain, « Allusion, citation, inter-textualité », *in* Fs. Winter, *AegTrev* 7 (1994), 72–73 et *AnnEPHE* V^e sect. 103 (1994–1995), 146.

34 R. El-Sayed, « Deux statues inédites du Musée du Caire », *BIFAO* 84 (1984), 127–146, pl. XXXVII–XXXIX.

35 El-Sayed, *BIFAO* 84, 146.

36 PM II^2, 184 ; texte publié par G. Daressy, *ASAE* 22 (1922), 265–266 [4].

37 On peut invoquer à la fois la similitude des titres et de la phraséologie.

38 El-Sayed, *BIFAO* 84 (1984), 134, C, l. 3–4.

39 L'interprétation de R. El-Sayed (« le savant dans la Place inaccessible ») ne tient pas au vu des parallèles cités *infra*.

40 Col. 14 de l'inscription ; cf. Chassinat, *Khoïak*, I, 196 = *Dendara* X, 28, 6–7.

41 Col. 31 de l'inscription ; cf. Chassinat, *Khoïak*, I, 270 = *Dendara* X, 31, 2–3.

42 *Dendara* II, 155, 13–14. Cf. Cauville, *RdE* 32 (1980), 51–52 (texte no 4). Pour la traduction, voir id., *Dendara II. Traduction*, OLA 88 (Le Caire, 1999), 238–239. Voir aussi le titre de la scène en *Dendara* II, 155, 9–10.

43 XVI, 9 et XVII, 4 : *t3 k3t nn rḫ s(y)*. Cf. Ph. Derchain, *Le papyrus Salt 825*, (Bruxelles, 1965), 17*–18*.

44 Herbin, *LPE*, 56.

New Archaeological Evidence from Bakchias (Kom Umm al-Atl, Fayum)

Paola Davoli
Bologna University

Bakchias is a Greco-Roman town in the northeast of the Fayum, 12 kilometers southeast of Karanis. It was probably founded during the project of land reclamation completed during the reign of Ptolemy II. In fact, papyrological evidence attests to its existence between the third and fourth centuries CE.

From an archaeological standpoint, Bakchias is yet not well known.[1] The existing area is oval in shape and covers 340,000 m² but only part is fairly well preserved. As with every other archaeological site in the Fayum, Bakchias was plundered from the time it was abandoned right up until the 1970s. The more destructive activities were those of the *sebbakhin* and local people searching for stones. The former probably worked at Bakchias during the first 30 years of the twentieth century. They leveled all the southern part of the area, close to where the modern village now stands, as well as the greater part of the center of the archaeological site, where a large number of exposed buildings can be seen. The stone-hunters continued their activities until the Supreme Council of Antiquities started to control the area in 1971.

The Joint Archaeological Mission of Bologna and Lecce Universities has been working at Bakchias since 1993. For the first three years we explored an area on the northern boundary of the *kom*. There we found three different levels of houses dating from the second century BCE to the third century CE.[2] Since 1996 the Mission has worked, under my direction, in the main temple of the town, a mud-brick building 41 meters long, 26 meters wide, and 10 meters high. This imposing building captured our interest for a number of reasons, above all because it is decaying due to being entirely exposed.[3]

B. P. Grenfell, A. S. Hunt, and D. G. Hogarth excavated the temple in 1896 and its plan, the only one to have been published when we started our excavation, appeared in *Fayûm Towns* in 1900.[4] The description of the temple given by the English explorers does not exactly correspond to the present situation.[5] In fact, the area around the temple was exploited by the *sebbakhin* some years after Grenfell's excavation and at present the door of the temple is

147

8 m above ground level and it is necessary to climb a high mound in order to go inside.

The first question we asked ourselves was, why does the temple have such deep foundations (more than 8 m because the end of the walls are not exposed) and what its relationship to the different levels and buildings around it? At the beginning we concentrated on both inside, on the temple, and outside, on the mound. The mound is 60 m long from north to south and 10 m high. In four campaigns we explored all the rooms and corridors of the temple (25 in total), and reached the floors. The rooms were completely filled with sand and mudbricks fallen from the walls; at present these reach a maximum height of 1.5 meters, instead of the 3 meters Hogarth mentioned a century ago. On the well-preserved walls there is thick mud plaster with a coat of light paint, as seen in rooms B and C.

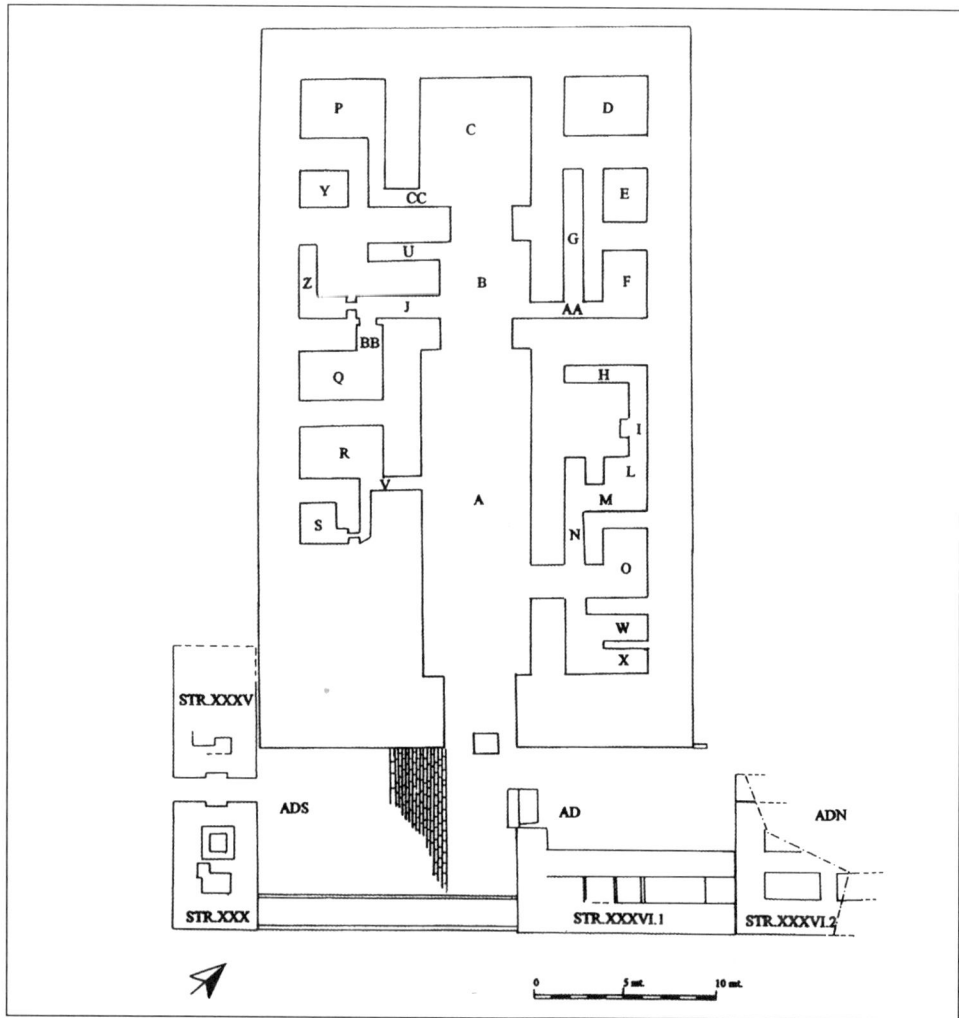

Fig. 1: Schematic plan of the Soknobkonneus temple.

The three central rooms (A, B, and C) were originally paved with sandstone blocks that were partially removed by the stone hunters. The well-preserved pavement is in room A, where we found two layers of sandstone blocks covered with a coat of pinkish plaster.[6] On this floor there are traces left by the people that occupied the temple after it was abandoned, probably the plunderers of what was left inside, for example, furniture and statues.

The work done by Grenfell and Hogarth was incomplete because floor level was not reached everywhere. For this reason some mistakes were made when the plan was drawn and many interesting objects were left behind. The objects we found testify that some of the side rooms were used as storerooms, at least during the Roman Period. In fact, we found many fragmented amphorae (imperial Egyptian amphorae), mud stoppers and a great number of mud seals. The plugs and the seals were impressed with various stamps, in Greek, hieroglyphic, and with motifs from Classical and Egyptian iconography.

Some of the side-rooms were modified during the Roman Period with the construction of new walls and pavements and as a result became real cellars (this is the case with rooms S, O, W, and X) like those in private buildings, with vaulting and a small entrance in the top. A rough staircase gave access to Storeroom R. Here we found two of the most interesting objects, dating back to the Hellenistic period: a small bronze statue representing a dancing ithyphalic dwarf,[7] hidden in the filling of the staircase, and the front part of a lion or sphinx with a Demotic inscription that mentions the name of the donor, Neferpetesukho, son of Hor.[8]

In front of the temple, the area we have explored is about 40 m from north to south and 15 m from east to west. The stratigraphy of the mound is quite complex because it is formed by buildings from different periods that were partly destroyed, covered and uncovered during antiquity and in some cases up until the 1970s. Although the excavation is not yet finished, we will attempt to describe what was found.

The first one and a half meters, beginning from the top, was composed of sand and a mixture of material such as mudbrick and a great quantity of mortar and sandstone fragments originating from the destruction of the buildings.[9] This is proof of the presence of stone buildings nearby. In the lower layers of this heap of debris were many fragments of the original furniture of the temple,[10] papyri,[11] broken statues made of different kinds of stone, and faïence and pottery.

Under this heap we also found a mud-brick floor (fig. 2) on the south side of the entrance of the temple. This was very fragile and partly destroyed. It was the last pavement used before the sanctuary was closed, probably at the end of the third century CE or at the beginning of the fourth. This was the floor of a courtyard closed to the east by a sandstone wall, of which only the mudbrick foundations survive. This structure consists of two parallel walls, completely plastered like the floor, and filled with clean sand. On the south side, the sandstone wall ends where it abuts the foundations of a massive building made of sandstone blocks dating back to the same period. Although heavily dismantled, the building is clearly recognizable as a pylon (str. XXX, XXXV), with the eastern tower the best-preserved part (fig. 3). In it there is at least one small room and the base of a staircase.[12]

From an architectural point of view, this find is of particular interest because it allows us to study the foundations of stone buildings as well as ancient construction techniques. The pylon was built on a thick layer of clean sand and the foundation trenches were filled with crushed stone derived from the cutting of the blocks. There is no mortar between the blocks of the foundation course, but it becomes ever more abundant in subsequent courses. The upper surface of each course was completely leveled, and along the perimeter we can see a setting line scratched in the stone. The front faces of the foundations of the pylon were not finished and show extra

Fig. 2: The entrance of the Soknobkonneus temple: mud-brick floor in front of it and the threshold blocks.

Fig. 3: The Ptolemaic building and the eastern tower of the pylon from north.

stone bosses. We do not know the final appearance of the pylon, but it is possible it was completely finished and decorated with light bosses. In fact, in the layers near the pylon we found some blocks finished this way.[13]

150

The study of the measurements and proportions of the building allowed us to attempt a hypothetical reconstruction of the complete pylon.[14] It seems that the unit of measurement employed in the construction of the pylon was a cubit of 53 cm and that it was combined to form squares with sides of 3 cubits each. The base of the pylon was 33 cubits long (= 17.80 m) and 9 cubits wide (= 4.78 m). As we know, thanks to the metrological studies of J.-F. Carlotti,[15] the Egyptian pylons were erected according to precise proportions between their parts. On the basis of all the measurements and proportions of the surviving parts of our pylon, we came to the conclusion that its height could originally have been about 18 cubits (= 9.50 m). Its entrance was about 4 m high and had double doors, as we can infer from the presence of niches on both sides of the passage.[16]

Fig. 4: Part of the structure XXXVI from south.

The pylon stands in front of a building (str. XXXVI) (fig. 1) the foundations of which we found last season.[17] This building was erected at the same time as the pylon and the enclosing wall, probably during the first or second century CE. The same kind of stone masonry was used and it is evidently part of a single architectural plan that completely changed the function and situation of the area in front of the temple. Grenfell, Hunt, and Hogarth were completely unaware of the presence of these stone buildings. In fact, they described the area in front of the temple as an open space and suggested that it might have been a sort of *agora*.[18] For this reason we can say that the buildings were dismantled in ancient times and what was left was then covered by sand. During our excavation we found proof that the foundations continued to be plundered until the 1970s.

At present we have brought to light only the forepart of a building that is 12 m wide. At this stage we are unable to determine its length (18 m of it has been uncovered). Unfortunately the stone-hunters completely destroyed its western wall, (of which we have found only a few blocks), and they managed to reach the lowest layers almost everywhere. What are left are parts of the foundations of an important building with a roughly recognizable plan (fig. 4). The walls of the foundations of this building were bordered by two mud-brick walls that delimited, respectively, the east and west sides of the foundation trench.

Between the two sandstone walls that run north-south on the eastern side of the exposed building, is the bottom of a staircase and three small, roughly-built rooms (1.5 x 2 m), probably crypts. Northward we have located three rooms; one was completely excavated and it turned out to be a foundation room. The central area of this part of the building is filled with clean sand. During the 1996 season we found a few sandstone blocks on this sand, which in my opinion were part of a double-layered floor. These blocks are the only ones to have survived the most ancient spoliation of the building. They were buried under five floors, built one on top of the other, and were composed of mud and waste matter containing many bits of broken furniture and objects.[19]

In the debris that covered all this area there were other architectural elements such as 15 blocks of more than 2 m in length, probably lintels or parts of ceilings, two cornices, six fragments of cavetto cornice or torus molding, and two *uraei* in sandstone that were part of a freeze. Though the excavation has not been finished yet, the architectural elements and the position of this building, near a temple and in front of a pylon, seem to suggest that it could also be a temple. The area explored corresponds to the first room; there are blocks that were part of the foundations of the door and north of them was the room paved in sandstone blocks. These were removed after the building was abandoned and the people that lived inside made new mud floors to cover the foundation sand.

In the area around the pylon there are buildings in mud brick that were partially explored in 1998 and dated to the Hellenistic period (str. XXXIV, XXVIII). They were partially destroyed and covered with sand when the stone buildings were erected. They constituted a group of houses directly connected with the temple of Sokanobkonneus, probably founded in the third century BCE. One of them (str. XXXIV) was razed during the second century BCE and then covered with a thick deposit of waste material. The floor level of this house seems to suggest that in the Hellenistic period the floor level of the temple and its entrance were lower than in the Roman Period.[20]

We still have a lot of work to do before we can obtain a clear idea of the buildings and the activities that took place in this area between the third century BCE and the beginning of the fourth century CE. During the next seasons we will continue the excavation in this area, both inside and outside the main temple, to try to understand the use of the numerous buildings and the dates of their construction and destruction.

Notes:

1 Cf. P. Davoli, *L'archeologia urbana nel Fayyum di età ellenistica e romana*, (Napoli, 1998), 117–137.

2 S. Pernigotti and M. Capasso (eds.), *Bakchias I. Rapporto Preliminare della Campagna di Scavo del 1993*, (Pisa, 1994); S. Pernigotti and M. Capasso (eds.), *Bakchias II. Rapporto Preliminare della Campagna di Scavo del 1994*, (Pisa 1995); S. Pernigotti and M. Capasso (eds.) *Bakchias III. Rapporto Preliminare della Campagna di Scavo del 1995*, (Pisa, 1996).

3 P. Davoli, "L' area templare di Bakchias," *Archeologia e papiri nel Fayyum. Atti del Convegno Internazionale (Siracusa, 1996),* (Siracusa 1997), 243–260; S. Pernigotti and M. Capasso (eds.), *Bakchias IV. Rapporto Preliminare della Campagna di Scavo del 1996,* (Pisa-Roma, 1997); P. Pernigotti and M. Capasso (eds.), *Bakchias V. Rapporto Preliminare della Campagna di Scavo del 1997,* (Pisa-Roma. 1998); S. Pernigotti, M. Capasso, and P. Davoli (eds.), *Bakchias VI. Rapporto Preliminare della Campagna di Scavo del 1998,* (Pisa-Roma, 1999); S. Pernigotti, M. Capasso, and P. Davoli (eds.), *Bakchias VII. Rapporto Preliminare della Campagna di Scavo del 1999,* (Imola, 2000).

4 B. P. Grenfell, A. S. Hunt, and D. G. Hogarth, *Fayûm Towns and Their Papyri,* (London, 1900), Pl. III.

5 Grenfell, Hunt, and Hogarth, *Fayûm Towns,* 36–38; D. Montserrat, "No Papyrus and No Portraits: Hogarth, Grenfell and the First Season in the Fayum, 1895-6," *BASP* 33 (1996), 148–161.

6 P. Davoli, *Lo scavo 1997. Relazione preliminare,* in Pernigotti and Capasso, *Bakchias V* 7–20.

7 S. De Maria, "Un bronzetto da Bakchias (Fayyum) e la serie dei nani danzanti ellenistici," *OCNUS* 7 (1999), 45–68.

8 G. Vittmann, "L'iscrizione demotica," in Pernigotti and Capasso, *Bakchias V,* 85–86.

9 Davoli, *Lo scavo 1997,* 39–55.

10 P. Davoli, "Mobili in legno dal tempio di Soknobkonneus a Bakchias (Fayyum)," in *Studies Sliwa* (in press).

11 The catalogues and the editions of the papyri are published in the annual *Rapporto Preliminare.* On the bibliography about Bakchias cf. P. Davoli, "Bibliografia relativa a Bakchias," in Pernigotti, Capasso, Davoli, *Bakchias I,* 77–87; M. Mengoli, S. Dellamore, *Bibliografia su Bakchias. II (1994–1999),* in Pernigotti, Capasso, Davoli, *Bakchias VII,* 125–133.

12 P. Davoli, "Lo scavo 1998, Relazione preliminare," in Pernigotti, Capasso, Davoli, *Bakchias VI,* 17–67.

13 The side walls of the south temple of Karanis are finished with light bosses; cf. A.E.R. Boak, *Karanis. The Temples, Coin Hoards, Botanical and Zoological Reports. Seasons 1924-31,* (Ann Arbor, 1933), Pls. X, XXVI and fig. 48; D. Arnold, *Temples of the Last Pharaohs,* (New York and Oxford, 1999), 255–256.

14 C. Tassinari, "Studio metrico del pilone Sud del tempio di Soknobkonneus," in Pernigotti, Capasso, Davoli, *Bakchias VI,* 69–80.

15 J.-F. Carlotti, "Contribution à l'étude métrologique de quelques monuments du temple d'Amon-Rê à Karnak," *Cah. de Karnak* X (1995). 65–94; J.-F. Carlotti, "Quelques réflexions sur les unités de mesure utilisées en architecture à l'époque pharaonique," *Cah. de Karnak* X (1995), 127–140.

16 S. Sauneron, *La porte Ptolémaique de l'enceinte de Mout à Karnak,* (Le Caire, 1983), 10–18.

17 P. Davoli, "Lo scavo 1999. Relazione preliminare," in Pernigotti, Capasso, Davoli, *Bakchias VI,* 15–62.

18 Grenfell, Hunt, and Hogarth, *Fayûm Towns,* 36.

19 Davoli, *Lo scavo 1996. Relazione preliminare,* in Pernigotti, Capasso, Davoli, *Bakchias VI,* 35–45.

20 Davoli, *Lo scavo 1998,* 54–56.

La nécropole d''Ayn el-Labakha (Oasis de Kharga): Recherches archéologiques et anthropologiques

Françoise Dunand, Jean-Louis Heim, Roger Lichtenberg

Université Marc Bloch, Strasbourg; Musée de l'Homme, Paris; Institut Arthur Vernes, Paris

La nécropole d''Ayn el-Labakha a été explorée entre 1992 et 1994 par l'Organisation égyptienne des antiquités. En 1994, nous avons convenu avec Adel Hussein Mohammed, alors inspecteur en chef des oasis, de travailler avec lui et ses collaborateurs, les inspecteurs de Kharga, sur le matériel humain et archéologique qu'ils avaient exhumé à 'Ayn el-Labakha. Ce travail s'est poursuivi de l'automne 1994 à l'automne 1997, après le départ d'Adel Hussein Mohammed, en collaboration avec les inspecteurs de l'OAE à Kharga, Bahgat Ahmed Ibrahim et Magdi Hussein.

'Ayn el-Labakha est situé à 30 km à vol d'oiseau au nord de la ville de Kharga, au pied de l'escarpement qui limite, au NO, la dépression constituant la Grande Oasis. Le site, dont le nom antique est à ce jour inconnu, occupe une superficie relativement vaste (150 *feddans*, soit environ 63 hectares) et comporte plusieurs groupes de monuments : deux temples, l'un en briques crues, l'autre hémispéos, dédié à un homme divinisé, Piyris[1] ; les vestiges arasés d'un édifice en briques crues (église ?) ; une forteresse romaine assez bien conservée, avec quatre tours d'angle ; un ensemble d'habitations.

La nécropole est située à quelques centaines de mètres de la forteresse, sur un escarpement constitué de bancs de grès alternant avec des couches de marne, le tout envahi par le sable, conditions particulièrement favorables à la bonne conservation du matériel humain et archéologique. Bien entendu, cette nécropole n'a pas échappé aux pillages, antiques ou modernes.

Nous n'avons que peu d'informations sur ce site, probablement occupé depuis l'époque ptolémaïque jusqu'au IVe siècle. Les graffiti grecs du temple hémispéos ont été datés des IIe-IIIe siècles[2]. La rareté des informations rendait d'autant plus utile l'exploration de la source inestimable de données que constituent les tombes, leurs occupants et leur mobilier. C'est ce que nous avons fait au cours de quatre campagnes, de 1994 à 1997, dont nous présentons ici les premiers résultats.

53 tombes ont été dégagées par les inspecteurs de l'OAE sur la falaise d''Ayn el-Labakha, dans des conditions de travail assez difficiles (forte déclivité, sable et déblais recouvrant l'ensemble du

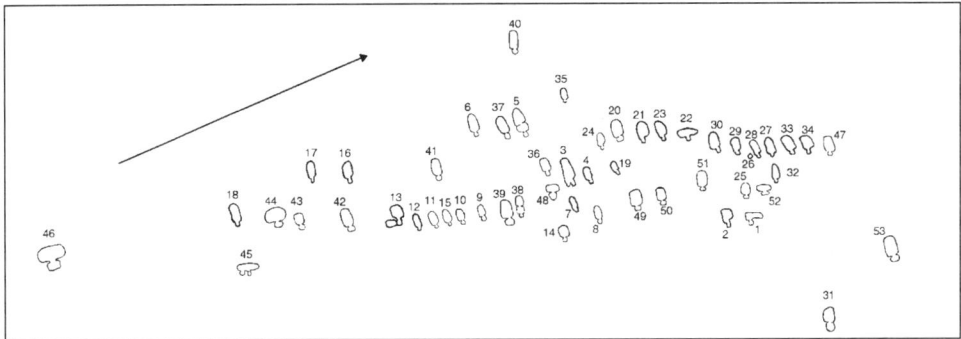

Fig. 1: Situation respective des tombes de Ayn el-Labakha d'après les données de l'Organisation Egyptienne des Antiquités. (La flèche indique le nord)

site). Creusées assez près les unes des autres, les tombes sont alignées irrégulièrement, leurs entrées débouchant sur de petites corniches étroites, grossièrement parallèles d'est en ouest. La plupart se conforment à un schéma simple : un puits peu profond, de petites dimensions, donne directement accès à un caveau creusé dans le rocher, généralement orienté SO-NE. Comme dans beaucoup d'autres nécropoles de cette époque, on a creusé les tombes dans la falaise en fonction de la nature du terrain et des possibilités d'accès, sans se soucier d'aménager ration-nellement l'espace. Les caveaux sont pour la plupart sommairement taillés, les parois irrégulières, les plafonds bas (en moyenne 1 m à 1,20 m) ; les ouvertures, de petites dimensions, devaient être fermées par des dalles (qui n'ont pas été retrouvées).

L'objectif de notre travail a été déterminé dès le départ en accord avec les inspecteurs de Kharga. Il s'agissait d'effectuer, à partir des restes humains, une étude de population (analogue à celle que nous avions effectuée à Douch)[3] utilisant la radiographie pour les momies et la technique anthropologique « classique » pour les squelettes. Nous voulions étudier sur le plan anthropologique et démographique la population antique d''Ayn el-Labakha et déterminer son état sanitaire : maladies, infirmités, régime alimentaire, causes de décès... Bien entendu, pour avoir une compréhension globale de cette population, il était indispensable d'étudier parallèlement le matériel déposé dans les tombes et constituant l'environnement des momies : objets révélateurs de leur culture matérielle, de leurs techniques et de leurs modes de vie. L'étude des procédés de momification, alliée à celle du mobilier funéraire, nous est évidemment apparue essentielle pour la compréhension des rites et des croyances à cette époque relativement tardive de la civilisation égyptienne qu'est l'époque romaine (mais il semble bien que l'occupation de certaines tombes remonte à l'époque ptolémaïque).

Matériel archéologique

Le mobilier des tombes est un bon révélateur du mode de vie de la population et, bien entendu, de ses croyances. De nombreux objets sont en rapport avec le rituel funéraire : masques, cartonnages de momies, statuettes de divinités. D'autres évoquent l'environnement quotidien des habitants d''Ayn el-Labakha : bijoux, objets de toilette, « vaisselle » en terre cuite ou en verre...

Matériel à caractère religieux et rituel

On n'a pas retrouvé trace de sarcophages en bois (peut-être récupérés par les pillards), mais des cartonnages (en tissu aggloméré recouvert de stuc peint) étaient présents, à l'état plus ou moins

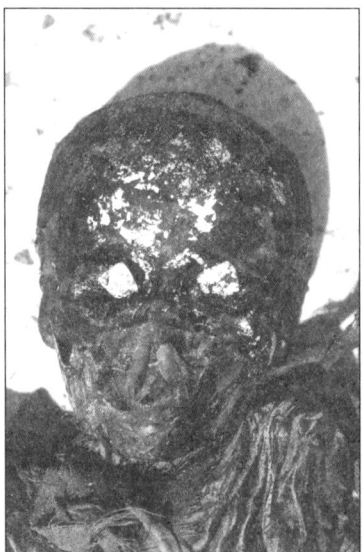

Planche 1: Momie d'un petit garçon (AL 06.1.06.) portant des feuilles d'or sur le visage, des plaques de cuir doré sur les yeux et les traces d'un bandeau métallique sur le front.

Planche 2: Cartonnage d'une jeune fille (Inv. 3446) représentée en Osiris, revêtue du linceul losangé caractéristique et portant les deux sceptres du dieu.

fragmentaire, dans 20 tombes sur 53 : cela suppose, chez leurs propriétaires, une relative aisance. Par ailleurs, de nombreuses momies devaient être déposées dans les tombes simplement enveloppées de linceuls et de bandelettes. Ces derniers sont souvent très bien conservés et très soignés. Ainsi, dans la tombe 51, sur 17 momies étudiées, 7 étaient entièrement bandelettées, 3 l'étaient encore en grande partie ; des fragments de masques et de cartonnages, des bijoux ont été retrouvés dans le caveau. En outre, la présence d'or cutané était visible sur 6 individus, ce qui est en faveur d'une bonne qualité de momification. On peut donc en déduire qu'il s'agissait d'une tombe « riche », probablement celle de notables locaux. La tombe 6 était certainement moins riche, mais on y a retrouvé 3 « momies dorées » dont celle, particulièrement remarquable, d'un garçon de 7 ans (AL.06.1.06), au visage presque entièrement doré et avec, sur les yeux, de petites plaques de cuir doré et sur le front les traces d'un bandeau, probablement en cuivre et or.

Deux cartonnages bien conservés (Inv. 3445 et 3446) sont particulièrement intéressants : ils figurent un défunt et une défunte (des adolescents, au vu de la taille) sous les traits d'Osiris ; la jeune fille n'a pas été figurée, comme c'est le cas pour le garçon, avec la couronne et la barbe d'Osiris, mais avec une perruque féminine ; en revanche, elle est vêtue du linceul losangé caractéristique du dieu et tous deux portent les deux sceptres qui sont ses attributs habituels. Plusieurs très beaux masques sont de type égyptien avec visage doré, perruque et plastron décoré de motifs traditionnels (en particulier Inv. 3447). La plupart paraissent datables des Ier-IIe siècles, mais des plaques de cartonnage découpé et deux « boîtes à pieds » ayant appartenu à des momies d'enfants peuvent remonter à la fin de l'époque ptolémaïque.

De façon assez surprenante dans l'environnement des momies, les amulettes paraissent avoir été très rares : ont-elles été emportées par les voleurs ? Ou bien la pratique était-elle en voie de disparition ? Nous avons fait la même constatation dans la nécropole de Douch.

Des statuettes de bois stuqué et peint évoquent des divinités funéraires et constituent pour le mort une présence protectrice : c'est le cas d'Anubis. D'autres se réfèrent au devenir du défunt et aux formes qu'il est censé prendre dans l'au-delà : 7 figurines représentent l'oiseau-âme, à tête humaine, c'est-à-dire le *ba*, cet élément que la mort sépare du corps mais qui doit nécessairement le rejoindre. D'autres représentent un faucon qui doit évoquer la « transformation en faucon » du défunt, mentionnée dans deux chapitres du *Livre des Morts*.

Objets de la vie quotidienne

Divers types d'objets trouvés dans les tombes évoquent la vie et les activités quotidiennes des habitants d''Ayn el-Labakha. Les bijoux, trouvés bien souvent sur les momies elles-mêmes, étaient particulièrement nombreux, ce qui semble correspondre à un pillage moins sévère que dans d'autres nécropoles. Ces bijoux, bien sûr, ne sont pas de grande valeur (perles de verre doré, pâte de verre, mais aussi cornaline et argent). En revanche, ils sont d'un style tout à fait comparable à celui des bijoux beaucoup plus riches que portent les femmes représentées sur les portraits du Fayoum entre le Ier et le IIIe siècle de notre ère. On peut noter que sur les momies que nous avons étudiées ce sont essentiellement des enfants qui étaient parés de bijoux, certains de ceux-ci étant des bijoux d'adultes. La momie AL 38.1.02., une fillette de 13 ans, portait deux colliers de grande taille, deux bracelets et cinq bagues, manifestement trop larges pour ses doigts.

Quelques objets de toilettes ont été trouvés : peignes, bâtonnets à khôl. La céramique était assez abondante, encore que peu diversifiée. Comme partout les types les plus représentés étaient les pots globulaires, les gobelets « tulipes » et les écuelles à fond plat, en un mot, la vaisselle de tous les jours. Si certains « pots » ont servi aux offrandes funéraires, d'autres, conservant des dépôts de ce produit noir, épais, que l'on retrouve sur les momies, ont dû servir aux embaumeurs.

La verrerie est relativement importante et de bonne qualité. Elle peut être l'indice d'un « niveau de vie » relativement élevé, car il ne s'agit pas d'une production locale.

Au total, le mobilier des tombes semble indiquer une certaine aisance chez la population d''Ayn el-Labakha, compte tenu bien entendu de différences sensibles aussi bien dans la présentation des momies (enveloppes, bijoux...) que dans les objets constituant leur environnement, différences qui reflètent certainement des clivages sociaux. Mais qu'en est-il des habitants eux-mêmes ?

Le matériel humain

Compte tenu de l'étendue de la nécropole et des dégradations et pillages qu'elle a subis, nous pouvons estimer à 450 ou 500 le nombre de sujets inhumés. En fait, les restes humains que nous avons pu identifier correspondent à plus d'une centaine d'individus pouvant être répartie de la façon suivante :

- 94 individus représentés par des momies (72) et des crânes isolés (22) recueillis dans plusieurs tombes et permettant une étude ostéométrique et radiologique ainsi que des observations anatomiques et paléopathologiques ;
- 41 os longs se rapportant à environ 37 sujets.

Globalement, nous avons affaire à des corps en bon état, ce dont témoigne également le fait que 20 % des momies sont encore bandelettés. Nous avons essayé de faire un bilan de cette population, en particulier sur le plan des maladies observées, des causes de la mort et même de l'âge au décès, constituant ainsi une esquisse de paléo-démographie. L'âge au décès est d'environ 32 ans, tous sujets confondus. Ce chiffre relativement bas reflète essentiellement la présence d'assez nombreux enfants.

Étude anthropologique

L'étude anthropologique de la nécropole porte sur 72 momies assez complètes pour permettre des radiographies, des observations anatomiques et des mensurations. D'autre part, 20 têtes isolées, réduites presque toutes à l'état osseux et provenant des tombes 6 (4 sujets), 29 (3 sujets), 41 (5 sujets), 42 (5 sujets), 50 (2 sujets) et 51 (1 sujet) ont donné lieu à des observations crâniométriques, anatomiques et pathologiques satisfaisantes en raison de la facilité d'examen des pièces.

Le crâne

Les crânes isolés sont le plus souvent dépourvus de leurs mandibules. 10 mandibules ont pu toutefois faire l'objet de mensurations et d'observations. Les crânes présentent une morphologie traduisant une population de type méditerranéen comme c'est le cas dans les autres sites de la New Valley. On note toutefois certaines particularités locales qui tiennent davantage aux conditions de vie, à l'état de santé et à la variabilité intra-professionnelle. Les crânes offrent une nette tendance dolicho-mésocrâne malgré des variations qui s'étendent individuellement de l'ultra-dolichocrânie à l'hyper-brachycrânie. Au total, 32 sujets, soit près de 30 % de la population, présentent un crâne à tendance allongée ou étroite, la moitié présentant un crâne moyen et près de 15 % un crâne à tendance courte ou large.

À titre comparatif, les sites de Douch et d'El-Deir fournissent la même distribution des classes de l'indice, malgré quelques différences portant sur les classes de part et d'autre des valeurs centrales. On note une légère tendance, compte tenu du faible nombre de sujets, au raccourcissement de la voûte crânienne chez le sexe féminin et à la tendance inverse chez les hommes. Les crânes sont généralement hauts avec un front moyennement large ; la face offre une tendance étroite et moyennement haute.

La face

Elle est le plus souvent orthognathe : le prognathisme est rare et limité à la région alvéolaire. Les pommettes peuvent être parfois assez saillantes mais la face n'est pas à proprement parler aplatie dans sa région supérieure ; elle est toutefois légèrement plus proéminente dans la région moyenne.

L'ouverture nasale est modérément large (mésorhinie) : sur 25 crânes examinés, 11 sont typiquement mésorhiniens, 10 présentent une ouverture nasale large (chamærhiniens) et 4 offrent une ouverture étroite (leptorhinie). Ici, on note une légère différence avec les crânes de Douch, situé à 150 km plus au sud, chez qui la largeur de l'ouverture nasale est plus grande. Mais le nombre de sujets examinés est différent.

Sur les crânes secs, le sillon ou la fossette prénasale intéresse 8 crânes sur les 22 observés, soit plus de 36 % de notre échantillon. Il convient de préciser que l'association dolicho-mésocrânie + chamærhinie + sillon ou fossette prénasale est généralement considérée comme représentative de populations qualifiées de « négroïdes » ; 2 crânes seulement associent ces trois caractères : 2 de la tombe 41 et 2 de la tombe 46.

Le palais est large, les orbites sont moyennement hautes et de contour sub-quadrangulaire.

Mandibules

Elles n'offrent pas de caractères particuliers. Le menton est généralement bien marqué, parfois nettement saillant lorsque la résorption du bord alvéolaire est présente. Les gonions (angles mandibulaires) montrent 27 cas d'extroversion relevés principalement chez les sujets masculins (19), ce qui est d'autant plus notable que cette population présente une tendance à la gracilité du squelette.

Squelette post-crânien

Les habitants d''Ayn el-Labakha présentent une tendance longiligne et une stature modérée, mais relativement plus élevée que celle qui a été mesurée ou calculée dans les deux autres nécropoles de l'oasis de Kharga, et ceci autant d'après les os isolés que sur les radiographies des momies. Dans les deux cas, les résultats sont pratiquement semblables. Les statures calculées par les os du membre supérieur sont généralement plus fortes que celles qui sont calculées par le membre inférieur, ce qui est une tendance observée dans les autres sites de l'Égypte antique et correspond à une morphologie longiforme. Aussi est-il préférable de ne tenir compte que du membre inférieur. Dans ce cas, la stature moyenne de la population atteint 158 cm pour les femmes et 163,5 cm pour les hommes, l'écart constaté entre les sexes étant de moitié plus faible que celui de Douch. En revanche, la taille mesurée sur les momies, pour les sujets d'âge supérieur à 15 ans, est de 143,95 cm pour les femmes et de 154,5 cm pour les hommes.

Dans l'état actuel de nos recherches, la population d''Ayn el-Labakha apparaît comme relativement gracile, avec une stature moyenne, mais supérieure à celle des autres sites de la Vallée. La morphologie à tendance longiforme correspond à un type « méditerranéen », peu différent de ce que l'on peut observer de nos jours, la diversité actuelle étant liée à un apport plus tardif de populations nouvelles. On peut ainsi définir la population d''Ayn el-Labakha par une prédominance de crânes mésocéphales ou dolichocéphales avec une face moyennement étroite, une ouverture nasale modérée ou large, des superstructures crâniennes assez faibles ou peu accusées, une gracilité relative du squelette. Ces caractères qui apparaissent à l'étude des os se confirment par l'observation des momies aux cheveux ondulés, jamais crépus. Ces caractères évoquent étroitement ceux que l'on a observés dans les autres sites de la Vallée, hormis un état de santé qui semble répondre, comme nous le verrons, à des conditions de vie plus favorables.

Étude paléopathologique

Elle s'est avérée riche, mais, contrairement à nos attentes, dans une large mesure différente de celle que l'on avait décelée à Douch. Bien sûr, on a observé des lésions de type traumatique, mais elles sont relativement rares. Un cas toutefois est exemplaire : celui de la momie AL 25.1.12. Ce garçon de 12 ans a dû tomber d'un lieu élevé ou subir un traumatisme très violent. Il est victime de nombreuses fractures, celle qui touche le crâne ayant entraîné la mort. Un enfant de 5 ans est également porteur d'une fracture du crâne.

L'arthrose, qui était très représentée à Douch, est beaucoup plus rare ici : l'on trouve seulement des lésions peu évoluées. Un homme de 60 ans présente néanmoins une arthrose très développée.

La pathologie infectieuse est fort représentée. La tuberculose osseuse (mal de Pott), souvent signalée par les auteurs, est présente à 'Ayn el-Labakha sous la forme d'un exemplaire malheureusement trouvé en surface. Par ailleurs, des lésions indiscutables de tuberculose pulmonaire ont été découvertes à 7 reprises. Il s'agit d'images pulmonaires calcifiées. On constate ainsi l'intérêt qu'offrent les momies non éviscérées pour l'opportunité de tels diagnostics. Il est intéressant de préciser que sur les 7 cas observés, 3 appartiennent à la tombe n° 20. Étant donné le caractère contagieux de la maladie, cela confirme, si besoin était, le caractère familial des tombes.

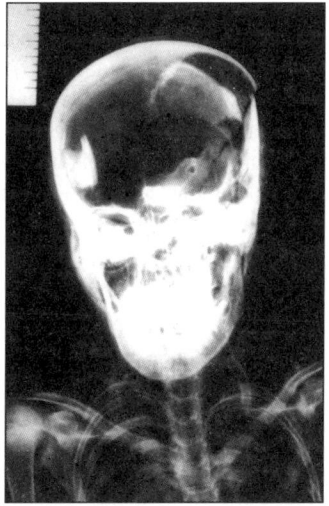

Planche 3: Radiographie du crâne de la momie AL 25.1.12., montrant la fracture complexe ayant certainement entraîné la mort.

159

La bilharziose a été retrouvée chez 14 individus. Si la répartition est moins étroite que pour la tuberculose, là encore la tombe n⁰ 20 se distingue : la moitié des sujets est victime de la bilharziose, 2 d'entre eux présentant aussi des signes de tuberculose.

La pathologie tumorale a pu être observée sur au moins deux enfants, une fille de 12 ans et un garçon de 8 ans. La fille présente des signes osseux en faveur d'un gliome du chiasma (tumeur maligne développée sur les voies optiques) tandis que le garçon semble victime d'une tumeur de l'hypophyse. Il est également porteur de signes de bilharziose. Un troisième enfant, âgé de 5 ans, est hydrocéphale.

Un crâne de la tombe 29 présente un aspect de *cribra orbitalia,* peut-être en rapport avec une thalassémie.

On relève un nombre notable de sujets portant des caries dentaires : au moins 17 sujets, 10 hommes, 5 femmes et 2 adolescents d'une quinzaine d'années. La fréquence des caries se répète principalement dans les tombes 6, 42 et 51, les 3 cas les plus atteints provenant de la tombe 42. Les caries affectent surtout des sujets relativement âgés : 12 cas de carie sur des sujets dont l'âge moyen est de 40 ans. La fréquence des caries à 'Ayn el-Labakha (18,1 %) dépasse très sensiblement les fréquences observées à Douch (12,7 %) et à El-Deir (près de 13 %), exprimant une alimentation plus riche en hydrates de carbone et probablement de meilleure qualité.

Les maxillaires sont dans 7 cas le siège de kystes ou d'abcès, auxquels dans 5 cas sont associées des caries. L'agénésie des M3 n'est observable que dans 1 cas (tombe 20). Une résorption dentaire plus ou moins avancée a été relevée sur 11 crânes, essentiellement des hommes.

État de santé et différenciation sociale

L'étude radiologique des momies (et des squelettes) permet de déceler en particulier les stries d'arrêt de croissance (ou « de Harris ») qui constituent un excellent révélateur du « niveau de vie » des populations. Ces stries, qui reflètent des périodes de malnutrition ou de maladie prolongée, sont très rares chez les pharaons, un peu plus fréquentes chez les notables et infiniment plus chez les populations paysannes. À Douch, nous les avions observées dans 48 % des cas, soit 63 % chez les femmes et 41 % chez les hommes. À 'Ayn el-Labakha, la proportion est assez voisine, 58 %, soit 60 % chez les femmes et 57 % chez les hommes.

Pour notre étude de la population d''Ayn el-Labakha, nous avons choisi un petit nombre de tombes dans lesquelles nous avons examiné un nombre relativement important de sujets, en espérant ainsi faire apparaître des parentés ou des différences d'une tombe à l'autre. Ainsi, nous avons examiné 58 sujets complets appartenant à 5 tombes. Parmi ces tombes, deux se distinguent : la tombe n⁰51 et la tombe n⁰ 20. La tombe n⁰ 51 est occupée par des momies de bonne facture, présentant peu de lésions pathologiques, ce qui est en accord avec sa richesse relative sur le plan du mobilier. La tombe n⁰ 20, en revanche, est occupée par des momies de qualité médiocre présentant des lésions pathologiques nettement plus marquées.

La momification

L'ensemble de la population en ayant bénéficié, il n'est pas étonnant qu'elle soit de qualité variable. Toutefois, elle est globalement assez bonne avec éviscération crânienne dépassant 75 % des sujets, éviscération abdominale de l'ordre de 20 % et présence d'or cutané sur 18 %. Ces données sont nettement « meilleures » qu'à Douch.

Conclusion

L'étude du site d''Ayn el-Labakha révèle une population homogène, de type méditerranéen, au niveau de vie relativement élevé, compte tenu d'une différenciation sociale clairement repérable à partir du mobilier des tombes et de la présentation des momies. Toutefois, ces résultats doivent s'intégrer dans une étude plus globale des populations de l'Oasis. Ils prendront toute leur valeur par la comparaison avec les résultats déjà obtenus à partir de la population de Douch et avec ceux que nous attendons de l'exploration en cours de la nécropole d'El-Deir.

Notes:

1 A. Hussein, *Le sanctuaire rupestre de Piyris à Ayn al-Labakha*, MIFAO 116, (Le Caire, 2000).

2 G. Wagner, *Les inscriptions grecques*, dans Adel Hussein, *ibid.*, 69–89.

3 Fr. Dunand, J.-L. Heim, N. Henein, R. Lichtenberg, *La Nécropole de Douch (tombes 1 à 72)*, FIFAO 26, (Le Caire, 1992).

Tell Ibrahim Awad:
A Sequence of Temple Buildings from
Dynasty 0 to the Middle Kingdom

Dieter Eigner

The first two seasons of excavation (1988–89) by The Netherlands Foundation for Archaeological Research in Egypt (NEFARE) in area A of Tell Ibrahim Awad revealed the massive mud-brick foundations of a building complex measuring about 35 by 70 meters. The building was identified as a temple from the Eleventh Dynasty probably founded by Mentuhotep II. The sanctuary possessed limestone walls of considerable thickness, resting on a bed of clean sand which filled a 90 cm deep rectangular pit.[1] In and near this pit were found the remains of mud-brick walls of an older date, obviously belonging to a predecessor of the Middle Kingdom temple.

The following seasons of excavation, up to 1999, uncovered remains of a temple dating to the Old Kingdom, and later on, the remains of buildings from the Early Dynastic and Protodynastic periods.

In accordance with the preliminary chronology developed by Van den Brink for Tell Ibrahim Awad,[2] a chronological chart for the temple site (squares A 130–140/190) is proposed below:

Phase	Date	Remains
1b	Eleventh Dynasty	temple
2a	Sixth Dynasty–First Intermediate Period	temple
2b	Fifth (– Sixth) Dynasty	temple
2c	Fourth Dynasty	temple
3	(Second –) Third Dynasty	temple
4	Second Dynasty	settlement deposits
5a–b	First Dynasty	2 phases of temple
5c–d	Dynasty 0–First Dynasty	2 phases of temple
6a	Dynasty 0	temple
6b	Dynasty 0	temple
6c	Dynasty 0 (Naqada IIIb)	fireplaces
6d	Dynasty 0 (Naqada IIIa?)	(temple-) enclosure

It must be noted that this detailed chronology is a preliminary one. Further study and evaluation of the ceramics could result in some modifications, but the framework of the main periods is attested by the stratigraphy and by finds which were *ad hoc* datable.

Phase 2a (Late Old Kingdom–First Intermediate Period)

The larger part of the temple built during this phase was dismantled before or destroyed by construction of the Middle Kingdom temple, especially by excavation of the pit holding foundation sand for the Middle Kingdom sanctuary. A typical feature of Phase 2a is large areas of mud-brick pavement that also cover the remains of Phase 2b. Part of an enclosure wall is preserved.

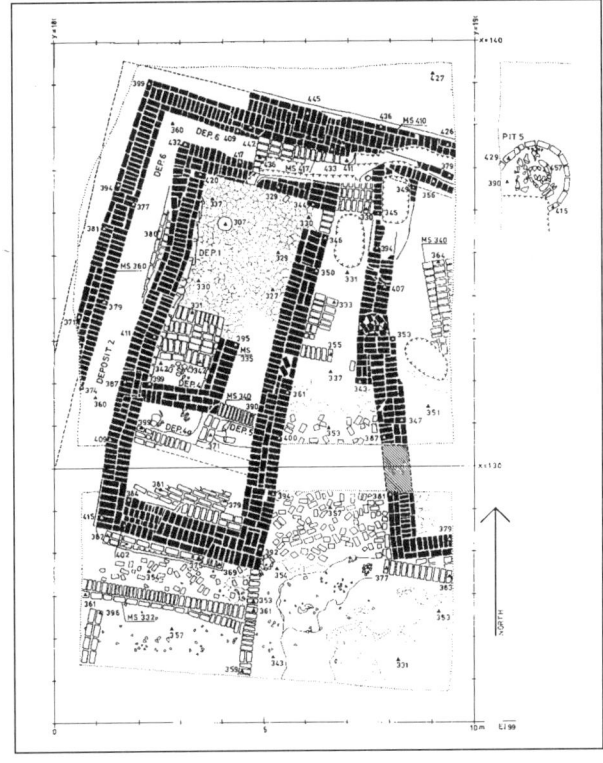

Fig. 1: Tell Ibrahim Awad, squares A 130–140/190: Temple of the Old Kingdom, Phase 2b (Dyn. 5 –6). Of Phase 2a (Dyn. 6 - First Intermediate Period) the outline of the enclosure wall, part of the brickwork of its northern section and of the adjoining pavement are indicated. Levels give elevation in cm above actual mean sealevel. "ME" indicates bottom levels of the walls.

Phase 2b (Fifth–Sixth Dynasty)

During the 1993 season the complete plan of the Old Kingdom temple was revealed. It is an elongated rectangle with a narrow corridor running between the building and the enclosure-wall. To the east, a wall borders an access passage, widening to a kind of forecourt in the south. South of the building, separated by a small alley, there is an enclosure, perhaps for a priest's house. The forecourt and alley are paved with bricks and brick fragments. Access to the passage leading to the entrance of the building is blocked by a little wall, leaving only a small gap for ingress.

The building is of modest size, the interior measuring 5 by 15 cubits. In view of such small dimensions, the designation "shrine" appears more appropriate than "temple." The room is divided into three sections: The northern entrance section is an open space with elaborate floor construction. In the middle section, an L-shaped wall embraces a collection of votive objects, thus forming a kind of sanctuary. A circular sand-filled pit cuts into the floor of the northern section; this was probably intended to hold an offering stand or serve as a foundation for some other installation (an altar?). Along the west wall fourteen offering stands of various sizes and shapes lay in a long row just as they had fallen when the wall bulged in. The southern section of the room contains a number of small compartments for various objects. These compartments rise about 60 cm above floor level, making most of the southern section appear to be occupied by a kind of bench.

Walls are almost uniformly two bricks (about 65 cm) wide. The brick sizes themselves vary from 27 by 13 cm to 30 by 15 cm. The material is mainly ochre silt, but bricks of mud and clay also occur. The walls are preserved up to a height of 1 m, including remains of Phase 2c. The brickwork gives a general impression of sloppy craftsmanship. This, together with fill accumulating in the corridor, might have caused the bulging of the western wall. The row of offering stands is partly buried under this wall, indicating that the accident happened when the building was still functioning. Some repair work appears to have been attempted in the northwestern corner, but sooner or later the building was deserted, filled with debris and the construction of Phase 2a on a higher level began.

Phase 2c (Fourth–Fifth [?] Dynasty)

In this phase the original plan of the complex becomes apparent. It differs only slightly from Phase 2b. The enclosure wall now has a curved outline and the corridor is closed at both ends. An additional paving of bricks covers the forecourt and extends into the passage, where a kind of *mastaba* forms a narrow gateway. Inside the building another layer of compacted mud, not as elaborately executed as the later one, forms the floor.

The size and material of which the bricks were made is generally the same as seen in Phase 2b. The brickwork demonstrates better workmanship; special care was taken in the layout of foundation layers, where small bricks—from 25 by 12 cm to 28 by 14 cm—were mostly used. In these foundation layers it definitely becomes evident that the chambers for deposits were part of the original plan.

Fig. 2: Tell Ibrahim Awad, squares A 130–140/190: Temple of the Old Kingdom, Phase 2b–c. Position of deposits of votive and other objects. Bottom levels of deposits are given, in some cases also top levels. Not shown are deposits nos. 8 and 11, which belong to other phases. Floor level of Phase 2b is 330, of Phase 2c it is 315.

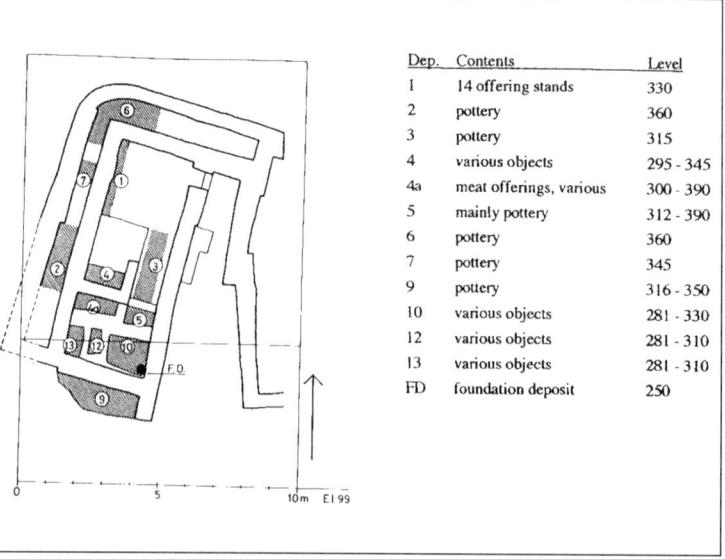

Dep.	Contents	Level
1	14 offering stands	330
2	pottery	360
3	pottery	315
4	various objects	295 - 345
4a	meat offerings, various	300 - 390
5	mainly pottery	312 - 390
6	pottery	360
7	pottery	345
9	pottery	316 - 350
10	various objects	281 - 330
12	various objects	281 - 310
13	various objects	281 - 310
FD	foundation deposit	250

The Deposits in the Old Kingdom Temple of Phase 2c-b

Tell Ibrahim Awad is, along with Elephantine, Hierakonpolis and Abydos, the fourth temple site in Egypt to contain deposits of a large number of votive and other objects. Fig. 2 presents an overview of the location of deposits and provides very general information on their contents. Deposit 1 is not a "deposit" in the same sense as the others, as the row of offering stands was meant for actual use. The "foundation deposit" can be designated as such according to position and contents: One ceramic bowl containing 21 objects, mainly made of faience, and one ceramic plate containing six objects, accompanying a unique three-dimensional faience representation of the Archaic *pr-nw* shrine.[3] No other object could be better suited for the foundation deposit of a temple/shrine in the Nile Delta. Placing the objects in ceramic containers stressed their special meaning. The deposits from Elephantine, Hierakonpolis, and Abydos are considered to be the predecessors of later foundation deposits;[4] the "foundation deposit" of Tell Ibrahim Awad appears to be a prototype.

The compartments for deposits 4, 4a, 10, 12, and 13 belong to the original architectural concept. Their walls are part of the foundation layout. Deposits 10, 12, and 13 are sealed on top by a double layer of bricks, in the style of a vault. It is quite improbable that objects were added to these deposits during the functional phase of the building. During the Old Kingdom votive objects were probably deposited on the bench and removed when the building was abandoned. Deposit 9 mainly contains offering stands. They were probably used in ceremonies taking place in or in front of the small paved forecourt and received a ritual burial after they had been used. The uppermost piece is an offering stand of huge dimensions and must have been a permanent installation in this court. (For the contents of the deposits see the contribution by Van Haarlem in this volume).

The Old Kingdom Shrine of Tell Ibrahim Awad

Fig. 3 is a reconstruction of the Old Kingdom shrine. It is a somewhat idealized picture, combining elements of both Phases 2c and 2b. Walls of the oblong room are reconstructed to a height of 7 cubits (3.67 m). Peaked corners have a long tradition in Egyptian domestic architecture from the Predynastic to the present day; they are added here as a very probable feature. Enclosure walls are reconstructed as 6 cubits (3.14 m) high. This would also be the inner height of the shrine from floor to ceil-

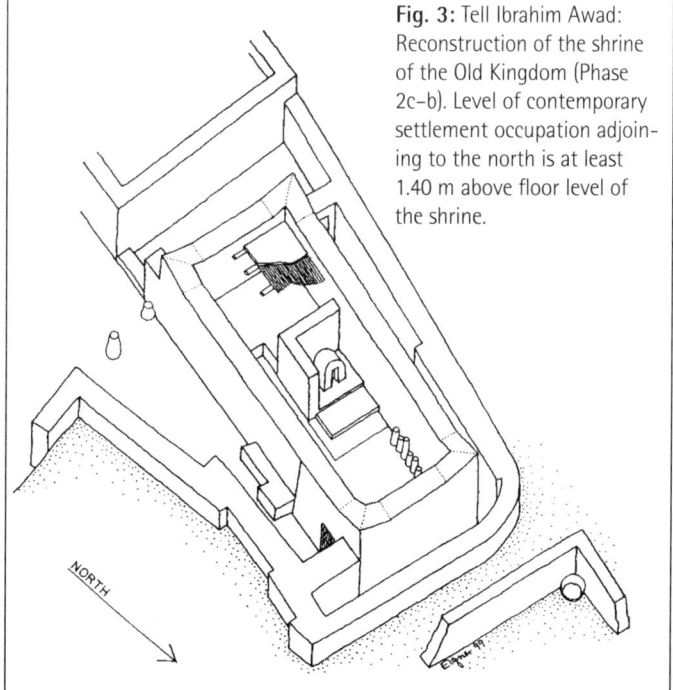

Fig. 3: Tell Ibrahim Awad: Reconstruction of the shrine of the Old Kingdom (Phase 2c–b). Level of contemporary settlement occupation adjoining to the north is at least 1.40 m above floor level of the shrine.

NORTH

ing. A roof of the usual construction—beams covered with a mesh of palm fronds, finally a covering of compacted loam—is indicated. There were probably also openings in the walls directly under the ceiling to admit light and air (not shown).

In the northern section of the room, a row of offering stands ranged along the western wall—Deposit 1—is depicted. The southern section is almost completely filled by the bench covering the compartments of deposits. The central section is occupied by the L-shaped wall forming the sanctuary and by the stepped platform in front of it. A *naos* of the same size and shape as the one dedicated by Pepi I to Satet on Elephantine has been added for demonstrative purposes.

At the entrance to the small eastern court, the large offering stand from Deposit 9 and a presumed water vessel of Phase 2b are represented. The "priest's house" of Phase 2b adjoins in the south. Part of a hypothetical domestic enclosure is added in the north to demonstrate the difference in level between the shrine and the neighboring settlement.

The most striking feature of the building is the complete absence of any monumentality. It is simply the domicile of a deity (whose identity will probably never be known) within a settlement context. What at first glance appears to be a simple mud-brick hut turns out to be a carefully planned building, in terms of its measurements in cubits and proportions of the plan.[5] The plan comprises three squares measuring 5 by 5 cubits, forming a long rectangular room measuring 5 by 15 cubits. The northern square is dedicated to cult ritual, the central square houses the deity in a protective niche at the end of a brick platform, while the southern square is dedicated to deposits of objects from earlier phases of the building. This complete and emphatic integration of deposits into the architecture is unique. At our present state of research, almost all the items in deposits (except pottery deposits) seem to come from Phases 4, 5, and 6 (Early Dynastic and Dynasty 0). On Elephantine as well, the vast majority of objects is dated to a period before the Old Kingdom.[6]

There is no trace of the cult statue that once stood in the protective shelter of the niche, probably in its own small shrine or *naos*. The niche itself might have been decorated by faience tiles, at least in the older phases. Van Haarlem proposed that tiles found at the site come from a small *naos* housing the deity.

Phase 3 (Early Old Kingdom, Second [?]–Third Dynasty)

Practically on the same level with the foundations of Phase 2c, the scanty remains of another foundation layer came to light, yet enough was present to prove that here was a building of the same type, almost completely destroyed by or dismantled before construction of Phase 2c.

Of Phase 3, there remained only the northwestern corner of the shrine and a longer stretch of its western wall. Significant are parallels to Phase 2c; a brick platform in front of a pit for a deposit still containing four faience objects and one very unusual stone. This indicates that the deposit was once full of objects and that the remaining objects were overlooked (or left behind on purpose?) in the process of transferring the contents to deposits of Phase 2c.

The building of Phase 3 is still more modest. The walls are only 1 and a half bricks (45 cm) wide. The brick size is 28 by 14 cm. Some walls in the northern part of square A 140/190 might belong to Phase 3, as well as the brick paving in square A 130/190.

Phase 4 (Second Dynasty)

There is a curious gap in the sequence of sacred buildings somewhere during the Second Dynasty, approximately between levels 265 and 300. A layer of dark settlement deposits, marked by numerous vessel emplacements lined with clay, covers the whole excavation floor, but no walls of domestic buildings exist. The vessel emplacements cut into the walls of Phase 5a–b. Is this gap in "sacred" occupation only due to a building process? Or was the site moved temporarily to another place outside the excavation area? In any case the votive and ceremonial objects of Phases 5 and 6 did survive to be put into the deposits of the Old Kingdom shrine.

Phase 5a–b and 5c–d (Dynasty 0–First Dynasty)

Surprisingly, under the settlement deposits of Phase 4, the remains of four subsequent buildings, carefully constructed of loam and silt-clay bricks, (measuring 26–33 by 13–16 cm) appeared. All four buildings are 5.5 cubits wide and of unknown length. Their relation to the Old Kingdom plan is evident, and identifies the buildings as shrines. An oblong transverse room, entered near the end of one long side, and the remains of a brick pavement, may well come from a platform in front of a sanctuary. Fragments of faience objects provide additional testimony for the character of the buildings. The buildings are dated by a tomb next to them that turned up completely unexpectedly. It is a small pit-grave containing the body of a male adolescent arranged in an extremely contracted position. The pottery accompanying the body was dated by Dr. Vera Müller to the period between kings Djer and Den.

Phase 6a (Dynasty 0)

In this Phase once again an oblong building appears, 5.5 cubits wide and of unknown length. Part of a brick pavement is preserved at one end of the room. The brick size is 31 by 15 cm. An ancillary building of several rooms adjoins the shrine on its southern side, and there are remains of an enclosure wall to the northwest.

On and in the floor of room R were found some small bag-shaped and globular ceramic vessels, typical of Naqada III.[7] Also in this room were some small shells, a deposit of about 50 small shells, a small stone vessel, about 100 faience beads, a stone palette, and a piece of kohl (antimony). These finds hint of the room functioning as robing room for the priest or sacristy. In the shrine itself, the most important find was the head of a pottery baboon (FR no. 298).

Phase 6b (Dynasty 0)

This is the oldest shrine of oblong plan, again 5.5 cubits wide and of unknown length. The bricks of ochre loam measure 31 by 15 cm and 35 by 17 cm. A prominent feature is a wall of L-shaped plan, projecting into the room, just as in Old Kingdom shrines. No doubt this wall was also meant to provide shelter for the divine image, enclosing a space 1 by 2 cubits. It is built of special bricks (28 by 14 cm) containing a high proportion of clay. The use of special bricks for this architectural element served several purposes; to stress the importance of this element, ensure better stability and perhaps even provide a suitable surface for fixing faience tiles.

The deposit of Detail 2 contains an offering stand decorated with incised triangles, a small globular ceramic vessel, a curious small ceramic vessel with three compartments,[8] and a "lotus shaped" bowl with flaring sides and flat bottom, typical for Dynasty 0/Naqada III.[9] Significant is the find of a small faience baboon's head (FR no. 321) in a floor of compacted loam. The same type of votive objects was encountered in the deposits of the Old Kingdom shrine.

North of the shrine at 5 cubits distant, an enclosure wall follows the same orientation, but a southern wall forms an irregular outline for the compound.

Phase 6c (Dynasty 0/Naqada IIIb)

This phase exhibits no architectural remains. A prominent feature is a number of circular and subrectangular fire-pits. At first glance there is no evidence for their function, neither as cooking nor industrial installations. There are no vessel emplacements, so abundant in some earlier strata. Altogether the phase of fire-pits seems to be only a short interlude. The pits are arranged in two rows along the walls of the later shrine; perhaps they served some function in the building process.

Object FR no. 406, a jar, was found buried vertically in the ground next to a fire-pit. It is about 45 cm tall. Since the high cylindrical neck is too narrow for a water container the vessel must have contained some substance that could be taken out by hand. This type of vessel is dated by Köhler to Naqada IIIb.[10]

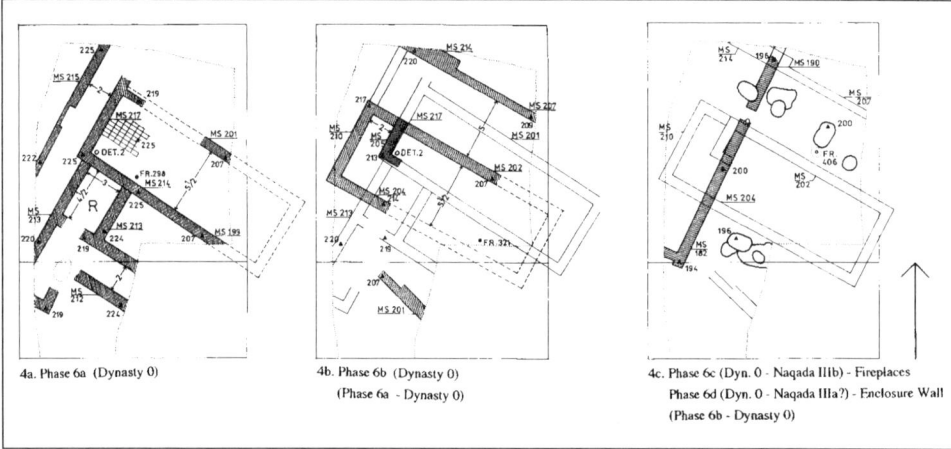

4a. Phase 6a (Dynasty 0)

4b. Phase 6b (Dynasty 0)
(Phase 6a - Dynasty 0)

4c. Phase 6c (Dyn. 0 - Naqada IIIb) - Fireplaces
Phase 6d (Dyn. 0 - Naqada IIIa?) - Enclosure Wall
(Phase 6b - Dynasty 0)

Fig. 4: Tell Ibrahim Awad, squares A 130–140/190: Shrines of Phase 6 (Dynasty 0). Levels give elevation in cm above actual mean sea level. "MS" indicates bottom levels of walls. Measurements are given in cubits. The walls of each phase are rendered in hatching, while walls of the following younger phase are given in outline.

Phase 6d (Dynasty 0/Naqada IIIa?)

This phase immediately precedes that of the fire-pits. A fundamental change in architectural conception marks the transition from Phase 6d to Phase 6b, or perhaps it was just at a shift of the sacred site. In any case, the architectural remains for Phase 6d consist of the front wall of an enclosure that is, assuming the door is in the central position, 25 cubits (13.10 m) wide. The wall is 1.5 bricks (45 cm) thick. The bricks of ochre loam measure 28 by 14 cm. The door is only one cubit wide. The socket for the door-pivot is a small circular pit filled with clay. The wall, preserved in one to two layers, was dismantled before the phase of fire-pits set in.

The change of architecture—or just of site—may tentatively be dated to the transition from Naqada IIIa to Naqada IIIb. The presumed shrine within the enclosure lies under the orchard which cuts the Tel.

Conclusion

The Old Kingdom shrine at Tell Ibrahim Awad can be recognized as the third example of the "Preformal" temple of this period,[11] the others are at Elephantine and Medamud. These differ greatly in their architectural conception from each other as well as from the shrine at Tell Ibrahim

Awad. In contrast to these two examples, the shrine at Tell Ibrahim Awad can be considered the standard type of Preformal temple in a provincial town. It has an architectural design of general validity, demonstrated by the relation of the plan to the hieroglyphic signs ⬚ and ⌓. In spite of its modest attitude, the architecture of the building is the result of careful and well-considered planning.

Deposits of votive and other objects are known only at Elephantine, Hierakonpolis, and Abydos. Most of them are "ill-defined heaps" or irregular pits in the ground without architectural context.[12] The complete incorporation of deposits into the architecture of the shrine is a unique feature of Tell Ibrahim Awad.

Based on evidence from Elephantine, Kemp has developed the idea of a "Preformal" shrine which was not patronized by the court and served the local cult in provincial towns throughout the Old Kingdom. It was replaced by the "Early Formal" temple of the Middle Kingdom.[13] The evidence from Tell Ibrahim Awad confirms Kemp's ideas of cultural dichotomy and transformation of temple buildings in an extensive and most impressive way.

On Elephantine the earliest phase of the Satet shrine dates back to the First Dynasty. At Tell Ibrahim Awad an architectural shape for the Preformal shrine was created at the time of early Dynasty 0 and persisted for about twelve centuries. The shrine of Phase 6b is the oldest brick temple so far ever excavated in Egypt. Excavation has not yet reached the *gezira*; in several more strata of occupation earlier phases of the shrine can be expected. There are good opportunities to recover the traces of the wood and mat (reed?) construction of an archaic *pr-nw* in the sand of the "primeval hill" of the *gezira*.

Notes:

1 D. Eigner, "A Temple of the Early Middle Kingdom at Tell Ibrahim Awad," in E.C.M. Van den Brink, (ed.), *The Nile Delta in Transition: 4th–3rd Millennium B.C.* (Tel Aviv, 1992), 69–78.

2 E.C.M. Van den Brink, "*Preliminary Report on the Excavations at Tell Ibrahim Awad, Seasons 1988 - 1990,*" in Van den Brink 1992, 43–68.

3 W. M. Van Haarlem, "Archaic Shrine Models from Tell Ibrahim Awad," *MDAIK* 54 (1998), 183 ff.

4 G. Dreyer, "Elephantine VIII. Der Tempel der Satet - Die Funde der Frühzeit und des Alten Reiches," *AV* 39 (1986), 59.

5 D. Eigner, "Tell Ibrahim Awad - Divine Residence from Dynasty 0 until Dynasty 11," *Ägypten und Levante* 10 (2000), *in press*.

6 Dreyer, *Elephantine*, 59 ff.

7 Ch. Köhler, *The Pre- and Early Dynastic Pottery of Tell el Fara'in / Buto*, in Van den Brink, *Nile Delta*, fig. 1, Stratum III and fig. 7.

8 Van Haarlem, "A Predynastic Triple Vessel from Tell Ibrahim Awad," *Göttinger Miszellen* 173 (1999), 193–195.

9 Ch. Köhler, *Pottery*, fig. 1, Stratum III, and fig. 4.

10 Ch. Köhler, *Tell el Fara'in – Buto III, AV* 94 (Mainz, 1998), Tafel 11.2, form 6A.

11 B. J. Kemp, *Ancient Egypt - Anatomy of a Civilisation* (London, 1991), 66.

12 Kemp, *Anatomy*, 75.

13 Kemp, *Anatomy*, 64 ff.

Die Treppe des Hinaufsteigens zum Dach des Tempels von Dendera am Neujahrsfest

Mamdouh Mohamed Eldamaty
Ain Shams University

In seinem Buch "Dendara et le temple d'Hathor" erwähnt F. Daumas, daß die westliche Treppe im Tempel von Dendera die Treppe des Hinaufsteigens zum Dach des Tempels am Neujahrsfest gewesen sei[1]. Diese These wird bis heute immer wieder übernommen. Wenn man aber die Inschriften und die Architektur der beiden Treppen des Tempels und die Position des Haupteingangs des Kiosks, in dem die Hauptzeremonien des Neujahrsfestes durchgeführt wurden, genauer betrachtet, stellt man fest, daß die östliche Treppe diejenige des Hinaufsteigens zum Dach war[2]. Meine These begründe ich mit den folgenden Feststellungen und Überlegungen:

I. Die Architektur der beiden Treppen

Die architektonische Form jeder Treppe (Fig. 1, W und X) richtet sich selbstverständlich nach deren Funktion. Die Ost-Treppe (W), die sich auf der rechten Seite des Tempels befindet, ist eine gerade Treppe, die keinen Lichtdurchlaß hat. Das heißt, daß die auf dieser Treppe ziehende Prozession kein Tageslicht benutzte; aus diesem Grund ist sie auch gerade gebaut, um den Zug der Prozession vor Hindernissen zu bewahren und zu erleichtern. Die Treppe auf der linken (= westlichen) Seite des Tempels verläuft dagegen gewunden, mit quadratischen Absätzen und Richtungswechseln. Diese Treppe (X) hat einige Lichtdurchlässe bzw. Fenster (Fig. 2) für das Tageslicht. Sie hat die eckige Zickzackform, damit große Teile von ihr vom Tageslicht erhellt werden. Aufgrund dieses Befundes weiß man, daß die Prozession der Hathor während der Feier des Neujahrsfestes die östliche Treppe im Dunkeln bzw. während der Nacht benutzte und durch die westliche Treppe bei Tageslicht zog. Da die Feier am Abend begann und die Prozession der Hathor im Kiosk auf dem Dach des Tempels bei Sonnenaufgang zugegen war, wurde die östliche Treppe folglich für den Aufstieg in der Dunkelheit der Nacht gebraucht. Nachdem die Sonne aufgegangen und die Zeremonien der Feier auf dem Dach vollzogen worden waren, nutzte die Prozession das Sonnenlicht und bewegte sich weiter nach unten auf der westlichen Treppe.

Des weiteren findet man eine Treppenkapelle (Fig. 1, V) als Passage und Stationskapelle für die Prozession der Hathor auf ihrem Weg auf das Dach während der Feier des Neujahrsfestes; jene Kapelle ist der Eingang zur Ost-Treppe. Die Prozession hielt also in dieser Kapelle, bevor sie auf der östlichen Treppe zum Dach hinaufstieg, was auch durch die Inschriften dieser Kapelle betont wird (siehe unten).

II. Die Inschriften

Die Inschriften, die sich auf die Funktion der beiden Treppen des Tempels beziehen, befinden sich hauptsächlich an ihren Wänden und an den Wänden der Treppenkapelle (V). Diese Inschriften könnten in zwei Gruppen eingeteilt werden, je nach Richtung des Prozessionsverlaufs.

1. Die erste Gruppe berichtet davon, daß die Ost-Treppe die Treppe des Hinaufstei-gens[3] und die West-Treppe die des Hinabsteigens war[4].

1.1. Texte an den Wänden der Treppenkapelle (V):

- ḏd mdw wȝt nt ns r ẖnd wr in ȝḫtit ẖnt ȝḫt-ḥḥ wȝt n wḏȝ r st mȝȝ itn in ḥt-ḥr wrt nbt iwnt[5]

Rezitation: Der Weg des Hinführens zu der großen Treppe durch die, die zum Horizont gehören, an der Spitze des Horizonts der Ewigkeit (= Dendera[6]. Der Weg des Gehens zum Platz des Sehens der Sonnenscheibe durch Hathor, die Große, die Herrin von Dendera.

- wȝt.s r ẖnm it.s hrw wp-rnpt ꜥk.s wȝḏit m rš sp-sn[7]

Ihr Weg, um sich mit ihrem Vater zu vereinigen am Tag des Neujahres. Sie tritt in die Dachkapelle (wȝḏit) mit Freude ein, zweimal.

- ḏd mdw in Ist wrt mwt-nṯr nbt iȝt-di ḥrit-ib iwnt špct wcrt ẖnt pr-špst spdt wbn m pt tp-rnpt in ḥꜥpi r bꜥḥ ȝḫt[8]

Rezitation von Isis, der Großen, der Gottesmutter, der Herrin von Dendera, inmitten von Dendera, der Erhabenen, der Mächtigen in Dendera, dem Sirius-Stern, der am Himmel am Tag des Neujahres erscheint, der den Nil bringt, um das Fruchtland zu überfluten.

1.2. Texte an den Wänden der östlichen Treppe (W):

- ḥt-ḥr wrt nbt iwnt irt-Rꜥ nbt pt ḥnwt nṯrw nbw špst wsrt ȝḫtit ḥȝitit sšp itrti m nfrw.s ẖnd ḥr ẖnd.s r ẖnm it.s r mȝȝ [itn] m wbn.f[9]

Hathor, die Große, die Herrin von Dendera, das Auge des Re, die Herrin des Himmels, die Gebieterin aller Götter, die Erhabene, die Mächtige, die zum Horizont gehörende, die Leuchtende, die die beiden Heiligtümer mit ihrer Schönheit erleuchtet, die auf ihrer Treppe emporsteigt, um sich mit ihrem Vater zu vereinigen und [die Sonne] bei ihrem Aufgehen zu sehen.

- ẖnm.t it.t Rꜥ m ḥȝit.t ḥr.t nfr rsi[10]

Du vereinigst dich mit deinem Vater Re in deiner Dachkapelle, indem dein schönes Gesicht nach Süden weist.

- ḥm-nṯr fdw n nbit sȝt-Rꜥ n pr-špst di-ꜥ.i r-tp ḥt-sššt ẖnd ḥr ḥȝt.s ḥr ẖnd n ḥmt.s r mȝȝ stwt it.s m wbn.f ẖnd.i ḥr ẖnd r (tp) pr-špst r snsn.s stwt n it.s[11]

Der vierte Priester der Goldenen, der Tochter des Re in Dendera: "Ich gehe zum Dach des Tempels von Dendera; ich gehe vor ihr auf der Treppe ihrer Majestät, damit (sie) die Strahlen ihres Vaters bei seinem Aufgang sieht. Ich betrete die Treppe zum Dach des Tempels von Dendera, damit sie sich mit den Strahlen ihres Vaters vereint".

172

1.3. Texte an den Wänden des westlichen Treppe (X):

- *ḥws.n.f ḫnd nt wbn-m-nbw m sni r ḥit ʿpi ḫnd.s r ḥmt.s tp-ʿ psḏt.s r-s3 m33 it.s Rʿ wp-rnpt*[12]

Er (der König) hat die Treppe derjenigen, die als Gold erglänzen, gebaut, als etwas, das dem Himmel der Flügelsonne gleicht, damit sie ihre Kultstätte vor ihrer Neunheit betritt, nach dem Sehen ihres Vaters Re am Neujahrsfest.

- *ḏd mdw mi m ḥtp ḥr ḫnd r sḫm.t ḥt-ḥr wrt nbt iwnt m-ḫt sm3.t stwt n Rʿ tp ḥt.t ḥnʿ psḏt*[13]

Rezitation: Komm in Frieden auf der Treppe zu deiner Kapelle, Hathor, die Große, die Herrin von Dendera, nachdem du dich mit den Strahlen des Re vereinigt hast, auf dem Dach mit der Neunheit.

- *isi m ḥtp r ḫnt ḥt-wʿbt m-ḫt ḥnmt.t it.t m tp-ḥt ḥt-nṯr.t*[14]

Gehe in Frieden in die Reinigungskapelle, nachdem du dich mit deinem Vather auf dem Dach deines Tempels vereinigt hast.

- *iḫ.sn m-ḫt.s r ḫnt ḥt-sššt ḥr-s3 m33.s ḥʿʿ itn m hrw wp-rnpt*[15]

Sie (= die großen K3w) gehen hinter ihr (=Hathor) zum Haus des Sistrums (=Tempel-gemach von Dendera)[16], nachdem sie die Strahlen der Sonne gesehen hat, am Tag des Neujahrsfests.

- *ḥm n ḥrit-tp ḳbḥ ʿ3 ʿk rwd m swt-št3w st3 m ḥʿʿ r h3it m ḳbb nmt ḥr ḥd wr ḥr 3b n ḥt-nṯr dsr w3t ḥr ḥʿt nṯrt tn r pr.s m hrw pn nfr ḥb Rʿ m wp-rnpt*[17]

Priester der Uräusschlange (=Hathor), der große Wasserspender. Die Treppe betreten zu den Stätten des Geheimnisses (=Krypten). Rückkehr mit Jubel zum Tempelgemach mit langsamen Schritten auf der großen Treppe auf der linken Seite des heiligen Tempels. Der Weg vor dieser Göttin zu ihrem Haus an diesem schönen Tag des Festes des Re am Neujahrfest.

Die eben erwähnten Inschriften setzen uns davon in Kenntnis, daß die östliche Treppe (W) die Treppe des Hinaufsteigens zum Dach des Tempels am Tag des Neujahres war, um die Statue der Göttin Hathor beim Sonnenaufgang im Kiosk (Dachkapelle) mit den Sonnenstrahlen zu vereini-gen und um die Sonnenscheibe zu sehen (*r ḫnm it.s r m33 [itn] m wbn.f*). Danach stieg die Hathor-Prozession durch die westliche Treppe (X) hinunter zum Tempelgemach "Haus des Sistrums (*r ḫnt ḥt-sššt ḥr-s3 m33.s ḥʿʿ itn m hrw wp-rnpt*).

2. Die zweite Gruppe von Inschriften legt dar, daß die West-Treppe die Treppe des Hinaufsteigens war[18], und die Ost-Treppe die des Hinabsteigens.

2.1. An den Wänden des westlichen Treppe (X):

- *w3t n msbb r st m33 itn r ḥnmt it.s (m) hrw wp-rnpt*[19]

Der Weg des Gelangens zum Sitz des Sehens der Sonnenscheibe, um sich mit ihrem Vater zu vereinigen (am) Tag des Neujahrfestes.

- *sps.n.f ḫnd wr nt 3ḫtit m iwnt r ḫnd r tp ḥt-nṯr.s im.f ḥʿ in ḥmt.s ḫnt pr-wr m hrw pn nfr ḥb Rʿ m wp-rnpt ḥtp m h3it.s tn nfrt ḥr.s nfr r rsi*[20]

Er (= der König) hat die große Treppe der zum Horizont Gehörigen in Dendera gebaut, um darauf auf das Dach ihres Tempels zu steigen. Erscheinen von ihrer Majestät an der Spitze des *pr-wr*, an diesem schönen Tag des Festes des Re, am Neujahrsfest, ruhe in dieser ihrer schönen Dachkapelle. Ihr schönes Gesicht ist nach Süden gerichtet.

- šmsw nbt ḥt-ḥr ḫnt iwnt pr m-ḫt.s r tp-ḥt ḥt-nṯr.s r ḥnm it.s hrw wp-rnpt ḥtp.sn ḥnꜥ.s m itrti ḥmt.s wn-ḥr ḥr.sn m ḥbw.sn ꜥrk.tw n.s irw štꜣ (m) st-ḥb-tpi[21]

Das Gefolge der Herrin, Hathor, an der Spitze von Dendera, geht hinter ihr hinaus zum Dach ihres Tempels, um sich mit ihrem Vater (am) Tag des Neujahrsfestes zu vereinigen. Sie ruhen mit ihr an der Seite ihrer Majestät. Das Gesicht auf sie öffnen (= sie sehen sie) an ihren Festen, um ihr die geheimen Zeremonien am Platz des ersten Festes zu vollenden.

2.2. An den Wänden der östlichen Treppe (W):

- pẖr ḥmt.s r st.s m ḫnt tꜣ-rrt r-sꜣ smꜣ stwt.s ḥnꜥ it.s[22]

Ihre Majestät umgibt ihren Platz in Dendera, nachdem ihre Strahlen sich mit ihrem Vater vereinigt haben.

- ḥt-ḥr nbt iwnt ḥrit-tp n Rꜥ twꜣ.n.i tmm ḥr ḥrit-tp n Rꜥ ḥt mꜣꜣ.c it.c m ḥrit[23]

Hathor, die Herrin von Dendera, die Uräusschlange des Re. Ich (= der Priester der Hathor) habe den Götterschrein unter der Uräusschlange des Re getragen, nachdem sie ihren Vater im Himmel gesehen hatte.

- ḥt-ḥr nbt iwnt irt-Rꜥ ḥrit st-wrt twꜣ.n.i ḥd ḥr ḥnwt n ḥt-sššt ḥr-sꜣ mꜣꜣ it.s m hrw pn nfr ms itn[24]

Hathor, die Herrin von Dendera, das Auge des Re, auf dem großen Platz. Ich (= der Priester der Hathor) habe den Prozessionsschrein unter der Gebieterin im Haus des Sistrums (= Dendera) getragen, nach dem Sehen ihres Vaters an diesem schönen Tag der Geburt der Sonne.

Die Inschriften dieser Gruppe berichten, daß die westliche Treppe (X) auch gebaut wurde, damit auf ihr die Prozession am Tag des Neujarsfestes auf das Dach des Tempels steige. Dieses Mal fand die Vereinigung mit den Sonnenstrahlen nicht beim Sonnenaufgang statt (*pr m-ḫt.s r tp-ḥt ḥt-nṯr.s r ḥnm it.s hrw wp-rnpt*), wie es in den Texten der ersten Gruppe erwähnt wird. Bei ihrer Rückkehr begab sich die Hathor-Prozession über die östliche Treppe (W) hinunter zum Tempelgemach (*twꜣ.n.i ḥd ḥr ḥnwt n ḥt-sššt ḥr-sꜣ mꜣꜣ it.s m hrw pn nfr ms itn*).

III. Die Position des Haupteingangs des Kiosks

Der inhaltliche Aufbau der Szenen an den Wänden des Kiosks ist selbstverständlich der traditionellen Ritualabfolge nachgeordnet. Der Kiosk, also die Dachkapelle, hat zwei Eingänge. Der Ost-Eingang ist der Haupteingang, wie sich aus der Szenenverteilung der Kapelle ergibt. Besondere Aufmerksamkeit verdienen die mittig auf der Innen- und Außenseite der Westwand der Dachkapelle angebrachten Szenen. Die inneren Szenen sind die *wn ḥr*–Szenen, "das Gesicht öffnen" an Hathor (Fig. 3 "5; 12"). Die äußeren Szenen sind die *dwꜣ nṯr*–Szenen, "den Gott preisen" vor dem Hathor-Symbol (Fig. 3 "18; 24"). Als erste Zeremonie fand in der Dachkapelle das Ritual des "Öffnen des Gesichts" statt, das auf der Mitte der Westwand gegenüber vom Haupteingang dargestellt ist. Zusätzlich determiniert das sich auf der Mitte der Außenwand befindliche Hathor-Symbol die Hauptachse der Kapelle, genau wie die Hathor-Symbol-Szene in der Hauptachse auf der Außenseite der südlichen Mauer des großen Tempels. Es handelt sich bei der Hauptachse also um die Ost-West-Achse des Kiosks.

Die Richtungsangabe *rsi* = Süden, die in den Inschriften (siehe oben "1. 2"; "2, 1") erwähnt wird, beschreibt die Ausrichtung der Hathor-Statue. Bei der Angabe der Himmelsrichtung "Süden" hat der Ägypter wegen der Lage des Tempels an der Nilschleife bei Qena aus religiösen Gründen bewußt die ideale Ausrichtung gewählt; gemeint ist mit dem "Süden" in Wirklichkeit der geographische Osten[25]. Der Ägypter hat sich also nach dem Nil ausgerichtet, der von Süden nach Norden fließt, wobei die rechte Seite des Nils Westen ist, und die linke Seite der Osten. Die Statue der Hathor muß nach den Inschriften die Sonne beim Aufgang (d. h. im Osten) erblicken. Sie schaut also in Richtung des Osteinganges.

Hieran zeigt sich, daß der Osteingang der Haupteingang dieser Kapelle war, durch den die Hathor-Prozession am Tag des Neujahrsfestes bei Sonnenaufgang eintrat. Da die östliche Treppe in den Haupteingang (an der Ostseite) des Kiosks mündet (siehe Fig. 4), kann man infolgedessen darauf schließen, daß es sich bei der Osttreppe des Tempels um die Treppe des Hinaufsteigens am Tag des Neujahrsfestes handelte.

IV. Edfu

Von den noch gut erhaltenen ägyptischen Tempeln aus der griechisch-römischen Zeit[26] sind nur die Tempel von Edfu und Dendera für diese Untersuchung geeignet, denn beide weisen jeweils zwei Treppenhäuser auf, die zum Dach des Tempels führen, wogegen es in Philae und Kalabscha nur je eine Treppe gibt. Wie es in Dendera der Fall ist, hat der Tempel von Edfu eine gerade Treppe ohne Lichtdurchlässe auf der rechten (= westlichen) Seite des Tempels. Diese Treppe beginnt auch mit einer Treppenkapelle, in der die Prozession der Göttin Hathor während der Feier des Neujahrsfests für einige Zeremonien vor dem Aufstieg auf das Dach Halt machte. Eine eckige Zickzacktreppe, die einige Durchlässe für das Tageslicht hat, befindet sich auf seiner linken (= östlichen) Seite; ein Durchgang verbindet diese Treppe mit der Erscheinungskapelle. Die Inschriften der beiden Treppen und der Treppenkapelle erwähnen, daß die beiden Treppen für das Hinaufsteigen auf das Tempeldach angelegt worden sind[27], was der Funktion der beiden Treppen von Dendera entspricht.

Schließlich kann man noch den Verlauf der Hathor-Prozession und die Funktion der beiden Treppen am Tag des Neujahrsfestes darstellen:

Am Abend des Neujahrsfestes begann die Feier mit dem Zug der Hathor-Prozession von den Krypten, dann begab sie sich zur Wabet-Kapelle. Nachdem die Zeremonien der Reinigung in der Wabet-Kapelle ausgeführt worden waren, steuerte der Zug auf verschiedene Kapellen im Tempelinneren und dann auf die Osttreppe zu. Die Prozession gelangte auf die Terrasse und betrat den Kiosk durch seinen Osteingang. Dort fand die Vereinigung mit der Sonnenscheibe am Morgen statt. Die goldenen Statuetten wurden also vom Sonnenlicht überflutet, das ihnen das Leben brachte, wie die Texte kommentieren: "Ihr Ba vereint sich mit ihrer Bes-Statue"[28]. Der allgemeine Ausdruck *ḥnm itn*, "sich mit der Sonnenscheibe vereinigen", bezeichnet diese Zeremonie. An anderer Stelle wird er durch *m33 itn* ersetzt: "die Sonnenscheibe sehen".

Anschließend stieg die Prozession durch die Westtreppe hinunter, damit das Volk auch an der Feier teilnehmen konnte. Danach kehrte der Zug wieder nach oben auf das Dach zurück; dieses Mal benutzte die Prozession die Westtreppe zum Hinaufsteigen. Die Zeremonien wurden im Kiosk vollendet; dann steuerte der Zug über die Osttreppe nach unten auf das Tempelinnere zu.

Die beiden Treppen wurden also für das Hinauf- und Hinabsteigen der Prozession im Neujahrsfest gebraucht. Die Osttreppe diente für das erste Hinaufsteigen kurz vor Sonnenaufgang, um die Statue der Göttin Hathor mit den Sonnenstrahlen zu vereinigen. Sie wurde auch für das Hinabsteigen der Prozession während der Rückkehr gebraucht. Die Westtreppe wurde jedoch hauptsächlich für das Hinabsteigen verwendet, nachdem Hathor sich mit den Strahlen des Re vereinigt und ihren Vater Re gesehen hatte. Sie wurde auch für das Hinaufsteigen während der Rückkehr der Prozession zum Dach benutzt.

Es genügt, die Festkalender der Hathor und des Horus durchzugehen, um zu sehen, daß sich die Liturgie des Neujahrsfestes häufig im Laufe des Jahres wiederholte. Die Säulen des Kiosks von Dendera geben viele Daten, an welchen die Prozession den Kiosk benutzte. Unter ihnen nehmen die Epagomenentage und das Fest der Trunkenheiten einen besonderen Platz ein[29].

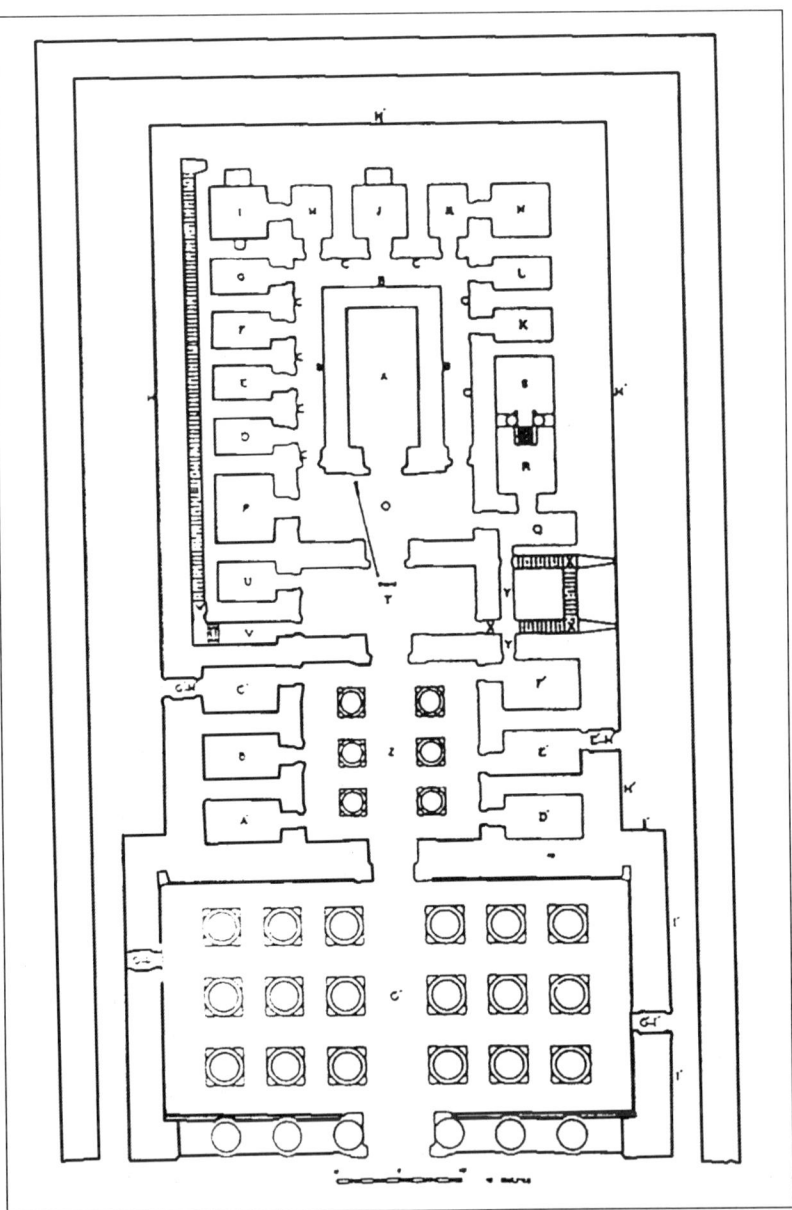

Fig. 1: Grundriß des Tempels von Dendera.

176

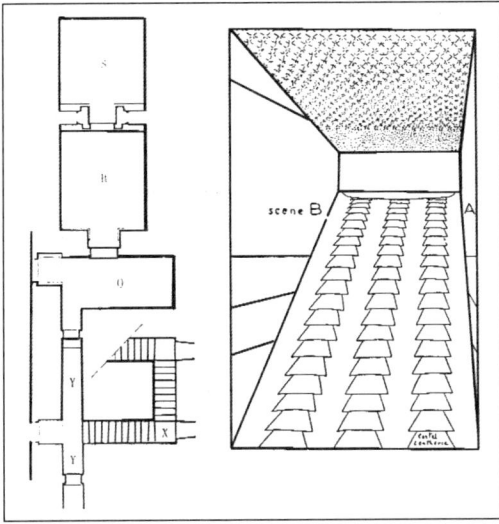

Fig. 2: Grundriß der Westtreppe von Dendera und einer ihrer Lichtdurchlässe.

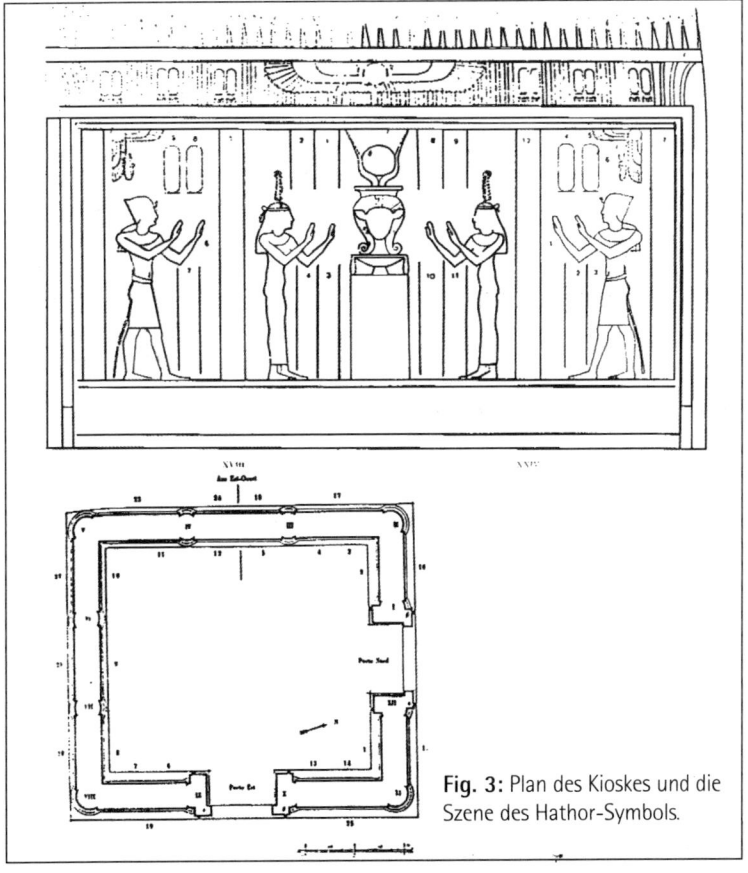

Fig. 3: Plan des Kioskes und die Szene des Hathor-Symbols.

177

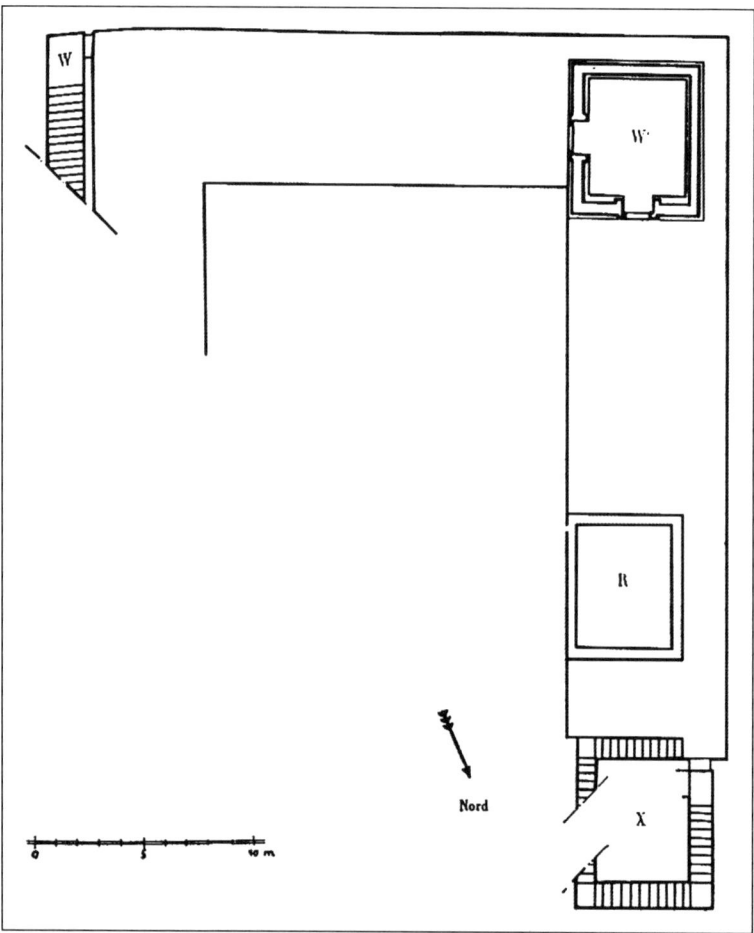

Fig. 4: Plan des Kioskes und der beiden Treppen.

Notes:

1 François Daumas, Dendara et le temple d'Hathor, Le Caire 1969, 63.

2 Vgl. Wolfgang Helck, Treppe, in: LÄ VI, 758.

3 Vgl. auch Dendara VII, 145, 7-8; 145, 14-15; 169, 3-4; 177, 10-11; 178, 3-8; 179, 7-11; siehe auch S. Cauville, Les inscriptions dédicatoires du Temple d'Hathor à Dendera, in: BIFAO 90 (1990), 103f.

4 Vgl. Auch Dendara VIII, 73, 13-14; 86, 14-15; 88, 8-10; 96, 9; 98, 13-14; 99, 1-8.

5 Dendara VIII, 142, 18-143.

6 Als Name des Tempels siehe Dendara VI, 169, 1.

7 Dendara VIII, 143, 3.

8 Dendara VIII, 157, 10-11.

9 Dendara VII, 168, 5-7.

10 Dendara VII, 178 , 8.

11 Dendara VII, 182, 12-14.

12 Dendara VIII, 85, 11-12.

13 Dendara VIII, 75, 5-6.

14 Dendara VIII, 90, 3-4.

15 Dendara VIII, 96, 15-97,1.

16 Als Name des Tempels siehe Dendara VI, 166, 1-2.

17 Dendara VIII, 97, 13-98, 1.

18 Siehe auch Dendara VIII, 113, 15-16.

19 Dendara VIII, 73, 8.

20 Dendara VIII, 100, 5-7.

21 Dendara VIII, 121, 2-4.

22 Dendara VII, 201, 1.

23 Dendara VII, 202, 7-8.

24 Dendara VII, 203, 1-2.

25 Dazu siehe M. M. Eldamaty, Sokar-Osiris-Kapelle im Tempel von Dendera, Hamburg 1995, 5 (2); 129 (5).

26 Diese Tempel sind der Mandulis-Tempel von Kalabscha, der Isis-Tempel von Philae, der Horus-Tempel von Edfu, der Hathor-Tempel von Dendera und der Doppeltempel für Haroëris und Sobek von Kom-Ombo.

27 Siehe an den Wänden der Treppenkapelle, Edfou I, 513, 11-13; 515, 4; und auf den Wänden der West-Treppe, Edfou I, 536, 6-7; 537, 7-8; 541, 6-7; 545, 18-19; 546, 2-3; sowie auf den Wänden der Ost-Treppe, Edfou I, 549, 2-4; 551, 6; 554, 16-17; 557, 4-5. Vgl. auch Dieter Kurth, Treffpunkt der Götter, Düsseldorf/Zürich 1998, 76f. und 107f.

28 Dendara VIII, 32, 6; vgl. auch Edfou I, 549, 5-6; M. Alliot, Le culte d'Horus à Edfou au temps des Ptolémées, Le Caire1979, 380-381.

29 François Daumas, Neujahr, in: LÄ IV, 470.

Une nouvelle enquête sur les tombes civiles et anonymes de la Vallée des Rois

Magdi Mohammed Fekri
Université de Munofiya

Bien que consacrée nécropole pour l'inhumation des souverains du Nouvel Empire, la Vallée des Rois comprend également dans ses flancs un certain nombre de sépultures de particuliers, voire de tombes enregistrées jusqu'à présent comme étant « anonymes ».

Pour celles dont on connaît les propriétaires, la liste ainsi que l'examen du matériel archéologique et épigraphique permettent déjà de mieux mettre en évidence les relations qui existaient entre ces personnages et la cour royale et donc, de mieux comprendre la faveur *post-mortem* dont ils ont bénéficié.

Pour les tombes « anonymes », un certain nombre de remarques peuvent être formulées à partir des fouilles et des constatations qui ont été faites par les archéologues et les historiens : s'agissait-il de tombes également aménagées pour des proches du roi régnant, ou bien de sépultures royales, voire princières, dont les projets ont avorté?

Notre propos, s'appuyant sur toutes les informations rassemblées par nos prédécesseurs, se fondant sur l'étude architecturale de ces tombes ainsi que sur le mobilier funéraire qu'elles ont pu livrer au cours des fouilles et qui est le plus souvent dispersé dans les collections égyptologiques internationales, a pour but de faire le point des connaissances acquises. Et c'est à partir de ces données, de leur analyse et des observations que nous y ajouterons, que l'on pourra suggérer dans cet exposé, quelques retouches à certaines pages de l'histoire de la Vallée des Rois.

Dans la nécropole sont, jusqu'à présent, inventoriées vingt-quatre tombes non-royales : cinq d'entre elles appartiennent à des particuliers, quinze sont considérées comme étant « anonymes » et les autres ont été préparées pour l'inhumation d'animaux, plus spécialement des singes. Nous n'évoquerons dans cet exposé que les cinq tombes de particuliers.

La plus célèbre de ces sépultures est connue pour être celle des beaux-parents d'Aménophis III, Youya et Touya. Elle porte le n° 46.

La tombe de Youya et de Touya (KV 46)[1]

La tombe de Youya et de son épouse Touya, parents de la reine Tiyi, célèbre grande épouse du roi Amenhotep III, fut découverte en 1905, dans la Vallée des Rois, entre la tombe n° 3 attribuée à Ramsès III et la tombe n° 4 appartenant à Ramsès XI.

Tout le mobilier funéraire était entassé dans une chambre unique, grossièrement taillée dans le calcaire et sans décoration[2].

L'entrée de la chambre était fermée par un blocage de pierre sèche et crépie d'un enduit de boue qui portait les empreintes du sceau officiel de la nécropole, ce qui indique clairement que la sépulture avait été réalisée en ce lieu avec l'autorisation officielle du pharaon.

Comme dans la tombe de Toutankhamon, l'équipement comprenait notamment trois cercueils anthropoïdes placés dans un sarcophage rectangulaire, coutume exclusivement royale puisque nous ne l'observons jamais dans les tombes privées de cette époque. Les viscères de Youya, comme ceux d'Amenhotep II, étaient contenus dans des vases canopes enfermés dans un coffre rectangulaire, tandis que pour Akhenaton, Toutankhamon et Horemheb, il s'agissait plutôt d'un réceptacle monolithe, muni de cavités cylindriques creusées directement dans le bloc.

Parmi le mobilier funéraire, figuraient deux coffrets à bijoux portant les noms d'Amenhotep III et de la reine Tiyi, ainsi que deux chaises en bois portant celui d'une princesse nommée Satamon, dont l'une avait visiblement été fabriquée pour un enfant. Satamon est qualifiée de *s3t nswt wrt mryt.f*, « fille aînée du roi, son aimée », sur la plus petite de ces chaises, tandis que sur l'autre, de dimensions normales, elle est mentionnée avec le titre de *ḥmt nswt wrt*, « grande épouse royale ». On sait, en effet, que vers la fin du règne d'Amenhotep III, cette princesse mise au monde par Tiyi, épousa son père.

Quant à Youya lui-même, le mobilier de la tombe nous indique qu'il était possesseur d'éminents titres et fonctions :

rpʿt ḥ3ty-ʿ smr ʿ3 n mrt smr wʿty n mrt smr tpy mrrw nswt mrrw bity sḏ3wty bity it nṯr it nṯr n nb t3wy ḥm nṯr n Mnw imy-r ssmt, ḥsy n nb.f, « prince gouverneur, grand ami bien-aimé, ami unique bien-aimé, premier ami aimé du roi de Haute-Égypte, aimé du roi de Basse-Égypte, chancelier du roi de Basse-Égypte, père divin, père divin du maître des Deux Terres, prêtre du dieu Min, directeur de la cavalerie, favori de son maître ».

Son épouse, Touya, était également dotée de titres prestigieux :

mwt n ḥmt nswt wrt, šmʿyt n Jmn, nbt pr, wrt ḥnrt n Jmn wrt ḥnrt n Mnw, ḥsyt n nṯr nfr ḥsyt n ḥt-ḥr et *ḥkrt nswt*, c'est-à-dire « mère de grande épouse royale, chanteuse d'Amon, maîtresse de maison, supérieure du harem d'Amon, supérieure du harem de Min, favorite du dieu bon, favorite d'Hathor et la protectrice royale ». Ce dernier titre, de *khekeret nesout*, a été parfois traduit par « ornée du roi » ou encore plus récemment par « ornement du roi ». En fait, les titulaires de cette qualité étaient la providence de la famille royale et exerçaient une présence tutélaire auprès de la reine, des enfants royaux et même du roi. La traduction la plus appropriée serait donc plutôt celle de « protectrice royale »[3].

À propos de Touya, la protectrice royale et future belle-mère d'Aménophisd'Aménophis III, W. Helck avance l'hypothèse qu'elle aurait « eu la chance de voir sa fille Tiyi acceptée – peut-être comme *khekeret nesout* – dans le harem du prince héritier qui l'aurait exceptionnellement élevée au rang d'épouse légitime après son accession au trône »[4]. Nous pensons que Tiyi, plus vraisemblablement, fut grâce à sa mère élevée à la cour parmi les princesses avant d'y être remarquée par le futur roi.

Ce fut probablement grâce à leurs titres et leur statut social, qu'ils eurent la possibilité de faire creuser, à l'égal d'Amenhotep III, une tombe dans la Vallée des Rois.

La tombe de Maiherprê (KV 36)[5]

La tombe fut découverte dans la Vallée des Rois en 1899, par Victor Loret, entre la tombe n° 35 d'Amenhotep II et la tombe n° 13 du chancelier Bay.

Maiherprê était le fils d'une nourrice royale et occupait notamment la fonction de porte-éventail.

Il était probablement d'origine nubienne en raison de la couleur noire de son visage qui figure sur une copie du *Livre des Morts* retrouvée dans sa tombe. Cette origine a été d'ailleurs confirmée par l'examen de sa momie réalisée en 1901, et G. Maspero a même suggéré que le propriétaire de la tombe n° 36 devait être le fils d'une reine noire. Puisqu'il est appelé « enfant du *Kap* » (de la nurserie royale), il avait été visiblement éduqué à la cour d'Égypte et avait dû devenir par la suite un proche ami de l'un des rois au début de la XVIIIe dynastie. C'est d'ailleurs probablement cette position qui dut être à l'origine de la faveur dont il bénéficia pour faire mettre en chantier sa sépulture dans la nécropole royale.

La tombe d'Ouserhat (KV 45)[6]

La tombe a été retrouvée en 1902, par Howard Carter. Des fragments de vases-canopes de la XVIIIe dynastie découverts à l'intérieur de la tombe mentionnent le nom de son propriétaire. Il s'agissait d'un certain Ouserhat, qui portait le titre de *imy-r 3hwt n Jmn* « directeur des champs d'Amon ». Mais la tombe a été réutilisée à la Troisième Période intermédiaire et plus précisément au cours de la XXIIe dynastie.

On sait qu'Ouserhat avait fait également préparer une autre tombe à Cheikh Abd el-Gourna, celle qui porte le n° 56[7]. Dans cette dernière, ses titres sont beaucoup plus développés et permettent de mieux connaître le personnage. Il occupait les fonctions de *sš nswt sš hsbt n šm'w mhw imy-r nfrw n Jmn imy-r k3w n Jmn,* « scribe royal, scribe des comptes de Haute et de Basse-Égypte, directeur du bétail d'Amon et directeur des bovidés d'Amon ». De plus, nous savons de lui qu'il était aussi : *hsy n ntr nfr hrd n k3p* : « favori du dieu bon, enfant du *Kap* ».

Son épouse, Moutnéferet, porte les titres *nbt pr hsyt n ht-hr hsyt n ht-hr nbt Jwnt hkr.t nswt,* « maîtresse de maison, favorite d'Hathor, favorite d'Hathor maîtresse de Dendara et protectrice royale »[8]. Dans la même sépulture, avait été également inhumée sa fille, Henoutnéferet, qui est pourvue des titres de *nbt pr hsyt n ntr nfr hsyt n ht-hr nbt Jwnt mrrt ht-hr nbt t3wy mryt nb.s hkr.t nswt,* « maîtresse de maison, favorite du dieu bon, favorite d'Hathor maîtresse de Dendara, bien aimée d'Hathor maîtresse des Deux Terres, aimée de son maître (à savoir : « aimée du roi ») et protectrice royale », qualité particulière qui était aussi celle de sa mère[9].

La tombe d'Amenemopet (KV 48)[10]

Cette tombe fut découverte en 1906 par Edward R. Ayrton. Amenemopet dit « Pa-iry » était l'un des hauts fonctionnaires à l'époque d'Amenhotep II. Il avait également une autre tombe à Cheikh Abd el-Gourna inventoriée sous le n° 29, où ce personnage porte les titres de *imy-r niwt t3ty imy-r hwt wrwt* 6, « gouverneur de la ville, vizir et directeur de six grandes cours de justice ». Son épouse Ouretmaâtef était, quant à elle, investie de la qualité de *khekeret nesout*, « protectrice royale ».

Amenemopet était d'une famille au statut social très élevé. Son père, Âhmose dit « Hemy », propriétaire de la tombe n° 224 de Cheikh Abd el-Gourna[11] *imy-r pr n hmt ntr rp't h3ty-',* « directeur de la propriété de l'épouse du dieu, prince gouverneur ». Quant à sa mère, la dame Nebou, elle portait, comme l'épouse d'Amonemopet, le titre de *hkrt nswt*, « protectrice royale »[12].

Le frère d'Amenemopet, s'appelait Sennefer et occupait la charge de « gouverneur de la Haute-Égypte ». Celui-ci était propriétaire de la célèbre tombe « aux vignes » qui porte le n° 96 dans la nécropole de Cheikh Abd el-Gourna. Sennefer ainsi que son épouse Senetnay semblent, cependant, avoir occupé finalement la tombe n° 42 de la Vallée des Rois qui, à l'origine, aurait pu appartenir à Thoutmosis II, bien que des dépôts de fondation retrouvés près de la descenderie de cette tombe, soient au nom de Merytrê-Hatshepsout, épouse de Thoutmosis III[13].

Dans la tombe KV 42 ont été notamment découverts des vestiges du mobilier funéraire de Sennefer, de Senetnay et d'un autre personnage, peut-être membre de cette famille, qui portait le nom de Baketrê. Parmi ces objets figuraient des vases-canopes au nom de Senetnay, au nom de son époux mais également portant l'identité de la dame Baketrê.

Deux des vases-canopes de Senetnay[14] font état du titre de *khekeret nesout* « protectrice royale »[15]. Sur les récipients placés sous la protection conjointe d'Isis et de Hâpy d'une part, et de Nephthys et de Qebehsenouf d'autre part, elle est désignée comme étant *im3ḥyt ḥr Wsir ḥkr.t nswt snt-n3y m3ˁt ḥrw* «la bienheureuse auprès d'Osiris, la nourrice royale, Senetnay, justifiée ». Sur les deux autres vases, le texte la cite comme *im3ḥyt ḥr Wsir mnˁt nswt snt-n3y m3ˁt ḥrw* « la bienheureuse auprès d'Osiris, la nourrice royale, Senetnay, justifiée » (musée du Caire : JE 36369-36372 et CGC 24974).

Pour ce qui concerne la dame Baketrê[16], dont le lien de parenté avec Sennefer n'est pas établi de façon sûre, il existe deux fragments appartenant à ses vases-canopes et qui la mentionnent comme étant *khekeret nesout*. Sur l'un d'eux, on peut lire : *im3ḥyt ḥr Wsir ḥkrt nswt b3kt Rˁ m3ˁt ḥrw* xrw « la bienheureuse auprès d'Osiris, la protectrice royale, Baketrê, justifiée » ; sur l'autre, est inscrit le même texte, simplement complété par la mention de *ḥr nṯr ˁ3*, qui la justifie « auprès du grand dieu » (musée du Caire : JE 3399-3400).

La tombe de Bay (KV 13)[17]

Bay était un haut fonctionnaire sous le règne de Séthy II et de Ramsès-Siptah, vers la fin de la XIXe dynastie. Il était « chancelier du roi de Basse-Égypte, porteur du sceau à la droite du roi, scribe royal », mais surtout l'éminence grise de la Couronne.

Le statut social de Bay et sa relation particulière avec la reine Taousert, sont incontestablement à l'origine de la faveur royale qui lui a été octroyée en vue de faire préparer sa « demeure d'éternité » dans la Vallée des Rois. Cette sépulture, néanmoins, n'a jamais été achevée et l'on sait, de surcroît, qu'elle a été finalement réutilisée pour l'inhumation de deux princes de la XXe dynastie : un certain Amonherkhepshef dont le nom figure sur le premier sarcophage qui appartenait à l'origine à la reine Taousert, et un autre prince portant le nom de Montouherkhepshef. qui pourrait être un fils de Ramsès VI[18]. Ces deux monuments, en granite, sont toujours *in situ* dans la tombe de Bay.

Ces cinq tombes apportent, comme on peut le voir, d'intéressantes indications sur leurs propriétaires. Leurs fonctions à la cour royale étaient importantes et permettent de comprendre la faveur dont ils ont pu bénéficier en se faisant inhumer dans une nécropole royale, près de leur maître. Ce privilège a même rejailli sur les membres de leurs familles puisque, pour la plupart, ces tombes étaient collectives, destinées non seulement au haut fonctionnaire élu, mais encore à son épouse et aux éventuels enfants du couple. Il est, à ce propos, intéressant d'observer que les femmes enterrées dans la nécropole portaient le titre de *khekeret nesout,* qualité remarquable qui, par sa spécificité, en faisaient des proches de la famille royale.

Notes:

1 N. Reeves - R. H. Wilkinson, *The Complete Valley of the Kings*, (Le Caire, 1996), 174–178 ; J. Romer, *Valley of the Kings*, (Londres, 1981), 197–210 ; E. Hornung, *The Valley of the Kings Horizon of Eternity*, (New York, 1990), 166, 169, 185, 186.

2 Th. Davis, G. Maspero, P. E. Newberry, H. Carter, *The tomb of Iouiya and Touiyou. The finding of the tomb*, (Londres, 1907) ; J. E. Quibell, *The tomb of Yuaa and Thuiu*, (Le Caire, 1908).

3 Cf. M. Fekri, *Les khekerout nesout dans l'Égypte ancienne*, thèse de doctorat inédite, université de Paris-Sorbonne (Paris IV, s.d.), 306.

4 W. Helck, *Der Einfluss der Militärführer in der 18. ägyptischen Dynastie*, (Hildesheim, 1964), 62.

5 N. Reeves - R. H. Wilkinson, *op. cit.*, 179–181 ; J. Romer, *op. cit.*, 171–173, 177, 178 ; E. Hornung, *op. cit.*, 166, 169, 185, 186.

6 N. Reeves - R. H. Wilkinson, *op. cit.*, 184 ; J. Romer, *op. cit.*, 185.

7 *PM* I/1, no 56, 111–112 ; Chr. Beinlich-Seeber - A. Shedid, *Das Grab des Userhat*, *ArchVer* 50, (Mayence, 1987).

8 W. Helck, *Urk.* IV, 1478 ; Chr. Beinlich-Seeber - A. Shedid, *op. cit.*, 49, 153.

9 W. Helck, *Urk.* IV, 1478, 1479, 1480 ; Chr. Beinlich-Seeber - A. Shedid, *op. cit.*, 43, 44, 55, 72, 153.

10 N. Reeves - R. H. Wilkinson, *op. cit.*, 184, 185 ; J. Romer, *op. cit.*, 209, 210 ; E. Hornung, *op. cit.*, 189.

11 *PM* I/1 no 224, 325.

12 W. Helck, *Urk.* IV, 1432 ; *LD* text III, no 85, 286 ; A. Weil, *Die Veziere des Pharaonenreiches. Chronologisch angeordnet von Arthur Weil*, (Leipzig, 1908), 79.

13 E. Hornung, *op. cit.*, 189 ; M. El-Bialy, « Récentes recherches effectuées dans la tombe no 42 de la Vallée des Rois », dans *Memnonia* X, 161–178.

14 Cat. expo. *Ägyptens Aufstieg zur Weltmacht. Ausstellung, Roemer- und Pelizaeus-Museum, Hildesheim, 3 August – 29 November 1987*, (Hildesheim, 1987), 304, no 258.

15 Carter a, par erreur, remplacé le signe *ẖkr* par le signe *sn* : cf. H. Carter, « Report on Tomb-pit opened on the 26th January 1901 in the Valley of the Tombes of the Kings between no 4 and no 28 », *ASAE* 2 (1901), 144–145.

16 A. Mariette, *Monuments divers recueillis en Égypte et en Nubie*, (Paris, 1872), pl. 36 b, c ; H. Carter, *op. cit.*, 198, 200 ; G. Legrain, *Répertoire généalogique et onomastique du musée du Caire. Monuments de la XVIIe et de la XVIIIe dynastie*, (Genève, 1908), 114, no 205 ; G. A. Reisner, *Canopics. (CGC nos 4001–4740 and 4977–5033)*, (Le Caire, 1967), 282.

17 N. Reeves - R. H. Wilkinson, *op. cit.*, 154 ; J. Romer, *op. cit.*, 98 ; H. Altenmüller, « Das Graffito 551 aus der thebanischen Nekropole », *SAK* 21 (1994), 1–19.

18 Ces deux sarcophages ont été découverts par H. Altenmüller : *ibid.*, 1–18 ; Chr. Leblanc, « La véritable identité de Pentauret, le "prince maudit" », *RdE* à paraître.

Tell al-Dab'a: Two Execration Pits and a Foundation Deposit

Perla Fuscaldo[1]

Consejo Nacional de Investigaciones Científicas, Buenos Aires

During the excavations carried out at Tell al-Dab'a / Avaris in the eastern Delta in 1997 by the Austrian Archaeological Institute in Egypt under the direction of Manfred Bietak, another part of the Eighteenth Dynasty palace district was uncovered at Ezbet Helmi. In the southeastern part of Ezbet Helmi, Area H/III, a foundation deposit and two execration pits dating to the beginning of the Eighteenth Dynasty were found between the late Hyksos complex (stratum D/2) and the palace (stratum C).[2]

The foundation deposit, contained a small collection of clay votive objects, one with a very badly-preserved hieratic inscription. The small execration pit, Locus 1055, included human skulls and finger bones. The large execration pit, Locus 1016, contained two human skeletons and a large amount of broken pottery. All of these pits belong to the very beginning of the Eighteenth Dynasty, to the transitional stratum D/1. The foundation deposit and the small execration pit belong to stratum D/1.2 and the large execration pit to stratum D/1.1. Locus 1055 is earlier than Locus 1016, but both execration pits probably had a connection with the historical events of the Ahmose occupation of the Hyksos city of Avaris.

The foundation deposit, Locus 1057, is an oval pit, 25 cm by 30 cm, and 15 cm deep, dug into a mud layer and filled with objects made of Nile silt; a fine bowl, model pottery, symbolic offerings, an agricultural tool, and a lump of mud. The deposit is associated with a large storage building with silos. The objects from this deposit are, a ring-base bowl, a model basket, two model sieves, a model basket with a sieve, a model *mr* hoe, a model mortar with a pestle, a model piece of bread, a model piece of meat, all of them in Nile B_2 fabric, and a cylindrical lump of mud with a basket impression on the top.

The ring-based bowl with red-slipped rim is found in the Hyksos period as well as throughout the Eighteenth Dynasty. The model *mr* hoe represents a wooden hoe with a blade inserted in the handle and tied with a cord to make it stronger. It is used to excavate the foundation trenches for a building as well as to cultivate the fields. The model sieves and the basket with a sieve represent the basketry sieves used to sift sand and also to separate the grain from the husk. The mortar and pestle are for grinding the grain to make flour for offering ceremonies like the piece of model bread found in this deposit. The basket is used as a food-tray. The model piece of meat represents another food offering. The lump of mud could symbolize the fertile soil, which allows plants to grow.

A foundation deposit is a type of votive offering placed in or beneath the foundation of a building to purify the area where the construction will take place. It is filled during the ceremonies connected with the building activities. The objects from the foundation deposit at Tell al-Dab'a are unusual in that all of them are made of clay. This is unknown during the Eighteenth Dynasty except for the foundation deposit of the Horus temple at Aniba, where all 116 objects were made of clay. The kind of objects from the foundation deposit at Tell al-Dab'a is related to the function of the structure to which they belong; a royal storage building probably used to store food to supply the Egyptian army during the campaigns against the Hyksos settlements between Avaris and Sharuhen.

The small execration pit, Locus 1055, is an oval pit 40 by 50 cm wide and 15 to 20 cm deep. It contained three male skulls, the bones from nine fingers and some pottery shards. One skull was lying on its left side facing south-east, the second was on its back and the third on its face. Two skulls belong to two immature males and the third one to a mature adult. One skull has a hole on the right side above the ear indicating a blow which probably also damaged his temple. The finger bones belong to three right hands. No traces of cuts were observed. Fragments of two drop jars and a cooking pot were found in the pit, probably used for filling material.

The large pit, Locus 1016 is, in my opinion, an execration pit. It is oval, measuring 2.20 m north-south and 1.90 m east-west (maximum diameter), 0.45 m deep at the edge and 1.10 m in the middle, and cuts the mud-brick pavement of M 1029. At the bottom of the pit, two male human skeletons were laid face down, facing south. Skeleton number one belongs to a young adult. The right arm and hand are raised. Skeleton number two, belonging to a mature male, lay parallel to number one, and had the arms extended along the body. No injuries made by an axe, knife, sword, or spear were observed on either skeleton.[3] A large amount of broken pottery, comprising around 380 vessels, and different kinds of stones, mainly limestone chips, were thrown inside the pit. Of the pottery, 92.0% belongs to the late Hyksos Period, and 8.0% to the early Eighteenth Dynasty. Most of the shapes (78.60%) are of Egyptian origin (Corpus A), 20.95% from the Middle Bronze Age II B-C tradition (Corpus B), and one, a wheel-made bichrome shard, is imported from Cyprus (0.45%; Corpus C). No Nubian pottery was present.

The late Hyksos Period ceramic material from Corpus A (163 vessels) is mostly domestic pottery (98%), and includes a model bowl (2%). The fabric is Nile silt, mostly Nile B_2 in the Vienna System, with some shapes in Egyptian marls, mainly Marl F. Most of these vessels are shaped on a low simple wheel (W_1). The shapes of the fine ware of domestic type are cups (12.5%) and bowls (87.5%); deep bowls, small bowls, ring-based bowls, small carinated bowls, and large bowls with ring base .

The general household ware from the late Hyksos Period is mainly jars (76%), some bowls (19%), and a few potstands (5%), all of Nile silt. The shapes of the jars are drop jars, bag-shaped jars, jars with direct rim, with exterior lip, with interior and exterior lip, with complex rim, and imitation *zir*. The bowls are flat-based bowls, carinated bowls, large bowls, bowls with complex rim, and footed bowls. Some bowls and jars are made of Marl F, and fragments of *zir* in Marl C_2 were found. Some potstands and model bowls were also present.

From the vessels of Corpus B, 56% were locally made and 44% were imported. The locally-made pottery includes fine ware in a single shape, the dipper juglet. The general household ware was comprised of cooking pots and storage jars in the same quantity (42%), and Egyptian amphorae (16%). The imported ceramics from the Levant are all amphorae (95%), used as containers for commodities, and one hand-made cooking pot (5%). The amphora fabric is mostly IV.02, but IV.01, IV.04, IV.08, IV.09, IV.10, IV.17, and IV.21[4] are also present.

The early Eighteenth Dynasty pottery found in this context includes seventeen vessels, 94% domestic pottery, with only one votive vessel, a model bowl. The fabric is mostly Nile silt, especially Nile B_2, some Nile B_2 sandy (Nile E_4),[5] Nile E_1, and one Nile C_1. Two jars are made of Marl F. Among the early Eighteenth Dynasty ceramic material, there are some shapes already known from the stratum D/2, such as flat-bottomed cups and round-based drop jars. But these shapes are now made mostly of Nile B_2 sandy (Nile E_4) and Nile E_1, or with a thick and slightly darker red slip. The cups can also be shaped in a slightly improved tall-stemmed wheel, and the drop jars can have flat bases. There are new types of jars, with exterior lip and long neck in Nile silt, and short-necked carinated jars in Marl F. The only Cypriot shard is wheel-made Bichrome ware with no decoration preserved.

The pottery assemblage from Locus 1016 indicates local ceramic production, mostly vessels of Egyptian tradition and some of Middle Bronze Age II B-C origin. These were probably made by Egyptianized Canaanites during the last years of the Hyksos rule in Avaris, and reused at the beginning of the Eighteenth Dynasty. The appearance of new shapes and fabrics, and the more frequent use of a slightly improved tall-stemmed wheel show the ceramic changes produced in Avaris in the transitional period at the end of the Fifteenth Dynasty and the beginning of the Eighteenth Dynasty.

The execration pits preserved the skeletons or parts of the skeletons of defeated enemies. The pit with the three skulls represents sacrificed enemies, local or foreigners, buried in connection with the construction of new buildings after the occupation of Avaris by Ahmose, as part of an execration ritual to purify the area in the recently conquered Hyksos palace district. I think that the pit, Locus 1016, with the two skeletons and the large amount of pottery, could have had the same meaning. figurines of the enemies were usually used as substitutes for the real body of these enemies, with their names and the so-called execration texts, written on them, as well as on pottery vessels. In the execration ritual these figurines and the vessels with the names of the enemies were broken, with the aim of destroying the person named.

In the Middle Kingdom fortress at Mirgissa, figurines and jars were found in situ inside two pits.[6] On three stone statuettes representing prisoners buried in sandy soil, and on a large amount of broken pottery placed in a pit, "execration texts" were written. In another pit a human skull was found. At Mirgissa not only human figurines and broken pottery but also human remains were buried, which means that an actual human sacrifice could have been made during this execration ritual.

The two execration pits at Tell al-Dab'a are similar to those found at Mirgissa. The execration pit, Locus 1055, with the three human skulls is similar to the Mirgissa pit containing a human skull. The execration pit, Locus 1016, with the two human skeletons and the broken pottery, could be similar to those with three limestone figurines embedded in sand, and to the pit with the inscribed broken pottery.

The special feature of the execration pit, Locus 1016 at Tell al-Dab'a, is that the figurines with the name of the defeated enemies were substituted with the sacrifices of two defeated enemies, the non-inscribed pottery probably broken on them and their bodies covered with it and with fragments of different stones and objects, as if they had been stoned (even though there is no evidence of injuries). If this had happened, we do not know why the Egyptians sacrificed enemies in Avaris instead of using substitute figurines as usual. This ritual of the destruction of pottery and the actual execution of prisoners, as happened with the rebels, could have been an execration ritual performed as part of the ceremonies for the celebration of the conquest of the city and for the construction of new buildings.

Notes:

1 CONICET, Buenos Aires

2 See P. Fuscaldo, "The Palace District of Avaris. The Pottery of the Hyksos Period and the New Kingdom (Areas H/III and H/VI), Part II: "Two Execration Pits and a Foundation Deposit," *Tell al-Dab'a* X, forthcoming.

3 From the preliminary report on the human remains from both pits made by the Mission's anthropologist, Karl Großschmidt.

4 According to a classification by Irmgard Hein.

5 According to the classification of the New Kingdom fabric made by I. Hein.

6 A. Vila, "Un dépot de textes d'envoûtement au Moyen Empire," *Journal des Savants* 153 (1963), 135–160, figs. 3–4; J. Vercoutter, "Fouilles à Mirgissa (Octobre-Novembre 1961)," *RdE* 15 (1963), 69–75, plate II, A. G. Posener, "Les Textes d' envoutement de Mergissa," (Syria), and "Cinq Figurines d'envoutement," *CBdE* 101, IFAO 1987.

A Preliminary Report on the Pottery from Tell al-Ghaba, a Saite Settlement in North Sinai

P. Fuscaldo, S. Basílico, B. Cremonte, S. Lupo
Consejo Nacional de Investigaciones Científicas, Buenos Aires

Since 1995 the Argentine Archaeological Mission in Egypt has been excavating the Saite settlement of Tell al-Ghaba in North Sinai as a joint project of the National Scientific Council (CONICET) and the University of Buenos Aires. The project is part of the Supreme Council of Antiquities' Archaeological Salvage Project of the Monuments in North Sinai.

In antiquity, North Sinai was part of the eastern Delta plain irrigated by the former Pelusiac branch of the Nile. It was a frontier area, the land bridge between Egypt and the Levant, the so-called "Ways of Horus," where many settlements were founded. Tell al-Ghaba is one of these sites, located on the north shore of a lagoon between Tell Hebua to the west and Tell Kedwa to the east.

The fieldwork was done under the direction of Eduardo Crivelli, and the geophysical survey was carried out by Jorge Trench. Their work shows that the site covered 12 hectares and was 500 m long by 250 m wide. The stratigraphic sequence is around 1.80 m deep; the sediments are salt-rich and the water table is quite high. The organic material is badly preserved and the upper layer was swept away by erosion. Only the base of the mudbrick structures remain. Eight areas were excavated or surveyed. There are four occupation levels containing the remains of at least nine mudbrick buildings, a large amount of small finds (mainly amulets), pottery, and lithics, and some bronze and one iron tool.

In Area I the sequence of occupation in chronological order is as follows: Above the sterile soil, stratum I, with the remains of some pottery shards, represents the first occupation of the site. stratum II preserved the foundation trenches for walls of a flimsy structure, "Building A" which was burnt. This rectangular building had at least two rooms. stratum III reveals a period of intensive occupation of the site. To this stratum belongs mudbrick "Building B," with four rooms, a storage facility, and two open courtyards with two large ovens. The ovens served both a domestic and industrial function, and were built directly above the remains of "Building A." Stratum IV is a destruction layer which appears not only here but also in other areas of the settlement. It is represented by Locus 1. In this locus no formal architectonic structures were identified, but abundant pottery shards, faunal remains (especially fish), and small finds were preserved. Locus 1 is separated from the modern topsoil by a sandy fill almost devoid of archaeological material.

The preliminary report on the pottery from Tell al-Ghaba presented here focuses on the ceramic material from the floors belonging to the buildings in the different strata in Area I and Locus 1. It includes the analysis of shapes, fabrics, and wares. The fabric analysis was made with a 10–20x hand-lens and a 20–40x microscope for the Nile silt clays and the Egyptian marls. The fabrics were classified according to the Vienna system. A preliminary fabric typology was established based on binocular microscope characterizations (10–40x) and thin section petrographic analyses done by Beatriz Cremonte,[1] with the co-operation of Maciej Pawlikowski[2] for the geological studies.

The local fabrics found in Tell al-Ghaba are mainly Nile silt, especially Nile B_2 in the Vienna system. They are very well levigated and fired. Most of the vessels are uncoated, only very few are red-slipped. Other fabrics are Nile C_1 and C_2, and Nile E. The local marl, Marl F, was frequently used. Three different types were recorded based on the amount of sand in the fabrics, classified as "Marl F," "Marl F sandy," and "Marl F very sandy." Beside this there are four marls that could be from the eastern Sinai, mainly used for shaping vessels that are imitations of imported pottery. A couple of shards were made of *Bir al-Abd* clay,[3] and closed and open vessels of Marl A_4 from Upper Egypt.

There are Levantine, Cypriot, and Aegean fabrics classified as IV, VI, and VII. Fifteen fabrics are Levantine, eight of them already known in the Middle and Late Bronze Age such as IV.01, 02, 08, 09, 12, 14, 19, and 20.[4] Most of the Levantine pottery (30%) was shaped in only four fabrics, classified as IV.TG.03, IV.TG.07, IV.TG.11, and IV.TG.23.[5] Two of the Levantine fabrics are Phoenician (IV.Phoen.01 and IV.Phoen.02), and possibly a third (IV. Phoen.?.03).

Eight fabric groups seem to be Cypriot, VI.TG.01, VI.TG.04, VI.TG.21, VI.TG.39, VI.TG.40, VI.TG.42, VI.TG.43, and VI.TG.49. Some of these fabrics were used for shaping fine vessels in the Cypriot-Phoenician "Black-on-red" ware (styles I, II, and III), mainly style II. The decoration of this ware is characterized by horizontally black painted bands and concentric circles on the body of juglets, jugs, and open shapes. The "Black-on-red" ware is found in many sites of the Eastern Mediterranean, after the installation of Phoenician factories in the area, mainly in Cyprus and exported from Cyprus to the Levantine coast and Egypt until the sixth century BCE. The styles I, II, and III correspond to the Cypriot period-styles III, IV, and V. There are a few shards from the Cypriot Period IV in the "Red Slip," "White Painted," "Black Slip" and Bichrome wares, and a combined style of White Painted outside and Bichrome inside.

Two fabrics could be from Samos, and one is from Chios. Three fabrics are probably from other parts of the Aegean (VII.TG.41, VII.TG.45, and VII.TG.58), two of them are very fine fabrics used for the Cypriot-Phoenician "Black-on-red" ware.

The comparison of the ceramics from the different strata of Area I shows an increase in imports. In stratum II, the pottery from Locus 40, a "Building A" floor, is 86% Egyptian and 13% import-

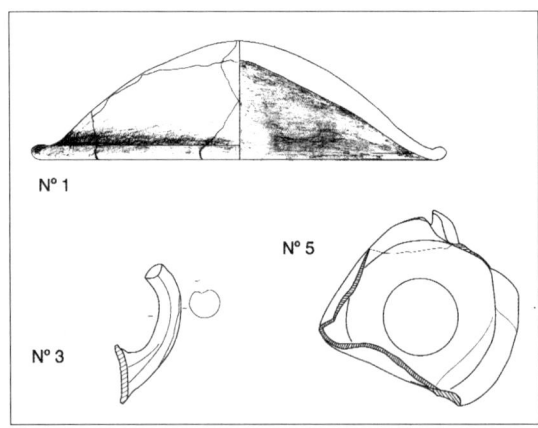

Figure 1

ed (1% is unknown); in stratum III, the pottery from loci 84 and 271, two floors of "Building B," is 84% is Egyptian and 12% imported (4% is unknown), and in stratum IV, Locus 1, 71% of the pottery is Egyptian and 28% imported.

If we compare the local pottery made in Nile silt clays, Marl F and in the marls probably coming from the eastern Sinai and/or south Palestine, with that made of Marl A_4, the percentage of the Upper Egypt Marl A_4 ceramics increases in strata II and III, but decreases in stratum IV. In stratum II, Locus 40, the pottery is 96% locally made and 4% is made of Marl A_4; in stratum III, loci 84 and 271, 93% is local and 7% is made of Marl A_4. In stratum IV (Locus 1) 96% is local and 4% is Marl A_4.

In stratum II, Locus 40, the imported pottery is 79% Levantine, 9% Phoenician, and 12% Cypriot. In stratum III, loci 84 and 271, the ceramics are 93% Levantine and 7% Aegean, and in stratum IV, Locus 1, 77% is Levantine, 7% Phoenician, 11% Cypriot, and 4% Aegean.

Locus 40 has preserved a small collection of very fragmentary pottery.[6] In local clays, some of the following shapes were found: a round-based bowl used as a lid (No. 1),[7] a bowl with flat rim inside and a cup with pointed base, in an uncoated ware in Nile B_2, and a burnished red-slipped bowl in the same fabric,[8] and the handle of a jug in Marl F (No. 2).[9] Among the imported ceramics from the Levant there are a handle of a "torpedo" amphora,[10] and an oil lamp (No. 3)[11] in IV.TG.36 fabric.

Some pottery shapes from loci 84 and 271 are: a cup (No. 4),[12] a fine deep-bowl with pointed base and grooves on the base (No. 5),[13] a jug with an angular shoulder,[14] two jars of a globular type (Nos. 8 and 10)[15] with the throwing lines visible on the exterior surface, and the lower part of a storage jar (No. 6),[16] all of them made of Nile B_2. A bowl in Nile E_1 was used as a cooking pot.[17] The Marl A_4 vessels are a deep bowl (No. 7),[18] a bowl, jars (Nos. 9 and 11),[19] and fragments of an amphora with grooves on the surface.[20] Two typical imported vessels are represented by a fragment of a Levantine "torpedo" amphora[21] and a fine Cypriot-Phoenician "Black-on-red" II (IV) juglet.[22]

In Locus 1, some of the shapes made of Nile clays include a Nile E_2 hand-made, ring-based juglet with very thick walls,[23] a footed cup,[24] a jar with grooves on the surface,[25] a pot (No. 12),[26] a pot for unguents,[27] and a model storage jar, all of them made of Nile B_2, and a bakery tray in Nile C_1. There are three types of pilgrim flasks, one in Nile E_2, another in Nile B_2 with three handles, and the third one is lentil-shaped[28] in C_1. There are two Aegean vessels, a jug with pinched rim and a black-painted band on the rim and neck, and a juglet with horizontally black painted bands and a circle on the body,[29] in VII.TG.45 fabric. A fragment of a *Chian* amphora,[30] with a red-painted band on a creamy slip around the handle (not preserved);[31] a Levantine "torpedo" shoulder made of IV.TG.03,[32] and the rim of another in IV.TG.24. The fine Cypriot imports are mainly "Black-on-red" ware; all of the

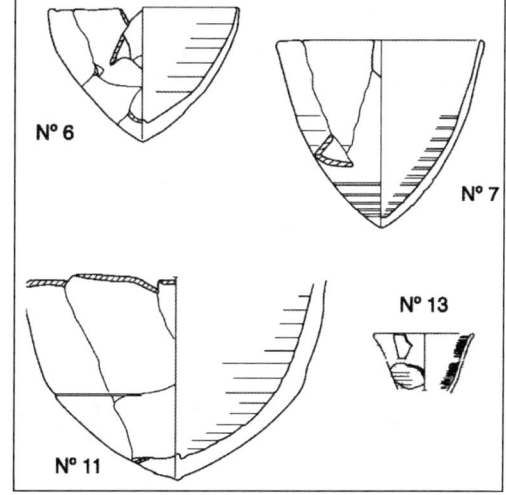

N° 6

N° 7

N° 13

N° 11

Figure 2

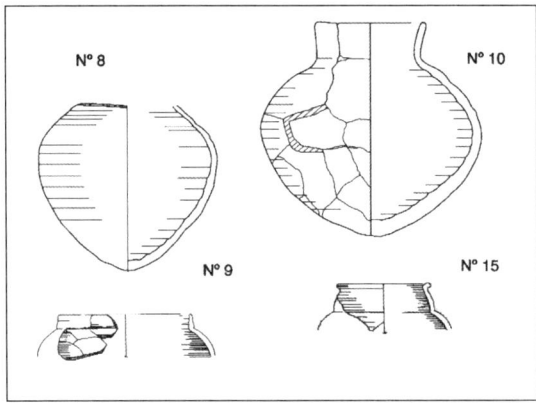

Figure 3

juglets are decorated with horizontal dark grey, dark reddish brown, or black painted bands on the rim, neck, body, and handle, and concentric circles. One is "Black-on-red" I (III),[33] three (e.g. No. 14)[34] are "Black-on-red" II (IV), and another (No. 13)[35] is a "Black-on-red" III (V) ware. All are made of the same fabric, VI.TG.39. The other Cypriot fine wares are, a White Painted IV bowl (No. 33),[36] a bowl with horizontal handles,[37] probably "Black-on-red" ware, in VI.TG.49 fabric, and a Bichrome shard from a bowl (No. 15),[38] and a compound neck of a Cypriot jug ("Plain White" ware?) in VI.TG.01. A barrel-shaped juglet,[39] in a marl probably from the eastern Sinai classified as II.TG.14, is an Egyptian imitation of a Cypriot vessel.

If we compare the pottery associated with the different buildings in areas I, II, and VI, the percentage of the Egyptian pottery in relation to the imported in the fortification structure called "Building C" (Area II) is higher than in "Building B" (Area I). "Building C" has a predominance of storage jars, *zirs*, and bakery trays. "Building D" (Area II), which probably had an administrative function, used many imported amphorae as containers. The pottery from "Building F" (Area VI) presents mainly a large amount, more than in other areas, of large storage jars and oven lids, bakery trays, and trays, in a very coarse Nile C_2.

In Tell al-Ghaba we also found some bowls, jars, and pilgrim flasks made of Nile B_2, in a style we have called "Black-on-red." It is characterized by horizontal black bands painted on a red slip outside and inside the open shapes, as shown on jar Inv. No. 868. There is also an unprecedented fine-Marl A_4 deep bowl (Inv. No. 1122), with an decorative pattern of horizontal, vertical, and oblique bands and lines, painted in black and red.

The Egyptian pottery from Tell al-Ghaba corresponds to a ceramic phase classified by David Aston as "Phase IV North."[40] The imported pottery is Iron Age III, which shows the connection between Egypt and the Eastern Mediterranean, especially the Levant. The "Phase IV North" includes the second part of the reign of Psamtik I until the beginning of that of Psamtik II. It is probably before the Saite expansion on the Levant, which started with the capture of the harbor of Ashdod by Psamtik I in Year Twenty-nine of his reign (635 BCE). The Twenty-sixth Dynasty kings built some forts and settlements along the "Ways of Horus" for campaigns in Judah. Tell al-Ghaba could have been one of these sites. The large amount of Levantine amphorae point to an important land-trade with Judah and Israel, which might have

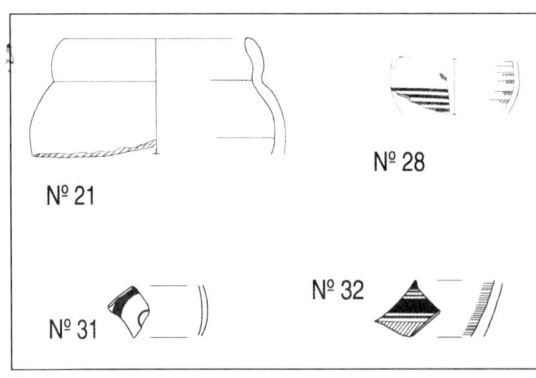

Figure 4

increased in connection with the expansion to the Euphrates by Necho II (609–659), who fought in Meggido against Judah and was defeated by the Babylonians in Karkemish.

A clay plaque,[41] with the representation of a nude female with Nubian features, probably a fertility goddess, and a pottery fragment with a cloth imprint inside, both from Locus 1, could be connected with the campaign of Psamtik II against Nubia at the beginning of his reign. Tell al-Ghaba could have been abandoned before the development of Naukratis,[42] before the expansion of the Greek trade in Egypt, because of the lack of pottery found in this area.

The pottery used to date this site indicates that Tell al-Ghaba was a Saite settlement of the beginning of the Twenty-sixth Dynasty, from the second half of the reign of Psamtik I to the beginning of the Psamtik II.

Notes:

1 CONICET

2 Polish Academy of Sciences, Cracow.

3 Y. Goren, E. Oren, and R. Feinstein, "The Archaeological and Ethno-archaeological Interpretation of a Ceramological Enigma: Pottery Production in Sinai (Egypt) during the New Kingdom," *KUHAA Konferenze* 34 (1995), 101–112.

4 We adopted the classification used in Tell el-Dab'a for the same fabrics.

5 The first fabric classification encompassed TG from 1 to 50, although some are being collected according to common characteristics for a definitive typology. A high number of fabric groups are temporally in use. This is the reason why such high numbers are temporarily used.

6 The corpus of Egyptian shapes was made by Silvia Lupo (CONICET) and that of the imported by Susana Basílico (CONICET).

7 Inv. No.1116; Rd: 28.5 cm; Wd: 1.2; H_1: 8.

8 Inv. No. 1109; Rd: 12 cm 1/16; Wd: 0.6; H_1: 2.5 + x; slip: 10R 4/8; burnished horizontally, high luster.

9 Inv. No. 861; Wd: 1.8 cm; Hd: 1.8–0.6; double strap; slip: 10YR 8/3; smoothed by hand.

10 Inv. No. 1273; Wd: 1 cm; H_1: 6.7 + x; Hd: 3 x 2.4; 10YR 8/3.

11 Inv. No. 761; length: 13.3 cm; width: 12 + x; height: 5.1; 5YR 6/6; smoothed by hand; rim modeled by hand; smoked inside; oil spots.

12 Inv. No. 35; Rd: 11 cm; Wd: 0.3; H_1: 7.5; 7.5YR 6/4.

13 Inv. No. 18; Rd: 12 cm; Wd: 0.35; H_1: 10.5; 10R 5/6; wheel smoothed.

14 Inv. No. 350; some crushed limestone inclusions; Nd: 6.5 cm; Md: 11; Wd: 0.6; H_1: 7.2 + x; H_2: 5.3; Hd: 1.5 x 0.8; 10R 4/6; wheel smoothed.

15 No. 9, Inv. No. 19; Md: 27 cm; Wd: 0.75; H_1: 23.8 + x; H_2: 13; 2.5YR 5/6–5/6; wheel smoothed. No.10, Inv. No. 41; Rd: 8.0 cm; Nd: 7.5; Md: 16.5; Wd: 0.7; H_1: 15.8; H_2: 8.0; 2.5YR 5/4.

16 Inv. No. 562; Md: 17 + x cm; Wd: 0.55; H_1: 11 + x; 7.5YR 5/3; smoothed.

17 Inv. No. 510; Rd: 22 cm 5/64; Md: 24; Wd: 0.75; H_1: 10 + x; H_2: 5 + x; 5YR 6/3; wheel smoothed.

18 Inv. No. 1245; Rd: 5.8 cm 1/32; Wd: 0.25; H_1: 3 + x; slip: 2.5YR 7/2; fine ridges outside.

19 No.14, Inv. No. 1203; Rd: 10.5 cm 1/32; Nd: 10; Md: 14 + x; Wd: 0.3; H_1: 3 + x; slip: 2.5Y 7/3; fine

ridges outside and inside. No.15, Inv. No. 832; Rd: 7 cm; 3/16; Nd: 7–8; Wd: 0.3; H_1: 3.5 + x; slip: 10YR 7/2; fine ridges inside and outside.

20 Inv. No. 1242; Md: 10 cm; Wd: 0.35; H_1: 8.0 + x; slip: 7.5YR 7/3–6/3; grooves on the exterior surface.

21 Inv. No. 719; Md: 32 cm; Wd: 1; H_1: 55.5 + x; H_2: 26; 7.5YR 7/4.

22 E. Gjerstad, "The Cypro-Geometric, Cypro-Archaic and Cypro-Classical Periods," *SCE* IV 2 (1948); I. Finkelstein, O. Zimhoni and A. Kafri, "The Iron Age Pottery Assemblages from Areas F, K and H and their Stratigraphic and Chronological Implications," in *Megiddo III: The 1992–1996 Seasons*, I. Finkelstein, D. Ussishkin and B. Halpern, (eds.), (1998), 244–324; P. Bikai, *The Phoenician Pottery of Cyprus* (1987).

23 Inv. No. 1057; Md: 9 cm; Wd: 0.9–1.45; H_1: 8 + x.; H_2: 3; Bd: 3; slip: 10R 5/6; polished, low luster.

24 Inv. No. 212; Fd: 4 cm 1/8; Wd: 0.55; H_4: 3.5; 10R 6/8.

25 Inv. No. 223; some crushed limestone inclusions; Rd: 10 cm 1/8; Md: 12 + x; Wd: 0.5; H_1: 7 + x; 2.5YR 5/8; horizontal grooves.

26 Inv. No. 164; Rd: 9.0 cm 3/16; Wd: 0.4; H_1: 6 + x; 10R 6/6; wheel smoothed.

27 Inv. No. 13; Rd: 3.4 cm; Md: 4.4; Wd: 0.38; H_1: 6; H_2: 2.2; 5YR 5/6; wheel smoothed.

28 Inv. No. 1173; made on the wheel in two parts; Rd: 4.5 cm; Nd: 3.3; Wd: 0.7; H_1: 6 + x; H_4: 5; Hd: 1.2 x 0.6; slip: 2.5YR 5/6.

29 Inv. No. 2028; Md: 5.0 cm 5/32; Wd: 0.3; H_1: 1.9 + x; slip: 5YR 4/4; polished, high luster.

30 This is the "type A" of Oren, (E. Oren, "Migdol: A New Fortress on the Edge of the Eastern Nile Delta," *BASOR* 256 (1984), 24, fig. 22, 1 and 4.

31 Inv. No. 48; Wd: 0.65 cm; H_1: 3.5 + x; slip: 10YR 7/4; painted lincs: 2.5YR 4/8.

32 Inv. No.1069; Md: 26 cm 1/16; Wd: 0.85; H_1: 5.1 + x; 2.5YR 6/8; wheel smoothed.

33 Inv. No. 362; Rd: 3 cm ?; Nd: 1.4–1.7; Md: 5 + x; Wd: 0.35; H_1: 4.8 + x; Hd: 0.7 x 0.6; slip: 10YR 4/4; painted decoration: 5YR 3/1.

34 No. 28: Inv. No. 778; Md: 6 cm; Wd: 0.3; H_1: 2.2 + x; slip: 2.5YR 5/8; decoration: 2.5YR 3/1; polished, medium luster. No.29, Inv. No. 1097; Rd: 3.6 cm 1/1; Nd: 1.2; Wd: 0.2; H_3: 1.80 + x; slip: 2.5YR 6/6; polished, low luster. No.30, Inv. No. 1041; Rd: 3.5 cm 1/16; Wd: 0.3; H_3: 2.9 + x; slip: 2.5YR 5/8; polished, medium luster.

35 Inv. No. 771; Md: 8 + x cm; Wd: 0.35; H_1: 2.4 + x; slip: 5YR 4/3; polished, high luster; decoration: 5YR 3/2.

36 Inv. No. 208; Rd: 21 cm; Wd: 0.65; H_1: 7.3 + x; slip: 2.5YR 8/3; decoration: 10YR 3/2.

37 Inv. No. 703; Rd: c. 30 cm; Wd: 0.4; H_1: 4.5 + x; Hd: 0.8 x 0.8; 1 strap; slip: 2.5YR 6/6; decoration: 5YR; polished, low luster.

38 Inv. No. 365; Wd: 0.45 cm; H_1: 2.55 + x; slip: 5YR 7/6; decoration: 5YR 2.5/1 and 10R 4/4.

39 Inv. No. 845; length: 10 cm; Wd: 0.4; H_1: 10 + x; slip: 2.5YR 7/6; smoothed.

40 D. Aston, *Egyptian Pottery of the Late New Kingdom and Third Intermediate Period (Twelfth-Seventh Centuries BC)* (1996).

41 Inv. No. 2019.

42 R. Sullivan, "Psammetichus I and the Foundation of Naukratis," in W. Coulson, *Ancient Naukratis* II, I (1987).

The Nabataean Temple at Qasrawet

Michal Gawlikowski
PCMA

The Nabataean site at Qasrawet (North Sinai) has been excavated by the IFAO at the beginning of this century, and again, illegally, during the Israeli occupation of the area. In both cases, the excavations were incomplete and the existing publications very preliminary. As I could see during a short visit in 1998, the ruins were already covered with sand, allowing only a cursory inspection.

Among the visible ruins, the temple is most conspicuous. There are four gabled facades turned inward, forming a square. The architectural form of the building was never clearly understood. Some monuments in Jordan, such as temples in Wadi Rumm, Khirbet ed-Dharih, and the so-called temple of the Winged Lions in Petra, can be usefully compared to Qasrawet. In this light, I intend to propose that this temple also had a central courtyard open to the sky. In my opinion, the temple of Qasrawet deserves to be systematically excavated.

Some 50 km east from al-Qantara, among the moving sand dunes beyond the new al-Salam Canal, are the seldom-visited ruins of a Roman Period settlement including two temples and a monumental enclosure. The site was first investigated in the beginning of the twentieth century by Jean Clédat,[1] who spelled the name as Qasr-Gheit. Clédat saw correctly that it must have been a Nabataean station on a secondary caravan route from Arabia to Egypt.

Clédat cleared the interior of the smaller of the two temples from sand; it is a rectangular building divided by an interior colonnade and includes a cult niche at the far end. The architectural decoration of this temple is Egyptian in style. Just in front of this monument another one, bigger and more remarkable, could not be excavated on that occasion. In the 1970s both temples were cleared again by E. Netzer but not published except for some cursory notes.[2] They are now filled once more with sand allowing only the tops of walls to be seen.

The main temple is usually described as two buildings encased one within the other. The outer walls form a square 19 m to a side, while in the middle there is another square structure, 7.40 m wide, resting on columns and pillars, the four angle pillars with half-columns and pilasters

195

Fig. 1: The temple of Qasrawet, seen from the south.

attached. The entablature presents on each side a gabled broken pediment turned inwards, which is a very exceptional feature in ancient architecture in general. The stone walls were reinforced with massive wooden beams, having left horizontal grooves above the capitals. According to earlier and recent excavators, the square temple was covered with a flat terrace roof resting on beams of which some remains were found in the fill.

The square plan with an inner building open on all sides strongly suggests that the main point of interest was to be found in the middle, enhanced by the magnificent architectural frame and surrounded by a circumambulation *(tawwaf)*. As several other Nabataean shrines are also square, it could be supposed that we have put a finger here on an ancient Arab religious tradition of pilgrimage, attached in this case to a desert sanctuary frequented by caravans coming from the depths of Arabia.

For several reasons, such conclusions seem too hasty to me. While there is no doubt about the Arab character of the Nabataeans, and no reason to quarrel with their supposed inclination to circular processions, it is hard to imagine such rituals taking place under a roof. Moreover, the architectural form of the building, with the central square reserved and set aside, can be envisaged with difficulty as equal in height to the surrounding covered space of the outer square.

Two possible schemes can be considered. The central colonnaded square could have been covered in the middle of an open enclosure, or it could form a light well in the middle of a large roofed *cella*. Both solutions seem satisfactory from the architectural point of view, and both are certainly feasible. The choice between them should be not arbitrary, however, but depend on comparison with other similar monuments in the Nabataean realm.

Indeed, closely similar arrangements have been recently identified in several Nabataean temples in Petra and elsewhere.[3] Philip Hammond some years ago excavated a shrine in Petra which he called the "Temple of the Winged Lions," after the griffin figures adorning the column capitals of this monument. The square *cella* included right and left lateral porticoes, and in the middle, a platform surrounded by columns that were not linked to the side walls of the building. It does not seem that the mode of covering was seriously studied by the excavators. As far as we can judge from the sketchy plan available, the platform should rather be open to the sky.

Much better studied is another Nabataean temple now under excavation in Khirbet ed-Dharih in central Jordan.[4] François Villeneuve has already published some preliminary observations and graphic documents, which enable me to show here not only a plan but also a tentative section across the *cella* (slightly modified). As I have recently proposed,[5] the *cella* must have been open, and also open was the square platform at the back, surrounded by columns carrying a heavy and elaborate entablature reaching the full height of the building. Emboldened by a good reception of this idea by the excavator, I am now more ready to see similar arrangements in other places.

One of them is a remote desert sanctuary in Wadi Rumm in southern Jordan.[6] A raised platform there supported a small building which has been seen as a chapel but appears more probably to be an altar. Whatever it might be, this feature stood quite obviously in the open. It was surrounded by columns with curtain walls between them, and later with a row of rooms, but remained at all times accessible from the front by means of some steps. Also this temple is being currently excavated and my conclusions must remain preliminary pending a fuller publication.

It has recently been proposed that the square platforms of these temples might be "thrones" of Nabataean deities.[7] In fact, such a seat *(motab)* is mentioned in the extant inscriptions only twice in relation to Dushara, the main god of the Nabataeans, and the meaning of the word remains far from certain. In this hypothesis, of course, the columns surrounding the platform

Fig. 2: A glimpse of the inner pediment.

should have supported a dais for the supposed throne. Their relation to the building as a whole would be rather awkward, however, because of the apparently equal height of the inner and outer structures.

It seems more likely that the central space was open to the sky, being a kind of peristyle within the square building. Its floor is, however, usually raised and should have supported altars rather than idols. Temples of this kind would provide a monumental frame for open-air sacrificial places of the ancestral nomad tradition of the Nabataeans and other desert tribes of Northern Arabia.

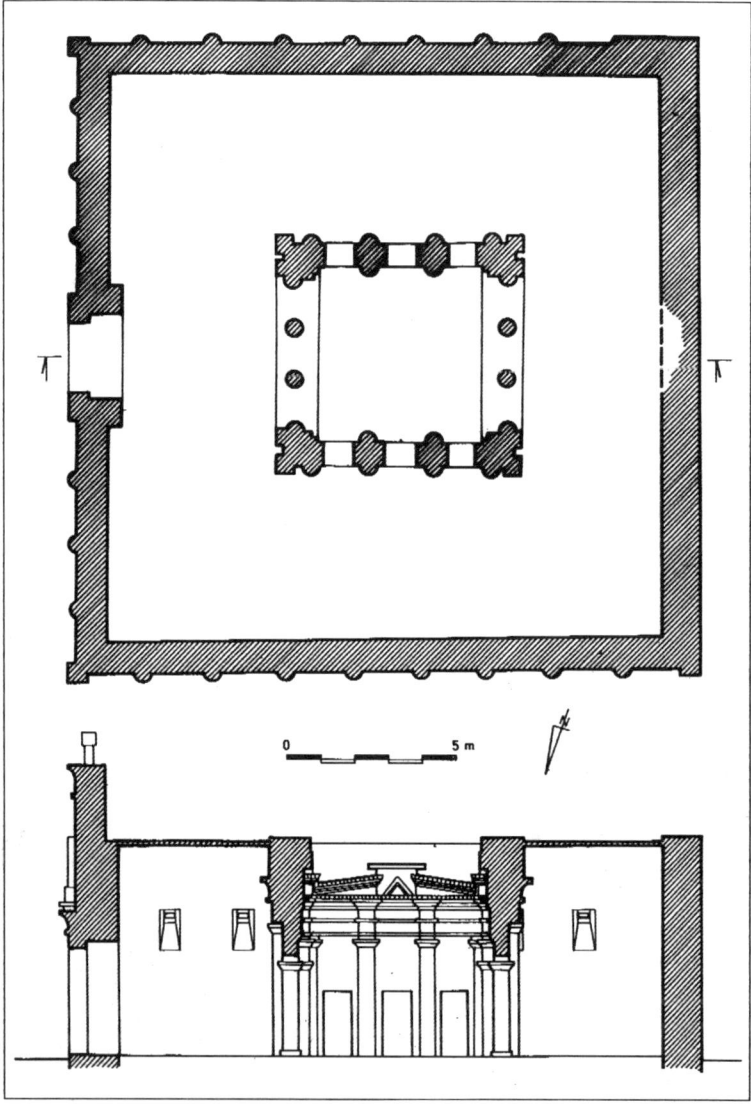

Fig. 3: A restored plan and section of the Temple of Qasrawet.

198

Qasrawet appears to be the closest parallel to some recently discovered sanctuaries in Jordan, and is certainly the best preserved of all. In fact it is the only ancient Arab temple preserved nearly complete.

Notes:

1 J. Clédat, "Fouilles à Qasr-Gheit (mai 1911)" *ASAE* 11 (1911), 145 sq.

2 E. D. Oren, "Excavations at Qasrawet in North-Western Sinai, Preliminary Report," *IEJ* 32 (1982), 203 sq.

3 Cf. M. Gawlikowski, "Les sanctuaires du Proche-Orient romain dans la recherche récente," *Topoi* 8 (1998), 31–52.

4 F. Villeneuve and Z. al-Moheisen, "Fouilles à Khirbet edh-Dharih (Jordanie), 1984–1987," *CRAI* (1988), 458–479; F. Villeneuve, *Liber Annuus* 42 (1993), 356–359; *Liber Annuus* 43 (1994), 486–489; *AJA* 98 (1994), 540–542; *AJA* 99 (1995), 521–522; F. Villeneuve, communication, 7th International Conference on History and Archaeology of Jordan, Copenhagen, 1998.

5 M. Gawlikowski, "Motab et hamana. Sur quelques monuments religieux du Levant," Conference "Temples et sanctuaires", Institut français d'archéologie du Proche-Orient, Beyrouth, 1999.

6 R. Savignac and G. Horsfield, "Le temple de Ramm," *RB* 44 (1935), 245–278; R. Savignac, "Le dieu nabatéen de Laban et son temple," *RB* 46 (1937), 401–416; D. *Kirkbride*, "Le temple nabatéen de Ramm. Son évolution architecturale," *RB* 67 (1960), 65–92; L. Tholbecq, "Les sanctuaires des Nabatéens. Etat de la question à la lumière de recherches archéologiques récentes," *Topoi* 7/2 (1997), 1069–1095.

7 E. Will, "Du môtab de Dusarès au trône d'Astarte," *Syria* 63 (1986), 343–351.

Les travaux récents du Centre polonais d'archéologie méditerranéenne en Égypte

Michal Gawlikowski
PCMA

Monsieur le Président, Mesdames, Messieurs

Je tiens d'abord à remercier M. Bernard Mathieu, qui a bien voulu me céder un quart d'heure de son temps pour que je puisse présenter un bref rapport sur les activités polonaises en Égypte. La coopération et la bonne entente entre l'Ifao et l'archéologie polonaise, entamée voilà soixante ans à Edfou, ne se démentit donc pas.

Le centre polonais, tel qu'il existe aujourd'hui, a été fondé au Caire il y a quarante ans par Kazimierz Michalowski, maître de tous ceux qui, parmi les archéologues de mon pays présents ici, ne sont plus tout jeunes. Il reste le patron de notre maison à Héliopolis. C'est dire l'émotion qui nous a saisi tout à l'heure en voyant sa mémoire honorée. L'Égypte a reconnu ainsi les mérites de son grand ami, un ami qui a su transmettre son attachement à ce pays à plusieurs générations de ses élèves.

Notre centre conduit actuellement des travaux de fouille et de restauration sur une vingtaine de sites dans cinq pays du Proche-Orient. En Égypte même, nous comptons en ce moment huit chantiers. Il n'est évidemment pas possible de les traiter maintenant en détail, mais on parlera de certains d'entre eux au cours de ce congrès.

Alexandrie d'abord, qui a été, dès le début, et qui reste toujours, l'une des pièces maîtresses de notre activité en Égypte. Au bout de longues années de fouilles, des dizaines de milliers de mètres cubes de déblais enlevés de ce qui était, au cœur de la ville moderne, le Kôm el-Dikka, c'est tout un quartier antique qui revoit le jour et qui est remonté dans une entreprise conjointe avec le Conseil suprême des antiquités. Les thermes, le théâtre, des maisons romaines ont été découverts, puis restaurés. Très bientôt, tout cet ensemble sera ouvert au public, grâce au dévouement de Wojciech Kolataj et Grzegorz Majcherek. Tout récemment, de belles mosaïques d'époque romaine y ont été mises en valeur grâce au financement de l'ARCE.

Une centaine de kilomètres vers l'ouest, sur la côte, c'est une petite Alexandrie qui a été découverte, il y a quinze ans, sur le chantier du site estival de Marina, près d'El-Alamein. Cette petite ville gréco-romaine, pour le moment anonyme, est fouillée depuis par Wiktor Daszewski, mon prédécesseur à la direction de notre centre, et restaurée par une équipe de l'École d'architecture de Wroclaw dirigée par Stanislaw Medeksza. Les tombeaux de Marina ressemblent à ceux d'Alexandrie, ses maisons nous donnent aussi un reflet de la métropole. Ses monuments publics attendent encore leur tour d'être fouillés.

Les travaux polonais portant sur l'Égypte ancienne sont trop nombreux pour que je sois en mesure de les énumérer tous. Je ne dirai rien d'un établissement prédynastique de Tell el-Farkha, qui sera présenté ici. Vous allez également entendre sous peu une conférence sur les nouvelles fouilles de Saqqara par Karol Mysliwiec. Vous allez aussi visiter le temple d'Hatshepsout où la terrasse supérieure et le sanctuaire sont enfin prêts à s'ouvrir au public. Ce grand travail de restauration, mené pour le compte du CSA successivement par Zygmunt Wysocki, par Franciszek Pawlicki, et terminé cette année par Zbigniew Szafranski et Rajmund Gazda, a complètement transformé le site du monastère de St. Phoebamon, le Deir el-Bahari comme il est connu généralement. Ses colonnes et ses murs remontés, ses statues et ses bas-reliefs reconstitués à partir de milliers de fragments, rendent un peu d'éclat d'origine à ce monument hors pair.

D'autres travaux ont été entrepris l'automne dernier au-dessus de Deir el-Bahari, haut dans la falaise : de nombreux graffiti hiératiques et coptes ont pu y être identifiés, suggérant une activité ancienne dans ces lieux inaccessibles qui surmontent le temple d'Hatshepsout et celui de Thoutmosis III. C'est un autre projet conjoint polono-égyptien. Depuis peu, nous sommes également associés à la fouille française de Dendara. En revanche, la fouille de Tell-Atrib dans le Delta vient d'être close. Ce site a fourni ces dernières années des témoignages abondants de caractère très particulier d'une installation hellénistique.

Les époques plus récentes sont représentées notamment par les travaux dans le monastère de Naqloni et dans les ermitages dispersés dans le gebel voisin à la lisière du Fayoum. Le site est fouillé depuis une quinzaine d'années par Wlodzimierz Godlewski qui a mis au jour, entre autres, d'importants documents sur papyrus et sur parchemin. Récemment, des peintures datant du XIe siècle sont apparues sous le crépi dans l'église conventuelle toujours en service, et déjà restaurées par nos soins.

Encore plus près de nous, le mausolée de l'émir Qurqumas, mort en 1510, objet de l'attention des restaurateurs polonais. Ce monument de la grande nécropole mamelouke du Caire sera lui aussi bientôt rendu au public, avec ses dépendances et sa mosquée.

Neues zu Pap.Gardiner II (BM EA 10676)

Louise Gestermann
Universität Bonn

Der Papyrus, um den es im folgenden gehen soll (P.Gard.II), ist an sich hinlänglich bekannt und für die Forschung zugänglich. Tatsächlich trifft dies jedoch nur auf die Texte des Papyrus zu, die—in einer überaus zuverlässigen Abschrift—in die Edition der Sargtexte aufgenommen wurden, die Adriaan de Buck zusammengestellt und seit 1935 veröffentlicht hat. Der Papyrus selbst muß demgegenüber nach wie vor als unpubliziert gelten.[1] Dieser Umstand dürfte mit dazu beigetragen haben, daß verschiedene Fragen zum Papyrus, wie z.B. die nach seinem Alter oder auch nach seiner Herkunft, kontrovers diskutiert werden und/oder als nicht geklärt angesehen werden müssen. Die Publikation des Papyrus, der sich heute im British Museum (BM) in London befindet, soll dazu beitragen, die Erforschung dieses überaus interessanten Papyrus voranzutreiben.[2] Und in der Tat hat bereits die Durchsicht der archivierten Unterlagen im BM manch bedeutsames Detail für die Bewertung des Papyrus erbracht, dazu im folgenden.

Es waren ursprünglich drei Papyri, die Alan H. Gardiner sehr wahrscheinlich im Winter 1929/1930 in Kairo erwarb (P.Gard.II-IV).[3] Alle drei Papyri beinhalten Sargtexte, und zwar mit einem Spruchmaterial, das in weiten Teilen Überschneidungen zeigt, und alle drei Papyri sollen auch aus derselben Quelle stammen. Die Papyri wurden von Gardiner mit nach London genommen, wo sie allem Anschein nach von Hugo Ibscher aufgerollt und hinter Glas gebracht wurden. Es läßt sich zudem rekonstruieren, daß die Papyri (II-IV) danach an Adriaan de Buck gingen, der sie für seine Sargtextedition bearbeitete.[4] Die drei Papyri wurden schließlich 1933 von Gardiner den Museen in London (P.Gard.II/BM EA 10676), Chicago (P.Gard.III/OIM 14059-87) und Paris (P.Gard.IV/Louvre E 14703) als Geschenk überlassen.

P.Gard.II bzw. EA 10676 nach der derzeit geltenden Inventarnummer des BM ist der am besten erhaltene und längste der drei Gardinerpapyri. Für ihn läßt sich eine Höhe von 21 cm (oder etwas mehr) und eine Gesamtlänge von ca. 10 m rekonstruieren. Der Papyrus enthält 73 Texte (nach der Zählung von de Buck), 51 auf dem rc. und 22 auf dem vs., wobei etwa ein Fünftel des Papyrus nur einseitig, d.h. auf der Vorderseite beschriftet ist.

Die Texte des Papyrus wurden formal wie auch inhaltlich klar gegliedert niedergeschrieben. Der Text der einzelnen Sprüche ist in senkrechten Kolumnen auf den Papyrus übertragen worden. Sofern vorhanden, sind Titel in eine waagerechte Zeile über den jeweiligen Spruch gesetzt, und zwar in der Regel mit roter Tinte. Eine weitere formale Gliederung wurde durch die Einfügung von Trennlinien erreicht. Senkrechte Trennlinien, die über die gesamte beschriftete Höhe gehen, also auch die Kopfzeile mit einschließen, grenzen einzelne Sprüche gegeneinander ab. Trennlinien, die unterhalb der Kopfzeile beginnen, subsumieren demzufolge einzelne Textelemente oder auch mehrere Sprüche unter einem Titel. Auch die Titelzeile kann durch eine obere und eine untere Linie gegen den Haupttext des daruntergeschriebenen Spruchs abgehoben sein. Ebenso wird das beschriebene Feld am unteren Rand mit einer Linie markiert.

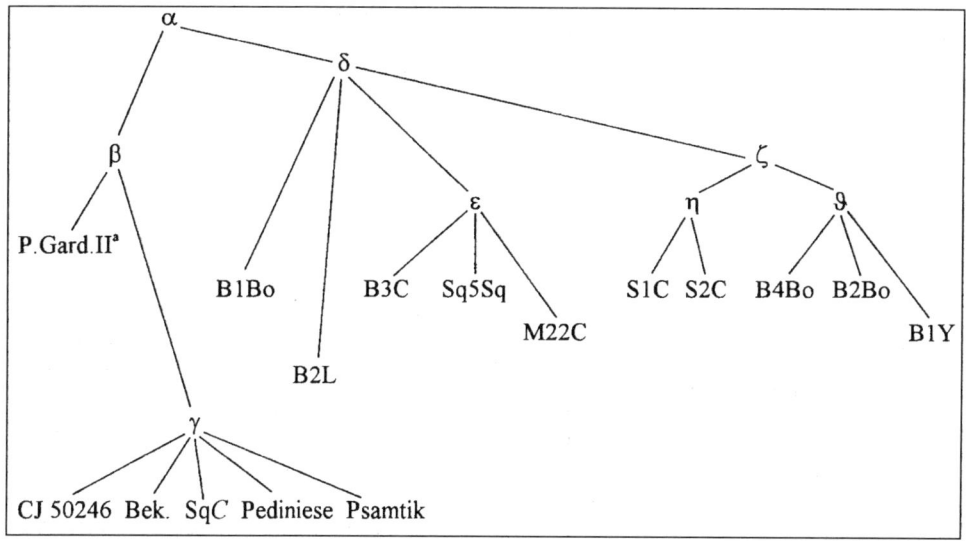

Abb. 1: Stemma zu CT 215.

Dieses deutlich erkennbare Grundschema kann allerdings unterschiedlich ausgearbeitet sein und weist auch gewisse Inkonsequenzen auf. Auffällig ist vor allem, daß die Kopfzeile zwar über weite Strecken durch jeweils eine Linie oben und unten eingeschlossen ist, daß dann aber wieder auf diese Abgrenzung verzichtet wird.[5] An einzelnen Stellen fehlt auch die senkrechte Trennlinie innerhalb einer Spruchsequenz, wo man sie eigentlich erwarten würde.[6] Hierfür wird man zumindest teilweise Nachlässigkeiten des Schreibers verantwortlich machen können.

Aber auch inhaltlich ist der Papyrus einem klaren Aufbau unterworfen. Und zwar sind auf dem Papyrus jeweils mehrere Texte hintereinandergesetzt, die sich unter einem Thema zusammenfassen lassen. So beginnt der Papyrus mit neun Transformations- oder Verwandlungssprüchen, abzulesen an der Verwendung des Terminus *ḫpr m* "(sich) verwandeln in" (CT 986–988, CT 288, CT 989–993). Auf sie folgen zwei Sprüche, die sich mit Thot beschäftigen (CT 994–995), zu denen möglicherweise auch noch CT 996 zu zählen ist. Der sich anschließende Text (CT 997) läßt sich wegen seines hohen Zerstörungsgrades nicht zwingend zuordnen. Es folgen CT 120–128, neun Texte, die den Himmelsaufstieg des Verstorbenen thematisieren und denen zugleich ein Wortspiel um die Zahlenkette bis neun immanent ist. Diese Sequenz ist im übrigen bereits in Pyramiden des

Alten Reiches belegt (s. auch noch im folgenden). Daran wiederum schließen sich zwei Texte an (CT 998–999), die als Gemeinsamkeit die beiden einleitenden Worte *rḫ rn* haben, also "den Namen kennen" (usw.). An drei Stellen des Papyrus sind Sprüche zur Zeit noch unter "Varia" zusammengefaßt, da sich der Zusammenhalt der Texte noch nicht gänzlich erschließt. Es gibt aber bereits Hinweise darauf, daß auch diese Einteilung noch zu revidieren bzw. zu konkretisieren ist.

Wir haben demzufolge mit P.Gard.II eine Textsammlung vor uns, in der die Sprüche nach Themen gegliedert erfaßt sind. Diese Ordnung ist anderen Kriterien zur Seite zu stellen, mit denen für die Funktion des Papyrus als Vorlagenpapyrus ("master copy") argumentiert werden kann. Die zumindest beabsichtigte Verwendung aller drei Gardinerpapyri zum Zweck der Weitergabe von Texten ist ja bereits früher angenommen worden.[7] Indiz hierfür ist zum einen die Verwendung von Papyrus als Textträger. An dieser Einschätzung ändert auch die Tatsache nichts, daß bei wenigstens einem Papyrus mit Sargtexten (dem Berliner Sargtextpapyrus 10482) davon auszugehen ist, daß er als Grabbeigabe diente.[8] Zum anderen ist darauf hinzuweisen, daß der Papyrus durchgängig in der 1. Person (Singular) formuliert ist und darüber hinaus keinerlei Dedikation enthält.

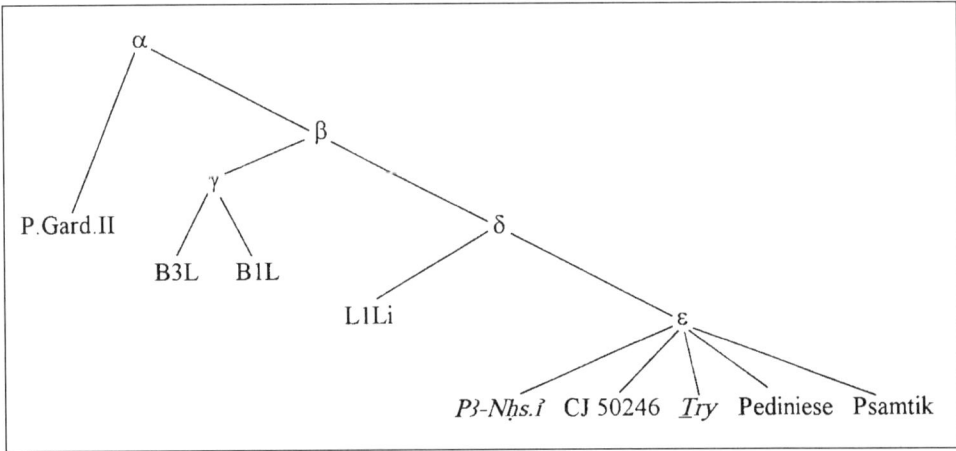

Abb. 2: Stemma zu CT 301.

Direkte Abschriften von P.Gard.II sind—dies sei vorweggenommen—nicht belegt. Es läßt sich aber die überlieferungsgeschichtliche Stellung von P.Gard.II recht klar bestimmen, die Stellung also, die der Papyrus bei der Weitergabe der Texte einnahm, die auf ihm belegt sind. Allerdings ist textkritisches Arbeiten, das allein eine entsprechende Aussage erlaubt, in nur eingeschränktem Maße möglich. Dies ist darin begründet, daß von den 73 Texten auf dem Papyrus 36 (und somit die Hälfte) überhaupt nur hier belegt sind, sonst aber nicht mehr. 15 weitere Texte kennen wir bislang nur von P.Gard.II und III, womit auch diese Texte für eine textkritische Analyse ausfallen. Es bleiben demnach 22 Sprüche, die mehr als zweimal überliefert sind und damit zumindest eine der Bedingungen für textkritisches Arbeiten erfüllen. Von diesen 22 Sprüchen eignen sich nicht alle in gleichem Maß für eine textkritische Analyse, einige aber eben doch, und darunter auch CT 215, dazu Abb. 1.[9] Wie das Stemma zu CT 215 erkennen läßt, steht P.Gard.II recht weit oben im Stemma und damit früh innerhalb der Überlieferung des Textes. Vorlage b ist einzig mit einigen Textabweichungen zu begründen, die P.Gard.II mit diversen spätzeitlichen Textzeugen teilt, die aus Saqqâra bzw. aus Heliopolis stammen. Ohne diese spätzeitlichen Abschriften würde die Vorlage b entfallen und P.Gard.II wäre direkt von a abhängig. Es ist außerdem erkennbar, daß P.Gard.II von der Tradition in Mittelägypten etwas separiert steht. Andere Sprüche wie z.B. CT 227 oder CT 301 (dazu Abb. 2, s. a. Anm. 9) bestätigen diese Einschätzungen, wonach P.Gard.II für eine recht frühe Überlieferung steht und zugleich keine besondere Nähe zu Textzeugen aus Mittelägypten aufweist. Besonders aufschlußreich ist allerdings die Spruchfolge CT 120 -128, die auch schon aus dem Alten Reich überliefert ist (dazu Abb. 3).[10] Wie schon kurz erwähnt, kleidet diese Sequenz das behandelte Thema, den Himmelsaufstieg des Verstorbenen, in ein Wortspiel ein. P.Gard.II nimmt bei dieser Spruchfolge eine Mittlerstellung zwischen den Textbezeugungen aus der 6. Dynastie in Saqqâra - dies sind Phiops I. und Neith - und solchen aus dem Mittleren Reich in Ober- und Mittelägypten ein. G2T (aus al-Gabalain) steht dabei bekanntermaßen für eine frühe Tradition der Sargtexte.

Diese Ergebnisse der textkritischen Arbeiten an P.Gard.II ließen zwei Fragen immer dringlicher werden, und zwar die nach dem Alter des Papyrus sowie die nach seiner Herkunft.

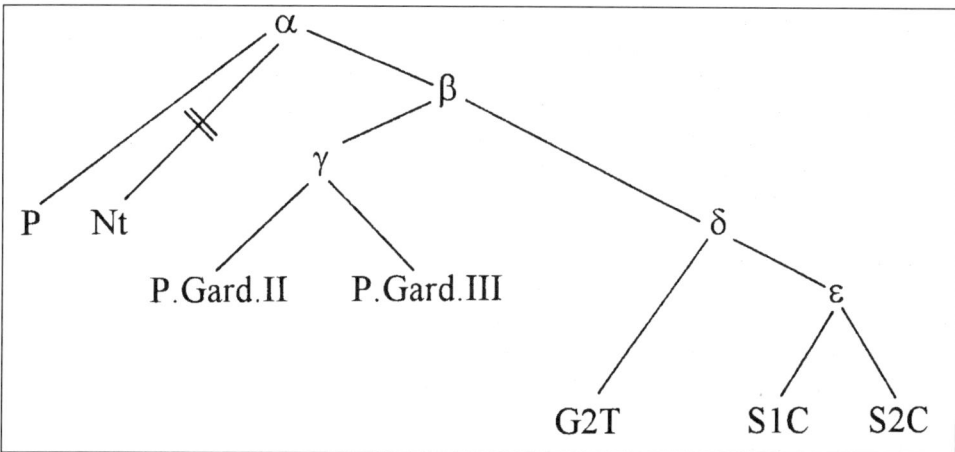

Abb. 3: Stemma zu CT 120–128.

Was den Entstehungszeitpunkt des Papyrus anbelangt, so stehen zwei Datierungsvorschläge im Raum, die verhältnismäßig stark voneinander abweichen. Gardiner war in einer Beschreibung des Papyrus für das BM davon ausgegangen, daß er aus dem Ende des Alten Reiches stammt.[11] Diese Einschätzung ist auch von anderen Wissenschaftlern und bis heute vertreten worden,[12] doch hat sich zugleich eine zweite Meinung in dieser Frage herauskristallisiert, die für den Beginn der 12. Dynastie als Entstehungszeitpunkt des Papyrus plädiert.[13] In beiden Fällen, d.h. sowohl bei der frühen wie auch der späten Datierung (relativ gesehen natürlich) wird mit der Paläographie der Texte argumentiert, die eben in die eine oder andere Richtung weisen soll.

Das Stichwort "Datierung" ist in diesem Kontext letztlich mehrdeutig und somit auch etwas ungenau, denn Bezugsgröße kann der Textträger, können aber auch die Texte selbst sein. Wie bereits dargelegt, läßt sich für die textkritisch bearbeiteten Sprüche eine Zugehörigkeit der Versionen von P.Gard.II zu einer frühen Überlieferungsphase der jeweiligen Texte ableiten. Dies ist m.E. für alle Texte auf dem Papyrus anzunehmen. Grob läßt sich etwa das Ende der 6. Dynastie in Betracht ziehen. Auch einzelne Schreibungen deuten auf eine Abfassung der Texte – frühestens – zu diesem Zeitpunkt hin, z. B. die Schreibung der Pronomen der 1. Person (Singular) mit Schilfblatt und sitzendem Mann. Sie kommt beim absoluten bzw. selbständigen Pronomen erst nach der 6. Dynastie auf.[14] Ob damit aber zugleich der Zeitpunkt der Niederschrift der Texte auf dem Papyrus bestimmt werden kann, ist durchaus fraglich. Denn diese könnte auch noch später und dann auf der Grundlage einer relativ alten Vorlage erfolgt sein. Die Paläographie ist in dieser Situation natürlich das gefragte Kriterium.[15] Eine Beurteilung der Handschrift fällt indes schwer, was einerseits auf Eigentümlichkeiten der Handschrift bei der Wiedergabe der einzelnen Zeichen und andererseits auf das nur in geringem Umfang vorhandene und nicht immer sicher datierte Vergleichsmaterial zurückzuführen ist. Nach einem ersten Durchgang durch die Paläographie des Papyrus und auf der Grundlage eines Vergleichs einzelner hieratischer Zeichen möchte ich derzeit davon ausgehen, daß auch die Beschriftung des Papyrus zum Ende der 6. Dynastie, wahrscheinlicher zu Beginn der "1. Zwischenzeit" erfolgte. Diese Frage kann aber noch nicht als abschließend behandelt angesehen werden, sondern erfordert weitere Arbeiten.

Eine Angabe dazu, woher P.Gard.II stammt, wurde von de Buck bei der Veröffentlichung der Texte des Papyrus nicht gemacht ("Provenience unknown").[16] Dessen ungeachtet hat sich die Meinung etabliert, P.Gard.II würde aus Asyūṭ stammen[17] – anfänglich offensichtlich angeregt durch den Berliner Sargtextpapyrus 10482, der nach Händlerangaben von dort stammen soll.[18] Eine angenommene Herkunft von P.Gard.II aus Asyūṭ fügt sich jedoch nicht oder nur schwer nachvollziehbar zu den Resultaten der zuvor dargelegten textkritischen Arbeit an dem Papyrus. Erfreulicherweise brachte dann auch die Suche in den Unterlagen des BM in dieser Frage einen weiterführenden Hinweis. Wie Gardiner in der schon zitierten Beschreibung des Papyrus für das BM ebenfalls mitteilte, hatte er, als er die Papyri erhielt, für diese auch eine Herkunftsangabe bekommen. Sie sollen aus Saqqāra stammen.[19] Dies fügt sich nun in geradezu vortrefflicher Weise nicht nur zu der zeitlichen Stellung, die m.E. für P.Gard.II anzunehmen ist, sondern auch zu dem Platz, den der Papyrus bei der Weitergabe einzelner - oder vielleicht auch aller- Texte einnimmt. Es ist ja (s. zuvor) für den Papyrus nicht nur eine Mittlerstellung zwischen Altem und Mittleren Reich zu beobachten, sondern auch zwischen der Überlieferung im Norden, d. h. in Saqqāra, und im Süden des Landes.[20]

Wir haben also mit P.Gard.II eine Sammlung von Sargtextsprüchen vor uns, die mit einiger Wahrscheinlichkeit in Saqqāra und möglicherweise schon zum Ende der 6. Dynastie oder dem Beginn der "1. Zwischenzeit" angefertigt wurde. Die Texte selbst werden aus der ausgehenden 6. Dynastie stammen.[21] Der formale Aufbau des Papyrus wie auch seine inhaltliche Gliederung legen nahe, in ihm einen Vorlagenpapyrus zu sehen, der dazu diente, Texte von einem Textträger auf einen zweiten zu übertragen. Ob dieser Papyrus letztendlich auch tatsächlich dafür benutzt wurde (und nicht z. B. als Grabbeigabe Verwendung fand), läßt sich nicht mehr feststellen. Direkte Abschriften vom Papyrus jedenfalls sind nicht nachweisbar.

Manche Frage zu P.Gard.II wird man derzeit als noch nicht definitiv geklärt ansehen müssen, und manches ist noch weiter zu prüfen. So können diese Ausführungen nur eine Art Zwischenbericht sein. Für alles weitere ist auf die Publikation von P.Gard.II verweisen, die sich in Arbeit befindet.

Notes:

1 Die photographische Wiedergabe eines einzelnen Blattes des Papyrus findet sich bei Janine Bourriau, Pharaohs and Mortals. Egyptian art in the Middle Kingdom, Cambridge 1988, Abb. zu Nr. 64, S. 82.

2 Zu danken habe ich schon jetzt dem BM, London, und insbesondere William V. Davies für die erteilte Publikationserlaubnis sowie Richard B. Parkinson für seine stete und hilfsbereite Unterstützung bei meiner Arbei an dem Papyrus.

3 Dies geht aus der Korrespondenz zwischen Gardiner und James H. Breasted hervor, die im Oriental Institute Museum (OIM), Chicago, aufbewahrt wird. Karen L. Wilson und John A. Larson vom OIM waren so freundlich, mir die entsprechenden Auszüge zukommen zu lassen, wofür ihnen gleichfalls schon an dieser Stelle gedankt sei.

4 Die entsprechenden Auskünfte verdanke ich zum Teil wiederum der im OIM archivierten Korrespondenz zwischen Gardiner und Breasted (s. die vorangehende Anm.) sowie Informationen aus den im BM aufbewahrten Unterlagen (vgl. Anm. 2).

5 Dies ist u.a. auf dem Verso der Fall.

6 Z. B. nach dem Spruch 125 (Kol. 164) der Sequenz CT 120–128.

7 Zu dieser Einschätzung vgl. u. a. Dieter Müller, Rezension von Adriaan de Buck, The Egyptian Coffin Texts VII, OIP LXXXVII, Chicago/Illinois 1961, in: BiOr XX, 1963, S. 246–250 (S. 248); Dino Bidoli, Die Sprüche der Fangnetze in den altägyptischen Sargtexten, ADAIK 9, Glückstadt 1976, S. 18 und S. 25; Günter Lapp, Die Papyrusvorlagen der Sargtexte, in: SAK 16, 1989, S. 171–202 (S. 172); Bourriau, Pharaohs and Mortals (s. Anm. 1), S. 82.

8 Vgl. hierzu Peter Jürgens, Der Tote als Mittler zwischen Mensch und Göttern im Berliner Sargtexte-Papyrus. Ein Zeugnis inoffizieller Religion aus dem Mittleren Reich, in: GM 116, 1990, S. 51–63.

9 Für die Details der textkritischen Bearbeitung von CT 215, CT 227 und CT 301 (dazu im folgenden und Abb. 2) vgl. Louise Gestermann, Die Überlieferung ausgewählter Texte altägyptischer Totenliteratur ("Sargtexte") in spätzeitlichen Grabanlagen (wird in ÄA erscheinen).

10 Eine Bearbeitung dieser Spruchgruppe durch die Verf. soll demnächst vorgelegt werden.

11 Dies geht aus den Unterlagen hervor, die ich im BM, London, einsehen konnte, s. Anm. 2.

12 Für eine Datierung in die 6. Dynastie s. Thomas G. Allen, The Occurrences of Pyramid Texts with Cross Indexes of These and Other Egyptian Mortuary Texts, SAOC 27, Chicago/Illinois 1950, S. 30f.; Alessandro Roccati, La littérature historique sous l'Ancien Empire égyptien, LAPO 11, Paris 1982, S. 18.

13 S. z. B. Bourriau, Pharaohs and Mortals (s. Anm. 1), S. 81f.

14 Elmar Edel, Altägyptische Grammatik, AnOr 34/39, Roma 1955/1964, § 173, S. 79f.; s.a. Wolfgang Schenkel, Eine Konkordanz zu den Sargtexten und die Graphien der 1. Person Singular, in: Harco Willems (Hrg.), The World of the Coffin Texts. Proceedings of the Symposium Held on the Occasion of the 100th Birthday of Adriaan de Buck, Leiden, December 17–19, 1992, Egyptologische Uitgaven IX, Leiden 1996, S. 115–127 (S. 122ff.).

15 Vgl. neben Georg Möller, Hieratische Paläographie. Die ägyptische Buchschrift in ihrer Entwicklung von der frühen Dynastie bis zur römischen Kaiserzeit I, Leipzig 1909, auch Hans Goedicke, Old Hieratic Paleography, Baltimore/Maryland 1988, der die Gardinerpapyri mit aufgenommen hat.

16 Adriaan de Buck, The Egyptian Coffin Texts II, OIP XLIX, Chicago/Illinois 1938, S. XII.

17 So z. B. D. Bidoli, Die Sprüche der Fangnetze (s. Anm. 7), S. 25; W. Schenkel, in: The World of the Coffin Texts (s. Anm. 14), S. 124f.

18 Hermann Grapow, Über einen ägyptischen Totenpapyrus aus dem frühen mittleren Reich, in: SPAW XXV, Berlin 1915, S. 376–384 (S. 377).

19 S. A. Alessandro Roccati, Magia e letteratura Nell'Egitto del II millenio A.C., in: Melanges Adolphe

Gutbub, OrMonsp 2, Montpellier 1984, S. 201-210 (S. 208, Anm. 3).

20 Warum Gardiner bzw. de Buck den Hinweis auf Saqqāra nicht weitergaben, ließ sich bislang leider nicht klären.

21 Gleiche Eckdaten dürften für P.Gard.III und IV gelten, was aber noch genauer untersucht werden müßte.

An Analysis of Various Anatomical Parts of Egyptian Mummies from Museum Collections in Spain*

Ángel González y Arema
International Association of Egyptologists

The purpose of this work is to study some anatomical remains of ancient Egypt. Each one of these is from a separate and anonymous individual, although the final of the four crania included in this study could possibly be identified among the members of the family of Sennedjem. This hypothesis will be put forward here. Each of these relics were brought to Spain as a result of the work of three men whose collections were developed almost contiguously.

Pedro González de Velasco (1815–1882)

At the middle of the last century, the ideas expressed by Charles Darwin were causing considerable agitation among the intellectual Spaniards, and it was in this context that the Museo Antropológico in Madrid was founded in 1875 to house the private collection of its founder, Dr. Velasco. In time, the Sección de Antropología Física of the museum brought together a noteworthy collection of items related to the human body. The presentation of two mummified heads from this collection will form part of this paper.

Eduard Toda i Güell (1859–1941)

Eduard Toda i Güell served in Egypt as a member of the diplomatic corps from 1884 to 1886. He was present when the excavation of the tomb of Sennedjem was undertaken in 1886. On his return to Spain, he donated his personal collection of Egyptian antiquities with half given to the Museo Arqueológico Nacional in Madrid, including the foot that will be analyzed in this paper, and the remainder donated to the Museu Víctor Balaguer in Vilanova i la Geltrú (Barcelone), whose skulls and hand will be included in this study.

Tomás de Asensi[1]

Tomás de Asensi traveled widely in Africa and Asia and on these journeys he accumulated an impressive number of antiquities and items of ethnographic interest destined for the Museo

Arqueológico Nacional. There were 417 Egyptian pieces including a hand with a carnelian ring on its little finger. This item will be discussed below.

Case no. 1

Hand currently in the collection of the Museo Arqueológico Nacional (inventory number 15120), whose identity, age at time of death, gender, and provenance in Egypt remain unknown. It date probably spans the Late Period. It was donated among the personal collection of Tomás de Asensi and measures 18.5 cm in length and 7.5 in width. The surface is entirely black and is hard and brittle. There are several cracks on the fingers and the palm. The epidermis has been lost on the exterior except for the fingertips. The dermatoglyphs and nails are present on all of the fingers. There are a number of remains of hardened bandage fragments still attached as well as impressions of where these had been. Muscular fibers are reddish, filiform and are firmly adhered. The tendons are easy to see on the back. This hand was cut from the corpse near the wrist, against which some kind of instrument was used as a lever. There are a number of small whitish spots scattered across the hand; it is possible that this results from fungi. The little finger has been completely detached. An amber-brown carnelian ring, in a very good state of preservation, was placed on that finger. It has been carved from a single piece using emery. The date of this piece is also the Late Period. It seems doubtful that the ring originally belonged to this hand given that the surface shows no signs of staining from the substances used during the embalming process nor the remains of a ring print.

Case no. 2

Hand currently in the collection of the Museu Víctor Balaguer (inv. no. 3982), whose identity and age at time of death remain unknown. According to Eduard Toda, the hand belonged to a woman from the Twelfth Dynasty. He obtained this piece during his stay in Gebelein between 1884 and 1886. The surface is covered with a resinous substance and natron salts were detected. This is a common characteristic of the mummies from the Middle Kingdom, so it is feasible to establish a dating within this period. No exhaustive investigation work was previously carried out on this hand nor has the piece has undergone any operation to restore or consolidate it. Indeed, at the present time, all that remains is a quantity of disarticulated bones gradually being reduced to dust in a process of continuous decay. In 1887, the hand still preserved its integrity, however 100 years later its fragmentary state and deterioration are clearly evident and is acknowledged in the museum's current catalog.

Case no. 3

Foot currently in the collection of the Museo Arqueológico Nacional (inv. no. 15211), whose identity, age, and gender remain uncertain. Eduard Toda obtained it somewhere in the Theban region on 1877. He dated it to the Twenty-sixth Dynasty, though this dating could be broadened to cover the whole of the Late Period. This foot has not previously been published. It retains the same aspect it had when it came to the museum. Its principal measurements are 21.5 cm in length and 7 cm in width. Traces of the ingredients used during embalming operations still remain, mainly on the surfaces of the toes and the tendons. Fingerprints are present on the toes with the exception of the second and third; all of the toenails are also preserved. This foot is classified among the denominated 'Egyptian Feet' because its big toe is shorter than the second one. Likewise, it could be classified as a 'Concave Foot,' although this observation should be made with some reservation because it could possibly have been deformed by the pressure of the bandaging. The skin is brittle and similar to papier mâché and it is completely split open in large cracks in numerous areas. A fragment of epidermis is missing on the sole and the tendons are totally exposed. Indeed, the calcaneus bone is almost entirely visible. This must have happened when the corpse was being handled by embalmers, because the tone of this bone is blackish due to direct contact with the compound also poured over the skin. Also, the only remains of wrapping on the foot are stuck to the bone itself with no skin layer in between. The most significant damage suffered by this piece took place when it was exposed to the open air and severed from the rest of the body.

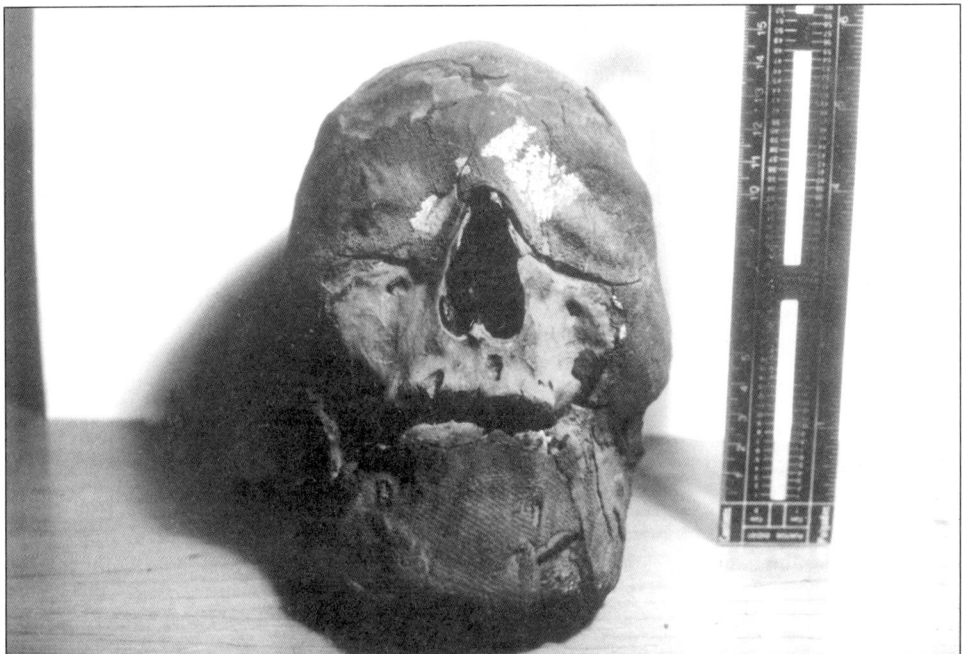

Figure 1

Case no. 4

Head currently in the collection of the Museo Nacional de Antropología (inv. no. 9529 [fig. 1]), whose identity remains unknown. This piece dates from the first half of the Roman Period (first-second centuries CE). With regard to the gender, we conclude the subject to be female because there is no prominent frontal and occipital protuberances and the mastoid apophyses are not large. Her age at time of death is possible to discern if we consider the degree of dental wear. When these pieces are compared with a group of samples whose age is confirmed, it is possible to infer that this person would have died at between 45 to 60 years of age. Its provenance is from one of the Theban cemeteries. The mouth is open; the opening possibly results from some form of ritual. The lips are entirely missing. There are no teeth left on the upper maxilla, but all teeth and molars present in the lower jaw show wear on the cutting edges. The second premolar and the first, second, and third molars on both sides of the upper jaw; the first molar on the right side of the lower maxilla, and the first and second premolars of both ascending rami of the lower jaw were lost prior to death; in each of these cases, alveolar absorption can be clearly discerned. The mesial and distal incisors, the first molar of both sides, and the left canine on the upper maxilla are missing, and alveoli present. On the right side, above the mesial and distal incisors and the canine there are root abscesses. There are also two abscesses over the first premolars on both sides. These can be caused by a severe dental attrition and relates to the condition in which we find the remaining teeth on the lower jaw. Given that abscesses are, in effect, deposits of pus, septicaemia could be concluded as one of the causes of death. The septum nasi and the bridge of the nose are completely absent. The ethmoid bone appears intact as the practice of excerebration was not performed. The eyes are entirely covered by wrappings. There are objects made of an unknown material placed over the eye sockets. Both ears are presents, but hidden by the linen of the wrappings. There is no sign of any hair on the exposed parts of the head. The aspect of the scalp is very fragile and brittle. If we look at the inner part of the cranial cavity through the foramen magnum, again it is clear that no brain evisceration was performed. In fact, parts of the encephalic mass are still adhered to the inner walls of the cranial cavity. There are also no cervical vertebrae present. It is feasible to affirm that this head belonged to a Mediterranean individual, slender and small, similar to those of other studied previously belonging to this period and general location. The bandages are soaked in a resinous substance. They appear to be adhered to the epidermis, in those places where skin remains and, if not, directly to the bone. They have been made from fine linen. It is possible to observe three gold leaf stuck onto these bandages. The injuries caused after death have been caused mainly by carelessness in the treatment of the corpse during the embalming process and the plundering suffered later on the body. It is highly probable that barely a disarticulated skeleton from the body when the preparation began. This would explain why the drainage of the brain was not carried out and also why the gold leaf is stuck to the wrappings and not directly to skin.

Case no. 5

Skull currently in the collection of the Museo Nacional de Antropología (inv. no. 9528 [fig. 2]), whose identity remains unknown. This skull can be dated within the first half of the Roman Period (first-second centuries CE). With regard to its gender, once we take into account that the

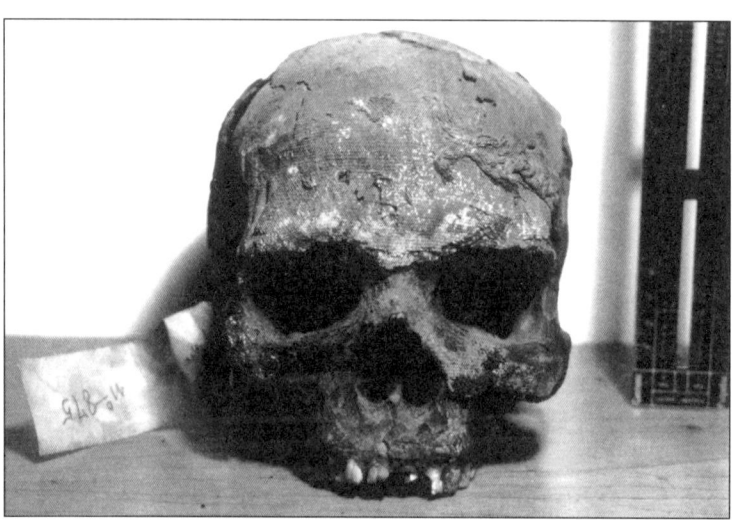

Figure 2

frontal protuberance is very prominent, as is the case with the occipital as well, and mastoid apophyses are well developed, it can be affirmed that this cranium belongs to a male. His age at time of death is possible to discern if we analyze the sagital suture, the only one visible. In this way it is possible to tell that the end of this individual's life came some time between the ages of 18 and 29. This fact is confirmed by the degree of dental wear when compared with the state of teeth of a number of specimens, all of them persons whose death has been verified to have occurred between these ages. It is known that its provenance in Egypt is the archaeological site of Thebes, perhaps from Deir al-Bahari, if we take into account the degree of similarity between this piece and two other specimens whose provenance from this area is well known. It has remained unstudied until this time. The lower mandible is missing. The mesial and distal incisors of both sides as well as the right canine show their pulp chambers as a consequence of traumatic lesions suffered after death. Complete alveolar absorption is perceptible in the first and second molars of both sides of the upper jaw; these molars were lost during the individual's lifetime. There is no evidence of the ethmoid bone having received any damage. The eye sockets are empty. Also, there are no vestiges of the outer ears. The hair and traces of epidermis could not be seen. If some of these were still preserved, it would have to be in the part of the cranial vault which is still wrapped. After the observation of the inner part of the cranial cavity, through the foramen magnum, it is clear that the brain had never in fact been removed. None of the cervical vertebrae are present. This piece also belongs to a Mediterranean, slender, small type of person. The wrappings are made of linen bandages soaked in resin to the extent that those in contact with the cranium form a true amalgam with it. These bandages currently present a cracked appearance and a tendency to fall off in fragments. Postmortem damage must have been exacerbated by the poor quality of the embalming work, whereby the decayed state of the corpse would explain why excerebration was not practiced.

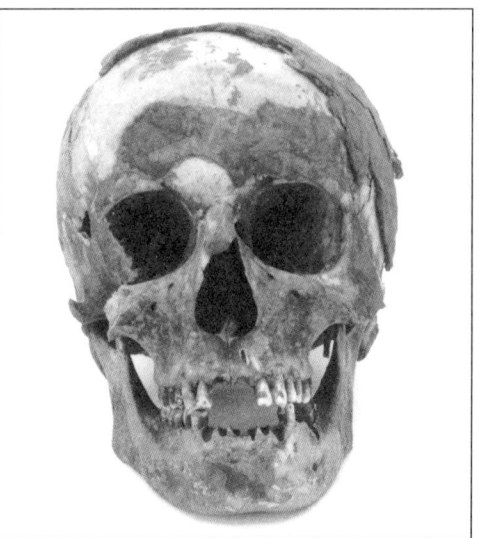

Figure 3

Case no. 6

This skull, whose identity remains unknown, is in the collection of the Biblioteca-Museu Víctor Balaguer (inv. no. 3977 [fig. 3]). This piece was dated in the Ptolemaic Period by Eduard Toda. This age can be validated and indeed extended to the first half of the Roman Period (first–second centuries CE). During this period, the absence of incisors in both maxillars is very frequent in contemporary mummies, perhaps due to carelessness or to a ritual connected with the ceremony of the Opening of the Mouth, as could have happened with piece no. 4 among those presented in this paper. Its identity remains un known. With regard to its gender, this skull was classified as that of a male. Its approximate age at the time of death corresponds to an individual who was in the third decade of his life, according to the analysis of dental wear and the phase of external closing of cranial sutures. This skull was acquired in Saqqara. This piece has been investigated by Dr. Domingo Campillo, a medical forensic and anthropologist, and was also referred to briefly in two books.[2] The loss of all incisors in both jaws might have resulted from the inserting of stuffing into the interior of the mouth. Some wear is evident on the cutting edges of the remaining teeth. Tooth losses with alveoli remaining are the mesial and distal incisors from the right and left sides of both maxillars and both canines of the lower mandible. The teeth in which apical holes are evident are the second pre-molar and the first molar from the left ascending ramus of the lower maxillar: in both of these latter cases, pus infection has been highly severe, connecting both adjoining cavities before coming to the surface and destroying part of the maxillar tissue, just above the chin cavity. There is the possibility that the infection caused by these abscesses became generalized and could have proved the cause of the death. Also, it is necessary to emphasize the presence of a slow alveolar resorption in all premolars and molars of both ascending rami of the lower maxillar. This process commonly originates from periodontal disease. Also, the apical alveolar side of the mesial and distal incisors of the upper left jaw show irregularly-edged and elongated perforations produced by post-mortem erosion in this area. Both horizontal portions of palatine bone are completely lacking. Their removal was due to the evisceration of the brain. On the other hand, it is possible that this situation is connected with the presence of an irregular hole at the back to the right of the foramen magnum because there is no sign of cicatrization in this perforation. Both the palatal region and the surrounding area, appear covered with a resinous substance. It was precisely in the first half of the Roman Period that a number of archaic practices were carried out on mummies. Specifically, this trepanation, if of funerary origin, would go back to the Middle Kingdom. The nasal fossae are visible. The septum nasi has been broken as has the lower part of the left nasal bone. The ethmoidal cribriform plate has been pierced because excerebration was done through this passage. The eye sockets are empty and both septa have been deliberately broken. The medial part of the left zygomatic arch and, to the right, this bone with the complete malar, have disappeared. Both losses could be related to these holes from the septa of both eye sockets. Some fragments of epicranial tissue are still adhered, and cover most of the lower part of the forehead. There are two perforations, produced post-mortem, which run through the right temporal squama following the line of the temporoparietal suture. The entire temporoccipital region is covered in cracks; this appears to be due to negligent post-mortem treatment. A large extent of the cranial vault is still covered by a very thin layer of linen, protecting what remains of the hair and scalp. These appear impregnated by a resinous substance which has solidified. The hair is straight, with an average length of some two centimeters. Their color goes from dark brown to reddish, but these alterations in the color of the hair are due to the dyeing properties of some substances used during the embalming process. The hair must originally have been black. The radiographic examination confirms the extraction of the brain through the nasal passage. The interior of the cranial cavity is covered uniformly with resin and there are remains of the encephalic mass left inside. This individual has been classified as a slender, small, Mediterranean-type person. The rest of the injuries received after death would appear to be connected with the sacking of the tomb or with the conditions in which the mummy was transported from Egypt.

Case no. 7

Skull currently in the collection of the Biblioteca-Museu Víctor Balaguer (inv. no. 3978 [fig. 4]), whose identity remains unknown. Its date and provenance in Egypt are known with certainty: this individual lived during the Nineteenth Dynasty, precisely during the reign of Userma'atre'setepenre Ramses II. The corpse was found in the tomb of Sennedjem, in Deir al-Medina (TT 1). We know that it belongs to a female. However, the further re-examination of the lower mandible suggests that this last could come from a male corpse, so the present piece could be the result of an assemblage made some time after excavation. With regard to her age at the time of death, she was in her thirties. This assertion is confirmed by the analysis of her cranial sutures and the study of the wear on the remaining teeth. All of the teeth of the upper arcade are lost. Dental loss where the corresponding alveoli remain is the case with all of the pieces in the upper jaw with the exception of the first premolar because it appears that the alveolar absorption had begun here. We deduce from this that the woman lost this piece during her lifetime. The remaining teeth mentioned could have fallen out after death. The only dental remain present is one root of the distal incisor of the left side of the upper jaw because its outer part was broken down. Also, there is a hole, situated over the apical side of the first premolar, of post-mortem origin due to erosion. The

Figure 4

back half of the right canine fosse has been lost due to traumatic post-mortem injury. With regard to the lower mandible, 13 of the 16 teeth remain in place, but those missing, all molars, give the appearance of never having come through, due to congenital factors. All of the teeth show a moderate amount of wear on their cutting edges. There are remains of some form of resinous material accumulated below the alveolar insertions. There are only traces of the soft parts of the head, located mainly running from the symphysis of the chin to the beginning of the left coronoid apophysis. Otherwise, this skull appears clean. The nassal fossae have been altered because of the deliberate breaking of the septum nasi and the piercing of the cribriform plate of the ethmoid from the practice of excerebration through the nose. In fact, the whole of this area is pierced through to the inner zone of the cranial cavity as seen in the radiographic examination. There are remains of the brain left inside after draining. This woman also belongs to a slender, small, Mediterranean group of people. There are no traces of bandages stuck on the head. This mummification was carelessly done. Possibly, it was reduced to a skeleton when the treatment began.

With regard to identification among the relatives of Sennedjem, Eduard Toda wrote a complete account of the items from Sennedjem's hypogeum, which included a list of the mummies found there.[3] He classified them into two groups. The first group was composed of nine corpses with their own sarcophagi, with inscriptions giving their names. From this list we can discard the following: Sennedjem; Ii-neferti, his wife; Rahotep and Khonsw, their sons; Tamaket, Khonsw's wife; Isis, their daughter and probable wife of Khabekhnet, another son; Hathor, another daughter; Rames, a son or grandson of the proprietor; and Taaskhsen, who possibly shared a common father with Sennedjem. The second group is composed of eleven mummies, none of them with any sarcophagi. Toda affirmed that he ordered that only the heads be preserved for their potential ethnographical interest.[4] He referred literally to Neferirut, a daughter of Sennedjem; Khabekhnet, a son; Ranekhu, a son or grandson of the proprietor; Hetepet, a daughter or a granddaughter; Piay and Anhotep, sons of Khabekhnet and Sahte; Amennakht, a son of Khonsw and

Tamaket; Khahetepneferrempet, Habekent and Mesu, men; and Mess Ruther, gender uncertain. All males and the gender-uncertain case can be ruled out, so the only two remaining females to whom the cranium could be possibly attributed are Neferirut and Hetepet, and this suggestion is advanced here.

Conclusions

These anatomical pieces were all brought to Spain during the last quarter of the nineteenth century, reflecting a desire to acquire specimens for scientific study as a part of the new discipline of the age, anthropology. This was demonstrably the motive for the acquisitions of the head and the skull belonging to the Museo Nacional de Antropología, and that of the female cranium in the Museu Víctor Balaguer, and possibly also that of the skull of a male belonging to the same collection. Collecting items from ancient Egypt was part of the common fashion of the time and this was the case with the two hands and the foot included in this paper. There was also a desire to aquire specimens for scientific study as part of the new discipline of the age, anthropology. This was demonstrably the motive for the acquisition of the head and skull belonging to the Museo Nacional de Antropología, the female cranium of the Museu Víctor Balaguer, and perhaps also the skull of a male in the same collection.

Each of these remains originate from the mummies of separate and anonymous individuals. The only one to have a possible identity attributed to it is the last of the crania discussed here, which could belong to Neferirut, a daughter of Sennedjem, or Hetepet, a daughter or granddaughter of this man. Only four mummies remain from this tomb: Sennedjem, Ii-neferti, Khonsw and Isis, apart from this cranium. This surely augments the important value of this relic.

Each of these pieces has a different provenance within Egypt: Gebelein, Saqqara, and the region of Thebes, especially the area around Deir al-Medina and perhaps, Deir al-Bahari, if not of unknown origin.

With regard to the causes of death, the poor condition of the teeth, with several infected abscesses which would have provoked septicaemiae, could have influenced the exitus letalis of two of these cases, since the rest do not present obvious symptoms from which to draw any conclusion.

Taken as a whole, these can be considered patent testimony to the preoccupation of Spain's intellectuals of the time, as well as to their desire to take on the study of these two newly created sciences, Egyptology and anthropology, clearly related in two of these cases to the diffusion of Charles Darwin's evolutionist theories across Europe.

Notes:

[*] Due to limitations of space, complete endnotes listing the pieces and documents used as a basis for comparison with those discussed in this paper could not be included in this publication.

1 It has not been possible to confirm the dates of birth or death nor the second surname, customarily given

216

in Spain, as this information is not recorded in the archives of Tomás de Asensi in the Museo Arqueológico Nacional.

2 E. Toda i Güell, *Biblioteca-Museu Balaguer: Catálogo de la Colección Egipcia* (Madrid, 1887); T. Montero and J. Padró, *Catalèg del Museu Balaguer: 2 Collecció Egipcia* (Barcelone, 1987).

3 E. Toda i Güell, "Son Notém en Tebas. Inventario y textos de un sepulcro de la XX dinastía," *Estudios Egptológicos* (Madrid, 1887), 22–23.

4 Toda i Güell, "Son Notém en Tebas," 22–23.

Un cas de méningocèle chez un nouveau-né égyptien de la XIe dynastie

R. Grilletto,* E. Fulcheri,** R. Boano,* E. Leospo,*** E. Rabino Massa*

Département de biologie animale et de l'homme - Université de Turin,
*** Département D.I.C.M.I. de l'université de Gênes, *** Musée égyptien de Turin*

La collection ostéologique égyptienne du musée d'Anthropologie de l'université de Turin (Italie) comprend, entre les squelettes complets (611) et les crânes isolés (447), 1058 sujets ; le musée possède également 80 vestiges partiels de momies humaines et 25 momies complètes.

Tous ces exemplaires ont été recueillis par l'anthropologue Giovanni Marro lors des fouilles que le professeur Ernesto Schiaparelli, en premier, et le professeur Giulio Farina, ensuite, avaient conduites en Égypte entre 1911 et 1937.

C'est au cours d'une de ces campagnes archéologiques, à Assiout, que fut trouvée la sépulture d'un enfant de la XIe dynastie (2100–1955 av. J.-C.). Dans sa relation de fouilles, Marro (1952) dit textuellement que cette découverte « concerne la sépulture d'un enfant à l'intérieur d'un panier où le petit cadavre avait été déposé en position fœtale, après avoir été dûment enserré d'étoffes de lin . . . On remarque un grand prolapsus rectal typique, ou, pour mieux dire, le prolapsus d'un considérable segment de la muqueuse rectale, qui a glissé sur la couche musculaire à cause de la lenteur de la sous-muqueuse, naturellement concomitante à l'atonie des sphincters anaux : une incidence qui n'est pas rare de nos jours, dans les premières années de vie de sujets mal nourris ».

Le professeur Marro s'étant limité, pour différentes raisons, à une analyse macroscopique, nous avons donc décidé, dans le but de parvenir à un diagnostic définitif, de soumettre le corps à une étude plus approfondie, qui comprenait des examens radiologiques et histologiques, dont les résultats font l'objet du présent travail.

Matériaux

Le professeur Marro, ayant établi la taille de l'enfant à 70–75 cm, déduisit qu'il était en présence d'« un enfant âgé d'environ un an ».

L'examen de l'état des sutures crâniennes, de la morphologie dentaire et de la taille, qui, après une nouvelle mesuration plus rigoureuse correspond à 55 cm, nous porte à croire qu'il s'agit d'un nouveau-né.

Le petit « est sur le ventre, la tête posée sur la joue gauche, les genoux appuyés sur le fond du panier, le dos fortement cambré ...»

Cette position « met en relief une saillie jaunâtre, bien visible, en direction longitudinale de forme ovale, presque réniforme (de 5,5 cm de long, 2,3 cm de haut et de 3 cm de largeur max.) ; une lésion accidentelle, provoquée lors de notre déplacement, permet de relever l'extrême minceur de la paroi, presque transparente et fortement racornie ... ; cette saillie est entièrement vide ».

Cette lésion se situe toutefois dans la région lombo-sacrée et non, comme l'avait décrit Marro, « vers le centre, dans la fente des fesses ».

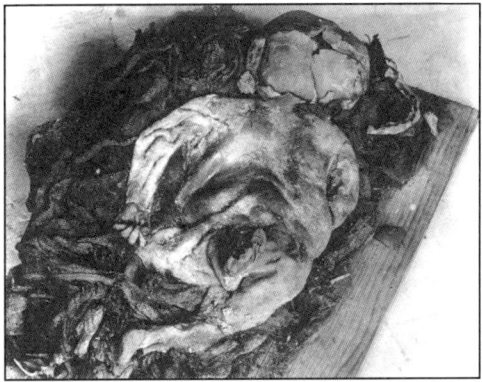

Fig. 1 : Sépulture d'un enfant de la XIe dynastie.

Actuellement cette coupole est cassée et, à sa base, on voit un tissu très compact, sillonné de fines dépressions qui confluent dans une zone centrale déprimée, comme un cratère.

Méthodes

Étude radiologique : l'enfant reposait sur une épaisse couche de sable qui formait, avec le petit corps, un seul bloc ; ceci avait empêché d'obtenir de bonnes radiographies.

Nous avons donc, en premier lieu, enlevé la couche de sable aussi soigneusement et délicatement que possible, puis nous avons réalisé des radiographies selon les paramètres suivants : 180 mA, 39 KV, temps 0,04.

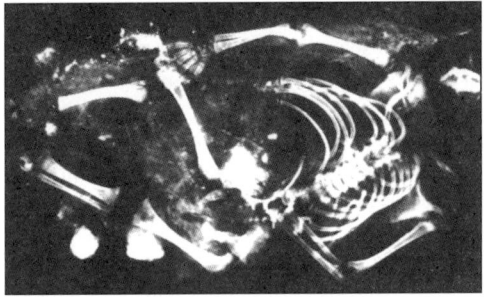

Fig. 2 : Étude radiologique.

Étude histologique : nous avons procédé à l'examen histologique du tissu qui constitue la paroi de la petite coupole. Ce tissu étant extrêmement fragile, nous l'avons d'abord fixé, puis réhydraté selon une technique que nous avons récemment mise au point.

L'échantillon a été fixé dans des vapeurs de formol à 60° C pendant trois heures et réhydraté à 4° C pour une durée variable de quelques minutes à quelques heures, selon la nécessité, dans du plasma humain rendu inactif à 56° C pendant 30 minutes.

Après l'habituelle inclusion en paraffine, nous avons obtenu des coupes microtomiques colorées avec hématoxyline-éosine, Van Gieson, Trichromique de Masson, Toluidin Blue, Weigert.

Résultats

Le nouveau-né avait été placé sur le ventre, avec la main droite sous la région pubienne ; par conséquent la radiographie a donné des résultats peu lisibles, mais nous pouvons néanmoins remarquer un désordre architectural avec disjénésie des dernières vertèbres lombaires et des premières du sacrum.

L'autre partie du sacrum ne présente aucune anomalie, ainsi que les autres vertèbres lombaires et thoraciques.

La radiographie permet de relever une bonne ossification au niveau de tous les os, longs et courts, ce qui exclut une insuffisance alimentaire. Les épiphyses sont encore assez transparentes en accord avec l'âge du sujet. En général, le squelette du nouveau-né ne présente aucune anomalie, si ce n'est l'anomalie vertébrale déjà signalée.

L'analyse histologique révèle une structure composée de faisceaux de fibres de collagène épaisses qui se séparent très facilement.

Les structures musculaires, glandulaires et nerveuses ne sont pas visibles. Il est possible d'identifier un petit vaisseau dans une zone. Il s'agit donc vraisemblablement d'un fragment de peau, présentant le derme papillaire ou réticulaire très mince, dû soit à la distension du tissu, soit au jeune âge du sujet ; nous avons également relevé une totale épidermolyse. Cet état est évidemment plus accentué puisqu'il s'agit de la peau d'un nouveau-né et non de celle d'un adulte.

Discussion

L'examen macroscopique, au vu de la localisation de la lésion et de la conformation de la masse, nous fait pencher pour un diagnostic de méningocèle. La masse est constituée d'une coupole de peau très mince et vide, et présente à sa base une zone d'installation déprimée avec une excavation en cratère qui pourrait être le point de communication avec le canal médullaire. Comme nous l'avons déjà mentionné, l'analyse radiographique a mis en évidence, bien que partiellement, un défaut des dernières vertèbres lombaires et, peut-être, des premières sacrées.

À la base de la coupole, nous n'avons relevé aucun poil ; de même, à l'intérieur, nous n'avons pas trouvé de structures nerveuses qui nous autorisent à penser à un myélo-ménongocèle.

Enfin, pour être exhaustifs, nous pouvons également affirmer, grâce à nos recherches, qu'il ne peut s'agir d'une tumeur tératoïde ou d'un hygroma cystique lymphostatique.

Nous pouvons finalement exclure le prolapsus de l'anus dont parle Marro, soit dans la forme des prolapsus muqueux typiques des nouveaux-nés, soit dans la forme de prolapsus total du rectum, dû aux phénomènes *post mortem*.

Nous sommes donc portés à diagnostiquer un méningocèle qui se présente, à notre avis, comme la plus ancienne attestation, sûre et complète, de cette pathologie qui avait été, auparavant, uniquement supposée et partiellement documentée. Rappelons, en effet, que plusieurs auteurs avaient mis en évidence dans un matériau ostéologique, même très ancien, une schise partielle ou totale d'un groupe de vertèbres qui aurait pu originer un méningocèle ou un myélo-méningocèle.

Bibliographie

Busingo A., Orlandi N, Manzini C., 1946 = *Sistema Nervoso*, dans *Trattato di Anatomia Patologica Speciale,* (Milan).

Cecconi A., Micheli F., 1940 = *Medicina Interna*, (Turin).

De Vecchi B., 1923 = *Teratologia generale*, (Turin).

Gallone L., 1975 = *Patologia chirurgica*, (Milan).

Kaufmann E., 1970 = *Trattato di Anatomia Patologica Speciale*, (Milan).

Lancereaux E., 1875 = *Traité d'anatomie pathologique*, (Paris).

Lunghetti B., 1938 = *Anatomia patologica del midollo spinale*, dans *Trattato Italiano di Anatomia Patologica*, (Turin).

Marro G., 1952 = Documentazioni morbose finora ignorate nell'Antico Egitto, XLIIᵉ année, Vol. 1/39, (Turin).

Quaternary Geology of Kafr Hassan Dawood, East Nile Delta, Egypt

Mohamed A. Hamdan

Geology Department, Faculty of Science, Cairo University

Introduction

Kafr Hassan Dawood (KHD) is a Late Predynastic to Early Dynastic site (ca. 3200–2900 BCE) located in the Eastern Nile Delta, near the southwestern part of Wadi Tumilat (see fig. 1). In antiquity, the Wadi Tumilat was part of major trade route between Africa and Asia, in particular Egypt and the Levant.

The Quaternary evolution of the Nile Delta has been discussed in general by Butzer[1] and Said.[2] More detailed paleo-geographical investigations mainly focused on the northern and eastern Nile Delta.[3] The present study aims to provide a paleoenvironmental interpretation of KHD and to correlate it with the other sites in the Nile Valley in general and the Delta in particular.

Method of Study

The late Quaternary stratigraphy of the KHD is reconstructed in the basis of data collected from four different sources: 1) about 28 mechanically-drilled cores

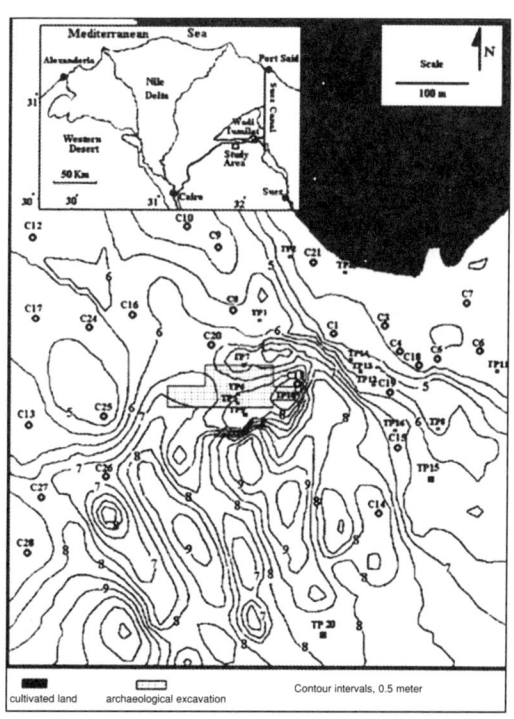

Fig. 1: Contour map of KHD showing location of test pits (TP) and cores (C).

221

(referred herein as "C"); 2) test pits (hereafter TP) that are usually two meters deep and one meter in diameter. However, TP18 is 3.5 m deep; 3) about 20 hand augered cores, about three meters in depth, usually located in the floor of the test pits; 4) archaeological excavations, which took place from 1988 until 1994, and were carried out by a team from the Egyptian Supreme Council of Antiquity (SCA). Since 1995 it has been headed by Fekri Hassan. A total area of 11,700 m^2 has been excavated down to an average depth of about 1.5 m. Of this, 9,900 m^2 is in the main Predynastic to Early Dynastic cemetery; the remaining 1,800 m^2 is in the Late Period to Ptolemaic area to the east of the main cemetery.

Lithostratigraphy

The late Quaternary and Holocene sediments of the KHD are represented by a complex sequence of both local and Nilotic deposits. The stratigraphy comprises five sedimentary units. Each of these is made up of several types of deposits, reflecting the variability of the environment of deposition during the various epochs. These units show a great thickness variabilty facies changes throughout the drilled cores (see fig. 2).

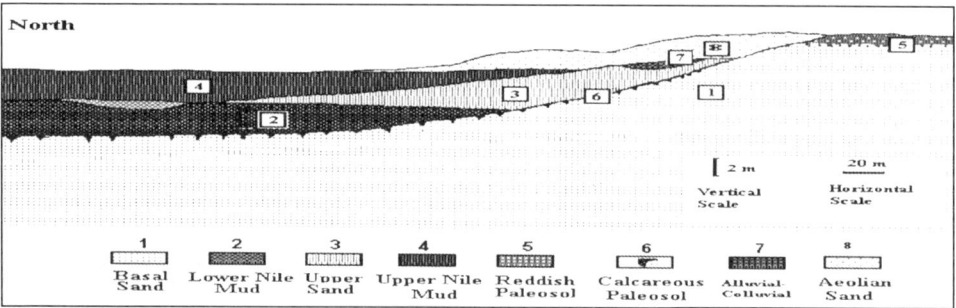

Fig. 2: North-south geological cross-section at KHD site, showing the vertical and lateral distribution of the different sedimentary units.

Basal Sand

This unit is recorded at the base of several cores at depths ranging from five to seven meters below the present flood plain surface (e.g. C 1, 4, 18, fig. 1). The basal sand is also exposed on the surface at the southern terrace of Wadi Tumilat (e.g. TP 20, fig. 1). At TP 20, it represented by very pale brown (10 YR 7/4), quartzose gravely sand, poorly sorted, cross-stratified, with foresets in a 60° NE direction. Ripple and microripple lamination with thin mud drapes are also observed. A few well-rounded limestone pebbles and gravel of local origin are scattered throughout the lower part. The sand is rich with heavy minerals. The heavy mineral assemblage is represented, in decreasing order of abundance, by opaques, amphiboles, pyroxene, epidotes, metamorphic minerals, and metastable minerals.

This unit is overlain, where exposed in the south, by 80 cm thick, brownish-yellow (10 YR 7/6) pebbly coarse to fine-grained sand, poorly sorted, with abundant angular limestone rock fragments of local origin and well-rounded quartz and basement rock fragments reworked from the older Quaternary deposits exposed further south and southwest. The upper 30 cm is highly calcareous and the top is covered with lag gravel. This layer is dated to post Late Pleistocene due to sharp erosional unconformity surface separating it from the underlying Basal Sand Unit sand and the presence of pottery dating from the Late Period to the Ptolemaic.

222

At the northern end of KHD, below the surface this unit is represented by very pale brown (10 YR 7/4), cross-stratified, poorly sorted, quartzose gravely sand, The mineral grains are rounded quartz, basement rock fragments and a few angular chert and limestone rock fragments. The upper surface of this sand is sounded at different levels in the drilled cores and in the north-south geoelectric resistively section (fig. 3). The heavy mineral assemblage is represented by opaques (44.8%), amphiboles (20.55%), pyroxene (12.47%), and epidotes (7.2%), as well as lesser amounts of rutile, tourmaline, zircon, and metamorphic minerals.

The top part of this unit is characterized by the existence of a thin white calcareous layer (ranging in thickness from 10 to 40 cm). This layer is white (10 YR 8/1), highly calcareous, silty, fine quartzose sand, and consists mainly of subangular to angular quartz, limestone rock fragments, and pale olive (5 Y 6/3) reworked mud clasts. Few milky quartz pebbles also occur. The local angular limestone clasts and their occurrence in a relatively low paleorelief area suggest that the soil formation was related to high water influx in the wetter conditions.

Based on their mineralogy, lithology, and stratigraphic position, these deposits are correlated with Qena sand, in Upper Egypt,[4] and with the Sath Ghorab Formation of Late Pleistocene age in Middle Egypt.[5] (see fig. 3)

Lower Mud Unit

This unit is recorded in all drilled cores, but with remarkably pronounced variation in thickness and lithology. In general, the thickness increases northward to more than 300 cm at C2, and more where the base is not reached in the northern cores, such as C21 (fig. 1). The lithology also shows little variation southward. This unit is represented by 150 cm (C5) to 300 cm (C2) thick, dark yellowish brown (10 YR 4/4) silty clay, which is hard, massive, slightly calcareous, and highly gypsiferous where fine acicular and columnar gypsum crystals fill the fractures and joints, especially in the upper two meters. This unit is nonfossiliferous; however, poorly-preserved root casts are represented in certain horizons. The unit also contains fine-grained calcareous concretions. Thin black Manganese cortex and yellowish ocher coat some of the concretions, which also exist along fissures.

In some cores (C18, C22, C6, fig. 1), a different unit is recovered. This unit is represented by about 30 to 50 cm thick (at a depth of about three meters from the present surface), very pale brown (10 YR 7/3), thin laminated, very fine to fine-grained quartzose sand. The sand is highly micaceous, non-calcareous, soft, and semi-consolidated.

The geoeresistivity soundings show that this unit is monotonous in thickness and homogeneous in composition in the northern part. However, the unit decreases in thickness and changes in composition, as it moves southward. Generally the mud of this unit is characterized by relatively low resistivity values (fig. 3), which range from 5–22 Ohm-m (but are still higher than the overlying unit). The difference in resistivity may be due to the degree of salinity and percentage of evaporites.

Phosphate analysis reveals that the Lower Mud Unit has less phosphate than the Upper Mud Unit, and is relatively higher than the underlying basal sands. The heavy mineral assemblage of this layer is represented, in decreasing order of abundance, by opaques (28.83%), amphiboles (27. 28%), Mica flakes (17.82%), pyroxene (9.33%), epidotes (4.68%), as well as some metamorphic minerals. The homogeneous Lower Mud Unit with relatively high organic matter content, may indicate that they were deposited in floodplain basins or in back swamps in the flood basin, whereas the very fine to fine sand were deposited in a levee environment.

The lower contact of this unit is sharp and highly undulated indicating that the base of the Holocene Nile Delta is an erosional surface formed during the low sea level stand of the last glaciation, which reached its maximum between 25,000 and 18,000 BP.[6] During the glacial maximum, the sea level was over 100 meters lower than at present.[7] The central part of the Nile Delta basin may have been excavated out as much as 40–80 below the present surface.[8] The intensity of paleorelief decreases gradually to zero at the Delta edges,[9] the Wadi Tumilat's paleorelief was in range of five meters in the north – south direction. The Lower Mud Unit is equivalent to the humic clay facies of Nile Formation in the Eastern Nile Delta[10] and Basal Clay south of Minshat Abu Omar, a Pre-dynastic site in the East Nile Delta.[11]

Upper Sand Unit

These deposits are exposed in the southern part of KHD, where the Predynastic and Late Period to Ptolemaic graves were dug. They are exposed on the ground surface in the form of a small terrace, about two meters above the cultivation surface, and disappear in the north. This unit unconformably overlies the Lower Mud Unit in all encountered test pits and is overlain by different lithologies. Upper sand deposits are also sounded in subsurface through some cores (e.g. C1). In Core C1, these deposits are sounded at a depth of one meter below the ground surface and lies underneath the Upper Mud Unit.

The exposed section of the Upper Sand Unit at TP7 is represented by 250 cm thick, very pale brown (10 YR 7/3), fine to very coarse-grained cross-stratified, micaceous quartzose, loose, friable sand. This unit consists of thin finning upward co-sets with low-angle cross-stratification. The set is about 10 cm in thickness and grades in grain-size from very coarse to fine-grained. The sets dip to the south at an angle of 10°. They are truncated with inclined reactivation surfaces with single grain-thick lag gravel. The gravels consist of sub-angular chert, limestone, and basement rock fragments. The Upper Sand Unit overlies unconformably the Lower Mud Unit and underlies abandoned channel deposits.

At Core C1, the Upper Sand Unit is sounded about 100 cm below the surface. It underlies unconformably the Upper Mud Unit and overlies the Lower Mud Unit. They are represented by about 300 cm thick, light yellowish brown (10 YR 7/4) fine-grained micaceous quartzose sand, with occasional pebbly horizons at different levels.

The Upper Sand Unit is represented by a thin, long veneer with irregular lower sole, indicating erosional unconformity surface separating it from the underlying Lower Mud Unit. The sand of this unit shows a high resistivity value like the Basal Sand Unit, but its upper part has very high resistivity (ranging from 46–100 Ohm-m and from 100 to 460 Ohm-m in the upper part).

The heavy mineral assemblages of the Upper Sand Unit are represented in decreasing order of abundance by opaques (55.48%), amphiboles (10.00%), pyroxene (4.7%), epidotes (3.68%), micas (2.43%), as well as metamorphic minerals and metastable minerals. It is obvious from the lithological and mineralogical studies that there is a great similarity between the Upper Sand Unit and the basal Pleistocene sand.

The Upper Sand Unit may be correlated with the fan–like deposits in the south part of Minshat Abu Omar.[12] It could be also correlated with the "Wild Nile" phase.[13]

Upper Mud Unit

The Upper Mud Unit is recovered only in the cores, which were drilled to the north of the KHD cemetery. It has more or less monotonous thickness but the lithology shows great variability. In general, It is represented by about two meter thick, pale brown (10 YR 6/3), hard, heterogeneous, sandy silt, sometimes gravely, and calcareous. The sand grains are represented by well sub-rounded to subangular quartz, rounded basement rock fragment and mica flakes. Calcareous nodules and concretions, as well as calcified root casts are abundant and concentrated in certain horizons (e.g. at a depth between 110 to 130 and 266 to 290 cm below the present ground surface). Along these horizons black Mn_2O_3 coat the carbonate nodules and yellow ocher fills the microfractures. Fresh water molluscan shells are represented mainly by gastropod tests. Most of these shells are broken.

The Upper Mud Unit is highly gypsiferous, where gypsum crystals occurred as veinlets filling the microfractures, rounded reworked grains and as fine-grained cementing material.

From an archaeological point of view, this unit is very interesting. At least three horizons exhibit anthropogenic remains (mainly pottery shards and stone artifacts). The anthropogenic remains were encountered at 40–80 cm, 120–190 cm, 23–270 cm, and 390–400 cm below the surface (C15, C3, C2, C4; fig. 1).

Fluvial-Colluvial Sediments

These deposits were formed shortly prior to the excavation of the graves at the cemetery or coeval with the early settlements in KHD, where the main large graves were dug through (the western part of the cemetery). This unit comprises both fluvial and colluvial sediments. It includes a gravel, sand and silt complex filling a small channel or ditch; the latter consists of a white ash layer and rubble lag gravel layer covering the graves. The microstratigraphy and the lithology of this unit were recovered through archaeological excavation which provided about 150 cm thick and more than 100m lateral extended sections. Lateral and vertical extensions of this unit throughout the whole area were followed through series of test pits and hand auger holes.

In TP1 (fig. 1), this unit is represented by three layers. These are, 30 cm thick, yellowish brown (10 YR 6/4) sandy silt, calcareous with white carbonate spots and calcified root casts as well as brownish yellow ocher stain. This unit shows an uncomformity erosive contact with the underlying Upper Sand Unit, with single grain-thick lag gravel. The deposits of this unit taper off both to the east and west for about 10 m, before they completely disappear (TP4, and 5; fig. 1). Stratigraphically, it seems that this unit represents an *in situ* abandoned channel unconformably overlying the Upper Sand Unit with single grain-thick lag gravel. This unit is overlain by a 15 cm, white to very pale brown color (10 YR 8/3–7/3), ash layer with randomly distributed reworked sand. Under the microscope, the ash consists of fine-grained angular quartz fragments, burned phytolith[14] as well as clay minerals. EDX-analysis shows that the ash layer consists predominantly of Si, Ca, Fe and Al, and differs from the volcanic ash in other areas in the Nile Delta in its great thickness, rich quartz and lower Al, K, and Na content. The lower boundary of the ash unit is sharp and straight The upper surface, by contrast, is gradational and highly irregular, reflecting disturbance under damp conditions.

Late Predynastic graves are dug into the sand of this unit. This unit disappears completely in the southern area of the site where it is covered with reworked mud and ash layers. The sand from this unit was used in constructing the superstructures of the graves.

To the north of TP1, the lower sandy silt layer changes to sand (TP2), the sand in turn changes to gravel in TP7, where the ash layer completely disappears. At TP7, the Alluvial-Colluvial unit is represented by 60 cm, brown to dark brown (10 YR 5/3–4/3), sandy silt with scattered quartz pebbles, hard and massive. This unit is equivalent to the lower sandy silt of TP1. White carbonate nodules and fragmented large bivalve shells (the same species silt exists in the irrigation canals) are also observed. Large numbers of these shell are also found in the Late Predynastic and Early Dynastic graves as offerings.

Late Quaternary Evolution of KHD

Based on the results of fieldwork, laboratory analyses and correlation with other areas in the Nile Delta, a model of the Late Quaternary paleoenvironmental evolution of KHD, may be constructed (fig. 4). This model is valid for Wadi Tumilat and the east Nile Delta as well. The main features of the model are as follows:

The older deposits in KHD consist of the Basal Sand Unit, which is exposed on the surface as a terrace delimiting the southern border of the site, or sounded on the cores, underneath the Nile mud at different levels. This sand is related to the Pre-Nile phase,[15] which forms the low terraces on both sides of the River Nile and its delta. Said assigns these deposits to the Middle Pleistocene.

These deposits are also correlated with the late Pleistocene Sath Ghorab Formation,[16] exposed in the Nile Valley in Lower Egypt. On the basis of grain-size and the sedimentary structures exposed in TP18, it seems that the Basal Sand Unit was deposited by a meandering river of African origin. The heavy mineral assemblage of these deposits may indicate that they were derived from Equatorial East Central Africa.[17] During the maximum of the last glaciation (18,000 to ca. 10,000 BP), the sea level dropped to about 100 meters below the present level.[18] As a result of this drop, deep erosion prevailed over the whole Nile Delta. The incision and lateral degradation eroded the subaerially exposed older Pleistocene deposits. Wunderlich and Andres dated the calcic paleosol from Buto to 13,000 ± 600 and 14,315 ± 285 BP (uncalibrated radiocarbon years).[19]

During the post-glacial period (14,000–10,000 BP), the sea level rose again accompanied by Nile aggradation. Sediments began to accumulate in the eroded basin, gradually burying the paleorelief. Coutellier and Stanley described basal Neo-Nile clays of the Central Delta dated to *ca* 10,000 BP.[20] Nile water reached the area of KHD through a permanent channel, which may represent a distributary of the Pelusiac branch. This channel was capable of carrying high quantities of sand and silt (the Lower Nile Mud Unit) from very remote areas of the Upper Nile Basin (as indicated by the heavy mineral assemblage). At that time, swamps and lakes covered the area of the Wadi Tumilat with dense vegetation.

The calcified root casts within the lower Nile mud as well as the reworked limestone rock fragments of local origin, may indicate contributions by runoff from the surrounding highlands. The climate was semiarid and wetter than at present. Horowitz postulated a similar paleoenvironment for the Middle East during Early and Middle Holocene times.[21] The Lower Nile Mud is correlated with the Darau Member of the Gebel Silsla Formation,[22] the Sahaba Formation (Wendorf and Schild and the Wadi Kubbanya.[23]

The upper boundary of the Lower Mud Unit is a sharp undulated erosive surface. The existence of a thin layer of lag gravel of black and white cortex may be interpreted as deflation by wind and/or rainwater. The cortex may be also interpreted as desert varnish. There are remarkable differences in lithology and environment of deposition between the Lower and the Upper Nile Mud units, which may indicate a time gap between. From 8,000 to 6,000 BP, a drop in sea level accelerated the degradation of the floodplain of the Wadi Tumilat.

Medium-grained sands were deposited by vigorous Nile courses in the central and western Nile Delta.[24] This high Nile phase is called Wild Nile by Butzer,[25] and dated to about 12,000 BP. In the area of KHD, the Wild Nile phase is represented by an active stream of African origin and draining parts of Pleistocene terraces. The wadi channels and runnels reworked the older Pleistocene sand, over the Lower Mud Unit (the Upper Sand Unit). The presence of reddish paleosol as a well-dissected caliche layer at the top of the Upper Sand Unit may indicate that the wet period, which was responsible for its formation, was followed by an arid period, or drier conditions and warmer summers.

The paleotopography of Kafr Hassan Dawood during the Predynastic to Early Dynastic period of human occupation, more or less resembled the present topography. The southern territories were occupied by sand hills (the Pleistocene terraces and Upper Sand Unit at its northern foot). The upper flat surface was used as a cemetery. The northern part of KHD was occupied by a very broad floodplain, which is covered with water during high floods. Swamps and *sabkhas* developed in the depression along the margin of the floodplain, frequently with vegetation cover.

Fig. 3: North-south resistivity cross section. Wenner inverted 2D Model (rms 72.4%).

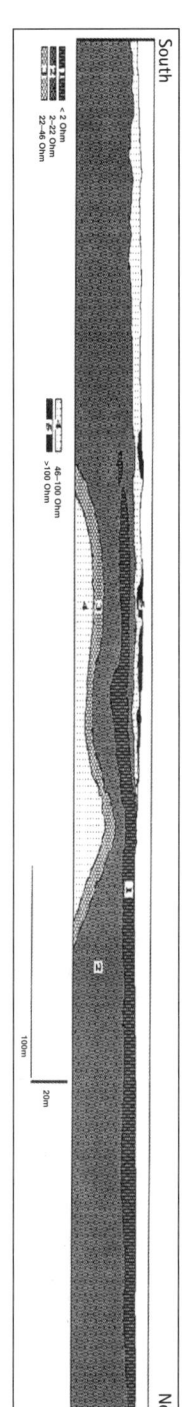

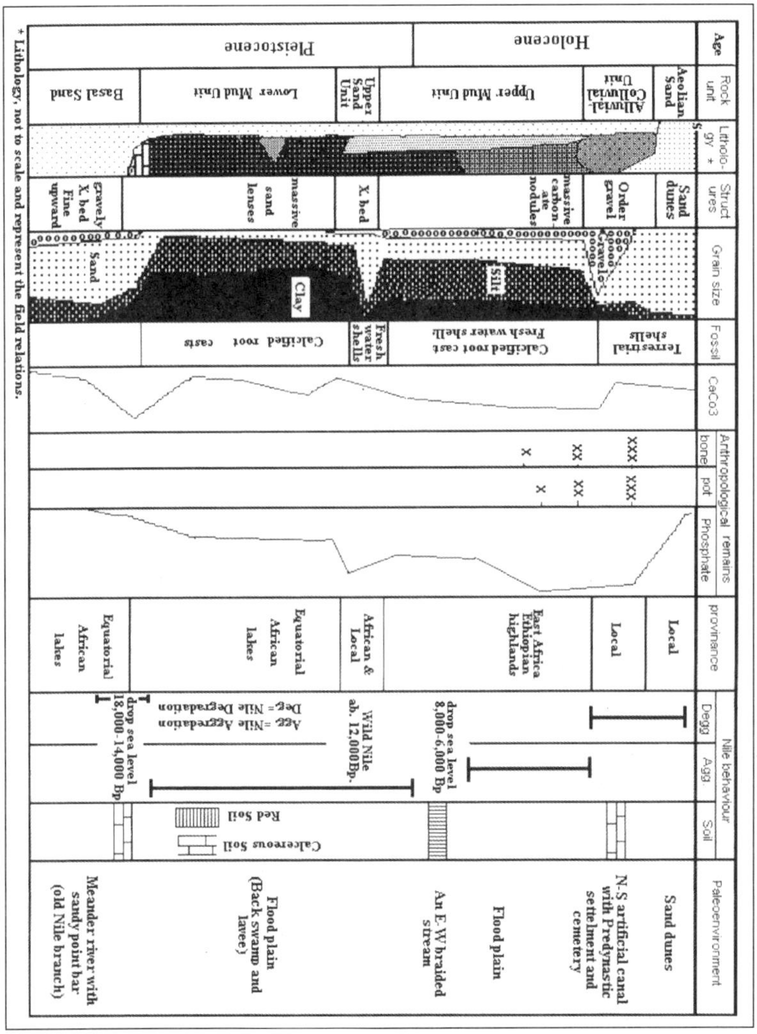

Fig. 4: Geological model of Kafr Hassan Dawood Site, East Nile Delta, Egypt.

Notes:

1 K. W. Butzer, "Delta," *Lexikon der Aegyptologie* 1 (1975), 1043-1052; K. W. Butzer, "Late Quaternary
  Problems of the Egyptian Nile: Stratigraphy, Environments, Prehistory," *Paleorien* 23/2 (1998), 151-173.

2 R. Said, *The Geological Evolution of the River Nile* (New York, 1981), 151.

3 D. J. Stanley, "Sediments transport on the coast and shelf between the Nile Delta and Israel margin as
  determined by heavy mineral," *Journal of Coastal Research*, 5/4 (1989), 813-828; A. Sneh, T.
  Weissbrod, S. Horowitz S. Moshkovitz, and A. Rosenfeld, "Holocene evolution of the Northeastern cor-
  ner of the Nile Delta," *Quaternary Research* 26 (1986), 194-206; H. E. Wit and L. V. Stralen,
  "Geoarchaeology and ancient distributaries in the Eastern Nile Delta," *Reports of the Laboratory of
  Physical Geography and Soil Science, University of Amsterdam* 34 (1988), 56.

4 Said, *Evolution*, 151.

5 M. A. Hamdan, *Pliocene and Quaternary sediments of Beni Suef-East Faiyum area and their relationship
  to the geologic evolution of the River Nile*, unpublished PhD thesis, Cairo University (Cairo, 1993), 240.

6 V. Coultellier and D. J. Stanley, "Late Quaternary stratigraphy and paleogeography of the Eastern Nile
  Delta, Egypt," *Marine Geology* 44 (1987), 257-275.

7 Butzer, "Delta," 117-131; A. Horowitz, *The Quaternary of Israel* (New York, 1979), 394.

8 Butzer, "Delta," 1043-1052; A. G. Madkour, *Boreholes Catalogue: Mansoura University Project* (Cairo,
  1988), 132; Stanley, *Sediments*, 813-828.

9 Wit and Stralen, *Geoarchaeology*, 56.

10 H. E. Wit, *The evolution of the Eastern Nile Delta as a factor in the development of Human culture
   Environmental change and human culture in the Nile Basin and Northern Africa* (Poznan, 1992), 305-320.

11 W. Andres and J. Wunderlich, "Untersuchungen zur Palaogerahie des westlichen im Holozan.
   Marbung/Lahn," *Marburger Geograpische Schriften* 100 (1986), 117-131.

12 W. Andres and J. Wunderlich, "*Untersuchungen,*" 117-131.

13 F. A. Hassan, "Holocene climatic changes and riverine dynamics in Nile Valley," in *Before Food
   Production in North Africa*, S. di Lernia and G. Manzi (eds.) (London, 1998) 43-51; K. W. Butzer, *Late
   Quaternary*, 152-173.

14 Arlene Rosen, personal communication.

15 Said, *Evolution*, 151.

16 Hamdan, *Pliocene,* 240.

17 Butzer, "Delta," 117-131; Said, *Evolution*, 151; H. A. Hamroush and D. J. Stanley, "Paleoclimatic oscillations
   in East Africa interpreted by analysis of trace elements in the Nile Delta sediments," *Episodes* 13 (1990),
   264-269; Hamdan, *Pliocene.*

18 Horowitz, *The Quaternary*; D. J. Stanley and A. G. Warne, "Nile Delta, recent geological evolution and
   human impact," *Science* 60 (1993), 628-634.

19 J. Wunderlich and A. Andres, "Late Pleistocene and Holocene evolution of the Western Nile Delta and
   implications for its future development," in H. Brückner and U. Radtke (eds.), *Von der Nordsee bis zum
   Indischen Ozean* (Stuttgart, 1991), 162-180.

20 Coultellier and Stanley, *Late Quaternary,* 257-275.

21 Wit, *Evolution*, 305-320.

22 K. W. Butzer and C. L. Hansen, *Desert and River in Nubia: Geomorphology and Prehistoric
   Environmemts at Aswan Reservoir* (Madison, 1968), 562.

23 F. Wendorf and R. Schild, "Prehistory of the River Nile," (New York, 1976), 387; R. Schild and F.
   Wendorf, "The Late Pleistocene in Wadi Kubbania," in *The Prehistory of Wadi Kubbania*, F. Wendorf, R.
   F. Schild, and A. Close (South Methodist University Press, 1989), 15-100.

24 Wunderlich and Andres, *Late Pleistocene*, 162-180.

25 Butzer, "Late Quaternary," 152-173.

The New Kingdom Necropolis at Dahshur

So Hasegawa
Waseda University

Introduction

General knowledge about the Memphite necropolis in the New Kingdom has been based on the area around Teti's pyramid, excavated by Firth and Gunn, and recently by the Supreme Council of Antiquities. The area below the eastern cliff has been excavated by the French Mission (under the direction of Alain Zivie). More information resulted from the rediscovery and excavation of tombs at the south of the Unas causeway, by the Egypt Exploration Society/Leiden Expedition (now Leiden Museum and Leiden University) and by Cairo University (fig.1: A, B). There has been considerable speculation about the formation of the necropolis during the New Kingdom.

A team from Waseda University* carried out research in an area some two kilometers north of the Red Pyramid of Snefru, after the area was vacated by the military and became available for excavation. Excavation unexpectedly revealed that a New Kingdom necropolis had been established at Dahshur (fig.1: Excavation Area).

A number of tomb-shafts became evident, and on the southernmost hilltop, the brick foundation of a tomb was uncovered (Pl. 1). The entire superstructure had been leveled to the mud-brick foundation in antiquity, but the scale of the tomb is comparable to that of Horemheb at Saqqara. Its plan comprised a ramp, courts, and a cult chapel. The tomb would seem to have originally belonged to one "Ipay, the Royal Scribe," or "Ipay, the Royal Scribe, Royal Butler," whose name and titles were found on a stamped brick.

Construction of the Tomb in the Post-Amarna Period

A deep rectangular shaft led to a series of roughly-hewn subterranean rooms 13 m in depth. The shaft (Shaft A) seems to have been covered by stone blocks measuring 52.5 by 26 by 22 cm—*talatat* size—which helped to date the construction. Several of the underground rooms (Rooms A–G) had been disturbed in antiquity, but systematic clearance of the debris was still carried out.

229

The original plan of the subterranean rooms seems to have only included Rooms A to E, with Rooms F and G added later.

Removal of the debris in Room F revealed Shaft A2, leading to a lower level. A number of stone blocks filled this shaft, and after their removal, the innermost Room H, containing a granite sarcophagus, was revealed. The sarcophagus had been lowered through the narrow Shaft A1, as demonstrated by its apparent original width (fig. 2).

Fragments of relief blocks were recovered from the debris. These no doubt originated in the walls of the courts and cult chapel of the New Kingdom sepulchers excavated at Saqqara—Horemheb, Maya, Tia and Tia, and so on. In fact, one of the relief fragments bore the cartouche of Horemheb. Some of these fragments have been reconstructed to form a "Window of Appearance," showing an unnamed pharaoh bestowing garlands on his subordinates.

Evidence of activity in the area was indicated by the objects around Shaft A and from the subterranean rooms. A head of a small limestone statue wearing the *atef* crown, a shard with the jackal and nine captives necropolis seal, a faience ring with a lotus design, the upper portion of a stirrup jar (Mycenean) painted red, and a shard from a blue-painted vessel, were characteristic of this period. Then faience rings with Tutankhamun's prenomen, and the cartouche of his Great Royal Wife Ankhesenamun, were unearthed, confirming the date.

Re-use of the tomb in the Ramesside Period

Besides the group of objects dated to the reign of Tutankhamun, scarabs bearing the name of Ramesses II on their bases suggested a date for the reuse of the tomb. This is also supported by the unfinished sarcophagus, which was found in the innermost part of the subterranean rooms.

The lid of the sarcophagus seems too large for the trough, which may be due to the fact that the work on the object was suspended because of the premature death of the owner. On the lid, a bearded face had been carved, but there had been insufficient time to complete the carving, and the dressed hair and collar around the crossed arms were instead painted black or red. On the foot end are texts of "Osiris Mes."

Examination of the undersurface of the lid made it clear that the carving had only just begun; however, the trough seems to have been mostly completed, except for a mortise for the lid pivot, where preliminary drill holes can still be seen. The decoration on the exterior is in sunk relief. The images of Isis and Nephthys at the head and the foot, and the Mes, the owner of the sarcophagus, are represented in front of Osiris and Anubis and accompanied by other gods of the underworld, which have been colored with yellow pigments.

The sarcophagus had been disturbed, and much sand was found inside, covering fragments of a wooden coffin, including part of a mummy-mask. Several *ushabtis* were also retrieved from the debris of the room. One group of small *ushabtis* is made of faience in the daily life style. Another group of pieces of wood coated with resin was retrieved, along with several sets of Canopic jars.

One fine complete sandstone *ushabti* of Mes is 36 cm in height and has its surface painted brown. It wears a Nubian wig and long kilt, on which the name and titles of Mes, "Royal Scribe" and "Steward" are engraved. The stylistic feature of the sarcophagus would suggest that it was made in the Ramesside period, and a hieratic jar docket—"Year 7 of Ramesses-Meryamun"—may point to a date early in the reign of Ramesses II.

Chronological subject of the area

The tomb of Ipay is surrounded by numerous shafts, and we have excavated the tomb of Ipay and its vicinity for the past six seasons (fig. 3). Each grid measures 10 by 10 m, and 3,000 square meters in total have been surveyed. The chronological framework of this area will suggest the dating of the whole necropolis area at Dahshur North, as represented by the objects observed on the surface and the probable similar distribution of the shafts.

In this site, the NW area is most remarkable. Objects recovered from the area are rich, such as a jar stopper with the cartouche of Tutankhamun, a faience broad-collar consisting of various kinds of beads in the style of the late Eighteenth Dynasty, a golden finger ring inset with a carnelian *udjat* eye; parts of an ivory *senet* game-box, found with playing pieces and knucklebones, and a narrow-waisted wooden headrest, all of which suggest use of this necropolis around the reign of Tutankhamun. It also implies the date when the necropolis was established, though some objects, such as a stele, had a characteristic Pre-Amarna Period motif, and an amulet bearing the name of Amenhotep III shows an earlier context.

In the NE corner of the tomb of Ipay, a small-sized tomb with a shaft numbered 22, which predated Ipay's tomb, was revealed, and the shaft was unfinished. Here also, a tripartite plan around the cult chapel was observed, and the brick size was different from that in Ipay's tomb. After this tomb had been abandoned, Ipay's tomb was constructed in its place. Ipay's tomb does not seem to be contemporary, and brick walls were evidently constructed on the debris of the shafts around it.

Whether the seemingly original owner of the tomb, the Royal Butler Ipay, was ever actually buried there is not clear. No funeral objects of his, or at least bearing his name, have been found, although *ushabtis* inscribed for a Huy, Amenemopet, and Pashedw were recovered, suggesting multiple burials or a complicated serial use of the tomb. Other numerous *ushabtis* for a Pipwy, Henwtmira, and Khentykhetyhotep, from the several shafts distributed around Ipay's tomb, would seem to confirm this. In addition, some wooden coffins and pottery coffins indicate use of the area until a later time, probably the Third Intermediate Period.

Preliminary Conclusions

During these seasons, we have concentrated our research on the tomb of Ipay and its vicinity, and the exploration of the area is mostly completed. The necropolis contains many shaft tombs, and some of the larger ones could have had superstructures comparable to those at Saqqara. The objects assemblage picked up from the vast area indicates that, although previously well-known for monuments of the Old and the Middle Kingdoms, Dahshur has now also been shown to have been the site of New Kingdom activity.

The use of the Ipay's tomb in the Post-Amarna Period implies the same formation and use of the necropolis as the area south of the Unas causeway at Saqqara. The results of our research have proved that the area extending more than five kilometers south from Saqqara to Dahshur must be considered, and it is hoped that our work will encourage discussion on the extent and disposition of the New Kingdom Memphite necropolis, particularly during the years when Memphis recovered its political status after the end of Amarna Period.

*Institute of Egyptology; General Director, Sakuji Yoshimura; Field Director, So Hasegawa; Epigrapher, Jiro Kondo; Architecture, Takeshi Nakagawa and Shin-ichi Nishimoto.

Pl. 1: General view of Ipay's tomb from S-E.

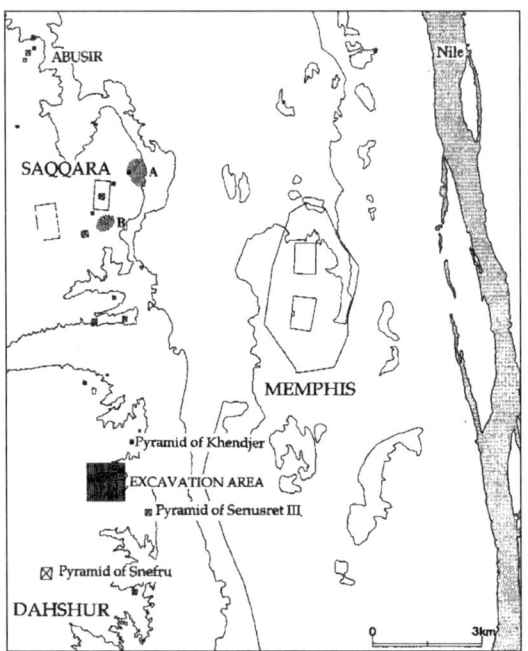

Fig. 1: Map of
Memphite area.

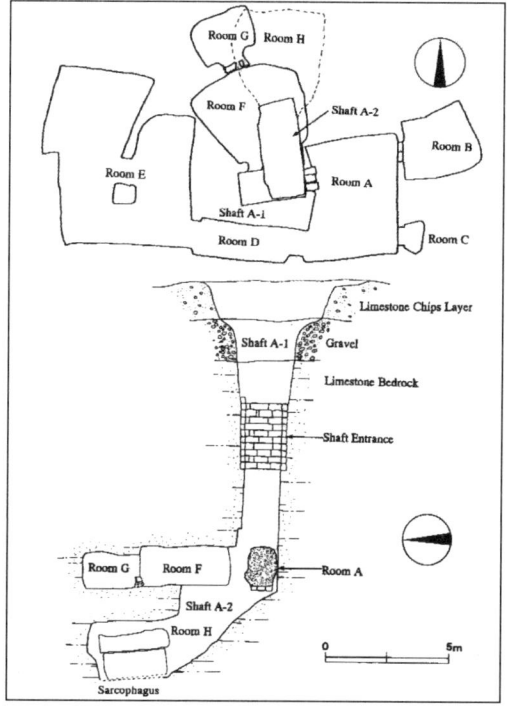

Fig. 2: Plan and section of shaft A.

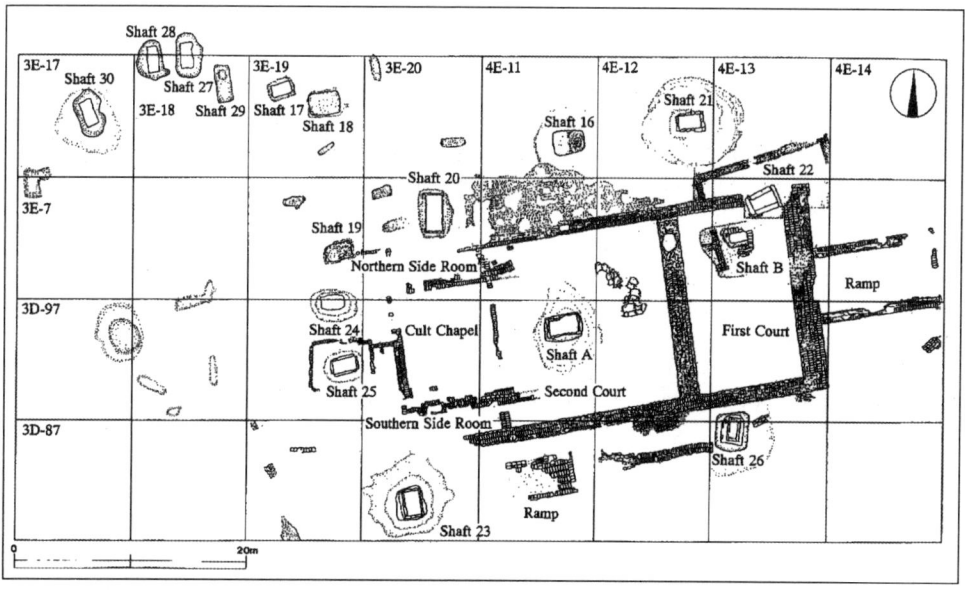

Fig. 3: Ipay's tomb and its vicinity.

233

The Mortuary Temple of Merenptah at Qurna and Its Building Phases

Horst Jaritz
Swiss Institute

After completing the architectural investigation of the mortuary temple of Amenhotep III at Kôm al-Hettan, the Swiss Institute began reinvestigating the neighboring "House of a Million Years" of Merenptah. Petrie had already excavated this temple about one hundred years ago, and had only left a sketch plan and rather limited description.[1]

Fifteen seasons of work at this temple have now passed.[2] Petrie's plan proved to be somewhat correct, although a great number of clarifications and additions could be made. At first sight, the final layout of the temple (fig. 1), which must be considered the link in the architectural development of mortuary temples from the Nineteenth to the Twentieth Dynasty, seemed to differ only slightly from these latter ones. However, our investigations revealed that the temple, before being completed after the fifth year of Merenptah's reign, was a constantly changing building site, where a series of sections and particular rooms were added to the primary layout.

Reconsidering our observations made so far, the original layout of the temple (fig. 2), and thus its first building phase, appears to be rather simple. Obviously it was restricted to a minimum of sections and rooms sufficient to serve the basic form of the mortuary cult. Excluding later additions from the existing plan of the temple, we seem to be confronted with the apparent prototype of a mortuary temple: It consists of a pylon as the entrance leading to a first courtyard for the Royal Presence and the mortuary palace of the deceased king. Then, behind a separating wall, a second courtyard on a higher level follows. This is a festival court with an Osiris-pillared portico in front of the temple façade. This portico leads to a first hypostyle hall, as the place where Amun and the king were united, and where the barques of the Theban triad and the king assembled for the barque procession. This hall is followed by a second hypostyle hall where the offerings were presented to the divine barques. And finally, the shrines for the barques of the Theban triad, Amun, Mut, and Khonsu, form the western end of the temple.

Subsidiary buildings in mud brick to the north and south of the temple, an essential part of this primary building phase and necessary for the support of the cult, were already completely erected.

234

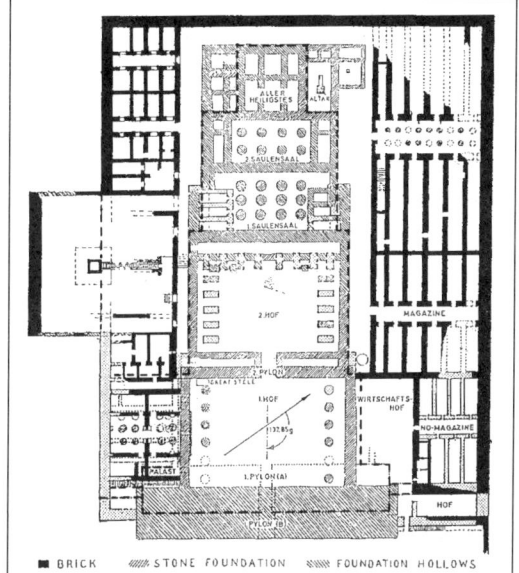

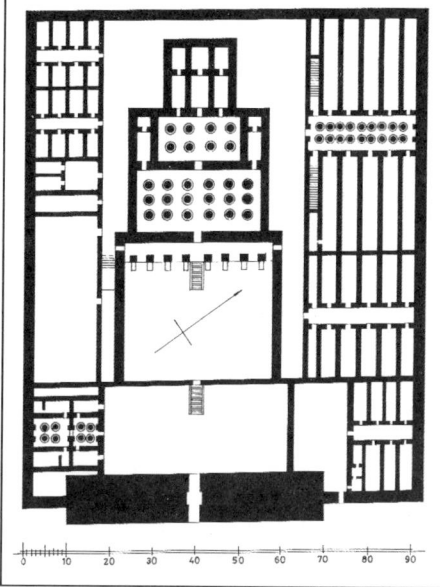

Fig. 1: Mortuary Temple of Merenptah, final layout of the temple plan (cf. William M. Flinders Petrie, Six Temples at Thebes. 1896, London 1897, pl. 25, with corrections and additions 1971–2000).

Fig. 2: Mortuary Temple of Merenptah, first building phase, plan reconstructed (cf. William M. Flinders Petrie, Six Temples at Thebes. 1896, London 1897, pl. 25).

To the north of the temple, three complexes of magazines of different sizes extended over the whole length of the temple. They were entered from the east by a gate just north of the pylon that led into a small courtyard, probably for supervising and registering the incoming goods. Attached to this courtyard, the first complex of storerooms of a comparatively small dimension was situated, supposedly connected by a staircase or ramp to the two larger complexes of storerooms on a higher level further west. Goods were transferred from this courtyard to these western storerooms. While the particular function of the two eastern complexes of storerooms remains unknown, the northwestern complex of storerooms was the treasury of the temple, according to an inscription on the lintel of its entrance and on a stele erected at the rear of its distribution hall.

South of the temple, the palace of the deceased king is connected to the first courtyard so that the king as a statue, when taken to the window of appearances, might participate in the ceremonies taking place there. West of the palace, there is a large, open court possibly subdivided into three parts, extending between the southern passage of the temple and the southern enclosure wall of the temenos. At the southwestern corner of the temenos, there is a complex of rooms which might have been used partly as storerooms and partly as the ateliers and the administrative complex of the temple.

While the pylon, sidewalls of the first and second courtyard, the palace, and the wall dividing the first and second courtyard, were constructed with mud brick bearing a variety of royal seals of Amenhotep III, the temple proper and its Osiris-pillared portico were built of stone masonry. For the foundation of this part, Merenptah reused Amenhotep III's material, such as limestone blocks from two small gates, anthrosphinxes, and jackal sphinxes made of limestone and sandstone respectively.

235

As far as we know now, it appears that the intended primary layout of the temple was never completed, perhaps due to time constraints as a result of the delayed succession of Merenptah. It was altered in certain parts during a second building phase. While the construction of the temenos wall, the northern magazines, and the southwestern administrative building were completed, other parts of the temple had already been changed during the laying of their foundations or after their walls had reached a certain height. The first alteration seems to have occurred in the first hypostyle hall, where the foundation trenches of the outer lateral walls had already been dug in the direction of those of the second hypostyle hall, and the foundations partly laid. In order to introduce three lateral rooms on each side of the hall, these walls were given up and redirected to the outer lateral walls of the second courtyard. It is interesting to note that this alteration took place even before foundation pits to support a third row of columns on each side of the hall were dug. At the same time, however, plans were changed again, and, instead of three northern side rooms, only two were constructed, one small eastern and one larger western one, judging from the reconstructed decoration of the southern inner wall of the latter.

It appears that almost the whole temple east of the first hypostyle hall underwent considerable alterations within the same scheme and during the same period. To the east, the Osiris-pillared portico of the temple façade was supplemented by two additional porticoes in front of the southern and northern lateral walls of the second courtyard, as seen on the plan of the first building stage. In consequence, the lateral walls of the second courtyard, which must have originally been built of mud brick, were now replaced in stone in order to carry the heavy stone roof of each of the colonnades and to properly attach it to a second pylon replacing the simultaneously demolished mud-brick wall dividing both courtyards.

As the alteration of the once-intended temple progressed eastwards, the following complex (fig. 3), comprising the lateral walls of the first courtyard and including the façade of the palace and the first pylon which were all constructed in mud brick, at least to a certain height, was demolished and replaced by enlarged constructions in stone. Only the inner part of the palace between its façade and the southern temenos wall was replaced by another slightly enlarged mud-brick construction. Together with the lateral stone walls of the first courtyard, lateral colonnades with open papyrus columns were introduced. While the southern one formed the portico of the palace façade, the columns of the northern one formed the backing for royal statues on low pedestals. The first pylon was rebuilt further east.

As long as it was available, building material originating from the neighboring temple of Amenhotep III was reused for the newly conceived stone constructions. The limestone blocks of a monumental gateway were taken for the first hypostyle hall and the temple façade as well as for the foundations of the second pylon, which were constructed simultaneously.

Besides sandstone material taken from some buildings of Tuthmose III and Akhenaten, Merenptah seems to have also used sandstone quarried from Silsileh for his temple, after reopening the neglected quarries.

For the foundations of the two colonnades of the first courtyard and probably for the core masonry of the first pylon, a number of rather small limestone blocks of a building of Hatshepsut were reused along with other kinds of stones. When the foundations of the lateral walls of the first courtyard were laid, material from preceding buildings seem to have become scarce and locally-obtained flint/chert boulders had to be included as well. According to this observation, three other parts of the temple must have been added to the primary layout during the same time, as their foundations show the same kind of flint/chert boulders; first, the rooms of the cult for the royal ancestors at the southwestern corner of the temple, and second, the courtyard and

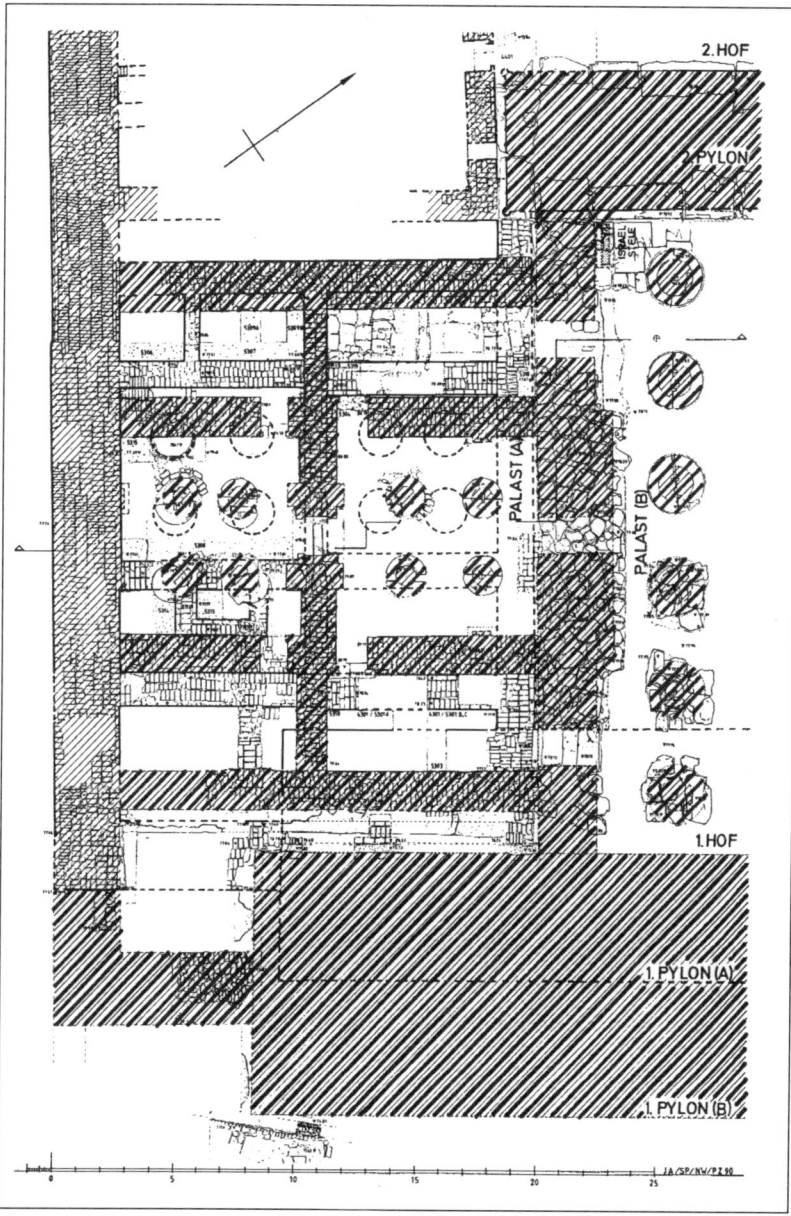

Fig. 3: First courtyard with palace, first courtyard, first and second pylon; first and second
building phases superimposed.

rooms for the cult of Re and the slaughter house at the northwestern corner of the temple. As for
the latter, a change in the already-excavated foundations took place during this building phase.
Instead of two longitudinal units of rooms, we find this complex changed into a hall with four

237

pillars and a small room at the rear, where there are traces of the positioning of a statue on the remaining floor slabs.

Finally, the construction of a well (fig. 4) still missing in the primary plan, must be mentioned. For its emplacement, the open space or court south of the second courtyard was chosen. However, preceding its excavation and the construction of the second pylon, we find the following layout of the area south of the second courtyard: From the southern passage of the temple an axial entrance leads into a central, almost square courtyard (14 x 16 m), probably planned for the emplacement of a first well. East of the courtyard, the area is occupied by a building (fig. 4) which

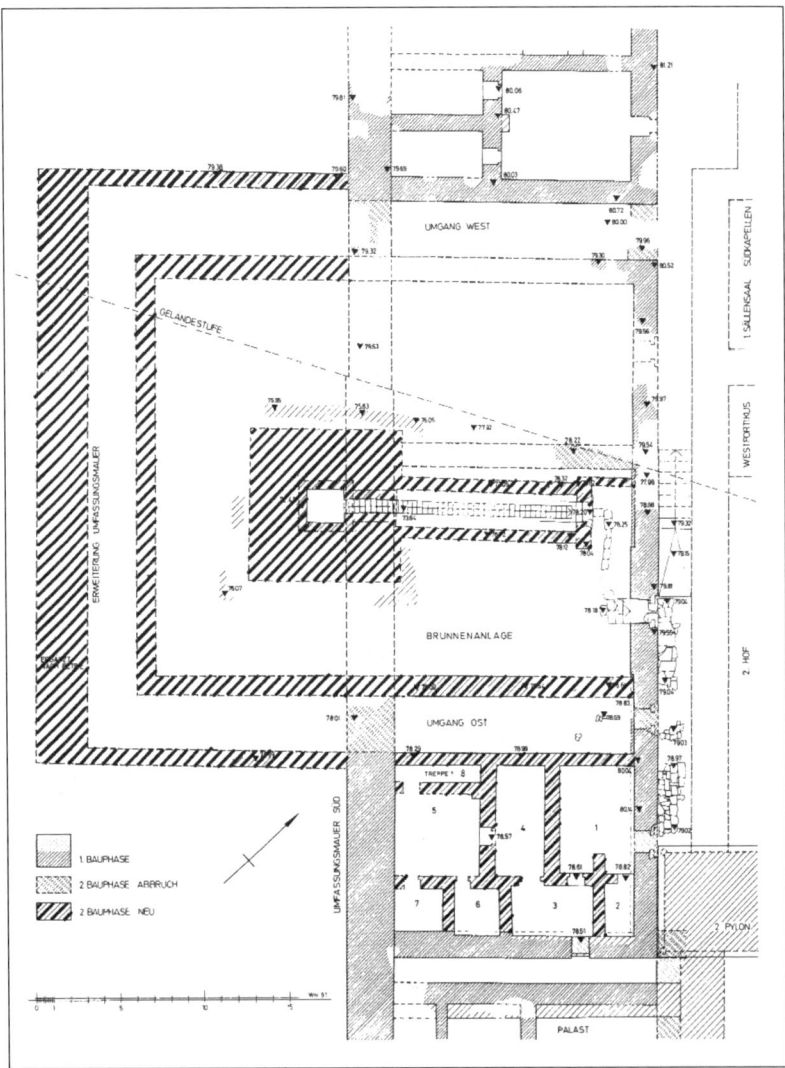

Fig. 4: Area south of second courtyard with temple well of the second building phase; first and second building phases superimposed.

may be interpreted as a priests' house. The area west of the courtyard, lying on higher ground and having the same dimensions as the priests' house, was found to be devoid of building remains.

The placement of the well in the courtyard described took this particular layout of the temple into consideration. Respecting the position of the priests' house and the western upper terrain, its staircase followed the eastern retaining wall of the latter. The complex as a whole, including an open space around the well and an outer passage, was doubled in size towards the south, displacing the southern enclosure wall. As access to the staircase of the well, the former entrance of the courtyard remained in use, and for communication between the passage around the well and the southern temple passage, two new doors were broken through the existing wall.

With the planned and partly-executed first version of the "House of a Million Years" of Merenptah (fig. 2), we are presented with almost the same layout as is known from the foundation trenches of the mortuary temple of Siptah.[3] This is the first temple we can trace succeeding the one of Merenptah. The impression given is that this temple was started and finished with only the elements necessary for the mortuary cult. Like the initial layout of the temple of Merenptah, it is also lacking the triple partition of its rear part. It only shows the barque shrines of the Theban triad; the rooms for the cult of the royal ancestors to the south and the cult of Re to their north are missing.

Concerning this triple order, Merenptah had apparently neglected the two important temples preceding, those of his grandfather Sety I and his father Ramesses II just to the north. However, he went back to the similar and reduced layout of the mortuary temple of Tuthmose III:[4] It consisted, from east to west, of one mud-brick pylon, two courtyards on mounting levels divided by a mud-brick wall, followed by the temple house with a single Osiris-pillared portico, two hypostyle halls, and finally, the triple partition of the rear part of the temple. The latter is different from that in the temple of Merenptah, but shows the same arrangement of the barque shrines.

The subsidiary structures of the first building phase, including the palace, had already been constructed in larger dimensions in the mortuary temples of Sety I and Ramesses II.[5] They were not changed during the second building phase, except for the palace which was rebuilt slightly larger (fig. 3), but retaining the same layout. Additional installations like the well and the priests' house west of the palace were built into the formerly open areas south of the second courtyard.

The aforementioned alterations carried out during a second building phase are partly additions to the primary layout and partly replacements of earlier structures in mud brick. Merenptah's primary intention may have been to accomplish the program of rooms necessary for the proper functioning of the cult, and also to upgrade and embellish his "House of a Million Years."

In answer to the question about the origin of the ideas for the alterations, and to what extent so far unknown novelties were introduced, we find that the introduction of three chapels on each side of the first hypostyle hall may have been based on the existence of chapels of the same kind at the same emplacement in the temple of Sety I,[6] the classical prototype of mortuary temples of the Nineteenth Dynasty. Later on, the same layout is found in the temple of Ramesses III at Medinet Habu, where one of the chapels kept the barque of the deceased king. The second hypostyle hall remained unaltered except for its side rooms; the rear rooms must have been changed into passages when further rooms were added to both sides of the barque shrines.

The alterations of the second courtyard, and the erection of two lateral Osiris-pillared colonnades, can only be seen in connection with the construction in stone masonry of a second pylon and the lateral walls of the courtyard, as mentioned above. Any previous arrangement of three

Osiris-pillared colonnades is unknown. The Ramesseum instead shows two opposing colonnades,[7] repeated at Medinet Habu.[8]

A second pylon goes back to the plan of the temple of Sety I,[9] later on an integrated part of the mortuary temple of Ramesses III at Medinet Habu.[10] The particular order of the complex east of the second pylon, comprising the first courtyard with its colonnaded halls and the palace, as well as the first pylon, is known from the Ramesseum, the mortuary temple of his father. In Merenptah's, the dimensions of the whole setting is smaller. Instead of the two rows of columns of the palace façade, the southern colonnade of the first courtyard shows a single row of columns. On its northern side, statues of the living king seem to have been placed in front of columns instead of pillars as in the mortuary temples of Ramesses II and Ramesses III.[11]

As reconstructed in the mortuary temple of Tuthmose III as well as the Ramesseum,[12] and later found in front of the temple of Ramesses III,[13] we have to also imagine the existence of a dromos leading to a tribune at its eastern end, long vanished under the cultivation.

Finally, looking at the altered layout of the rooms for the mortuary cult of the royal ancestors, added to the southwestern corner of the temple, this form, a four-pillared hall with a back room, though unknown in the temple of Sety I, where the cult already seems to have existed, can be seen in a similar layout at the Ramesseum (contiguous temple).[14] At the succeeding temple of Ramesses III, this layout is missing. Instead the layout resembles the two longitudinal rooms abolished at Merenptah's temple.

The sun court for the cult of Re with its central altar and subdivided room at the rear, seems to derive directly from the temple of Hatshepsut.[15] Neither the temple of Sety I nor the one of Ramesses II seem to have had the same layout. Only later on, in the temple of Medinet Habu, do we find a rear room. The slaughterhouse, which was finally erected outside the northwestern corner of the temple just beside the sun court, consisted of a courtyard accessed at its southeastern corner, a semicovered portico with one pillar and a room at its rear.

As the slaughterhouse of the temple of Sety I seems to have been situated at the southwestern corner of the temple,[16] it could have been located in the same place at the Ramesseum, where a complex subdivided into a courtyard, an antechamber, and two rooms at the rear, could be interpreted as such.

At the temple of Medinet Habu, the slaughterhouse, following exactly the same layout as the one in the temple of Merenptah, is situated on the north side as well. Here it has already become integrated with the temple.

While the plan of the first building stage seems to primarily follow the basic needs of the mortuary cult as established in the temple of Tuthmose III, only the final plan of the mortuary temple of Merenptah (fig. 1) with its alterations and additions in the second building stage, appears as a link between those of the Nineteenth and Twentieth Dynasties. Like this, the temple of Merenptah adapts itself to the temples of its immediate predecessors. By adding newly-conceived elements such as the Re cult complex and the slaughterhouse, as well as the rooms for the cult of the royal ancestors, it bridges the succeeding mortuary temple of Ramesses III, the latest of the monumental "Houses of a Million Years," where these elements already form part of the temple plan.

Notes:

1 W. M. Flinders Petrie, *Six Temples at Thebes 1896* (London, 1897), 10ff.

2 1.-4. Grabungsbericht, in: *MDAIK* 48, 1992, 65–91; *MDAIK* 51, 1995, 57–83; *MDAIK* 52, 1996, 201–232; *MDAIK* 55, 1999, 13–62.

3 Petrie, *Six Temples*, pl. 26.

4 H. Ricke, "Der Totentempel Amenophis' III," in *Bf* 11 (Wiesbaden, 1981), pl. 6.

5 R. Stadelmann, *MDAIK* 29, 2, 1973, Abb. 3; resp. Abb. 4, cf. U. Hölscher, *The Excavation of Medinet Habu* III (Chicago, 1941), fig. 53.

6 R. Lepsius, *Denkmäler aus Aegypten und Aethipien* (Berlin, 1849), Bl. 86; Hölscher, *Medinet Habu* III, 23, pl. 2; R. Stadelmann, *MDAIK* 35, 1979, 313.

7 Hölscher, *Medinet Habu* III, 73, pls. 10, 39A.

8 U. Hölscher, *The Excavation of Medinet Habu* I (Chicago, 1934), pl. 2; III, 8, pl. 20B.

9 LD 1, 86; at the temple of Sety I still constructed in mud brick, see R. Stadelmann, *MDAIK* 35, 1979, 310.

10 Hölscher, *Medinet Habu* I, pls. 1f.

11 Hölscher, *Medinet Habu* III, 73, pl. 10, for the temple of Ramesses II explained, however, as "Osiride pillars"; for the temple of Ramesses III, see Hölscher, *Medinet Habu* I, pls. 2, 20; III, 7f., fig. 3, pl. 18B.

12 J.-Cl. Golvin, "La restitution architecturale du Ramesseum," *Memnonia* I–II (Le Caire, 1991), pl. VII.

13 U. Hölscher, *The Excavation of Medinet Habu* IV (Chicago, 1951), 11–13, figs. 11–13.

14 Hölscher, *Medinet Habu* III, 23, 30, 74, figs. 45f., pl. 10.

15 E. Naville, *The Temple of Deir el-Bahari I* (London, 1895), pl. 1; VI (London, 1908), pl. 174; Hölscher, *Medinet Habu* III, pl. 2.

16 Hölscher, *Medinet Habu III*, 23f., pl. 2, 10.

The First *Serekhs*: Political Change and Regional Conventions[1]

Alejandro Jiménez-Serrano
Asociación Española de Egiptología

Introduction

Over the last 20 years, two different models[2] of the development of *serekhs* have been proposed. This study presents a critical discussion of both. The analysis and study of all the royal representations of the Late Predynastic and First Dynasty have provided evidence which permits the construction of an alternative model based on regional concepts of the image of power.

Contextualization

Late Predynastic Egypt needed writing, as did many other civilizations. Until recently it was assumed that the hieroglyphic system appeared as a consequence of the influences of neighboring regions (the Lower Euphrates or Susa),[3] it now seems that writing had a local origin.[4] However, it is a fact that some architectural concepts[5] or symbols had their origin in Uruk.

The geographical origin of the palace-façade is still under discussion, but does not affect this investigation, which assumes the reality of its existence and does not discuss the place where it first appeared.

The process of unifying the Nile Valley is also still being discussed, but there is some archaeological evidence that permits affirmation of the following:

- Since the middle of the Naqada II Period, at least one proto-state existed in Upper Egypt, whose elite were buried in Cemetery U at Abydos.
- At the end of the Naqada II period, the whole Nile Valley from Elephantine northward possessed more or less the same material culture.[6]
- Egypt maintained trade contacts with all neighboring regions: Nubia, the Western and Eastern Deserts, Sinai, Southern Canaan, and Mesopotamia. In the Naqada III Period, those contacts included two more areas: Phoenicia (mainly Byblos) and the Central Nile Valley.

Although social differentiation existed earlier than the Naqada III period, it is at that time when it is possible to detect the appearance of the representations of Egyptian and Nubian elites as a distinct class. All of them developed different types of iconography that became part of both cultures. Those local variations in the iconography are explained by the existence of different elites (for example, at Abydos and Qustul), although in other cases it could be explained by the ignorance of writing[7] or different traditions in the administration.

All the representations have been analyzed under a classification that has been specifically created. This classification is based on the different elements that constitute the "clasical" *serekh*, the falcon, palace-façade, and the phonogram. It has permitted the division of *serekhs* into six different categories: (A) phonograms, (B) a phonogram surmounted by a falcon, (C) a building surmounted by a falcon, (D) "classical" *serekhs* (phonogram plus a palace-façade surmounted by a falcon), (E) a palace-façade with phonograms in the interior, and (F) palace-façade.

From this classification, a typology of the royal representations of the Late Predynastic and Early First Dynasty has been created. The typology consists of one of the four periods into which have been divided the evolution of the royal representations (1–4). After one of those numbers, follows one of the letters of the classification (A–F), then the number of the site where the representation was found, as they appear listed on the pages following. In some cases, if there is more than one example from the same site, a letter has been suffixed (from "a"). For example, 4D35b means:

4: number of table

D: type of royal representation

35: Hierakonpolis

b: example

The Evolution of the Representation of the Royal Name in the Late Predynastic and Early Part of the First Dynasty in Egypt

Since the discovery of tomb U-j, it has been known that the administration of the elite at Abydos was in its developmental stages at the beginning of the Naqada III Period. We can presume that this process has parallels in some parts of the Delta, as well as in other parts of the Nile Valley (for example, Lower Nubia).

In Upper Egypt, it is possible that the necessity of a complex instrument of management implied the creation of writing, which was shortly after used to represent the leader. In some parts of the Delta and its neighboring regions (the region of Memphis, "The Ways of Horus" and Southern Canaan),[8] other systems of representing the elite were developed. In this case, it was used as a container to represent the contents, in other words, the image of the palace-façade was used to refer to the person who held the power there.

After the reign of Scorpion I, some depictions that evolved directly from the ones created in the Delta (palace-façades) appeared at Abydos, which indicates the exchange of concepts between the two regions. Probably this type was created in Lower Egypt, because this design appeared later with phonograms inside.

In Lower Nubia, a similar system was developed. From the seal impressions and reliefs in the incensaries found at Qustul,[9] it can be assumed that the Nubian elite were always represented in relation to a building, but in those cases, it was not a palace-façade, but a temple with a falcon (Horus or Dedwen) on the top.

Therefore, in this early phase, Naqada IIIa.2/b.1, the three elements that constitute the "classic" *serekh* (phonogram, palace-façade, and falcon) have already appeared in the Nile Valley.

During the next phase, the period of Naqada IIIb.1(/2), coincidental with the expansion of the protostate of Qustul,[10] the systems of representing the elite began to intermix in Egypt. In Upper

243

Egypt, the system of representation with a phonetic sign evolved and took an element (the falcon) that appeared in Lower Nubia. In this new system, the typical Nubian building is deleted (which has no meaning in Upper Egypt), but received a new element—a phonogram (for example, Iri Hor). It could explain the appearance of the so-called Double Falcon, in an area influenced by trade, such as the Sinai, as the spread of Upper Egyptian religious concepts based on duality.[11]

In Lower Egypt and in its surrounding areas, the system of representing the power of the palace-façade emerged with a new element from Upper Egypt, the phonogram (Ni and Hat). Because they never appeared under the protection of the god Horus, they could not be titled "Horus."

During the next phase (Scorpion II-Narmer), and due to unknown reasons but probably related to the unification process, the "classic" serekh appeared. At the same time, all the types continued to be represented in their original locations. There are important differences concerning the materials or contexts in which the contemporary serekhs appeared outside of Egypt. In Southern Canaan and Northern Sinai all the representations appeared on pottery (a royal propaganda artifact-gifts), in Lower Nubia, these are related to military records. Other cases are those representations in the deserts, which are closer in the case of Canaan and Sinai. It might be inferred that those are samples of the royal propaganda directed at intimidating the nomads of the desert, showing the power of the Egyptian king, who could organize expeditions to those territories.

There is a question that derives from all of this analysis; can it be assumed that the different types of representation were diverse political entities? The answer is affirmative, but must distinguish the different phases. In the first and in the second phases (Naqada IIIa.2/b.1/2), the majority of the representations might correspond to states, coalitions, or others. Upper Egypt, under the rule of Scorpion I, can be considered a unified state, after the conflicts between the protostates in the second half of the Naqada II Period.[12] It is very plausible that the system of writing—with an Upper Egyptian origin—spread out at the same time as the Upper Egyptian State, although it could be faster than the political expansion. The unification was not a single event; rather, it should be understood as a long process of integration which had conflicts and numerous centrifugal movements, whose causes would have diverse origins: pest infections, invasions, debility of the central government, and so on.

Sites:

Palestine & Sinai (1-10):

Tell Erani.-	1.
Nahal Tillah.-	2.
Arad.-	3.
Raffiah.-	4.
Beda.-	5.
Sinai.-	6.
Tel Malhata	7.
En Besor	8.

Delta (11-20):

Kafr Hassan Daud.-	11.
Ezbet el-Tell.-	12.
Minshat Abu Omar.-	13.
Tell Ibrahim Awad.-	14.
Tell el-Farkha.-	15.
Tell el-Fara'in (Buto).-	16.
Lower Egypt.-	17.

Memphite region (21-30):

Abu Rawash.-	21.
Zawiyet el-Aryan.-	22.
Tura.-	23.
Saqqara.-	24.
Helwan.-	25.
Tarkhan.-	26.
Abusir el-Meleq.-	27.

Upper Egypt (31-40):

Umm el-Qaab.-	31.
Temenos of Abido.-	32.
Coptos.-	33.
Wadi el-Qash.-	34.
Hierakonpolis.-	35.
Adaima.-	36.

Lower Nubia (41-50):

Siali.-	41.
Qustul.-	42.
Faras.-	43.
Djebel Sheikh Suleiman.-	44.

Sites	A	B	C	D	E	F
Raffiah						1F4a 1F4b
Beda						 1F5a
Ezbet el-Tell						1F12a 1F12b 1F12c
Tell el-Farkha						1F15a-d (unpub.)
Abusir el-Meleq						1F27a 1F27b
Umm el-Qaab	1A31A-kk2					
Siali			1C41a 1C41b			
Qustul			1C42a 1C42b 1C42c 1C42d			
Faras			1C43a			

Table 1: Different types of royal representations in the Naqada IIIa2/b1 period.

Yacimientos	A	B	C	D	E	F
Tel Malhata					2E7a	2F7a 2F7b
Sinai			2C6a			
Beda			2C5a 2C5b			
Tell Ibrahim Awad			2C14a			
Tell el–Fara'in (Buto)					2E16a	
Zawiyet el–Aryan		2B22a				
Tura			2C23a		2E23a 2E23b	
Tarjan					2E26a	
Umm el-Qaab		2B31a-o				2F31a 2F31b 2F31c 2F31d
Hierakopolis		2B35-a-c				

Table 2: Different types of royal representations in the Naqada IIIb.1(/2) period.

Sites	A	B	C	D	E	F
Minshat Abu Omar				3D13a		3F13a
Tell Ibrahim Awad					3E14a	
Kafr Hassan Daud					3E11a	
Lower Egypt			3C17a			
Helwan				3D25a 3D25b 3D25c		
Tarkhan	3A26a			3D26a 3D26b 3D26c		
Umm el-Qa'ab				3D31a-aa	3E231a-j	
Temenos of Abidos	3A32a					
Wadi el-Qash			3C34a			
Hierakonpolis	3A35a 3A35b 3A35c	3B35a 3B35b				2F35a
Qustul			3C42a			
Djebel Sheikh Suleiman	3A44Aa		3C44a			

Table 3: Different types of royal representations in the Naqada IIIe period.

Sites	A	B	C	D	E	F
Tel Erani					4E1a	
Nahal Tillah					4E2a	
En Besor				4D8a		
Arad				4D3a		
Minshat Abu Omar				4D13a		4F13a
Tell Ibrahim Awad					4E14a	
Ezbet el-Tell				4D12a	4E12a	
Lower Egypt					4E17a	
Abu Rauash						4F21a
Zawiyet el-Aryan				4D22a		4F22a
Saqqara				4D24a		
Helwan		4B25a			4E25a	
Tarkhan				4D26a	4E26a	
Umm el-Qaab	4A31a	4B31a 4B31a		4D31a	4E31a	4F31a
						4F32a

Sites	A	B	C	D	E	F
Temenos of Abydos						
Wadi el-Qash				4D34a 4D34b[1]		
Adaima				4D36a y b[2]		
Hierakonpolis	4A35a 4A35b			4D35a	4E35a 4E35b	
Djebel Sheikh Suleiman			4C42a			

Table 4: Different types of royal representations in the First Dynasty.

Notes:

1 The present paper is a summary of my Ph.D thesis, *La evolución del nombre real en Egipto desde el final del Predinástico hasta principios de la Primera Dinastía*, defended at the University de Jaén (Spain) in 2000.

2 W. Kaiser and G. Dreyer, "Umm el-Qaab. Nachuntersuchungen im frühzeitlichen Königsfriedhof 2," *MDAIK* 38 (1982), 211–269; E.C.M. van den Brink, "The incised *serekh* signs of Dynasties 0-1. Part I; complete vessels," in J. Spencer (ed.), *Aspects of Early Egypt* (London, 1996), 140–158.

3 B. G. Trigger *et al., Ancient Egypt. A Social History* (Cambridge, 1983), 40; J. R. Ray, "The Emergence of Writing in Egypt," *World Archaeology* 17/3 (1986), 309; J. Vercoutter, *La Prédynastie égyptienne. Anciens et nouveaux concepts* (CRIPEL 13; Lille, 1991), 144; A. J. Spencer, *Early Egypt. The Rise of Civilisation in the Nile Valley* (London, 1993), 61–62; H. G. Fischer, "The Origin of Egyptian Hieroglyphs," in W. M. Senner (ed.), *The Origins of Writing* (Nebraska, 1989) 61; A. Jiménez Serrano, "Las rutas del comercio de Egipto con Mesopotamia a finales del IV Milenio a. C.," *Jornadas de Arqueología Subacuática* III (1998), 231–235.

4 P. Vernus, "La naissance de l'ecriture dans l'Egypte Ancienne," *Archeo-Nil* 3 (1993), 79, 89; J. Cervelló Autuori, *Egipto y África. Origen de la civilización y la mlonarquía faraónicas en su contexto africano,* (Barcelona, 1996), 108, n. 324; earlier, see W. S. Arnett, *The Predynastic origin of Egyptian Hieroglyphs,* (Washington, 1982).

5 T. von der Way, "Indications of Architecture with Niches at Buto," in R. Friedman and B. Adams (eds.) *The Followers of Horus* (Oxford, 1992), 220, 223,

6 von der Way, "Indications," 217, fig. 1.

7 We have to assume that many pot marks were made before the piece was fired. In this context, if a potter made pot marks, it was not necessary for him to be able to read and write.

8 It is possible that the high number of *serekhs* found in "The Ways of Horus" and in the sites at Southern Canaan might be due to research attention being focused on those regions in contrast to the recent and difficult excavations in the Delta. I can assume that this high frequency of representations of Egyptian power was Egyptian propaganda directed to the foreign lands.

9 B. B. Williams, *The A-Group Royal Cemetery at Qustul: Cemetery L* (Chicago, 1986).

10 A. Jiménez Serrano, *La transición del cuarto al tercer milenio a. C. en la Baja Nubia,* Memoria de Licenciatura, Universidad de Jaén, 1997 (unpublished).

11 There are many mentions of Horus and Set as *Nebuy* ("The Two Lords"). The ideograms of this word consist of two falcons, see Autuori, *Egipto y África,* 200–203, with references.

12 A. Pérez Largacha, *El nacimiento del Estado en Egipto* (Madrid, 1993).

The Work of the American Research Center in Egypt in the Tomb of Sety I in the Valley of the Kings, 1998–1999

Michael Jones

American Research Center in Egypt, Cairo.

During 1998 and 1999 the American Research Center in Egypt carried out a series of conservation studies in the Tomb of Sety I (KV 17) in the Valley of the Kings.[1] The scope of the work was a technical study and a touristic presentation plan with the following components:

1. Geotechnical evaluation leading to a study of the structural stability of the tomb.
2. Study and evaluation of the conservation needs of the mural decoration.
3. Study and evaluation of the current display of the tomb to visitors with proposals for suitable site presentation including lighting, walkways, protection, environmental monitoring and control and signage.

The project did not call for actual intervention as its purpose was to examine existing conditions in the tomb in order to understand how it reached its present state, and to use this to formulate an appropriate plan for possible future restoration work.

The project was divided into the following separate components, each of which was a specific activity completed with a comprehensive report.

1. Photographic documentation in 35 mm color slides and 35 mm black and white film before the project began and during its implementation. (Robert Vincent and Michael Jones; Cairo.)
2. Three-dimensional survey. (Jim McLane and Brad Porter; San Francisco.)
3. Geotechnical study. (Jim McLane and Raphael Wüst; San Francisco and Vancouver.)
4. Evaluation of the mural decoration. (Cristina Vazio, Silvia Boria, Fabio Porzio, and Marina Possehl; Rome.)
5. Egyptological study to collect all the published material on the tomb and its contents, and to provide an interpretation of the tomb to use as a source for signs, brochures, and other information for visitors. (Bojana Mojsov; Cairo.)
6. A display and presentation plan with visitor quotas and designs for access, walkways, information, lighting, ventilation, and safety. (Shari Saunders; Cairo.)

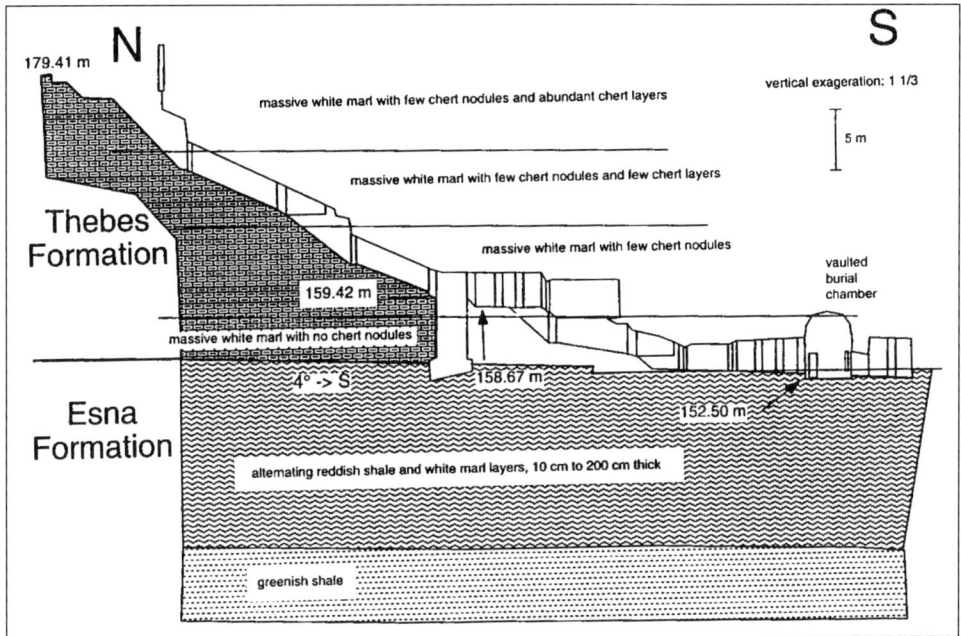

Fig. 1: Cross section through KV 17 showing the lithological composition. (After McLane and Wüst.)

Recent History of the Tomb

Giovanni Belzoni discovered the Tomb of Sety I in October 1817 and left a detailed narrative complete with colored illustrations.[2] He and Alessandro Ricci also made over three hundred drawings and watercolor paintings which provide a unique record of the condition in which they found the tomb.[3] Following its discovery, the tomb became the most famous and consequently the most visited in the Valley. As a result, the processes of destruction and decay rapidly accelerated until the monument faced a series of crises at the beginning of the twentieth century. Belzoni himself set this process in motion in two ways. By filling up the well (Room D) to facilitate removal of the sarcophagus, now in the Sir John Soane Museum, London, he changed the drainage system and created a potential watercourse so that the lower chambers of the tomb flooded during heavy rains in 1818. For his pioneering "publication," in the form of the celebrated replica of the tomb in London, he needed impressions of the painted reliefs. The numerous wax and papier maché squeezes eroded the paint and left deposits on the reliefs. Soon afterward, the actual removal of selected reliefs by Champollion and Rosellini and others throughout the nineteenth century defaced the walls of the tomb irreversibly. In 1901 Carter installed electric lights, walkways, and railings. Two years later, following the collapse of Pillar E in Room J, he restored the broken and eroded walls with red brick and constructed supports in Rooms I, J, and K. Shortly thereafter sections of the vaulted astronomical ceiling of Room K collapsed. Additional steel frame supports were added in Room J in 1981 and, following a further collapse of the east end of the vaulted ceiling 1988 and finally in Room K in 1991, the tomb has been closed to visitors.[4]

The next serious attempt to record the tomb in detail after Belzoni was made by Harry Burton, whose comprehensive photographic documentation from 1921–28 covers all 16 rooms.[5]

These photographs have proven essential for understanding the progress of decay on the mural paintings and deterioration in the tomb's geology.[6]

The Geotechnical Evaluation

This includes an assessment of how the tomb fits into the general geological structure and records the faults, major cracks, and lithology of the tomb. Rock samples were taken from the pit in Room K and from fallen pieces of Room P for swelling tests and compressive strength tests.

The geological composition of the bedrock of Western Thebes consists of three formations.[7] Stratigraphically lowest is the Tarawan Formation which is composed of chalk, also referred to as "Dakhlah Chalk." It is visible in the area around the private tombs and the Deir al-Bahri Temples, where its thickness is greater than 30 m. Lying over the Tarawan Chalk is the Esna shale. The Esna Formation is in two distinct units of which the lower, composed entirely of shale, is approximately 40 m deep, while the upper layer is a series of interleaved beds of shales and marls 16 m deep. The most striking exposure of the Esna shale is to be seen in the lower parts of the cliffs around Deir al-Bahri, where it appears as a dark gray loose rock with narrow white bands. The Esna shales are overlain by the Thebes Formation, composed of marine limestone and marls more than 350 m thick. The Thebes Formation is divided into four main layers (Members I–IV) according to variations in their lithology and weathering patterns. The lowest, Member I, is a marl layer 75 m deep topped by 12 m of alternating marls and limestone. Members II–IV are alternating layers of limestone, marl, shale, and nodular chalk containing chert nodules and interbedded chert bands more than 270 m thick.

The tomb was cut straight into the lowermost unit of the Thebes Formation, through a stratum of marls with frequent nodules and bands of chert. These are clearly visible in the walls of Corridors A and B. The ancient masons had trouble cutting through the hard chert to make the walls even. In some places the chert is left standing proud, while elsewhere it was cut back into the wall or extracted and the resulting cavities filled with plaster. Large lacunae in the reliefs occur where the plaster filling has fallen out. At the depth of Rooms C to G the chert is far less frequent, as at this level the tomb was cut through a solid marl layer. The well (Room D) descends more than 11 m vertically through the marl. The lower part is now filled with over a meter of fine silty flash flood deposits which have almost completely buried the two side chambers at the base of the shaft. In 1994 about 85 cm of flood water collected in the shaft, equivalent to approximately 13 cubic m, which were eventually absorbed by the fill and bedrock. The interface between the Thebes Formation marl and underlying Esna shale is about 1 m below the top of the present fill of the well.

Throughout the marls there is a system of natural joints which are clearly visible in the ceilings of Rooms E, F, and G. At the corner of the walls between Room D (well) and Room E, large triangular sections of rock have fallen away and in Room F a section of the ceiling has detached and fallen at the intersection of two open joints. The joints sometimes show traces of sediments, probably brought in by rainwater seeping through from the surface, indicating that some of the joints run through the rock in the form of open cracks to the surface of the Valley. In Room G, adjacent to Room F, considerable ceiling damage has occurred where sections of rock have fallen, and the damage was enlarged when Champollion and Rosselini extracted the doorjambs at the base of the stairs.[8] Rooms G, H, and I have been cut through the deepest part of Member I of the Thebes Formation with the upper surface of the Esna shale only a few centimeters below the floor. The significance of this becomes clearer in the innermost rooms of the tomb. In Room I the ceiling is poorly preserved, but only a few joints can be seen because large segments have

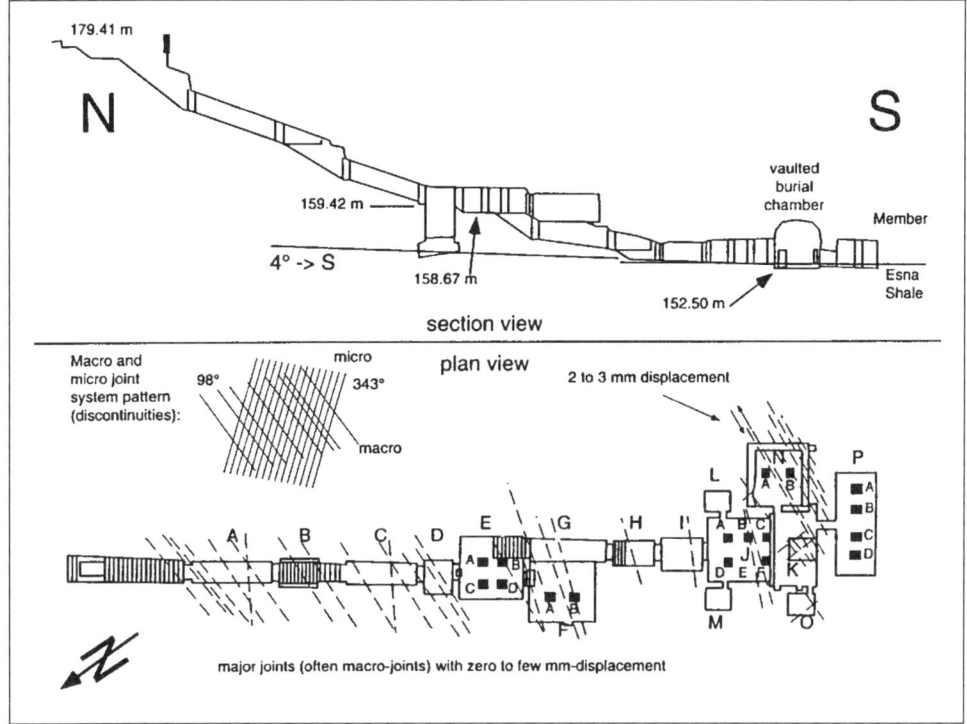

Fig. 2: Cross section through KV 17 showing the system of micro- and macro-joints. The major joint system runs between 90° and 110° (macro-joints) and 345° (micro-joints). The micro-joint system has a spacing of 1.0 to 5.0 cm. (After McLane and Wüst.)

detached and fallen, mostly on the western side. The top of the Esna shale emerges at the base of the west wall and there has been extensive collapse of the jambs between Rooms I and J, which are now repaired with Carter's brickwork. Nevertheless, crack monitors which have been attached to the walls and ceiling at various times since 1961 show that very little movement has occurred since then.

Rooms J and K and the rooms opening off of them show increasing signs of stress, which undoubtedly began as soon as the first major rainfall hit the region after the tomb was quarried. The excavation of the tomb to its lowest levels penetrated the Esna shale which is visible at the bases of the walls and pillars to a height of over 1.5 m in Room K. Severe erosion of the soft shale caused by flooding and wear and tear during the nineteenth century is now marked by the extensive red brick repairs mentioned above. On the west side of Room J the ceiling is now supported by steel beams erected before Burton took his photographs in the 1920s. These were augmented in 1990. It was on this side that column E collapsed in 1901. In Room K extensive cracking is visible on all the walls,[9] and large sections of the vaulted astronomical ceiling fell in two major collapses in 1902 and 1988. Steel beams now support the east end of this Room. Room P, situated beyond the burial chamber (Room K) is, however, the most severely ruined room. This room is still filled with collapsed masonry from the walls, ceiling, and one of the columns. The western end of this room lies immediately over the enigmatic 100 meter-long tunnel which opens off the pit in the floor of Room K and descends steeply into the shale on the same alignment as the main part of the tomb itself. It is not known whether the tunnel cuts completely through the Esna shale into the Tarawan Chalk.

A comparison between conditions shown in the Harry Burton photographs and the state of the tomb today has proved invaluable. An important detail shown in Burton's photographs is that there were many more cracks and holes in the walls than are apparent today, particularly in the upper rooms of the tomb. These holes and cracks were filled during various unrecorded small scale conservation works that have been carried out during the 1980s and 1990s, thereby obscuring important evidence for the structural state of the walls. Because of this activity, very little difference can be seen now between present conditions and those of 80 years ago in the cracks or dislodged sections of masonry in Rooms A to I. In Room J, however, cracks on the west side of the room are now more visible. In Room K, there is striking evidence for significant deterioration, since cracks have become more numerous and visible, some cracks show displacement and a large section of rock has detached from the south side of the vaulted ceiling.

The greater damage in the lowermost rooms is the result of their position at the interface between the marls of the Thebes Formation and the underlying Esna shales combined with the effect of water that has been introduced both by direct flooding and seepage through joints. Analyses of tests on rock samples from the tomb show that the rocks are highly absorbent. The shale beneath the floors of the lower rooms of the tomb swell and shrink during saturation and desiccation and are more likely to shear than to crack, thus applying enormous stress on the marl above. The marl, which is more rigid and has a huge overburden of rock above, will crack under pressure. Swelling and shrinkage in the period since the tomb was cut in the early Nineteenth Dynasty has occurred with a sufficient combination of upward force and downward compression to cause the alternating build-up of stress and stress release, which has in turn led to the cracking, fissuring, and breakage visible in the rock today.

Evaluation of the Mural Decoration of the Tomb

This study was carried out by a team from Rome led by Cristina Vazio.[10] Every decorated surface in the tomb was examined in detail and data were collected based on a close visual examination. Following this first phase, trial conservation tests were carried out on six decorated surfaces in different parts of the tomb.

The process by which the ancient craftsmen prepared the walls, pillars and ceilings for decorating was begun by leveling the bedrock into a flat surface and then filling any cavities with a gray plaster composed of a mixture of gypsum, anhydrite, and silt. The surfaces were then coated in a very smooth plaster layer 1 to 2 mm thick, the same mixture but with more gypsum added to give it a whiter and less coarse finish.

Preliminary drawings, of which a considerable amount survive in the tomb, were then made, laid out first in red and then "formalized" in a more finished style in black. The outlines of the drawings on the walls and pillars, but not the ceilings, which were left flat, were carved out and the surrounding surfaces cut away to leave the plaster layer attached only to the parts in raised relief. The interrupted progress of the carving in the lower end of Corridor B provides a clear insight into the technique: The ancient sculptors began at the bottom of the wall and worked upwards, so that the upper half of the walls on both sides is still completely covered in the plaster. Room F, where almost no carving took place, is in the same condition. Once the walls had been carved, a white preparatory wash made from a mixture of potassium salts, calcium, magnesium, and arabinose acid was applied to the whole surface to provide a uniform background

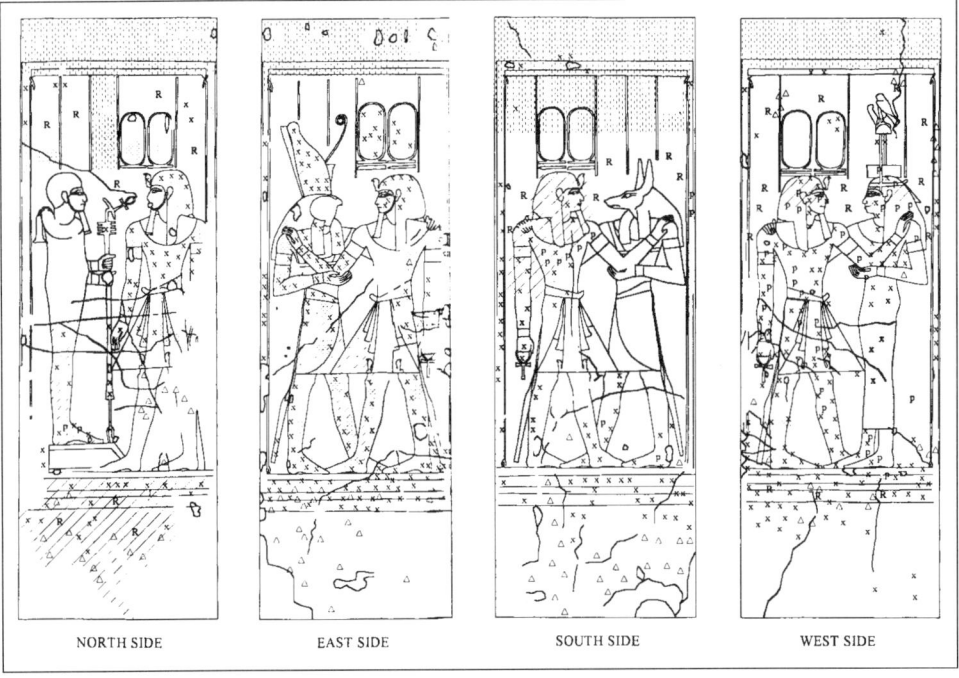

NORTH SIDE	EAST SIDE	SOUTH SIDE	WEST SIDE

KEY OF STATE OF CONSERVATION DRAWINGS

AREA OF SQUEEZES

GIPSUM	▨
WAX	▢
WAX AND RESIN	▢
PAPIER-MACHE	▢
PALE MORTAR	▥

SUPPORT

LACUNAE OF DEPT	⬭
CRACKS	⬭

PLASTER LAYER

LACK OF ADHESION	▵▵▵▵

PICTORIAL LAYER

ABRASION	▨
FLAKING	▦
LOSSES	▢
MACULAR CHROMATIC ALTERATION	▨
FOREIGN SUBSTANCES	▢
NATURAL DEPOSIT	▦

PREVIOUS INTERVENTIONS

FILLINGS OF LACUNAE AND CRACKS	▢
READHESION OF DETACHED FRAGMENTS	▨
CLEANING	▢
RETOUCHES	▢
FACING	▢

OTHER

DEVICES FOR MONITORING STRUCTURAL MOVEMENT:

GLASS/PERSPEX	▭
GYPSUM/PAPER	▭
IRON OBJECTS	▨
INSCRIPTION	▨

Fig. 3: Room E, Pillar A; diagram showing the present state of conservation of all four faces. (After Vazio.)

for the paint layer. Even where the background color was yellow, as in Rooms J and K, there is an underlying white preparatory layer to give the yellow surface greater luminosity. The binding medium for this layer, as for all the colors used in the paintings, was gum arabic. In Rooms E and I an unusual phenomenon was observed: Here a gray layer composed of charcoal and gum arabic was applied before the white preparatory layer, either to provide a contrasting shade of white or to stand for an aspect of the mythology of these rooms which has yet to be understood.

Detailed examination of the walls revealed that an astonishing number of alterations took place during work on the murals, not only in the preliminary drafting stages but also during the work of carving and painting the reliefs. This is all the more remarkable given the fact that there was never any scope for improvisation in the designs beyond the most basic selection of subjects. An example is on the first pillar in Room F where a pale wash was applied over the initial drawings to erase them so that parts of the figures could be drawn again. On the famous scene of Sety I presented to Osiris and Hathor by Horus in Room E,[11] the legs of the king were first painted in Egyptian blue and those of Horus were first painted in Egyptian green. Both were then overpainted in red. It is not clear whether this was an intentional sequence of colors that was necessary for the complete identification of these two figures, or whether this represents a mistake that was subsequently covered over.

The principal colors used throughout the tomb were white (huntite), black (charcoal, lampblack or wine-black carbon obtained by burning grapevines), red (red ochre comprised of mostly iron oxide mixed with varying quantities of clay or chalk), yellow (orpiment; asrsenic trisulphide in monoclinic crystalline form), blue (Egyptian blue; a synthetic pigment obtained from the fusion of silica, calcium carbonate, sodium carbonate, and copper), and green (Egyptian green, obtained by the same process as Egyptian blue but with a different oxidation). The reds and yellows were finished with a coat of varnish made of gum arabic.[12] Its purpose was probably to enhance the depth of color so that the red and yellow surfaces would not be overpowered by the lustrous effect of the Egyptian blue and green, and the striking contrast of white and black.

Despite the high quality of the original craftsmanship, the decorated surfaces in KV 17 are on the whole in a poor state of preservation. This emerges clearly from the study of the existing conditions carried out to determine the causes of decay and deterioration, and to provide recommendations for future restoration work. Nevertheless, even though some parts of the tomb may appear to be seriously damaged, an appropriate intervention process could reverse many of the problems encountered. On the other hand, in some areas where damage appears to be superficially light, closer examination will show that restoration could accomplish very little.

The following is a summary of the main causes of decay in order of seriousness, as reflected by their impact on the walls of the tomb:

1. Squeezes and the removal of actual fragments have accounted for the most serious and widespread damage. Squeezes were taken in some 880 places throughout the tomb and in many places multiple squeezes were taken of the same subject. They can be quantified as follows:

    Squeezes using beeswax: about 510.

    Squeezes using a mixture of beeswax, resin and vegetable fibers: about 140.

    Squeezes using papier maché: about 130.

    Squeezes using gypsum: about 100.

    Squeezes using pale mortar: 3.

    The earliest squeezes were made by Belzoni using the first two methods listed. The effect of squeezes containing wax was to leave a residue in the form of dark wax and resin drips on the wall surface or a thin yellowish-brown coating which has adhered strongly to the wall and hardened into a flaky discoloration. This is especially clear where the underlying pictorial layer has absorbed some of the substances used in the squeezing mixture.[13] These substances have, however, served to protect the paint beneath, so that, in places where wax squeezes were taken, the original decoration is relatively well preserved.

The squeezes taken using gypsum, probably by Hay and others, were lethal for the pictorial layer. The gypsum was mixed with water which dissolved the pigments on contact so that walls subjected to this treatment are now stripped down to the bedrock surface. They are usually disfigured with drips of hardened gypsum.

Papier maché squeezes also caused numerous abrasions to the surfaces. The process involved the application of numerous layers of wet paper to the surface, which, after they had dried, could be removed as a mold bearing an imprint of the relief. The original paint layer was often protected from the water by an application of wax prior to the wet paper and traces of gray wax can be seen in the areas squeezed in papier maché. Once the paper was dry, remains of wax and paper were generally left stuck on the wall for fear of removing the paint, but many of these have been recently pulled off with the expected losses to the paint layer. In other areas they remain and the pigments are generally well- preserved beneath. A very few mortar squeezes were made that have caused abrasions to the walls.

2. Flooding. The walls of the entrance corridors, Rooms A, B and C, and part of the well, Room D, were scoured clean by flooding both before and after Belzoni's time. Mud traces still adhere to the walls in the first corridor and staining from dampness after flooding is visible elsewhere.

3. Inappropriate conservation and restoration. Examples of over-zealous cleaning can be seen in parts of Room K and the south wall of Room J where the yellow background has been over-cleaned so that the ancient varnish has been removed and the white underpainting shows through in some places. Other areas show modern repainting of damaged pictorial surfaces and refilling of cracks in unsuitable materials. Both these interventions can be reversed and replaced by more appropriate measures.

4. The presence of visitors and tourists. Numerous graffiti and blackened walls from candle and torch smoke date to the nineteenth century when this was the only means of lighting the interior prior to the introduction of electricity. The tomb was inhabited by travelers during the century, and Champollion organized a great banquet in the tomb in honor of Belzoni during which fires were lit. Most of these traces can be easily removed, indeed many of those visible in Burton's photographs have already been wiped off. However, more serious damage has been done by people rubbing against and touching the walls which are irreparably disfigured in many of the most vulnerable places in the tomb.

5. Cleaning tests were carried out on the south wall of Room E, on the west wall of Room I, on the east wall of Room K and on one area on each of the two pillars in Room N. The particular surfaces were chosen because they were considered typical of the original techniques, and the range of deterioration and kinds of decay, and in order to ascertain the materials and methodologies that would be suitable for a future restoration of the mural decoration.

The studies undertaken by this project have shown that, although a complete conservation of KV 17 is possible, it would be extremely difficult, complex, and expensive. The scale of the undertaking should not be underestimated. A full structural stability survey would be needed and its findings and recommendations assessed before further work is planned. The lower parts of the tomb are potentially dangerous and Room P should be considered an hazardous area in its present condition. The unexcavated sections of the tomb, Rooms D (well), O, and P should be carefully excavated by archaeologists working with a structural engineer.

Only after the excavation work and sufficient structural intervention have been accomplished would it be possible to begin work on the conservation of the mural decoration. The tomb contains about 2,350 square m of painted reliefs on walls and pillars, painted ceilings, and preliminary drawings in Corridor B and Room F. Based on the observations made during test cleanings, an estimated ten years would be needed for a complete conservation of all the decorated parts of the tomb.

Presentation of the Tomb to Visitors

The tomb should be opened to visitors only after it has been made safe by the completion of structural engineering work and a comprehensive conservation project. The damage caused to the interior environment by uncontrolled access is well documented. Therefore, a visitor quota must be imposed and adhered to, which will not only ease the environmental pollution inside the tomb (temperature, humidity, and carbon dioxide levels) but will also improve the quality of a visit. Discreet barriers should be installed to protect the paintings. Raised floors to prevent visitors from walking on the bedrock pavements will be needed to reduce erosion. Limited and carefully-positioned signs should be installed that will not obscure views or hinder circulation. Extensive, well-positioned low-temperature lighting will be needed together with a ventilation system that will not disturb the atmosphere of the tomb.

Visitors to any ancient monument should be encouraged to participate in the preservation of the monument itself. This can be achieved through successful site management. One significant way in which they might do so is to avoid entering the original altogether and, having experienced the place where it is located, proceed to an accurate replica. For tomb as large as that of Sety I the replica might comprise only its most important parts. It could be sited close to the actual tomb and form the core of a visitors center focused on the Valley of the Kings in both its ancient and modern contexts. The replica would be successful only by faithfully reproducing portions of the actual tomb as precisely as possible and, if well maintained, would become a major attraction that would contribute to saving the original monument.[14]

Notes:

1 The work was carried out by the Antiquities Development Project (ADP) of ARCE with funding from the United States Agency for International Development (USAID) under Grant No. 263–G–00–96–00016–00, "Promotion of Sustainable Tourism Cultural Activities," also known as the Mubarak–Gore Agreement, in collaboration with the Supreme Council of Antiquities. The Project Officers were Thomas Dailey and Anne Patterson, and the Grant Administrator for the ADP was Brian Martinson.

We are grateful to the SCA for permission to do this work and to Secretary General Professor Dr. Abd el-Halim Nur el Din and his successor, Professor Dr. Gaballah Ali Gaballah, Chief Inspector of Luxor Antiquities Mohammed Nasr, and on the West Bank Sabri Abd el-Aziz, Mohammed el-Bialy and Ibrahim Soliman. ARCE is supporting another project in the Valley of the Kings, focusing on floodwater control, sponsored by the California Academy of Sciences; J. McLane and R. Wüst, "Flood Hazards and Protection Measures in the Valley of the Kings," *Cultural Resource Management* 23, 6 (2000), 35–38.

2 G. Belzoni, *Narrative of Operations and Recent Discoveries within the Pyramids, Temples, Tombs and Excavations,* in *Egypt and Nubia,* 1821 (London, 1822) 230–246. PM I^2, (1973), 528 (plan) and 535–545. References to rooms and scenes here are those in PM.

3 These are now in the Bristol City Art Gallery and Museum. I am grateful to Sue Giles for permission to examine them in August of 1996. Examples are reproduced in color in E. Hornung, *The Valley of the Kings* (New York, 1990), 133.

4 J. Romer, *Valley of the Kings* (New York, 1981), 123, 126, 178. Interventions in the tomb during the twentieth century have been summarized in a report by John Rutherford submitted to the Egyptian Antiquities Organization, in J. Rutherford *et al., Damage in the Royal Tombs in the Valley of the Kings at Thebes,* 1977 (unpublished).

5 The photographs are in the archives of the Metropolitan Museum of Art, New York. All but four photographs are published in E. Hornung, *The Tomb of Pharaoh Seti I. Das Grab von Sethos' I* (Basel, 1991). We are indebted to Susan Allen for providing the project with copies of the four unpublished photographs.

6 The most recent publication of KV 17 is the survey in K. Weeks (ed.) *Atlas of the Valley of the Kings,* Publications of the Theban Mapping Project I (Cairo, 2000), sheets 34–36. A description with plans, views and bibliography can be found at www.kv5.com/html/data_kv17.html

7 The following geological and geotechnical descriptions are derived from the report by Raphael Wüst presented in J. McLane, R. Wüst, et al., *Geotechnical Evaluation Tomb of Seti I Valley of the Kings* (1999), for the Antiquities Development Project (ADP) of ARCE.

8 PM I^2, 539; the east jamb is in Florence and the west jamb is in the Louvre. A drawing by Hay showing these walls intact is reproduced in Romer, *Valley,* 123. A fragment with the head of the goddess Maat removed at the same time from the entrance jamb of Room N is also in Florence.

9 Clear color photographs showing cracks in Room K are reproduced in R. H. Wilkinson and C. N. Reeves, *The Complete Valley of the Kings* (London, 1996), 136.

10 Cristina Vazio's illustrated report entitled *Study of the State of Preservation of the Decoration of the Tomb of Seti I* was submitted to the American Research Center in Egypt in May, 1999.

11 PM I^2, 537; 16.

12 The practice may be more widespread than has been generally recognized and deserves to be studied further. For example, the glossy burnished effect visible on the red surfaces in the wall reliefs at the Temple of Sety I at Abydos was probably accomplished in the same way and for the same reason.

13 The same accretions are visible on fragments in collections that were removed from the tomb later in the nineteenth century. I am grateful to Pamela Hatchfield and Susanne Gansicke of the Museum of Fine Arts Boston, Conservation Section, for the analysis of a sample of a "dark, thick accretion" on a fragment from the tomb (MFA accession no. 72.648) which was subjected to infrared spectroscopy, confirming that its major component is beeswax.

14 The best known and one of the most successful examples is Lascaux II in France; C. Lahanier, "La reconstruction photogrammétrique de la grotte de Lascaux" in Preprints of the 6th *Triennial Meeting* ICOM, Committee for Conservation, 3/4, 1981, 29–34. J. Brunet and J. Vouvé, *La Conservation des Grottes Ornées,* CNRS (1996), 127–246.

Tell el-Farkha 1998–1999: Pottery from Predynastic and Early Dynastic Strata

Mariusz Jucha
Jagiellonian University, Cracow

In the following report I focus on the pottery found during the 1998–1999 excavations at Tell el-Farkha. The resulting data allow us to date this site from the Predynastic to Old Kingdom times.[1] I pay particular attention to the pottery found at the Western Tell, which was dated to Predynastic, Protodynastic, and to the beginning of Early Dynastic periods (Phases 1–5). Only a few examples of the pottery presented here come from the Central Tell. While the lowermost Phase 1 belongs to the Lower Egyptian Culture, the following Phase 2, at the present state of research, seems to be representative of the beginning of the transition between the Lower and Upper Egyptian material. Our Phase 3 can be connected with the end of Naqada II and the beginning of Naqada III, while the subsequent Phases 4 and 5are characteristic for the period of state formation in Egypt.

Predynastic Phases 1 to 3 (Naqada IIc–IIIa)

The majority of the pottery discovered in the Predynastic phases can be categorized as Rough ware. From Phase 1 comes a few brown or reddish-brown coated shards with burnished surface. These shards seem to be similar to Maadi reddish-brown ware (Ware Ib) with burnished surface. But in contrast with Maadi where they are common, at Tell el-Farkha (Tell W) they are rare.

The pottery with temper that looks like hair-fine lines is present mostly in Phase 1. This kind of temper is very thin but it is usually very long and occurs on the pottery that belongs to the Lower Egyptian Culture.[2] A few shards of this type were also collected from subsequent Phase 2.

The pottery with incised or impressed zigzag pattern (fig. 1:1) is also very characteristic for Phase 1. This kind of decoration is absent in the subsequent phases, as it is at other archaeological sites in the Nile Delta such as Tell Ibrahim Awad,[3] Tell el-Iswid (South),[4] and Buto.[5] This kind of decorated pottery at the Western Tell is represented both in the upper Lower Egyptian strata of

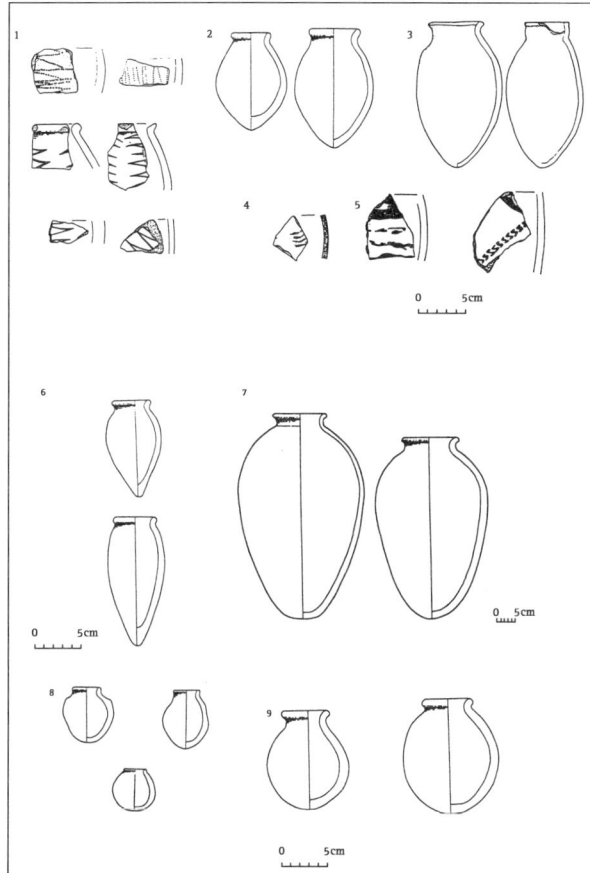

Fig. 1: Pottery fragments with zig-zag decoration and complete vessels from phase 1 (1-3); Pottery fragments with painted decoration from phase 1 (4) and phase 2 (5); Complete vessels from phase 3 (6-9).

Phase 1 and in the lowermost levels of the Tell that have been discovered up to now. It seems to be similar to its presence at Buto schicht II[6]—dated to Naqada IIc-d1[7]—and comparable with presence of Lower Egyptian Culture at other archeological sites in the region of Tell el-Farkha; for instance Tell el-Iswid South[8] or Tell Ibrahim Awad[9] situated respectively about 17.5 km and 25 km from Tell el-Farkha.[10] A similar decorative technique (the rocker stamp and related decoration techniques) was also attested in a few Late Naqada II settlements in Middle Egypt (Harageh) and Southern Egypt (Matmar, Badari, Hamammiya, el-Tarif, Armant).[11] A zigzag pattern is also present on a few shards from Hierakonpolis.[12]

From Phase 1 also come some small bag-shaped Rough-ware vessels with slightly pointed bottoms (fig. 1:2)[13] and oval vessels (lemon jars) with pointed base, straight (or concave) neck and simple rim (or slightly thickened external extension) (fig. 1:3).

Shards with painted decoration, very characteristic for the Predynastic Naqada (NII) Culture of Upper Egypt, are represented in Phases 1–2 only by a few shards with, for example, spiral motif, wavy line pattern, or the "s" decorative pattern (fig. 1:4–5). Those, according to Kaiser's classification, fit well into the second half of the Naqada II tradition.[14] The pottery with a similar decorative pattern is attested, for instance, in Minshat Abu Omar, where it belongs to graves of group I.[15]

As the material is still under investigation, what we can say presently about Phase 2 should be considered a preliminary conclusion. In this phase rough ware forms occur which are generally unknown in the previous Phase 1. Those forms of closed types and thickened external rim seems to be similar to Petrie's type R84[16] which, according to Kaiser, is connected with the Naqada IIc-IIIa1 Periods.[17] According to Hendrickx, some subtypes of this group can occur both earlier[18] and later[19] but generally are no longer present in the second half of Naqada IIIa2.[20] This type is mostly popular in Naqada IId1 and Naqada IId2-IIIa1.[21] Different fragments could also quite well belong also to other jars, as for instance R85 or R86 which are generally of a date similar to the previous one.[22] At Tell el-Farkha fragments of those forms are more numerous in the subsequent phase. A few fragments, similar, but more narrow, seem to belong to Petrie's type R76.[23] Those in Kaiser's classification are generally connected with Naqada IId2[24] and according to Hendrickx, different subtypes of this group can be dated from Naqada IIb to Naqada IIIa1.[25] Moreover in the material of Phase 2, a few examples of "hair tempered" pottery were also found.

Probably shards of hole mouth jars also found in subsequent Phases 3 and 4 belong to the local tradition. This kind of pottery is sporadically represented in Petrie's older corpuses dealing with Upper Egypt.[26] Those forms were presented among the corpus of shapes coming from Hicrakonpolis localities of Naqada II date and were connected with Predynastic settlement at this site.[27] At Mendes these were found in units 2 and 3 (Area B) correlated with Buto schicht III dated to Naqada IId2–Naqada III.[28] At Buto similar forms were attested at schicht III[29] and occur, for instance, in the transitional Naqada IId2 schicht IIIa[30] and also in the Naqada IIIa2 dated schicht IIId–e[31] which seems to be

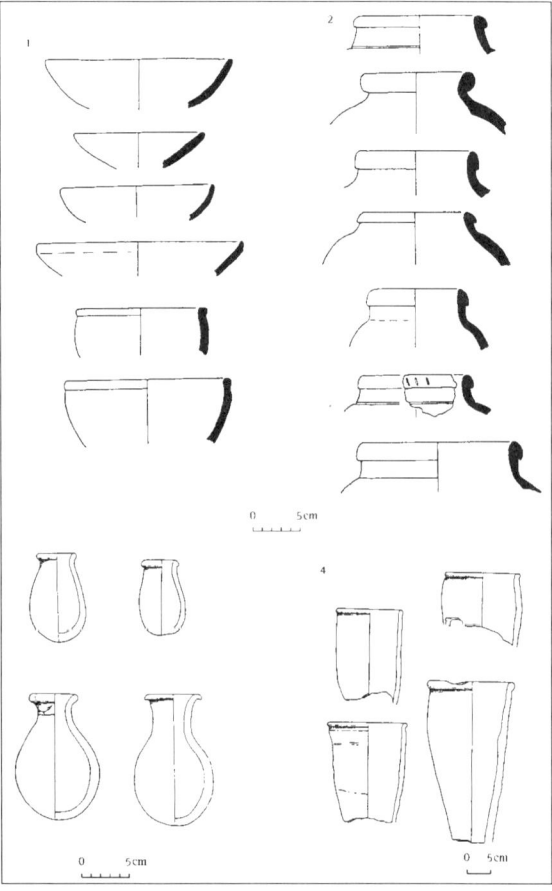

Fig. 2: Fragments of bowls and jars and complete vessels from phases 4-5.

similar to the occurrence of these forms in phases at Tell el-Farkha.

More examples of new types of pottery, which occurred in the previous phase, were found in Phase 3. From this Phase come also two complete, small pointed jars (fig. 1:6), two large oval vessels (fig. 1:7)[32] and miniature vessels (fig. 1:8) (a few were also found in the subsequent phases). Small miniature vessels[33] are known from the Predynastic and mostly from the Protodynastic Period in Buto.[34] A few examples are also known from Tell Ibrahim Awad.[35] Similar were found even in Upper Egypt at Hierakonpolis at Locality 29A in a pit associated with a re-use of this area in Protodynastic-Early Dynastic times.[36]

From the end of the Predynastic (Phase 3) and the beginning of the subsequent Protodynastic Period (Phase 4) come fragments and complete examples of simple rough small bag-shaped jars (fig. 1:9) similar to Petrie's type R65. This type of pottery is attested for a long span of time and can occur in Naqada II and at the beginning of the Naqada III Periods.[37] They are known also from other sites of these periods situated in Delta; for instance Buto,[38] Beni Amir,[39] and Minshat Abu Omar.[40]

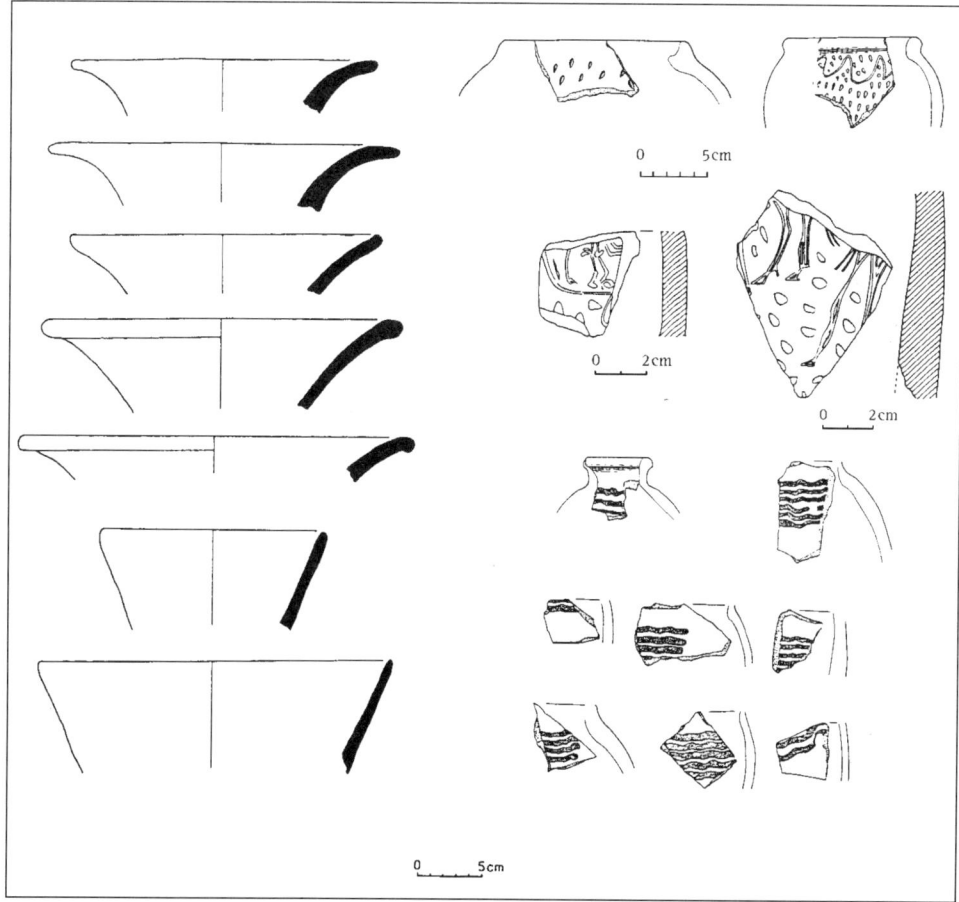

Fig. 3: Fragments of bowls and sherds with punctuated and painted decoration from phases 4-5.

Protodynastic/Early Dynastic Phases 4–5 (Naqada IIIa–c1)

In the strata belonging to this period we found a lot of fragments of rough, thick-walled bread-molds and large trays. The number of these forms increases from Protodynastic to Early Dynastic times. At the Western Tell most shards of this kind of pottery belong to spherical forms with rounded bases. Shallow forms, sometimes with flattened bases, are also present but they appear in lesser quantities. The rim top is mostly simple and rounded. There are also known examples with flattened or concave rim tops but these are fewer in number than those with rounded tops. Some potmarks have been recorded on the sides of the bread-molds.

Fragments of different types of fine ware bowls (fig. 2:1) are also present in these phases. Most of these bowls are red or reddish-brown coated both inside and outside and burnished. Very characteristic are vertically burnished bowls. They are sometimes horizontally burnished outside and vertically inside. In a few examples also the upper part of the inner surface just below the rim is also horizontally burnished but the lower part is still vertically burnished.

265

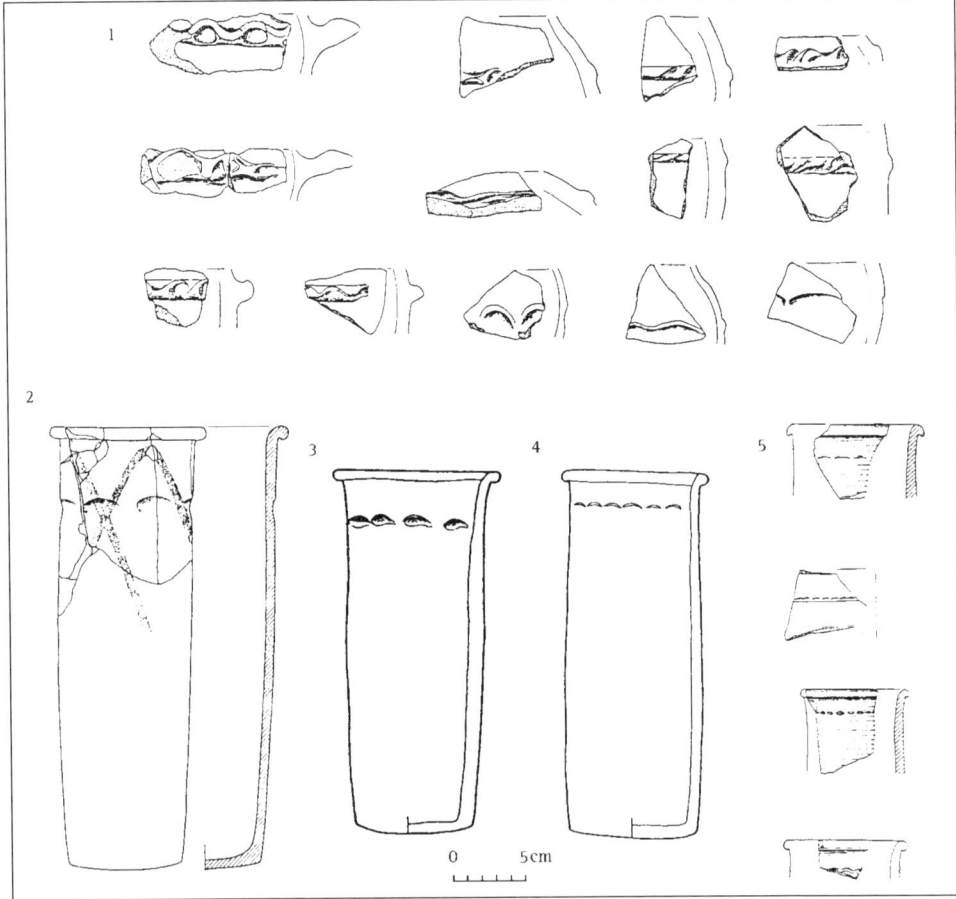

Fig. 4: Decorated sherds and cylindrical jars from phases 4–5.

Strata of Phases 4–5 also contain fragments of very hard, fine pottery made of Nile silt (untempered or with very fine sand inclusions). A few specimens are also made of marl clay. The surface of this pottery is very well/hard-smoothed. In most cases there are fragments of jars (fig. 2:2) which sometimes have marks of the turning device on the neck. Potmarks also occur on a few examples. In most cases they probably belong to the so-called wine jars and are similar to those found, for instance, at Tell Ibrahim Awad[41] on the Dynasty 0–beginning of the First Dynasty–pottery.

Among material of Phases 4–5 there are a few fragments and complete examples of small drop-shaped vessels (fig. 2:3). Similar examples are known from the Naqada III Period[42] and they are present at other archaeological sites in the Delta, including Tell Ibrahim Awad[43] and Buto.[44]

Dated mostly to Phase 4 are rough tall tapering vessels (height from 16 to 32 cm) without a bottom which was probably narrow and flattened (fig. 2:4). They were found abandoned in different fireplaces (hearths) of Naqada III date. Similar vessels were found in similar contexts at Tell Ibrahim Awad in Predynastic layers and were connected with a Phase which is contemporary with Naqada IId1.[45] But this type was probably not restricted only to the late Naqada II in Upper and Lower Egypt but was also in use later.[46] The question is, what was the function of this kind of pottery? Possibly after the breaking of the bottom of the pots, they could have been used as stands for cooking pots. It is possible also that they were more directly connected with food production and could have been used as vessels to dry corn. Differing heights of these pots could have been caused by continued re-use. The bottoms could have been broken off several times.

From Phase 4 come small rounded jars of pale brown polished pottery with narrow and high necks and rounded external rims (fig. 2:5). In this phase and subsequent ones there also occur Rough ware bowls (fig. 3:1) with concave walls and simply rounded or slightly thickened external extensions, and cups with straight sides and simple rims.

A few shards collected from Phases 4–5 exhibit punctuate decoration (fig. 3:2). This kind of decoration is known from Predynastic times as well as from the Naqada III Period. A similar kind of decoration is also present at other archaeological sites in the Delta, for instance, Buto.[47]

We also found fragments of pottery decorated with impressed dots and incised pictures (figs. 3:3–4). They generally can be dated to the end of the Protodynastic and the beginning of the First Dynasty. On the first example we can probably see a lower part of a human figure standing behind an animal, only partially preserved (fig. 3:4). On the second one there is a partially-preserved man standing in the boat with an oar (?) in his hand (fig. 3:3). A similar kind of decorative technique was represented on the material from Tell el-Farkha found by the Italian Mission in the upper strata of the Protodynastic Period and the lower strata of the Early Dynastic Period. But there were only examples decorated with impressed dots and incised lines.[48] The pottery decorated in a similar way (punctuate decoration connected with pictures) was also found for instance at Tell Ibrahim Awad[49] and among the Egyptian Protodynastic/Early Dynastic material in southern Canaan.[50]

Most fragments of D-ware from the Western Tell and which occur in Phase 4 and sporadically also in Phase 5 are decorated with so called "water lines" (fig. 3:5). This kind of decoration is well-attested in the Protodynastic Period. It can occur both earlier as well as later.[51] According to Kaiser, it occurs in Naqada IIIa–b[52] though according to Hendrickx, it is more popular in the Naqada IIIa2, but the same types of D-ware occur also later (in his Naqada IIIB–which can be comparable to Kaiser's Naqada IIIb–c1).[53] Similar examples are known also from Buto–stratum IIId–e dated to Naqada IIIa2[54] and Tell el-Iswid (South)–stratum VII dated to Naqada III/Dynasty 0.[55] Also at Tell el-Farkha this pattern appears both in upper and lower strata of Protodynastic phase attested on the Western Tell.

Shards with different plastic decoration (fig. 4:1) were found mostly in Phases 4 and 5. They belong generally to fine ware made of Nile silt or marl clay. They are locally produced in Egypt but there are also a few examples of protruding well-modeled wavy-handles of Canaanite origin. A few body shards with plastic rope band decoration (characteristic for the so-called wine jars) were found mostly in the layers of Phase 5 and generally can be connected with the end of the Protodynastic and the beginning of the First Dynasty. In the collected material there are also a few potshards with a lightly-impressed or cut row of arches on the shoulder, a motif which generally predates the First Dynasty.

Among the pottery of Phases 4–5 there are a few cylindrical jars made of marl clay. Three complete or reconstructable pots (figs.4:2–4) were found together in the layers of Phase 4. The vessels were decorated with a degenerated version of the wavy-handle design. One of the above-mentioned cylindrical vessels has painted net decoration characteristic of Naqada IIIa2[56] and a wavy design made by pushing up the wet clay slightly from the body toward the neck (fig. 4:2). Similar examples or fragments come from excavated sites in the Nile Delta; Minshat Abu Omar,[57] Tell Ibrahim Awad,[58] and Buto.[59] The second cylindrical vessel has a wavy design made by pushing up the wet clay slightly from the body toward the neck (fig. 4:3) which is characteristic for the period of unification;[60] the third one has a raised band of decoration, formed by pushing the clay upwards with the fingernail (fig. 4:4) which is characteristic for the period of transition between Dynasty 0 and the First Dynasty.[61]

Different fragments of cylindrical vessels (fig. 4:5) with decoration similar to the above-described or decorated with impressed dots, with an incised line and upper edge pushed into a wavy line or both upper and lower edges pushed into wavy lines, are present in material belonging to Phase 5. Generally, fragments with this kind of decoration are younger then the net-painted design[62] and come mostly from Naqada IIIb/c1 strata, which are the uppermost levels of the Western Tell. Examples of this kind of decoration are known from Protodynastic/Early Dynastic layers, at, for instance, Buto,[63] Tell el-Iswid (South)[64] and Minshat Abu Omar.[65]

As only part of the Western Tell has been investigated up until now and the pottery is being examined, our suggestions dealing with chronology of the site (e.g. Western Tell) should be considered as a preliminary.

At the beginning, the Western Tell was inhabited by people of the Lower Egyptian Culture (from Phase 1). This occupation lasted probably from the later stage of this culture, which is contemporary to the Naqada (IIb?)IIc-d1 culture of Upper Egypt, and which seems to be similar to the situation at Eastern Delta sites such as Tell Ibrahim Awad and Tell el-Iswid (South) in contrast to earlier occupation of the Western Delta site at Buto. On the basis of our present research we can tentatively suggest the following dating for subsequent phases: Phase 2: NIId2 or the beginning of NIID2, Phase 3: NIId2/IIIa1–IIIa2(?) or the end of NIID2–beginning of NIIIA1(?) and Phase 4: NIIIa2–IIIb or NIIIA1–IIIB. The end of the occupation on the Western Tell took place probably somewhere at the end of Protodynastic and the beginning of the Early Dynastic Period (Phase 5: NIIIb/IIIc1 or the end of NIIIB to NIIIC1). As only a few surface finds seem to belong to later pottery we can tentatively suggest that the Western Tell was abandoned some time during the First Dynasty, probably at its beginning.

After the fall of the settlement on the Western Tell, the inhabited area became concentrated on the Central and the Eastern Tells. Both those Tells were probably inhabited from the Predynastic Phase 1—belonging to Lower Egyptian Culture— through the Predynastic Naqada II/III phases to Old Kingdom times.

Addendum: Three tombs were discovered on the Eastern Tell during the excavation season in 2001.

Notes:

1. M. Chlodnicki, R. Fattovich and S. Salvatori, "Italian Excavations in the Nile Delta and New Hypotheses on the 4th Millennium Cultural Development of Egyptian Prehistory," *Rivista di Archeologia*, 15, (1991), 5-33; M. Chlodnicki, R. Fattovich and S. Salvatori, "The Nile Delta in Transition: A View from Tell el-Farkha," in E.C.M. van den Brink (ed.), *The Nile Delta in Transition: 4th-3rd Millenium BC*, (Tel-Aviv, 1992), 171-190; M. Chlodnicki, R. Fattovich, and S. Salvatori, "The Italian Archaeological Mission of the C.S.R.L-Venice to the Eastern Nile Delta: A preliminary report of the 1987-1988 field seasons," *CRIPEL* 14 (1992), 45-62; M. Chlodnicki, K. Cialowicz, "Tell el-Farkha. Explorations, 1998," *PAM* (1999), 63-70.

2. Ch. Köhler, "The Pre- and Early Dynastic Pottery of Tell el-Fara'în (Buto)," in van den Brink, *Nile Delta*, 16-17

3. E.C.M. van den Brink, "Preliminary Report on the Excavations at Tell Ibrahim Awad, Seasons 1988-1990," in van den Brink, *Nile Delta*, fig 10.

4. E.C.M. van den Brink, "A Transitional Late Predynastic-Early Dynastic Settlement Site in the Northeastern Nile Delta, Egypt," *MDAIK* 45 (1989), fig. 10, 11.

5. Th. von der Way, *Tell el-Fara'în. Buto I. Ergebnisse zum frühen Kontext während der Jahre 1983-1989*, (*AVDAIK* 83; Cairo, 1997), Taf.39

6. Th. von der Way, *Untersuchungen zur Spätvor-und Früfgeschichte Unterägyptens*, (*SAGA* 8; Heidelberg, 1993), 19, Abb.5.

7. von der Way, *Tell el-Fara'în*, Buto I, 80.

8. von der Way, *Untersuhungen*, Abb.26.

9. van den Brink, "A Transitional Late Predynastic," Tab. 1.

10. E.C.M. van den Brink, "Settlement patterns in the Northeastern Nile Delta during the fourth-second milleniuma B.C.," in L. Krzyzaniak, M. Kobusiewicz, J. Alexander (eds.), *Environmental Change and Human Culture in the Nile Basin and Northern Africa until the second Milleniuim B.C.*, (Poznan, 1993), figs. 6-7, Tab. 3.

11. van den Brink, "A Transitional Late Predynastic," 70-71, n. 26.

12. B. Adams, R. Friedman, "Imports and Influences in the Predynatsic and Protodynastic Settlement and Funerary Assemblages at Hierakonpolis," in van den Brink (ed.), *Nile Delta*, fig. 3a.

13. W. Kaiser, "Zur inneren Chronologie der Naqadakultur," *Archaeologia Geographica* 6 (1957), Taf. 22, 23; W.M.F. Petrie, *Corpus of Prehistoric Pottery and Palettes*, (London, 1921), Tab. XL; T. Wilkinson, *State Formation in Egypt. Chronology and Society*, (Cambridge Monographs in African Archaeology 40; Oxford 1996), P075.

14. Kaiser, "Zur inneren Chronologie," Taf. 22, 23

15. K. Kroeper, "The Excavations of the Munich east Delta expedition in Minshat Abu Omar," in E.C.M. van den Brink (ed.), *The archaeology of the Nile Delta. Problems and Priorities*, (Amsterdam, 1988), figs. 23-25.

16. Petrie, *Prehistoric Pottery*, Tab.XLII-XLIII.

17. Kaiser, "Zur inneren Chronologie," Taf. 23, 24.

18. St. Hendrickx, "The relative chronology of the Naqada culture: problems and possibilities," unpublished version of the text delivered at the British Museum colloquium on Early Egypt, London, July 22nd, 1993, (herein after referred to as "Chronology") 34, 83.

19. Hendrickx, "Chronology," 83.

20. Hendrickx, "Chronology," 38.

21. Hendrickx, "Chronology," 35-36, 84.

22. Hendrickx, "Chronology," 83.

23. Petrie, *Prehistoric Pottery*, Tab. XLI.

24. Kaiser, "Zur inneren Chronologie," Taf. 23.

25. Hendrickx, "Chronology," 82.

26. Petrie, *Prehistoric Pottery*, Tab. XLIV: R89p, R100; W.M.F. Petrie, *Corpus of Proto-Dynastic Pottery*, (BSEA LXVI (B); London, 1953), Tab. XXV: 83s.

27. Adams and Friedman, "Imports," 324–326, fig 7.

28. R. Friedman, "The Early Dynastic and Transitional Pottery of Mendes: the 1990 season," in van den Brink, *Nile Delta*, 200–204, figs. 2:d and 4:d.

29. Ch. K^hler, *Tell el-Fara'in-Buto III*, (Mainz, 1998), 21.

30. Köhler, *Buto III*, 120, Taf. 20:2.

31. Köhler, *Buto III*, 120, Taf. 20:1, 3.

32. Petrie, *Proto-Dynastic Pottery*, Tab. XXIV; Wilkinson, *State Formation*, P116.

33. Petrie, *Proto-Dynastic Pottery*, Tab. XXVI .

34. Köhler, "The Pre- and Early Dynastic," fig. 7:5–8, 11–16, 22–25; K^hler, *Buto III*, 20, Abb. 14, Taf. 18.

35. van den Brink, "Preliminary Report," 53, Pl. 21.

36. Adams and Friedman, "Imports," 327, fig. 8:f.

37. Kaiser, "Zur inneren Chronologie," Taf.23, 24; Petrie, *Prehistoric Pottery*, Tab. XL; Wilkinson, *State Formation*, Pl.074.

38. Köhler, "The Pre- and Early Dynastic," fig. 7.

39. M. Adel M. Ahd el-Moneim, "Der Säpatvordynastische–Frühdynastische Tell von Beni Amir (Ost-Delta)," *Journal of Historical and Archaeological Researches* I (1993), Abb. 29:XI

40. Kroeper, "Excavations," figs. 63, 64.

41. E.C.M. van den Brink, "The Amsterdam University Survey Expedition to the Northeastern Nile Delta (1984–1986)," in: van den Brink (ed.), *Archaeology*, figs. 13–16.

42. Petrie, *Prehistoric Pottery*, Tab. L; Wilkinson, *State Formation*, P134.

43. van den Brink, "Preliminary Report," 53, figs. 7:2, Pl. 18:1–3.

44. K^hler, *Buto III*, Tab. 16:13–15 and 54:1.

45. van den Brink, "Preliminary Report," 53–54, fig. 11, Pl. 22.

46. Petrie, *Prehistoric Pottery*, Tab. XLVI.

47. K^hler, *Buto III*, 138, Taf. 57:3–5.

48. Chlodnicki et al., "Italian Excavations," 23, fig 15: 36, 38, 40–42.

49. W. M. van Haarlem, "The Excavations at Tell Ibrahim Awad: (Sharqiya Province)," Paper presented to The Eighth International Congress of Egyptologists, Cairo, 28 March-3 April 2000, forthcoming.

50. T. E. Levy, "Egyptian-Canannite Interaction at Nahal Tillah, Israel (ca. 4500–3000 BCE): An Interim Report on the 1994–1995 Excavations," *BASOR* 307, 1997, 20–21, fig 17:4.

51. Petrie, *Prehistoric Pottery*, Tab. XXXII:D20,D21 = S. D. 62–75; *Idem, Proto-Dynastic Pottery*, Tab. XXVI:87k, Tab. XXVII:91D7 = S. D. 77, Tab. XXIX:94k = S. D. 77; Tab.IX:53f = S. D. 80; Tab. XXVIII:92g = S. D. 80.

52. Kaiser, "Zur inneren Chronologie," Taf. 24.

53 Hendrickx, "Chronology," 37–38.

54. Köhler, "The Pre- and Early Dynastic," figs. 3:6–8.

55. van den Brink, "A Transitional Late Predynastic," figs. 14, 12.

56. St. Hendrickx, "The relative chronology of the Naqada culture: problems and possibilities," in A. J. Spencer, *Aspects of Early Egypt*, (London, 1996), Tab. 7; Kaiser, "Zur inneren Chronologie," Taf. 24; Petrie, *Prehistoric Pottery*, Tab. XXX; *Idem, Proto-Dynastic Pottery*, Tab. VIII, Wilkinson, *State Formation*, P050.

57. Kroeper, "Excavations," fig. 78.

58 van den Brink, "Preliminary Report," 52–53.

59. Kˆhler, *Buto III*, 47, Taf. 64: 9–12.

60. Petrie, *Proto-Dynastic Pottery*, Tab. VIII, IX; Wilkinson, *State Formation*, Pl. 050.

61. Petrie, *Prehistoric Pottery*, Tab. XXX; *Idem, Proto-Dynastic Pottery*, Tab. VIII, IX; Wilkinson, *State Formation*, P052; Hendrickx, "Chronology," Tab.7.

62. Petrie, *Proto-Dynastic Pottery*, Tab. VIII, IX; Wilkinson, *State Formation*, P052.

63. Köhler, *Buto III*, Taf. 58, Abb. 24.

64. van den Brink, "A Transitional Late Predynastic," 77, figs. 14:13, 14.

65. Kroeper, "Excavations," figs. 86–88.

Djara: Prehistoric Links between the Desert and the Nile

Karin Kindermann
Heinrich-Barth-Institut, Universität zu Köln

Anumber of links—particularly several artifact types and technological features—point to contacts between Neolithic and Predynastic sites in the Nile Valley and Mid-Holocene groups in the Western Desert. This part of the desert stretches westward from the Nile Valley to the borders of Libya and embraces more than two-thirds of the whole area of Egypt. The so-called Limestone, or Egyptian Plateau (formerly also called Libyan Plateau), lying between the Egyptian oases and the Nile Valley is a component of the Western Desert.[1] This relatively monotonous high plain is covered in most parts with *hamada*.[2] The Abu-Muhariq-dune train—with a length of more than 500 km, stretching from Bahariya Oasis in the northwest to Kharga Oasis in the southeast—divides this plateau into two parts. Directly in the

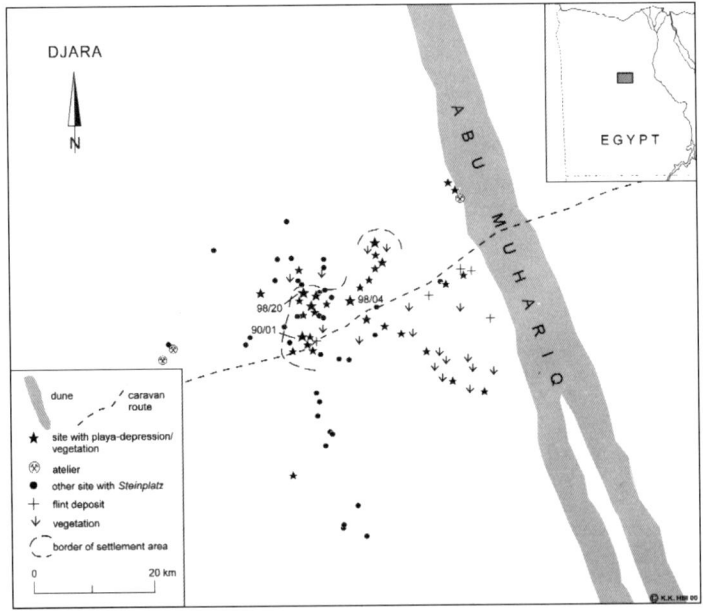

Fig. 1: Djara settlement area (Limestone Plateau).

272

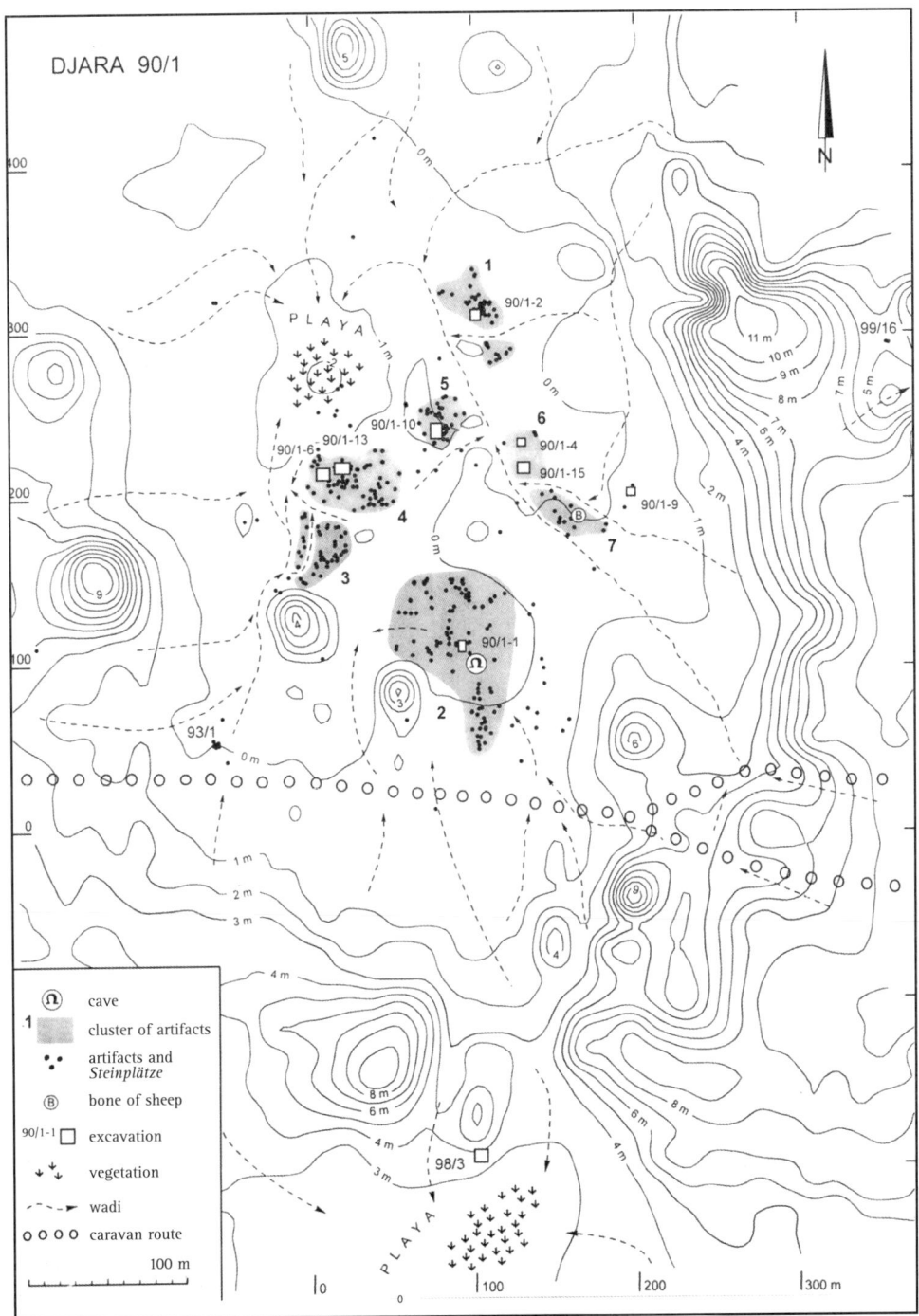

Fig. 2: Archaeological site Djara 90/1.

centre of the Limestone-Plateau, only 15 km away from the dune, the archaeological region of Djara is situated in a landscape dominated by small limestone hills (fig. 1).

This place was first mentioned by the German explorer Gerhard Rohlfs in his travelogue, *Drei Monate in der Libyschen Wüste*.[3] His interdisciplinary expedition, with the objective of exploring the Libyan Desert, followed the caravan route from Assiut to Farafra Oasis. On Christmas Eve, 1873, they reached a spacious dripstone cave called Djara. He added a detailed map to his book, with the exact traveling route and an annotation that the ground in this region was covered by flint splinters. Though archaeology played only a minor role in this early enterprise, his remark is the first published indication of prehistoric artifacts in this region. Subsequently the cave sank into oblivion for more than 100 years. In 1989 Djara was rediscovered by Carlo Bergmann, a modern camel nomad, who roves together with his caravan hundreds of kilometers through the desert each winter. For the first time he reported on neolithic stone artifacts around the cavern entrance and also described rock engravings inside the Djara cave. In 1990 a small interdisciplinary group of geographers, egyptologists, and archaeologists visited this site together with Bergmann for scientific research. Different archaeological and interdisciplinary expeditions were realized from 1993 until 1999 through the Heinrich-Barth-Institut and the *ACACIA* project.[4]

Other parts of this plateau remained an archaeological *terra incognita* for a long time. In spite of the fact that it is situated relatively close to the Nile Valley, little attention was focused on research. Apart from the Rohlfs expedition, the famous archaeologist Gertrude Caton-Thompson crossed the Limestone Plateau in 1928 further to the south, between Abydos and Kharga Oasis. As she wrote, "Anxious to trace [...]

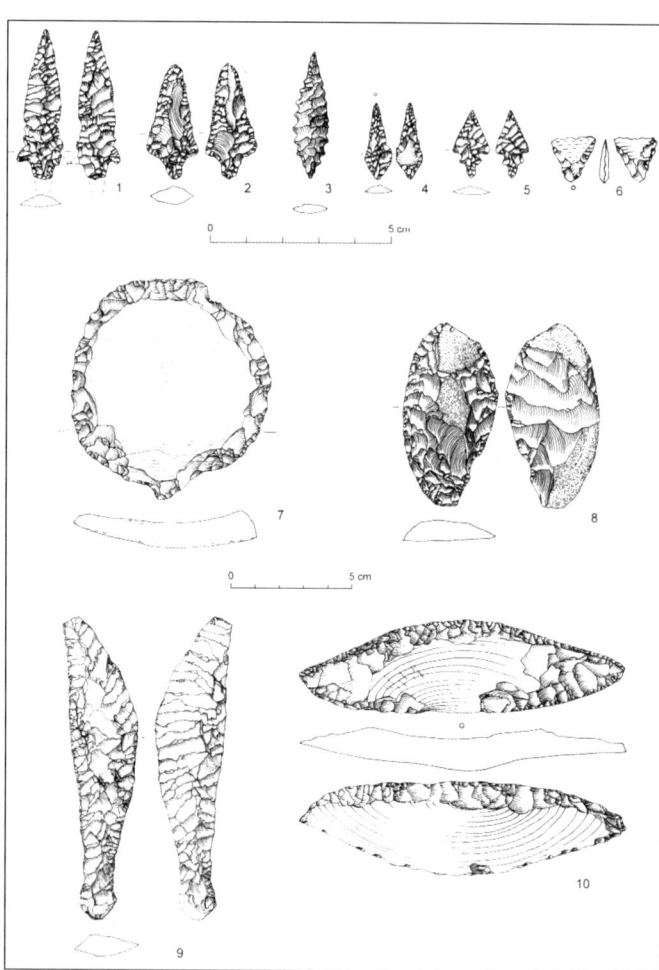

Fig. 3: Artifacts from Djara 90/1: 1–5 bifacially retouched arrowheads; 6 transverse arrowhead; 7 circular scraper; 8 side-scraper (excavation Djara 90/1–1); 9 knife; 10 side-blow flake.

contacts between Kharga Oasis and the Nile Valley in postpalaeolithic times [...]."[5] Several neolithic stone artifacts from various surface collections were observed, for example different bifacially retouched projectile points and side-blow flakes. Her research must be seen as one of the earliest efforts to query prehistoric contacts between the Western Desert and the Nile region. During our explorations and surveys on the Egyptian Plateau, undertaken by the *ACACIA* project, numerous Mid-Holocene sites were discovered on the plateau, contributing to this discussion. The archaeological sites from the Djara region are of particular scientific interest.

The site Djara 90/1, is situated in a shallow depression, 400 m in diameter, surrounded by small limestone hills. Sparse vegetation grows near playa-sediments in the north-western part,[6] into which a centripetal wadi system once drained in (fig. 2). Foremost, the site is characterized by the dripstone cave with its impressive stalagmites and rock engravings. Mainly animals like ostriches, antelopes, and bovids, but also human beings and symbols are depicted.[7] Around the entrance the ground is scattered with hundreds of lithic artifacts. Seven different concentrations have been distinguished. Altogether nine excavations-areas were carried out on site Djara 90/1 and in addition to that various fireplaces, so-called *Steinplätze*,[8] were excavated (fig. 2). The archaeological ground survey and the excavations should help to separate dissimilar activity areas and phases of use. The assemblages consist of diversified artifact *spectra*, which let us presume a longer stay of people, with various activity areas, as is known from so-called base camps.

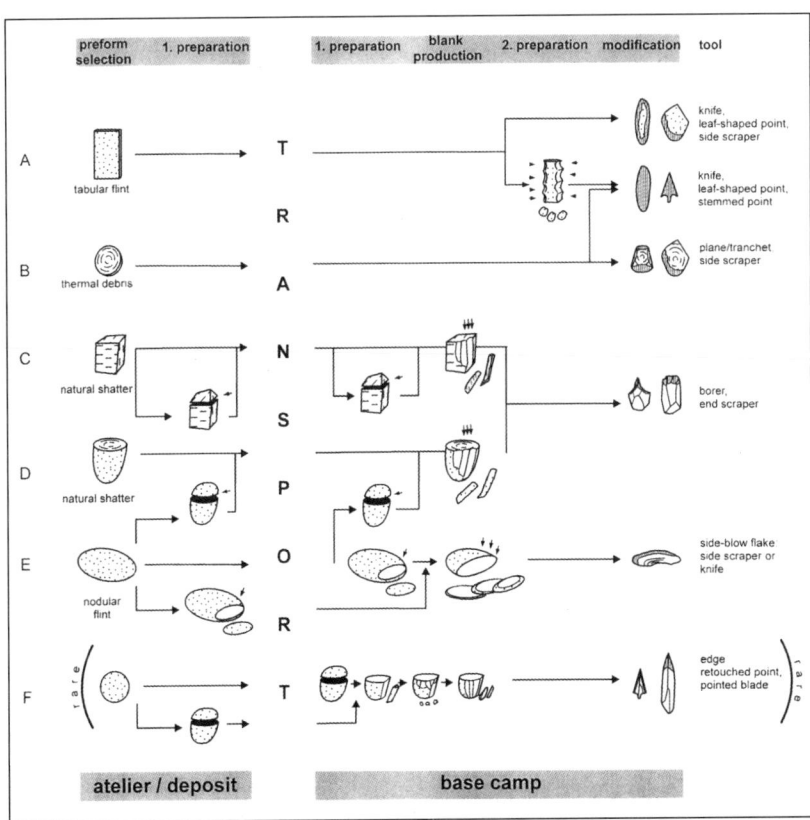

Fig. 4: Production sequence of mid-Holocene inventories from Djara sites.

This includes, for example, the production of stone artifacts, the use of rubbing stones and mill-stones, the preparation of wild animals, and the manufacture of beads from ostrich eggshell.

Ceramics are rare and only small pieces were observed near the old caravan route, which transverses Djara 90/1 to the south. All shards seem to belong to younger time periods, when caravans passed through this region regularly. One shard with an impression of a grain of rice (*Oryza sp.*)[9] gave a radiocarbon date of 1,200 CE, while definite evidence for prehistoric pottery is lacking. Lithics make up the largest group of artifacts. The tool kit is dominated by bifacially-retouched pieces, often made by a fine pressure flaking technique (fig. 3). Facially-retouched stone implements like knives (fig. 3.9), leaf-shaped points and especially arrowheads in all sizes, including stemmed, winged, side-notched, and bipointed varieties are common (figs. 3.1–3.5). Hollow-based forms, which are typical for the Fayum Neolithic (*Fayum A*),[10] were not observed in this region until now. Transverse arrowheads were rarely found, only three are known from Djara 90/1 (fig. 3.6). Side-blow flakes (fig. 3.10), side and circular scrapers are well-documented (figs. 3.7–3.8), as are borers and planes. Concerning the raw material, local flint with a wide range of different colors—from yellow upon red to brown—dominates the assemblage, with more than 90% in the inventories. Only very few lithic tools are made of quartzite or limestone.

Tabular flint was also used for the production of stone artifacts as well as flint nodules and flint splinters of all sizes, naturally produced by frost and salt weathering. First examination led to the assumption that special natural flint blanks were used for particular tool types. The tabular flint was above all applied to produce thin forms, which were preferred for knives, because an additional reduction during the manufacturing process was not necessary anymore (fig. 4A). Thermal debris were preferred for planes, because often the blank has one naturally convex side just as the final tool product does (fig. 4B). Over and above that, the artifact material of Djara is dominated by a chipped stone industry, predominantly flake-based. Flakes with a great width and short length were often used for side-blow flakes. This special tool is defined by its elegantly curved form, comparable to a wing. Alternate retouch runs along the edges and sometimes also facial retouch occurs. Caton-Thompson already suggested that these tools are side scrapers,[11] but knives or a multifunctional use is also conceivable (fig. 4E). From the current point of view, side-blow flakes show a special regional distribution over the Western Desert, including the Egyptian Oases and a specific chronological intensity, covering the later Neolithic time periods. Only very few exotic pieces are known from sites in the Nile Valley. So far workshops are documented only from Kharga Oasis,[11] the Nabta Playa region (site E 75–8)[12] and now from a site in the Djara region, named Djara 90/1–6. Here a whole reduction sequence could be conjoined. An affiliated charcoal sample from this site was dated 5,700 BCE (6,800 BP) and is consequently much older than the previously-presumed dating of the later Neolithic periods.

For the absolute dating of Djara's facially-retouched artifacts, site Djara 90/1–1 is of interest, situated 14 m north of the cave entrance. It was selected because many different facially-retouched tools as well as flakes and lithic chips were observed on the ground. Two fireplaces filled with black charcoal produced bifacially-retouched arrowheads and one side scraper found *in situ* (figure 3.2, 3.4, 3.5, and 3.8). That this artifact collection consisted of nearly all arrowheads is not astonishing, because projectile points are the predominant tool category for this excavation unit. They are very common at all sites in the whole settlement area. Comparable points are known, for example, from neolithic sites of the Kharga Oasis (*Umm el-Dabadib*)[13] and Dakhla Oasis (*Bashendi units*),[14] from the Western Desert, B.O.S. site *Lobo 81/55* in the Abu Minqar area,[15] from the Nabta Playa region site E75–8,[12] and the Fayoum Depression.[10] Two radiocarbon dates from the hearths of Djara 90/1–1 dated these bifacially-retouched tools to between 5,600 and 5,400 BCE (6,700 and 6,500 BP), chronologically comparable to the so-called

Middle Neolithic of the Nabta Playa and Bir Kiseiba region and the Bashendi unit of the Dakhla Oasis. On the basis of typological considerations and 11 different C14 dates from Djara site 90/1, all in a period from 6,700 to 5,400 BCE, (7,800 to 6,500 BP), the vast array of lithic implements can be correlated with the so-called Middle Neolithic.[16] For a few implements from the surface, an absolute allocation is difficult. Sometimes it is hard to separate features from one another because of the dense artifact scatters.

Djara 90/1 belongs to a settlement area with an extent of approximately 10 by 5 km, in which several sites with an extraordinary richness of mid-Holocene stone artifacts were observed (fig. 1). Even though we surveyed some epipalaeolithic sites on the Egyptian Plateau, older than 6,700 BCE (7,600 BP), their number is quite low—only 5 percent—in comparison with sites from younger periods. The vast amount of archaeological sites from the Djara region also belong into the mid-Holocene. There is more than one reason for this agglomeration directly in the middle of the Egyptian Plateau; several natural favorable factors occur. The extent of this settlement area covers exactly the dimension of small depressions with living vegetation. In former times, open water was temporarily available here in good years. Today playa-sediments witness these ephemeral lakes only. Over and above this, various local flint deposits and work-shops document a surplus of raw material for stone artifact-production. Exploitable flint deposits were observed foremost within the Minia Formation at the level of Djara 90/1 and also in smaller quantities within the Naqb Formation (Thebes Group) a little bit further to the south. Mostly the flint weathered out of small limestone hills; at most sites flint blanks are naturally produced by frost-and salt weathering. Due to a clever choice, blank preparation is not necessary anymore.

Atelier sites are characterized by a special human exploitation, which at all sites is conspicuously uniform. A great number of artificially-tested and prepared flint nodules or natural shatters were found. Here and there a few blank products and scarce modified pieces were registered. Archaeological remains, which could give us a piece of advice for a longer settlement, such as an intensive artifact production with stone tools, rubbing stones, and millstones or ceramic fragments, are completely absent. Accordingly, the people stayed only for a short time at these deposit sites. In the nearer surroundings, probably within a perimeter of a day's walk, the camp sites must be within reach. For the Djara region the distances are easy to estimate. Atelier sites or flint deposits lay in distances of up to 15 km from the camp sites of the Djara settlement area. It can be established that archaeological sites are tied to the sources of raw material deposits (fig. 1).

Only little is known about the economic and environmental conditions of the Djara region. Although most sites belong to the so-called mid-Holocene, it is uncertain when and where exactly the nomadic way of life replaced the hunter-gatherer subsistence. The domestication of cattle is assumed already before 8,000 BCE (9,000 BP) for the ecologically-favorable regions of south-east Egypt.[17] In and around the Dakhla Oasis the introduction of domesticated animals is verified for the first time between 5,500 and 4,900 BCE (6,600 and 6,000 BP).[18] At Djara 90/1 a bone fragment of a domesticated sheep was found in a mid-Holocene surface concentration. Radiocarbon analyses should provide further information. Apart from that, only bones of wild animals, like *Gazella dorcas* and *Gazella dama* are the most dominant ones.[19] The archaeobotanical determination of charcoals shows a broad spectrum of different plants. Beyond the typical desert vegetation of *Acacia* and *Tamarisk* species, many different kinds of *Capparaceae*-taxa were identified, an indicator for groundwater resources.

In conclusion, it can be said that the Egyptian Plateau, just as other parts of the Western Desert during the Early and the mid-Holocene, was not an easy environment to live or even survive in. The vegetation was sparse and concentrated around ephemeral lakes, as evidenced by the settlement area of Djara. In the Western Desert most of the Holocene sites were also discovered near these playa-sediments.

Returning to the links between the Western Desert and the Nile Valley, it must be emphasized that a direct comparison between the sites of the Djara region and mid-Holocene inventories from the Nile Valley is difficult. Between the latest palaeolithic and the earliest neolithic sites, a chronological hiatus of several centuries from about 6,000 to 5,200 BCE (7,200 to 6,350 BP) is obvious for the Nile Valley. According to Fekri Hassan, an explanation could be seen in the Middle Holocene drop of the Nile level, reaching a minimum about 5,900 BCE (7,000 BP) and lasting until 5,500 BCE (6,600 BP). The aridity and the simultaneous decrease in rain were responsible for the movement of groups down to the Nile channel. Such sites would have been destroyed by the higher flood-level between 5,300 and 3,800 BCE (6,350 and 5,000 BP).[20] Another fact is that the common traits appear in some cases a millennium earlier on the Limestone Plateau and in the Egyptian Oases, than they do within the Nile Valley. It was often suggested that the onset of this drying trend at the end of the sixth millennium may have played an important role in the population transfer to the Nile Valley about 5,900 BCE (7,000 BP).

According to the C14 dates, the traits common to the two regions appear some time earlier in the Djara region and the Egyptian Oases than in the Nile Valley. In both areas a predominantly flake-based chipped stone industry is usual. The local flint material from the Limestone Plateau was the dominant raw material in both regions. The tabular flint was often used for tall bifacial implements. The facial retouch technique became important for producing a great variety of different tools, which ended up in the beautiful Gerzean flint knives classified as Naqada II.[21] Various artifact forms were shared by the two areas including bifacially-retouched knives, planes, circular scrapers, and lens-shaped or transverse arrowheads. Traits exist in the Nile Valley as well as very intensively into the Egyptian Oases. The special attraction of the Djara region consists of the abundance of readily-available raw material—flint—and especially favorable environmental circumstances.

Notes:

1 R. Said, "Geomorphology," in: R. Said (ed.), *The Geology of Egypt* (Rotterdam, 1990), 9–25.

2 This means a light-colored hummocky landscape with small rocky outcrops, the result of weathering; S. Kröpelin, "Geomorphology, Landscape Evolution and Paleoclimates of Southwest Egypt," *Catena Supplement* 26 (1993), 31–65.

3 G. Rohlfs, *Drei Monate in der libyschen Wüste* (Heinrich-Barth-Institut; Köln, 1875, Reprinted 1996): 59–60.

4 *ACACIA* is the abbreviation for, "Arid Climate Adaptation and Cultural Innovation in Africa." The scientific research in 1993 was carried out under the direction of Rudolph Kuper and was supported by the Fritz Thyssen Foundation. The expeditions of 1995/96, 1998 and 1999, funded by the Deutsche Forschungsgemeinschaft (DFG), were organized by the Cooperative Research Center 389 *ACACIA* , sec-

tion A1 (R. Kuper/H. Besler)–"Regional climatic changes and human settlement between the Nile Valley and the Central Sahara"–at the University of Cologne.

5 G. Caton-Thompson, "Royal Anthropological Institute's prehistoric research expedition to Kharga oasis Egypt. Preliminary outline of the season's work," *MAN* 31 (1932), 77–85.

6 *Playas* are the deepest parts of depressions (clay pan) without any drainage in arid regions. After periodic or episodic precipitation events, clay sediments were deposited here. S. Kröpelin, "Untersuchungen zum Sedimentationsmilieu von Playas im Gilf Kebir Südwest-Ägypten," in: R. Kuper, (ed.), *Forschungen zur Umweltgeschichte der Ostsahara* (Africa Praehistorica 2; Köln, 1989), 183–305.

7 A small collection of rock art from the Djara cave can be found at:
http:\\www.uni-koeln.de\sfb389\sectionA\A1-section.htm.

8 For the definition of Steinplatz, see B. Gabriel, "Neuere Ergebnisse der Vorgeschichtsforschung in der östlichen Zentralsahara," *Berliner Geogr. Abhandlungen* 16 (1972) 153–156.

9 All archaebotanical determinations were done by Barbara Zach and Stefanie Nußbaum.

10 G. Caton-Thompson and E. W. Gardner, *The Desert Fayum* (Gloucester, 1934).

11 G. Caton-Thompson, *Kharga Oasis in Prehistory* (London, 1952).

12 F. Wendorf, and R. Schild, *Prehistory of the Eastern Sahara* (London, 1980), 148–165.

13 D. L. Holmes, "Analysis and Comparison of Some Prehistoric Projectile Points from Egypt," *Institute of Archaeology Bulletin* (1991) 28: 99–132.

14 M.M.A. McDonald, "Dakhleh Oasis Project, Third preliminary report on the lithic industries in the Dakhleh Oasis," *JSSEA* 12 (1982), 115–138, Pl. VII–XVII.

15 F. Klees, "Lobo: a contribution to the prehistory of the eastern Sand Sea and the Egyptian oases," in L. Krzyzaniak and M. Kobusiewicz, (eds.), *Late Prehistory of the Nile Basin and the Sahara* (Poznan, 1989), 223–231.

16 The chronological differentiation of Nabta Playa and Bir Kiseiba is established by the CPE (*Combined Prehistoric Expedition*). F. Wendorf, and R. Schild, *Cattle-keepers of the Eastern Sahara* (Dallas, 1984); F. Wendorf. and R. Schild, "Nabta Playa and its role in Northeastern African Prehistory," *Journal of Anthr. Arch.* 17 (1998), 97–123. The prehistoric period system of the Dakhla oasis subdivides into *Masara, Bashendi A,* and *B* unit; M.M.A. McDonald, "The Late prehistoric radiocarbon chronology for Dakhla oasis within the wider environmental and cultural setting of the Egyptian Western desert," in M. Marlow, (ed.), *Proceedings of the First Dakhla Oasis Project seminar* (Oxford, 1994, *in press*); M.M.A. MacDonald, "Early African Pastoralism: View from Dakhla Oasis (South Central Egypt)," *Journal of Anthr. Arch.* 17 (1998), 124–142.

17 F. Wendorf and R. Schild, "Conclusions," in, F. Wendorf, R. Schild, and A. E. Close, (eds.), *Cattle-keepers of the Eastern Sahara: the Neolithic of Bir Kiseiba* (Dallas, 1984), 404–428.

18 M.M.A. McDonald, "Early African Pastoralism," 124–142.

19 All archaezoological determination were done by Hubert Berke.

20 F. A. Hassan, "The predynastic of Egypt," *Journal of World Prehistory* 2 (1998), 136–185.

21 P. Kelterborn, "Towards Replicating Egyptian Predynastic Flint Knives," *Journal of Archaeological Science* 11 (1984), 433–453.

Appearance of the Abusir Pyramid Necropolis during the Old Kingdom*

Jaromír Krejčí

Czech Institute of Egyptology, Charles University, Prague

During the last two decades, the use of up-to-date techniques and approaches has been developed to a high degree in Egyptology. Among these new technologies may be counted computer-assisted design software (CAD). This software is used for making three-dimensional reconstructions of ancient monuments in addition to its everyday use in architectural firms and the building industry.

The present paper concerns applying this new technology to some of the conclusions reached in my PhD thesis about the Abusir pyramid field during the Old Kingdom. My first step in this project was to complete a thorough analysis of written, epigraphic, archaeological, and architectural data with the aim of providing a new view of the historic and building development of the pyramid field.[1] The second step was to prepare new, computerized, three-dimensional reconstructions of the royal mortuary monuments in the necropolis.[2] This work was an attempt to follow up on already existing projects, especially those concerning the Old Kingdom pyramid complexes and necropolises being studied at the Oriental Institute, University of Chicago,[3] and the Institute Français d'Archéologie Orientale, Cairo,[4] and others.[5]

History of Research on the Abusir Pyramid Necropolis

The Abusir necropolis was virtually ignored by early explorers and researchers until the 1830s and the advent of J. S. Perring.[6] Further work was done by the Lepsius expedition in 1840s.[7] In the area of Niuserre's sun sanctuary, the British military officer H.W.V. Stuart worked very briefly in 1882.[8] The French archaeologist J. de Morgan also devoted his attention to this site.[9]

Between the years 1898–1901, an expedition financed by W. von Bissing, under the direction of L. Borchardt, von Bissing, and H. Schäfer, preceded the archaeological excavations of the *Deutsche Orient-Gesellschaft* (DOG) in the area of Niuserre's sun sanctuary.[10] These archaeological excavations, under the auspices of the DOG, moved to the area of the pyramid field proper at Abusir over the years 1900–1908[11] and carried out trial excavation, especially around

Userkaf's sun sanctuary (1913). That expedition was also the first occasion of work on the Unfinished (Neferefre's) Pyramid.[12] It was not until the 1950s that valuable finds were made by the joint Swiss-German Expedition in Userkaf's sun sanctuary.[13]

The appearance of the Abusir necropolis was further altered when work by the Czechoslovak (from 1993 *Czech*) Institute of Egyptology from Charles University, Prague, began in 1960. The mission completed the cleaning already begun by de Morgan in the mastaba of Ptahshepses,[14] dedicating its attention to this monument until 1974.[15] The year 1976 was a crux in the research, as the Institute's expedition opened a new archaeological concession in the southern part of the royal necropolis at Abusir. During the first seasons, the mission excavated a group of graves, in which some members of the family of King Djedkare were buried, supplementing this work with investigation of the pyramid complex of Queen Khentkaus II.

The years 1980–1998 brought further new and very important finds from the area of Neferefre's mortuary complex.[16] Due to its unique situation, Neferefre's mortuary temple was better preserved than most other royal mortuary temples. Most of it was not built in stone, but due to the king's early demise, with mud-brick masonry. In the area of the mortuary temple, some very important finds were made: The Third Papyrus Archive of Abusir[17] which, like the other two Abusir archives,[18] revealed many significant facts concerning the functioning of the ruler's mortuary cult.

Another important discovery concerns other monuments on the site and in the vicinity. Among these finds were a group of royal statues, inlays made of faience, mud seals, fragments of stone and ceramic vessels. The discovery of parts of the king's anatomical remains in 1997 was also of a great significance.[19] Besides the mortuary complex, other monuments were explored from 1980 to 1998: the pyramid complex of queens (Lepsius no. XXIV), the mastaba of Princess Nebtyemneferes[20] and the mastaba of Prince Nakhtkare.[21] Among the most important discoveries made concerning ancient architecture were Neferefre's ritual slaughterhouse[22] and the hypostyle hall in Neferefre's mortuary temple. We also had the a rare opportunity to examine the core masonry of Pyramid Lepsius XXIV.[23]

A Short History of the Abusir Pyramid Necropolis

We can only speculate as to why the necropolis was founded where it was because the reasons are no longer clear.[24] The first royal monument was a sun sanctuary erected for the first ruler of the Fifth Dynasty, Userkaf. At the same time he built his pyramid complex in Saqqara, beside Netjerykhet Djoser's Step Pyramid. Possibly one of the reasons (apart from the availability of building material and religious concerns) why his successor, Sahure, chose Abusir as a place of his last repose, was the fact that Userkaf's sun sanctuary stood on the northern border of the future necropolis.

It is Sahure's cult complex that shows us how pyramid complexes of the Fifth Dynasty were designed and built. Their focal parts—the pyramids—were not built as solidly as the great pyramids of Dahshur or Giza of the previous dynasty. On the other hand, the other parts of the complexes, especially the mortuary and valley temples, were much more elaborate, incorporating greater amounts of valuable materials such as red granite, basalt, Egyptian alabaster (calcite), and quartzite in their construction. We can only hypothesize that religion was among the reasons for this change of emphasis from the pyramid to the associated buildings, or else it was an attempt to build the royal graves in more economical way.

After Sahure, Neferirkare became ruler, but it appears this was not the result of direct lineage: Among Sahure's four sons, Neferirkare was not mentioned.[25] Furthermore, Neferirkare's name, added to some figures on the reliefs in Sahure's mortuary temple, was carved in such a way that he may not have been the expected successor.[26] Neferirkare probably chose an unusual form for his monument—a stepped pyramid[27] (see figs. 1, 3, 4). We can only speculate why he did this, whether the structure in northern Abusir was really started for him, and if it was indeed a pyramid.

His successors Neferefre and Shepseskare[28] also died young. Both Neferefre's (see fig. 2) and Neferirkare's mortuary complexes were therefore finished by another son of Neferirkare (and Neferefre's brother), Niuserre. Niuserre's pyramid complex had little room for its layout and it was virtually jammed between Neferirkare's complex and the private tombs that had already been built in the cemetery before that time.

Niuserre's successor, Menkauhor, chose another place for his grave[29] and the use of Abusir as a royal necropolis was then discontinued.

Borchardt's Three-Dimensional Reconstruction of the Abusir Pyramid Necropolis

On the basis of his excavations, Borchardt made an ideal three-dimensional reconstruction of the appearance of the Old Kingdom pyramid necropolis.[30] That reconstruction was published before the archaeological work on Neferirkare and Sahure's complexes had been finished. Concerning this he said, "We, in this ideal reconstruction, came to the work with all care, we followed discovered data unconditionally and it was complemented only there, where the analogies of other buildings were presented . . . ."[31] Despite such care, we found in this reconstruction a considerable number of mistakes. In part, these inaccuracies were caused by the incomplete state of the excavation of several monuments. It is reflected, for example, in the omission of the second southern entrance and the ramp belonging to Sahure's valley temple. Furthermore, Sahure's satellite pyramid has been omitted; it should have been depicted next to the southeastern corner of Sahure's pyramid. Also, the wall around the "queen's pyramid" (today, we know it is the king's satellite pyramid), located by the southeast corner of Niuserre's pyramid, is omitted. Nonetheless, Borchardt correctly guessed its position, thanks to the work already done.

On the grounds of recent research, we are able to suggest that Neferirkare's pyramid could have been a step pyramid in the process of being converted into a true pyramid.[32] The final appearance of this monument was apparently affected by the death of the king. Regrettably, we are not able to suggest the height this reconstruction project might have reached.

Another detail not present in the reconstruction is the foundations of the causeway leading to Neferirkare's mortuary temple. Its approximate route had to be known to Borchardt and should have been included. Borchardt probably wanted to depict the state of the necropolis immediately after the completion of the royal pyramid complexes. Therefore, the private tombs, built in later periods of development (from the latter part of the Fifth Dynasty and onwards) on top of the track of Neferirkare's causeway, could not be represented. Borchardt generally focused his attention on the royal monuments. Because of this, the private tombs were represented fairly randomly on the drawing. Only the mastaba of Ptahshepses and mastabas to the northeast of Niuserre's mortuary temple were positioned relatively accurately. Those tombs that Borchardt did not excavate were missed out or are depicted too schematically, possibly because Borchardt considered his reconstruction to be idealized. Neither did he incorporate the part of the necropolis south of Neferirkare's complex despite the fact it could have been done on the basis of the surface survey. The pyramid of Queen Khentkaus II, which he considered to be a "double mastaba"[33] was also shown as this reconstruction.

The depiction of the terrain and also the neighborhood of the necropolis do not correspond to reality, so this, too, seems to be fairly schematicized. However, we should note that it is not possible to reconstruct the geomorphology of the near neighborhood and the region between the pyramids themselves. The majority of that terrain is covered by Borchardt's own excavation dumps.

Behind the pyramids at Abusir, towards Giza, other buildings are depicted. Closest to the south, we see Userkaf's sun sanctuary, whose final three-dimensional reconstruction Borchardt could not prepare. This was due to the lack of archaeological excavation at the time of publication. Behind Userkaf's sun sanctuary, we can see Niuserre's sun sanctuary. The question is, whether the structure depicted to the right of the latter temple was intended to represent a further hypothetical sun sanctuary, a hypothetical pyramid dated to the Thirteenth Dynasty,[34] or even one of the pyramid complexes at Zawiet al-Aryan. Again, we must conclude Borchardt prepared his reconstruction as an "ideal" one.

Using CAD Programs in Everyday Work

Unfortunately, the use of CAD software in Egyptology at present depends on chance, due to the choice of program. Therefore, unfortunately, the results of projects[35] carried out up until now vary greatly in quality. The need for discussion in the field of three-dimensional reconstructions and visualizations of the buildings amongst scholars is becoming more and more necessary.[36]

Despite the fact that CAD programs are fully-professional tools for documenting in pen-and-ink, I found them to be "user friendly" once I mastered the program. At the beginning the user is confronted with a blank, white, working space, which is a counterpart of the drawing table. On this "draughtsman's desk," the floor plan of the building is made. It is possible to use many tools—from a simple drawing facility to copying or transferring separate items or groups of items. The "plan" can be zoomed practically without restriction and transformed into different scales. Apart from this, it is possible to place into the plan items like walls, slabs, columns, roofs, doors, windows, and other openings, even special types of lighting fixtures and other items, from predesigned libraries employed by professional architects. It is possible to change the parameters of these items (such as width, height, "material," level above the project zero) without any great problems. The CAD programs are based on the use of vectors for any item of the project. These data specify length, width, azimuth, height, and level above the project zero of the items concerned. These data have to be mathematically logical; if incorrect data are used, the program cannot operate properly. It follows that all the data put into the computer have to be prepared very carefully: "Bad data" could destroy a draughtsman's work and force him to retrace his steps.

When work on the ground plan is finished, a view over the reconstruction can be selected. There are predefined perspective views (parallel projections: axonometric views, side, top, bottom, and front views, etc.) and it is also possible to choose the perspective from any particular place (or geographical location on the site). One can also select the date or time—between night and day—the height of the sun above the horizon, the "angle" of the view, and more.

Four variants can define the graphic output: a wire frame model with all the edges visible (fig. 1); its derivation, a wire frame model where invisible edges are not depicted (fig 2.); a shaded model with all visible surfaces shaded according to the pre-set lighting direction, and lastly, a photorealistic model of the building (fig. 3). In many cases, it is necessary to use other graphic software to finish the figures, enabling one to enhance the quality of the figures, to add some special effects, and so on.

The CAD programs, however, have some restrictions. For example, D. Arnold, in his article on the *mammisi* at Armant temple,[37] concedes that the software which is now available on the market unfortunately does not let the user model some items of ancient Egyptian architecture.[38]

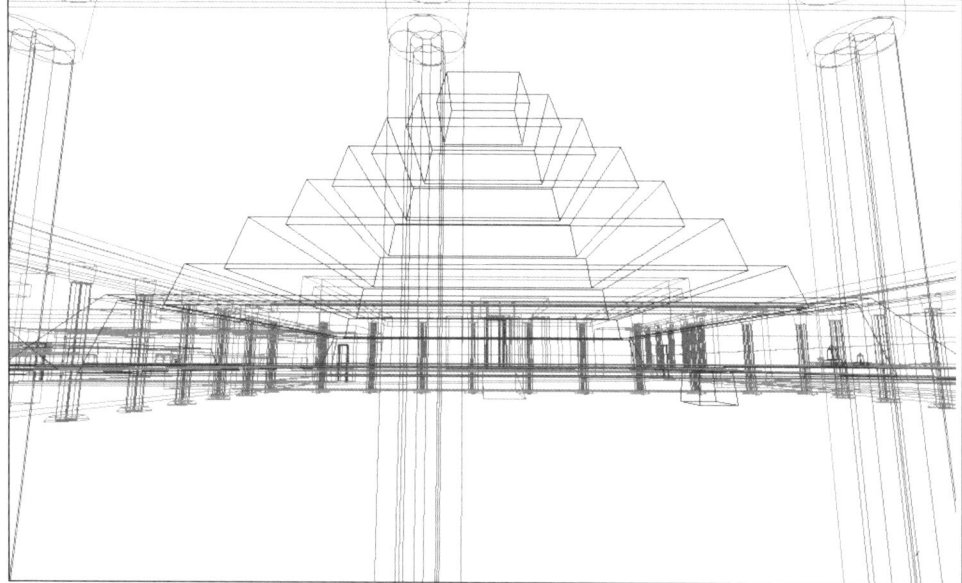

Fig. 1: Wireframe computer model with all the edges visible (courtyard and pyramid of Neferirkare).

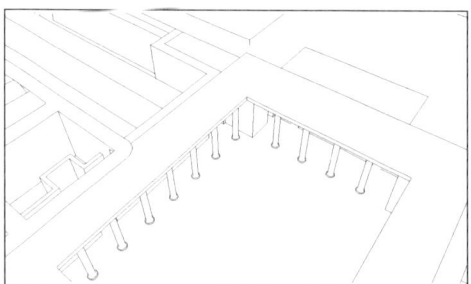

Fig. 2: Wireframe computer model, where invisible edges are not depicted (open courtyard of Neferefre's mortuary temple; view from above).

Fig. 3: Photorealistic computer model of a part of Niuserre's mortuary temple, Neferirkare's pyramid and other monuments in the southern part of the necropolis (from the northeast).

New Three-Dimensional Reconstruction of the Abusir Pyramid Field

The excavations of Lepsius, Borchardt, and Verner brought many important, unique, and in the case of the Czech Mission, also new pieces of information to the study of Old Kingdom architecture and the development of the necropolis. Therefore, it was necessary to prepare another three-dimensional reconstruction of the necropolis. Some of the figures prepared in the course of the first stage of the work on the Abusir pyramid necropolis were selected, as we see in figures 3 and 4. Only the measured data, or data gained by scientific analytical work, were used in order to come as close as possible to ancient reality.

In comparison to Borchardt's three-dimensional reconstruction in fig. 4 we can see the necropolis from nearly the same direction as it was shown by Borchardt more than 90 years ago.

As a matter of course, recently excavated monuments have been added—the mortuary complexes of Khentkaus II, Neferefre (see fig. 2), Lepsius structures XXIV and XXV, the mastabas to the south of Neferefre's mortuary temple,[39] and (more schematically) the mastabas to the east of Niuserre's pyramid, and the group of mastabas belonging to members of Djedkare's family.

As mentioned above, Borchardt's refuse heaps covered the vicinity close to the pyramid complexes to such a extent that it is not possible to visualize many private tombs. Seeing that the project of the three-dimensional reconstruction is only just beginning, it has not been possible to prepare the three-dimensional model of the terrain. That will be done in the near future and will be connected with the reconstruction of the ancient monuments.

This and other figures showing some separate monuments document the potential contribution of CAD (and other graphic software) to the study of Egyptian architecture. Consequently, it shows great promise for communicating aspects of Egyptology to the broader public.

Fig. 4: Overview of the Abusir pyramid field as seen from the southeast (photorealistic computer model).

Notes:

*Through a post-doctoral grant from the Grant Agency of the Czech Republic, 404/99/D003. Part of this article was written during my study stay at Hamburg University. I would like to acknowledge the assistance of Prof. Dr. Hartwig Altenmüller, Dr. Eva Pardey, and Dr. K. Martin. I would also like to thank Dr. Vivienne Gae Callender for her valuable help with my English and discussion concerning this topic.

1 See J. Krejčí, "The origins and development of the royal necropolis at Abusir during the Old Kingdom," in M. Bárta and J. Krejčí, (eds.), *Abusir and Saqqara in the Year 2000, Archiv orientální Supplementa* IX (Prague, 2000), 467–484.

2 The reconstructions are included in my yet-unpublished PhD thesis, *Building and Historic Development of the Abusir Royal Necropolis during the Old Kingdom*, Faculty of Arts, Charles University in Prague, 1999 [in Czech]. Thanks go to the Centrum pro podporu počítačové grafiky *v* ČR, especially to Ing. Tomáš Lejsek, for his generous loan of the ArchiCAD® 5.0 program produced by the Hungarian software company GraphiSoft®, Ltd., Budapest. I would like also to thank Ing. Vladimír Hamata, member of the Computer Center of the Czech Technical University, Prague, for his valuable help in the course of preparing the computer visualizations.

3 M. Lehner, *The Complete Pyramids* (Cairo, 1997), 106–107, 202–226, 230–239; M. Lehner, J. Sanders, et al.: http://www-oi.uchicago.edu/OI/PROJ/GIZ/Giza.html.

4 A. Labrousse, *Regards sur une Pyramide* (Paris, 1991); A. Labrousse, "Discovery of the Pyramid of Queen Ankhesenpepy II," *EA* 13 (1998), 9; A. Labrousse, *Les pyramides des reines. Une nouvelle nécropole à Saqqâra* (Paris, 1999).

5 We can also mention here a project not connected with questions about the pyramid complexes, e.g., the reconstruction of the temple at Musawwarat al-Sufra by S. Kirchner, http://www.vordenker.de/tempelvr/heute.htm, or the illustration of B. Girsh accompanying the article of D. Arnold, "Zum Geburtshaus von Armant," in H. Guksch und D. Polz (eds.), *Stationen. Beiträge zur Kulturgeschichte Ägyptens. Rainer Stadelmann gewidmet* (Mainz, 1998), 427–432.

6 J. S. Perring and H. Vyse, *Appendix to Operations Carried on at the Pyramids of Gizeh in 1837* (London, 1842), 6, 12–22, map of the pyramid field, 13.

7 *LD* Text I, 129–139; *LD* I, pl. 32.

8 These trial diggings were mentioned briefly by H. Schäfer in "Bericht über die Ausgrabungen bei Abusir im Winter 1898/99," *ZÄS* 27 (1899), 7.

9 J. de Morgan, "Découverte du mastaba de Ptah-chepsés dans la nécropole d'Abou-Sir," *RevArch* 24, 3 (1894), 18–33; despite the fact that de Morgan must have known the terrain and monuments of the Memphite necropolis very well, his *Carte de la nécropole memphite. Dahschour, Sakkarah, Abou-Sir* (Le Caire, 1897) contains many mistakes and is not recommended for today's scientific work.

10 L. Borchardt, *Das Re' Heiligtum des Königs Ne-woser-re' (Rathures). Band I, Der Bau* (Berlin, 1905); F. W. von Bissing and H. Kees, *Das Re-Heiligtum des Königs Ne-woser-re (Rathures). Band II. Die kleine Festdarstellung* (Leipzig, 1923).

11 L. Borchardt, *Das Grabdenkmal des Königs Nefer-ir-ke³-re^c* (WVDOG 11; Leipzig, 1909); L. Borchardt, *Das Grabdenkmal des Königs Ne-user-re^c* (WVDOG 7; Leipzig, 1907); L. Borchardt, *Das Grabdenkmal des König Sa³-hu-re^c*, Band I – Bau (WVDOG 14; Leipzig, 1910); L. Borchardt, *Das Grabdenkmal des Königs Sa³-hu-re^c*, Band II – Die Wandbilder (WVDOG 26; Leipzig, 1913).

12 Borchardt, *Sa³-hu-re^c, Band* I, 146.

13 See H. Ricke, "Erster Grabungsbericht über das Sonnenheligtum des Königs Userkaf bei Abusir," "Zweiter Grabungsbericht über das Sonnenheligtum des Königs Userkaf bei Abusir," *ASAE* 54 (1957), 75–82;

305-316; "Dritter Grabungsbericht über das Sonnenheligtum des Königs Userkaf bei Abusir," *ASAE* 55 (1958), 73-77; H. Ricke et al., *Das Sonnenheiligtum des Königs Userkaf. Beiträg, Bf 7/8* (1965, 1969).

14 M. Verner (ed.), *Preliminary Report on Czechoslovak Excavations in the Mastaba of Ptahshepses at Abusir* (Prague, 1976). A list with short description of each archaeological season up to 1987 can be found in: M. Verner (ed.), *Objevování starého Egypta/Unearthing of Ancient Egypt* (Praha, 1990), 47-52; see also M. Verner, *Forgotten Pharaohs, Lost Pyramids. Abusir* (Prague, 1994), 20-180; M. Bárta, "The Czech Institute of Egyptology. Bibliography 1958-1997," *ArOr* 66 (1998), 17-26.

15 See Verner, *Unearthing*. Thereafter the mission took part in the UNESCO Monuments of Nubia Salvage Campaign: H. Žába, *The Rock Inscriptions of Lower Nubia, Czechoslovak Concession*, (Prague, 1974); E. Strouhal, *Wadi Qitna and Kalabsha South, Vol. I: Archaeology*, (Prague, 1984).

16 For the most recent works in the complex see M. Verner, "Excavations at Abusir. Preliminary Report 1997/8," *ZÄS* 126 (1999), 70-76.

17 M. Verner, "Excavations at Abusir. Season 1982: Preliminary Report," *ZÄS* 111 (1984), 70-78; P. Posener-Kriegér, "Remarques préliminaires sur les nouveaux papyrus d'Abousir," in H. R. Roemer et al., *Ägypten. Dauer und Wandel*, (SDAIK 18; Mainz, 1985), 35-43; Verner, *Abusir*, 157-170; P. Posener-Kriegér, "News from Abusir," in S. Quirke (ed.), *The Temple in Ancient Egypt* (London, 1997), 17-23.

18 For other two see, P. Posener-Kriegér J. L. de Cenival, *Hieratic Papyri in the British Museum. Fifth Series. The Abu Sir Papyri*, (London, 1968); P. Posener-Kriegér, *Les archives du temple du Neferirkarê-Kakaï (Les papyrus d'Abousir), Traduction et commentaire I-II*, (Le Caire, 1976), and "Fragments de Papyrus," in M. Verner, *Abusir III. The Pyramid Complex of Khentkaus* (Prague, 1995), 133-142.

19 Verner, *ZÄS* 126 (1999), 70-76.

20 Verner, *ZÄS* 115 (1988), 167-168; see ground-plan published in Verner, *Abusir*, 84.

21 M. Verner, "Excavations at Abusir. Seasons of 1994/95 and 1995/96," *ZÄS* 124 (1997), 71-85.

22 M. Verner, "A Slaughterhouse from the Old Kingdom," *MDAIK* 42 (1986), 181-189.

23 M. Verner, "Pyramid Lepsius no. XXIV. Notes on the Construction of the Pyramid's Core," in *Stationen*, 145-150; J. Krejčí, 'The hypostyle hall of Neferefra's mortuary temple," in preparation.

24 See further, J. Krejčí, "Origins and the Development of the Royal Necropolis at Abusir During the Old Kingdom," in Abusir and Saqqara in the year 2000, in press.

25 Borchardt, *Saʾ-hu-reᶜ* II, 112, 115, 119, Bl. 33, 44, 49; PM III2, 332. cf. M. Verner, "Shepseskare, who was he and when did he reign?," in *Abusir* 2000.

26 It seems that in at least one case the former name depicting the figure on the relief was chiseled and smoothed and Neferirkare's name was introduced there. For these deletions see: Borchardt, *Saʾ-hu-reᶜ* II, 90, 111, 116; Bl. 17, 34, 48.

27 M. Verner, "Remarks on the Pyramid of Neferirkare," *MDAIK* 47, 1991, 72-78.

28 In the case of Shepseskare we are not quite sure if the unfinished monument between Userkaf's sun sanctuary and Sahure's pyramid should be ascribed to him. We leave aside the question of Neferikare's successor for the moment (cf. M. Verner, in *Abusir* 2000, 581-602)

29 Concerning this problem there was a long discussion. The place where his pyramid complex was built is not generally accepted—it could be in northern Saqqara (Berlandini), or at Dahsur (Stadelmann).

30 The first reconstruction was published in 1904 (L. Borchardt, "Ausgrabungen der Deutschen Orient-Gesselschaft bei Abusir im Winter 1903/4," *MDOG* 24 [1904], pl. 2), with the final form appearing in 1907 (Borchardt, *Ne-user-reᶜ*, pl. 1).

31 Translation from German; Borchardt, *Ne-user-reᶜ*, 9.

32 M. Verner, "Remarks on the Pyramid of Neferirkare," *MDAIK* 47 (1991), 411-418.

33 Borchardt, *Saʾ-hu-reᶜ* I, 145.

34 After A. Dodson. The sandy hills visible on the edge of the desert were the pyramid complexes. A. Dodson, "Two Thirteenth Dynasty Pyramids at Abusir?" *VA* 3 (1987), 231-232; A. Dodson, "From Dahshur to Dra

Abu al-Naga: The Decline and Fall of the Royal Pyramid," *KMT* 5/3 (1994), 25–39. From satellite photographs, it does not follow that it was the remains of a pyramid. The question is whether it is not a sun sanctuary. However, this is, in comparison to the archaeologically known sun sanctuaries, located too close to the edge of the cultivation and not at a high enough level. The question is whether or not this structure represents a cemetery for the surrounding settlements from the later periods, as a Greek or Roman sarcophagus lay on the surface of this structure. We can mention here also the problem of Lepsius' "pyramid No. XXVIII." As the excavations done by Borchardt's expedition established that the hill consisted of layers of petrified clay sediments—*tafl*—and also that there were mud brick structures present. However, the use of clay sediments for the construction of the royal pyramids cannot be taken seriously. See also L. Bares, "A Note to the Thirteenth Dynasty at Abusir," *VA* 4 (1988), 117–119.

35 See notes 3–5.

36 However, for example, in the framework of prehistoric archaeology such discussing groups do exist. These problems are also solved on mailing lists on the Internet.

37 Arnold, *Stationen*, 427–432

38 Arnold, *Stationen*, 427, n. 5.

39 Only the first *mastaba* in this row, that of prince Nakhtkare, has been excavated. In the terrain it can be seen that the *mastabas* were probably built using one layout and all at one time.

The Potential of Egyptian-Russian Cooperation in Underwater Archaeology: An Historical Perspective

Victor V. Lebedinsky
Russian Academy of Sciences

Although underwater archaeology is a relatively new discipline in Egypt, it has become a sophisticated and methodical area of scientific development. The first research concerning underwater archaeological objects in Egypt was made by Port Engineer Gaston Jondet. Before constructing breakwater facilities for the new harbor in Alexandria in 1916, he thoroughly examined the region to the west of Pharos (Qait Bay), discovering an ancient port, striking for its scale and complicated construction.[1] The remains were located only a few meters below the surface and could be discerned with the naked eye. For this reason the researchers used divers for drawing their plans, only a few times. The report, made by Gaston Jondet, gave a detailed description of the construction of an ancient port.

In 1961 Kamal Abu el Sadat, a professional diver and amateur archaeologist, discovered architectural elements and fragments of a large sculpture seven m high and weighing 25 tons not far from Fort Qait Bay. In 1962 the sculpture was lifted from the seabed with the help of Egyptian naval officers. The sculpture probably represents Isida (Isida-Faria), Mistress of Pharos, and once adorned the Alexandria Park. The statue is now located in the garden of Alexandria Naval Museum.

In 1968 Kamal Abu el Sadat received a grant from UNESCO to draw up a plan with the description of all fragments of architectural monuments, mainly on the location of the ancient lighthouse. UNESCO sent Russian archaeologist, V. Nesterov, and specialist in underwater archaeology, H. Frost, for scientific and technical support. They located the ancient monuments under the water and took their measurements with ordinary instruments. Frost drew up the first map of the region and united numerous architectural fragments. In 1976 she published sketches of the monuments discovered as well as a description of the region.[2]

At the beginning of the 1990s, interest in underwater monuments in Alexandria grew tremendously. In 1992 Franck Goddio, supported by Ibrahim Darwish, director of Egypt's Department of Underwater Archaeology, received a license to examine the seabed near Alexandria. With the help of new and unique electronic devices (a nuclear magnetometer and sensitive sonars) Goddio carried out an underwater archaeological inspection of the eastern port of Alexandria. The results of his research implied prospects for further excavations.[3]

In 1994 underwater archaeological research was begun near Fort Qait Bay.[4] The main tasks of the expedition included drawing up detailed topographical and illustrative descriptions of the region within an area of more than two hectares adjoining Fort Qait Bay, as well as the lifting and restoring of the most important finds. Research was carried out both by ordinary methods and with the help of computer technology and sensitive sonar devices.

In 1994–96 dozens of unique sculptures and fragments were discovered, including the granite colossus of Ptolemy. This statue was part of a sculptural group including the statue of Isida found there in 1961. Twelve sphinxes were also discovered, some of them bearing the titles of Ramesses II and Psamtik II and fragments of obelisks with the names of Sety I, Ramsses II, and Psamtik II. Hundreds of columns, bases, and capitals were examined, and earlier Egyptian monuments were found alongside Greek ones. A large number of ancient Egyptian monuments, belonging to pre-Ptolemaic periods, proved the Ptolemies loved to steal well-known monuments from the older cities of Egypt to decorate their own capital. In this case, judging by the inscriptions on the discovered monuments, they were taken from Heliopolis.

The discovery of huge stone blocks weighing up to 75 tons led the scientists to theorize that they had discovered fragments of the ancient Pharos lighthouse. No other mention of any other monumental construction in the eastern part of the island exists. The fact that the blocks probably fell from a considerable height increases the probability they belonged to the Pharos lighthouse.

In 1996 Frank Goddio and the European Institute of Marine Archaeology which he founded, resumed their search of the eastern port of Alexandria.[5] The project involved topographic research and archaeological excavation in the flooded area of Alexandria's eastern harbor; i.e., the palace areas and port structures of the ancient city that were probably engulfed by the sea at the end of the sixth century CE. Until recently, scientists had only theorized about the topography of that region based on classical texts. The work is being carried out with the help of the yacht *Oceanex* and the catamaran *Caimiloya*, both specially-equipped for underwater archaeological research.

Scientists use unique methods and technical facilities to examine underwater archaeological objects, i.e. super-sensitive side-scan sonar, special devices for determining the seabed profile and nuclear magnetometers. All data coming from the seabed are processed by computer and their coordinates established with the help of the Global Positioning System (GPS) satellite navigation system This is very important for the further identification and locating of all finds.

Under the agreement with the Egyptian government, it was decided not to lift from the seabed objects weighing more than 500 kg, but to leave them for a future underwater museum. As many of the architectural fragments found which exceed the above figure bear inscriptions and reliefs, the scientists decided to try a new method of casting molds underwater. As a result of this research, the ancient topography of the eastern port of Alexandria was reproduced and exact maps with the ancient coast line and flooded territories drawn up. It turned out that the whole port and ancient harbors of Alexandria, as well as the island of Antirodos, are underwater. This new information supports and supplements the reports of ancient authors concerning the topography of that region. The finds discovered on the island of Antirodos are of considerable interest: Flooded territories and ancient constructions of the island were covered with a thin layer of white sand and limestone concretions. An ancient ship and a large number of whole and fragmented amphorae of various kinds, were preserved in the internal part of the ancient harbor.[6]

During the research carried out in Abu Qir Bay near Alexandria in 1983, scientists discovered the remains of almost all of Napoleon's fleet, sunk by a British squadron under the command of Admiral Nelson. During the work, many interesting elements were lifted from the seabed. In May 1986 the French ship *Patriot* was discovered. It is a three-masted vessel of 580 tons displacement, the largest transport ship to follow Napoleon on his Egyptian expedition. A large part of the scientific equipment belonging to the men who accompanied Napoleon was on board. As a result, brass scientific instruments, writing materials, and other technical artifacts were lifted from the seabed.[7] The Government of the Arab Republic of Egypt has demonstrated great interest in underwater research. Some special state institutions have been established, such as the Department of Underwater Archaeology of the State Committee of Antiquities, for excavations dealing with problems of underwater archaeology. The successful underwater research being conducted now in the ARE integrates all the experience gained since the advent of this science more that one hundred years ago.

Underwater archaeological research started in the Black Sea earlier than in Egypt. In 1905 Russian engineer L. P. Kolli worked in Feodosia, a large port dating from ancient times to the Middle Ages (6th century BCE–4th century CE) He discovered amphorae and quay piles from ancient times (4th–3rd century BCE). Samples of the ground turned out to be identical to that of the coastline. That enabled him to gauge the extent of the Black Sea in ancient times (6th century BCE–4th century CE).[8] In the middle of the nineteenth century, Count A. S. Uvarov, who examined archaeological monuments of the Northern parts adjoining the Black Sea, suggested that the coastal area of ancient Olvia was flooded with the waters of the Bugsky estuary.[9] Count Uvarov's suggestion was proven during archaeological research carried out by B. V. Farmakovsky.[10] In 1913–1916 on his commission, V. I. Derenkin examined the submerged constructions of ancient Olvia.[11] Thus, underwater archaeological research had already been carried out in the northern parts of the Black Sea coastal area at the beginning of the twentieth century. At the end of the 1930s, the famous Soviet professor R. A. Orbeli focused on underwater archaeological research.[12] Orbeli was one of the first to try to clear underwater monuments with the help of suction pumps. He paid considerable attention to theoretical methods of underwater archaeology. His textbook, *Researches and Discoveries* is the first on underwater archaeology and his research methods for underwater archaeology are still used today.[13] Orbeli planned to establish a museum and institute for underwater archaeology in the USSR.[14]

After World War II, professor V. D. Blavatsky resumed research in the Black Sea. In 1957–1965, under his guidance, scientists examined a number of ancient cities on the northern coasts of the Black Sea, such as Nimfey, Pantikapei, Germonas, Fanagoriya, Hersones, and Olvia, and carried out underwater excavation.[15] As a result, it became clear that the Black Sea level rose by four meters compared to its level in the middle of the first millenium, and the sea absorbed about one-third of the original area of ancient cities, including city buildings and port facilities. For the first time it was possible to see the real dimensions, structure, and number of inhabitants of centers on the northern parts of the Black Sea area. During research by Blavatsky, new methods for underwater study of cultural layers were established. During this work the scientists used the most advanced technical facilities, e.g. echo-sounding locators and underwater television.

In August of 1962, S. F. Strzheletsky and A. I. Tsekhovoy organized an underwater archaeological expedition in the area of ancient Hersones. The aim of the expedition was to examine the submerged part of Hersones in Karantine Bay and Cossack Bay.[16] After examining the western part of Karantine Bay, the researchers came to the conclusion that what they saw were port buildings of ancient Hersones. In 1964–1966 the Hersones area was examined by an underwater archaeological expedition headed by V. I. Kadeev.[17] The aim of the expedition was to determine the purpose of constructions discovered in the Karantine Bay and to date them. The expedition faced unexpected problems. The remains in the western part of the Karantine Bay turned out to be the defense towers of Hersones in the Middle Ages. Exploring the shafts also revealed the remains of an earlier cultural layer. The expedition also discovered what was left of a defense tower on the bottom of the bay, dated to the fourth to fifth centuries CE, thus the question about the location of port facilities from the ancient and medieval Hersones remains open.

During research in the Round and Sand Bays, ancient amphorae and fragments dating from the fourth century BCE to the third century CE were discovered, and also fragments of jugs and amphorae dating from the ninth to the eleventh centuries CE. The finds, undoubtedly representing a ship cargo, proved that shipwrecks caused by a sandbar in the center of the bay were a frequent occurrence. The attempt to trace the ancient wharf in the Sand Bay, mentioned by Z. Arkas, was not successful, although two stone blocks found on the sea bottom could belong to that wharf. The searchers found a shipwreck 35 meters from the shore and five meters deep in the Sand Bay dating to the first century CE. In August 1974, the Hersones Museum carried out underwater research in the western bay of Archer Bay.[18] The scientists discovered a large number of ceramic fragments, dating from the fourth to the third centuries BCE and to the thirteenth to fourteenth centuries CE. Ancient ships, caught in a storm, usually took refuge in nearby bays, including Archer Bay. Ships often failed to make the correct turn and sunk. At the beginning of the 1980s, underwater archaeological research was carried out on the sea bottom of the Kerch strait, near the Zavetnoye village. During this exploration, scientists discovered and examined ancient Akra, a populated area of the European Bosporus, mentioned by Starbon, Pliny, and Pseudo-Arrian.[19] Scientists had failed to locate that area for more than a century. The research proved that today ancient Akra is deep under water. Fortress walls, towers, and other city buildings were discovered on the seabed, including a square stone well, 3 m down and about 170 m from shore. A narrow stone ridge was discovered about 600 m from the shore and 10 m down; lead and stone remains of anchors were found nearby, as well as ancient iron anchors. That ridge probably served as a defensive pier for Akra's harbor. During the research and excavations, scientists drew the plan of a city that had been flooded, and lifted various archaeological finds.

Underwater research carried out in the 1990s, enabled a large number of archaeological objects to be located. In 1995 the city archives of ancient Hersones were discovered among flooded remains in the Karantine Bay. A Venetian ship, dated to the fourteenth century, was found in Sudak Bay and examined. In 1999 a Byzantine ship was found near the Meganom Horn. The presence of a large number of flooded settlements and port facilities is explained by the fact that the level of the Black Sea rose more than four meters during the last two thousand years.

It is interesting to note that more than 15 ships, sunk during the Crimean War (1854–1856), were discovered here. For example, the ships of a British squadron were found near Balaklava and French ships near the Hersones lighthouse and Eupatoria. Russian ships were sunk in the Sevastopol Bay, blocking its entrance.

At present the Black Sea coast is a very promising area for underwater archaeological exploration. Evidence for contacts between Egypt and the northern part of the Black Sea in ancient times exist in the ancient records and also in the archaeological monuments found during excavations, for example, an urn from Alexandria and various Egyptian ceramics and other objects.[20] This allows us to hope that Egyptian monuments will be found underwater. The types and conditions of the location of underwater archaeological monuments in the Black sea are close to Egyptian ones, which enables us to apply methods and techniques used in one area, to the other.

In this connection, the Center for Egyptological Studies of the Russian Academy of Sciences, together with the National Preserve Hersones Tavrichesky, started underwater archaeological research in the Black Sea in 1999, beginning with the drawing-up of an precise underwater archaeological map of the Black Sea.

Notes:

1 J. Taylor, ed., *Marine Archaeology* (London, 1965), 160–162.

2 W. La Riche, *Alexandria* (Gedeon, 1996), 125.

3 F. Goddio, A. Bernard, *Alexandria. The Submerged Royal Quarters* (London, 1998), 1–4.

4 J. Y. Empereur, "Alexandria: The Underwater Site near Qaitbay Fort," *Egyptian Archaeology* 8 (1996), 7–10.

5 F. Goddio, A Bernand, "*Alexandria,*" 6–58.

6 S. A. Ezzat, "2000-year-old shipwreck found in Alexandria near Cleopatra's palace," *The Egyptian Gazette* (November 5, 1998), 7.

7 A. V. Okorokov, ed., *Podvodnay razvedka pamyatnikov istorii i kultury* (Moscow, 1988), 8–9.

8 L. P. Kolli, "Sledy drevnei kulturi na dne morskom," *Izvestiy Tavricheskoi uchenoi arhivnoi komissii* 43 (1909), 125–137.

9 A. S. Uvarov, *Issledovanie o drevnostyh Yzhnoi Rossii i beregov Chernogo moriy* (St. Petersburg, 1851), 40.

10 B. V. Farmakovsky, *Olviy* (Moscow, 1915), 23.

11 B. V. Farmakovsky, "Otchet o raskopkah v Olviy v 1924g," *SGAIMK* 1 (1924), 145 (fig.3). A. I. Karasev, "Oboronitelnie sooruzheniy Olvii," *KSIIMK* XXII (1948), 32.

12 R. A. Orbeli, "Gidroarheologiy – Podvodnie istoricheskie iziskaniy bliz drevnih grecheskih gorodov na Chernomorscom poberezhie," *Sudopodiem* 1 (1945), 140–176. R. A. Orbeli, "Podvodnye istoricheskie izyskaniy i zadachi EPRONa," *EPRON* XXIII–XXV (1938), 343–346. R. A. Orbeli, "Gidroarheologicheskaya karta SSSR," *EPRON* XXVI–XXVII (1940), 177–187. R. A. Orbeli, "Cheln (drevnyy lodka-odnoderevka)," *EPRON* XXIII–XXV (1938), 345–357.

13 R. A. Orbeli, *Issledovaniy i izhyskaniy. Materialy po istorii podvoodnogo truda s drevneishih vremen do nashih dney* (Moscow, 1947) 283.

14 R. A. Orbeli, "Za razvitie podvoodnoi arheologii," *EPRON* XXIII–XXV (1938), 359–365.

15 V. D. Blavatsky, "O podvodnoi arheologii," *Sovetskay Archeologia* 3 (1958), 73–89; V. D. Blavatsky and V. I. Kuzishin, "Podvodnye razvedki v 1958g," *Kratkie Soobscheniy Instituta Archeologii* 83 (1961); V. D. Blavatsky and V. I. Kuzishin, "Podvodnye razvedki drevney Fanagorii," *Vesnik AN SSSR* 1 (1959); V. D. Blavatsky "Podvodnye raskopki Fanagorii v 1959g," *Sovetskay Arheologia* 1 (1961), 277–279; V. D. Blavatsky, "Raboty podvodnoy Azovo-Chernomorskoi ekspeditsii 1960g," *Sovetskay Archeologia* 4 (1961), 150; V. D. Blavatsky, "Podvodno-archeologicheskay ekspiditsiy 1962g," *Sovetskay Archeologia* 1 (1965) 272–275; V. D. Blavatsky, "Podvodnye razvedky v Olvii," *Sovetskay Archeologia* 3 (1962), 225–234; V. D. Blavatsky, "Technika podvodnyh arheologicheskih rabot," *Arheologia i estestvennye nauki,* (Moscow, 1965), 268–278; V. D. Blavatsky and B. G. Peters, "Podvodnye archeologicheskie issledoivaniy v rayone Evpatorii," *Kratkie Soobscheniy Instituta Archeologii* 104 (1967), 73–78; V. D. Blavatsky and B. G. Peters, "Korablekrusheniy kontsa IV-nachala III vv. do N.E. okolo Donuzlava," *Sovetskay Arheollogia,* 3 (1969),

293

151–158. V. D. Blavatsky and B.G. Peters, "Priemy podvodnyh arheologicheskih rabot pry izuchenii ostatkov drevnego korablekrushenia," *Morskie podvodnnye issledovaniy* (Moscow, 1969), 339–342.

16 Archive State Reserve "Hersones Tavricheskiy," D. N 819.

17 Archive State Reserve "Hersones Tavricheskiy," D. N 1400, D. N 1189, D. N 1606.

18 Archive State Reserve "Hersones Tavricheskiy," D. N 2079.

19 K. K. Shilik, "Issledovaniy antichnoi Akry, " *Arheologicheskie otkritiy (1985)g* (Moscow, 1987), 632; K. K. Shilik, "Lokalizitsia antichnoi Akry kak primer kompleksnogo analiza v istorico-geografichedskih issledovaniyh," *Kompleksnye metody v izuchennii istorii s drevneishih vremen do nashih dney* (Moscow, 1984), 108–111; K. K. Shilik, "Reaboty Bosporskogo otryda," *Arheologicheskie otkritiy 1984g* (Moscow, 1986), 493.

20 State Reserve "Hersones Tavricheskiy," Inv. N 34/37074, Inv. N 144/37080.

Données nouvelles sur les inhumations de figurines osiriennes : le tombeau d'Osiris à Karnak

François Leclère
Ifao

Les recherches menées depuis 1993 dans le secteur du tombeau d'Osiris à Karnak au nord du temple de l'est[1], nous ont permis jusqu'à présent de repérer trois phases de développement d'un cimetière de figurines osiriennes ayant fonctionné pendant tout le Ier millénaire av. J.-C. L'état le plus tardif correspond à des « catacombes » en briques cuites, composées de longs couloirs voûtés parallèles, aux parois enduites de chaux et pourvue sous le règne de Ptolémée IV d'une décoration peinte à caractère osirien. Les centaines de niches qui s'ouvraient dans ces parois devaient à l'origine contenir des figurines enterrées à l'occasion de la célébration de mystères osiriens, mais aucune d'entre elles n'a été retrouvée.

Parallèlement à l'assemblage des milliers de fragments d'enduit peint provenant de ce bâtiment, la fouille s'est poursuivie dans le secteur immédiatement à l'est où un autre édifice, construit également en briques cuites et comportant plusieurs chambres voûtées, correspond à une phase antérieure du cimetière. Son exploration partielle au moment de son premier dégagement en 1950 avait alors montré qu'il datait au moins de l'époque saïte et contenait des figurines osiriennes. Un sondage récent entre les deux constructions a révélé un état encore antérieur du cimetière, constitué d'une accumulation plus ou moins désordonnée de niches individuelles en briques cuites contenant chacune une figurine osirienne.

Les dernières campagnes de fouilles ont été consacrées à ces deux premières phases. Bien que l'exploration reste encore très limitée, les premiers résultats obtenus apportent déjà des éléments nouveaux susceptibles d'être confrontés à ce que nous pouvons connaître par ailleurs des rites d'inhumation de simulacres osiriens, d'après les textes et quelques autres exemples archéologiques concrets.

I. Structures
A. *Le cimetière primitif*
Dans la zone explorée du cimetière primitif, sur la quinzaine de sépultures miniatures reconnues

jusqu'à présent, quatre ont été fouillées intégralement. La zone d'inhumation dépasse largement l'emprise limitée du sondage puisque des traces de sépultures ont été repérées en surface jusqu'à une quinzaine de mètres plus à l'est. Ces sépultures en briques cuites sont empilées les unes au-dessus des autres, sur plusieurs niveaux, sans organisation apparente, avec une orientation différente presque à chaque fois. À défaut de véritables sols, on a pu observer des niveaux de remblais successifs, qui semblent indiquer un enterrement progressif. L'analyse stratigraphique est rendue complexe par le fait que certaines niches ont parfois été implantées dans des fosses qui se recoupent les unes les autres. Longs de 75 cm à 1 m environ, les édicules ont la forme de niches couvertes d'une voûte sommaire composée principalement de briques disposées en bâtière. Quelques variantes apparaissent dans la typologie de construction (fig. 1).

Fig. 1 : Tombe-niche du cimetière primitif, en cours de démontage (cliché A. Chéné).

Du point de vue de la datation, l'analyse stratigraphique du terrain montre que ces tombes-niches se trouvent pour la plupart dans des niveaux antérieurs au tombeau dit saïte. En plusieurs endroits, les murs de celui-ci les oblitèrent. Des dispositifs particuliers de briques ont parfois été aménagés à la base des parois, dans le but de les enjamber sans les détruire, et témoignent du respect dévolu aux sépultures anciennes. En outre, les remblais qui recouvrent les sépultures les plus basses ont été recoupés par la tranchée de fondation d'un vaste massif de briques crues correspondant à un bastion d'angle de l'un des anciens murs d'enceinte du temple d'Amon, dans un état que nous avons attribué au règne de Psousennès, en raison de la présence dans la maçonnerie de briques estampillées au nom du grand prêtre d'Amon Menkheperrê[2]. Si ces briques n'ont pas été remployées à une époque ultérieure, les enterrements auraient donc commencé au moins au début de la Troisième Période intermédiaire, ce que tendrait à confirmer le matériel céramique contenu dans les strates remblayant les niches. Néanmoins, en surface, quelques sépultures pourraient dater de la Troisième Période intermédiaire et de la Basse Époque. La fouille est encore trop peu étendue pour qu'il soit possible de déterminer dans quel ordre précis les enterrements se sont succédé ni à quel rythme. Compte tenu de ce que nous savons par ailleurs des rites osiriens, il est raisonnable de penser à un rythme annuel d'enterrement.

À la Basse Époque, le mode d'inhumation a partiellement changé. Les sépultures osiriennes présentent une forme similaire, mais elles ont été cette fois-ci installées au sein d'un édifice spécialement conçu à cet effet et bâti sur l'ancien cimetière.

B. Le « tombeau voûté » saïte

Au moment de son dégagement en 1950, l'édifice était alors enfoui sous plusieurs mètres de remblais qui ont été totalement enlevés par le fouilleur, parfois jusque sous la base de la construction, ce qui nous prive malheureusement aujourd'hui d'informations stratigraphiques capitales. Le bâtiment, qui s'étend sur environ 8 m de long, est construit en briques cuites du même type que celles des anciennes niches. Il est composé de plusieurs éléments aboutés les uns aux autres et se répartissant en deux zones majeures :

• un corps principal orienté nord-sud, constitué de deux sections voûtées bout à bout, pourvue chacune d'une chambre latérale secondaire du côté ouest, également voûtée, et de dimensions plus petites ;

• un long bras de plan plus irrégulier, accolé au corps

Fig. 2 : Vue verticale du "tombeau voûté" saïte (cliché A. Chéné).

principal du côté nord, perpendiculaire à l'axe de celui-ci et pourvu à l'ouest d'une sorte de puits carré. Il était également couvert, au moins partiellement, de voûtes sommaires qui ont disparu depuis leur dégagement, il y a 50 ans. L'analyse architecturale indique que l'édifice n'a pas été construit en une seule fois mais par éléments juxtaposés de façon diachronique. Les espaces intérieurs sont remplis de tombes-niches indépendantes, de structure similaire à celle des petites tombes du cimetière primitif, mais rangées, cette fois, les unes à côté des autres et en plusieurs couches successives. Elles sont chacune pourvues d'une couverture en bâtière comme les niches du cimetière primitif et présentent de semblables variantes de construction.

L'exploration, cette année[3], de la chambre latérale nord (fig. 3) a révélé trois étages de niches superposés, remblayés successivement, mais laissant, à chacun des deux niveaux inférieurs, un espace de circulation accessible par une ouverture à l'ouest, partiellement bouchée à chaque changement de niveau. La disposition des niches plus nombreuses de l'étage supérieur a montré que la voûte n'a pu être mise en place qu'après le remplissage total de la chambre.

Dans le bras nord-est, nettoyé en 1999, la densité des sépultures est plus importante. Il est possible qu'il ait lui-même été construit par ajouts de sections successives, trop étroites pour que l'on ait pu y circuler, et couvert, après remplissage de niches par le dessus, d'une voûte générale très irrégulière. Une semelle dans la maçonnerie est peut-être l'indice du sol de circulation extérieur. Les niches étaient remblayées d'une *mouna* très compacte, parfois couverte d'un lait de chaux préparant une surface de pose pour les sépultures d'un nouvel étage. En revanche, et bien qu'elles n'aient pas encore été ré-ouvertes, il semble que les chambres du corps principal étaient voûtées dès l'origine et qu'on y installait

Fig. 3 : Vue des figurines osiriennes de la partie supérieure de la chambre 2 du "tombeau voûté" saïte (cliché Fr. Leclère).

progressivement les sépultures en accédant à l'intérieur par des portes cintrées, dont trois sont visibles, au nord, au sud et à l'est.

Néanmoins, il semble bien qu'au moment de son fonctionnement, l'édifice n'était pas totalement enterré. L'épais remblai qui couvrait l'ensemble de l'édifice avant 1950 n'a été déposé que plus tardivement, sans doute avant l'édification des catacombes de Ptolémée IV.

La datation saïte de l'édifice a été suggérée par la présence de briques cuites estampillées au nom de Néchao II, signalées par le fouilleur en 1950 et encore visibles aujourd'hui dans plusieurs parties du monument. Elles ont pu être remployées plus tardivement. Des tessons de calage entre les briques de voûtes tendent à confirmer une datation au moins saïte. Le nombre potentiel de niches contenues dans la construction, dans l'hypothèse d'un rythme annuel d'enterrement, dépasse de toute façon le seul règne de ce roi et l'édifice a pu fonctionner pendant toute la Basse Époque et jusqu'à son remplacement sous Ptolémée IV par les nouvelles « catacombes », édifice construit d'un seul tenant et de manière plus rationalisée.

II. Les simulacres osiriens

Chacune des tombes-niches des deux phases du cimetière renferme une figurine osirienne flanquée d'« accessoires » divers. Elles sont toutes semblables à quelques variantes près. Leur état de conservation particulièrement médiocre fait de leur fouille une opération très délicate et méticuleuse.

La figurine principale, longue d'une cinquantaine de centimètres au maximum, est réduite à une silhouette très sommaire, momiforme, de face, et coiffée de la couronne blanche. Elle est composée d'une très mince coque de plâtre renfermant du sable pur et finement tamisé. De faibles traces de pigments sur la coque témoignent de l'existence d'une décoration peinte. Dans un cas, la figurine était dotée d'yeux en calcite et obsidienne. De part et d'autre, quatre simulacres plus petits (une dizaine de centimètres), mais de composition identique, figurent des substituts des réceptacles-canopes assimilés aux quatre fils d'Horus. Leur modelé et leur état trop sommaires empêchent d'identifier chacun d'entre eux. Parfois, un objet arrondi de même composition, vraisemblablement un scarabée, est placé près de la tête (cf. *infra*).

L'état de conservation médiocre de ces figurines est lié à la fois à leur procédé de fabrication et aux agressions naturelles : on peut supposer que le sable était au départ aggloméré avec une sorte de liant organique qui a permis de modeler ou de mouler la figurine puis de l'enduire de plâtre mais qui a dû disparaître assez rapidement. La coque n'a en général pas résisté aux tassements de terrain, aux infiltrations de boue, aux remontées périodiques de la nappe phréatique ou encore au continuel cheminement de racines et de petits vers (fig. 4).

Les simulacres mis au jour dans le tombeau saïte présentent des caractéristiques supplémentaires. Certains d'entre eux, dans le bras nord-est de l'édifice, ont fait l'objet d'une sorte de momification : ils sont emmaillotés dans une sorte de gangue noirâtre dont l'aspect (empreintes de tissu, pliures) évoque celui d'un linge imbibé de bitume ou de résine aujourd'hui très dégradée. De minuscules perles tubulaires et annulaires en faïence et en terre cuite, retrouvées en grand nombre et en tas désordonnés de part et d'autre des figurines, appartenaient sans aucun doute, à l'origine, à une résille décorant la surface des pseudo-momies[4]. En plusieurs endroits à l'intérieur comme à l'extérieur des niches, ont été retrouvées des balles en argile compacte d'environ 2 à 3 cm de diamètre, anépigraphes (cf. *infra*). L'une des figurines était accompagnée de deux amulettes osiriennes en pierre et en bronze. Sous une autre se trouvait une petite feuille d'or chiffonnée d'environ 5 mm de diamètre, qui avait peut-être une fonction analogue à un dépôt de fondation.

Certaines figurines découvertes cette année, dans la pièce latérale nord, nous ont apporté des informations capitales permettant de reconstituer en partie le processus de fabrication : le noyau de

sable, sans doute durci à l'origine par une résine, a été enfermé
dans un emballage végétal constitué de feuilles longues et
étroites (papyrus ou sorte d'alfa)
jointes les unes à côté des autres
comme des bandelettes et serrées
par des liens. Le végétal a disparu mais a laissé son empreinte
dans la couche de plâtre dont a
été enduite la figurine. Celle-ci a
été entourée d'un tissu léger de
type gaze, lui-même enduit
d'une nouvelle couche de plâtre
bien lissée en surface. Là encore,
l'information nous est parvenue
en négatif. La figurine a alors été
peinte sur les deux faces : un
collier, avec à l'arrière son contrepoids, et, sur le torse et le dos,
deux lignes rouge croisées,
figurant l'étole caractéristique
non seulement des représentations osiriennes mais de toutes
les divinités momiformes ainsi
que des cercueils anthropoïdes
de la Troisième Période intermédiaire[5]. Des fragments assez
larges de pâte verte, trop
dégradés pour être reconnaiss-
ables, nous autorise cependant à
supposer que le visage et peut-
être des mains étaient figurés en
cire. Le simulacre était enfin
éventuellement emmailloté dans
un linge imbibé de résine.

Le matériel ainsi réuni peut
être confronté aux informations
que quelques textes et des trou-

Fig. 4 : Détail de la partie supérieure des figurines de la chambre 2
(cliché Fr. Leclère).

vailles archéologiques anciennes pouvaient jusqu'à présent nous apporter sur les rites d'inhumation de figurines osiriennes.

III. Éléments de comparaison
A. Archéologie
Des figurines ont en effet été mises au jour entre le début et le milieu du siècle sur quatre sites :
Le Ouâdi Qoubbanet el-Qouroud à Thèbes ouest, Tehneh el-Gebel, Touna el-Gebel et Cheikh Fadl

300

en Moyenne Égypte). Martin Raven les a récemment réétudiées[6]. Celles de Tehneh étaient contenues dans un cercueil hiéracocéphale en bois peint et inscrit, lui-même placé dans un sarcophage en calcaire ou en terre cuite inséré dans une cavité creusée dans la roche. Quatre boules de résine, en forme de tête de lion ou inscrites au nom de quatre déesses léonines, accompagnaient le simulacre. Christiane Ziegler les a identifiées à ce que des rituels apotropaïques sur papyrus définissent comme les boules chargées de protéger Osiris au moment de sa résurrection[7]. Celles que nous avons retrouvées dans les sépultures du tombeau saïte sont similaires mais anépigraphes. À l'intérieur du cercueil de bois, la figurine est flanquée de quatre petits simulacres, substituts des canopes fils d'Horus, et souvent d'un scarabée placé généralement près de la tête. C'est ce qui nous a permis d'identifier comme tel un accessoire trouvé dans certaines des sépultures de Karnak, près de la tête de la figurine. Il est intéressant de noter à ce propos que, dans le décor des catacombes ptolémaïques voisines, à l'extrémité ouest de la partie sud de la voûte du couloir sud, Osiris est figuré assis sur son trône, suivi des quatre fils d'Horus et d'une divinité dont la tête est surmontée d'un scarabée, appelée le « scarabée vénérable » (ḫprr šps). Sur une autre figurine de Tehneh, le scarabée est placé sur la poitrine de la figurine, ce qui peut faire penser au scarabée de cœur caractéristique de l'équipement funéraire royal. Sur le plan de la forme générale, les figurines sont similaires aux nôtres :
- le corps est composé d'une silhouette momiforme ; les dimensions sont proches (une coudée de long) ;
- elles sont coiffées la plupart du temps de la couronne blanche ou de la couronne atef ;
- l'équipement est comparable ;
- certains détails sont fabriqués en cire (visage de la figurine et des fils d'Horus, couronne, mains, sceptres, scarabée) et parfois rehaussés de dorures.

Malgré ces ressemblances, les divergences sont nombreuses :
- outre leur contexte d'inhumation différent (sarcophages, nécropole de la bordure désertique), elles sont presque toutes ithyphalliques, ce qui n'est jamais le cas à Karnak, et leur facture est très dissemblable ;
- figurine et simulacres sont généralement composés d'un noyau de sable, de terre ou de résine d'une part, et d'orge d'autre part, contenus dans un linceul de toile imbibée de bitume ou de résine, et/ou entourés de bandelettes de lin ;
- les figurines sont toutes plutôt datées de l'époque gréco-romaine, d'après les inscriptions des sarcophages et le style des visages.

B. Textes

Deux sources majeures sont à mentionner : d'une part, les textes des chapelles osiriennes de Dendara, d'autre part le Papyrus Salt 825.

Les textes de Dendara[8], notamment ceux de la chapelle orientale, décrivent précisément les ingrédients nécessaires à la fabrication annuelle de figurines à l'occasion de la célébration des fêtes de Khoïak et certaines étapes de la fabrication de deux types de figurines. Celle du Khenti Imentet est un mélange de sable et d'orge placés dans deux demi-moules latéraux tapissés d'une étoffe, arrosé et mis à germer dans une cuve. Les deux parties sont ensuite démoulées et assemblées avec de la myrrhe sèche et des serre-joints constitués de quatre cordelettes, puis la figurine est emmaillotée après séchage au soleil. Elle a la forme d'Osiris momiforme à face humaine et coiffé de la couronne blanche. L'autre figurine, celle de Sokar, est un mélange de terre et d'une série de matériaux différents parmi lesquels des substances organiques (pulpe de dattes, myrrhe sèche, encens frais, une douzaine d'aromates) et, en très faible quantité, plus d'une vingtaine de minéraux précieux, le tout mélangé avec de l'eau pour former une pâte. Celle-ci est placée ensuite dans deux demi-moules en forme de cuve et de couvercle, préalablement oints d'huile. La pâte sèche quelques jours dans le moule puis au soleil. La figurine a visage humain coiffé d'une perruque pourvue d'un *uræus* et les mains tiennent les sceptres sur la poitrine. Toute une série d'amulettes étaient ajoutées dont quatre figurines momiformes figurant les fils d'Horus. Les figurines fabriquées participent, au même titre que les statues de culte, aux grandes fêtes, avant d'être enterrées définitivement, au bout d'une année, dans la nécropole. Le texte ne nous dit rien des conditions exactes d'inhumation, sinon que les figurines devaient être placées dans un sarcophage de bois à figure humaine.

Le pSalt 825[9] un manuscrit probablement abydénien et datant de la fin de la Basse Époque ou de l'époque ptolémaïque, indique que le Khenti Imentet était modelé à partir d'une pâte plastique à base de sable, d'argile et de différentes gommes et résines, puis enduit, selon Ph. Derchain, d'au moins deux couches d'onguents composés, la première à chaud, à base de cire et de résines, la seconde à froid, à base de résines mélangées à des dissolvants liquides, chacune étant ensuite recouverte de tissu. Interprété autrement[10], le texte pourrait faire référence à la fabrication de deux figurines différentes.

De la même manière que les figurines retrouvées en fouille, celles qui sont décrites dans ces deux textes présentent des points de convergence avec nos simulacres de Karnak, notamment l'emploi de sable et de résine, mais aussi beaucoup de différences. L'absence d'orge dans les figurines de Karnak n'est finalement pas parlante : de même que l'emballage végétal détecté, les graines, si elles étaient présentes, ont pu disparaître totalement. Il est donc bien difficile de rattacher les figurines de Karnak à telle ou telle tradition.

Conclusions

Le site de Karnak nous offre la possibilité peu courante d'étudier en détail le fonctionnement d'un cimetière osirien, fonctionnement qui s'inscrit dans la durée, avec trois phases de développement, et de mieux appréhender la réalité des rites osiriens du mois de Khoïak. La comparaison avec d'autres témoignages archéologiques et textuels permet de mettre en évidence l'originalité de ceux-ci à Karnak, tout au moins pour ce qui concerne la fabrication et les conditions d'inhumation des figurines. Il est clair que selon l'endroit et l'époque, les recettes ont dû beaucoup varier, ce que confirme encore, dans le texte de Dendara, la liste des figurines fabriquées dans telle ou telle localité.

Notes:

1 Recherches effectuées dans le cadre du CFEETK. Voir L. Coulon, Fr. Leclère, S. Marchand, «"Catacombes" osiriennes de Ptolémée IV à Karnak. Rapport préliminaire de la campagne de fouilles 1993», *CahKarn* 10 (1995), 205–238 ; Fr. Leclère – L. Coulon, « Fouilles dans la nécropole osirienne du secteur nord-est du temple de Karnak », in C. J. Eyre (éd.), *VIIth International Congress of Egyptologists, Cambridge, 3–9*

September 1995, Abstracts of Papers, (Oxford, 1995), 104-105 ; id., « La nécropole osirienne de la "Grande Place" à Karnak. Fouilles dans le secteur nord-est du temple d'Amon », *in* C. J. Eyre (éd.), *Proceedings of the VIIth International Congress of Egyptologists, Cambridge, 3-9 September 1995, OLA* 82 (1998), 649-659 ; Fr. Leclère, « A Cemetery of Osirid Figurines at Karnak », *EgArch* 9 (octobre 1996), 9-12 ; voir aussi D. Lefur, « Conservation des fragments peints des catacombes osiriennes de Karnak », in R. Tefnin (éd.), *La peinture égyptienne ancienne. Un monde de signes à préserver. Actes du colloque international de Bruxelles, avril 1994, Monumenta Aegyptiaca* VII, (Bruxelles, 1997), 85-95, et les comptes rendus donnés, d'après nos rapports, par J. Leclant , G. Clerc, *Orientalia* 63 (1994), 408-409, § l, *Orientalia* 64 (1995), 284-286, § k, *Orientalia* 65 (1996), 289-291, *Orientalia* 67 (1998), 376-377, § l, et J. Leclant - A. Gout, *Orientalia* 68 (1999), 380-382.

2 L. Coulon, Fr. Leclère, S. Marchand, *CahKarn* 10 (1995), 223-225.

3 Entre la communication au congrès et la remise de cet article.

4 Comme sur les momies humaines à partir de l'époque saïte, cf. par exemple M. J. Raven *De dedencultus van het Oude Egypte,* (Amsterdam, 1992), 64-65, no 25.

5 Sur le sens de cette étole, cf. R. Van Walsem, *The Coffin of Djedmonthuiufankh in the National Museum of Antiquities at Leiden,* (Leyde, 1997), 116-119, n. c.

6 M. J. Raven, « Corn-Mummies », *OMRO* 63 (1982), 7-38 ; id., « Four Corn-Mummies in the Archaeological Museum at Cracow », Materialy Archeologiczne 30 (1997), 5-23, auquel on ajoutera *Egyptian Classical and Western Asiatic Antiquities, Sotheby Parke Bernet Inc.,* (New York, Friday May 16, 1980), n°s 405-407 ; on ajoutera à la bibliographie des objets déjà mentionnés par M. J. Raven : G. Galliano, *Musée des Beaux-arts de Lyon. Les antiquités. Guide des collections,* (Paris, 1997), 33 ; Fr. Tiradritti (éd.), *Il Cammino di Harwa. L'uome di fronte al mistero : l'Egitto,* (Milan, 1999), 116, 169, n° 119 ; *Christie's Antiquities Auction,* (13th June 2000), 21, n° 227 ; pour des figurines d'un type un peu différent, voir id., « A New Type of Osiris Burials », *Egyptian Religion. The Last Thousand Years. Studies dedicated to the memory of J. Quagebeur, OLA* 84 (1998), 227-239, auquel on ajoutera *Auction Antiquities Christie's,* (New York, Friday, 30 May 1997), 32, n° 59.

7 J.-Cl. Goyon, « Textes mythologiques. II. Les révélations du mystère des quatre boules », *BIFAO* 75 (1975), 349-399 ; *id., Le papyrus d'Imouthès, fils de Psintaês,* (New York, 1999), 63-73 ; Chr. Ziegler, « À propos du rite des quatres boules », *BIFAO* 79 (1979), 437-439 ; cf. également M. J. Raven, *OMRO* 63 (1982), 24, n°s 207-211. Des boules d'argile d'un type similaire ont été trouvées dans le temple d'Osiris à 'Ayn Manawir (oasis de Douch), cf. N. Grimal « Travaux de l'Ifao en 1994-1995 », *BIFAO* 95 (1995), 570-571 ; M. Wuttman et al., « Premier rapport préliminaire sur le site de 'Ayn Manawir », *BIFAO* 96 (1996), 393, 398, 435-436.

8 É. Chassinat, *Le mystère d'Osiris au mois de Khoiak,* (Le Caire, 1966) ; S. Cauville, « Les mystères d'Osiris à Dendera. Interprétation des chapelles osiriennes », *BSFE* 112 (1988), 23-36 ; id., *Le temple de Dendara. Les chapelles osiriennes. Transcriptions et traduction, BdE* 117 (Le Caire, 1997), notamment 14-28, *Commentaire, BdE* 118 (Le Caire, 1997), 17-19, 220-224.

9 Ph. Derchain, *Le papyrus Salt 825 (BM 10051). Rituel pour la conservation de la vie en Égypte,* (Bruxelles, 1965), 79-95, 143-145 ; Fr.-R. Herbin, « Les premières pages du Papyrus Salt 825 », *BIFAO* 88 (1988), 95-112 ; sur l'évocation de simulacres de type probablement différent, cf. Favard-Meeks, « Behbeit el-Hagara. Le "temple de la fête" et la famille osirienne », *in* R. Gundlach - M. Rochholz, 4. *Ägyptologische Tempeltagung. Feste im Tempel, Ägypten und Altes Testament* 33/2, (Wiesbaden, 1998), 130.

10 Suggestion faite par Laurent Coulon.

Letters to the Dead in Ancient
and Modern Egypt

Hisham El-Leithy
SCA Center of Scientific Publication, Egypt

Comparative studies in Egyptology attract many Egyptian as well as foreign scholars. This paper concerns letters to the dead, an ancient practice that has parallels in modern Egypt. I have studied these modern letters through Sayyed Uways Publications such as "Letters to Emem Esh Shafe'ee's tomb."

Fifteen letters written in hieratic from the Old Kingdom[1] till the second half of the seventh century BCE[2] were sent to deceased relatives. The same type of letter has been found but directed to Egyptian deified humans such as Hekayeb, from the Middle Kingdom, and to Amenhotep son of Hapu, from the New Kingdom. There are also many letters sent to gods, written in Demotic. Letters to gods and saints overlapped for a while with, and then replaced, the ancient letters to the dead written during the late New Kingdom or Third Intermediate Period. In modern Egypt, we find this phenomenon in the tomb of the Imam Esh-Shafe'ee.[3]

It is not unusual for Egyptians to communicate with their dead relatives. Their "letters" were not meant to send greetings, but to ask for assistance.[4] Letters to the dead show that living persons who had experienced injustice turned to the dead for help. They could expect them to act on their behalf if they had been slighted. They also felt they might be persecuted by the dead whether or not it was justified by the actions of the living.[5]

Why Did People Communicate with the Dead?
Letters to the dead exhibit a fundamental distrust of law courts and civil authorities.[6] In ancient times as in modern, it is noticeable that those who tried to obtain their rights could become the victims of double-dealing. In the event of mistreatment, common people preferred to seek the aid of a strong and influential acquaintance.

Why Did People Turn to Saints and Gods in Later Periods?
The transfer of practices that could be deduced from people changing from appealing to dead

human beings to appealing to gods is, however, complicated by factors such as the new kingdom prominence of intermediary statues which appear to receive the complaints and intercede on behalf of the living. During the New Kingdom and Late Periods, Egypt was probably more urban and sophisticated than during earlier periods. Later religion seem to display more faith and piety, and perhaps this was the reason saints and gods were appealed to in later periods.

Material Evidence for the Letters to the Dead

Letters to the dead were written in hieratic on bowls, linen, papyrus, and ostraca and were deposited in the tomb whenever the sender experienced particular difficulty. We find that the Egyptians chose bowls (Fig. 1) to write their letters, to be sure that the spirit would read what is written when it went out to receive offerings.[7] Modern Egyptians use paper to write their letters to the Imam Es-Shafe'ee.

Receptacles for Letters

Where did the living they put their letters to the dead? In ancient Egypt, an inscribed bowl would be placed near the deceased. Letters on linen were placed on top of the corpse before interment. In modern times, letters to the sheik's tomb were sent by ordinary mail; such letters have been found. Sometimes the people themselves put the letters beside the tomb or gave them to the tomb's custodian. The letters that were laid beside the tomb stayed for a night and after that were burnt,

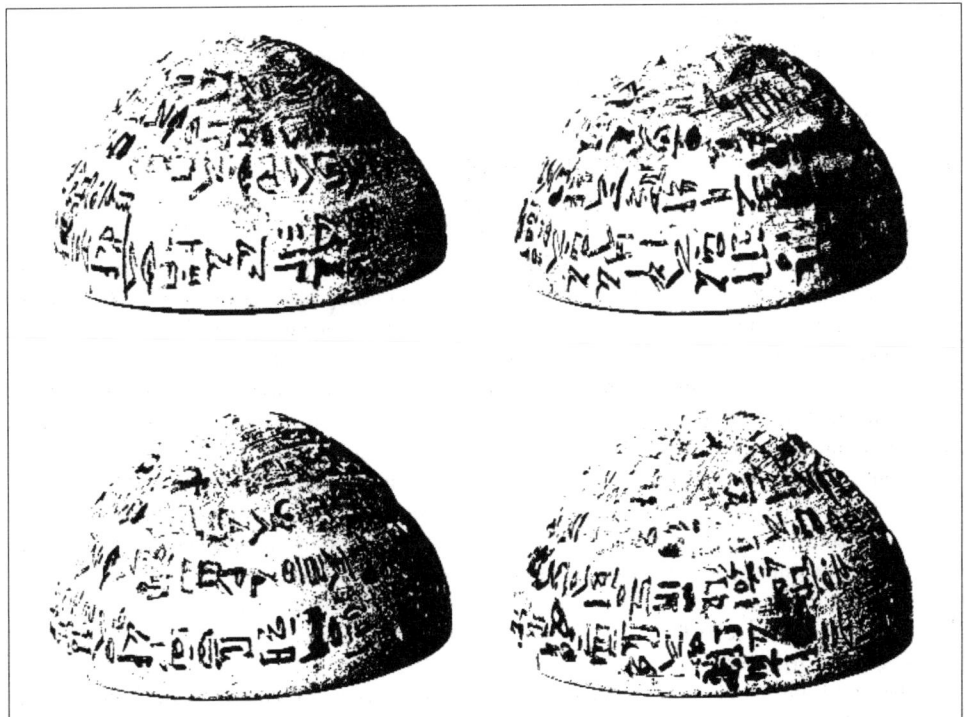

Fig. 1: Letter on bowl in Louvre E6134 (From A. Piankoff & J. J. Clere, "A Letter to the Dead on a Bowl in the Louvre," JEA, 20, (1934). 157–169.)

according to the decision of the custodian. According to Sayyed Uways, the author of the book "Letters to Emam Esh-Shafe'ee,"[8] the custodian received a lot of letters on Fridays (1952–1957).[9]

Who wrote the Letters to the Dead?

People from all walks of life and from different places in Egypt wrote to the dead. We know little about the ancient writers, but from the content of some letters we can guess the position of the sender. For example, in a letter sent by a widower to his dead wife ꜥnḫ Iry in the Nineteenth Dynasty (P. Leiden I371),[10] he mentioned that when she was alive he reached a high-ranking position with the pharaoh and was following him everywhere (perhaps as a member of the pharaoh's guards). Another example from the Twenty-first Dynasty is a letter on an ostracon written by the scribe of the tomb of Butehamon to his dead wife Iḥt3y, Chantress of Amon, and left with her coffin.

Modern letters to the dead were written by people of all levels of society, educated—teachers and state employees—and uneducated and common people. For example we found a teacher writing to Imam Es-Shafe'ee in order to complain about his wife. We know from the context of the letter that the sender hired a man to write it. In another example, a man wrote a letter on behalf of a woman to Imam Es-Shafe'ee: "This woman was away from her house, which has been stolen, and I want you to return back her property from a woman or a man."

It was observed that the senders of these "modern" letters came from different places all over Egypt, while all ancient letters were found in Upper Egypt. But this was probably because the major sites yielding antiquities were mainly in Upper Egypt, and conditions of preservation were better there and there are more excavations. Modern letters to the dead came from all over Egypt, but the percentage of Lower Egyptian ones is little bit higher than those of Upper Egypt, because of the concentration of population in the Delta.

The Formulae of Letters to the Dead

The formulae of letters to the dead are somewhat similar to ordinary letters. The address is the first element, the greeting formula the second element, the principal contents the third element, any statement of injury as the fourth element, and the appeal to the deceased is the fifth element. We may or may not find all these elements in one letter, but the basic elements like address, statement of injury, and appeal should be in the letter. Sometimes, we do not have a statement of the injury because the sender thought that the addressee was already aware of it. A great number came from the late Old Kingdom and the First Intermediate Period, because the country suffered civil wars and social disorder, and the people felt insecure, which led them to communicate with the dead in order to solve their problems. Similarly, a great number of letters to Imam Es-Shafe'ee were sent between the years 1952 to 1957, a time of trouble and injustice in Egypt. Both ancient and modern letters to the dead addressed the same subjects, such as asking for children, getting rid of enemies, recovering from illness, complaining of sorrows and grievances caused by wives and fathers, and matters related to stealing and revenge, or trouble at work.

Purpose of the Letters
Asking for Children

A: Jar-stand from the First Intermediate Period from the Haskel Museum in Chicago bears a letter to the dead, a son writing to (Fig. 2) his dead father asking him for a child for himself and one for his sister: "Let a healthy son be born for me (and) it is for your daughter that I'm begging a second healthy son."[11]

B: We also found the same appeal had been sent to Amenhotep son of Hapu, who was venerated in the Late and Ptolemaic Periods, who was called upon to provide children. We found that *Wsr wr* sent him a letter in order to let his wife become pregnant: "If it happens that Taipet becomes pregnant and if she gives birth to a child, I shall give one more *deben* together with two *deben* for the good treatment."[12]

I have not yet found a letter to Imam Es-Shafe'ee concerning this matter, but pieces of paper concerning requests for a child are known. We do have modern letters concerning *Nadr* or reward if he did what they asked.

Recovering from Illness

Ancient Letters

A: Cairo bowl in the Egyptian Museum, Cat. General 25375, with a letter to the dead with an appeal for recovering from illness. In the early Twelfth Dynasty, someone wrote to his dead relative to stand beside the maidservant *Im^w* who is ill: "What about the maidservant *Im^w* who is ill? Aren't you fighting on her behalf night and day with whomever, male or female, is acting against her?"

B: Letter in hieroglyphics addressed to Amenhotep son of Hapu written on the base of a statue, from the Twenty-sixth Dynasty. We found that people such as the daughter of King Psamtik sent letters to this late noble, addressing him as a great physician. She complained about trouble with her eyes and dedicated the statue, apparently representing the deceased

Fig. 2: Letter on jar stand in the Haskell Museum of Chicago (From A. H. Gardiner, "A New Letter to the Dead," JEA, 16, (1930). 19–22.)

himself and designed for his cult place, to cure the disability:[13] "I suffer from my eyes, may you cause that I be healthy at once. I have made this 'statue' as reward for you."[14]

Modern Letters

C: Letter addressed to Imam Es-Shafe'ee, November, 1957 CE, sent from the al-Sharqia district: "May you cure my eyes because I'm an old man and you should punish the one who afflicted (injured) me."

Vanquishing Enemies

A: Naga ed-Deir letter N 3500, from the Ninth Dynasty, is a letter sent to two dead relatives: "Both of you protect your offspring! Indeed, take hold of this dead man and dead woman."[15]

B: Bowl from the First Intermediate Period, Louvre, E 6134:A mother sent to her dead son, in order to act against their enemies: "May you make obstruction against male and female enemies who are evilly-disposed towards your household."[16]

C: Bowl from Hu, First Intermediate Period, located in Edwards Library, University College of London: A sister sent to her dead brother, in order that he might act against the enemies: "So punish the one who is doing what is distressing to me since I'll triumph over whatever dead man and dead woman acting against my daughter."

D: Cairo, No. 25375, bowl from the early Twelfth Dynasty which bears a letter to the dead concerning an appeal for acting against the enemies: "What about the maidservant *Imʿw* who is ill? Aren't you fighting on her behalf night and day with whoever male or female is acting against her?"

E: Coptic letter sent by a woman saying: "It's Esrmpe the daughter of Kllaouc who is complaining about *hr*, the son of Tanesneau, I complain to you, do justice to me and *hr* the son of Tanesneau concerning what I have done to him and what he has done to me namely he does not cohabit with me."

Modern

F: A man wrote this letter in behalf of a woman to Imam Esh-Shafe'ee: "This woman was away from her house which has been stolen and I want you to return back her from any woman or man (who stole it)."

Fig. 3: Letter on base of statue (From H. Wild, "Ex-voto d'une princesse sait a l'adresse d'Amen-hotep-fils de Hapou," MDAIK 16 (1958), 406–413, pl. XXXIII.)

G: A man sent this letter concerning a complaint against enemies: "I want you to revenge me from the one who injured me, man or woman."

H: Three sisters sent a letter against someone who accused them of taking his money: "They want the Imam to revenge them from the one who took the money, woman or man." This letter is to be compared with the Cairo letter to the dead on linen about the fact the sender is more than one person. (A mother and her son are sending to their father.)

308

I: Another woman sent a letter in order to ask for revenge for a thief who stole her jewelry: "you judge with fairness, you should get rid of him or her."[17]

Expressing Sorrow and Grievance
Ancient

A: (P. Leiden I371). Letter sent by a widower to his dead wife ʿnḫ Iry from the Nineteenth Dynasty: The widower tries to express to his departed wife the troubles which her spirit caused him and how he suffered since she died and the sorrows which faced him, saying: "What have I done against you? What you have done is that you have put your hands on me although I had done nothing evil against you, from the time that I was living with you as husband until now."[18]

B: A letter had been written by the scribe of the tomb of Butehamon to his dead wife iḥt3y, the Chantress of Amon, on an ostracon with her coffin from the Twenty-first Dynasty: "It is you who should speak well within the necropolis since I committed no abomination against you while you were on earth."[19]

C: From the late Ptolemaic Period a letter had been sent to Thoth by a girl and a boy including a complaint against their father who mistreated them after their mother's death and after their father's remarriage: "He has not been merciful to us with whom our mother spent many years, he caused our mother's death while we were small. He took another one into his house and he cast us out from it. It's you (Thoth) who saved us. If he takes the oath before you may you interrogate him and may you judge between us and this man. Many are the wrongs which he inflicts on us. If a strong man beats us in the street he says 'Beat them,' he does not say 'Don't.' When he sees us at the door of his house, he hurls an oipe container after us."[20]

Modern
We have a letter sent by a teacher appealing to Imam Es-Shafe'ee against his wife saying: "She didn't take care of my rights and my children's and she took my money and gave it to her mother. She served the others and she didn't do for me and she laughed at me and let the people laugh at me and she made me bad reputation, judge between me and her and return back my children."

Revenge
We found Coptic letters concerned with revenge upon the persons who hurt the sender, such as:

A: Moscow, letter with appeal for revenge: "May you get rid of Prostasin and Tontia at once. May you get rid of the one who raped. May you destroy those persons who raped."[21]

B: Oxford Bodliean papyrus bearing an appeal to saints: "I cry unto you, the righteous, look in my case and achieve my appeal and revenge me from Maria daughter of Tospeil and Andrias son of Martha at once. Bring damnation, pains, hot fever, madness, and death upon Maria daughter of Tospeil and their children and get rid of them and beat them at once."[22]

C: P. Berlin 10587: "I cry unto you the right name Rafeil, Adonay, and Sabawt, send me Temo Lokhious who beats with stroke and I want you to revenge me from those who lied. I cry unto you in the name of the son whose name is right who is Seth the Living Christ. You should bring blind[ness] and wounds upon them and destroy them."[23]

309

We note here that Egyptian Copts had Seth the Living as the evil foil for Christ, as Allah has in His Names the name and its opposite.

D: BM 6162: "Make her without hope in this world, make her barren, cause her to devour the fruit of her womb. Bring a demon upon her who shall cast her into a heavy sickness and great distress and bring a fever upon her."[24]

E: P. Cambridge University: "You may bind the mouth and the tongue of Gharib son of Sitt al-Kull that he be not able to have power to speak an evil word against Thijar, I conjure you by the voice which went up from the cross, until the seven unbroken seals depart from him I adjure you, I conjure you that."[25]

Modern

F: A man sent to Imam Es-Shafe'ee from al-Monuofia district (Fig. 4): "I cry unto the court to be fast in taking my right in revenge for me from the one who mistreated me and brought without my being able to do anything upon him."[26]

G: Another letter from al Fayum: "May you revenge me in (harming) the body of every one who did wrong against me and in his body and his children's."

H: Tanta: "I cry unto you to bring damnation upon the one who took the hen."[27]

I: A woman sent her letter to Imam Es-Shafe'ee saying: "revenge me from them to be died."

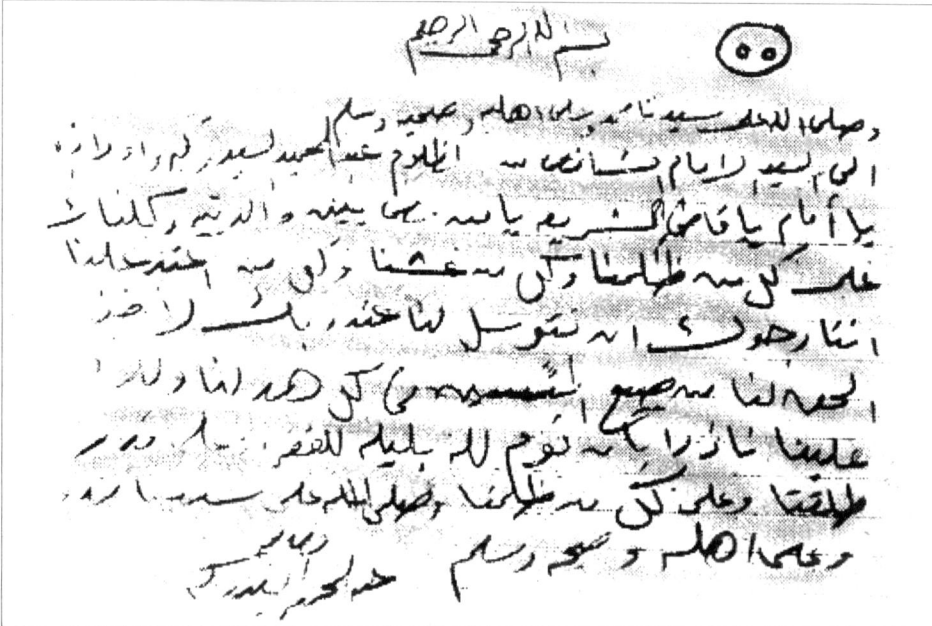

Figure 4

Robbery and Inheritance Matters

A: Letter on a bowl from Kâw by a son to his dead father Inekhenmut: "Now my fields have been taken possession of by Sher's son Henu, now my brother is with you in the same city of the dead, you must institute litigation with him since you have witnesses at hand in the same city."[28]

B: A plea from the servant *irtw r.w* daughter of *p3 ti p3 nb* to *tnhm* her husband: "I'm victimized at the hand of *ns hr* son of *hr s3 ist* his mother being *irt.w*. He robbed me, and he took your clothing by force and he stole your copper together with three pieces of cloth."[29]

C: A letter has been sent by a woman to Imam Es-Shafe'ee: "I appeal to you with this petition from Ihinasia in Beni Suef; there is a male son of a male from my city threatening me with beating and abusing me and he is Tag al-Eslam son of Ali and a female who took my cotton crop in year 1952 moreover they stole the field and they took what they wanted unlawfully."

Letters of Complaint Concerning Work

We found that there are letters sent to the dead, gods, and saints concerning problems with work.

Ancient

A: Demotic letter to Thoth, the sender is *iw.f ʿ3w* son of *hr nfr hby* asking him to protect him from his fellow at work whose name is *p3 šr t3 iht* son of *mntw htp*, saying: "He does nothing for Ibis except to eat its food nor does he even have a guard kept over it. He has stolen my money and wheat, he has had my servant slain. He has stolen for himself everything that I possessed. Let me be protected from *p3 šr t3 iht*, son of *mntw htp*."[30]

Modern

B: We have one letter of this kind in the letters to Imam Es-Shafe'ee; it is from a man who says: "A man complained from a man (unnamed) who always hurt me and I'll act against him and I'll let God be angry with him by my doings against him."

Conclusions

After all these examples we come to the conclusion that, although letters to the dead have a long history dating back to the Old Kingdom, letters to gods and saints appear to be a later development which first overlapped then replaced the letters to the dead.

From this comparative study, we found that the idea of Egyptian letters to the dead is still used in modern days, but in different ways as we mentioned before. In this context, I would like to refer to some habits in modern life, such as the Egyptians' writing in the last two pages of some newspapers which is another form of letter to the dead. They believe the dead will read these words and reply to them. In such cases the living request the dead to, "Pray for us and remember us in your world before the Christ."

The mentality and the thoughts of ancient Egyptians were similar. Our modern lives and emotions are still affected by social matters and administrative conflicts. There is another element affecting Egyptian thought, namely religion, both in ancient and modern Egypt. We found that the letters to the dead were affected in the use of some expression and spells in their letters to the dead by the Pyramid Texts, Coffin Texts, and Book of the Dead; the same is happening in modern days but in different ways, because now we have the Holy Bible and the Koran, although these religions forbid such communication, as the Bible makes plain: "There shall not be found with you anyone that made his son or his daughter to pass through the fire, one that used divination, one that practices augury, or an enchanter, or a sorcerer or an enchanter, or to be able to consult with a familiar spirit, or a wizard or necromancer. For whoever does these things is an abomination unto one Lord."(Deuteronomy, 18, 10–12). In the Koran we find several written texts forbidding any appeal to the dead since appeals should be made only to God.

Acknowledgements

I would like to thank Prof. Ola Alagizy and Prof. Fayza Haikal, who encouraged me to study this topic. Dr. Heikal is particularly interested in researching Egyptian customs and traditions and believes Egyptians are well-suited to do this kind of study because of their links with the past and ability to investigate surviving customs such as the letters to the dead.

Notes:

1 A. H. Gardiner and K. Sethe, *Egyptian Letters to the Dead: Mainly from the Old and Middle Kingdoms* (London, 1928).

2 Jasnow and Vittman, "An Abnormal Hieratic letter to the dead, P. Brooklyn (371799E)," *Enchoria* 19/20 (1992/1993), 23.

3 S. 'Uways, *Hadith 'an al-mar'ah al-Misirrah al-mu'asirah*, ["Talk about the Modern Egyptian Woman"] (Cairo, 1913), 12. See also S. Uways, *Ata al-mu'damin*, ["The Dead Giving"] (Beirut, 1973), 22, and S. 'Uways, *Letters to the tomb of the Emam Esh-Shafe'ee*, (Cairo,1978).

4 E. Wente, *Letters from Ancient Egypt*, (1991), 211ff.

5 J. Baines, "Practical Religion and Piety," *JEA* 73 (1993), 79–98.

6 G. Hughes, "A Demotic Letter to Thoth," *JNES* 17 (1958) 1–12.

7 Gardiner and Sethe, *Egyptian Letters*, 3.

8 S. 'Uways, *Letters*, 154ff.

9 Ezat El Saadani, letter written to Al-Ahram, Cairo, 17/01/1960.

10 Gardiner and Sethe, *Egyptian Letters*, 7.

11 A. H. Gardiner, "A New Letter to the Dead," *JEA* 16 (1930), 19–22.

12 M. Malinine, "Une Lettre Demotique a Amenothes fils de Hapu," *Rde* 14 (1962), 37ff.

13 H. Wild, "Ex-voto d'une princesse saite a l'adresse d'Amen-hotep-fils de Hapu," *MDAIK* 16 (1958), 406–413 (Pl. XXXIII).

14 Wild, "Ex-voto," 06–413 (Pl.XXXIII). 408.

15 W. K. Simpson, "A Late Old Kingdom Letter to the Dead from 'Nag 'Ed-Deir N 3500," *JEA* 56 (1970), 58–64. 60.

16 A. Piankoff and J. Clere, "A Letter to the Dead on a Bowl in the Louvre," *JEA* 20 (1934), 157–169, 159.

17 S. 'Uways, *Letters*, 154

18 Gardiner and Sethe, *Egyptian Letters*, 7

19 A. H. Gardiner and J. Černy, *Hieratic Ostraca* 22, Vol. 1 (Griffith Institute, Oxford 1957). Pl. LXXX, LXXXa; J. Černy, *The Comunity of Workmen at Thebes During the Ramesside Period*, Bd'E 50, IFAO;

Cairo, 1973) 369ff; J. Frandsen, "The letter of Ikhtay's coffin: O Louvre. 698," in *Village Voice,* R. J. Demaree and Egberts eds. (Leiden, 1991), 31–49.

20 G. Hughes, "The Cruel Father: A demotic Papyrus in the Library of G. Michaelides," *Studies in Honour of J. A. Wilson* (London, 1971), 43–54.

21 A. Turaje, Koptische Aupsäge, *Abhandlungen der Kaiserlicher Preussicher Archaeologischer Gesellschaft,* 8d XVIII (1907), 28–32.

22 W. Crum, "Eine Verfluchung," *ZÄS* 34 (1896), 85–89.

23 A. M. Kropp, *Ausgewählte Koptische Zaubertexte* II (Bruxelles, 1931), 238–243.

24 W. Crum, *Catalogue of Coptic Manuscripts in the British Museum* N.1223 (London, 1905), 505.

25 W. Crum, "A Bilingual Charm," *PsBa* 24 (1902), 328ff.

26 S. 'Uways, *Letters,* 169.

27 S. 'Uways, *Letters,* 189.

28 Gardiner and Sethe, *Egyptian Letters,* 3.

29 Jasnow and Vittman, "An Abnormal Hieratic Letter," 23.

30 Hughes, "A Demotic Letter," 5.

Nubian Influence on the Later Versions of the Book of the Dead

Leonard H. Lesko
Brown University

The Egyptian Book of the Dead has been known and studied for a very long time, but in spite of the fact that it had some antecedents in Middle Kingdom coffins that occasionally seem more meaningful, it still had an extensive period of development on its own, and several different standardized versions evolved in later periods. Clearly, the papyri that are lumped together as the Book of the Dead are often quite different books, not just variations of the same work. When Lepsius published the Turin Ptolemaic papyrus of Iwef-ankh in 1842, he not only provided a useful facsimile of a major Late Period document, but also established the standard order of chapters that is still followed today, albeit with numerous additions.[1]

Because Brown University also has a Ptolemaic Book of the Dead of the God's Father Hor (one that Stephen Thompson and I are preparing for publication), I have become somewhat involved in the discussion and controversy about where and how the Book of the Dead actually ends. The four concluding chapters in the Turin papyrus, 162–165, were later additions not found in New Kingdom examples of the Book of the Dead, but the majority of the late manuscripts, like the Brown example, has these same spells in the order 163–165 with 162 being the final chapter. I wrote an article four years ago for the Wente *Festschrift* entitled "Some Further Thoughts on Chapter 162 of the Book of the Dead."[2] These thoughts were further to Jean Yoyotte's "Contribution à l'histoire du chapitre 162," in *Revue d'égyptologie* 29 (1977) and Malcolm Mosher's "Theban and Memphite Book of the Dead Traditions in the Late Period," in *JARCE* 29 (1992). I essentially agreed with Yoyotte about the canonical and deutero-canonical traditions, with the Turin papyrus a representative of the former and the Brown papyrus an example of the latter. Mosher's "Memphite" and "Theban" traditions cover essentially the same ground, but his terminology unfortunately seemed reminiscent of Budge's "recensions" and not in agreement with either the contents of the chapters or the interesting additions found on several examples.

Now all four of these spells have something in common with these Late Period manuscripts, even if Chapter 162 had an earlier source in a different context in the Twenty-first Dynasty and also survives separately on at least 72 later *hypochephali*.[3] For one thing, all of these chapters, unlike the older portions of the Book of the Dead found earlier in these manuscripts, are concerned with Amun-Re, and we also find Neith here, and a cow-goddess named *ȝḥȝt* or *iḥȝt*. A Theban origin would indeed seem arguable, and a note at the beginning of Chapter 166 (which occurred together with Chapter 162 in its earliest Twenty-first Dynasty form) refers to discovery in a Ramesside royal burial context,[4] but another note at the end of P. Marseille 91 says that this supplement to the Book of Going Forth by Day was found at Tanis in the temple of Amun-Re.[5] Having several different notations on these manuscripts makes it necessary indeed either to try to accomodate all the variations, to explain their separate origins, or to assume that one or the other attribution was purely pseudepigraphic. Yoyotte wanted to be accomodating and tried to fit Neith and a cow goddess nicely into a Delta-Tanite context.[6] The untranslatable phrases in several of these spells, widely thought to be Semitic (as suggested by Pleyte and restated by T. George Allen),[7] could even enhance the argument for this northeastern connection. The efforts of Twenty-first Dynasty priests to preserve the mummies of earlier New Kingdom royalty could have resulted in the discovery of some portion of these texts in an Amun temple, at Tanis as claimed on P. Marseille 91, or Thebes for that matter. On the other hand, none of these chapters occur on any of numerous known Book of the Dead examples made for important representatives of the priestly side of the Twenty-first Dynasty. These spells came into the canon later, sometime in the Twenty-sixth Dynasty, and survived through the Ptolemaic period.

Two other significant additions to these texts are, 1) the colophon which may or may not follow Chapter 161 occasionally,[8] and could have marked an earlier *end* of the Book of Going Forth by Day, but more frequently occurs after Chapter 162, which then would have concluded either the complete earlier work, the single Chapter 162, or this whole group (163–162); and 2) the prefatory title to Chapter 163 in P. Marseille 91 that indicates these were, "spells added from another book as a supplement to Going Forth by Day." While the latter could refer to the three Spells 163–165, it seemed more likely to me that it referred to the group of four spells, and this addition was probably labled "Mistress of the hidden place (*st*) [or] temple (*ḥwt*)," which title occurs at the end of Chapter 162.[9]

This is essentially where I left my case for this supplement to the Book of the Dead in my article for the Wente *Festschrift*, but today I would like to call attention to a few references in Chapters 163 and 164 that may shed some light on the source of Yoyotte's deutero-canonical tradition. The first point is that all four of these spells have highly unusual, untranslatable names and phrases that have long been thought to be Semitic.

For example, Chapter 162 has the *names ḥȝ-ḳdt, iw-riȝ, ḥȝ-ḳȝ-r-sȝ-inw-ḳ-rw-rw-ḥȝi* (a group writing that could as well be read *ḥḳrs-inḳ-rrḥ*), *srpt-mȝ-is-riw, ḥȝ-rw-sȝy* (or *ḥr-sy*), and *bȝ-r-kȝti-tȝ-wȝy* (or *br-kt-ṭwy*) in addition to the *ȝḥȝt* cow and an apparently sportive writing of Atum's name that might combine individually-translatable elements in its acrophonic selections [hieroglyphs].[10] Chapter 163 has a combination of names and places including *ḥȝrti* (or *ḥrt*), Lord of Motion, who causes rest in the marshes of *ḥȝ-ḳr-ḳȝ-nȝ-mw* (or *ḥḳr-ḳnm*) and a corpse resting in *sn-ḥȝ-gȝ-r-ḥȝ-nȝ-mw* (or *snhg-rhnm*), and later "the one who is hidden within the pupil of the *udjat*-eye, whose name is *šȝr-šȝr-ḥt-šȝ-pw-nṯr-kȝ-ir.t-kȝ* (or *šr-šr-ḥt-šp-nṯr-kirt-k*)," and "He is the one who sets in the northwest of the mountain-peak of Napata (*ṯhnt n ipt*) in the land of the tribesmen (*n pȝ tȝ iwn-tyw*), and does not cross to the west."[11] The spell goes on to address, "Amun the Bull and Kheprer the Lord of the Two *Udjat*-Eyes . . . , whose names are *šȝr-šȝr-ḥt* and *šȝ-pw-nṯr-nṯr-irt-kȝ-rn-n-kt*. He is *šȝy-šȝ-kȝ-imn-šȝ-kȝ-nȝ-sȝ-r-ḥȝwt*, 'Atum has illuminated the two lands for him,' is his name."

Chapter 163 has three aspects of the sun god (Kheper, Amun, and Atum) with Amun central and Gebel Barkal in Nubia as his locus. Chapter 164, in addition to its well-known vignette of Sekhmet-Bastet-Raet, mistress of the gods, wherein he calls her "the mother of the divine king, *p3-š3-k3-s3* (or *pšks*) and royal wife of *p3-rw-h3-ḳw* (or *Prhḳ*)" who are, unfortunately, otherwise unknown. Others on the barque of the god include "*s3-pwy-tk-h3-r-s3-pw-s3-r-m-k3-k3-rmt*, the *srhp* (or *srk.fy*) flame of *r͐-s3-k3-n3tt* in the prow of the barque, and *ḫ3-r-pw-ḳ3-k3-š3r-bw-š3-b3-š3-k3ty* in the speech (*m ḏd*) of the *Nehsyw* (mistakenly written as *͐mw* in the Hay papyrus), the tribes-men of Nubia (*iwntyw nw t3 stt*)."[12] Here we have reference to at least one, if not quite a few more, Nubian words among the untranslatable phrases of these spells.

Finally, Chapter 165 has the names "*rw-ty-k3-s3, k3-s3-k3-k3*, Amun of the *iwn.w k3-tik-iw-š3r, rw-k3ti-š3-k3-b3-yr-ḳti, m͐-iw-r-rw-ḳ3t, rwty-n3-s3-ḳb, b3-i-k3*, and a *sk3ty* in the netherworld."[13] Again being from the same Book, these phrases are likely linked to the others.

I wish I could give a smooth translation or even a few intelligent guesses about the meanings of our Napatan phrases in these spells, but that will take a little longer. It seems likely that some portions of these "Nubian" phrases included Egyptian loan words, e.g., *imn* and *nṯr*.

What we can do now is consider some ramifications of the occurrence of "Nubian" phrases in this Late Period supplement to the end of the traditional Book of the Dead. Niwinski noted con-siderable changes to the Book of the Dead that occurred in the Twenty-first Dynasty,[14] and I have argued that both the large number of copies belonging to Chantresses of Amun, and the contents of these works, point to feminine interest and involvement in some of the compositional changes encountered at that time.[15] Some Books of the Dead of the High Priests, on the other hand, have notable deficiencies, including spells partially or totally missing.[16] The fact that Chapter 162 seems to have originated in that same period, is interesting because that earliest example was probably not a real Book of Going Forth by Day at all[17] but a separate collection of spells.

If, however, the earliest examples of Chapters 163 and 164, which were also Amun- centered and can both be shown to have Nubian connections, yet first appear in the Twenty-sixth Dynasty, then their origins can quite easily be ascribed either to the members of the Twenty-fifth (Nubian) Dynasty or to their descendents. These include, of course, the Napatan kings and the famous Divine Adoratresses of Amun (Amenirdis I, sister of Kings Piyyi or Piankhy and Shabaka, and Piankhy's children Shepenwepet II, and her brothers, the kings Shebitku and Taharqa); these fam-ilies were even larger.

We are all familiar with Piankhy's piety and devotion to Amun-Re of Karnak. But it was Shabaka who revived the office of High Priest and bestowed it upon his son Horemakhet.[18] And, of course, Taharqa in his 26-year reign was able to accomplish a great program of major con-struction projects in Nubia and also in Upper Egypt, particularly at Karnak temple. He inaugu-rated an archaizing, purifying, artistic, and religious renaissance, harking back to the Old Kingdom, but also undertook a number of restoration projects.

In 664 BCE Ashurbanipal conquered Egypt from Tanuatamun (or Tantamani) of the Twenty-fifth Dynasty, and Thebes was sacked, thus ending Nubian domination of Egypt, but despite the terrible destruction, the first ever so far south, the Assyrians and their Saite lackies did not imme-diately take away control of Karnak Temple from its Nubian priesthood.

We know that the Divine Adoratress Shepenwepet II remained in control of this major reli-gious center and Montuemhet, the Fourth Prophet of Amun, continued as mayor of Thebes. We don't know whether Montuemhet would have considered himself a Nubian, (although he was married to at least two Nubian women *wḏ3-rn.s*, (Udjarenes) another daughter of the royal fami-ly as Jean LeClant has shown,[19] and Shepen-mwt, whose portrait my wife Barbara discovered in Seattle.[20] But, clearly Shepenwepet was not the only ranking Nubian in the temple. We can see

316

from the very interesting vignette of the Saite Oracle Papyrus now in Brooklyn published by Parker,[21] that the Karnak temple had many light-skinned God's Fathers who were witnesses to the oracle, and also three Prophets whose skin color gets progressively darker as their rank increases. In particular, Harkhebi, the darkest-skinned priest in the vignette was the First Prophet of Amun in Year 14 of Psametik I (651 BCE) and he was the son of the earlier first prophet, Horemakhet, and grandson of Shabaka himself.

Now in Year 9 of his reign, Psametik I had had his daughter Nitocris adopted by the reigning Nubian God's Wife Shepenwepet II and her heiress-apparent Amenirdis II (who was a daughter of Taharqa) to be their successor as Divine Adoratress, but he did not remove either of them or Harkhebi from their Theban priestly positions. When Montuemhet died in Year 17 of Psametik I, he was succeeded by one of his two sons named Nesptah as Fourth Prophet and Governor of the South, and this Nesptah served till he died in Year 25. In spite of the fact that we have no evidence for a successor to Harkhebi as High Priest, and Kitchen suggests that the office was abandoned for two generations,[22] it is actually quite possible that a Nubian First Prophet would have remained in office through the reign of Necho II until the reign of Psametik II, and this might even account for the fact that in his first year this Saite king had his own daughter Ankhnesneferibre not only adopted by Nitocris to be the future Divine Adoratress, but he also immediately appointed her to be the First Prophet of Amun. Of course, by Year 3 of his reign, Psametik II had sent a full-scale expedition against Nubia, and at about the same time, the names of Taharka and his predecessors began to be systematically erased from their monuments in Egypt.

The point is that Nubian priests were in control of the temple of Amun-Re at Karnak, if not the entire south, for perhaps 120 years, and it does seem that during this time they were responsible for changing the traditional ending of the Book of the Dead to incorporate Amun, or, at the very least, one of them or someone present might have included some Nubian phrases in the work in deference to these Nubians, and, interestingly, these additions remained part of the canonical work for perhaps five more centuries.

Postscript

In conclusion, I would like to make a comment in response to what I understood as a criticism of "reductionism" in the general session on religion at this Congress. It really does seem to me that the "religionists" have had far too much to say already about ancient Egyptian religion. The texts were not divinely written; and we generally do not have original documents, but rather badly-copied versions that had been edited inadequately and remain for the most part undifferentiated. Their context is at least as important as their contents. What we need most now is a strong dose of textual criticism, and perhaps more "reductionism." After the general session on "literature," which did not include religious literature, I would nonetheless suggest that Fayza Haikal's remarks on the "manipulation of texts" and the importance of "ethno-Egyptology" for literature may be just as significant, if not more so, for religious literature.

Notes:

1 K. R. Lepsius, *Das Todtenbuch der Ägypter nach dem hieroglyphischen Papyrus in Turin* (Berlin, 1842).

2 L. H. Lesko, "Some Further Thoughts on Chapter 162 of the *Book of the Dead*," in E. Teeter and J. A. Larson (eds.), *Gold of Praise: Studies on Ancient Egypt in Honor of Edward F. Wente* (Studies in Ancient Oriental Civilisation 58; Chicago, 1999), 255-259.

3 E. Varga, "Les travaux préliminaires de la monographie sur les hypocéphales," *Acta Orientalia* 12 (1961) 235-247.

4 W. Pleyte, *Chapitres supplémentaires du livre des morts, 162, 162,* 163, [164 à 174]*, 3 vols (Leiden, 1881), 3, Pl. 111; J. Yoyotte, "Contribution à l'histoire du chapitre 162 du livre des morts," *Revue d'égyptologie* 29 (1977), 197.

5 Yoyotte, "Contribution," 198-199.

6 Yoyotte, "Contribution," 201-202.

7 Pleyte, *Chapitres* 1, 48-55; T. G. Allen, *The Book of the Dead or Going Forth by Day: Ideas of the Ancient Egyptians Concerning the Hereafter as Expressed in Their Own Terms* (Studies in Ancient Oriental Civilization 37; Chicago, 1974), 157-158.

8 Yoyotte, "Contribution," 196, n 14, but see also Malcolm Mosher, "Theban and Memphite Book of the Dead Traditions in the Late Period," *JARCE* 29 (1992), 135, n 60.

9 Pleyte, *Chapitres*, 3, Pl. 33.

10 Pleyte, *Chapitres*, 1, 54, and 3, Pl. 21.

11 Pleyte, *Chapitres*, 3, Pls. 54-56.

12 Pleyte, *Chapitres*, 3, Pls. 74-76.

13 Pleyte, *Chapitres*, 3, Pls. 89-109.

14 A. Niwinski, *Studies on the Illustrated Theban Funerary Papyri of the 11th and 10th Centuries B.C.*, (Orbis Biblicus et Orientalis, 86; Freiburg, 1989); and "The Solar-Osirian Unity as Principle of the Theology of the 'State of Amun' in Thebes in the Twenty-first Dynasty," *Jaarbericht van het Vooraziatisch-Egyptische Genootschap Ex Oriente Lux* 30 (1987–1988), 89-106.

15 L. H. Lesko, "Some Remarks on the Books of the Dead Composed for the High Priests Pinedjem I and II," in D. P. Silverman, (ed.), *For His Ka: Essays Offered in Memory of Klaus Baer* (Studies in Ancient Oriental Civilization, 55; Oriental Institute, Chicago, 1994), 183-184.

16 Lesko, "Some Remarks," 181-183.

17 Yoyotte, "Contribution," 198.

18 K. Kitchen, *The Third Intermediate Period in Egypt (1100-650 B.C.)* (Warminster, 1973), 382.

19 J. Leclant, *Montouemhat: Quatrième Prophéte d'Amun, Prince de Ville* (Bibliothèque d'Étude 35; IFAO, Cairo, 1961), 263-265.

20 Barbara S. Lesko, "Three Reliefs from the Tomb of Mentuemhet," *JARCE* 9 (1971-72), 87, fig. 3.

21 R. A. Parker, *A Saite Oracle Papyrus from Thebes in the Brooklyn Museum (Pap. Brooklyn 47.218.3)* (Brown Egyptological Studies 4; Providence, 1962), 3-6, Pl. 1.

22 Kitchen, *Third Intermediate Period*, 405, 480.

Mosaic Floors from Roman *Triclinia* in Alexandria: Evolution of Techniques and Design

Grzegorz Majcherek

Polish Center of Mediterranean Archaeology, Warsaw University

It seems that mosaics never gained the same kind of popularity in Greco-Roman Egypt as in other areas of the Mediterranean. Alexandria certainly was the exception. Wiktor A. Daszewski, who has studied the subject for many years, has been able to catalog and document some 70 mosaics and mosaic fragments found in the city and its near vicinity.[1] But this relative abundance of mosaic floors is unfortunately illusory; most of these finds were usually deprived of their original architectural and chronological context. The Alexandrian mosaic repertoire has grown in recent years as a consequence of archaeological investigations in the modern city. In contrast to the earlier finds, these new pieces come from well-documented contexts and constitute notable material for a study of their chronology and development.

In the last few campaigns, excavation work carried out by the Polish Center of Archaeology in cooperation with the Supreme Council of Antiquities at the site of Kom al-Dikka in Alexandria has concentrated on the study of the still mostly-unknown residential architecture of Alexandria in the Early Roman Period (first to third centuries CE). This research has already resulted in the uncovering of large fragments of several relatively well preserved houses situated in different parts of the site. It comes as no surprise, that the five houses that were explored reveal a similar architectural layout, strongly rooted in the Greco-Roman tradition.[2] The focal point is a large inner, usually pseudo-peristyled courtyard, which provides internal communication and lightning for the varied rooms grouped around it. The houses were as a rule lavishly decorated. Excavations have brought to light extensive evidence of the original interior decoration in the form of painted plastering, stuccowork, architectural elements, and so on. Several pieces of marble statues representing both gods and mortals have been discovered in adjacent layers, including a portrait of the city's founder, Alexander the Great.[3] Mosaic floors are perhaps the best illustration of the affluence of the residents of these houses. They are found in all the buildings and represent different techniques of execution and styles of decoration. Of special interest are the floors decorating the *triclinia* of these houses; they take on an unique and distinctive character that sets them apart from other mosaics.

319

All the *triclinia*, undoubtedly the most imposing rooms of the investigated houses, are similar in plan and size (up to 6 x 7 m). They are entered usually from a courtyard through a monumental tripartite entrance placed between columns or pillars. All the mosaic floors follow a typical Roman design: U-shaped border, intended to accommodate the banquet couches, running around a T-shaped center field.

Fig. 1: Mosaic from House M (northern triclinium). Photo by W. Jerke, Polish Centre of Archaeology in Cairo.

The Early Roman house uncovered near the Theater (House M) comprised two *triclinia* situated on opposite sides of a big court.[4] The larger, northern one preceded by a portico, is decorated with a mosaic floor showing the typical U+T design. This fine tessellated floor has survived in relatively good condition, including the decorative panel, practically wholly preserved, although the *emblema* itself is much damaged (fig. 1). The ample space along the walls (*ca.* 1.45 m wide) was paved with small, irregular stones with no pattern to them. The mosaic proper combines juxtaposed surfaces and lateral extensions. The exceptionally simple and sparing orthogonal pattern in front consists of tangent octagons outlined in black on a white background. Each octagon has small black squares set into it. Large lozenges appear in both lateral extensions. The central square field (1.90 x 1.90 m) is framed by a black band. A shield of bichrome, chromatically interchanging scales edged by a triple black fillet is inscribed in a square field. In the corners of the latter, there are dolphins placed symmetrically on either side of a trident. The fragmentarily preserved, small (*ca.* 0.35 m in diameter), multicolored *opus vermiculatum emblema*, shows three birds.

The subject of the *emblema* makes it one of only a few figural mosaics known from Roman Alexandria.[5] It brings to mind associations with representations of various species of birds depicted on separate panels of yet another mosaic discovered at the site.[6] Bird images in themselves are among the most popular themes on Egyptian mosaics. We find them represented also on the fragmentarily preserved mosaic floor from Abukir (Canopus), where they constitute part of a Nilotic landscape decoration.[7] Our emblema, however, reveals a striking similarity with another *emblema* from Kom Truga (Psenemphaia), also representing three birds in almost identical composition. This piece, dated to the last quarter of the first century BCE, was found inserted in a much later tessellated floor of the second century CE.[8] Perhaps in our case we are also dealing with a similar phenomenon. As there is another, earlier mosaic floor below our mosaic, this would indicate that our *emblema* may have originally come from this earlier floor. Our mosaic has yet to be dated precisely and excavations are in progress, but we are inclined to date it to the turn of the first century CE. By the same token, it would be the oldest example among those presented here.

Shield-of-scales panels are exceptionally popular in Egypt and are evident in number.[9] The motif is to be seen on two Hellenistic floors; one from Tell Timai (Thmuis) with a representation of Berenike II,[10] the other from Gabbari.[11] In the Roman Period, it appears also on mosaics from Alexandria (Moharrem Bey),[12] Canopus,[13] and Memphis.[14] Another example of similar design is provided by a second century CE floor discovered in 1895 by Hogarth and Benson at Kom al-Dikka, and depicting a variant of the geometrized shield composed of triangles.[15] This last example is all the more interesting to us, as according to the discoverer it had contained a bird *emblema*. All these examples however, are multicolored. On the other hand, our piece fits very well into the bichrome, mostly black and white style that became prevalent in Alexandria from the first century CE onwards. The composition itself of a circle inscribed into a square, so exceptionally popular in Egypt, is considered as distinctive of the Alexandrian style.[16]

Oddly enough, this piece reveals a certain conservatism exemplified by the aesthetic principle proper to Hellenistic mosaics. A gradual rise in the quality of materials and the technique of executing from the outside in, seems to be characteristic of this principle. In other words, the outer border of Hellenistic mosaic floors is often made quite randomly of irregular stones, while the central part could have been executed in the *tessellatum* technique and the *emblema* itself in *opus vermiculatum*.

While immensely popular in Alexandria, black and white mosaics do not seem to be typical of *triclinium* decoration, giving way definitely to the colored mosaic floors. Color is actually what decided the case in favor of the latter, as it revealed in incomparably better light the affluence and high social status of the house owner. The two kinds of mosaic floors presumably coexisted, although their development was mutually interconnected, taking advantage of similar decorative motifs.

A polychrome tessellated floor from the late second or early third century was uncovered in the Early Roman house F at Kom al-Dikka.[17] Although fragmentarily preserved, there is no doubt that it must have been also the typical *triclinium* mosaic, as shown in a graphic reconstruction (fig. 2). The preserved fragment measuring some 2.20–3.80 m consisted of the main multicolored paneled carpet with bichrome extensions. The two panels at the bottom were originally subdivided into smaller squares, each featuring a different geometric pattern. The panels in the right fragment contained alternately either an inscribed sexfoil or poised concave squares. The left panel is similar with alternating fields filled with a checker-pattern of intersecting squares, the colors counterchanged, or polychrome intersecting circles. Three rows of four-pointed stars enclosing hexagons with inscribed crosslets appear in the upper left bichrome field.

The central panel, however, is different. It is bordered with a simple, tight, asymmetrically-shaded guilloche on a black ground. The corners of the square are filled with ivy scroll and *hederae*. There is little doubt that originally it must have enclosed a circular scaled-shield panel with counterchanged colors, now very poorly-preserved with merely a few tiny fragments surviving. There is equally little doubt that a panel thus composed must have framed an *emblema* of some

Fig. 2: Mosaic from House F. Drawing by the author.

kind. Other mosaics from Alexandria confirm this hypothesis. Only the *emblema* itself remains a mystery. Was it like the examples discussed already? Or did it perhaps repeat the gorgoneion motif as on the mosaic recently discovered during French rescue excavations on the site of the Cinema Diana. The latter offers perhaps the best parallel, for particular decorative motifs, as well as for the composition as a whole. A graphic reconstruction published by A.-M. Guimier-Sorbets shows clearly an almost identical design of the central panel. Moreover, the U-shaped bichrome extensions in both cases are filled with rows of very similar four-pointed stars.[18] The mosaic from Kom al-Dikka is distinguished by an exceptionally developed geometrical carpet design in the front part, inspired most probably by floors executed in the *opus sectile* technique. This hypothesis, although very tempting, ought yet to be tested against a broader background. Examples of the *opus sectile* floors with geometric design seem to be quite common in the Mediterranean, but fortunately our site has also produced some direct parallels.

A small fragment of the mosaic floor decorating the so called Villa of the Birds (House *alpha*) had been excavated in the eastern part of our site in the early 1970s.[19] Last year, as part of a special ARCE/EAP Mosaics Conservation Project funded from the USAID Grant,[20] it was possible to clear the whole extent of this enormous floor, which measures roughly 7.50 by 6.20 m. This mosaic is a particularly interesting and unique case of a composition consisting of two clearly separated fields; one in *opus tesselatum* and the other in *opus sectile*, forming again the customary U+T design (fig. 3). The tessellated border alongside three of the walls presents a plain carpet decorated with semis of small black crosslets formed by four poised tesserae on a neutral white background. The well-balanced *opus tessellatum* border constitutes an intended contrast for the lively and colorful design of the central panel executed in the *opus sectile* technique which was undoubtedly the main ornamental feature of the floor, emphasizing the fineness of the arrangement as a whole. Unfortunately, the *opus sectile* mosaic is quite damaged. Traces of particular pieces are nonetheless clearly discernible as impressions in the bedding, permitting a very precise reconstruction of the design.

The composition of this strictly geometrical decoration is based on the division of a central field into square and triangular elements of different size. Dominating the design are six large square panels in an oblique arrangement; each square containing an inscribed red circle and a

Fig. 3: Mosaic from the Villa of the Birds. Photo by W. Jerke, Polish Centre of Archaeology in Cairo.

wreath of white heart-shaped elements outside it. Inside each circle there is yet another square inside a colorful frame. Linear white eight-pointed stars on a yellow ground fill the spaces between the large squares. The sides of the central design were framed with bands of plain grey marble tiles. The elaborate coloring is due to the use of different colored, mostly imported stones; Lacedaemonian green porphyry, *pavonazetto*, Numidian *giallo antico*, white Thasian marble, *breccia, rosso antico,* and local limestone.

The few examples of opus sectile mosaic floors known from Egypt decorated rooms serving other than *triclinium* purposes like, for instance, the roundel from Kom Trouga,[21] found in a bath and dated to the late first century BCE, or a floor discovered in the Late Roman (fifth century CE) *hospitium* at Huwariya.[22] Another fragmentarily preserved but very fine mosaic floor was discovered at Kom al-Dikka in the neighboring Early Roman House *gamma* (third century CE), but it does not appear to have had a tessellated border.[23] Fragments of marble floors with *opus sectile* elements were also found in one of the rooms of House F,[24] and in the vestibule of the Theater.[25] One should remember that Alexandrian workshops are also believed to have produced the *opus sectile* glass panels found at Corinth.[26] While finds from Egypt do not necessarily offer direct parallels for the combined *tesselatum*-and-*sectile* floor from the *triclinium* of Villa of the Birds, Cirenaica is another case altogether. The nearest analogy to this system of decoration combining two different techniques are pavements from the *triclinium* at the Palazzo dei Colonne,[27] and the *triclinium* from the "Roman Villa" in Ptolemais.[28] A similar system of decoration is to be seen also in pavements discovered at the House of Giasone Magno in Cyrene,[29] and in building "W" in Berenice.[30] The overall stratigraphical evidence inclines us to date this floor to the end of the first century CE, the beginning of the second century CE at the latest.[31]

Fig. 4: Mosaic from House M (southern triclinium). Photo by W. Jerke, Polish Centre of Archaeology in Cairo.

The artistic effect of *sectile* floors must have made them extremely popular. And indeed, their popularity in Roman Alexandria is evidenced not only by the numerous finds of loose profiled marble tiles all over the Kom al-Dikka site, but also by yet another, although simpler fragment, discovered in the previously-mentioned House M, located in the vicinity of the theater.[32] In the large southern hall of this house, sumptuously decorated with pairs of engaged columns and entered through a traditional tripartite entrance flanked with two columns, the floor again reveals the typical *triclinium* design, although with a pattern that is not as clear and visibly inferior in execution (fig.4).

The space along the walls was paved with small irregular pieces of multi-colored stones set in red lime mortar, recalling the *opus signinum* technique. The central part was made of multi-colored marble tiles arranged in a simple geometric design; a combination of squares, triangles and lozenges framed by a wide band of black marble tiles. The lateral panels are very interesting, forming as they do the horizontal bar of the letter T. While made of small irregular marble pieces, it is an obvious, even if not very successful imitation, of the circle-in-square motif represented by the other opus sectile mosaic. Dated to the early second century CE, this mosaic is far from the refined and almost perfect aesthetics of the previous floors. We are apparently dealing with an obviously simplified, hence cheaper transposition of the composition from the Villa of the Birds, that was easier to make by less skilled artisans.

All the four *triclinia* mosaic floors presented here fall into two clearly distinct types, but the essence of the division is not so much the obviously different execution (*sectile* and *tessellatum*), as it is the nature of the composition itself, respecting the functionally imposed U+T arrangement. The composition and the aesthetics of sectile floors are based on a distinct contrast between the two component parts, a contrast frequently emphasized by the choice of two different techniques. The main decorative panel in these mosaics, usually forms a repetitive carpet design without any central dominating motif. On the other hand, tessellated floors feature a combination of the typical central composition, represented by a circle-in-square design containing an *emblema*, and a geometrical carpet derived from the *opus sectile* floor designs. The effect of distinguishing the center field in this kind of mosaic floor is usually achieved by contrasting the color panels with a black and white or neutral border.

In general, the *triclinia* mosaic floors from Kom al-Dikka fit very well into the mosaic art of Roman Alexandrian, testifying also to the popularity of the two phenomena that are typical of this center; a predilection for the circle-in-square design and the fashion for black and white decoration.

Notes:

1 W. A. Daszewski, "From Hellenistic Polychromy of Sculptures to Roman Mosaics, Alexandria and Alexandrinism," *Papers delivered at a Symposium Organized by The J.Paul Getty Museum and the Getty Center for the History of Art and the Humanities and Held at the Museum*, April 22–25, 1993 (1996), 145.

2 For a brief discussion on Alexandrian domestic architecture cf. G. Majcherek, "Notes on Alexandrian habitat, Roman and Byzantine houses from Kom al-Dikka," *TOPOI* 5/1 (1995), 133–150. For individual hous-

es see preliminary reports; G. Majcherek, "Alexandria 1994; Archaeological Excavations," *PAM* VI (1995), 11–20; G. Majcherek, "Excavations at Kom al-Dikka 1995," *PAM* VII (1996), 13–22; G. Majcherek, "Kom al-Dikka, Excavations 1995-96," *PAM* VIII (1997), 17–31; G. Majcherek, "Kom al-Dikka, Excavations 1997, " *PAM* IX (1998), 23–36.

3 G. Majcherek, "Excavations 1995–96," fig. 2; Z. Kiss, "Un portrait d'Alexandre le Grand rècement trouvè à Alexandrie," *Swiatowit* I XLII (1999), 34–36.

4 G. Majcherek, "Excavations 1994," 11–20, fig. 1. The northern triclinium was uncovered in the spring of 2000.

5 For mosaics with figural representations cf. Daszewski, "Hellenistic Polychromy," 147, n. 19. This list can now be extended to include yet another mosaic with figural emblema representing a panther (mosaic a-6) found in the "Villa of the Birds" during the ARCE/EAP Conservation Project. For *emblemata* in Alexandria cf. Daszewski, *Corpus*, 84–86; W. A. Daszewski, "An Old Question in Light of New Evidence," in G. Grimm *et al.* (eds.), *Das Römisch-Byzantinische Ägypten*, Akten des internationalen Symposions, 26–30 Sept. 1978, Trier; (Aegyptiaca Treverensia 2, Mainz, 1983), 161–165, Pl. 28–31.

6 "Villa of the Birds," mosaic a-5, cf. M. Rodziewicz, "Un quartier d'habitation grèco-romain à Kom al-Dikka," *Etudes et Travaux* IX (1976), 179, figs. 11–14.

7 E. Breccia, *Monuments de l'Egypte Grèco-Romain* (Bergamo, 1926), 81–82, Pl. XLVII, 3–6; W. A. Daszewski, *Corpus of Mosaics from Egypt, I, Hellenistic and Early Roman Period*, (Mainz, 1985), 136–138, cat. nn. 30, 32.

8 A. Khashab, Les hammams du Kom Trougah, *ASAE* LIV (1956), 118, n. 1; M. Abd er-Rahman, "Les premiers fouilles du Kom Trougah," *ASAE* LV (1958), 356, Pl. VIb; Daszewski, *Corpus*, 172–173, cat. no. 47. pl. D1; fig. 12.

9 For a detailed discussion of the motif cf. Daszewski, *Corpus*, 63–65.

10 E. Breccia, *Le Musèe Grèco-Romain au cours de l'annèe 1925–1931* (Bergamo, 1932), 194, Pl. 53; Daszewski, *Corpus*, 158–160, cat. no. 39, Pls. B; 33.

11 G. Botti, *Catalog des monuments exposès au Musèe Grèco-Romain d'Alexandrie* (Alexandrie, 1901), 520f; Daszewski, *Corpus*, 120–128, cat. no. 20, Pl. 22–23; fig. 6.

12 G. Botti, *Le Musèe Grèco-Romain d'Alexandrie (1892–1898)* (Venue: Alexandrie, 1899) 20; E. Breccia, *Alexandrea ad Aegyptum* (1914), 190.

13. Breccia, *Catalog des Monuments*, 81–82, Pl. XLV.

14 Stored in the CIBA building in Basel, CIBA-Blätter 19, n. 175 (Sept./Oct 1961); K. Parlasca, "Hellenistische und Römische Mosaiken aus Ägypten," *La mosaïque Grèco-Romaine, IIe Colloque international pour l'Ètude de la mosaïque antique, Vienne 1971* (Paris, 1975), 363–68, Pl. H (color plate).

15 D. G. Hogarth, E. F. Benson, "Report on Prospects of Research in Alexandria with Note on Excavations in Alexandrian Cemeteries," *Egypt Exploration Fund Archeological Report* (1894–1895), 16; A. Adriani, *Repertorio d'arte dell'Egitto greco-romano*, Serie C, I/II (Palermo, 1966), 83, n. 44A, tav. 23; 86.

16 Daszewski, "Hellenistic Polychromy," 146.

17 G. Majcherek, "Excavations 1994," 18.

18 A.-M. Guimier-Sorbets, "Le pavement à la Mèduse dans une maison d'epoque impèriale à Alexandrie," *Alexandrina I* (1998), 115–140, fig. 1.

19 Mosaic a-3, M. Rodziewicz, "Un quartier," 178–9, fig. 10.

20 The author wishes to express his thanks to Robert Vincent, EAP director, for the opportunity to present the newly discovered mosaic. For the final publication see; W. Kolataj, G. Majcherek, E. Parandowska; *ARCE/EA Conservation and Display of Roman Mosaics, Alexandria, Final Report 2000* (in press).

21. M. Abd-ur-Rahman, "Premiers fouilles," 356, fig.2, Pl.V; Daszewski, *Corpus*, 173, cat. n. 48, Pl. 24b, fig. 12.

22 M. Rodziewicz, "Opus sectile mosaics from Alexandria and Mareotis," in *Tesserae, Festschrift fur Josef Engemann, Jahrbuch fur Antike und Christentum* 18 (1991); 208–211, figs. 4–7.

23 Rodziewicz, "Un quartier," 186, figs. 22/4; Rodziewicz, "Opus sectile," 206–207, fig. 2.

24 Majcherek, "Excavations 1996–1997," 27–28, fig. 2

25 W. Kolataj, and T. Kolataj, "Polish Excavations at Kom el Dikka in Alexandria, 1967," *Bulletin de la SociÈte Archèologique d'Alexandrie*, 43 (1975), 79–97, Pl. VII.

26 L. Ibrahim *et al. Kenchreai - Eastern Port of Corinth 2. The Panels of Opus Sectile in Glass*, (Leiden, 1976). For the *sectile* glass panels in Egypt cf; M. -D. Nenna, "Les elèments d'incrustation; une industrie Ègyptienne du verre," *Alessandria e il Mondo ellenistico-romano, Atti del II Congresso Internazionale Italo-Egiziano 1992* (Rome, 1995), 377–384; cf. also H. W. Müller, "Koptische Glasintarsien mit figürlichen Darstellungen aus Antinoe/Mittel Ägypten," *Pantheon* 20 (1962), 13–18.

27 G. Pesce, *Il "Palazzo delle Colonne" in Tolemaide di Cirenaica* (Rome, 1950), 38, fig. 42.

28 C. Kraeling, *Ptolemais, City of the Libyan Pentapole* (Chicago, 1962), 138, fig. 68–69, Pl. 49A).

29 P. Mingazzini, *L'insula di Giasone Magno a Cirene* (Rome, 1966).

30 J. A. Lloyd, ed. *Excavations at Sidi Khrebish Benghazi (Berenice)* I (Supplement to Libya Antiqua V; Tripoli, 1978), 156–158, Pl. XIIb. "House of the Cascade" in Utica offers yet another example; cf. M. Alexander and M. Ennaifer, *Quelques prècisions à propos de la chronologie des mosaiques d'Utique* (La Mosaique Grèco-Romaine II, Paris, 1975), 31–39, Pl. XIII, 2.

31 Rodziewicz, "Opus sectile," 205, was inclined to date this mosaic floor on archaeological grounds to the second century CE. Daszewski, "Hellenistic Polychromy," 149, falls back on an analysis of the style to lower the dating even to the end of the first century CE.

32 G. Majcherek, "Excavations 1994," fig. 1.

La fibrose hépatique non cirrhotique dans l'ancienne Égypte des Pharaons

Elio Mantellini, Sergio Nappini

La discussion sur les maladies qui touchaient les anciennes populations du monde est difficile et se heurte à nombre d'obstacles. On peut cependant essayer de focaliser certains points fondamentaux, qui nous permettent d'affirmer et de démontrer indirectement que plusieurs maladies et, entre autres, la fibrose hépatique non cirrhotique, frappaient les anciens Égyptiens au temps des Pharaons[1].

La fibrose hépatique non cirrhotique est une maladie du foie en partie inconnue, ayant de multiples causes. Souvent cette fibrose est provoquée par une infestation intestinale due au Schistosome Mansoni, c'est-à-dire à un vermisseau, semblable à la Bilharzia, qui pénètre dans le corps par la peau et cause de nombreuses complications ; mais contrairement à la bilharziose, il épargne toujours la voie biliaire et l'appareil urinaire[2].

Le Schistosome Mansoni[3] est présent de nos jours au Moyen Orient et en Afrique Occidentale, surtout sur les rives du Nil. Il n'est donc pas erroné de soutenir que la fibrose hépatique non cirrhotique ainsi que la bilharziose furent parmi les maladies qui affligèrent les Égyptiens au temps des Pharaons.

La Schistosomiase Mansoni a une évolution très variable et elle est actuellement mortelle dans 25% des cas[4]. Dans un premier stade, l'infestation passe habituellement inaperçue, se développe ensuite une fibrose périportale, appelée fibrose de Symmers (v. stèle de Bak), la plus grave des complications causées par le Schistosome Mansoni. Cette fibrose de Symmers, dite aussi « en tuyau de pipe », provoque une hypertension portale avec hépatomégalie : le foie prend un aspect nodulaire et le lobe gauche grossit. Le tissu fibrotique occupe les espaces portals et cause un blocage présinusoïdal sans endommager les hépatocytes, contrairement à la cirrhose hépatique qui provoque un blocage postsinusoïdal et endommage le parenchyme.

L'hypertension portale est toujours présente, associée à : splénomégalie, varices œsophagiennes et gastriques avec fréquents épisodes d'hématémèse. La fonction hépatique reste inaltérée : ascite, œdèmes des membres inférieurs, gynécomastie et tous les autres symptômes d'hépatopathie chroniques sont rarement observés.

Les œufs du Schistosome Mansoni circulent dans le sang veineux et par conséquent ne sont pas toujours présents dans les selles ; en circulant dans le sang, ces œufs rejoignent les espaces portaux où ils causent une inflammation granulomateuse qui comprime les veinules portales en provoquant une hypertension typiquement présinusoïdale, la réduction du flux sinusoïdal et la rupture des veinules portales[5].

La néphrose, le coma hépatique et le cœur pulmonaire (complications tardives) sont observés uniquement dans les cas graves et de longue durée. Les complications neurologiques au contraire peuvent être précoces et causer des crises épileptiques.

De nos jours, en Égypte, le Schistosome Mansoni provoque très souvent un syndrome caractérisé par : diarrhée hématique et anémie, dues à une grave entéropathie granulomateuse qui peut simuler un cancer.

Les études récentes du professeur Sarin (1998)[6] démontrent que la fibrose hépatique atteint des personnes jeunes et se manifeste avec des épisodes d'hématémèse bien tolérés, anémie et tuméfaction de l'hypocondre gauche.

Nunn[7] confirme que 12% de la population égyptienne est touchée par la schistosomiase dans ses différentes formes. Selon Popper et Kent[8], cette maladie est de nos jours la cause la plus fréquente d'hypertension portale dans le monde.

Ruffer[9], Leca[10], Hart[11], Ghalioungui[12], Miller[13] et Nunn[14] sont convaincus que la schistosomiase et la bilharziose touchaient sans aucun doute la population de l'ancien Égypte, mais aucune preuve tangible ne peut le démontrer, car les rares organes conservés dans les vases canopes ou retrouvés dans les momies sont altérés par le temps.

La réfutation ou la confirmation de cette intéressante théorie sur la pathologie humaine d'il y a quatre mille ans dépendront des découvertes futures et en particulier des découvertes de momies aux organes mieux conservés.

Notes:

1 P. H. Gray, « Radiography of ancient egyptian mummies », Med. rad. and phot. 43 (1967), 34–44; G. Lefebvre, Essai sur la médicine égyptienne de l'Epoque Pharaonique, (Paris, 1956); E. G. Smith - W.R. Dawson, Egyptian Mummies, (Londres, 1924).

2 E. Mantellini - M. Tosi, « La calcolosi biliare in Egitto al tempo dei Faraoni », Atti VI Int. Congr. of Egyptologists, (Turin, 1993), 373; E. Mantellini et al., « La lithiase urinaire dans l'Antique Egypte des Pharaons », Proceedings of the VIIth Int. Congr. of Egyptologists, (Louvain, 1998) 7,73.

3 H. Grapow et al., Grundiss der Medizin der Alten Agypten, 8 Vol. (Berlin, 1954–1962).

4 M. A. Amin, « Infezioni e parassiti nell'Antico Egitto », Ureteral calculi, Br. J. Urol. 45 (1973), 192; C. Daglio, Infezioni e parassiti nell'antico Egitto, Cop. Sc. Univ., (Turin, 1981).

5 T. E. Nash, « Schistosomiasi », Harrisons principles of internaz. Medicine, (Milan, 1992), 1107; V. Teodori, Patologia Medica I (1987).

6 S. K. Sarin, « *Non cirrhotic portal hypertension* », *Atti postgraduate course advances in therapeutic heptatonique*, (Chicago, 1998), 111.

7 J. F. Nunn, *Ancient Egyptian Medicine*, (Londres, 1996), 71, 82, 91.

8 H. Popper – G. Kent, « *La fibrosi nelle epatopatie corniche* ». « *Cirrosi epatica* ». *Il pens. Scientifico*, (Roma, 1976), 112.

9 M. A. Ruffer, *Studies in the Paleopathology of Egypt*, (Chicago, 1921).

10 A. P. Leca, *La médecine égyptienne au temps des Pharaons*, (Paris, 1971–1986).

11 G. D. Hart *et al.*, « Autopsy of an egyptian mummy », *Canadian Medical Association Journal* 117 (1977), 461.

12 P. Ghalioungui, *La médecine des pharaons*, (Paris, 1983).

13 Miller R. L. *et al.*, « Palaeoepidemiology of schistosoma infection in mummies », *British Medical Journal* 304 (1992), 555; Miller R. L. *et al.*, « Predynastic schistosomiasis » *in* W. V. Davies – R. Walker (éd.), *Biological Anthropology and the Study of Ancient Egypt*, (Londres, 1993).

14 Nunn, *Ancient Egyptian Medicine*, 91.

Recent Explorations in the Ninth Nome of Upper Egypt

Yahia El-Masry
General Director, Sohag Zone

In the last ten years, we have carried out many soundings and
excavations in the district of modern Akhmim,[1] a region which corresponds to the Ninth Nome of
Upper Egypt.[2] In the course of this
work we have discovered a number
of archaeological sites (Fig. 1).
Some of these sites were previously unknown, others were known
from references in old Egyptological literature, but over the years
knowledge of their location had
become lost.

Between 1989 and 1999 work
was conducted at five sites on both
the east and west banks of the Nile.
The work at these sites revealed a
number of cemeteries; two date to
the end of the Old Kingdom (OK) and
the First Intermediate Period (FIP), a
third cemetery dates to as early as
the Fifth Dynasty, and a fourth is a
large cemetery of Ptolemaic date
where Maspero had done some work.

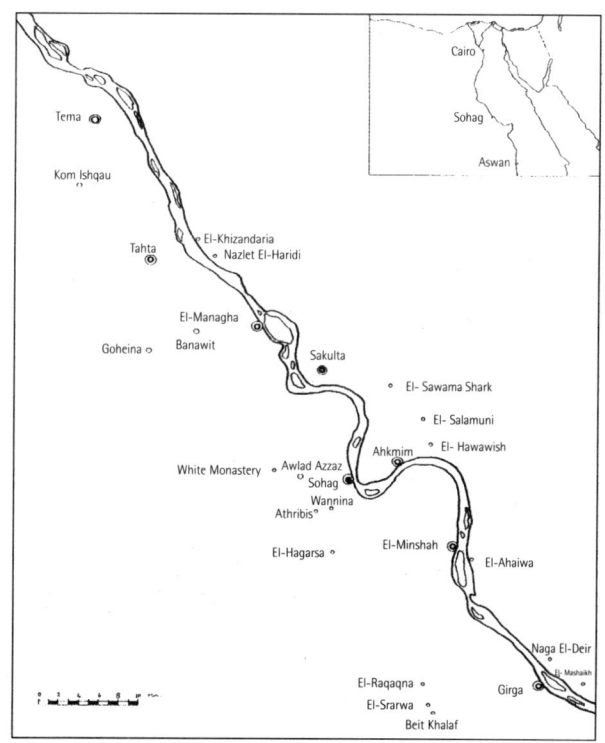

Fig. 1: Location of the nine nome sites.

331

In the last year of the last century we discovered a decree lying on a pavement of a Ptolemaic Period temple. A few meters from this temple we found the remains of a settlement. At the fifth site, located on the west bank some kilometers from Sohag, Coptic magazines and a gate of the Ptolemaic Period were discovered.

The Rock-Cut Tombs of Gohaina

In 1989, a survey was conducted in the mountains about seven kilometers from Gohaina,[3] a town which lies about 35 kilometers northwest of Sohag. The survey brought to light an ancient cemetery. It was used in the past as a quarry, but remains of a group of rock-cut tombs were found. It is clear that the earliest tombs are of OK date and that the cemetery was in use down to the Greco-Roman Period.

The tombs of the OK were cut into poor quality stone, and were plastered and painted. The general design of the tombs consists of an entrance leading to a small chapel. In the middle of the back wall of the chapel there is a shaft leading to a burial chamber. The only painted tombs were numbered G1 and G2. They were situated on the extreme north of the first level. The first tomb's interior was covered with white plaster, while the second's was covered with light brown plaster;[4] both were painted. In the first tomb, the majority of the scenes were preserved, while the decoration in the second tomb was in poorer condition. We know the name of the owner of the first tomb, G1, is ḥwi (Khui),[5] with the good name ṯti-iḳr (Thethi-iqer).[6] This name is attested in the OK in other provinces of Upper Egypt. The owner of the other tomb, G2, was probably named Resity.[7] This can be concluded from the discovery of a loose fragment, which was decorated with the same color scheme as tomb G2,[8] and on which was written the name of Resity. He is perhaps the third son of the owner of tomb G1, since the

Fig. 2: South wall, offering table scene. G1 tomb of ḥwi.

332

third son depicted behind the owner of tomb G1 in the fishing scene of that tomb bears the same name.

In the niche at the rear of the chapel of tomb G1, inscribed on the north wall, appears an offering list.[9] In the middle of the niche is the false door,[10] upon which the owner is said to be a priest of the god Min,[11] with the additional titles of *smr wᶜty, hᶜty-ᶜ* and *hk3 hwt*. The south wall of the niche includes a scene of the tomb owner in front of an offering table, which has some unique features (Fig. 2). The table does not contain the usual loaves of bread or straight reeds,[12] but sprouting seeds are depicted; these are gathered in a bunch at the bottom and the sprouting shoots splay outwards on both sides. This may be the result of the desire of the local artist to create a new type of offering table scene depicting the plants and the seeds from which bread is made.[13] This kind of depiction may relate to the notion of the Fields of Iaru.

The absolute date for both tombs is uncertain, but from their location and size and general architectural design,[14] in addition to the decoration of the tombs, as well as some other evidence, a date at the end of the OK may be suggested at least for Khui, more precisely between the end of the Sixth Dynasty and the beginning of the Eighth Dynasty. For tomb G2, the likely date is at the beginning of the Ninth Dynasty. We can judge the importance of this site from the number of other tombs located near it, and its use through pharaonic history, as in other cemeteries in Upper Egypt.

Fig. 3: Second site White Monastery Cemetery.

The Cemetery West of the White Monastery
The mountains west of Sohag City contain a number of cemeteries, located near each other, but dating to different historical periods. The sequence from south to north is, consecutively; The

Cemetery of Hagarsa,[15] Athribis,[16] The West Cemetery of the White Monastery, and Awlad Azaz.[17] The Cemetery of the White Monastery was not known previously and takes its name from its proximity to the White Monastery.

The cemetery on this site is divided into two sections separated by an old road leading to an old quarry, near the top of the desert mountain (Fig. 3). The design of the first of the northern group of tombs includes a vertical shaft leading to a burial chamber, which remains unexcavated. The second group of tombs, located to the south of the old road, is arranged in a number of levels and has a general design in the shape of the letter "L." In the lower levels the tombs are spaced several meters apart, while in the upper level they are very close togther. Those tombs with entrances facing east were excavated in 1989. In spite of the high quality of the stone cutting and the clear remains of the lintels and drums at the entrance, it seems that the stone surface was plastered before being inscribed. Only on the wall of one tomb are some incised inscriptions still visible.[18] The traces give the name of the *im3ḫw ḫwi*.[19] In spite of the fact that these tombs were full of debris, it seems that many years ago they were known to robbers, since during the course of cleaning the tombs, empty match boxes made in Sweden were found, as well as part of a

Fig. 4: Mummy of *šnkri*.

kerosene lamp, and some empty cigarette boxes. Nevertheless, we found parts of wooden coffins, linen, cartonnage, and a Coptic papyrus that contains about 40 lines of inscription in black ink.

The most important discovery was five wooden coffins[20] inside the shaft of a tomb in which no traces of any decorated surface remains. This tomb was located at the extreme north of the southern group and was numbered E17. The design of the tomb consists of a square entrance leading to a slanting passage, which opens onto a rectangular burial chamber. On the north wall of this chamber is an opening leading to a very small room that contained one coffin, while the main room contained two coffins, and the sloping passage also contained two coffins.

The coffin in the small northern room was inscribed in hieroglyphs for its owner *šnkri* (Senkeri),[21] with the good name *Jti* (Iti),[22] with the titles *ḥ3ti-ʿ3 sḏ3wti-biti* (Fig. 4), and "The Honored One Before the God Min, Lord of Akhmim."

The two coffins in the passage were also inscribed. The first one was for a lady with the name *ʿnḥ-sn* (Ankh-sen),[23] with the title of *ḥkrt nswt wʿtt*. She was also a priestess of the goddess Hathor, Lady of the city of Philae, which suggests she originated from there. The second coffin was inscribed for a girl with the name *ʿnḥ-sn-ikrt* (Ankh-senikeret).[24] She carries the same titles as the woman who may be her mother, and appears to have been named after her mother, with the distinguishing epithet of *ikrt*.[25]

Inside each coffin were a mummy and some funerary equipment. Three of the mummies were covered in cartonnage and linen.[26] The linen was tied with the knot of Isis. Two wooden coffins were inscribed only with *wḏ3t*-eyes, and their mummies had no cartonnage. Finding this number of coffins inside a small tomb, the hasty manner in which the burials appear to have been done—two of the coffins were not inscribed, and two of the mummies were not provided with cartonnage—in addition to the presence of a small girl together with the adults, all suggest that the deaths happened suddenly. This evidence, in addition to the style of the hieroglyphic signs, indicates a date in the FIP. The whole find complex recalls that found in the cemetery of Hagarsah.[27]

The Cemetery of Naga al-Diabat

Between 1989 and 1999 the Supreme Council of Antiquities carried out some soundings after a survey of this area, which is located facing the mountain of the cemetery of Hawawish. Maspero wrote of a large cemetery in Akhmim that was two kilometers long.[28] Kuhlmann suggested that the hill upon which three monasteries were built might be the cemetery, which Maspero also mentions. He termed the cemetery in this hill "A" and the cemetery of the mountain of Hawawish "B."[29] Until our work, the exact location of the cemetery remained unknown.

About three seasons of work have been carried out in this area, and this has revealed a number of tombs, some part rock-cut and constructed of mud brick in combination. The tombs were found to contain some funerary objects, including the lid of a sarcophagus, made of good quality limestone and inscribed for a priest *ḏḥwti min* (Djehuti-Min).[30] He may be the son of the same priest (*ḥrw-m3ʿ-ḥrw*) who restored the chapel of King Ay in Salamoni.[31] Many stelae[32] and inscribed offering tables were found. In the last season, we found a tomb for ibis mummies. We may be able to define a sequence of the owners of the sarcophagi, offering tables, stelae, and wooden statues. Some of the tombs possessed a strange design, with shared stairs leading to separate burial chambers. Many of the objects from different periods currently in the Cairo Museum and other museums which are attributed to Akhmim are probably from this site,[33] since Hawawish contains only tombs of the OK. It seems that the first level of the cemetery, which lies between al-Deir al-Gibli and al-Deir al-Wastani, belongs to the Ptolemaic period. This site may also contain tombs of other periods, since Maspero also mentions the tomb of *Nḥt-Min* (Nakht-Min), architect of King Ay.[34]

Al-Khezanderia

This site contains a cemetery, a temple, and a settlement. Work started here in 1999, and to date only one season has been carried out. Al-Khezanderia is located northeast of Akhmim and comprises two sites, the mountain of Abu al-Nasr and the mountain of Jebel al-Haridi. Our work is located in Abu al-Nasr. A rock cut stela of Ramesses III is known at Gebel al-Haridi.[35] An English mission made a survey of both mountains.[36] The survey of the Supreme Council of Antiquities in Abu al-Nasr determined that it contained three archaeological sites. The first site contained tombs belonging to the OK, NK, and later. We began cleaning one large OK tomb. It has an impressive façade, with two sets of two statues on either side of a central entrance. A rectangular room was entered through the entrance from the east. In the north wall of the chamber were two small passages, which led to small rectangular rooms. The tomb is unfinished inside, as the rock remains unevenly cut in the northern half of the chapel. On the north wall of the court in front of the tomb is the figure of the tomb owner holding his staff, executed in raised relief. There are remains of some broken hieroglyphic signs, which may be read as *pr-nṯr*.[37] In the course of cleaning the forecourt, we found Islamic Period copper vessels and a large number of Ptolemaic coins.[38]

The second site at al-Khezanderia is located at the foot of the mountain, just behind a modern canal. Here a Ptolemaic temple was discovered, partially rock-cut and partially stone-built. The most important discovery was a large round-topped stela, 120 cm wide and 220 cm long, of good limestone, and with a high-quality hieroglyphic inscription. At the top of the stela are some figures, which represent, from the left, the queen, the king, the gods Osiris, Isis, Horus, and Min. Before them are the traces of an unfinished figure facing the others. The stela bears 21 lines of hieroglyphic text, with 17 lines of Demotic text following. At the end of the hieroglyphic text there is one line in cursive hieroglyphs. This stela contains many cartouches of Ptolemy III, his wife, and his sister Arsinoe.[39] On the top of the stela is a date of Year 5 in the reign of this king, which is written in both Egyptian and Greek. The stela includes references to very important historical events, relating to conflict between Egypt and Syria; to offerings to Egyptian temples and the creation of an order of priests for the cult of the king, as well as a new festival relating to this cult. There is also a reference to the correction of the Egyptian calendar. This stela is considered the most complete example which has been found to date.[40] Near this temple, about 25 meters away, we found a settlement built of red and mud brick, as well as stone.

This group of sites, the OK tombs, the Ptolemaic temple, as well as the settlement, may represent the boundary of the Ninth Nome.

Tell Edfa

Edfa[41] is located some 10 km northwest of Sohag, and 3 km south of the Red Monastery. Three successive seasons of excavation starting in 1992, revealed the different levels of the Tell to be as follows:
- The highest level contained a group of Coptic mud-brick tombs in which some Islamic coin and bracelets were found.
- The levels below this contain some Greco-Roman granaries of mud-brick, in which some big jars of red pottery set on pottery stands were found. Inside these storehouses the following objects were also found; a group of lamps, some Demotic and Coptic ostraca, and fragments of some Greco-Roman statues and terracotta figurines. To the west of these storehouses a stone gate was uncovered.

In fact, these excavations, which were carried out during the last decade, points out that Sohag is much more important than we previously thought, and a thorough archaeological survey is still needed.

Notes:

1 Akhmim is on the east bank of the Nile opposite modern Sohag, the capital of the Ninth Nome of Upper Egypt during the pharaonic period; see E. Brovarski, *Akhmim in the Old Kingdom and First Intermediate Period* (Melanges Gamal Eddin Mokhtar I; Cairo, 1985), 118-153; Y. El-Masry, "Seven Seasons of Excavation In Akhmim," in C. J. Eyre (ed.), *Proceedings of the Seventh International Congress of Egyptologists. Cambridge, 3–9 September 1995 (OLA 82*; Louvain, 1998), 760-765.

2 W. Helck, *Die Altagyptische Gaue* (Wiesbaden, 1974), 39-5; A. H. Gardiner, *Ancient Egyptian Onomastica* II (Oxford, 1947), 41; (for the limits of the Ninth Nome).

3 This site is not mentioned in *PM.*

4 Like the majority of other nome cemeteries; see N. Kanawati, *The Rock Tombs of Hawawish: The cemetery of Akhmim* (Sydney, 1980-1992).

5 H. Ranke, *Die Altagyptischen Personennamen* I (Gluckstadt, 1935-77), 267: 12

6 The epithet *ikr* in Thethi-iqer's name includes him amongst some of individuals with similar epithets like *k3-ḥp: ṭti-ikr* of the Hawawish reign of Pepy II or later, *ʿnḫ-ti-fi* who was also described as *ikr*, Eighth Dynasty, see Kanawati, *Hawawish* I, 12–14 and *šni-ikr* of Thebes may also be dated to the end of the Old Kingdom, Kanawati, *Hawawish* I, 35, n. 30.

7 Ranke, *PN* 1, 226: 29, the name is listed as *Rsy* (G2's name is *Rsiti*).

8 It caries the name *Rsiti* and if this is the owner of the tomb, he is probably a younger (?) son of *ḥwi*, since a son of this name appears in the end register of the north wall of G1, following another (elder?) son, whose name is now lost.

9 The same item is in Winifed Barta's work, *Die Altagyptische Opferliste von der Fruhzeit bis zur griechisch romischen Epoche* (Berlin, 1963).

10 The painted false door in G1 is of the type found at Hawawish at the very end of Dynasty Six, e.g., tombs C9, (Kanawati, *Hawawish* VII, fig. 8; H24) and G79, (Kanawati, *Hawawish* II), figs. 4, 23; Kanawati, *Hawawish* III, fig. 26. The same type of false door is seen in tombs from the later period in the neighboring nome of Abydos, e.g. in the tomb of an overseer of priests who is dated to the Ninth Dynasty; C. Peck, *Some Decorated Tombs at Naga ed-der*, Ph.D. Thesis, Brown University, 1958, 123ff., Pl. 12.

11 The name of the god *Min* (Min) appears in the tomb G1 (fiat sign for have appeared on the lower lintel of the false door) it is part of an epithet such as, "The Honored One Before the God Min."

12 Short reeds are depicted on the offering table in the tomb of *Mrii-ʿ3* at Hagarsa, which dates to the Eighth Dynasty; see N. Kanawati, *The Tombs of Hagarsa* (ACE 3, (Sydney, 1993-1995) 28–29, Pls. 38, 46.

13 E. Worsham, "A representation of the so-called bread loaves in Egyptian offering scenes," *JARCE XVI* (1979), 7–10.

14 The same design for G1 is found in the neighboring cemetery of Hawawish, e.g. *Ppy-ʿnḫ-ns*; Kanawati, *Hawawish* IX, fig.1.

15 M.F.W. Petrie, *Athribis* (London, 1988) for recent records see Kanawati, *Hagarsa* III, *passim.*

16 R. Al-Farag, P. Khulman, and U. Kaplony, "Recent Archaeological Explorations at Athribis in Upper Egypt," *MDAIK* 41 (1985), 1-8.

17 B. Ockinga, *A Tomb from the reign of Tutankhamun at Akhmim* (ACE Reports 10; [England, 1997]).

18 Still visible on the right wall is a figure of a man with his bow and arrows. For some examples see J. Vandier, *Moʿalla: la tomb Ankhtifi et la tombe de Sebekhotep* (Cairo, 1950), Pl. XXXV.

19 The writing of the epithet *im3ḫii*, with the name is a useful criterion for dating this tomb. Some examples in the neighboring cemetery of Hawawish are from the very end of the Sixth Dynasty or immediately after; see Kanawati, *Hawawish* VII, 25, fig. 16; Kanawati, *Hawawish* VIII, 27 fig. 10.

20 Similar wooden coffins (Eighth Dynasty) were found at Hagarsa by a team from the ACE in 1989; see Kanawati, *Hagarsa* II, 85–88.

21 The name as written here is unattested in Ranke.

22 Ranke, *PN* I, 52: 29.

23 The name not lisited in Ranke, *PN*.

24 The name is not listed in Ranke, for the term *ikrt*; see: Ranke, *PN* I, 47:20. Only *ikr-ʿnh* is attested, Ranke *PN* I, 47:18.

25 A name with the epithet *ikrt* is attested on a stela from Sheikh Farag, See D. Dunham, *Naga El-Der Stelae of the First Intermediate Period* (London, 1937) 37, no. 23. B.M.F.A. 25. 679.

26 DNA analysis and examination of the X-rays are necessary to determine the age and sex of the mummies and to identify any abnormal pathology and possible causes of death.

27 Kanawati, *Hagarsa* II, *passim*.

28 G. Maspero, *Etudes de mythologie et d'archeologie* I (Paris 1893), 215.

29 P. Kuhlman, *Materlallenzur Archaologle and Gexhichte des Raumes von Akhmim*, sonderschrift 11 (Mainz, 1983), 53ff.

30 The son bears the same titles of his father, *sm3 Mnw wr n snw hm ntrt m Jpw rh nswt*; see: P. Kuhlmann, "Der felstempel des Eje bei Achmim," *MDIAK* 35 (Cairo, 1979) 175–176, n. 39.

31 Kuhlmann, "Der felstempel," 175.

32 All of the hieroglyphs are incised, while the figures are executed in sunk relief. At the top of the stelae is represented the winged sun disc with uraeus, between which is written a royal title of "the Osiris, Bakhthis."

33 For some similar objects, see, S. Hodjash and O. Berlev, *The Egyptian Reliefs and Stelae in the Pushkin Museum of Fine Arts, Moscow* (Leningrad, 1982), 184ff; and see: also *PM* V, 20–26.

34 G. Maspero, *Histoire ancienne des peuples de l'Orient* II (Paris, 1909), 488, n. 3; G. Maspero, *Etudes de mythology et d'archeologie Egyptiennes* I (Paris, 1893), 216.

35 L. Habachi, "Three large rock stelae carved by Ramesses III near quarries," *JARCE* II (1974) 69–75.

36 C. J. Kirby, "Preliminary Report of the First Season of Work at Gebel al-Haridi, 1991–92," *JEA* 78 (1992) 19–27; C. J. Kirby, "Preliminary Report of the Second Survey Season at Gebel al-Haridi, 1993," *JEA* 80 (1994) 11–22.

37 Written *pr-ntr*, suggesting that the tomb owner had a position as a temple official.

38 May date to either Ptolemy VI or Ptolemy XI; See G. T. Martin, *The Sacred Animal Necropolis at North Saqqara* (London, 1981), 52–5, Pl. 45 for similar examples.

39 Ptolemy III Evergates I (246–222 BCE) *Jwʿ-n-ntrwi-snwi stp-(n)-Rʿ shm-ʿnh-n-Jmn* see A. E. von Beckerath, *Handbuch der ägyptischen Konigsnamen* (Berlin, 1984), 113, 289.

40 For the time being there are two complete and three fragmentary copies of the Canopus Decree; from Tanis see *Urk.* II, 124–154, now Cairo Mus. CG22-187; from Kom al-Hisn, now Cairo Mus. CG22-186. The fragment Louvre C.122 contains some lines of hieroglyphic texts (unpublished); A fragment from al-Kab in Upper Egypt contains some lines.

41 S. Sauneron, "Le village D'Edfa: son passe medieval, Greco Roman et pharaonique," *BIFAO* 62, (1946), 42–50; E. Amelineau, *La Geographie de l' egypte a l'epoque copte* (Paris, 1890), 155–157.

How Studies of Botanical Remains and Animal Bones Contribute to the Re-writing of the History of the Delta over Time

Samia El-Merghani
Center of Research and Conservation of Antiquities, Egypt

Introduction

In the excavation of sites, especially Prehistoric and Archaic ones, archaeologists often discover botanical and faunal remains. In the past, little attention was given to this material, but now this situation has changed in favor of laboratory and technical developments and the participation of specialists in archaeological fieldwork.

Botanical Remains

The Kafr Hassan Dawood cemetery in the East Delta belongs to the Predynastic and Archaic periods. Through my work in lifting bones from a human burial (No. 525), I discovered a deep pit beside the skeleton. This pit is vessel-shaped, 10 cm under the level of the skeleton. This pit was 16 cm diameter at the surface and 33 cm deep. It was attached to a tunnel that extended under the human remains. The dimensions of the tunnel were: diameter 13 cm, depth 20 cm. The pit and tunnel were full of seeds from plants mixed with a large amount of sand. When we extracted the contents of the pit and tunnel, we found pieces of plant cortex. This cortex was cylindrical in shape, 2–3 cm in length, but when exposed to air, it broke into very small pieces.

Experiment

On the site we examined the seeds with the naked eye; they were brown in color and very brittle, similar to each other in shape, and in two sizes, three and five mm in length.

With the help of paleobotanist, Prof. Wagieh El-Saadawi, I re-examined the seeds and cortex and made several comparative studies.

1) By comparing the ancient seeds with modern seeds according to morphological shape and size, I recorded the following:

    a) The ancient seeds are similar to seeds of the *Sesbania* plant in morphological shape. (figure 1)

b) When the modern seeds are left to dry, their size diminishes greatly.

c) The modern *Sesbania* plant is a corticate plant; the lagenostom seed belongs to the genus *Dicotyledon*.

2) Chemical analysis of the seeds indicates that the ancient seeds are composed only of inorganic materials.

3) By examining them with a stereomicroscope, using different power lenses, the ancient seeds appear to be composed of particles that are not similar.

4) Examination with electron stereomicroscope gave the same result.

5) Chemical analysis of the cortex indicates that it is organic material.

6) DNA analysis showed the presence of DNA still present in the cortex.

7) When the ancient cortex was sectioned, plant cells appeared. (fig. 2).

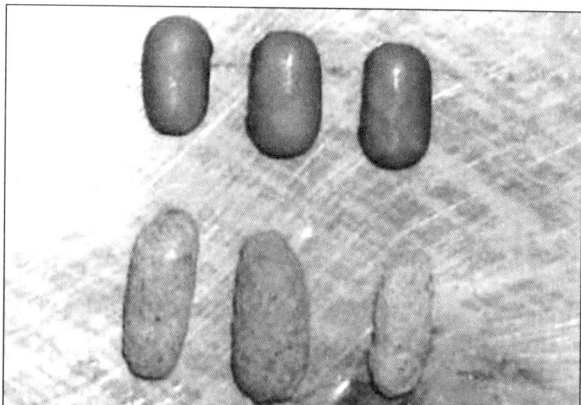

Figure 1

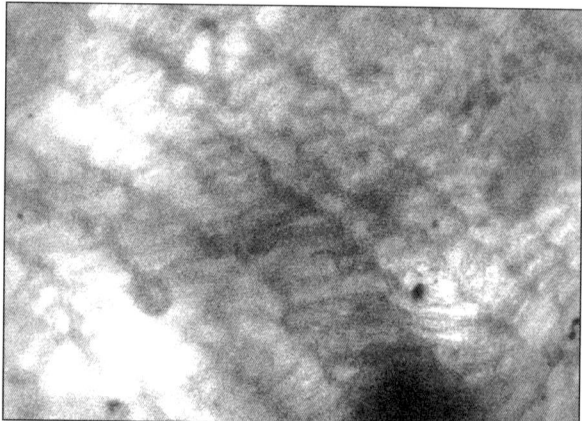

Figure 2

Results

1) The ancient seeds are similar to modern *Sesbania* seeds in morphological shape and size.

2) After dessication, the ancient seeds lost their organic matter but the shape was preserved in the form of the fossil plant, cast type.

3) The organic matter and DNA still remain in the cortex, which still contains plant cells.

4) We can assume that those ancient seeds and cortex belong to the same *Dicotyledon Sesbania* plant.

Discussion

The studies of these botanical remains demonstrated the changes the plants underwent through time. The following facts should be taken into consideration:

Upon the death of the plant, disintegration of organic matter starts to take place. However, if this disintegration is stopped at one stage or anther, a fossil plant will result. There are several types of fossil plants.

1) The chief factors governing tissue preservation in fossil plants are: a) the structure of the plant body, and b) the environmental conditions during fossilization.[1]

2) Some plants, chiefly algae, possess a hard exoskeleton most commonly composed of calcium carbonate or Cilica. This is part of the plant is resistant to decay and is preserved with little or no chemical or physical change.[2]

3) In our case study, the ancient seeds were the fossil plant, cast type. In this type, the casts of seeds are frequently formed when the plants decay, before any amount of compaction of sediments has taken place. The cavity or "mold" which subsequently becomes filled with sand or mud which upon hardening becomes a cast,[3] The hard part of the plant—the exoskeleton—is preserved but in a very dry state.

4) In Egypt there is species of *Sesbania* named *Sesbania aegyptica*. In Hierakopolis *Sesbania sesban* seeds from the Paeleolathic were recovered. These were used for food.[4] The ancient Egyptian used *Sesbania* fibers for making fishing nets.[5]

5) Recent studies in Biology and soil fertility prove that the nodules induced by Rhizobium on the *Sesbania sesban* affect fertility of soils as well as the fixation of nitrogen in soils.[6, 7]

Conclusion

The ancient Egyptians used legumes in their diet from the earliest times. This kind of food was nutritious and contributed to their good health. Teri Tucker, an American anthropologist, obtained these results by examining and studying 63 skeletons from the same cemetery.[8] This means that the ancient Egyptian made this botanical offering to the dead for more than one reason: for food for the deceased and to enable them to make fishing-nets in the next world.

Animal Burials

The ancient Egyptian loved many animals and had an acute knowledge of their characteristics. In ancient Egypt there were many sacred animals. The religious beliefs and concepts related to sacred animals developed during the earlier (primitive) Prehistoric Period. Our visual source of information about this subject is supplemented by varied textual material from early times, and of course by the physical remains of the animals themselves recovered from archaeological excavations, sometimes prepared for eternity as mummies.[9]

Cattle

The ancient Egyptians domesticated cattle very early on. The earliest archaeological evidence has been found in the Western Desert. Zoologists agree that the Egyptian domesticated cattle (*Bos taurus*) goes back to 9400–9000 BP.[10]

Egyptologists and all those interested in Egyptology are very well acquainted with the myth of Osiris and Isis and their son Horus. Through the course of Egyptian civilization, religious beliefs and concepts developed, and the events of this mythical story have been written down several times.[11] The myth tells us many events that happened in different places in Egypt; one of the important ones took place in the swamps of the Delta, where Isis hid her son Horus. In this part of the myth we know the important role the goddess Hathor (the cow) played in protecting and caring for Horus.

The Burials

In the Kafr Hassan Dawood cemetery, archaeologists discovered several child burials in separate areas; in the northern area of the cemetery three cows were found buried with them. In one case, a skeleton of a cow and a skeleton of a child about 5–6 years old were found. The child was arranged in the position of suckling the breast of the cow. (fig. 3)

Figure 3

Discussion

The archaeologists disagree about the dating of these burials; some of them believe they belong to the Predynastic Period, and saw this as evidence of sanctifying the goddess Hathor; others believed they dated to the Twenty-sixth Dynasty or the Greco-Roman Period. However, if we restudy the other prehistoric sites discovered before, we will find the following:

1) In the Badarian culture, many animals were discovered wrapped in linen as mummies, among them there are cows. Vandier believed that the interest in, and caring for cows by Badarian people was the start of sanctifying of the goddess Hathor.[12]

2) In the Naqada culture many examples of black-topped pottery were discovered. The lateral sides of the top of one of the pots has the shape of a cow-head with long horns and two human arms offering a breast. Jequier suggested that these lateral forms represent the symbol of goddess *Nbw*—the old name of the goddess Hathor.[13]

3) On the other hand, in the Kafr Hassan Dawood cemetery, about 1,000 skeletons, not including child skeletons, were discovered. Especially in the Prehistoric Period, child burials were placed inside/between the houses, as they were in the Merimde culture and Helwan I,[14] or were buried with their mothers.[15]

4) The myth of Osiris and Isis was closely related to the East Delta region and the province of Buto, which is near Kafr Hassan Dawood.

5) In the Dynastic Period we have some representative statues having the same form—the goddess Hathor in the form of a cow and the infant king suckling (e.g., Thutmose III and Psamtik I, in the Egyptian Museum).

Conclusion

In my opinion, the burials of children and cows in Kafr Hassan Dawood belong to the Predynastic

Period. This case not only represents the sanctifying of the goddess Hathor but also represents the original form and early manifestation of this myth. I can add that the Egyptians buried their children with cows which were considered as substitute mothers in the other world.

The Jackal

In ancient Egyptian civilization, the jackal was the symbol of the god Anubis. In Ancient Egyptian religion, Anubis represents the god of the cemetery and protector of the dead.

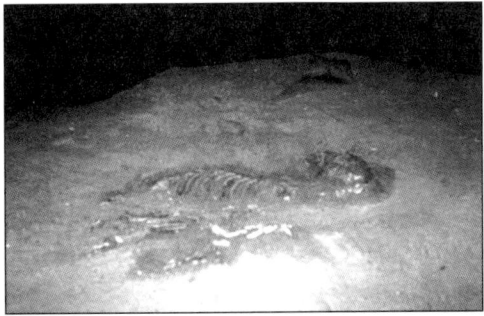

Figure 4

Adolf Erman suggested that Anubis originated in Middle Egypt, and became the god of the dead from Old Kingdom times onward.[16] Anubis was worshiped in Middle Egypt (province 12 Lycompolis, east Assiyut, and province 17, Cynopolis, (now called Alkis near al-Minya).[17]

During the dynastic period, Anubis was the essential god of mummification, and featured in the judgment of the dead, as in Chapter 125 of the Book of the Dead.[18]

The Burial

In Kafr Hassan Dawood a skeleton of a jackal was discovered in the northern part of the cemetery. It was was buried on a small hill about one meter above the human burials. (fig. 4).

Results and Discussion

It is not possible to determine the date when the ancient Egyptians started to sanctify the jackal as a symbol of the god Anubis. We are also unable to determine when Anubis became the god of the cemetery. Erman hypothesized it was in middle Egypt, during the Old Kingdom.

After the discovery of the Kafr Hassan Dawood cemetery we can refute this old hypothesis. We can also assume that the ancient Egyptians sanctified the jackal as the god of the cemetery very early, at least from the Predynastic Period onward, not only in Middle Egypt but also in the East Delta.

Conclusion

Ancient Egyptian beliefs and concepts started very early, in the Prehistoric Period. The newly discovered sites in the Delta shed light on this time. The physical remains of animals provide us with facts about the religious beliefs and gods in the Delta from the earliest times.

Notes:

1 W. El-Saadawi, "Lectures on Palaeobotany and Fossil Plants of Egypt for Geologists," (unpublished lecture notes form Ain Shams University, Cairo, 1997), 53, 54.

2 El-Saadawi, "Lectures," 58, 59.

3 El-Saadawi, "Lectures," 57.

4 S. Abrahim, *Plants of Ancient Egypt*, Academy of Scientific Research and Technology (Cairo, 1998) (in Arabic), 15.

5 Abrahim, *Plants,* 16, 17.

6 B. Dreyfus and Y. Dommergues, "Glomus fasciculatum alleviates transplantation shock of micropropagated *Sesbania* sesban," *FEMS Microbiological Letters* 10 (1981), 313–317.

7 H. Saint Macary, *et al.*, "Inorganic fertilizer enrichment of soil: effect on decompotision of plant litter under subhumid tropical conditions," *Philippine Journal of Crop Science* 10 (1985), 17–20.

8 T. Tucker, "Biocultural Investigation at Kafr Hassan Dawood," (paper presented at the Human Remains Workshop, Quantara, Egypt, April 2000).

9 P. Houlihan, *The Animal World of the Pharaohs* (Cairo, 1996), 2, 10.

10 C. Reed, *Archaeozoological Studies in the Near East*, 105 (Chicago, 1983), 527.

11 A. Erman, *The Religion of Ancient Egypt*, 2nd ed., translated by Abd Almanam Abu-Bakr (Cairo, 1997), 80–82.

12 A. Saleh, *Ancient Egyptian Culture and its Antiquities* 1 (Cairo, 1980) (in Arabic), 119, 120.

13 Saleh, *Ancient Egyptian Culture,* 137, 138.

14 Saleh, *Ancient Egyptian Culture,* 96, 102.

15 Saleh, *Ancient Egyptian Culture*, 99, 108.

16 Erman, *Religion*, 51.

17 J. Černy, *Ancient Egyptian Religion*, trans. by Ahmad Khadry (Cairo, 1987) (in Arabic), 227.

18 Erman, *Religion*, 256.

Polish–Egyptian Archaeological Activities in West Saqqara

Karol Myśliwiec

Polish Academy of Sciences and Warsaw University, Poland

In 1987, the Polish Center for Mediterranean Archaeology of Warsaw University made a geophysical survey of the desert area extending westwards from the Djoser pyramid enclosure and including the hill which runs southwards from the mastaba of Ptahhotep, comprising in total, the area between this tomb's latitude in the north and that of the Unis pyramid in the south.[1] This survey was followed by three trial pits (*ca.* 5 x 5 m each) which showed the area contained many tombs and burials dating from the Old Kingdom to the Byzantine Periods.[2]

Upon resuming this work in 1996 jointly with the Supreme Council for Egyptian Antiquities, the Mission concentrated its activities around trial pit no.1, located almost on the westward extension of the pyramid's east–west axis. Remains of constructions and objects dateable to the beginning of the Old Kingdom, were unearthed in 1987.[3] This pit was located *ca.* 120 m west of the western edge of the pyramid of Netjerikhet. In 1997, a small funerary chapel hewn in a rock shelf running north–south *ca.* 110 m west of the pyramid was found (fig. 1).[4] It belongs to a previously unknown vizier with three names: Meref-nebef, Unis-ankh, and Fefi. All of these names are found in his "ideal biography," an inscription forming the upper register on the chapel's façade.[5] The titles of the deceased and the decoration of the chapel suggest he lived during the reign of Teti, but he may have become a vizier late in his career, possibly after this king's death.[6]

The vizier and his tomb are unusual in many respects. At the moment of discovery, the chapel was found to be blocked with a huge agglomeration of mud bricks fallen from the superstructure. Parts are still preserved *in situ* over the chapel's architrave.[7] This superstructure was a mud-brick wall enclosing a kind of mastaba with a 14.5 m deep shaft in its northern part. The space between the wall and the shaft was filled with stone rubble, mostly flint, apparently the debris from hewing the shaft. It appears that the collapse of the front (western) wall occurred all at one time, and not necessarily from natural causes. Below the normal strata of fallen mud brick there is a stratum of regularly laid stones that seems to indicate an attempt to block the façade of the chapel. The latter was found filled, only in its lower part, with a mixture of mud brick, soil, and pottery. The façade was similarly filled to the ceiling of the entrance recess. Many fragments of pottery of ritual use were found in the fill, but none could be dated to later than Old Kingdom. This implies the chapel became inaccessible shortly after the death of the vizier and was never penetrated until our discovery.

The tomb's façade is a rectangular niche hewn in a rock shelf running north–south and parallel to the west side of the Step Pyramid. The long eastern wall of the niche bears a sophisticated decoration in three registers (fig. 2). Below the red-painted ceiling connecting this wall with an outer "lintel," is a long inscription in four lines. Each line ends with one of the three vizier's names.[8] A version of an "ideal biography," this inscription is carved in sunk relief, and the hieroglyphic signs, preserving fragments of their original blue-green filling, are reminiscent of the Pyramid Texts.[9] In every respect they contrast with those in the middle register of the decoration. This is a long "address to the living," composed in vertical columns and carved in raised relief. Parts of this text are badly damaged, mainly due to the extreme friability of the muddy limestone extant in this part of Saqqara. The lower register contains eight large-sized representations of the vizier striding toward the entrance, disposed symmetrically on both parts of the wall (fig. 2).

The paint in the chapel is much better preserved than in other tombs of the same period. There are many classic scenes,[10] and also some unusual ones. The number of women the vizier describes as wives is surprising, and it is unique that the four wives accompanying the vizier in several scenes are represented as a quartet of harpists. This is the case of the large scene of female dancers decorating the chapel's southern wall (fig. 3) where the vizier appears in the company of another lady whose name and title have unfortunately vanished. The relationship between the vizier and still another of his consorts, named Meres-ankh, who is represented without any title, is obscure. The representations of his sons are very indicative of the atmosphere within the fam-

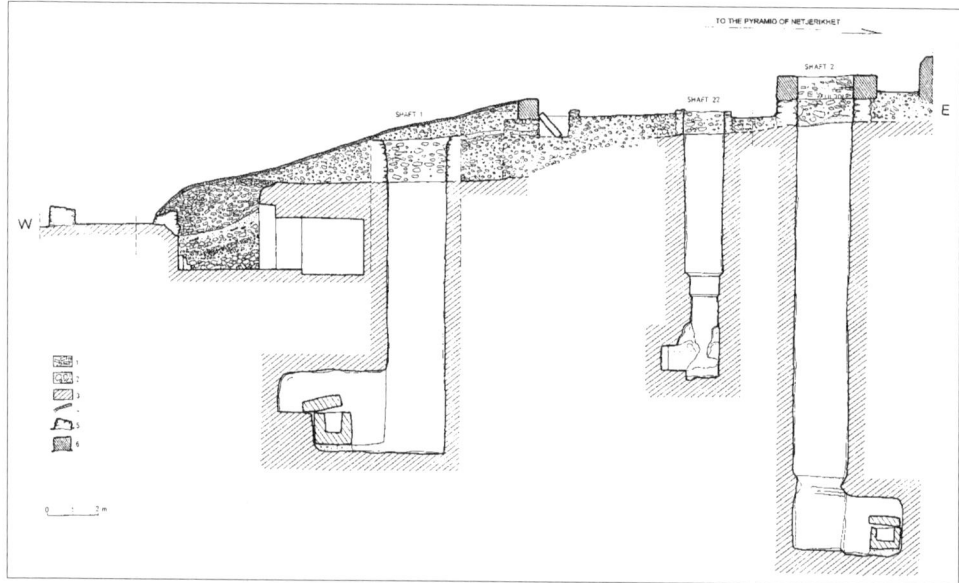

Fig. 1: East–west cross section of the area excavated in 1987 (trial pit I) and 1996–1998 west of the Djoser pyramid, showing the funerary chapel of Meref-nebef (early Sixth Dynasty) and shafts of late Old Kingdom mastabas.

Drawing: Marek Puszkarski.

ily, particularly after the vizier's death. All of them have been hammered out, except for those depicting a son bearing the father's name, Fefi. He was doubtless the winner in a conflict that must have ravaged the family. Those conflicts may have been one of the reasons why the tomb was never completed. The construction of a smaller chapel to adjoin that of Fefi on its southern side was abandoned just after the hewing of the entrance was begun. An additional small chapel was erected, probably at the end of the Old Kingdom, for the posthumous cult of vizier, at the eastern section of the wall surrounding the shaft.[11]

Another reason for the tomb's unfinished state may have been the political and social environment; the turbulent times may have affected the vizier's career. The extremely poor quality of the rock could also have contributed to the tomb's abandonment: permanent problems faced by the decorators of the chapel are evidenced by the multiple gypsum and mortar repairs to level uneven wall surfaces. As well, pieces of stone were inserted to complete the decoration in various areas.

Given the unfinished state of the tomb, the question arises as to whether the vizier was ever buried here. The only shaft visibly connected with his chapel, the one on the eastern side, is in an unusual location: 70 cm behind the chapel's northeastern corner. The limestone coffin found in the burial chamber was empty. Its roughly sculpted sides, as well the walls of the chamber itself, bear no traces of any decoration. It remains an open question, therefore, whether the shaft was hewn for Meref-nebef or was just an earlier structure later incorporated into the vizier's mastaba. It is also debatable whether his body was ever deposited in the coffin.

The extremely friable rock is a great challenge to the Polish conservators working on the reliefs and paintings of the chapel. Samples of rock, mortar, and pigments were examined in order to define the most appropriate methods of conservation.[12] Their work was complicated by the rock's extremely high saline content, which has a tendency to collect on the decorated surfaces. In order to secure durable protection for the chapel with the aim of creating a microclimate to stabilize climatic conditions inside, a solid shelter of stone blocks with ventilation holes was built above the chapel in 1999.[13] It also protects the remains of the tomb's mud-brick superstructure, which are still preserved *in situ*.

Further excavations, carried out from 1998–1999, extended our research in two directions: east, toward the Step Pyramid, and west, toward the desert. The aim was to obtain a broad cross-section of the area extending from the Step Pyramid to the western section of the alleged "dry moat."[14] We expected the

Fig. 2: Funerary chapel of Meref-nebef: North end of the façade with polychrome decoration in three registers. Missing parts of the inscription on the "outer lintel" (top of the photograph) were repaired in gypsum.
Photo: Stefan Sadowski, Polish Center of Mediterranean Archaeology, Warsaw University.

moat to be found in the longitudinal depression that runs on a north-south axis to the west of the Step Pyramid enclosure.

A dense agglomeration of shafts belonging to mud-brick mastabas of the late Sixth Dynasty and perhaps also the early First Intermediate Period fills the area between the rock shelf containing the tomb of Meref-nebef and the Step Pyramid.[15] These mastabas were so close together that some partly crossed over each other, revealing subsequent phases of use. Each mastaba had a narrow oblong chapel orientated north-south and bordered with a recessed mud-brick wall. Niches in western sections of these walls usually housed false doors of limestone. Not all were inscribed

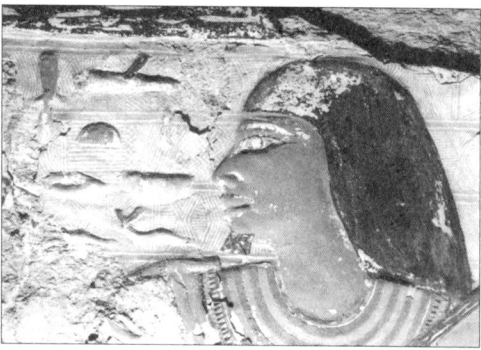

Fig. 3: Meref-nebef watching dancing girls in a large scene decorating the chapel's southern wall.
Photo: Zbigniew Kość, Polish Center of Mediterranean Archaeology, Warsaw University.

and only one was found *in situ*. It belongs to a Peh-en-Ptah, whose titles are not preserved.[16] Other stelae of this kind were found lying in the secondary filling of various shafts. Two priestesses of Hathor are named, Djesti and Kheti,[17] as well as various high officials including Ni-Pepy[18] and Teti-ankh.[19] The stela of Teti-ankh is the only one merely painted, while the others bear inscriptions and representations in sunk relief.

Each chapel adjoins a compound of one or more shafts, constituting the mastaba's western part. The superstructure of the shafts was built of bricks or stones. The space between the shafts and the girdle wall was filled with rubble made up of bricks, pottery, and other matter. A slight inclination of the upper part of some walls suggests the mastabas could have been domed.

The Old Kingdom structures were covered with a thick layer of pure sand, in which many burials of late, most probably Ptolemaic date, were found.[20] Most of these were simple mummies deposited in the sand or inserted into holes inside or between the walls of Old Kingdom structures. Some were wrapped in painted cartonnage;[21] a few were lying in wooden or terracotta coffins.[22]

The simplest burials consisted of just a skeleton wrapped in a mat, or placed in a depression bordered with reused mud bricks or stones.[23] These poor burials contain only exceptionally small objects like amulets or necklace beads.[24] Their dating is based on pottery found with the burials and the style of the painted decoration on the well-preserved cartonnage and wooden coffins. Some fragments of imported and stamped Greek amphorae were found in this stratum as well.

A large, unusual structure has been unearthed in the upper stratum in the southeast part of the excavated area close to the western wall of the Step Pyramid enclosure. It was composed of a large, long wall running north-south and some smaller perpendicular

Fig. 4: List of offerings above the offering table in the scene decorating the southern part of the chapel's western wall.
Photo: Zbigniew Kość, Polish Center of Mediterranean Archaeology, Warsaw University.

ones made of reused limestone blocks, doubtless originally belonging to the pyramid's west enclosure wall. In spite of their monumental appearance, the walls were simply built on a layer of pure sand without any foundations.[25] Further to the east, this structure includes a broad platform built of one layer of mud bricks set on a high bed of sand overlain with mud.[26] Extending further toward the pyramid, this enigmatic construction betrays hasty work aimed at creating an imposing building for ritual use.

In 1999, the excavation of a trial pit more than 30 m long west of the tomb of Meref-nebef (i.e., toward the alleged "dry moat"), brought a surprising discovery: An Old Kingdom shaft hewn in the rock was found to have a hole in its northern wall, providing a view into a long subterranean corridor running west–east, directly toward the Step Pyramid. Filled with sand almost up to the ceiling, this corridor was the subject of our research in the 2000 campaign.

This long trial pit has also revealed the terrace-like structure of this area, as well as the remains of stone and mud brick structures connected with the terraces. These are not natural, but rock-cut, although they do not run in a perfectly straight north–south line.[27] Also here the upper stratum contains many burials of Ptolemaic date, mainly mummies with or without cartonnage. It seems to be a specific feature of the stratigraphy in this part of Saqqara that Old Kingdom structures in the lower strata frequently coincide with undisturbed burials of Ptolemaic date lying almost directly above them. There are no traces of any activity during the two millennia separating these two chronological extremities of Pharaonic Egypt. Should the secondary burials be understood as a sign of respect for a particularly important part of the royal necropolis, or, contrarily, a sign of neglect? Why had this part of Saqqara become so "fashionable" in the Ptolemaic Period? These are just some of many questions that only systematic excavations in the area west of the Step Pyramid will be able to answer.

Notes:

1 J. Leclant, G. Clère, "Fouilles et Travaux en Egypte et au Soudan," *Or* 57 (1988), 329 (n); K. Myśliwiec, T. Herbich, with a contribution by A. Niwiński, "Polish Research at Saqqara in 1987," *Etudes et Travaux* 17 (1995), 177–203.

2 K. Myśliwiec *et al.*, *Etudes et Travaux* 17 (1995), 186–203.

3 K. Myśliwiec *et al.*, *Etudes et Travaux* 17 (1995), 186–195. For the 1996 campaign, see K. Myśliwiec, "Saqqara, Excavations 1996," *PAM* VIII (1997), 103–109.

4 "Saqqara, Excavations 1997," *PAM* IX (1998), 90–99; K. Myśliwiec, "A New Mastaba, A New Vizier," *Egyptian Archaeology* 13 (1998), 37–39; K. Myśliwiec, "Vizir de Saqqara, " *L'Archéologue, Archéologie Nouvelle*, 42, (juin-juillet, 1999), 47–49; K. Myśliwiec, "Le vizir retrouvé de Saqqara," *Le monde de la Bible* 115, (novembre-décembre, 1998), 74; Z. Szafrański, "Nieznany wezyr króla Teti; w cieniu najstarszej piramidy świata," *Archeologia Żywa* 1 (Warsaw, 1998), 2–8.

5 K. Myśliwiec, *New Faces of Saqqara-Recent Discoveries in West Saqqara* (Tuchów 1999), pl. 27 b; *Nowe oblicza Sakkary-rewelacyjne odkrycia polskich archeologów w Egipcie* (Tuchów, 1998), (Polish version of the previous publication), pl. 27 b.

6 K. Myśliwiec and K. Kuraszkiewicz, "Recent Polish-Egyptian Excavations in West Saqqara," *Abusir and*

Saqqara in the Year 2000, Archiv Orientalni Supplementa (ed. by M. Bárta and Y. Krejči) (Prague, 2000) 499–508.

7 K. Myśliwiec, "New Faces" pls. 16, 17, 18, 22–24, 26.

8 See n. 5.

9 For a facsimile of the text see "Nowe odkrycia przy najstarszej piramidzie świata," *Świat Nauki* 8 (1999), 32–35 (Polish edition of *Scientific American*). This article has also been published in the German; ("Meref-nebef: Berater des Pharaos, *Spektrum der Wissenschaft*," (December, 1999), 54–60, Italian ("Saqqara: una tomba piena di misteri," *Le Scienze* 337 (2000), 76–85), French ("La découverte d'un vizir," *Pour la Science,* (avril, 2000), 34–41), Greek ("O Tafos tou Archierea tou Farao," *Elliniki Ekdosi* (January, 2000), 51–60) and Japanese, "The newly-discovered Tomb hidden behind the world's oldest pyramid," *Nikei Science,* 30, 8 (2000) 48–58, editions of *Scientific American,* but only some of them repeat the facsimile of the inscription. For translation of the text (into Polish) see, "Aleja zasłużonych po zachodniej stronie najstarszej piramidy–odkrycia w Sakkarze," *Meander* 3 (1998), 239–243.

10 K. Myśliwiec, "Five Wives & A Girlfriend," *Discovering Archaeology,* (July/August, 1999), 54–67; "New Faces" pls. 28–52.

11 K. Myśliwiec, "Nowe odkrycia przy," 28–29; K. Myśliwiec, "Saqqara. Excavations 1998," *PAM* X (1999), 84, fig. 2–3; K. Kuraszkiewicz, "False-door stele of Meref-nebef," *PAM* X, 101–105; K. Myśliwiec and K. Kuraszkiewicz, "Recent Polish-Egyptian Excavations," 501, figs. 1, 2.

12 Z. Godziejewski, "Conservation work in the funerary chapel of Meref-nebef," *PAM* X (1999), 97–100; "Conservation Work," *PAM* XI (2000), 107–108.

13 K. Myśliwiec, "West Saqqara 1999," *PAM* XI, (2000), 90, fig. 1.

14 N. Swelim, "The Dry Moat of the Netjerykhet Complex," in John Baines, T.G.H. James, Anthony Leahy and A. F. Shore, (eds.), *Pyramid Studies and Other Esseys Presented to I.E.S. Edwards* (London, 1988), 12–22.

15 Cf. the reports of the author in *PAM* X (1999), 85–87, and *PAM* XI (2000), 91–96; "Five wives," 57; "West Saqqara 1999: Polish-Egyptian Mission," *ASAE (in press).*

16 K. Myśliwiec, *PAM* XI (2000), 92–93, fig. 1.

17 Myśliwiec, "Vizir de Saqqara," 48; "West Saqqara. Excavations, 1998," *PAM* X (1999), 87 (fig. 6); K. Myśliwiec and K. Kuraszkiewicz, "Two more Old Kingdom Priestesses of Hathor in Saqqara," *Les Civilisations du Bassin Méditerranéen. Hommage à Joachim Śliwa* (Cracovie, 2000), 145–153.

18 K. Kuraszkiewicz, "Two Fragments of false-door of Ni-Pepy from West Saqqara," *Etudes et Travaux* XIX *(in press).*

19 K. Myśliwiec, *PAM* X (1999), 87–88, fig. 7.

20 K. Myśliwiec "New Faces," pl. 4; K. Myśliwiec, "Nowe odkrycia," 31 (upper photo); K. Myśliwiec "Five Wives," 56, 60–61.

21 K. Myśliwiec, "New Faces," pls. 6–10; K. Myśliwiec," Five Wives," 58.

22 K. Myśliwiec "New Faces," pls. 4–7; K. Myśliwiec, "Five Wives," 58.

23 K. Myśliwiec, "New Faces," pl. 11; K. Myśliwiec, "Nowe odkrycia przy," 31, upper photo.

24 K. Myśliwiec, "New Faces," pl. 12.

25 K. Myśliwiec, "New Faces," pls. 19, 20, 22, 23.

26 K. Myśliwiec, *PAM* XI (2000), 95–96, fig. 5.

27 For stratigraphy and geology of the excavated area, see: Z. Szafrański, "Observations on Stratigraphy–Northwestern part of Area I/ E-F (former Pit I/E-F)," *PAM* X (1999), 91–96; E. Mycielska-Dowgiałło, Z. E. Szafrański, B. Woronko, "Reconstruction of morphodynamic processes during the last 4700 year period in archaeological site (Area I) at Saqqara (Egypt)," *Geoarqueologia I, Quaternari Litoral, Memorial Maria Pilar Fumanal, Universitat de València, Departament de Geografia* (1999),

167–178; A. Ćwiek, "Preliminary Remarks on the Stratigraphy of West Saqqara," *PAM* XI (2000), 109–117; E. Mycielska-Dowgiałło, B. Woronko, "Genetic-climatic Interpretation of Mineral Deposits Uncovered in Section N and Sections Perpendicular to It," *PAM* X (1999) 107–112.

Malkata, Site K:
The Aegean-Related Motifs in the Painted Decoration of a Demolished Building of Amenhotep III

Margarita Nicolakaki-Kentrou
University of Cambridge

In the vicinity of the royal building complex of Amenhotep III at Malkata, Western Thebes, lies Site K. This is a heap of about four and a half to five meters high, adjacent to the northwestern side of the ancient spoil mounds surrounding the artificial lake of Birket Habu.[1] It was initially investigated by Georges Daressy in 1888,[2] and was relocated in the early 1970s by the Pennsylvania University Museum Expedition directed by David O'Connor and Barry Kemp. The partial excavations of the 1973 season uncovered a thick layer of rubble filled with mud bricks, often stamped with the names of Amenhotep III and Tiye, sherds, mud jar-sealings from amphorae, pieces of mud from the roof of a building, and fragments of painted wall plaster. Site K was thus identified as a dump for the actual structure and contents of a grand building of Amenhotep III, which was built specifically for the purposes of the king's First Jubilee Festival, and was later demolished for the expansion of the Birket Habu basin.[3]

Throughout Site K's secondary deposit, approximately 800 fragments of painted mud plaster, for the most part small and friable, were distributed. The bulk of them appears to have derived from walls, or at least from a mud-brick surface, and perhaps, to a lesser extent, from ceilings. So far their study—still at a preliminary stage—has relied solely on color reproductions drawn by the expedition's artist, Lillian Concordia, supplemented, wherever possible, by on-the-spot photographs of the material.[4] The overall character of the surviving compositions seems to be purely Egyptian, in terms of subject matter, style, and technique, implying the Egyptian identity of the artists engaged. Most identified geometric and figurative elements, rich in human, animal, and plant figures, seem to have originated from scenes of two main iconographic cycles:

a. Compositions of tribute offering, foreign captives, and the theme of abundance serving the royal propagandistic policy; and

b. Nature scenes inspired from hunting or wild animal life.[5]

What strikes the student of this material first, is the fact that among the designs of indisputable Egyptian identity lies a limited, but significant, number of motifs totally alien to the indigenous iconography, some having absolutely no precedent in the tradition of Egyptian art. However, these designs are paralleled in motifs rooted in the artistic creation of the contemporary civilizations of the Aegean. In an attempt to unveil this, a portion of the color copies of the most representative and better-preserved fragments has been selected and sorted into three categories:[6]

1. Rosette Terrain (Pl. 1, figs. A–E)

No less than 50 of the fragments in question bear figurative or geometric elements combined with dotted rosettes on either brown-red or bright blue backgrounds. Among them, those deriving from costumes of Syrians or Nubians are easily recognizable.[7] On certain pieces, though, these stylized flowers are found associated with plants, animals in motion and at least one human in such a way as to designate the setting, a blossoming terrain, upon which the action unfolds.

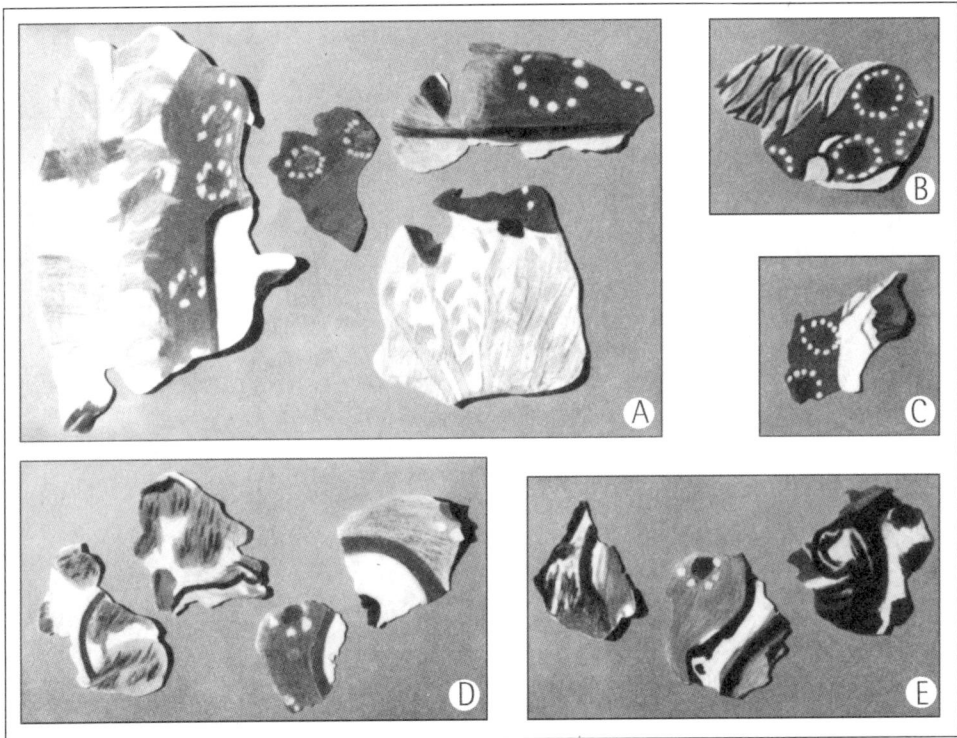

Plate 1: Facsimiles of painted mud-plaster fragments of hunting or wild animal life scene(s) on rosette-filled ground of brown-red color (except from 1D).

A: Landscape elements.

B: Lion's mane and fore paw.

C: Face of brown-red human figure.

D: Parts of the head, neck, and body of a brown-white bovine, possibly associated with clumps of papyri, against bright blue rosette-filled background.

E: Parts of the head, hind leg, and tail's end of a black-and-white leaping calf.

Pl. 1.A: The undulating edge of the brown-red field in the largest fragment shown implies the irregularity of the terrain that borders an area of white background upon which low leafy or bushy vegetation is painted.

Pl. 1.B and Fig. 1: The lower part of the rich and long mane of an impressively well-executed lion figure is formed with successive rows of yellow flame-like designs, finely outlined in black. Part of its inverted forepaw with a white, slightly hooked, claw has also been preserved. The paw's position in relation to the mane can only be justified on the assumption that the forelegs of the animal are shown bent. In Aegean as well as Egyptian hunting scenes, such is the usual rendering of subdued animals.[8] But in Egyptian art figures of subdued lions with their legs bent are rarely depicted. The few surviving examples are only slightly later in date, best represented on the painted scene on Tutankhamun's wooden chest.[9] On the contrary, defeated lions in dramatic postures have been preserved in Mycenaean renderings from as early as the mid-sixteenth century BCE, especially on minor works of art. The figure of a wounded lion on a golden cylinder seal from Grave Circle A at Mycenae[10] has been used to demonstrate the possible posture of the Site K animal and the proposed position of the fragment.

Fig. 1: Proposed posture of the lion in Plate 1.B based on the representation of a wounded animal on a golden cylinder seal from Grave Circle A at Mycenae.

Pl. 1.C: The preserved face of a human figure, presumably a hunter, headed towards the terrain, is remarkable for the fine, highly aesthetic outlines. The red preliminary sketch lines are still visible.

Pl. 1.D: A brown-white bovine is drawn against a bright-blue rosette-filled background, slightly preserved below the animal's muzzle. The clumps of papyri recall the bull scene from the North Waiting Room of Malkata Palace.[11] The bright-blue background is unusual for an Egyptian wall painting,[12] whereas vivid sky-blue backgrounds distinguish a great number of Aegean fresco compositions often including figures of bulls, the most distinct example being the "Bull-leaping fresco" from Knossos.[13]

Pl. 1.E and Fig. 2: A black-and-white leaping calf is rather crudely executed. Its reconstruction is based on the analogous figure in Malkata's Main Palace,[14] but the head is apparently depicted reversed, as in equivalent renderings from Amarna.[15]

Fig. 2: Reconstruction of the leaping calf in Plate 1.E.

Among Egyptian works of art there exists no visual evidence of a rosette-filled, undulating terrain serving as the background for hunting or wild animal life compositions. Paradoxically enough, merely a written record of such a rendering from the Audience Hall of the King's Palace at Malkata has come down to us through Daressy's report.[16] In Minoan and Mycenaean art, on the other hand, the dot-rosette motif is frequently seen in several variations as a filling ornament on the background of scenes of animal life. The "Partridges Frieze" from the "Caravanserai" in the wider area of the Palace at Knossos arises as the best fresco parallel.[17] Other close parallels lie among the animal-life scenes painted on a series of Mycenaean figurative vases, found widely spread in Cyprus and Syro-Palestine from the early fourteenth century BCE.[18] Although their

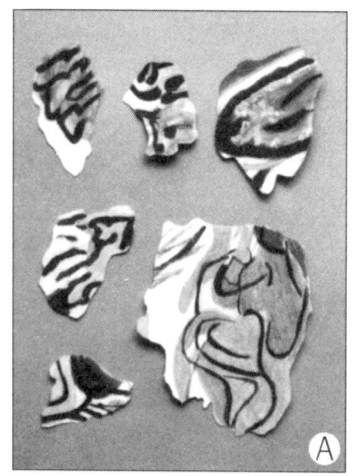

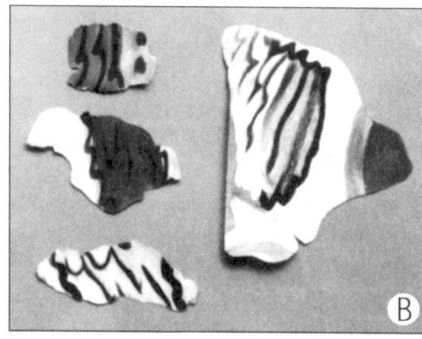

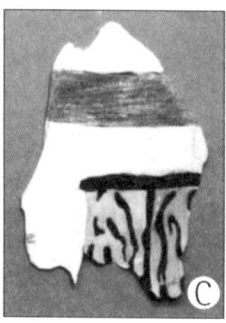

Plate 2:

A: Facsimiles of painted mud-plaster fragments of multicolored rocky formations.

B: Facsimiles of painted mud-plaster fragments of multicolored rocky formations.

C: Facsimile of marbling imitation fragment.

presence in Egypt is not archaeologically attested, the probability of their importation should not be ignored. An additional medium of the motif's diffusion should be looked for in textiles, a trading commodity of principal importance, but which is highly perishable.[19] The distribution of Aegean textiles in Egypt is manifested in the paintings of Menkheperresonb's tomb where Cretan envoys are shown carrying rolls of tasseled cloth.[20] The popularity of the dot-rosette motif in Minoan and Mycenaean fabric decoration is imprinted on the colorful garments worn by human figures in the frescoes like the Knossian "Cupbearer."[21]

At this point, one should also bear in mind the analogy between Site K's rosette terrain and Tell al-Dab'a's bull-leaping tableaux, where, in place of the dot-rosette pattern, the labyrinth or maze pattern, another typical Minoan motif, serves as the background for the animals in motion.[22]

2. Rockwork (Pl. 2.A–B)

The second group of Aegean-related fragments, about a dozen in number, comprises irregular, adjoining fields of red, blue, and yellow color on white ground. Their surface is covered with black striations and sinuous or crooked lines, mostly interweaving, usually in random order. On some fragments they are depicted in conjunction with floral motifs. These exact characteristics cannot be paralleled by any known figurative or non-figurative representations of ancient Egyptian art whatsoever. Serious analogies can again be detected in a multitude of artistic works from the Aegean, in which the mountains and craggy rocks dominating the Helladic landscape are conventionally rendered with asymmetrical, polychromatic fields covered with freehand lines in the form of striations or loops.[23] The designs in Pl. 2.A reflect the impressionistic spirit and vividness emerging from the rocky elevations in Cretan and Theran murals, such as the nature scenes from the House of the Frescoes at Knossos[24] or the Spring Fresco and the Miniature Frieze from Akrotiri.[25] The fragments in Pl. 2.B feature a stricter arrangement of the fields, clear and precise outlines, and highly stylized striations. These recall the austerity and stillness of Mycenaean renderings of the rockwork motif manifested, for example, in the Groom Fresco from Mycenae or the Bluebird Frieze from Pylos.[26]

A few adaptations of the variant Aegean rockwork motif are present in early New Kingdom art, the hanging isolated arcs on Ahmose's dagger being the most distinct.[27] Similar depictions, including irregular, trapezoidal or oval rocks in red and blue, although without striations, have also been identified in the Tell al-Dab'a material.[28]

3. Marbling (Pl. 3.C)

The last category, represented by a single piece originating from a corner mud brick, displays great morphological resemblance to the previous category. The dominant motif consists of two adjoining, rectangular, clearly defined fields of yellow and blue color, covered with black, asymmetrical, and randomly arranged striations. The clarity in shape and strict boundaries of the design imply an association with marbling, a motif of Minoan origin, imitating in paint the veining of luxurious orthostats of alabaster or gypsum, positioned along the bases of walls.[29] The marbling of these rocks is rendered on dado or border decoration in a great range of colors, shapes, and varieties, as evident in plentiful compositions from Crete and Thera[30] as well as the Mycenaean world.[31]

The great popularity of the marbling motif among the royal courts of the Eastern Mediterranean is conspicuous by its presence in the palaces of Mari,[32] Kabri,[33] Qatna,[34] and Alalakh, Level IV.[35] Site K's representation is the first marbling specimen to be recorded in Egypt. Yet it is not regarded as unique, since another example is believed to have survived among the Tell al-Dab'a findings. To be more specific, a set of fragments identified as depicting parts of a bull's coat[36] seems more comprehensible when juxtaposed against polychrome imitations of orthostat slabs from the Aegean. Their resemblance to the marbling panels from the West House at Akrotiri is indeed striking.[37]

The mechanisms of the artistic transference of Site K's Aegean motifs could be further elucidated if one crucial factor is born in mind: the chromatic code of red-blue-yellow applied to rockwork representations is met exclusively on fresco decoration in the Aegean. Monumental painting should thus be regarded as the principal agent of inspiration for the Malkata artists. Consequently their presupposed visual contact with the prototype material could have only been accomplished in its locus of origin. The high Egyptian toponymic, geographic, and politico-economic knowledge of the Aegean area under Amenhotep III, mirrored in finds from both regions,[38] has formed the theory of the consignment of one or more official Egyptian embassies to major trading posts in the Aegean.[39] The Site K evidence, demonstrating a considerable Egyptian familiarity with the artistic heritage of the Aegean, works in favor of this hypothesis. Given the accustomed exchange of artists between the royal courts of the Bronze Age Eastern Mediterranean[40] it would be reasonable to assume the partaking of palatial craftsmen in such a conceivable Egyptian mission. Thus, the Aegean motifs incorporated in the decoration of Amenhotep III's First Jubilee building may have been executed by Egyptian artists who had the opportunity to visit some of the Aegean palaces and to witness and study their highly esteemed monumental paintings.

Nevertheless, given the aforementioned correlation between the paintings from Site K and those from Tell al-Dab'a, we are also faced with another likelihood: the adaptation of a tradition-based iconographic program, possibly maintained through "pattern-books,"[41] rooted in the amplification of Minoan cultural expansion into Ahmose's Egypt. Although the chain of artistic continuity in the Egyptian palatial architecture has suffered serious losses, the presence of various Aegean motifs in the decoration of the three main domestic royal structures surviving from the Eighteenth Dynasty in Tell al-Dab'a, Malkata, and Amarna, gives credence to this possibility, too.

Out of the restrictions set by the source material itself and our limited comprehension of Egypto-Aegean interconnections during the Bronze Age, arise great difficulties in any scholarly attempt to give satisfactory answers to the emerging questions. It is hoped and believed that prospective research and future discoveries will reduce the perplexity of this field of cross-cultural studies.

Notes:

1 B. J. Kemp, "The discovery of the painted plaster fragments at Malkata," in A. Καρέτσου (ed.) Κρήτη-Αίγυπτος. Πολιτισμικοί Δεσμοί Τριών Χιλιετιών, Μελέτες, (Athens, 2000), 45–46; B. J. Kemp, and D. O'Connor, "Malkata and the Birket Habu," *Journal of Nautical and Underwater Archaeology* 13 (1974), 101–36, fig. 19.

2 G. Daressy, "Les Palais d' Amenophis III et le Birket Habu," *Annales du Service des Antiquités de l' Egypte* 4, (1903), 165–70.

3 Kemp, *Discovery*, 46.

4 Kemp, *Discovery*, 46.

5 M. Nicolakaki-Kentrou, "Amenhotep III and the Aegean, New Evidence on Intimacy: The painted plaster fragments from Site K at Malkata," in A. Καρέτσου (ed.) Κρήτη-Αίγυπτος. Πολιτισμικοί Δεσμοί Τριών Χιλιετιών, Μελέτες, (Athens, 2000), 47–51, 47–48.

6 For color illustrations see A. Καρέτσου et al. (eds.) Κρήτη-Αίγυπτος. Πολιτισμικοί Δεσμοί Τριών Χιλιετιών, Κατάλογος, (Ηράκλειο, 2000) Pl. 286–288.

7 See for example, N. M. Davies, and A. H. Gardiner, *Ancient Egyptian Paintings* III (Chicago, 1936), 115, 150–151, Pl. LX, LXXIX, LXXX.

8 On lion figures in Egyptian and Aegean iconography see J. C. Crawley, *The Aegean and the East. An Investigation into the Transference of Artistic Motifs between the Aegean, Egypt and the Near East in the Bronze Age*, SIMA 51, (Jonsered, 1989), 29–32, 36–38, 134–136, 164, 171–172, 175–176; M. Lurker, *The Gods and Symbols of Ancient Egypt*, (London, 1980), 77; N. Marinatos, "Celebrations of Death and the Symbolism of the Lion Hunt," in R. Hägg. and G. C. Nordquist, (eds.), *Celebrations of Death and Divinity in the Bronze Age Argolid*, (Stockholm, 1990), 143–147; L. Morgan, *The Miniature Wall Paintings of Thera. A Study in Aegean Culture and Iconography*, (Cambridge, 1988) 44–49; L. Morgan, "Of Animals and Men, The Symbolic Parallel," in C. Morris (ed.), *Klados. Essays in Honour of J.N. Coldstream*, (London, 1995), 171–184; L. Morgan, "Power of the Beast, Human-Animal Symbolism in Egyptian and Aegean Art," *Ägypten und Levante* VII (1997), 17–31, 29–31; D. J. Osborn, and J. Osbornová, *The Mammals of Ancient Egypt*, (Warminster, 1998), 113–119.

9 Osborn and Osbornová, *Mammals*, 115–118; Davies and Gardiner, *Paintings*, 146–147, Pl. LXXVII.

10 S. Hood, *The Arts in Prehistoric Greece*, (London, 1978), fig. 228 C.

11 W. S. Smith, *The Art and Architecture of Ancient Egypt*, 2nd edition, revised by W. K. Simpson, (London, 1981), 286, fig. 281.

12 T.G.H. James, *Egyptian Painting and Drawing in the British Museum*, (London, 1985), 13; Davies and Gardiner, *Paintings*, xxxix–xl.

13 Hood, *Arts*, 65, 85, fig. 48; S. Immerwahr, *Aegean Painting in the Bronze Age*, (Pennsylvania, 1990), 91–92, 110, 122, 132, 166, Pl. 41.

14 Smith, *Art and Architecture*, 286, fig. 282.

15 On the decorated floors of Amarna in the North Harim see, W.M.F. Petrie, *Tell al Amarna*, (London, 1894), 13–4, Pl. II–IV; J.D.S. Pendlebury, *The City of Akhenaten* III, (London, 1951), 40–1; Smith, *Art and Architecture*, 286; F. Weatherhead, "Painted pavements at the Great Palace at Amarna," *JEA* 78 (1992), 179–194; in the Maru Aten see, T. E. Peet and C. L. Woolley, *The City of Akhenaten* I, (London, 1923), 118–9, Pl. XXXIV–XXXIX.

16 Daressy, *Palais d' Amenophis*, 167; Smith, *Art and Architecture*, 291.

17 A. J. Evans, *The Palace of Minos at Knossos* I–IV, I, (1921–1935), 109–116, figs. 51–54, frontispiece; Immerwahr, *Aegean Painting*, 34, 78–79, 103, 174, Pl. 30.

18 E. Vermeule and V. Karageorghis, *Mycenean Pictorial Vase Painting*, (Cambridge, 1982), 1–3, 27–28, 153, cat. entries and Pl. III.29, IV.4, IV.71.

19 E.J.W. Barber, *Prehistoric Textiles. The Development of Cloth in the Neolithic and Bronze Ages with Special Reference to the Aegean*, (Princeton, 1991), 311–312, 345–346; Crawley, *The Aegean and the East*, 247.

20 S. Wachsmann, *Aegeans in the Theban Tombs*, (Leuven, 1987), 75, Pl. XXXV–XXXIX.

21 Barber, *Textiles*, 328, fig. 15.9; Evans, *Palace of Minos* II, Pl. XII.

22 M. Bietak, "Connections Between Egypt and the Minoan World: New Results from Tell el-Dab'a/Avaris," in W. V. Davies and L. Schofield, (eds.), *Egypt, the Aegean and the Levant*, cover and Pl. 1 (ill. L. P. Brock); M. Bietak, *Avaris, the capital of the Hyksos: Recent excavations at Tell el-Dab'a*, (London, 1996), Pl. IIIa–V; M. Bietak and N. Marinatos, "The Minoan wall-paintings from Avaris," *Ägypten und Levante* 5 (1995) 49–62, 51–54, fig. 4.

23 Crawley, *The Aegean and the East*, 146–147.

24 Evans, *Palace of Minos* II, 2, 431ff., figs. 262, 264, 270, 272, 275, Pl. X–XI; III, Pl. XXII; Hood, *Arts*, 48–53, 56, figs. 27, 28, 31, 32, 50; Immerwahr, *Aegean Painting*, 42–46, 170.

25 C. Doumas, *The Wall-Paintings of Thera*, (Athens, 1992), 47–49, 100, Pl. 26, 29, 36–38, 66–70.

26 Immerwahr, *Aegean Painting*, 123–4, 141, 192, 199, Pl. 64, 81.

27 H. Kantor, "The Aegean and the Orient in the second millennium BC," *AJA* 51 (1947) 1–103, 63–66, 71, 72, 74, Pl. XXI.A, B; Smith, *Art and Architecture*, 220–222, Pl. 215.

28 N. Marinatos, "The Tell al-Dab'a paintings. A Study in Pictorial Tradition," *Ägypten und Levante* 8 (1998), 83–99, 87, figs. 2, 22, 23.

29 Crawley, *The Aegean and the East*, 149–150;

30 Doumas, *Wall-Paintings*, 46, 46, 49, figs. 14–17, 24, 49–56, 63–64; Immerwahr, *Aegean Painting*, 22, 145, 178, 180, 187, 190, 204, Pl. 41, 42, 50–52.

31 Σ. Ε. Ιακωβίδης, *Γλας* II, (Athens, 1998), 183–187, Pl. VI.a, IX; Immerwahr, *Aegean Painting*, 145, Pl. 83.

32 A. Parrot, *Mission Archéologique de Mari II. Les Palais. Peintures murales*, Institut Francais d'Archéologie de Beyruth, (1958), 67–69, Pl. XV

33 Most recent, W. D. Niemeier, and B. Niemeier, "Minoan frescoes in the Eastern Mediterranean," *Aegaeum* 18 (1998), 69–97, esp. 71–78, 2–3, Pl. V.

359

34 Du Mensil Du Buisson, *Le site archeologique de Mishrife-Qatna*, (Paris, 1935), frontispiece; W. S. Smith, *Interconnections in the Ancient Near East: A Study on the Relationships between the Arts of Egypt, the Aegean and the Western Asia*, (New Haven, 1965), fig. 31.

35 L. Woolley, *Alalakh. An account of the excavations at Tell Atchana in the Hatay, 1937–49*, (Oxford, 1955) 92, 230-2.

36 M. Bietak, "Der Friedhof in einem Palast-garten aus der Zeit des späten Mittleren Reiches und andere Forschunsergebnisse aus dem östlichen Nildelta (Tell el-Dab'a 1984–87)," *Ägypten und Levante* 2 (1991), 47–110, 52, Pl. 20C.

37 Doumas, *Wall-Paintings*, 46, 49, Pl. 14–17, 24, 49–56, 63–64.

38 For references see Nicolakaki-Kentrou, *Painted plaster fragments from Site K*, 50.

39 E. H. Cline, *Sailing the Wine-Dark Sea. International trade and the Late Bronze Age Aegean*, BAR International Series 591 (1994), 38–48; E. H. Cline, "Amenhotep III, the Aegean and Anatolia," in D. O'Connor, and E. H. Cline, (eds.) *Amenhotep III. Perspectives on His Reign*, (Ann Arbor, 1998), 236–250.

40 Crawley, *The Aegean and the East*, 254–259; C. Zaccagnini, "Patterns of Mobility Among Ancient Near Eastern Craftsmen," *Journal of Near Eastern Studies* 42, (1983), 4.

41 Wachsmann, *Aegeans*, 12–17.

Geotechnical Survey at Tell Tabilla, Northeastern Nile Delta, Egypt

L. A. Pavlish,* G. Mumford,* and A. C. D'Andrea‡

*University of Toronto, ‡Simon Fraser University

Site Location

Tell Tabilla, variously known as Tell Balala, Billi, Tell Billeh, Tell Tébilleh, Tell Tibilla, Tell Tiblah, Tell Tibla, Tell el-Débéléh, Tell Debleh, or Tell Tabilla is located at latitude 31° 3' North and longitude 31° 36' East.[1] This site is in the province of Daqahliya in the district of al-Dikirnis in the northeast Delta, about 20 kilometers east of al-Mansura and the Damietta branch of the Nile, three kilometers to the south of Dikirnis, three kilometers northeast of Tanah, and three kilometers northwest of Mit Faris (Mit Fares). Although Tell Tabilla does not appear on a 1:25,000 scale map of the Delta, it is close to Dikirnis which is located at grid coordinate 93/660 on the Survey of Egypt 1948 map[2] (See figs. 1a and 1b).

Historical Context

The earliest occupation reported from Tell Tabilla dates to the Old Kingdom and First Intermediate Period. Other remains include Second Intermediate Period pottery (Tell-Yahudiya ware); scarabs of Thutmose III (Eighteenth Dynasty; probably late re-issues), a monument bearing a fragmentary prenomen cartouche best equated with Sheshonq I (Twenty-second Dynasty), a late Saite Period to early Ptolemaic Period statue of Sieset (Twenty-six to Thirtieth Dynasties), and other Late Period remains.[3] The remaining occupation mound encompasses a greatly diminished necropolis area with mudbrick tombs, and a citadel area with granite blocks and other traces of a temple. Blocks from the site and ex-situ monuments in the Cairo Museum and elsewhere provide the name of the temple: *ḥwt-ḥzi* (*ḥwt-ḥ3s*). The inscriptions from other monuments from Tabilla attest to the presence of other deities, such as Osiris, Osiris-Onnophris, Osiris-*ḥzi*, Isis, Horus, and Sobek.[4] Although it has been debated in the past,[5] most scholars now accept that "the district of Ro-nefer" (*R3-nfr; R-nfr*) (mentioned in inscriptions from Tell Tabilla) lay within the Sixteenth Lower Egyptian Nome in the east Delta rather than the Seventh Lower Egyptian Nome in the northwest Delta.[6]

Previous Excavation at Tell Tabilla

Relatively little excavation has been conducted at Tell Tabilla. In 1908 Hossein Abdallah
excavated in several areas of the ancient
necropolis at this site, discovering scarabs of
Thutmose III, bronze statuettes of Osiris, a
bronze box, a bronze axe, a limestone statuette, and brick tombs containing mummies
with terracotta masks.[7] Mohammed Effendi
Chaban and M.C.C. Edgar visited Tell Tabilla,
and continued the excavation work begun by
Abdallah.[8] Chaban found such items as a
large limestone sarcophagus, two bronze statuettes (Selket; serpent Ramen), a statuette of
Osiris, a bead necklace, and scarabs.[9] Chaban
also published a summary of the work begun
by Hossein Abdallah, providing a hieroglyphic inscription from one of the statuettes discovered in 1908, namely the Commander of
Troops and Mayor in Mendes, Osiris-nakht.[10]
In 1914 M.C.C. Edgar published a report concerning his archaeological discoveries in the
Delta, and mentioned the discovery at Tabilla
(in 1910 or later?) of a limestone block that
bore an inscription from a temple dedicated to
Osiris-Khes.[11] Edgar also mentioned the discovery of a limestone block with part of the
prenomen of Sheshonq I (?), which was found
in the necropolis at Tel Balala [Tabilla],[12] and
he discussed an inscription on a statuette

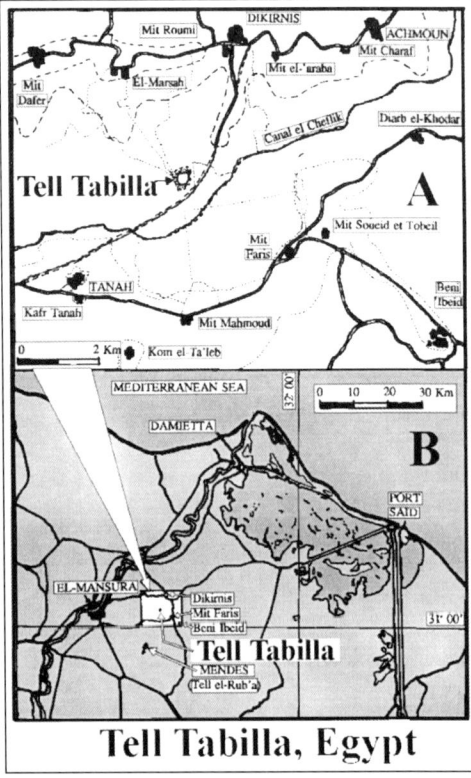

Fig. 1A: Location of Tell Tabilla with respect to Dikirnis.
Fig. 1B: General location of Tell Tabilla in the Eastern
Nile Delta, Egypt.

found by Hossein Abdallah in 1908.[13] More recent investigations by the Supreme Council of
Antiquities have revealed Old Kingdom remains below the Late Period necropolis area that occupied the location of the present-day water plant (Chief Inspector Selim El-Boghdady, personal
communication). The 1999 University of Toronto Winter expedition confirmed this observation.

Aside from reports from colleagues who have visited the site as tourists, a search through the
Egyptological literature and annual reports of archaeological excavations in Egypt[14] has revealed
no further archaeological excavation at Tell Tabilla.

An attempt to consolidate the evidence to-date from Tabilla reveals the remnants of monumental cultic and mortuary stone architecture across the mound's surface, consisting of pieces of
granite, limestone, diorite, and banded alabaster (calcite). The granite pieces are reported to have
lain on the surface for several decades and represent inscribed and plain fragmented pieces from
different parts of a shrine; wall blocks, a shrine/naos (?) corner, doorway fittings, and possibly
worn fragments of statuary. One granite L-shaped piece bore a fragmentary inscription: *mry*
[*Pt^c*]*h? di ^cnkh* ("Beloved of P[tah], given life"). Some granite and limestone pieces bear lines of
wedge-shaped indentations from the Roman Period or later caused by the dismantling and quarrying of the shrine for other construction purposes. The limestone pieces associated with this

362

structure include a large number of rectangular, dressed blocks (mainly from the water plant), a rectangular wall block re-cut with rounded edges (decorated with two kneeling figures), a long U-shaped drain-pipe, a large column base (77 cm in diameter), and three small column bases (43 cm in diameter). Votive statuary is represented by three pieces: The headless statue of a mayor of Mendes (originally dedicated or reused at Tabilla),[15] a worn alabaster piece resembling part of a limb, and a headless statue of a scribe with an inscribed backpillar (found recently in the water plant grounds by the SCA and awaiting examination).

Traces of the elite segment of Tabilla's population are reflected through the existence of five limestone sarcophagi removed from the water plant grounds. These containers still contain clay and silt filling and have rounded head ends (one yielded two burials and amulets). A Late Period diorite sarcophagus, recently moved to the southern end of the mound, is different in form, being roughly finished along most exterior sides with smoothing only at the head end and top ledges. From reports by local workmen and villagers, it would appear that the shrine once lay toward the northern end of the site. This area yielded limestone floor and wall blocks and column bases both within and without the water plant compound.[16] The elite sarcophagi reportedly come from the area immediately south of the shrine's precinct, in the southern environs of the water plant. Further investigation of the exposed sections south of the water plant yielded traces of burnt mudbrick walls, protruding bone fragments, and dense ash layers, possibly indicating the continuation of the necropolis discovered in 1908. Excavations along the northern end of the mound reveal an additional Late Period cemetery with massive blocks of mudbrick enclosing deep chambers. The overall dense clay debris covering the mound and noticeable inhibition of vegetation growth indicates the presence and erosion of massive, undoubtedly state-engineered mudbrick walling systems. The detrital evidence for a stone temple suggests the significance of Tabilla within the Third Intermediate Period and Late Period governmental and religious infrastructure.

Geotechnical Work

Three straightforward activities were carried out at Tell Tabilla prior to undertaking excavations:

1. A topographic map of the extant portions of the site was produced
2. Artifact density measurements were performed to ascertain the former extent of the site
3. A magnetometer survey was carried out on a portion of the site thought to have the best potential for substantive subsurface architecture.

Topographic Mapping

The Tell today is greatly reduced by intense agricultural activity in the region that consists of a three and a

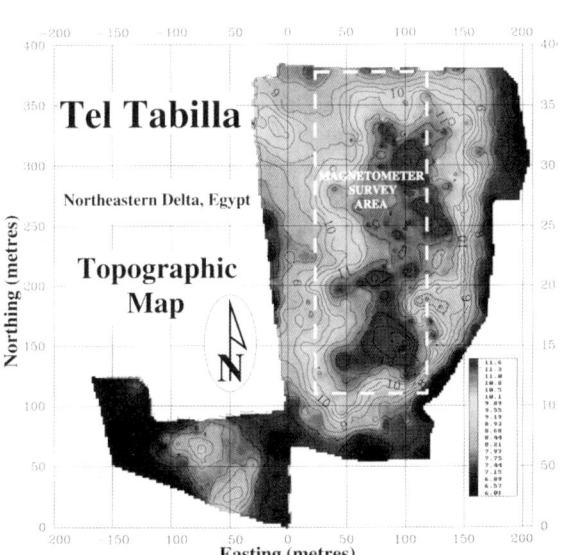

Fig. 2: Topographical Map of Tel Tabilla (elevation in meters asl) showing the magnetometer survey area.

half crop rotation per year with the summer crop being rice, which raises the water table to the surface. The average elevation of the agricultural land surface in the vicinity of the Tell is approximately 4.25 meters above sea level (asl). The surface gradient between Tell Tabilla and Tell el Rub'a (or Mendes) to the south suggests that the now-extinct Mendesian Branch of the Nile would have had a flow gradient of less than 1 in 20,000. Such a gradient would tend to produce both braided and meandering Mendesian channel components that undoubtedly influenced the degradation and final termination of this branch of the Nile.

The Tell Tabilla remnant rises to an elevation of approximately 13.5 meters asl, or a bit more than nine meters above the surrounding countryside. The "citadel" region of the Tell is a north-south ridge approximately 250 meters in length with a width between 50 and 100 meters. The surface area of the "citadel" is approximately 1.6 hectares [(16,300 square meters) calculated on the arbitrary base elevation of 10.5 meters asl] (fig. 2). The mean elevation of the Tell is 8.9 meters asl, and the total surface area of the Tell is approximately seven hectares (70,350 square meters). This surface area is distributed in a "J"-shaped pattern with a maximum north-south extent of 375 meters and a maximum east-west extent of approximately 250 meters. The volume of the Tell above the regional landscape is approximately 266,000 cubic meters. The rate of accretion of Nile alluvium in the general region prior to the building of the Low Dam at the turn of the last century and the High Dam in mid-century (1963) was about 1mm per year. Thus, in many locations at the site, Old Kingdom materials are well below the present-day land surface and water table, precluding their easy excavation. Sediment coring suggests a possible hiatus in occupation of the site for a period of approximately a millennium following the Old Kingdom.

Artifact Distribution

There is a great deal of confusion about the size of Tell Tabilla when it was an active community. It seems likely that the site, like its much larger sister site, Mendes, lying to the south, would have been a source of raw building materials from the Roman Period onward. Little evidence remains of these activities today except for a few massive stone blocks with characteristic lines of chiseled holes. Thus, the site's original extent probably encompasses many hectares of agricultural land surrounding the present-day remnant.

The earliest account of the site's size comes from a land registry carried out in 1375 by Ibn el-Ji'an.[17] He assessed "Dibleh" 15 dinars for a land area of 461 feddans.[18] This is equivalent to approximately 200 hectares or about 28 times the present site size. This is equivalent to a circular plot of land approximately 785 meters in radius or a square land parcel 1,400 meters on a side. In the context of the period, one may assume that the agricultural lands accruing to the thirteenth century Tell Tabilla occupation were included in the tax assessment. The Napoleonic map of 1800 published in the *Description de l'Egypte* located Mendes at the site of Tell Tabilla and appears to ascribe the former site's dimensions to it (2,000 meter long quadrilateral).[19] In 1841 de Bellefonds' map shows the Mendes North mound (Rub'a) to be about the same size as Tell "Debeleh" (1,500 meters N-S and 800 meters E-W: 120 hectares).[20] The Daressy map of *ca.* 1890 shows Mendes to be twice the size of Tell "Debeleh" (approximately 60 hectares). A report by Daressy in 1930 ascribes 225 feddans to Tabilla (approximately 96 hectares); but his accompanying map describes the site as a quadrilateral with a north side of 312 meters and the other three sides of 600 meters in extent that is equivalent to slightly more than 27 hectares.[21]

A series of sampling traverses were carried out, radiating from the extant Tell. Artifact densities per square meter unit were determined. The results indicated that a significant artifact occurrence was present in an 800 meter by 800 meter land parcel with the Tell roughly centrally located. These results suggest that Daressy's observations of modern site size and subsequent diminution due to agricultural impact are acceptable approximations. In addition, a random 0.1% sample of the artifact densities on the Tell was taken. The results showed clearly a positive correlation between sample location elevation and sample size per square meter. These results demonstrated that surface finds were gravity, sheetwash, and/or aeolian-assisted, implying that mass wasting was the dominant geomorphic force on the upper elevations of the extant Tell.

Magnetometer Survey

As a precursor to the planned excavations, a magnetic survey was carried out on the citadel portion of the remaining mound which, according to sample artifact density measurements, once measured at least 800m x 800m; but which is now much reduced to a "J"-shaped configuration facing to the north of 375m x 250m. The grid was set out on the stem of the "J" and ran 250m (N-S) and 100m (E-W) effectively covering the "citadel" region of the site. Line spacing was four meters and station spacing was one meter. The GSM-19T magnetometers (mobile and base station) from Gem Systems, Richmond Hill, Ontario, Canada generated data corrected for diurnal fluctuations in the earth's magnetic field. The mean magnetic value was approximately 43,000 gammas. Low magnetic readings are shown in black on fig. 3, a contour map. High magnetic values are shown in gray. Fig. 4 is a greyscale imaged map that clearly shows a 40 by 40 meter multi-roomed structure on the citadel centered on 120 north/50 east and aligned north northwest. Other smaller structures are also visible. These data were plotted using standard contour and imaging software packages. These geophysical targets will be integrated into the planning for future research- oriented excavation objectives. Results suggest a

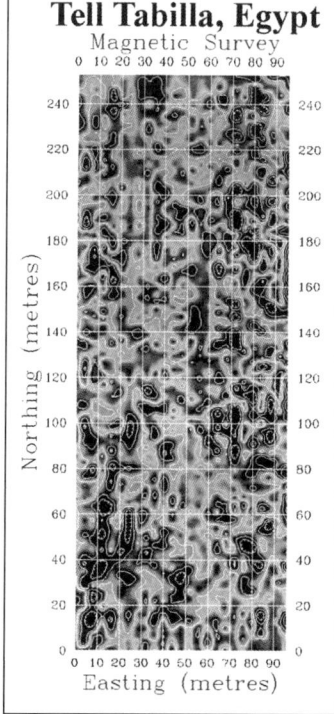

Fig. 3: The ntoured results f the magnetic urvey. The dark regions are magnetic lows.

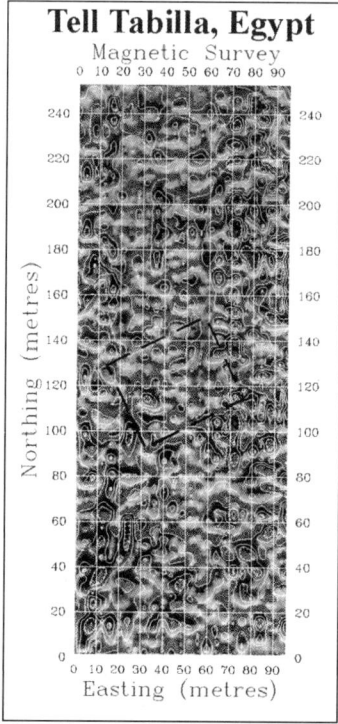

Fig. 4: The imaged and contoured results of the magnetic survey showing one region of interest.

365

substantial amount of subsurface architecture made of low iron limestone and mudbrick still exists at the site below surface. Temple precinct architecture is consistent with the magnetic anomalies. Several clusters of *ex-situ* limestone and granite blocks lie within the southern and northern parts of the site, while numerous limestone blocks lie in the water plant's enclosure. The surface finds of limestone shatter and slag at the site also bear out these observations.

Notes:

1 M. G. Daressy ,"Recherches géographiques," *ASAE* 30 (1930), 69–94 [map location of Tell Tebilleh, 89]; Kümmerly and Frey, *Égypten Egypte Egypt: Bildungs-und Kulturkarte; Carte educative et culturelle; Educational School-Map 1:950,000* (Cairo, 1989).

2 E.C.M. van den Brink, "Appendix A," in E.C.M. van den Brink (ed.), *The Archaeology of the Nile Delta: Problems and Priorities* (Amsterdam, 1988) 314, 321.

3 M. G. Lefebvre, *Textes Égyptiens du Louvre* (Revue d'Égyptologie 1; Paris, 1933) 87–90.

4 J. Malek, "Tell Tibilla," *LÄ* 6 (1985), 3, 39.

5 M.C.C. Edgar, "Notes from my inspectorate," *ASAE* 13 (1914) 277–84; H. Gauthier, *Dictionnaire des noms géographiques dans les textes hiéroglyphiques* III (Cairo, 1925), 121; [Tell Tebilla]; M.C.C. Edgar, *Dictionnaire des noms géographiques dans les textes hiéroglyphiques* IV (Cairo, 1925), 121 (Tell Tebilla).

6 H. Kees, "Mendes," in Pauly-Wissowa (ed.), *Realencyclopedie X* (Stuttgart, 1932), cols. 780–784; Reprinted in H. De Meulenaere and P. MacKay, *Mendes II* (Warminster, 1976), 148–50; K. A. Kitchen, *The Third Intermediate Period in Egypt (1100–650 B.C.)* (Warminster, 1986), 366, section 328, n. 710 (second edition with supplement); P. Montet, *Geographie de l'Égypte ancienne* 1 (Paris, 1957), see C. Klincksieck, nn. 140–41; Lefebvre, *Textes Égyptiens*, n. 1; Malek, "Tell Tibilla," 39.

7 M. E. Chaban, "Monuments recueillis pendant mes inspections," *ASAE* 10 (1910), 28–30.

8 Chaban, "Monuments recueillis," 29–30.

9 Chaban, "Monuments recueillis," 29–30.

10 Chaban, "Monuments recueillis," 29; Edgar, "Notes," 277; Lefebvre, *Textes Égyptiens*, 90–91, n. 8.

11 Edgar, "Notes," 277–78; Lefebvre, *Textes Égyptiens*, 91, n. 2.

12 Edgar, "Notes," 277–78; B. Porter and R. L. B. Moss, *Topographical Bibliography of Ancient Egyptian Hieroglyphic Texts, Reliefs, and Paintings: Lower and Middle Egypt (Delta and Cairo to Asyut)* IV (Oxford, 1934). Note Tell Balala (Tell 'Tebilla") is listed on page 39.

13 Edgar, "Notes," 277–78; Chaban, "Monuments recueillis," 29–30; Daressy, "Recherches géographiques," 78–94, 89 map).

14 *Orientalia*, Nova Series (1948–98), 17–67; *PM* 1934, 39).

15 J. Yoyotte, "La Ville de 'Taremou' (Tell el-Muqdam)," BIFAO 52 (1953), 180–181.

16 Three hundred and fifty-seven substantive blocks have been recorded at the Tell. None are found in their original setting, having been moved either during ancient activities, or modern ones associated with the construction of the water purification plant. One hundred and forty-six blocks were recorded within the confines of the water plant, and they are believed to be representative of a Late Period temple. Informants

recount the removal of the remnants of a limestone platform during plant construction. These blocks were placed along the inner margins of the outer wall of the plant. A percentage of the blocks found outside of the construction area may have been part of the structure, but to ascertain the number will require further research. Over 29 cubic meters of limestone were recorded within the plant walls. If the flooring were 36 cm in thickness, then the 35 blocks with that value for one of their dimensions would generate a little over 23 square meters of surface area. This would represent a small percentage of a normal temple floor (perhaps 10%). If the pavement stones for the temple floor had a thickness varying between 30 and 39 cm, then 81 blocks may have made up the remnant recovered, and 49 square meters of floor may be extant. Finally, if all the blocks not clearly defined as coming from other architectural context (i.e., non-floor) are used in the floor surface calculation, approximately 76 square meters of flooring were recovered.

17 Daressy ,"Recherches géographiques," 86–87, n. 3.

18 One often thinks that change of a real substantive nature is a phenomenon of our era and our era alone. But of course this is simply not true. Change is a constant factor in the human condition, and it is thus so with the life and times that surround the 1375 Land Registry Tax Assessment. There are always problems including an isolated report as if it is representative of a time and place. One is forced to face the question: Can a single account for a given year be used to characterize cultural trends for a time window of decades? Every reader must decide for themselves both the adequacy of the question and its answer.

Ibn Khaldun was one of the early scholars to enunciate 'Laffer's curve': "Dynasties obtain large revenues from low tax rate at their beginnings and small revenues from high tax rates at their ends." Thus, it was with the Land Registry of 1315. The assessment of 15 dinars for 461 feddans at Tabbila for the new Land Tax Registry of 1375, the penultimate year of Sultan Sha'ban II's reign (AH 764–778 / 1363–1376 CE), provides a perspective on the Egyptian economy of the last quarter of the fourteenth century and a direct insight into the number of people that were being supported at Tabilla at the time.

Sha'ban, the grandson of Sultan Mohammed Nasr (1310–1341; 3rd reign) was invested at 10 years of age. His vizier controlled the political and economic strings of the country. The Bahri Dynasty was under siege for a number of pressing reasons that did not create a crisis in a month or a year as happens in the twentieth century. The events of the fourteenth century culminated within the Egyptian context with the accession of the Burgi Mamluks in 1382. The events that led to this change of power occurred throughout the previous 80 years.

The Little Ice Age ruined economies throughout Europe which in turn destabilized economies and trading patterns within the known world (e.g., the Baltic froze over in 1303, 1306, and 1307). The flooding of the gold markets in Egypt and the Middle East with the Hadj of Mansa Musa from West Africa in the 1320s depressed gold values for the following decade. When the Western Mongol Empire collapsed in 1335, the trade links to the Far East were broken. With the destruction of the Mongol capital of Karakoram, the Ming Dynasty developed an isolationist policy that led to the expulsion of all foreigners by 1368. The presence of the Timur with their capital at Samarkand (1369–1500) combined with the constant warring after 1374 between the Mongols, Turkmans, and Kurds brought trading activities to a standstill. While trade with the Far East was maintained, the net balance of payments had remained positive in Egypt, but, with the trade to the Far East closed and the successive plagues (six between 1348 and 1400) that devastated the Egyptian population further disrupting the economy with its accompanying famines (1374) and food riots, the treasury of Sha'ban's time was severely compromised. This economic downturn occurred in spite of a relatively enlightened monetary policy that maintained the dinar at 98%–99% purity (4.25 grams gold) with a silver to gold ratio of 9.3 to 1. The devaluation of all European currencies at this time, the presence of these currencies in Egypt, and Egypt's in Europe almost guaranteed that Gresham's Law would apply to the Egyptian economic situation. Basically, bad money drives good money out of circulation. Thus the quality dinar would have been hoarded both at home and abroad. The actual value of the dinar is difficult to appraise; it had great value. Ibn Battuta noted in India that one dinar was worth 400,000 cowrie shells or 40,000 rupees. The purchasing power of a dinar was probably variable, as 1,100 cowries would buy a slave in Mali in the middle of the fourteenth century. At the time of the Tax Assessment at Tabilla, 100,000 dinars would purchase approximately 70,000 tons of wheat.

Thus, the tax burden of Tabilla was 2,100 pounds of wheat, or approximately 35 bushels. So, the tax was a bushel from every 13 feddans of land or approximately 4.5 pounds per feddan. While attempts have been made to determine the size of a feddan in antiquity, early nineteenth century French studies showed that there were differences between the feddan in the north and south of Egypt. Until recently, when it was defined to be a little less than an acre, it was to some extent arbitrary. A feddan was the amount of land that could be plowed with an ox in a workday. In addition, a land quantity could be divided into equal parts (feddan) so that all eligible were given a fair share. The male head of a household with an ox might receive two feddan while the head of household without an ox would receive only one. These estimates permit one to establish a range for the number of households at Tabilla in 1375. There must have been more than 230 and less than 922. These numbers imply that the population that contributed to the Tax Assessment must have been in the order of several thousand individuals.

19 E. F. Jomard, "Nome Mendésien," extracted from "Description des antiquités d'Athribis, de Thmuis et de plusiers nomes du Delta oriental," from *Description de l'Égypte ou Recueil des Observations et des Recherches qui ont été, faites en Égypte pendant l'Expédition de l'Armée Français* IX (Paris, 1829) 369–381, reprinted in H. De Meulenaere and P. MacKay, *Mendes* II (Warminster, 1976), 44–45.

20 R. K. Holz, D. Stieglitz, D. P. Hansen, and E. Ochsenschlager, *Mendes* I (Cairo, 1980), Plate 11d.

21 M. G. Daressy , "Recherches géographiques," 89, map.

Travaux récents (1995-1999)
à Ehnasya al-Médina
(Hérakléopolis Magna)

Maria Carmen Perez-Die
Museo Arqueologico Nacional, Madrid, Spain

La Mission archéologique espagnole a continué ses travaux sur le site d'Ehnasya al-Médina (Hérakléopolis Magna) sous la direction de M. Carmen Perez-Die depuis 1984[1]. La grande extension du site a exigé que l'on établisse un ordre de priorités dans les travaux et, pendant les quinze dernières années, on a fouillé principalement au sud-ouest de la ville, près de la muraille sud, à deux endroits différents où se trouvaient la nécropole de la Première Période intermédiaire et le cimetière de la Troisième Période intermédiaire, parfois superposés dans les deux secteurs.

Durant quinze années, nous avons fait des découvertes extraordinaires qui ont déjà été présentées au cours d'autres congrès et qui sont en partie publiées[2]. Nous reviendrons plus tard sur ces travaux ; dans la présente communication, nous souhaitons exposer les résultats obtenus entre 1995 et 1999 dans le cadre de la fouille, des études architectoniques et stratigraphiques, ainsi que certaines conclusions générales sur le site et la restauration de la nécropole.

Entre 1995-1999 nous avons fouillé toute la partie ouest, c'est-à-dire les secteurs que nous avons appelés L-49, L-55, et L-57. Dans le secteur L-55, les niveaux supérieurs avaient été fouillés dans les années 90. Nous avons trouvé dans les strates les plus profondes une tombe de la Première Période intermédiaire, complètement saccagée et sans couvercle, à l'exception d'un morceau de toit qui restait encore à sa place originelle. La tombe était scellée par un niveau stérile et avait été construite avec des blocs de pierre orientés nord-ouest/sud-ouest. Malheureusement, il n'y avait pas d'inscriptions nous informant du nom du propriétaire. Au sud, une chambre en brique cachait un très intéressant dépôt *in situ*, formé d'une table d'offrandes anépigraphe, de vases de libations, de bols, etc. D'autre part, la fouille de ce secteur nous a aussi permis de découvrir une série d'inhumations de la Deuxième Période intermédiaire sur lesquelles nous reviendrons.

Dans la zone la plus au sud-ouest, dans le secteur L-57 nous avons trouvé un complexe tombal, (Tombes 8-9) entouré d'un gros mur en brique crue, appartenant à la Troisième Période intermédiaire. On a pu documenter la fosse de ce mur qui coupait les niveaux les plus anciens.

Ainsi, nous avons vérifié que ce complexe était, par rapport à d'autres du cimetière de la Troisième Période intermédiaire, celui qui avait la chronologie la plus moderne, vers le VIIIe siècle av. J.-C. Le complexe est formé de deux chambres en pierre qui n'ont conservé aucun reste des dalles du toit et qui sont séparées par un mur en brique crue. La chambre la plus au nord était vide au moment de sa trouvaille et celle du sud était occupée par des individus qui ont réutilisé la tombe quelques années plus tard.

Les travaux les plus intéressants menés à Ehnasya durant les dernières années sont les études stratigraphiques du secteur fouillé auparavant. Nous avons commencé par l'étude systématique de la séquence stratigraphique des secteurs L-49 et L-55, et nous avons continué dans les autres secteurs. L'étude des matériaux archéologiques nous a permis d'établir la chronologie relative, en partant de la Première Période intermédiaire et en allant jusqu'à l'époque romaine. L'étude de la poterie, réalisée par David Aston a été fondamentale, et je lui reste très reconnaissante pour toute l'information qui sera publiée sous sa direction.

Jusqu'à présent nous avons pu établir différents niveaux archéologiques dans les secteurs fouillés par la Mission archéologique espagnole.

Premier Niveau

Il correspond au cimetière de la Première Période intermédiaire[3]. L'extension de cette nécropole est assez grande et est documentée depuis la muraille sud, dans la zone fouillée par Lopez et Presedo dans les années soixante, jusqu'à la zone où nous avons travaillé. Les tombes ont des chambres en pierres rectangulaires avec un trou dans le sol pour placer les offrandes et avec des murs en briques crues tout autour. À l'intérieur, nous avons trouvé dans un cas un beau sarcophage anépigraphe. Parfois, les tombes ont des reliefs dans les murs et une stèle de fausse-porte associée qui nous donne des renseignements très précis sur le propriétaire : nom, titre, etc. Les tables d'offrandes apparaissent devant la stèle de fausse-porte. De plus, nous avons aussi constaté que la nécropole a été détruite de façon intentionnelle et très peu d'objets ont été trouvés à leur place d'origine. La céramique apparaît à de nombreuses reprises, avec les jarres hérakléopolitaines et d'autres formes bien typiques de cette période. L'étude approfondie de cette nécropole est en train de se faire, avec toute la documentation trouvée, y compris les inscriptions inédites conservées au musée national d'Archéologie de Madrid et provenant des fouilles anciennes. Entre les personnages connus, on pourrait signaler Im, « connue véritable du roi », Ibenen, « contrôleur du palais », Ankhef, « général » ; Neferkhaou, « gouverneur du district » ; Herishefnakht, « surintendant des champs » ; Khety, « trésorier » ; Sakat, « connu véritable du roi » ; Satbahetep et Neferkhaou ; Sehu, « chef des secrets de la maison parfaite » ; Tjaiou, « concubine royale unique », etc.

Deuxieme Niveau

À partir du Moyen Empire, nous avons constaté une sorte d'abandon du site. Les tombes de la Première Période intermédiaire sont tombées en ruine, mais à la Deuxième Période intermédiaire l'espace est de nouveau réutilisé comme nécropole et lieu d'enterrement. Parfois, les individus sont placés sur les murs ou dans les chambres qui existaient déjà, à plat ventre, avec la tête tournée, les mains sur le bassin, et parfois en association avec de la poterie ou des scarabées.

Troisieme Niveau

Pendant le Nouvel Empire, le secteur est abandonné, et l'on oublie que des nécropoles anciennes ont existé. Cependant, nous avons trouvé un enterrement en jarre du Nouvel Empire avec un fœtus à l'intérieur. Nous avons localisé aussi d'autres inscriptions et objets réutilisés, comme le fragment d'une statue du Parahotep, vizir de Ramsès II, dont la tombe se trouve à Sedment[4].

Quatrieme Niveau

À partir de la XXe dynastie, le secteur est recoupé de nouveau, mais cette fois il s'agit d'une occupation de nature plus profane que religieuse, destinée à des activités artisanales : le secteur devait déjà être en ruine et il avait perdu son caractère religieux et funéraire ; ainsi, à partir de la XXe dynastie, la zone a été remplie de structures circulaires en brique crue, réutilisant aussi les pierres des tombes anciennes. Les structures circulaires ont livré des matériaux céramiques des phases I et parfois II d'Aston c'est-à-dire depuis la XXe jusqu'à la XXIIe dynastie : cette zone d'activité artisanale est caractérisée par la réutilisation systématique de l'espace qui a tendance à niveler la surface et à remplir les dénivellations du terrain. Ces structures circulaires ont été utilisées comme des récipients, des silos, des fours etc., ceci même s'il est bien difficile de leur assigner un rôle spécifique. Quant au matériel associé, apparu à l'intérieur ou à côté, il s'agit de mortiers, de meules faites en granit ou en quartzite, avec les faces aplanies et avec des traces de matériaux broyés. Les structures circulaires contenaient aussi beaucoup de charbon, terre brûlée, ossements d'animaux, instruments lithiques, etc.

Ce niveau a été très bouleversé par le suivant qui l'a fait disparaître dans plusieurs secteurs. On verra pourquoi.

Cinquieme Niveau

Il appartient à la nécropole de la Troisième Période intermédiaire, secteur où la fouille a été prioritaire. Ce niveau est défini d'abord par la construction, entre la XXIIe et la XXIIIe dynastie, des grands complexes tombaux destinés à des hauts dignitaires locaux : prêtres, prêtresses et chefs militaires ; à partir de la XXVe et jusqu'au début de la XXVIe dynastie, se produit la réutilisation de cet espace par des gens aux possibilités économiques moindres.

Chaque complexe tombal est formé, tel que nous l'avons trouvé, par une série de chambres, quelques-unes en pierre, d'autres en brique crue, parfois voûtées[5]. Les problèmes posés pendant la fouille ont été énormes, du fait des caractéristiques du terrain, des réutilisations anciennes, et du manque d'objets avec une chronologie absolue précise et de personnages déjà connus. On a seulement distingué le fils et la fille d'un premier prophète d'Amon, Smendès, que nous avons identifié avec précaution avec le Smendès III de K. A. Kitchen que l'auteur date du IXe siècle av. J.-C.

Les tombes ont été construites dans une fosse qui a cassé les niveaux archéologiques les plus anciens, aussi a-t-on parfois fouillé des stratigraphies inversées. Ainsi, le niveau IV, c'est-à-dire celui qui correspond à l'aire d'activité artisanale avec les structures circulaires, a été complètement démonté par les travaux de construction des grandes tombes. Parfois, la fosse est arrivée jusqu'au niveau de la Première Période intermédiaire, utilisant ses pierres comme sol pour la nouvelle tombe. Nous avons aussi constaté qu'entre les dallages des chambres en pierre existaient des éléments réutilisés appartenant à des tombes de la XXIe dynastie et dont on ne connaît pas l'emplacement d'origine.

Les dallages du sol et les blocs des murs des tombes ont été incrustés à l'intérieur de la fosse de construction, d'où leur aspect peu soigné. Les murs reposant sur le sable du désert, la fosse était ensuite remplie de morceaux de pierres de taille, de débris et, finalement, entourée par des murs en brique crue qui dépassaient les dalles du toit. Il est bien possible qu'initialement, et au moment de l'enterrement, soit restée seulement, à l'extérieur, la façade avec la porte d'accès devant laquelle il devait y avoir une sorte d'antichambre ; cette dernière aurait fonctionné à l'origine comme puits d'accès. On a pu constater que les tombes étaient assez profondes. L'hégémonie des éléments et des murs intérieurs, qui ont été polis et recouverts de peintures aujourd'hui presque complètement disparues, est manifeste.

Le problème des chapelles funéraires individuelles est toujours d'actualité. Existaient-elles à l'origine? Où étaient-elles situées? Nous n'avons trouvé aucun espace susceptible d'être une chapelle et nous avons seulement pu confirmer l'existence d'un culte dans une chambre rectangulaire qui, peut-être, a servi de chapelle funéraire commune pour toutes les tombes de la nécropole.

D'autre part, nous avons constaté que les tombes ont été réouvertes, réutilisées, et refaites pendant la Troisième Période intermédiaire, et que le cimetière a subi de profondes modifications architectoniques à différents moments de cette période. Les travaux de restauration et d'agrandissement de la nécropole pendant la Troisième Période intermédiaire peuvent être mis en évidence à plusieurs endroits. Malgré tout, beaucoup de tombes nous sont arrivées saccagées et assez détruites.

Quant aux chambres en brique crue, beaucoup sont voûtées mais, à l'exception de la voûte de la tombe 6, elles ont été rasées et occupées par des individus qui se sont fait enterrer à l'intérieur. Habituellement, il ne reste des voûtes que des traces dans les murs. Nous avons aussi noté de petits arcs, normalement dans les parois latérales des chambres voûtées, qui pourraient s'interpréter comme une sorte d'accès, malgré leur faible hauteur. Un point est confirmé : les voûtes sont construites *après* les chambres en pierre.

Faisons à présent quelques rappels.

Au nord

Tombe 1

Elle devait avoir trois chambres en pierre, mais elle n'en conserve actuellement plus que deux, car la chambre du sarcophage a disparu et ses pierres ont été volées. À l'intérieur, les *oushebtis* d'un certain Osorkon nous donnent le nom du propriétaire de la tombe[6]. Peut-être cet Osorkon est-il en relation avec le personnage du même nom qui apparaît sur un fragment de table d'offrandes située juste en face de la porte de la tombe, personnage dont on connaît la filiation puisqu'il était le fils d'un Nimlot[7]. À l'est, une chambre voûtée très détruite a été récupérée et fouillée en 1998.

Tombe 3

Elle est formée de trois chambres en pierre, la plus orientale contenant l'immense sarcophage en granit, anépigraphe, dont le couvercle était brisé et déplacé sur le côté. Le tour du sarcophage était occupé par des vases céramiques et par les *oushebtis* d'un personnage appelé Paenherishef qui était père divin de Khonsou[8]. On a constaté que la tombe a été réutilisée plusieurs fois.

À l'est

Tombe 4

Appartenant à Tanetamon, grande des recluses d'Herishef, fille du premier prophète d'Amon Smendès, et de la mère divine Ihé. À l'intérieur, elle conservait les *oushebtis* de la propriétaire et les vases canopes avec le nom et la filiation : appuyée sur le toit de la chambre funéraire, reposait une base avec des inscriptions qui mentionnaient Tanetamon, sa fille, l'« imyt-bah » de Herishef Tasheritenptah, et un certain Osorkon, peut-être familier de Tanetamon[9]. Au sud, on a trouvé une chambre voûtée remplie d'individus.

Tombe 2

À côté de la tombe de Tanetamon se situe la tombe d'un Osorkon, chef de l'armée, fils royal et prêtre d'Herishef, peut-être l'Osorkon de la base de Tanetamon, ou son frère si on l'identifie avec l'Osorkon fils de Smendès découvert dans l'inscription d'une table d'offrandes que nous n'avons pas trouvée *in situ*[10]. À l'intérieur de la chambre en pierre, on a trouvé les *oushebtis*[11] et les vases canopes anépigraphes. Dans l'antichambre ont été découvertes des inhumations secondaires, quelques-unes avec des *oushebtis*, comme ceux de la reine Shepensepedet, inconnue jusqu'à présent[12]. Au nord, une enceinte voûtée en brique crue abritait les corps de personnes décédées après Osorkon.

Tombe 5

Elle possédait trois chambres, dont une restait ouverte et une autre était saccagée, saccage remontant peut-être à l'époque romaine, d'après la poterie. On ne connaît pas son premier propriétaire et dans sa réutilisation, on a observé un individu portant un magnifique collier en or, lapis-lazuli, cornaline, et une petite statuette en or de déesse léontocéphale.

Tombe 6

Cette tombe appartient à Tcherit fils de Nimlot[13]. Tel que nous l'avons trouvé, le complexe était formé de trois chambres voûtées en brique crue, et d'une quatrième en pierre, très détruite.

À l'ouest
Tombe 7

Cette tombe était formée d'une chambre voûtée au nord et de trois enceintes en pierre dont deux sont conservées, l'antichambre étant démontée. Une dalle du toit, réutilisée, conservait une inscription qui mentionnait Imenhaemipet, prêtre d'Herishef, chef de l'armée et chef de la forteresse des Mashawesh, tribu libyenne installée en Égypte et berceau de la XXIIe dynastie, dont les liens avec Hérakléopolis sont maintenant hors de doute. D'autres dalles de la tombe du même personnage ont été découvertes dans une autre enceinte située au nord de cette sépulture[14]. Une des chambres en pierre conservait une inhumation accompagnée de vases canopes, le scarabée de cœur en place, avec le nom de la personne enterrée : le fils royal Osorkon[15].

La nécropole de la Troisième Période intermédiaire se prolonge encore dans la zone fouillée par nous récemment (tombes 8–9, voir plus haut), dans la zone plus au nord avec d'autres inhumations sans tombe spécifique[16], et dans le secteur fouillé par Lopez en 1966[17]. On a trouvé en outre d'autres inscriptions appartenant à des tombes qui n'ont pas encore été localisées, notamment sur le linteau du fils du chef des Mashawesh, Osorkon, premier prophète d'Herishef et chef de l'armée.

Grâce à l'épigraphie, on a pu connaître les noms et titres des personnes enterrées : il y a beaucoup d'Égyptiens, mais on constate une forte présence libyenne : Osorkon, Nimlot, Tcherit. On a relevé aussi la présence d'autres étrangers à Hérakléopolis : des Tuher, c'est-à -dire des soldats asiatiques installés en Égypte après la bataille de Qadesh[18], ou des commerçants phéniciens ; ceci grâce à la trouvaille des nombreux vases céramiques d'origine orientale[19].

Notons qu'à partir du VIIIe siècle av. J.-C., pendant toute la XXVe dynastie et le début de la XXVIe, on a constaté une réutilisation de la zone funéraire que nous venons de décrire. Parfois les murs sont refaits, les enceintes sont agrandies, parfois voûtées. Les inhumations, souvent très pauvres, se situent à l'intérieur des enceintes en brique, derrière, devant ou à côté des grandes tombes en pierre. L'anonymat de ces individus est total et leur statut social très bas, reflet des conditions historiques adverses dans des moments de déclin ou de décadence politique. Leur mobilier funéraire est très pauvre[20].

Les corps présentent à peine des traces de momification et l'inhumation est faite dans un sarcophage en bois ou en brique crue mais normalement dans de simples fosses. Les momies peuvent être couvertes par des cartonnages polychromes ou munies d'yeux incrustés en faïence ou en bronze. Elles sont accompagnées de diverses amulettes : Amon, Bès, Horus, déesse léontocéphale, œil-*oudjat* etc., et elles ont été parfois couvertes de résilles funéraires et dotées de scarabées. Concernant les *oushebtis*, nous avons pu réaliser une typologie spécifique qui établit la chronologie, et confirmer l'existence d'un atelier local qui à l'époque fabriquait des exemplaires. La poterie est associée aux inhumations ; il y a parfois des vases complets, mais surtout des fragments de coupes, des plateaux, des jattes etc.

Niveaux Superieurs

À certains endroits du secteur, du matériel appartenant aux VIIe et VIe siècles av. J.-C. a été découvert, de même que du matériel de l'époque gréco-romaine.

Restauration

De nombreuses tombes nous sont arrivées avec le toit cassé, ouvertes et saccagées. Aussi n'avons-nous pas oublié les travaux de restauration du cimetière, comme le Service des antiquités égyptiennes nous l'avait demandé[21]. L'idée initiale était de replacer les dalles à leur place d'origine, car la plupart des dalles calcaires du toit étaient cassées et tombées à l'intérieur des tombes.

Avant toute chose, on a décidé de faire des analyses chimiques et mécaniques de la pierre calcaire à l'Université du Caire, et les résultats obtenus nous ont confirmé la mauvaise qualité de cette pierre, ainsi que la facilité avec laquelle elle peut se détruire ; il a ainsi été impossible d'appliquer certaines solutions prévues initialement, telles que l'assemblage des pierres avec des barres d'acier, avant de les replacer sur les toits des tombes.

En fonction des résultats des analyses, nous avons adopté une solution beaucoup plus simple, complètement réversible, qui n'implique aucune intervention directe sur les dalles calcaires et qui reste en accord avec l'idée initiale de mettre les éléments en pierre à leur place.

Nous avons dessiné des éléments modulaires métalliques qui s'adaptent à toutes sortes de surfaces et qui s'appuient sur des supports télescopiques réglables en deux directions. Avec les modules métalliques, nous avons construit des structures qui ont été placées à l'intérieur des tombes et, sur ces structures, on a appuyé les dalles du toit ; entre les dalles, on a mis une sorte de mortier particulier qui imite celui d'origine mais qui reste suffisamment différent pour qu'on le distingue. L'aspect extérieur de ces tombes est maintenant bien plus compréhensible, même si, à l'intérieur, les supports sont visibles : mais cela ne constitue pas un grand problème, car il ne reste pas de traces de peinture à l'intérieur. Si dans l'avenir on trouve d'autres solutions pour restaurer les pierres, on pourra le faire sans le danger qu'elles se détruisent.

Pour préserver le secteur, nous avons mis une toile métallique tout autour qui le protège efficacement.

En conclusion, nous souhaitons signaler que les fouilles du cimetière de la Première Période intermédiaire et de la Troisième Période intermédiaire nous ont permis de reconstruire une partie de l'histoire d'Hérakléopolis Magna, inconnue jusqu'à présent. L'époque hérakléopolitaine est mieux connue depuis quelques années et la liste des gouverneurs locaux d'Hérakléopolis appartenant à la Troisième Période intermédiaire, établie par Kitchen, peut être complétée par des personnages trouvés dans la fouille de la Mission archéologique espagnole. Grâce à la découverte à Ehnasya de tous ces personnages, on leur a rendu leur mémoire historique et, dès lors, leurs noms ne tomberont jamais dans l'oubli.

Notes:

1 Entre 1966 et 1984, d'autres Espagnols ont travaillé à Ehnasya. Voir J. Lopez, « Rapport préliminaire sur les fouilles d'Hérakléopolis (1966) », *Oriens Antiquus* 13 (1975) 299–316 ; *id.*, « Rapport préliminaire sur les fouilles d'Hérakléopolis (1968) », *Oriens Antiquus* 14 (1976), 57–78 ; M. Almagro - F. J. Presedo, « Les fouilles à Hérakléopolis Magna (1976) », *in First International Congress of Egyptology, October 2–10 1976. Acts*, (Berlin, 1979), 67–71.

2 M. C. Perez-Die - P. Vernus, *Excavaciones en Ehnasya el Medina I, Introducción e Inscripciones*, (Madrid, 1992) ; M. J. Lopez, F. Quesada et M. A. Molinero, *Excavaciones en Ehnasya el Medina II, Cerámica y Recipientes en piedra*, (Madrid, 1995) ; M. C. Perez-Die, « Documents de la Troisième Période intermédiaire provenant d'Hérakléopolis Magna », *Actes du IV Congrès International d'Égyptologie* II, (Munich, 1985), 240–248 ; M. C. Perez-Die, « Hérakléopolis Magna et ses nécropoles : la Troisième Période Intermédiaire », *AEPHE* 97 (1988-89), 158–162 ; M. C. Perez-Die, « Fouilles récentes à Hérakléopolis Magna », *in Libya and Egypt, c1300–750 BC*, (Londres, 1990), 115–131 ; M. C. Perez-Die, « La necrópolis del Primer Período Intermedio. Estado de la cuestión », *Hathor* 2 (1990), 95–100 ; M. C. Perez-Die, *Heracleópolis Magna durante el Tercer Período Intermedio*, thèse de doctorat (Universidad Complutense, Madrid, 1992) ; M. C. Perez-Die, « Discoveries at Herakleopolis Magna », *EgArch* 6 (1995), 23–25 ; M. C. Perez-Die, « La réutilisation de la nécropole de la Troisième Période Intermédiaire/début de l'Époque Saïte à Ehnasya el Medina (Hérakléopolis Magna) », *Stationen. Beiträge zur Kulturgeschichte Ägyptens. Rainer Stadelmann gewidmet*, (Mayence, 1998), 473–483.

3 La nappe phréatique nous empêche d'arriver aux niveaux plus anciens. Voir Lopez, *Oriens Antiquus* 14, 57–78. Perez-Die, « La necrópolis del Primer Periodo Intermedio de Heracleópolis Magna », *Hathor* 3 (1991), 93–100. A. Roccati, « I testi dei sarcofagi di Eracleopoli », *Oriens Antiquus* 13 (1974), 161–197 ; Perez-Die - Vernus, *Excavaciones* I, doc. 1–4 ; H. Willems, « A note on the Date of the Early Middle Kingdom Cemetery at Ihnâsiya al-Madîna », *GM* 150 (1996), 99–109.

4 Perez-Die - Vernus, *Excavaciones* I , doc. 8–11

5 Phase de construction postérieure par rapport aux chambres en pierre. Possible réaménagement de la nécropole ? En cours d'étude.

6 Perez-Die - Vernus, *Excavaciones* I, doc. 38.

7 Perez-Die - Vernus, *Excavaciones* I, doc. 30.

8 Perez-Die - Vernus, *Excavaciones* I, doc. 51.

9 Perez-Die - Vernus, *Excavaciones* I, doc. 21–26.

10 Perez-Die - Vernus, *Excavaciones* I, doc. 20.

11 Perez-Die - Vernus, *Excavaciones* I, doc. 20.

12 Perez-Die - Vernus, *Excavaciones* I, doc. 39, 41 et 42.

13 Perez-Die - Vernus, *Excavaciones* I, doc. 28–30.

14 Perez-Die - Vernus, *Excavaciones* I, doc. 15.

15 Perez-Die - Vernus, *Excavaciones* I, doc. 53–54.

16 Perez-Die - Vernus, *Excavaciones* I, doc. 37, 40, 46, 49, 50, 52.

17 Lopez, « Rapport préliminaire », *Oriens Antiquus* 13, 291–316.

18 Perez-Die - Vernus, *Excavaciones* I, doc. 12, 16.

19 Lopez - Quesada, *Excavaciones* II, 106–108.

20 Perez-Die, *in Stationen*, 473–483.

21 Perez-Die, J. Medina, C. Davila et M. A. Moreno, « La Misión Arqueológica Española en Egipto. Trabajos de Conservación y Restauración en el yacimiento arqueológico de Ehnasya el-Medina », *IV Congreso Internacional de Rehabilitación del Patrimonio Arquitectónico y Edificación*, (Cuba, 1998), 296–299.

Some Remarks Concerning the Superstructure of Some Mastabas at Abusir

Ali Radwan

Cairo University

In this short paper I will deal with one feature of the mud architecture of the First Dynasty, namely the superstructure of some *mastaba*-tombs uncovered by the Cairo University Expedition to Abusir, north of the sun-temple of Niuserre. This burial site seems to be one of the principal cemeteries of the Early Dynastic Period in the Memphite region.[1] Some of the larger *mastabas* belong to a group of middle-class people who lived during the second half of the First Dynasty, as attested by two clay seals (stoppers) on storage jars, which carry the Horus-names of Dewen (*Mastaba* IV) and Qay-âa (*Mastaba* XIV).[2]

It is a fact that the inhabitants of the Delta had their own style of architecture during the Predynastic Period: The unification of the Two Lands was preceded by or based upon a phase of cultural similarity which prevailed throughout Egypt during the Naqada III Period (a period of cultural integration). The Early Dynastic Period was the era of creativity and the formation of different features and styles in art and architecture, although the establishment of the architectural tradition was the main task of the Third Dynasty and the Old Kingdom periods.

The fact that the Memphite region, by the beginning of the First Dynasty, was the main seat of the administration of the Two Lands speaks for itself. In this area we have indeed, as was later said, "the balance of the Two Lands."

In ancient Egypt, funerary customs and religious beliefs changed according to social and political events and led to cultural differences. Very important for studying the burial patterns in any cemetery are the above-ground structures (superstructures) of the tombs which can show not only the architectural style but also the afterlife concepts and mortuary customs of their owners. Normally we can discern two *mastaba* types for the Early Dynastic Period:[3]

1. The elaborate paneling system called "palace façade," confined to Lower Egypt. It might give the *mastaba*-tomb the shape of a house or even a palace.
2. The mound-shaped superstructure, which can only be traced in a very small number of *mastabas*, especially in the south (Abydos and Hierakonpolis), could have its ow

significance, namely its resemblance to the so-called "High-Sand" or "primeval hill," symbolizing regeneration.[4]

Mastaba IV, which is surrounded by a massive enclosure wall, shows the paneling only on the eastern side, in front of it we found a number of pottery vessels, which represent the usual offerings for the deceased. On the north side, the superstructure of this *mastaba* has a small rounded projection, which can be interpreted as a special cult-niche.[5]

Mastaba V (a stairway tomb) has on its eastern side an offering chapel consisting of a corridor with small cult-niche (facing east) and a small *serdab*-like room (facing north), the first known example of its kind in a private tomb.[6]

Mastaba XVII also has in its offering chapel a small sealed room (*serdab*)[7] which can only be the earliest form of the same feature found in the superstructure of some private tombs of the Old Kingdom. The tomb of Den at Abydos may have the first *serdab* in a royal tomb.[8] The reign of King Den appears to be a time of many innovations.[9]

The small burials for common people, of different types, were found scattered around the large *mastabas*. These could have been servants or members of the household of the *mastaba* owners. In some cases the subsidiary tomb could take the form of a small *mastaba* with two or even three steps. Only the eastern side is provided with two offering niches; the larger and most important one is located at the southern end.

Some large *mastabas* (e.g. numbers XXIV and XXVI) have solid superstructures without any kind of decoration. It seems likely a mound type was intended.

A boat pit was added to the complex of Mastaba XXVI and is situated (on a west-east axis) just to the north of the enclosure wall of the *mastaba*.[10] Mastaba XVII with all its elements (enclosure wall and paneled superstructure, offering chapel, dummy graves, bull's head, and subsidiary tombs) was the focus of a special article.[11]

In the hilly area between the Sun Temple of Userkaf and the Pyramid of Sahure we discovered a group of robbed burial shafts that can be dated to the Fifth Dynasty. I expect they may belong to the members of one family as they are all cut in a line behind a long wall, have false doors (in mud brick with mud plaster), and two offering tables (limestone—very simple types) still *in situ*, with the *ka* sign incised on the surface of one of them to indicate "offerings."[12]

Notes:

1 Cf. D. Jeffreys and A. Tavares, "The Historic Landscape of Early Dynastic Memphis," *MDAIK* 50 (1994), 143 ff. (esp. 146 ff.); H. Bonnet, *Ein frühgeschichtliches Gräberfeld bei Abusir* (Leipzig, 1928), 1 ff.

2 Cf. A. Radwan, "Ein Treppengrab der 1. Dynastie aus Abusir," *MDAIK* 47 (1991); A. Radwan, "A Cemetery of the 1st Dynasty," *MÄU* 4 (1995), 308, n. 7; D. Kessler and R. Schulz eds., *Gedenkschrift für W. Barta* (Frankfurt am Main, 1995), 312, n. 14; J. Leclant and G. Clerc, *Orientalia* 61 (1992), 242, fig. 17.

3 Cf. G. A. Reisner, *The History of the Egyptian Mastaba*, (Mélanges Maspero I; Cairo, 1935–38), 579 ff.; J. Brinks, "Mastaba," *LÄ* III (1980), 1214 ff.; H. W. Müller, "Gedanken zur Entstehung, Interpretation und

Rekonstruktion ältester ägyptischer Monumentalarchitektur," paper presented at the DAIK Symposium Okt. 1982, in W. Kaiser ed., *Ägypten–Dauer und Wandel*, (Main am Rheim, 1985), 7 ff.; W. Kaiser, *Zu Entwicklung und Vorformen der frühzeitlichen Gräber mit reichgegliederter Oberbaufassade*, (Mélanges G. Ed. Mokhtar II; Cairo, 1985), 25 ff.; G. Dreyer, "Zur Rekonstruktion der Oberbauten der Königsgräber der 1. Dynastie in Abydos," *MDAIK* 47 (1991), (Festschrift W. Kaiser), 93 ff.

4 Cf. e.g. A. Radwan, "Mastaba XVII," (Abusir and Saqqara in the year 2000, Archiv orientální, Supplementa IX; (Prague, 2000), 513, n.19.

5 Cf. Radwan, "A Cemetery," 312, n. 11; Cf. in this respect, P. Janosi, "Bemerkungen zu den Nordkapellen des Alten Reiches," *SAK* 22 (1995), 145 ff.

6 Cf. A. Radwan, "Ein Treppengrab," 305 ff., Abb. 2; M. Bárta, "*Serdab* and Statue Placement in the Private Tombs down to The Fourth Dynasty," *MDAIK* 54 (1998), 65 ff. fig. 2.

7 A. Radwan, "Mastaba XVII," 510.

8 Cf. G. Dreyer, "Umm el-Qaah," *MDAIK* 46 (1990) 77 f., Taf. 23, b, Abb.8.

9 Cf. e.g. W. Kaiser, "Ein Kultbezirk des Königs Den in Sakkara," *MDAIK* 41 (1985), 54, n. 43.

10 For similar boat-graves in Saqqara and Helwan see W.B. Emery, *Archaic Egypt*, (Harmondsworth, 1963), 54, fig. 17; 68, 131, fig. 78; Z. Y. Saad, *Excavations at Helwan* (1969), 23, 74 f., Pl. 105–108. For the complete report about the Abusir-boat and its funerary significance, see A. Radwan and J. Lindemann, in a forthcoming volume of *MDAIK*.

11 Radwan, "Mastaba XVII," 509 ff.

12 For the different types of offering tables of the Fifth Dynasty, see M.M.F. Mostafa, "Untersuchungen zu Opfertafeln im Alten Reich," *HÄB* 17 (1982), 97 ff.

La chapelle de Thot à Abou Simbel

Wagdy Ramadan
Ain Shams University

Cette chapelle est située au sud du grand temple d'Abou Simbel[1]. L'architecture de ce petit monument est des plus simples : il se compose d'une cour et d'un spéos. L'axe de la cour diffère sensiblement de l'axe du grand temple, alors que celui du spéos s'en rapproche. Le monument est orienté est-ouest. La chapelle est formée d'une cour unique à ciel ouvert. Elle est limitée des trois côtés par des murs de brique crue. À l'est, l'entrée principale est ménagée dans le mur. Si l'on en juge par la forme actuelle de son embrasure, elle était pourvue d'une porte à battant ouvrant vers l'extérieur (est).

Amelia Edwards[2] montre sur son plan l'existence de deux jambages en pierre accolés au mur, mais nous n'en avons pas retrouvé la trace sur les deux dalles de sol en grès qui précèdent l'embrasure. Au nord se trouve un mur de brique qui sépare la cour du parvis du grand temple. Il s'appuie à son extrémité ouest contre la falaise dont le plan incliné nous montre quel était le profil original de celle-ci. Cette cour en granite a été en partie restaurée au début du siècle. Elle se présentait à l'époque de nos relevés comme une véritable structure.

Au sud, la cour est limitée par un mur de brique auquel fait suite, vers l'est, un pylône. Le sol de la cour était originellement constitué, dans ses deux tiers est, par un dallage de briques crues de grandes dimensions. Une petite rampe, elle aussi ménagée dans le roc, donne accès à l'entrée du spéos. Cette rampe actuellement très usée ne présente aucun vestige de marches éventuelles.

La façade du spéos, taillée dans la falaise, présente une porte qui n'est surmontée d'aucune corniche. Le spéos est une salle rectangulaire (l.= 6,45 m. ; l.= 4,40 m.) et ses parois sont rectilignes et verticales. La paroi postérieure (ouest) n'est pas perpendiculaire à ses voisines. La paroi nord est pratiquement parallèle à la paroi sud du couloir sud du grand temple, ce qui viendrait appuyer l'hypothèse selon laquelle la chapelle de Thot aurait été construite après l'achèvement du grand temple[3]. Le plafond de la salle a la forme d'une voûte orientée est-ouest, son arc est très tendu et régulier.

Sur le montant gauche (sud = X 5) se trouve le roi Ramsès II vêtu d'un pagne court à devanteau et coiffé de la couronne blanche. Ses pieds sont chaussés de sandales et il tient une massue dans sa main gauche tandis que sa main droite est levée en signe d'adoration.

Devant le roi ,on lit :

« (...) l'eau divine[4] du maître de l'Univers, le maître des Deux Terres Ousermaâtrê Setepenrê, aimé de Thot, maître de Khemenou (Hermopolis), et d'Amon, qui réside à Imenherib[5]..., maître des couronnes[6], Ramsès II, aimé d'Amon-Rê , aimé de Rê-Horakhty qui réside en Ta-Séty ».

Derrière le roi :

« Grand officiant[7], toutes protection et vie sont derrière lui, comme Rê ».

Devant le roi, on lit (X,4) :

« Vive le dieu parfait[8], qui accomplit ce qui est utile[9] (les rites) dans le domaine de son père Amon, le maître des Deux Terres, Ousermaâtrê Setepenrê, aimé d'Amon-Rê, maître des trônes des Deux Terres, qui réside en Ta-Séty. Vive le dieu parfait qui a fait (ceci comme) un monument... sur son siège, le maître des couronnes Ramsès II, aimé d'Amon-Rê, aimé de Rê-Horakhty, le grand dieu, qui réside en Ta-Séty[10]. »

On pénètre à l'intérieur (Y) de la chapelle par une porte s'ouvrant au milieu. À l'intérieur, les montants sont simplement indiqués par la gravure et couronnés d'un linteau que décore un disque ailé flanqué d'uræi. La porte était pourvue d'un unique vantail qui venait se loger derrière le montant est.

Devant le roi sur le montant gauche (Y,4), on lit :

« Vive le dieu parfait, qui accomplit les rites, qui est riche en monuments dans *Per-Meses* ("La demeure de celui qui l'a enfanté")[11], fils de Rê, maître des couronnes, Ousermaâtrê Setepenrê, qu'il soit doué de vie, de force (pour) l'éternité des jubilés, maître des couronnes, Ramsès II, aimé d'Amon-Rê. »

Au -dessous du bras droit, on lit :

« Tout ce qui entre [dans] la demeure divine, pur, pur, pur, pur »[12]

Au-dessus des autels sur la paroi sud (Y.5), on lit dix colonnes :

« Vive le dieu parfait, qui accomplit les rites pour (son) père Thot, maître de Khemenou, qui réside à Imenherib. Il a fait un grand monument dont le sommet est pour l'éternité face à l'horizon du ciel (d'ou émerge le soleil). »[13]

« Paroles à dire par Thot, maître de Khemenou, qui réside à Imenherib, il dit : « (je) te donne l'éternité en tant que roi des Deux Terres, fils issu de (son) corps, Ramsès II, aimé d'Amon-Rê. J'ai fait (ceci) comme ce qui contente ton *ka*[14] (qui dit) : « je te donne une infinité de jubilés en tant que roi[15] et (tout) ce que le soleil entoure. »[16]

Devant le roi-dieu sur la paroi sud (Y.6), on lit quatre colonnes :

« Vive le dieu parfait, celui qui est riche en miracles divers[17] dans *Pr-Mss*, détenteur de la force[18], maître des Deux Terres, Ousermaâtrê Setepenrê, maître des couronnes, Ramsès II aimé d'Amon-Rê. »

Sur le mur nord, Ramsès II debout, faisant l'offrande devant sa barque sacrée. La proue et l'étrave de la barque sont ornées par une tête de faucon. La barque repose sur une base. Devant le roi se trouvent un guéridon, une table chargée d'offrandes, de fleurs, et un autel sur lequel se trouvent quatre vases *nmst*[19], un encensoir et trois fleurs de lotus[20].

Au-dessus des autels :

« Vive le dieu parfait qui a fait un monument pour son père Rê-Horakhty. Il a fait un grand temple pour la première fois en son nom[21], en beau grès blanc dont le sommet est aussi haut que le soleil se levant par amour pour lui. »[22]

Au-dessus des autels, sept colonnes sont inscrites :

« Paroles à dire par Amon-Rê, seigneur des trônes des Deux Terres, qui réside dans la terre méridionale, Ramsès II, aimé d'Amon-Rê, la barque pour son fils aimé, maître des Deux Terres, Ousermaâtrê Setepenrê, dit : « je te donne un grand âge[23] pour accéder au trône[24], et le temps de vie de Rê[25] quand tu es sur la terre, que (tu) paraisses sur le trône[26] d'Horus, comme Rê éternellement ».

Devant la déesse Ousermaâtrê, on lit :

« .... l'eau (divine) sortant du temple, née du[27] roi et de l'Ennéade au complet[28], le maître des Deux Terres, détenteur de la force, Ousermaâtrê Setepenrê, maître des couronnes, Ramsès II, aimé d'Amon-Rê, puisse-t-il donner toute vie et force éternellement. »

Une bande de hiéroglyphes est inscrite autour du plafond, on lit :

« Vive l'Horus, le taureau puissant, aimé de Maât, le dieu parfait (aimé) d'Amon-Rê et de Mout, maîtresse du ciel, qui gouverne les Deux Terres, le maître des couronnes, Ramsès II, aimé d'Amon-Rê. Il a fait un grand temple à nouveau en son nom, pour son père Amon-Rê qui réside en la terre méridionale, creusé dans la montagne sacrée[29] en beau grès blanc (comme un travail fait pour l'éternité). »

Conclusion

Je dirai en conclusion que l'étude de cette chapelle relative au dieu Thot est très intéressante dans la mesure où elle nous a conduit à préciser quelques informations sur son culte dans le territoire d'Abou-Simbel et de la Basse-Nubie.

On voit là combien les anciens Égyptiens étaient de très minutieux observateurs du monde astronomique. C'est la raison pour laquelle cette chapelle a été construite dans cet endroit d'où émerge le soleil. Cette idée est sûrement en relation avec le phénomène qui avait frappé certains archéologues et voyageurs du siècle passé[30]. Nous savons que les premiers rayons du soleil pénètrent deux fois l'an jusqu'au sanctuaire pour y éclairer la statue de Ramsès II divinisé. On sait que le roi Ramsès II fut divinisé dans plusieurs temples ; le culte se rapportait en ces lieux à l'aspect guerrier du roi conquérant[31].

L'examen des textes de cette chapelle fait le point sur quelques renseignements que nous avons été amené à rassembler sur le culte du roi Ramsès II. On voit sur le mur nord le roi faisant l'offrande devant sa barque sacrée et la légende est « Ramsès II, aimé d'Amon-Rê, dans la barque, le grand dieu ». Le second élément que nous ajouterons au sujet du culte est une mention du bâton auguste du roi, revêtu d'électrum et orné de toute pierre précieuse. De plus, la déesse Ouser-Maat-Rê qui fait partie du prénom du roi Ramsès est représentée debout derrière la barque sacrée. Devant elle, on lit que le roi est né de la Grande Ennéade.

La filiation du roi issu d'Amon-Rê et de Mout est mentionnée sur le mur ouest où il est dit : « fils d'Amon et né de Mout maîtresse du ciel ». On a pu remarquer que le roi Ramsès II, en tant que roi divinisé, offre, en la présence de Rê-Horakhty, son prénom sous la forme de l'image de Maât, c'est-à-dire « Ousermaâtrê »[32].

On peut mettre l'accent sur la relation entre le roi et les dieux, car il est mentionné comme un roi aimé de Thot et d'Amon-Rê qui réside en Ta-Séty. C'est pourquoi on trouve que le roi a fait à nouveau un sanctuaire pour son père Thot et Rê-Horakhty, en grès blanc, ainsi que le grand temple d'Abou Simbel qui a été creusé dans la montagne sacrée d'Abou Simbel.

Enfin, on sait que Thot est en relation avec le soleil, car il est le fils aîné de Rê et le cœur de Rê[33].

Notes:

1 Je remercie le directeur général du Centre d'étude et de documentation sur l'ancienne Égypte, pour les photos qu'il m'a données.

2 A. Edwards, *A Thousand Miles up the Nile*, (Londres, 1877), 494–519.

3 H. El-Achirie - J. Jacquet, *Le grand temple d'Abou Simbel* 1,1 *Architecture*, (Le Caire, 1984), 23–24.

4 Il s'agit d'une filiation divine du roi, voir J. Vandier, *La religion égyptienne*, (Paris, 1944)184, n. 2 ; Fr. Daumas, *La Civilisation de l'Égypte pharaonique*, (Paris, 1987), 144. Sur la filiation du pharaon, voir G. Posener, *De la divinité du pharaon*, (Paris, 1960), 34–5 ; S. Morenz, *La religion égyptienne. Essai d'interprétation*, (Paris, 1962), 197, n. 4. Dans le texte précédent, Ramsès II est semence du maître de l'Univers, voir J.-Cl. Goyon, *Confirmation du pouvoir royal au Nouvel An. [Brooklyn Museum 47.218.50]*, BdE 52, (Le Caire, 1974), 50 ; Fr. Le-Saout, « Fragments divers provenant de la cour du VIIIe pylône », *Karnak* VII, (1982), 267.

5 Une localité consacrée à la déesse Anouqit et au dieu Thot à Abou Simbel, voir G. Maspero, *Temples immergés de la Nubie* I, (Le Caire, 1911), 160. *Imn-hr-ib*, c'est-à-dire « Amon est satisfait », voir H. Gauthier, *DG* I, (Le Caire, 1925), 74.

6 Sur le sens de $ḥ^cy$, voir A. H. Gardiner, « Regnal years and civil calendar in pharaonic Egypt », *JEA* 31, (1945), 25 ; J. Leclant, « Sur un contrepoids de Menat au nom de Taharqa : allaitement et "apparition" royale », *Mélanges Mariette*, BdE 32 (1961), 265, n.1 ; D. B. Redford, *History and Chronology of the Eighteenth Dynastie of Egypt. Seven Studies*, (Toronto, 1967), 27.

7 Cette formule est connue dès la XIe dynastie, voir Chr. Desroches-Noblecourt - Ch. Kuentz, *Le petit temple d'Abou Simbel. «Nofretari pour qui se lève le dieu-soleil »*, 180, n. 219.

8 À partir de la XVIIIe dynastie, cette épithète se met avant le prénom. Elle apparaît sous la IVe dynastie., cf. R. El-Sayed, « Stèles de particuliers relatives au culte rendu aux statues royales de la XVIIIe à la XXe dynastie », *Mélanges Kuentz*, BIFAO 79, (1979), 171, n. e ; Desroches-Noblecourt - Kuentz, *op. cit.*, 131, n. 42. Notons que l'épithète était appliquée aussi aux rois vivants, cf. A. P. Zivie, « Un monument associant les noms de Ramsès I et de Séthi I », *BIFAO* 72, (1972), 105, n. 1.

9 Sur ce sens, voir D. Meeks, *AnLex* 77.0069.

10 Rê-Horakhty porte l'épithète *nb t3-sti*, voir Noblecourt-Kuentz, *op. cit.*, 62, 196, n. 273.

11 Sur *Pr-Mss*, voir Gauthier, *DG* II, 89 ; H. Brugsch, *Dictionnaire géographique de l'ancienne Égypte*, (Leipzig, 1879), 306–7. Pour *mswt* désignant « lever du soleil » voir Meeks, *AnLex* 78.1843.

12 Effectivement, à partir de l'époque ramesside, on trouve souvent cette formule sur les montants de porte et fréquemment accompagnant une représentation du roi debout, voir par exemple : la porte latérale du temple de Louqsor (côté ouest) = Al. Gayet, *Le temple de Luxor, MMAF* 15, (Le Caire, 1894), pl. 17 ; la porte du temple de Ptah à Karnak = G. Legrain, « Le temple de Ptah Rîs-anbou-f dans Thèbes », *ASAE* 3, (1902), 104 ; sur le montant du temple d'Amenophis à Giza, cette formule est inscrite devant le roi Merenptah, cf. Chr. Zivie, *Giza au Deuxième Millénaire*, BdE 70, (Le Caire, 1976), 114, n.a et fig. 22.

13 On remarque qu'il y a un lien entre cette phrase et le site sur lequel le grand temple d'Abou Simbel a été construit.

14 Sur *hr k3.f*, « ce qui contente son ka »,voir Meeks, *AnLex* 791835 ; *KRI* II, 387,16 ; 749,3. Pour *iry hrrt*, « faire ce qui plaît (à) », *ibid.*, 311,8 ; 483,13 ; 571,12.

15 Litt. « le souverain », pour désigner le roi d'Égypte, voir Meeks, *AnLex* 78.2829.

16 Sur le sens de *sn*, voir M. Gitton, « Variation sur le thème des titulatures de reines », *BIFAO* 78, (1978), 399 ; Meeks, *AnLex* 78.4133.

17 Meeks, *AnLex* 77.0753.

18 Litt. « celui qui possède un bras (ou un glaive) », voir Noblecourt-Kuentz, *op. cit.*, 133, n. 46.

19 Sur l'usage du vase *nmst*, voir E. Otto, *Das ägyptische Mundöffnungsritual*, *ÄgAbh* 3, (Wiesbaden, 1960), 37–8.

20 Sur le rôle du lotus comme une évocation de la naissance, cf. J. Yoyotte - S. Sauneron, « La naissance du monde selon l'Égypte ancienne », *La naissance du monde*, *SourcOr* 1, (Paris, 1959), 37.

21 Meeks, *AnLex* 78.1620.

22 Il existe une relation étroite entre le monument et la lumière qui pénètre dans le temple d'Abou Simbel.

23 Meeks, *AnLex* 78.0135 ; J. Assmann, « Eine Traumoffenbarung der Göttin Hathor. Zeugnisse "persönlicher Frömmigkeit" in thebanischen Privatgräbern der Ramessidenzeit », *RdE* 30, (1978), 26, col. 10.

24 Pour *zbi nst*, cf. Meeks, *AnLex* 79.2490.

25 Meeks, *AnLex* 79.0537.

26 Sur *ḫꜥi ḥr nst*, ibid., 79.2158.

27 *Ibid.*, 77.1857.

28 Sur *psḏt tmti*, ibid., 77.4810.

29 Cette montagne sacrée désigne ici Abou Simbel, voir S. Sauneron - J. Yoyotte, « La campagne nubienne de Psammétique II et sa signification historique », *BIFAO* 50, (1951), 203, n. 2.

30 Noblecourt-Kuentz, *op. cit.*,. 142 ; J. J. Ampère, *Voyage en Égypte et en Nubie*, (Paris, 1868), 515 ; A. Edwards, *A Thousand miles up the Nile*, (Londres, 1891), 303–4.

31 L. Habachi, *Features of the deification of Ramesses II*, ADAIK 5 (Glückstadt, 1969), 42–4 ; J. Leclant, *Recherches sur les monuments thébains de la XXVe dynastie dite éthiopienne*, BdE 36, (Le Caire, 1965), 327, n. 6 ; A. M. Blackman, *The temple of Derr*, (Le Caire, 1913), 97 ; D. Wildung, *Egyptians Saints. Deification in pharaonic Egypt*, (New York, 1977), 9, fig. 9 ; P. Vernus, *Athribis*, BdE 74, (1978), 36, n. a ; R. El-Sayed, *BIFAO* 79, (1979), 165. Sur le culte rendu aux statues royales de Ramsès II, voir J.J. Clère, « Nouveaux documents relatifs au culte des colosses de Ramsès II dans le delta », *Kêmi* XI, (1950), 34–5 ; L. Habachi, « Khatân'a-Qantîr : Importance », *ASAE* 52, (1954), 514 sq.

32 Maât symbolise pour le dieu, les offrandes, les amulettes, les membres mêmes du dieu, le sens de la justice, cf. Moret, *op. cit.*, 140 sq ; R. El-Sayed, « Nekhtefmout, supérieur des porte-encensoirs (II) », *ASAE* 70, (1984), 333, n. sss.

33 P. Boylan, *Thot, the Hermes of Egypt*, (Londres, 1922), 118–9 ; R. El-Sayed, « Thoth n'a-t-il vraiment pas de mère ? », *RdE* 21, (1969), 72, n. 3.

Twenty-five Years of Work in the New Kingdom Necropolis of Saqqara: Looking for Structure*

Maarten J. Raven
Rijks Museum Van Oudheden

In the year 2000, the Leiden mission in Saqqara is celebrating the fact that it has worked for a quarter of a century in the New Kingdom necropolis of that fascinating site. Starting in 1975, under the auspices of the Egyptian Antiquities Organization as a joint venture between the Egypt Exploration Society and the Leiden Museum of Antiquities, the project became a cooperation between the Leiden Museum and Leiden University in 1999. The current field directors are Dr. René van Walsem and the present author. Under the former directorship of Professor G. T. Martin, the mission has achieved several successes, foremost of which was the rediscovery of the long-lost tombs of Horemheb and Maya. During these 25 years, a total of 12 tombs were excavated.

The original objective of the Saqqara Mission was to find the tomb of Tutankhamun's famous treasurer Maya, part of which Lepsius saw in 1843. In view of the presence of three splendid tomb statues of the deceased and his wife Merit in the Leiden Museum, such a discovery, it was anticipated, would certainly provide additional information on the provenance and function of material in the Museum's collection. Using Lepsius' map, which proved to be slightly inaccurate, the expedition started work in the right general area but located the tomb of Horemheb instead. In 1986, with the discovery of Maya's tomb about 30 meters further north, the expedition's aim was realized. After that, one might have asked why we wanted to continue our fieldwork in the area.

The answer to that question is that only now have we started to understand some of the underlying structures of this part of the Saqqara necropolis. Instead of quitting once our original curiosity had been satisfied, we felt that we should continue to look for such patterns and structures which would provide an insight into the workings of Egyptian civilization as a whole. If we want to answer all the questions that still face us in this respect, we may well need yet another 25 years of work in the same area.

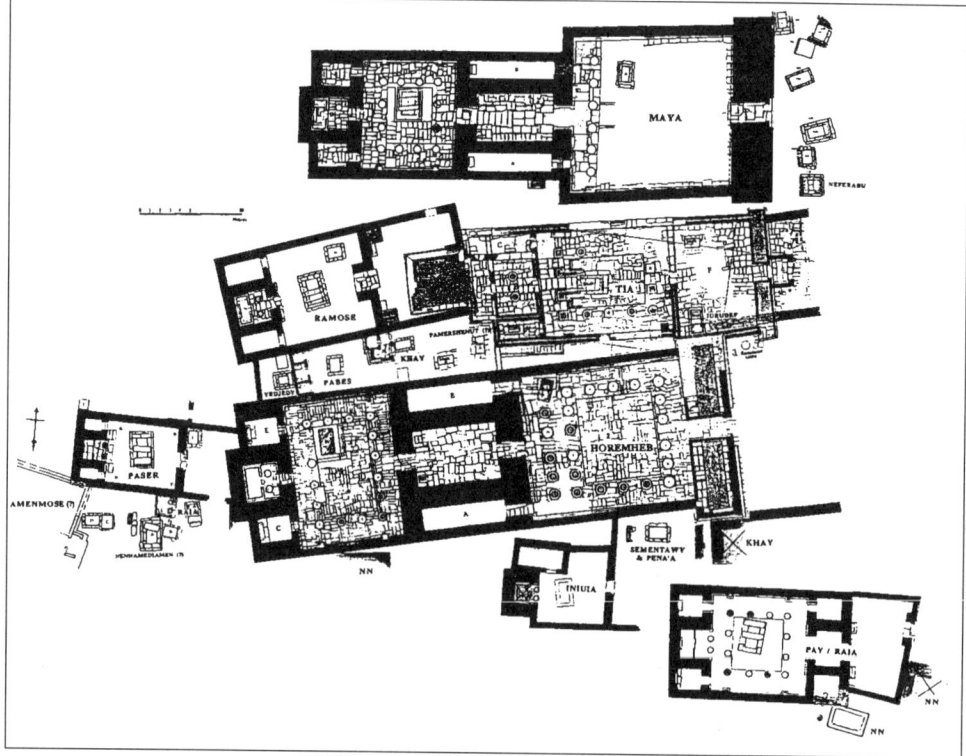

Fig. 1. New Kingdom necropolis of Saqqara, plan of Leiden Expedition concession.

Patterns of Distribution

There was not just one New Kingdom cemetery in the vast expanses of the Memphite necropolis, which certainly included areas at Giza, Zawyet al-Aryan, and Dahsur.[1] Even within the present site of Saqqara there are New Kingdom tombs scattered all over the place; in the escarpment close to the present-day village of Abusir, around the Teti pyramid, in the Bubastieion area, and of course south of the Unas causeway where both the Leiden mission and the former Cairo University Expedition have uncovered about 48 tombs.[2] Although the heyday of these cemeteries fell between the reign of Tutankhamun and the second half of the reign of Ramesses II, there are certainly both older and more recent New Kingdom tombs at Saqqara. In 1999, two pit graves with anepigraphic headstones were detected south of the tomb of Horemheb; these contained one decayed wooden coffin each and a number of burial gifts provisionally dated to the mid-Eighteenth Dynasty.[3] These finds suggest that an older cemetery had already existed on the spot later selected for the funerary monuments of Tutankhamun's top officials. At the other end of the chronological range, tombs have been attested dating to the reigns of Ramesses IV or even later.[4] All this shows that the vicinity of the royal residence was not the only factor deciding the importance of the Saqqara necropolis.[5]

What has not yet been elucidated by the joint efforts of all the expeditions working in the area is what defined the distribution of the various tombs over the individual cemeteries. It has been suggested that maybe the earliest monumental tombs were rock-cut structures in the eastern escarpment and the excavations by Zivie in this place certainly comprise some of the earliest New Kingdom tombs from Saqqara. Later Eighteenth Dynasty tombs have been found both in the area of the Leiden concession (Maya, Horemheb, Ramose, Iniuia, Pay) and around the Teti pyramid Ipuia, Amenemone),[6] which might suggest a gradual westward extension of these monumental tombs. During the Nineteenth Dynasty, however, the distribution was much more diverse, with new tombs being inserted between those of the Eighteenth Dynasty both in the Horemheb area (Tia, Paser, Racia, Khay, and Pabes) and along the escarpment (Nemtymes, Nakhtmin).[7] A quite new cemetery of this period was opened in the area of the Cairo University concession. Finally, for some reason, the only monumental Twentieth Dynasty tombs known to us are located in the Teti pyramid cemetery, where they were surrounded by monuments of almost two centuries earlier. All this shows that there was certainly no strict "horizontal stratification" attesting a chronological development, but that there must have been other patterns defining the distribution of the individual tombs.

Patterns of Association

Malek was the first to suggest that some of these distribution patterns may have lain in the sphere of professional association. The royal butlers of the Ramesside Period seem to have had a predilection for the cemetery near the Teti pyramid.[8] The terrain south of the Unas causeway counted no less than four tombs of overseers of the royal treasury (Maya, Tia, ST 101, ST 203). Still, this evidence is not very conclusive because many officials utilized several distinct titles in the course of their careers and it is not always clear which was considered to be their most important one. Moreover, the association is convincing only if the tombs were really situated side by side, which is not always the case. A good example of such a situation is the tomb of Tia, built next to that of his illustrious predecessor Maya. One may also compare the tomb of Pay, who started his career as "Overseer of the cattle of Amun-re." This made him a colleague (probably the successor)[9] of Iniuia, whose tomb is situated directly behind Pay's.

Adjacent tombs did not always belong to people of equal rank. Thus, there may have been patterns of patronage;[10] a superior official allowing a favorite assistant to be buried close to his own monument, or even within the precincts of his own funerary structure. A good example of the latter is the tomb of Iurudef, who was private secretary to the Overseer of the Treasury Tia, and was buried in a subsidiary shaft of that monument.[11] More common, however, was the solution to build the servant's tomb outside the monument of the superior in rank. A good example of this procedure is the tomb of the troop-commander Ramose, which adjoins Horemheb's monument in the north. It can hardly be doubted that this army officer should be identified with Horemheb's personal secretary who is depicted behind the general's chair in the latter's tomb.[12]

It is difficult to assess whether or not the same association existed between the tombs of Maya and Horemheb on the one hand, and the adjacent monuments of Iniuia, Pay, and Racia on the other. As "Scribe of the Treasury of the Lord of the Two Lands,"[13] Iniuia must have served under Maya's administration during at least part of his career, but of course we cannot prove how close their association really was. Pay combined the titles of "Overseer of the Cattle of Amun-re," "Overseer of Works of all the Monuments of His Majesty," and "Director of the *Harîm*,"[14] so that for him the situation was very similar. In his case, though, we can add that one of his sons, Nebrê, was a "Scribe of the Treasury of the Lord of the Two Lands" and is depicted as such in the tomb of his superior, Maya.[15] This suggests that rather intimate ties may have existed between the two officials and their respective families.

Another son of Pay, Racia, must have had links with Horemheb. Racia started his career as a military man and must have served under the general. This relationship may well have defined Racia's wish to be buried close to the tombs of the top official. Thus, the reason for the rather rare burial of father and son in a common tomb may well have lain outside the sphere of mere family ties.

A final pattern of association may be distinguished in the position of the tomb of Tia and Tia and the nearby burial of a Ramesside princess in one of the subsidiary shafts of the tomb of Horemheb.[16] Although Tia may have been attracted by the monument of his predecessor in the office of Overseer of the Treasury, Maya, the fact that his tomb was clearly designed to be a royal monument rather suggests that the proximity to the temple-tomb of Horemheb, who was regarded as the founding-father of the Nineteenth Dynasty, was considered to be of even greater importance.

Offering Cult

This brings us to the next issue of the cemetery as a place of veneration. Evidence for the actual performance of the mortuary cult has not often been recorded during previous excavations in Saqqara or elsewhere. During the clearance of the tomb of Horemheb, however, two limestone plinths were found in the statue room which were inscribed with the name of "the lector priest of Horemheb, Pehefnefer"; the same person engraved his name in front of a person represented on a relief in the entrance to the statue room.[17] Since the plinths in question (which must have carried two figures of the Anubis jackal) date to the Ramesside period, they prove that the cult of the deceased still flourished at the time. In Horemheb's case, the fact that the tomb owner was known to have become a pharaoh himself and was regarded as an ancestor of the ruling family, certainly favored the decision to continue the cult of the now deified general. This is also indicated by the fact that Pehefnefer gave his own son the unusual name "Horemheb-em-netjer."[18]

Still, such a prolonged survival of the offering cult was apparently not unique in Saqqara. A similar situation prevailed in the neighboring tomb of Maya. A barrel-vaulted chapel against the exterior south wall of the tomb has preserved a private altar and stela of one of Maya's mortuary priests, a lector priest called Yamen who is represented officiating before his deceased master.[19] There was at least one other stela niche or miniature chapel next to Yamen's, suggesting that the cult was indeed continued for some time. One of the stelae thought to have come from here is now in Warsaw (MN 142294). It depicts a "lector priest of the overseer of the treasury Maiay" who is called Peraca(er)neheh and clearly dates to the Ramesside period, attesting that the cult of the deceased was still very much alive at the time. A corroboration for the dating is the depiction in the second register of this stela, where we see a group of three persons offering to "the lady Tyia," doubtless the princess of that name who was buried with her like-named husband immediately to the south of Maya. Thus, the priests of the time seem to have combined the cultic obligations of various tombs in the area. The Warsaw monument thereby proves that such cults could survive for well over a generation.[20]

Access and Communication

A related question is how the traffic on the cemetery was regulated. During its centuries of operation there must have been quite a heavy stream of people moving up to the Saqqara plateau or returning home from there. These consisted of stone cutters and masons, artists and architects, priests and funeral cortèges, and finally, relatives and other visitors to the tombs. Clearly there must have been special installations to ensure the easy access to the necropolis for all these people with their different needs. Some of these installations must have lain outside the plateau itself, such as canals, harbors, and perhaps roads. For the heavy transport involved in the supply of bricks, architectural elements, and sarcophagi, as well as for the funeral cortèges themselves, there must have been a system of inclines and sloping roads; perhaps the remains of the Old Kingdom pyramid causeways still functioned to a certain extent, which might explain the concentration of activity around the pyramids of Unas and Teti. Finally, the necropolis itself must have formed a maze of minor roads and alleys providing access to each individual monument.

A study of this aspect of access and communication has been somewhat neglected so far and would certainly be most rewarding. Of course, it is intimately connected with the aspect of the spatial distribution of the various monuments themselves, and with the much more basic question of who controlled the layout and development of the cemetery as a whole.

For a better understanding of this aspect of "traffic control," full excavation of the area due east of the tombs of Maya, Horemheb, and Tia would be highly desirable. Partial investigation of Maya's forecourt has already demonstrated the presence of a number of later New Kingdom tomb chapels and shafts respecting the axial approach through Maya's monumental pylon gateway. In itself, this proves that originally Maya had a large open area in front of his tomb, and a similar situation prevailed for Horemheb's tomb. It would be most interesting to assess how these squares linked up with the main thoroughfares of the period and whether the principle of axiality was also observed there.

Design and Metrology

So far, the study of the remaining funerary architecture of the New Kingdom tombs at Saqqara has been descriptive rather than analytical. It is too early to state anything definite about what may be the earliest New Kingdom tombs at the site, i.e. the plain pit graves without any superstructure recently discovered by the Leiden Mission. A characterization of the rock tombs in the eastern escarpment is best left to the excavator of that specific area, since the data published thus far by Alain Zivie are rather scanty. What remains are the free-standing monuments. Here, Van Dijk is doubtless right in stressing their similarity to contemporary religious architecture and in interpreting them as private mortuary temples.[21] Within this framework, however, there is a dazzling variety from the most simple offering chapel to the other extreme of temple-like structures with a replication of the courtyard and other elements. This can be illustrated as follows:[22]

	rear chapel	pyramid	chapel	courtyard	side chapel	outer court	statue room	pylon	portico
Racia			x						
Tjay			x	x					
Amenemone			x	x	x				
Paser			x	x	x				
Iniuia			x	x	x				
ST 6			x	x	x			x	
ST 5		x	x	x	x			x	
ST 201			x	x	x			x	x
ST 7			x	x	x			?	x
Ramose			x	x	x	x			
Pay/Racia			x	x	x	x	x		
Horemheb			x	x	x	x	x	x	
Maya			x	x	x	x	x	x	
ST 217		x	x	x	x	x		x	

	rear chapel	pyramid	chapel	courtyard	side chapel	outer court	statue room	pylon	portico
ST 219		x	x	x	x	x	x	x	
ST 218		x	x	x	x	x			x
Tia	x	x	x	x	x	x		x	x
ST 0	x	x	x	x	x	x		x	x
ST 101	x	x	x	x	x	x		?	?

The basic nucleus of the temple-tomb is the offering chapel at the western end. Almost always the offering chapel is flanked by two side-chapels and preceded by a courtyard. There may be westward extensions consisting of additional chapels and a pyramid. During the Eighteenth Dynasty the tombs were built in mud brick with limestone revetment, so that the miniature pyramids could be built on the roof of the central chapel. When the construction changed to limestone paneling with rubble fill throughout, these pyramids would have become too heavy and accordingly were erected on the ground behind the central chapel.

The eastward extensions of the richer tombs could consist of a statue room or vestibule preceding the inner courtyard and usually flanked by lateral chapels. Both the earlier and the later tombs regularly have an outer courtyard preceded by a pylon gateway, whereas the Ramesside examples show a preference for entrance porticoes.

A final element which needs to be studied in the future is the metrology of these tombs. An analysis of the tomb of Pay has demonstrated that its dimensions can usually be expressed in multiples of the Egyptian cubit. Its width of about 10.50 m is the equivalent of 20 Egyptian cubits, and the inner courtyard was clearly conceived as a square of 18 x 18 cubits. Apparently, the exterior walls were planned to be 1 cubit thick. The doorways to the chapels were doubtless planned to be 2 cubits wide, the wider doorways at either end of the vestibule or statue room were 4 cubits wide. All this suggests that this tomb was planned very carefully. Similar measurements have been found in the other tombs. Thus, the proportions of the tombs of Maya and Horemheb are clearly based on a grid with squares of 6 x 6 cubits.[23]

Conclusion

Although the original aim of the joint expedition of the Egypt Exploration Society and the Leiden Museum of Antiquities—relocating the long-lost tomb of Maya—was realized in 1986, our 25-year commitment with this part of the Saqqara necropolis has made us aware that there are many aspects of these fascinating monuments which are not yet fully understood. By continuing our fieldwork, together with our new partner, Leiden University, we hope to be able to solve some of these questions which are relevant for the study of Egyptian society as a whole.

Notes:

*A fuller version of this article may be found in M. Bárta and J. Krejci (eds.), Abusir and Saqqara in the Year 2000 (Prague, 2000).

1 For Giza, cf. C. M. Zivie-Coche, "Aux marges de Memphis: Giza," in: A. P. Zivie (ed.), *Memphis et ses nécropoles au Nouvel Empire* (Paris, 1988), esp. 116-7. For Zawyet el-Aryan, see D. Dunham, *Zawyet el-Aryan, The Cemeteries Adjacent to the Layer Pyramid* (Boston, 1978), 37-73 and Pls. 28-69. For New Kingdom tombs recently found at Dahshur, see S. Yoshimura *et al.*, "A Preliminary Report of the General Survey at Dahshur North, Egypt," *Mediterraneus* 20 (1997), 3-24; "Preliminary Report of Excavations at Dahshur North, Egypt," *Mediterraneus* 21 (1998), 3-32.

2 Reports of the Anglo-Dutch mission are published in the *Excavation Memoirs* of the Egypt Exploration Society; preliminary reports in *JEA*, from 1995-1999 in *OMRO*. For the Cairo University mission there is only the article by S. Tawfik, "Recently Excavated Ramesside Tombs at Saqqara, 1: Architecture," *MDAIK* 47 (1991), 403-409.

3 See R. van Walsem *et al.*, "Preliminary Report on the Saqqara Excavations, Season 1999," *OMRO* 79 (1999), 23-4 and pls. 7-10.

4 J. Malek, "The Tomb-chapel of Hekamaetre-neheh at northern Saqqara," *SAK* 12 (1985), 43-60; id., "The Royal Butler Hori at Northern Saqqâra," *JEA* 74 (1988), 125-136.

5 Cf. already J. van Dijk, in Zivie, *Memphis*, 39.

6 Cf. Malek, *SAK* 12, 47 ns. 19-20 with ref. It should be noted that blue-painted sherds of pottery are rather common in the area north of the Teti pyramid (personal observation).

7 For the tomb of Nakhtmin, see J. Leclant and G. Clère, "Fouilles et travaux en Égypte et au Soudan, 1992-1993," *Orientalia* 63 (1994), 377 with ref. (ranged under the heading 'Abusir' but in fact cut in the escarpment of Saqqara-North).

8 Malek, *SAK* 12, 50; *JEA* 74, 136.

9 J. van Dijk in, H. D. Schneider *et al.*, "The Tomb-complex of Pay and Ra^{c}ia: Preliminary Report on the Saqqara Excavations, 1994 Season," *OMRO* 75 (1995), 19.

10 See already G. T. Martin, *The Hidden Tombs of Memphis, New Discoveries from the Time of Tutankhamun and Ramesses the Great*, (London, 1991), 117.

11 Cf. M. J. Raven *et al.*, *The Tomb of Iurudef, a Memphite Official in the Reign of Ramesses II* (EM 57, Leiden and London, 1991), 4-5 and Pl. 2.

12 J. van Dijk in, G. T. Martin *et al.*, *The Tombs of Three Memphite Officials: Ramose, Khay and Pabes* (EM 64, London, 1999), 9. For the original scenes, see Martin, *The Memphite Tomb of Horemheb* I, scenes [56] and [70].

13 J. van Dijk in, H. D. Schneider *et al.*, "The Tomb of Iniuia: Preliminary Report on the Saqqara Excavations, 1993," *JEA* 79 (1993), 7.

14 J. van Dijk in, Schneider *et al.*, *OMRO* 75 (1995), 19.

15 *LD* III, Pl. 241b; Cf. Van Dijk in, Schneider *et al.*, *OMRO* 75 (1995), 19.

16 For Tia, see Martin, *The Tomb of Tia and Tia*, 2; Van Dijk, 59-62. For princess Bentanat, see H. D. Schneider, *The Memphite Tomb of Horemheb, Commander-in-Chief of Tut^{c}ankhamûn, II: A Catalogue of the Finds* (EM 60, Leiden and London, 1996), 1-3 and 30, cat. 152-153.

17 Martin, *The Memphite Tomb of Horemheb, I*, scenes [65]-[66] and [56], respectively.

18 Martin, *The Memphite Tomb of Horemheb, I*, 71-3.

19 For this and the next stela, see now M. J. Raven, "A stela relocated," in: A. Niwinski (ed.), *Essays in Honour of Prof. Dr. Jadwiga Lipinska* (Warsaw Egyptological Studies I, Warsaw, 1997), 139-48, Pl. XVI.2-XIX.

20 The Tomb of Tia and Tia was decorated around year 20 of Ramesses II, and the husband seems to have

died shortly after (Van Dijk in, Martin, *The Tomb of Tia and Tia*, 59). Of course, the wife may have predeceased her husband.

21 J. van Dijk in, Zivie, *Memphis*, 42–45.

22 For convenient plans, see J. Malek, *JEA* 74, 126 fig. 1; Tawfik, *MDAIK* 47, fig. 1 opposite 408; and the various publications of the EES/Leiden mission quoted above.

23 A special article on this subject by the author is in preparation.

Notes on the Function
of the Great Hypostyle Hall
in the Egyptian Temple: A Theban Approach[*]

Hosam Refai
Helwan University, Cairo

In Thebes of the New Kingdom, the hypostyle hall of the Egyptian temple emerged as a result of religious and architectural considerations. There was, however, no homogeneous concept behind the classical form of the hypostyle hall. Quite dissimilar architectural backgrounds and building concepts defined the variety of forms brought forth[1] and whereas the function of each room of an Egyptian temple can normally be determined from its name and from the scenes on its walls, the hypostyle hall has no specific name,[2] nor is there a specific repertoire of scenes. Nevertheless, a decorative concept can be determined and shows that the decoration comprised mainly depictions of the royal cult contained in a variety of common offering and ritual scenes. Among the scenes of the royal cult, the coronation, legitimacy, and confirmation of king's sovereignty are of profound importance. The description of the hypostyle hall as a "Hall of Appearance" has hitherto been related to the processional scenes of the barques of the gods "appearing" during their processions in the hall.[3] Such scenes are found, however, only in the Great Hypostyle Hall at Karnak[4] and were perhaps also present in the festival hall of the Akhmenu.[5] In all other Theban hypostyle halls, scenes of barques are not included in the decorative repertoire but appear either at the front of or behind the hypostyle hall. In the Theban mortuary temples the barque processions clearly belong to the decoration of the open courts, as is the case in the Temple of Sety I (on the facade of the inner-temple)[6] and in Medinet Habu.[7] The side walls of the open courts, both in the Temple of Sety and the Ramesseum probably also had processional scenes similar to those of Medinet Habu. Taking into consideration that the festival hall of the Akhmenu and the Great Hypostyle Hall at Karnak were both open festival courts that were subsequently roofed, it becomes evident that the scenes of barque processions belong to the open court and not to the hypostyle hall.[8] Furthermore, scenes of the coronation rituals of the king are present in all non-Theban hypostyle halls, whereas scenes of barques appear only in the rock temples of Ramesses II in Wadi al-Sebu'a, al-Derr, and Abu Simbel.[9]

Thus the differences in the essential features of the decorative repertoire of the hypostyle hall and the festival court are clearly evident: in the hypostyle hall the coronation rituals and scenes related to the legitimacy of the king are dominant, whereas the festival court is dominated by scenes of the festivals to which the processional barque scenes belong. The similarity of the two buildings in architectural background, etymology, and function, however, allows decorative elements of the festival court to penetrate into the hypostyle hall, particularly because the barque cult is closely associated with the royal cult.

In trying to specify the function of the hypostyle halls of the Theban temples one has to distinguish between the temples of the east and west banks,[10] for while all the hypostyle halls of the temples of the west bank seem to have had a similar function, the function of those of the east bank was apparently contained in the overall function of each temple. Taking this into consideration, the function of the Theban hypostyle halls could be described as follows:

1. The function of the pillared festival hall of the Akhmenu is not easy to determine, as the function of the entire complex is still controversial.[11] While it is clear that the royal cult played a substantial role in the Akhmenu, arguments that the entire Akhmenu was a royal cult center[12] seem to ignore certain aspects of the Amun rituals and those of the Ennead of Karnak as well as the fact that the Akhmenu would in that case be unique in Egyptian temples.[13] It remains to be determined to what extent the royal cult was associated with the Akhmenu. Could the other aspects of the building be regarded as part of the royal cult or was it a place where both the royal and the divine cults met? The important role of the royal cult in the Akhmenu has already been referred to by Vandier, although he subordinated the royal cult to the divine cult and limited it to rooms XXIV and XXV.[14] Barguet offered a plausible explanation: "*Dans cet ensemble monumental, le culte divine est subordonné aux rites royaux, le roi tenant ici la première place.*"[15]

In light of Bell's research on Luxor Temple,[16] the Akhmenu may have been a predecessor of the Luxor Temple in its function, although the "renewal of the king" seems here to be associated with Sokar.[17] The idea of the "theological system of Luxor" was probably introduced by Hatshepsut, the need of an annual renewal festival being obvious to prove her legitimacy,[18] and it was under her reign that the Opet Festival became an annual event.[19] Thus it seems that the "renewal festival" in conjunction with the Opet Festival found its final site in Luxor under Amenhotep III, although it had been celebrated earlier in connection with the Akhmenu[20]—that is, if there were no earlier buildings of Hatshepsut or Thutmose III at Luxor suitable for this purpose which were subsequently replaced by Amenhotep III. The Akhmenu would thus have served as a point of departure for the barques and also as the place where the final rituals took place. The rites of the royal cult would probably have then been performed in the pillared hall and the adjoining rooms XXIII–XXV.[21] The pillared hall may have served as a *m3rw* or "Viewing Place" prior to that of Amenhotep III, which could perhaps be identified with the Hypostyle Hall of the Luxor Temple.[22]

The pillared hall of the Akhmenu was also a predecessor of the Great Hypostyle Hall at Karnak as an assembly place for the barques and point of departure for all festival processions. It is worth noting that the Akhmenu was ritually connected to the mortuary temple of Thutmose III in Deir al-Bahari, as was the case later with the Great Hypostyle Hall at Karnak and the Qurna-Temple of Sety I and with the court of Ramesses II in the Luxor Temple and the Ramesseum. The fact alone that the Akhmenu was point of departure for the divine barques and the Temple of Thutmose III was their final destination ritually united the two buildings. Furthermore, their architectural similarity cannot be overlooked, especially in the realization of the hypostyle hall and the location of the central chapels dedicated to Amun.[23]

2. In the Luxor Temple one has to regard the function of the hypostyle hall as part of the

"renewal festival" of the king in conjunction with the Opet Festival. As in the Akhmenu, most of the scenes of the hall are lost, making it difficult to tie the remaining scenes to a specific interpretation. As the remaining eastern wall of the hypostyle hall does not contain barque or festival scenes, the western wall would not have contained any either. The southern (rear) wall contained—as well as could be determined from the remains—large-scale scenes of the king, probably standing before Amun-Re.[24] Thus in general, the hall probably contained the standard repertoire of royal legitimacy scenes. The barque scenes are found in room VIII[25] (probably the barque chapel) and later in the colonnade,[26] which was built as a processional road for the barques. As the ceremonies in the temple must have been viewed by at least some representatives of the people, maybe the *rḫit*,[27] it is tempting to regard the hypostyle hall as the *mꜣrw* mentioned on the stela of Amenhotep III[28] found in his mortuary temple.[29] The hall would thus have served as a stage where the renewal of the king was presented to the public. It may also have had a similar function during the celebrations of the *Sed* Festival that Amenhotep III held in Thebes. During the Valley Festival the hall served as a barque station for the divine barques on the way to the west bank, a sort of second point of departure.[30]

    3. The function of the Great Hypostyle Hall at Karnak as an assembly hall and barque station for the divine barques is clearly identified by the inscriptions on the architraves, which describe the hall as "the Place of Appearance of the lord of the gods," at different festivals.[31] On almost every wall in the hall the procession of the barques is depicted,[32] making this hall the only one in Thebes—in addition to perhaps the Akhmenu[33]— where this "appearance" of the divine barques is present in the decoration. But the Great Hypostyle Hall was not only an assembly hall for the barques, it was *the* point of departure for all processions of the gods, who lived in Karnak. The description of the hall as *st ḫꜥit* clearly determines its practical function, as the first "appearance" of the barques actually took place here. The barque ritual was also performed here, as is evident from the scenes on the north and south walls—a ritual that was unlikely to have been held in any other Theban hypostyle hall. The Great Hypostyle Hall at Karnak is thus an exceptional one. The barque scenes here show events that actually took place in the hall and aim to emphasize Karnak as the point of departure and return of the divine barques, i.e., as their permanent residence.

    The overwhelming majority of the scenes in the hall are, however, dedicated to the royal cult. It even seems that they were meant to show each and every aspect related to it, culminating in the monumental scenes—the largest in the hall—of royal legitimacy and glorification found on both sides of the entrance wall.[34] Although clearly associated with the procession of the gods as they lie at the point where their barques leave the hall,[35] it is obviously the royal glorification that "appears" here. Furthermore, scenes of the divine birth of the king and his coronation rites are also present.[36] The legitimacy of the king is stressed through the depiction of the divine Sety I and his *ka*.[37] This particular scene appears on the south wall facing the Luxor Temple, probably alluding to the temple's function and the transference of the divine *ka*. Perhaps this is why the entire birth cycle is shown on that wall. A description of the complete repertoire of scenes related to the royal cult and depicted on the walls need not be repeated here, but one has to bear in mind that the barque processions are associated with the royal cult as they also serve as "glorification and perpetuation of royal power."[38] So not only the barques appear, but also the king "appears in the house of his father Amun."[39] The fact that the Hall was dedicated to Amun is not unusual, as all religious buildings, including those of the royal cult, were dedicated to gods.

    Particularly in the case of the Great Hypostyle Hall at Karnak one can differentiate between a practical and a ritual function. On the practical side, the hall served as an assembly point for the barques on their way to processions. The ritual function was closely related to the royal cult and the similarity of the names of both this hall and the Temple of Sety I in Qurna (*ḥwt-nṯr ȝḫ sthi mri n pth* or *mri n imn*) endorses this idea. This is not to say that the Great Hypostyle Hall was a mortuary temple;[40] it was more likely a "representative building" for the royal cult, representing the partial concept of the mortuary temple as a cult place of the deceased king, a sort of "royal temple within the divine temple."

4. The hypostyle halls of the mortuary temples of Sety I in Qurna, the Ramesseum and Medinet Habu all had similar functions. The Qurna Temple of Sety I initiated the form of the classical mortuary temple of the New Kingdom. The building was adequately adapted for the now fully-developed cult procedure and was merely copied and enlarged in the subsequent temples of Ramesses II and Ramesses III.[41] Side chapels were added to the Hypostyle Hall as a new architectural element. In the Temple of Sety there are three on each side, given the numbers I–VI in *PM*. Three of these (II, III, and V) are directly associated with the royal cult: Chapel II served as a purification chapel, Chapel III was the barque chapel of Sety-Amun and Chapel V a baptism chapel, where the king and Amun were being united.[42] The function of the other three chapels (I, IV, and VI) is difficult to specify as the wall scenes do not offer specific indications, but they probably had further functions related to the royal cult. The appearance of the female personification of the temple in Chapels III and V as mother of the king is noteworthy and underlines the role of the mortuary temple as place of rebirth and regeneration for the deceased king: "Behold, (I am) behind you, I am your temple, your mother."[43] The depiction of Hathor as Western Goddess,[44] probably a unique example in Theban temples, emphasizes this idea.

On the walls of the hypostyle hall scenes of the royal cult are dominant,[45] and although the inscriptions on the architrave describe the Hall as a "place of appearance of the lord of the gods on his Beautiful Feast of the Valley" or a "Hall of Appearance in the inside of his temple, a place of appearance for his splendid cult-statue on his Beautiful Feast of the Valley,"[46] one has to regard these descriptions in relation to the royal cult. The barques of the gods entered the hypostyle hall not merely to "appear" but to take the king's barque into procession. This coming together of the divine barques and the royal one was the most important ritual performance to take place in the hall. The fact that the royal barque now joined those of the gods probably alone attested to the legitimacy of the king and was a symbolic re-enthronement. The king now became divine, as the suckling scenes of the king by Hathor and Mut at both ends of the hypostyle hall[47] indicate. At this point the divine sphere begins and the king enters the rear part of the temple as a god, having been united with Amun in the hall previously, and their barques now join.[48] This was the main purpose of the "appearance" of the barques.

The wall scenes clearly support this idea. Depiction of the barques here was of no special importance; it was sufficient to depict them on the facade leading to the hall.[49] The wall scenes show the result of the rituals: the renewed confirmation of the king's rule. The function of the hall is thus closely associated with its side chambers. As a unit they were dedicated to the cult of the king, and Stadelmann's description, calling this part of the temple the "Identity Temple," "The place where the mystical union of Amun and the dead king takes place,"[50] is quite appropriate.

The hypostyle halls of both the Ramesseum and Medinet Habu could be regarded in the same manner. In the Ramesseum again the scenes of the barques do not appear in the hypostyle hall, but instead are found in the "Astronomical Room" behind it, which led Arnold to believe it functioned as the "Hall of Appearance."[51] As in the Temple of Sety, and later in Medinet Habu, the scenes of the barques are not inside the hypostyle hall but in the adjoining premises.[52] Here also the scenes on the walls are closely related to the royal cult and the legitimacy of the king.[53] Even the rare depiction of war scenes inside the hypostyle hall should be regarded as part of the royal cult, the "destruction of the enemies" and the triumph over chaos being of such importance during the war-intensive reign of Ramesses II that they could penetrate apotropaically to the inside of the temple.[54] Although Ramesses II describes the Great Hypostyle Hall at Karnak as *st ḥʿit*, as did his father,[55] the architrave inscriptions describe the hypostyle hall of the Ramesseum as *st ḥtp n nb nṯrw m ḥb =f n int*.[56] Thus the function of the hall, as far as the barques are concerned, is specified. The barques were placed here not to "appear" but to take the barque of the king into procession. The royal barque was undoubtedly placed in one of the unfortunately destroyed side chapels (perhaps in Chapel 6 on the north side, which has a wider entrance than that of the other chapels)[57] or in one of the two chapels of the northern part of the west wall (and if so probably the one to the north, which had direct access to it from the right entrance of the hypostyle). The function of the hypostyle hall of the Ramesseum is therefore identical to that of the Temple of Sety and this part of the temple could be described as an "Identity Temple" as well. The second hypostyle hall is also closely linked to the royal cult.[58] The barque scenes here merely demonstrate the result of the ritual which had previously taken place, the king's barque now joining those of the gods. The scenes on the west wall opposite the entrance confirm the legitimacy of the king.[59]

The same function could be assigned to the hypostyle hall of Medinet Habu. Here also, scenes of the legitimacy of the king dominate the wall decoration.[60] Unfortunately the inscriptions of the architraves are missing, but they would most probably have described the hall as a resting place for the barques as well. The specific function of each of the side chapels is difficult to determine, but at least Chapels 1–3 are directly associated with the royal cult.[61] Chapel 1 probably served as a purification chapel.[62] The somewhat larger Chapel 4, or possibly Chapel 7 in the right rear, could have served as a barque chapel.[63]

In an overall view then, the functions of all three hypostyle halls and the three mortuary temples in general were to a large extent identical.

Notes:

* The present study was originally part of my dissertation titled: *Untersuchungen zum Bildprogramm der großen Säulensäle in den thebanischen Templen des Neuen Reiches* (Beiträge zur Ägyptologie, Band 18; Wien, 2000).

1 For a detailed discussion of the architectural concepts see Refai, *Säulensäle*, 25–29.

2 For the etymological details see Refai, *Säulensäle*, 30–32.

3 D. Arnold, *Wandrelief und Raumfunktion in ägyptischen Tempeln des Neuen Reiches* (MÄS 2; Berlin, 1962), 94 f.

4 H. Nelson, *The Great Hypostyle Hall at Karnak 1, Part 1.The Wall Reliefs* (OIP 106; Chicago, 1981), Pls. 37, 38, 53, 76, 151, 152, (159), 178, 180, 197, and 226.

5 P. Barguet, *Le temple d'Amon-Rê à Karnak* (RAPH 21; Cairo, 1962), 175.

6 *PM* II, 408, n. 5–7.

7 *PM* II, 498 ff., n. 93–98; *Medinet Habu* IV, Pls. 227–232.

8 See also Arnold, *Wandrelief*, 106 ff. The festival court in the "Luxor Temple," also seems to have been decorated with scenes of barque processions, see Arnold, *Wandrelief*, 112; A. Gayet, *Le temple de Louxor I: Constructions d'Aménophis III* (MMAF 15; Paris, 1894), fig. 4.

9 Arnold, *Wandrelief*, 98 ff. It remains questionable, however, whether we should regard the second pillared halls in such temples as corresponding to the hypostyle halls of free-standing temples.

10 R. Stadelmann, "Totentempel und Millionen-jahrhaus in Theben," *MDAIK* 35 (1979), 313.

11 Vandier, Manuel II, 890 ff.; Barguet, *Temple d'Amon-Rê*, 157 ff. and 283 ff.; G. Haeny, *Basilikale Anlagen in der ägyptischen Baukunst des neuen Reiches* (BeiträgeBf 9; Wiesbaden, 1970), 13 ff.; F. Daumas, *L'interprétation des temples égyptiens anciens à la lumière des temples gréco-romains* (Cahiers de Karnak VI; Cairo, 1980), 274 ff.

12 Haeny, *Basilikale Anlagen*, 13 ff.

13 Daumas, *L'interprétation*, 266 and 274 f. The suggestions of Daumas, however, are mostly unsatisfactory, see Refai, *Säulensäle*, 49.

14 Vandier, *Manuel* II, 900 f.

15 Barguet, *Temple d'Amon-Rê*, 157. For more details cf. Refai, *Säulensäle*, 50.

16 L. Bell, "Luxor Temple and the Cult of the Royal Ka," *JNES* 44.4 (1985), 251–294; see also G. Haeny, "Zur Funktion der 'Häuser für Millionen Jahre'," in: *HÄB* 37 (1994), 101 f.

17 G. A. Gaballa and K. A. Kitchen, "The Festival of Sokar," *Or* 38 (1969), 27 f.; Barguet, *Temple d'Amon-Rê*, 284 f.

18 Bell, "Luxor Temple," 290 f.

19 Cf. W. J. Murnane, "Opetfest," *LÄ* IV, 574.

20 The scenes on the eastern wall of the pillared hall (*PM* II, 110, n. 334–336) seem to fit as depictions of the initial festival, for a detailed discussion cf. Refai, *Säulensäle*, 51, n. 142.

21 See also Arnold, *Wandrelief*, 65.

22 Refai, *Säulensäle*, 68f.

23 J. Lipinska, *Deir el-Bahari II, The Temple of Tuthmosis III, Architecture* (Warsaw, 1977), 26ff.

24 Arnold, *Wandrelief*, 100.

25 Gayet, *Temple de Louxor*, fig. 125–127; R. A. Schwaller De Lubicz, *Le temple de l'homme. Apet du sud a Louxor* II (Paris, 1957), Pl. XXXI.

26 W. Wolf, *Das schöne Fest von Opet* (Leipzig, 1931), Pls. 1 and 2; The Epigraphic Survey of the University of Chicago, *Reliefs and Inscriptions at Luxor Temple, Volume 1: The Festival Procession of Opet in the Colonnade Hall* (OIP 11 Chicago, 1994).

27 Arnold, *Wandrelief*, 95; Bell, "Luxor Temple," 275.

28 *Urk.* IV, 1651, 6 ff. For details cf. Refai, *Säulensäle*, 68 f.

29 R. Stadelmann, "Tempel und Tempelnamen in Theben-Ost und -West," *MDAIK* 34 (1978), 179; Bell, "Luxor Temple," 275.

30 Stadelmann, "Tempel und Tempelnamen," 180.

31 L.-A. Christophe, "La face sud des architraves surmontant les colonnes 74–80 de la grande salle hypostyle de Karnak," *BIFAO* 60 (1960), 76 and 77, n. 1; Haeny, *Basilikale Anlagen*, 59.

32 H. Nelson, *The Great Hypostyle Hall*, Pls. 37, 38, 53, 76, 151, 152, (159), 178, 180, 197, and 226.

33 *PM* II, 110, n. 334–336; Refai, *Säulensäle*, 51, n. 142.

34 Nelson, *Hypostyle Hall*, Pls. 7 and 137.

35 Arnold, *Wandrelief*, 104.

36 Nelson, *Hypostyle Hall*, Pls. 66, 67 and 70.

37 Nelson, *Hypostyle Hall*, Pl. 42.

38 Stadelmann, "Tempel und Tempelnamen," 177.

39 Nelson, *Hypostyle Hall*, Pl. 64.

40 As Haeny suggests, *Basilikale Anlagen*, 61. See also Stadelmann, "Tempel und Tempelnamen," 175 ff.

41 Cf. Stadelmann, *Totentempel*, 310.

42 For details cf. Refai, *Säulensäle*, 159 ff.

43 H. Refai, "Der Tempel als Mutter," *SAK* 30 (2001), 1–6.

44 *PM* II, 412, n. 45. For the function of the Western Goddess cf. H. Refai, *Die Göttin des Westens in den thebanischen Gräbern des Neuen Reiches* (ADAIK 12; Berlin, 1996), 25 ff.

45 *PM* II, 410.

46 *LD* III, 132 b and d (= 152 d).

47 *PM* II, 410, n. 21 and 26.

48 Stadelmann, *Totentempel*, 315 f.

49 *PM* II, 408, n. 6 and 7.

50 Stadelmann, *Totentempel*, 315.

51 Arnold, *Wandrelief*, 101.

52 In all three temples the side walls would have provided enough space for such scenes. It is very unlikely that the side walls in the Ramesseum contained any barque scenes because they were already present in the second hypostyle hall and also because this was the case in the Temple of Sety and in Medinet Habu, both of which have similar wall scenes and wall proportions to those in the Ramesseum.

53 *PM* II, 438.

54 E. Hornung, *Geschichte als Fest. Zwei Vorträge zum Geschichtsbild der frühen Menschheit* (Darmstadt, 1966), 17 and Arnold, *Wandrelief*, 109 f.

55 Christophe, "La face sud," 77 and n. 1.

56 W. Helck, *Die Ritualdarstellungen des Ramesseum* (ÄA 25; Wiesbaden, 1972), 136.

57 Hölscher, *Medinet Habu* III, 73.

58 Refai, *Säulensäle*, 189 f.

59 C. Sheikholeslami, "The Function of the Second Hypostyle Hall in the Ramesseum," *Memnonia* VI (1995), 101 ff; Refai, *Säulensäle*, 190.

60 *Medinet Habu* V, Pls. 303, 308–317, 338, and 348.

61 Stadelmann, *Totentempel*, 313; W. Murnane, *United with Eternity. A Concise Guide to the Monuments of Medinet Habu* (Chicago/Cairo, 1980), 43 ff.

62 Arnold, *Wandrelief*, 76. See also Hölscher, *Medinet Habu* III, 13.

63 Hölscher, Medinet Habu III, 13; Murnane, *United with Eternity*, 45 f.

The Abydos Cemeteries in
the Late Old Kingdom

Janet Richards
University of Michigan

In Egyptian archaeology, we are uniquely positioned to address the development and use of sacred landscapes over thousands of years, and to discuss the shifting pattern of access to them by different social and political groups. Furthermore, we can sometimes contextualize actual historical individuals within these ancient settings, and integrate the information they communicate through the medium of their inscriptions with the formal and spatial dimensions of their physical context. The archaeology of these individuals, seen within the local, regional, and state systems in which they operated, can refine our understanding of the ways in which archaeological remains complement historical data in pivotal periods of Egyptian history such as the late Old Kingdom.

Since the nineteenth century, scholars have known that an important cemetery of the Fifth and Sixth Dynasties was part of the long-lived sacred landscape at Abydos in an area called "the Middle Cemetery" by modern archaeologists. Lepsius documented the tomb of a vizier Iww in 1840.[1] Between 1858–1870 Mariette's activities at the site yielded false doors, stelae, and funerary equipment inscribed for other important officials.[2] The provenance of these discoveries seems to have been a prominent hill on the low desert plateau termed *la necropole du centre* by Mariette. One individual for whom several pieces of mortuary furniture emerged was the Governor of Upper Egypt, Weni the Elder, whose lengthy autobiography (CGC 1435) details his political career. Given the paucity of stratigraphic or locational data provided by Mariette, the spatial organization and general character of his *necropole du centre* has remained unknown, along with any specific context for Weni, whose inscription now figures prominently in the political history of the period. Brovarski has proposed a hypothetical reconstruction of the mortuary landscape and the tomb of this official, but this contextual discussion was of necessity tentative in scope.[3]

A preliminary picture of the wider Old Kingdom mortuary landscape can be pieced together from the publications of a series of excavations in the early twentieth century. We knew that during the early Old Kingdom, neither the Middle nor the Northern Cemetery were in use for private burials (this area being restricted to royal purposes); instead, a cemetery was located some distance further north, in Peet's Area D.[4] Here, Peet excavated about 45 shaft graves with small *mastabas* (brick-faced and sand-filled) clustered around one large chapel. The excavator believed that more graves were lost beneath the cultivation, but the cemetery was nonetheless relatively small.

During the Fifth Dynasty, however, the focus of private burial activity shifted to the northeastern ridge of the Middle Cemetery, where Ayrton, Garstang, Loat, Peet, and Frankfort excavated well over a thousand Fifth and Sixth Dynasty graves.[5] The predominant type of tomb was a square or rectangular shaft, often with a chamber cut at the bottom; simple surface graves were also excavated in the cemetery. These graves contained burials in loosely-contracted or extended positions with heads north, often in badly-preserved coffins, with a relatively limited range and number of artifacts, including head rests, mirrors, calcite and other stone vessels, pottery, jewelry, and copper objects. No surface architecture seems to have been preserved for any of the graves.

The burial ground shifted to Area E, a level stretch of the Middle Cemetery plateau, sometime during the Sixth Dynasty, when space in the northeastern ridge was exhausted. Peet excavated 129 Old Kingdom shaft graves here, plus several surface graves, and surmised that the cemetery in fact extended some distance to the west. Only one superstructure was preserved, a very small mud-brick *mastaba* of questionable date.[6]

The overall impression, then, of the Northeastern Ridge and Cemetery E, is of two areas of numerous, relatively modest burials, lacking surface architecture and inscribed stone elements, bracketing a steep hill where the elites of Mariette's excavations were buried. The sharp increase in the number of burials compared to the earlier Old Kingdom cemetery is striking, and may well relate to the growth in importance of the town of Abydos and its temples. Worth noting also, is that when this "middle-class" cemetery was originally established on the Northeastern Ridge in the Fifth Dynasty, it lay outside the restricted zone buffering the Early Dynastic royal remains, and was topographically distinct from the main plateau of the Middle Cemetery. It was only when space ran out that this kind of burial activity moved into the low desert, beyond the elite zone. These modest burials were spatially partitioned from the elite zone, both by distance and topography.

The questions raised by this synthesis are numerous. How does this "middle class" cemetery relate formally and chronologically to the mysterious zone it brackets, and what overall picture of the Old Kingdom mortuary landscape at Abydos results? What is the nature of the mysterious Mariette zone, both spatially and formally, and can the original contexts of the Mariette inscriptions, such as the autobiography of Weni the Elder, be identified? How did the cemetery as a whole articulate with the adjacent town and temple area, and how does it illuminate late Old Kingdom history?

Under the aegis of the University of Michigan and the Pennsylvania-Yale-New York University Expedition to Abydos, I initiated a reinvestigation of the Middle Cemetery in 1995, hoping to address these questions. It has so far comprised two survey seasons, one full season of excavation, and two productive study visits to the Egyptian Museum.[7]

The data gathered have already provided some answers to the questions raised above, information on previously unknown elites, and evidence for wholly unsuspected votive activity. Additionally, fresh facts have emerged regarding the career and family of Weni the Elder, and the disposition of his tomb in the Middle Cemetery.

The term "Middle Cemetery" refers generally to the 50-hectare low desert plateau which lies local south of the Royal Wadi in North Abydos (fig. 1). We created a detailed topographic map of this entire area, confirming that it is internally differentiated by varying topographic levels, including a prominent "hill" sloping off steeply on four sides. Originally the Middle Cemetery also included the Northeastern Ridge; it has now vanished beneath the modern villages, although Mr. Ahmed el-Khattib, then General Inspector of al-Balyana, has commented that vestiges remained visible in the early 1980s.

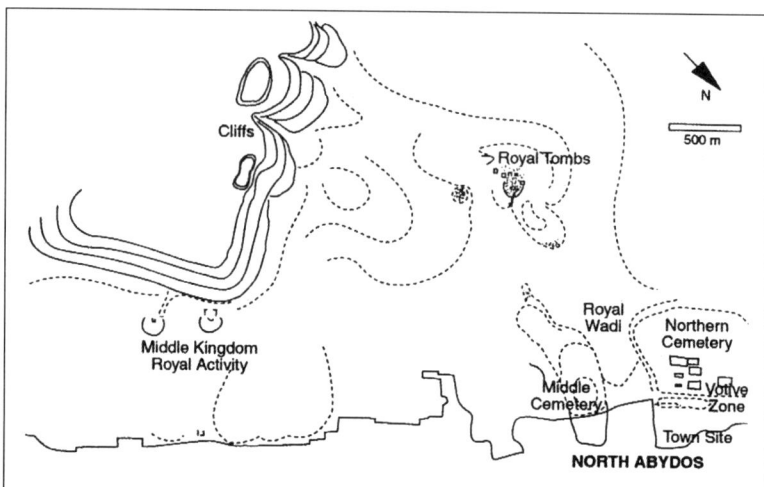

The steep escarpment now adjacent to the village of Beni Mansur fits most closely the description of Mariette's *necropole du centre*, and therefore after creation of our map, we intensified the collection and analysis of ceramics in that area to evaluate the chronological periods present. In this sample, Sixth Dynasty wares and shapes predominated, with coarse offering wares far out-numbering the finer red wares associated with burial chambers. The next time period documented on the surface was the Late through Ptolemaic Roman period, implying a nearly 1600 year hiatus in use of the cemetery. Also documented during survey were several large, ruined mud-brick *mastabas*, reinforcing the notion that Mariette's *necropole du centre* lay here.

During the first full excavation season, completed in December 1999, we returned to areas with the highest percentage of Old Kingdom ceramic and significant architectural remains. We opened a total of four areas, but here I will focus on the two most important areas in terms of understanding the late Old Kingdom cemetery. The first of these was a badly ruined *mastaba* that was initially the most visible chapel in the Mariette area. Excavation of this area revealed a large and elaborate complex focused on the mastaba, and a number of subsidiary monuments con-

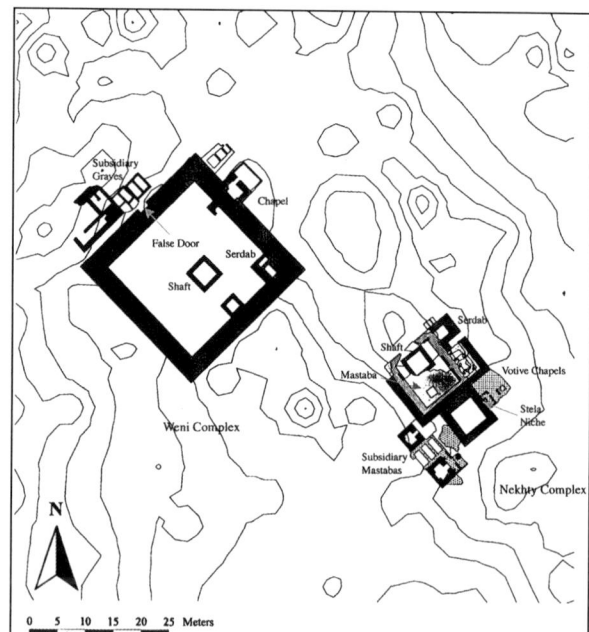

Fig. 2: Map of primary areas excavated, 1999 season (produced by G. Compton).

402

structed around it in the late Old Kingdom, the First Intermediate Period, the Middle Kingdom (surprisingly), and the Late Period (fig. 2).

The first phase of construction in this complex involved the excavation of a 3.30 m square deep shaft. Originally this shaft was completely covered by the construction of a solid *mastaba*, the original dimensions of which were 10 x 8 m, with a minimum height of 2.5 m. Previous excavators, however, destroyed nearly half the *mastaba* to gain access to the shaft. The complex belonged to an individual not otherwise documented at Abydos-Nekhty, a prince, count, sole companion, and chief priest, as attested on the lintel of his burial chamber.

The *mastaba* and its primary offering area (east of the structure) were subsequently enclosed by a wall measuring 13 x16 m. Both offering area and enclosure wall were badly destroyed, probably during the same episode that removed half the *mastaba*. Fragments of menu list reliefs of very high quality were found in this area. The local east wall incorporates a robbed-out *serdab* and limestone slabs *outside* the wall, implying an extension of the complex to local north.

To local south of the primary complex, a somewhat later building was added. This later building incorporated a niche for a stela on its local east exterior; although the stela was missing from the emplacement, its rough base stone was still *in situ*, as was a limestone offering table with a *htp* sign and two libation basins. The niche was the focus of a small walled courtyard, where fragments of late Old Kingdom beer jars were excavated. A comparison of the effective dimensions of the niche with those of the stela of Mezenet,[8] the granddaughter of the vizier Iww, offers a tempting fit between archaeological context and museum artifact.

In this area, 50 cm above the original Old Kingdom-use surface, small mud-brick votive chapels aligned with Nekhty's complex were constructed in the Middle Kingdom. We excavated an intact basalt pair statue here, inscribed for a man named Intef and his wife Ita. Small votive chapels of the Middle Kingdom period were discovered elsewhere during the excavations, indicating a wholly unsuspected level of votive activity during that period. It is possible that a refurbishment of this elite cemetery went hand-in-hand with Middle Kingdom royal activities at Umm al Qa'ab.

To the local west of the primary complex, we excavated two satellite *mastaba* chapels. Two door-jamb fragments were recovered from the northern chapel, inscribed for Nekhet-Kay. The southern chapel was generally better preserved, with a courtyard fronting its eastern entrance, bounded by a low mud-brick wall, two emplacements for mini-obelisks, a mud pavement, and a circular mud-plastered basin for burnt offerings placed directly opposite the entrance to the chapel. The chapel interior contained badly-deteriorated tomb paintings of activities on an elite estate, including a sequence of bread-making operations.

We exposed three shafts lying between the two *mastabas*, and excavated two. No *in situ* remains were found, apart from two model copper tools characteristic of the late Old Kingdom. The ceramic assemblage for the entire area indicates continuous use from the late Old Kingdom through the First Intermediate Period.

Finally, throughout the general vicinity of Nekhty's complex, we documented badly-disturbed Saite period vaulted tombs, constructed in alignment with the central Old Kingdom remains, but not encroaching on them. This pattern suggests that in the later periods of Egyptian history, local and perhaps regional populations of Abydos were not only aware of the Old Kingdom cemetery, but were still respectful of its importance, and careful to avoid intrusive building. That changed during the Ptolemaic-Roman period, when earlier remains were ruthlessly overbuilt.

Lying local north of this complex is an even larger structure (see fig. 2), which, during excavation, yielded similar kinds of diachronic patterning—late Old Kingdom through First Intermediate Period, respectful Late Period re-use, and Ptolemaic-Roman and Coptic recycling. It also provided new information on Weni the Elder, and most likely was the final resting place of that enterprising individual.

We already knew that by the end of the career described in his autobiography, Weni had attained the office of True Governor of Upper Egypt.[9] He also held other such titles such as Count, Chamberlain, and Overseer of the Scribes of the King's Documents, to name a few. The overall impression of Weni's narrative is that of upward mobility on the strength of his personal qualities and extraordinary service alone, identifying himself as one of Eyre's category of "new men."[10] Weni's high rank has led some scholars to hypothesize that he was not really buried at Abydos, and that his autobiography was placed within a votive chapel instead of a tomb.[11] A further layer of uncertainty lies in the not infrequent confusion in Mariette's records. A cogent example is a relief fragment of a tomb owner's upper torso (CGC 1670), which Borchardt assigned to Weni's Abydos assemblage, despite its designation as a Saqqara find.[12]

Our excavations have confirmed that Weni was buried at Abydos. In 1996, we documented what we believed to be a solid mud-brick *mastaba* about 16 m long on its local north face. Excavation, however, revealed it to be a massive enclosure, 29 m long on each side, 3 m thick, and with a perceptible batter to its exterior and interior surfaces (see fig. 2). It is preserved to a height of 5.5 m, but was certainly higher originally. The builders constructed a great burial shaft within this enclosure along with two other smaller shafts; the interior of the enclosure was then filled with clean sand, and possibly roofed to seal the shafts, and to present the appearance of a solid *mastaba*. This *mastaba* is situated at what would have been the highest point in the Middle Cemetery, and its visual impact on inhabitants of the town below would have echoed that of the Early Dynastic funerary enclosures across the wadi in the Northern Cemetery. Like them, it is so large that it is visible from the high cliffs more than half a mile away.

In the earliest levels, a small sample of Dynasty artifacts emerged: a model black stone vase from a Sixth Dynasty "Opening of the Mouth" assemblage, a fragment of a limestone bowl, and a number of inscribed relief fragments. These latter included two pieces which when joined together furnished the name "Weni the Elder."

Fig. 3: North wall of Weni the Elder's *mastaba* with false door *in situ.*

Further evidence emerged supporting this association. In a large niche on the north wall exterior, we excavated a damaged false door inscribed for Weni the Elder (fig. 3). Not only does this false door provide us with a "good name" for Weni (Nefer Nekhet Mery-ra), but it also documents his final career promotion, a fact not recorded in his autobiography: Chief Judge and Vizier.

A series of shaft and surface burials lay to local north of the false door. The central shaft contained the intact burial of an adult male, deposited in nested wooden coffins, with the remnants of a funerary mask in place over his head. Based upon associated ceramic, these burials ranged in date from the late Old Kingdom to the First Intermediate Period, suggesting that Weni's grave became the focus of a group cemetery—perhaps a kinship network.

On the east face of the *mastaba*, we discovered further evidence of Weni. In the surface fill, we excavated a square-sided limestone door jamb or pillar. Preserved to a length of two meters, it preserves probably two-thirds of its original height. It is inscribed for the same Vizier Iww documented by Lepsius, and on both sides of this jamb, male relatives present offerings to Iww. One of these relatives is identified as: "his eldest son, the governor of Upper Egypt Weni the Elder." Thus, despite the stress laid by Weni in his autobiography on personal merit as his road to success, it is clear that he belonged already to a powerful family—although he chose not to communicate this fact.

Also on the east, we excavated a small offering chapel constructed directly onto the wall of the *mastaba*. Entered through a narrow doorway on its east side, the chapel was originally completely decorated with painted low relief depicting offering bearers. Several blocks remained *in situ* on the walls and doorway; nine additional blocks were excavated in the center of the chapel. One exterior doorjamb was partially preserved, bearing a standing representation of the tomb owner, preserved from the waist down. Based upon the style and quality of the relief on this jamb and the other chapel reliefs, it is likely that this doorjamb was a gift from a royal workshop, while the scenes of offering bearers might have been produced locally. Comparison of the doorjamb relief with the disputed Weni relief in the Egyptian Museum (CGC 1670) suggests that we can re-situate the original placement of the former above the *in situ* torso and legs of the tomb owner. Other fragments of relief found in the same area display the same high quality of work.

It seems clear that this half-destroyed chapel is the original context of Weni's funerary furniture excavated by Mariette, and I propose the following reconstruction. Weni's first false door (CGC 1574), the pink-washed example in the Museum, was placed in the main niche of this chapel, the floors of which were also pink-washed to simulate red granite. I believe that the autobiography (CGC 1435) was mounted on the exterior face of the chapel, whose walls are sufficiently thick to have borne its undoubtedly great weight.[13] Such a placement would explain both the off-axial location of the chapel entrance—which was pushed north to accommodate the 2.75 m width of the autobiography—and the condition of the latter, which is extremely weathered. The two miniature obelisks inscribed for Weni (CGC 1309, 1310) would have been placed just outside the entrance to the chapel. Upon Weni's promotion to Chief Judge and Vizier at the very end of his career, he installed his second false door on the north face of his *mastaba*. Both false doors align with the probable location of Weni's burial chamber, on two crucial axes. The final piece of funerary architecture to be set into place, and the only piece bearing the rank *iry prt*, was a lintel dedicated by Weni's son Iww (CGC 1643), and most probably this too formed part of the eastern chapel.

In the *mastaba* interior, we excavated an extensive deposit of offering pottery around the mouth of the great shaft. A minimum of 508 Sixth Dynasty collared wine jars filled with mud were found in piles to the local east and west of the shaft, and laid out neatly to local north. Among this deposit of pottery, ten *in situ* coffin burials of the Late Period were excavated, indicating later re-use of the interior of Weni's *mastaba* as a small cemetery; the jumbled bones of at least 40 individuals piled against the interior face of the *mastaba*'s east wall were probably cleared away from the same area by Mariette's men.

A rectangular *serdab* in the southeast corner (see fig. 2) contained the deteriorated remains of more than 30 bases for wooden statues and production scenes. This mostly destroyed deposit yielded several disembodied elements of figures such as arms, hands, and animal fragments, as well as several painted limestone components of the production scenes. Also found was a beautifully-executed limestone statuette of the tomb owner as a young boy, identified as *ḥȝty-ꜥ* Weni (fig. 4).

This combined evidence strongly suggests that we have located Weni's tomb, the primary monument in an elite zone that was the first private activity in the Middle Cemetery proper after a restriction of nearly 700 years.[14] The tomb

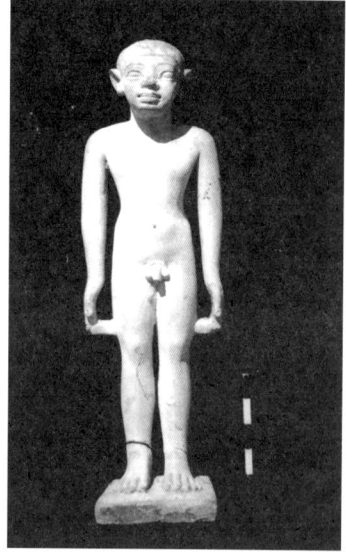

Fig. 4: Limestone statuette of Weni as a boy.

makes a striking visual statement of access, wealth, and political power, which may have mirrored a similar statement in the Old Kingdom town at Abydos.

Matthew Adams, who co-directs the settlement project with David O'Connor,[15] has commented on the presence there of a mysterious, massive building, which he suspects is the remains of a governor's palace. Given its scale, and the similarity of its construction techniques to those documented in Weni's tomb complex, it is tempting to attribute its existence to Weni's building activities at Abydos, which could then be seen as bridging town and cemetery, two parts of an active social and political landscape.

The picture which is emerging, based upon the results of this initial season of excavation, confirms the existence in the Abydos Middle Cemetery of large and elaborate burial complexes for prominent individuals of the late Old Kingdom, the context of Mariette's finds. This exclusive zone also included more modest burials contemporary with those in the Northeastern Ridge and Cemetery E, but perhaps representing kin or dependents of the officials here. The rise in importance of the cemetery may correspond to the accelerating prominence of Osiris at Abydos, and the growing political power of the great Abydene families, including those of Djau and Iww; and the Middle Kingdom votive attention and long-lived respect for the cemetery attests to the weight of local tradition at this regional and ceremonial center.

Notes:

1 R. Lepsius, *Denkmaler* I (Berlin, 1849–56), 65.

2 A. Mariette, Abydos I–II. *Description des fouilles executées sur l'emplacement de cette ville Tome II* (Paris, 1869, 1880), 38–41; *Catalogue générale des monuments d'Abydos* (Paris, 1880).

3 E. Brovarski, "Abydos in the Old Kingdom and First Intermediate Period," I, in *Hommages a Jean Leclant* I (IFAO Bibliotheque d'Etude 106/1, Cairo, 1994), 99–121.

4 T. E. Peet, *Cemeteries of Abydos* III (London, 1913), 8–22.

5 W.L.S. Loat, "A Sixth Dynasty Cemetery at Abydos," *JEA* 9 (1923), 161–63; J. Garstang, "Excavations at Abydos 1909," *LAAA* 2 (1909), 125–129; T. E. Peet, *Cemeteries of Abydos* II (London, 1914), 76–83; H. Frankfort, "The Cemeteries of Abydos: work of the season 1925–26," *JEA* 16 (1930), 213–219.

6 E. Naville, *Cemeteries of Abydos* I (London, 1914), 1–34; Peet, *Cemeteries of Abydos* II, 17–29.

7 This work has been made possible through the gracious permission of Dr. Gaballah Ali Gaballah and the Permanent Committee, and the kind support in Cairo of Drs. Mohammed Saleh and Mohammed el-Shimmy of the Egyptian Museum, Mr. Mahmoud el-Halwagy and his curatorial staff, and Mr. Mark Easton, Mme. Amira Khattab, and the staff of the American Research Center. In southern Egypt I am grateful to Dr. Yahia el-Sabry el-Misri, General Director of the Antiquities of Sohag Governorate, Mr. Ahmed el-Khattib, General Inspector of Balyana, and Mr. Adel Makary Zekery, who acted as Inspector for the project. I would also like to thank Drs. William Kelly Simpson and David O'Connor, co-directors of the Pennsylvania-Yale-New York University Expedition, and Drs. Günter Dreyer and Vera Muller of the German Institute for their great generosity with equipment. Last but not least, I am always grateful to my phenomenal house and field crews at Abydos.

8 CGC 1576

9 See M. Lichtheim, *Ancient Egyptian Literature* 1 (California, 1975), 18–23, for translation and bibliography.

10 C. Eyre, "Weni's career and Old Kingdom historiography," in C. Eyre et al, (eds.), *The Unbroken Reed* (London, 1994), 107–124.

11 Lichtheim, *Literature*, 18.

12 L. Borchardt, *Denkmaler des Alten Reiches* I (Berlin, 1937), teil II, 127, blatt 88.

13 This possibility was suggested by Brovarski in "Abydos," 115.

14 J. Richards, "Conceptual landscapes in the Egyptian Nile Valley," in W. Ashmore and B. Knapp, Eds., *Archaeologies of Landscape: Contemporary Perspectives* (Oxford, 1999).

15 M. Adams, "Community and societal organization in early historic Egypt," *Newsletter of the American Research Center in Egypt* 158/159 (1992), 1–10.

The "Re-conquest" of the Great Sand Sea

Heiko Riemer

Heinrich-Barth-Institut, Köln

This paper will focus on the very early origin of Egyptian civilization in the desert, which started with the climatic change at the beginning of the Holocene. At that time prehistoric people reoccupied—or re-conquered as mentioned above—the Great Sand Sea, which was one of the largest regions of the Libyan Desert without ground water or any other permanent water supply. Archaeological remains represent prehistoric occupation of the Libyan Desert during the Holocene "wet" period from the ninth to the sixth millennium BCE (calibrated).[1] Since 1995, the interdisciplinary Arid Climate, Adaptation and Cultural Innovation in Africa (ACACIA) project at the University of Cologne and the Heinrich Barth Institute has conducted archaeological fieldwork in desert areas to reconstruct this prehistoric occupation.[2] Research also took place in the southern Great Sand Sea where large longitudinal dunes run from north to south. Following a combined geographical-archaeological survey, carried out in the winter of 1995/96,[3] site surveys were conducted in the area of Regenfeld in 1996 and 1997 (fig. 1). Excavations and intensive surface collections were carried out at three major sites along an old water pool or "mud pan" (called playa), 50 km northwest of the so-called campsite Regenfeld—named by Gerhard Rohlfs during his desert expedition in 1873.[4]

Numerous artifact scatters (clusters) were situated between the shoreline of an old water pool and the eastern border of a large longitudinal sand dune. The sand dunes were built up during the Pleistocene. The upper reddish playa deposits of the depression were accumulated during the Holocene by successive rainfalls that filled a temporary lake inside the mud bowl. Moreover, the dune sands became stronger with humidity and stored the water, forming a fertile ground for sparse vegetation like grass shrubs, tamarisks, and acacia trees. These resources were most attractive for prehistoric campsites. Collection of surface and seven excavations revealed numerous occupation events from the early Epipaleolithic to the Ceramic. Radiocarbon analysis of 15 samples yielded a time span from 8700 to 5400 BCE (9300–6400 BP uncalibrated) (fig. 2).

Most of the prehistoric localities existed along the edge of the playa pool or on the old dune

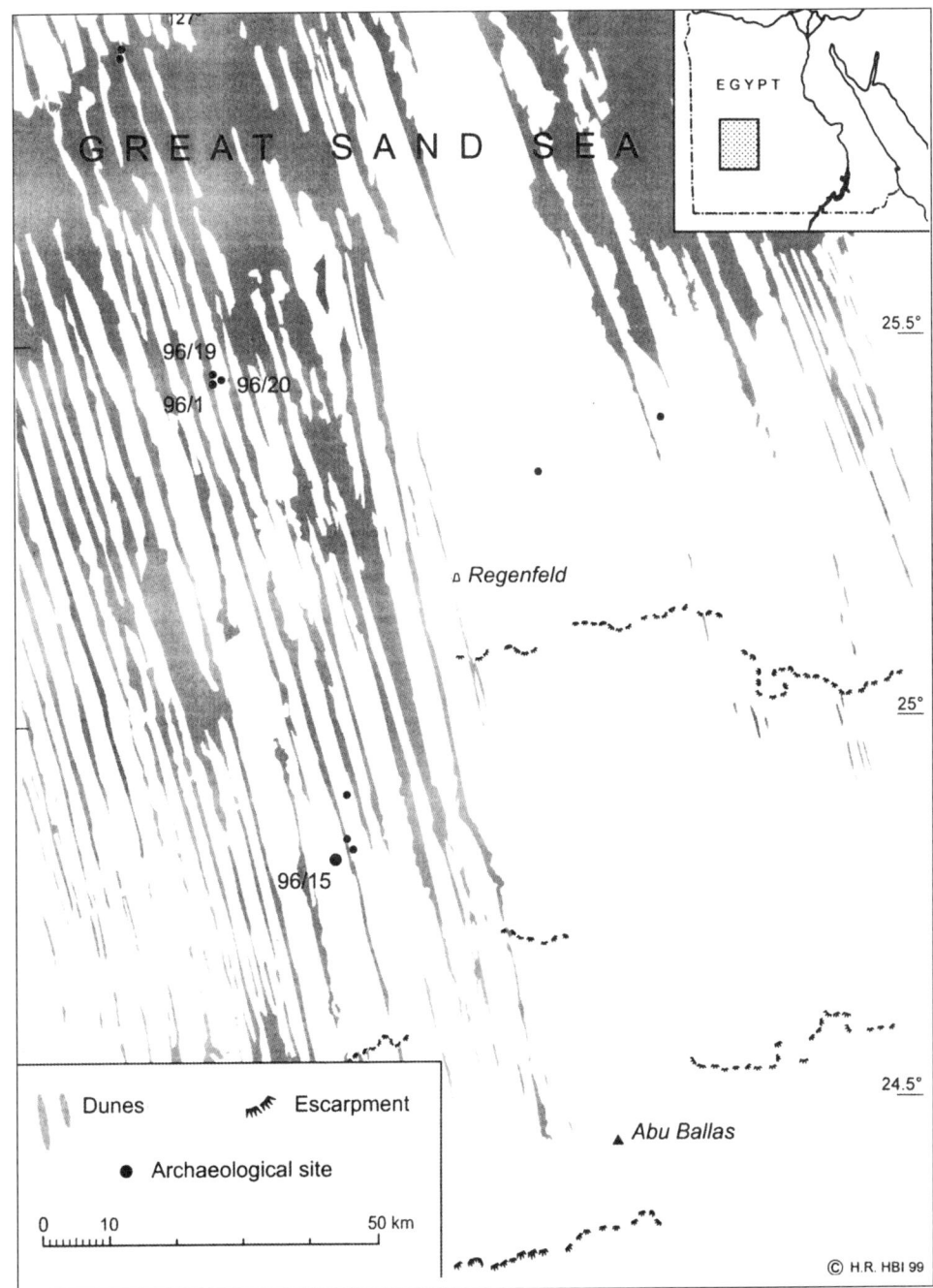

Fig. 1: Area of Regenfeld (Great Sand Sea) with archaeological sites mentioned in the text.

up to 50 m back from the playa. It is likely that the occupations took place at the beginning of, or during, the temporary inundation. Only the surface scatter of site 96/20—which yielded two older Epipalaeolithic dates around 8200 BCE (9000 BP)—was found in the center of the playa pool. At the time this site was occupied, the lake ran dry completely or only a small pond, less then 50 cm deep, remained.

The cultural remains along the edge of the playa yielded Epipalaeolithic events as well as younger events; those remains coming from the upper levels of the old dune behind the shore-line dated to events in the Ceramic period.

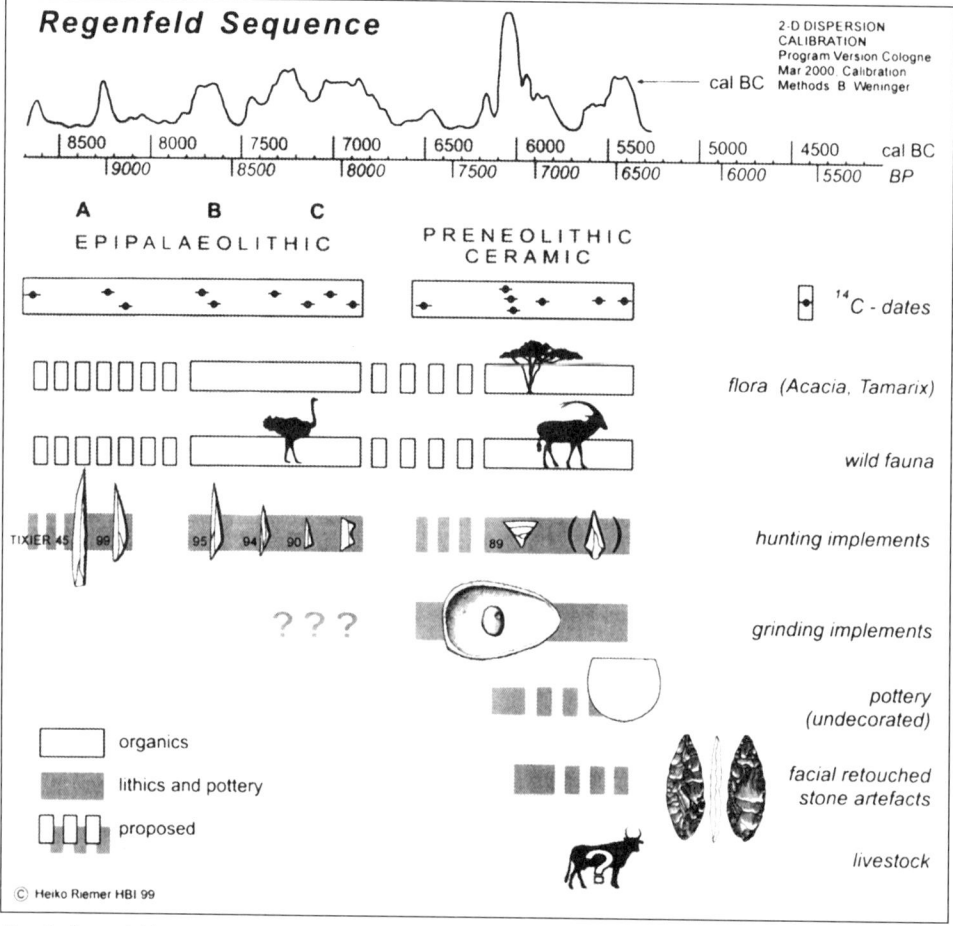

Fig. 2: Regenfeld sequence: cultural and environmental development.

The stratigraphic sequence, determined by an excavation trench running over 40 m from the playa edge to the upper levels of the old dune, indicated occupation events which were inter-rupted by Aolian sand deposits from 7100 to 6950 BCE and from 6950 to 5900 BCE (8200–8000 and 8000–7000 BP). These layers indicate dry events penetrating the Holocene wet period, which was far from being a period of continuously fertile conditions.

The reoccupation of the Great Sand Sea, indicated by a large amount of archaeological sites, coincides with the moving of the southern summer rain front (monsoon belt) toward the north in the ninth millennium BCE. The rains were probably sparse, never exceeding 100 mm per year. The earliest Epipalaeolithic occupiers came into the region as hunters and gatherers. The inventories carried out from Epipalaeolithic units yield many backed bladelets used as insets for hunting arrows (figure 2). The older Epipalaeolithic bladelets (Regenfeld A) were extremely elongated points with straight or rounded backs (Tixier types 45 and 99); younger Epipalaeolithic units (Regenfeld B–C) yielded elongated backed triangles (Tixier types 90, 94, and 95). After 6500 BCE (7600 BP) the archaeological sites showed different inventories of artifacts, suggesting a meaningful cultural and economic change which is up to now not clear in detail. During this time, which falls chronologically into the range of the al-Nabta and Bir Kiseiba Middle Neolithic, and the Dakhlah Bashendi unit, undecorated pottery was used in small amounts (figure 4.3). The question of economic change and the introduction of domestic animals and pastoralism may be discussed based on the evidence from plants and bones collected from the Regenfeld sites (fig. 3). As indicated by a survey of the faunal remains by Hubert Berke, gazelle (*Gazella leptoceros* and *Gazella dorcas*) dominated during all periods; addax antelope, hare, ostrich, and fennek were less frequent. These species were well adapted to very dry environments where open water was absent or available only at a distance. Cut marks from butchering and fire-blackened bones indicated that the animals were hunted and prepared for meals. Domestic fauna were not documented in the Epipaleolithic as well as in the younger inventories of the Regenfeld sites, except for a small site in the southern margins of the Great Sand Sea named 96/15 (fig. 1). A test excavation inside a stone circle yielded a mandible fragment (fig. 4.5). The size and shape fall within the range of domestic cattle, however, one could not exclude a very large *Oryx gazella dammah*, although the lower edge of the mandible seems to be more similar to *Bos taurus*. Less unspecific stone artifacts were uncovered nearby. A radiocarbon date of about 5500 BCE (6600 BP) was recorded.

Nevertheless, the data are ambiguous. One does not know exactly when the prehistoric inhabitants changed their economy from hunting and gathering to pastoralism, and if this process happened suddenly or continuously or fluctuated. Moreover, pastoralists also presumably nourished themselves by hunting and gathering. Thus it is difficult to use terms like "Neolithic," or "pastoral," for the areas of the "absolute desert," although pottery was known. It seems to be correct to classify the "post-Epipalaeolithic" period of Regenfeld, *ca.* 6500–5400 BCE (7600–6400 BP), as Preneolithic Ceramic.

On the other hand, McDonald suggested a date for the earliest caprovids in Dakhla, of about 5900 BCE (7000 BP / Late Bashendi A). A significant introduction of cattle and caprovids was documented for Bashendi B from 5400 BCE (6500 BP).[5] There the environmental conditions were more favored and water was available permanently from wells or natural springs. Outside of the oasis sheep and cattle were kept out at a playa-site in Eastpans, 80 km to the south of Dakhla, dating to around 4900 BCE (6000 BP). It might be that at this time the Great Sand Sea and neighboring desert areas were occupied by prehistoric groups specialized in hunting and gathering strategies (Preneolithic Ceramic), whereas pastoralists *(Neolithic Ceramic)* settled in the oasis and temporarily on their margins.

The data provided by plant remains in the Regenfeld area (fig. 3) provided some information about the environment and the plants gathered for subsistence. The analysis of charcoals by Barbara Eichhorn yield dominated taxa of acacia and tamarisk in all of the occupation. These dry land plants are characteristic of sparse vegetation north of 22° latitude focused on the edges of water pools and sand dunes.[6] However, there is a significant turning point for their subsistence

411

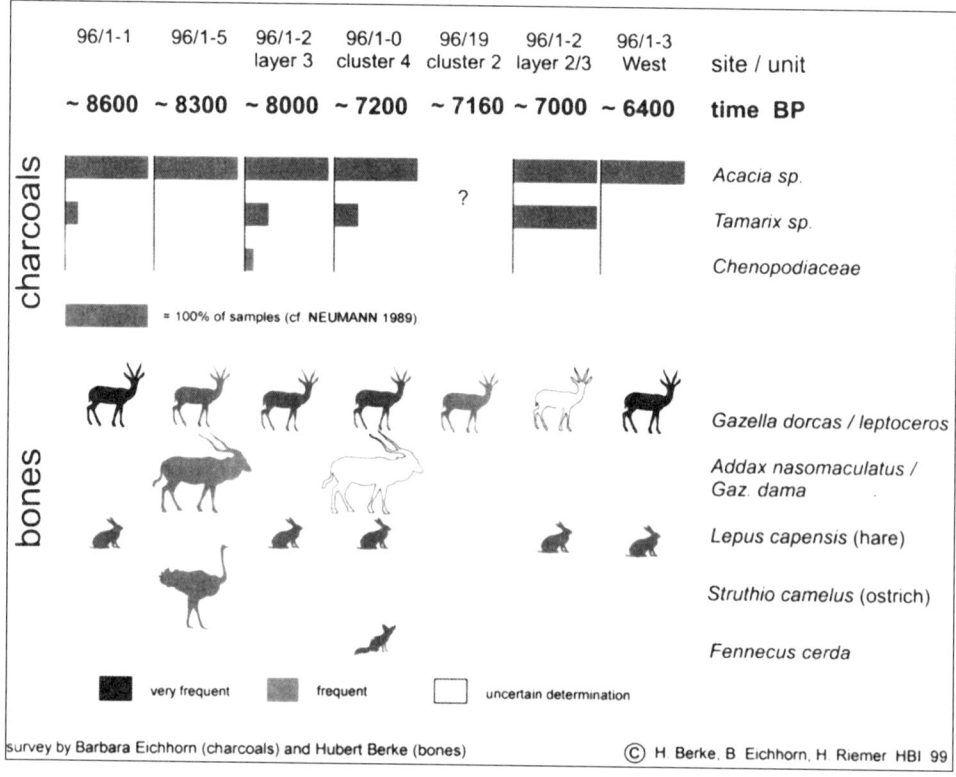

Fig. 3: (above) Sites Regenfeld 96/1 and 96/19: survey of bones and charcoals (by Hubert Berke and Barbara Eichhorn).

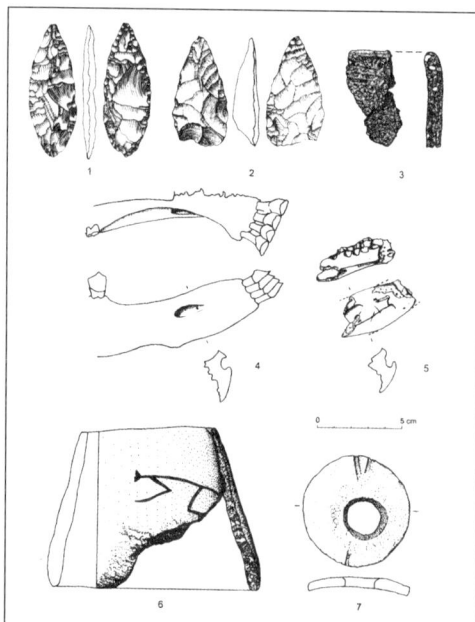

Fig. 4: (left) Artifacts and bone from Regenfeld: 1–2 bifaces (96/19); 3 undecorated pottery (96/1-cluster 4); 4 mandible of Bos taurus (comparative piece); 5 mandible fragment (96/15); 6–7 clay ring and disc (96/15).

strategy, marked by grinding equipment which appears less in the late Epipalaeolithic and increases to a large percentage after 7700 BP. These tools could be used for grinding wild grasses or roots.

Most archaeological remains—especially sites with large quantities of artifacts—are situated in favored locations, at old water pools with vegetation and temporary water. Moreover, water was stored in the dune sands, promoting good conditions for shrubs, tamarisks, and acacia to grow. The vegetation could be used for gathering wood and grass and perhaps to pasture herds, as nomads actually do in sahelian areas. Nevertheless the Great Sand Sea was far from being paradise during the so-called Holocene "wet" period. The Sand Sea was occupied, although the favored sites lack evidence for water. All lake deposits yield typical playa sediments without fossil remains of plants or animals. This was caused by sporadic episodes of water which evaporated before any bio-activity started. The prehistoric groups had to travel seasonally and camp temporarily on each site or move to more favored regions when the water pools ran dry and open water was not available. Hunter-gatherers as well as pastoralists were subject to these conditions.

Some "exotic" artifacts and raw materials focus on this movement. The sites of Regenfeld are favored for evidence of such transport activity, because less material for stone tool production were available in this region. Fossil wood, which is the only local material, has been used in large quantities for flaking stone tools in the older Epipalaeolithic. In the earlier Epipalaeolithic and the Ceramic Period silicified sandstone and flintstone dominated. The closest source of brownish silicified sandstone is along the escarpment of Abu Ballas, around 100 km to the south. Flintstones originate from the Limestone or Abu Muhariq Plateau and the oases. The distance between Regenfeld and the Oases of Dakhla or Abu Minqar is more than 100 km. Libyan desert glass or silica glass is another kind of raw material, worked in smaller quantities in Regenfeld. The actual distance between Regenfeld and the source of desert glass—the Glass Area at the western border of the Great Sand Sea—is about 150 km.

The impressive sand ridges impede the east-west crossing of the Great Sand Sea by cars as well as animals. Thus, the area has been long seen as a natural barrier between the East and West. However, the steeply sloped and soft sand dunes were formed after the last Holocene wet event and also after the prehistoric occupation. It does not seem unreasonable to suggest that prehistoric travelers moved quickly over the well-rounded and hardened ground of the older Pleistocene whale-back dunes. The distribution of raw materials shows the distance as well as the intensity of contacts and movement within the territories of the prehistoric groups. The large percentage of flint stone in the late Epipalaeolithic (Regenfeld C) and appearance of more in the Ceramic Period could be interpreted as increasing contacts with the oases.

Different influences are also observed on a few tools that were common in regions outside the Great Sand Sea; I will focus on an example which underlines the contacts in the Ceramic Period with the oases.

Six percent of the flaked stone tools of the dense artifact scatter of Site 96/19 consists of facially or bifacially-flaked tools (figure 4.1-2). Tools manufactured by this technique, leaves and a tranchet, were identified. The materials present were flint stone and silicified sandstone and local fossil wood. Facially flaked elements were frequently known from Farafra and Dakhla and the Limestone Plateau. The tools were brought from this region or made from local materials by people who brought this characteristic technique to the sites of Regenfeld. At the eastern margins of the Great Sand Sea some other sites were found near Abu Minqar, including the so-called Lobo site. These sites, less than 50 km away from Abu Minqar and Dakhla, indicate intensive contacts with the oasis and the Limestone plateau, evident from large quantities of facially and bifacially-retouched tools as well as from the high flint stone ratios.

In conclusion, the remains visible from activities from the Epipalaeolithic and the Ceramic Period indicate influences from diverse regions and human movement over long distances. When rainfall transformed the desert into a sparsely vegetated and locally-watered landscape, people entered the favored sites and moved on when the grass turned brown and the pools dried up. In the Ceramic Period the contacts between Regenfeld and the oases increased. Future research has to be clear about precisely when and under what circumstances contacts came close to the oases. Possibly this development was caused by the introduction of pastoralism which occurred on the periphery of the oases, where cattle were pastured temporarily on favored sites. In fact, it is an open question how far pastoralists entered the Great Sand Sea and other desert areas, and how pastoral dynamics probably affected the peripheral populations of hunters and gatherers and forced contacts between the oases and the desert.

In the fifth millennium BCE the Libyan Desert dried up and the people had to retire to the oases when rainfall failed to occur. This climatic change coincides with the archaeological data documented from the most desertic areas as well as from Regenfeld. The last event of Regenfeld related to archaeological remains happened about 5400 BCE (6400 BP). The count of dates from the desert areas outside Regenfeld belonging to the period after 5000 BCE (6100 BP) is very rare and limited to favored refugees from the mountainous relief of the Gilf Kebir. Curious pottery depots are the only remains from the Predynastic/Early Dynastic. The ceramics consisted of conical rings stored together with perforated clay discs. Such depots were discovered on the southern bank of the rocky inselberg of Regenfeld 96/15 (figure 4.6) as well as from other points in the Libyan Desert. A radiocarbon date related to a depot of Eastpans (95/3) falls into the Late Predynastic or Early Dynastic. These sparse remains from the desert are considerably fewer but indicate an increase in long-distance exchange by well-adapted travelers who passed through the desert while in the Nile Valley the dawn of Egyptian civilization was becoming visible.

Notes:

1 R. Kuper, "The Eastern Sahara from North to South: Data and dates from the B.O.S. Project," in L. Krzyzaniak and M. Kobusiewicz (eds.), *Late Prehistory of the Nile Basin and the Sahara* (Poznan, 1989) 197–203; R. Kuper, "Prehistoric research in the Southern Libyan Desert. A brief account and some conclusions of the B.O.S. project," *Cahier de Recherches de l'Institut de Papyrologie et d'Égyptologie de Lille* 17 (1995), 123–140.

2 ACACIA is funded as Collaborative Research Center 389 by the Deutsche Forschungsgemeinschaft (DFG). The Egyptian work is directed by R. Kuper and H. Besler under the label of Subproject A1: Climatic Change and Human Settlement between the Nile Valley and the Central Sahara.

3 H. Besler, "Aktuelle Paläoformung in der Großen Sandsee Ägyptens. Erste Ergebnisse aus dem Kölner SFB 389," *Zeitschrift für Geomorphologie* 111 (1997), 1–16.

4 G. Rohlfs, *Drei Monate in der libyschen Wüste* (Cassel: Theodor Fischer 1875; reprinted Köln: 1996), 160–177.

5 M.M.A. McDonald, "The Late Prehistoric Radiocarbon Chronology for Dakhleh Oasis within the Wider Environmental and Cultural Settings of the Egyptian Western Desert," in M. Marlow (ed.), *The Oasis Papers: Proceedings of the First International Symposium of the Dakhleh Oasis Project* (Dakleh Oasis Project Monograph 6; Oxford, 1998), 117–132; M.M.A. McDonald, "Early African Pastoralism: View

from Dakhleh Oasis (South Central Egypt)," *Journal of Anthropological Archaeology* 17 (1998), 124–142.

6 K. Neumann, "Vegetationsgeschichte der Ostsahara im Holozän. Holzkohlen aus prähistorischen Fundstellen," in R. Kuper (ed.) *Forschungen zur Umweltgeschichte der Ostsahara* (Africa Praehistorica 2; Köln: 1989), 13–181.

The Computerized Database and Potential for a Geographic Information System at Kafr Hassan Dawood

Joanne M. Rowland, Fekri A. Hassan

Institute of Archaeology, University College, London

The site of Kafr Hassan Dawood (KHD) lies in the east Delta, 8 km east of Tell al-Kebir and 40 km west of Ismailia, on the southern edge of the Wadi Tumilat.[1] The excavations at KHD were initiated in 1988 by the Egyptian Antiquities Organization (now the Supreme Council of Antiquities) and headed by M. Ilewa El-Musalami and M. S. El-Hanghouri as a result of a pre-developmental survey being carried out in the area. In 1995 Professor Fekri A. Hassan of the Institute of Archaeology, University College London (UCL), was invited to direct a joint SCA/UCL program of archaeological research, conservation and training at the site.

The cemetery at KHD consists of burials from the Terminal Predynastic/Early Dynastic and the Late Period/Ptolemaic Periods. At the end of the last full season of excavation (December 1998–January 1999) the site had yielded 1057 graves. The majority of these graves (744) form part of the Terminal Predynastic/Early Dynastic cemetery.

The original objectives of the SCA/UCL team at the site of KHD were: 1) excavation to provide an accurate record of all archaeological remains; 2) to ascertain the direction and extent of the growth of the two cemeteries and their relationships to one another; 3) on-site conservation; 4) training of Egyptian and Western personnel in excavation and conservation methods and theories; 5) creation of a database to aid statistical analysis of the archaeological material and data and establishing a Geographical Information System (GIS) for the site. The ultimate goal has been to further the understanding of the cultural and social mechanisms of the emergence of state society in Egypt.

One of the procedures was to create a computerized database for the site that could be linked to a Geographical Information System (GIS). This type of technology was chosen to help interpret socioeconomic/political development across the cemetery and to answer questions related to the distribution of wealth, in terms of grave size, variety, and number of artifacts, across the site.

The original computerized database for KHD was structured by Prof. Fekri A. Hassan in 1995 (in Lotus) and restructured by Joanne Rowland in 1998 (Excel).[2] The final restructuring will transfer the data into a relational database (Access) for better access and manipulation of the data. Information recorded in the database includes the results from previous excavations by the SCA, in particular M. S. El-Hanghouri, and we are very grateful to them for providing this information. A copy of the database is housed with the SCA.

The current database stores information that can be divided into the categories of: grave number and location; types of artifacts and numbers of artifacts within graves; totals of goods: pottery totals, totals of non-pottery or "status" artifacts; number of types of artifact present in each grave (between 0 and 7); social value score; presence of potmarks/serekhs; grave size, length, width and depth, and shape; presence of a coffin; human skeletal remains, orientation of the interred, and sex and age (where the information is available); and presence of a "symbolic" potsherd, where found in association with the skeletal remains.

The aims of employing the technology of a computerized database and GIS for the site were originally to facilitate enquiries into spatial distribution. The following categories of inquiry are among those that can be asked of the system: The distribution of artifact types; the placement of different types of graves; spatial location of graves of males, females, and children; spatial location of graves containing potmarks; spatial location of multiple burials; indication of association between certain types of burial and certain types of artifact; and visualization of inequality within the society as represented through the mortuary remains.

The types of data that we have to work with and some of the questions that we are interested in have briefly been stated. But the reasons for choosing this particular type of technology as a tool for handling this data, and helping to answer queries are discussed below.

Standing on its own, the database is a tool that is capable of storing the various categories of information concerning the cemetery and provides an instant recall of data, which is continually updatable with new data as the excavations progress and with new categories as different approaches are considered. In addition it presents the data in a form that facilitates its manipulation in a variety of ways that are appropriate for a diversity of research questions; the data is in a form that can be readily manipulated for statistical analyses. When stored within a relational database system (such as Access), the capability exists to store and display static visual data, for example, photographs of graves and artifacts, plans and sections of graves, and drawings of artifacts.

The data can be imported in tabular form from the database into a GIS (ArcView is used for the KHD information). The GIS for KHD currently contains a digitized plan of the site grid and graves located up until 1995. This GIS was created by Ahmed Saleh, a KHD trainee who was sent to Uppsala, Sweden for GIS training under the supervision of Dr. Lana Troy and Prof. Paul Sinclair. The updating of the GIS with the results of the subsequent seasons of excavation is in progress. The GIS enables the site data to be visualized and considered from a geographical perspective, and the visualization of the data opens up new possibilities for discussing temporal and spatial issues within the cemetery. The database holds the raw data from the site, the grid number, the position of the grave and its size, orientation and contents, and the GIS shows exactly where the grave is positioned within the cemetery, and highlights its possible relationships to other graves.

The GIS holds data within any number of different views/themes. For KHD the main two themes are currently the excavation grid and the position of the graves. From these initial two themes, additional themes have been added, including in one theme the graves of the Terminal Predynastic/Early Dynastic cemetery and in another the graves of the Late Period/Ptolemaic cemetery. A series of themes highlight the distribution of various types of artifact across the site, for example, graves containing potmarks/serekhs, graves containing one artifact type, and upwards to seven artifacts types, and so on. The main GIS themes will be extended in due course to include

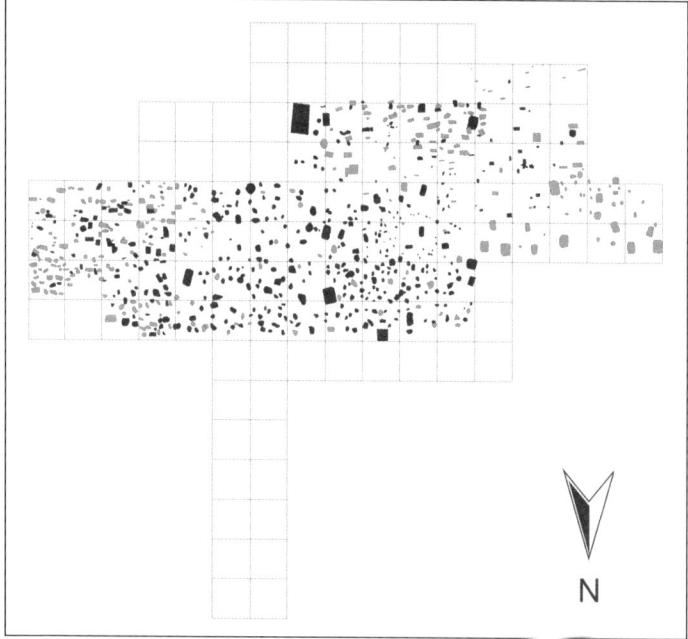

Fig. 1: GIS map showing both the Terminal Predynastic/Early Dynastic (in black) and the Late Period/Ptolemaic (in gray) graves at KHD (graves located between 1988 and 1995).

the positioning of test pits outside the excavated area, contour maps, digital elevation models (DEM), and details of the ancient topography, such as the location of waterways and the floodplain.

Within the GIS, each grave outline is created as a polygon, to which specific data is attached. There exists an intermediate table, the purpose of which is to directly link the database information for a given grave, with the polygon in the GIS. This table lists the grave number, period (whether Terminal Predynastic to Early Dynastic or Late Period/Ptolemaic), and the position of the grave within the excavation grid. At the point when the database table is imported into the GIS it is joined to this intermediate table through the common variable of grave number. The spatial data is then associated with the specifications for each grave. As each query is asked, new tables of results are created and may be stored within the GIS as a new theme if required, which presents the advantage of being able to run further analysis on an exclusive set of grave data.

The GIS is capable of reproducing plans of the site which are created from the information stored within any number of themes, as described above. However, in addition to the system responding to queries by visual presentation of the data in plan form, when the mouse is positioned over a specific grave it will bring up the information from the database on this particular grave displayed in tabular form on the screen, overlaying or alongside the site plan.

The accuracy of the results achieved by the database/GIS is naturally reliant on accurate information being gathered and input from the start. Inaccurate or incomplete data might not render this tool as the best choice. At KHD, to compliment the notebooks, plans, and photographs made during fieldwork, a special computer-friendly single context recording system was introduced in 1996. Each context is recorded separately to show its relationship to other contexts, a context being either a culturally or geologically formed stratigraphic record of activity. This recording system has made the storage and management of information much simpler. The site recording system, along with the presence of geoarchaeologists on site, enables the collection of data that will facilitate the visual recreation of the ancient landscape.

It is important to clarify, through the medium of spatial analysis, whether it is appropriate to make inferences about kinship, social inequality, wealth, and chronology from the spatial distribution of graves. In order to do this a number of issues need to be addressed. Four of these issues are considered: 1) Is the spatial distribution indicative of particular patterns of growth in the cemetery? 2) Does it suggest that graves may occupy certain positions for purely practical reasons, for example the spatial gap between two other known grave plots, to accommodate a further burial? Alternatively, does it suggest that the positioning of graves is tied to kinship? 3) Do clusters of graves provide any indications concerning social inequality? 4) Does the spatial distribution suggest that there was more spatial distinction in the early stages of growth of the Terminal Predynastic/Early Dynastic cemetery, coupled with a later, more random, approach to the location of graves as the availability of desirable space at the cemetery site became more of an issue? It is important that any potential patterns emerging from GIS analysis are subjected to further statistical analysis in order to confirm whether the patterns might be actual or random.

As stated above, the database/GIS system holds information pertaining to both the Terminal Predynastic/Early Dynastic cemetery and the Late Period/Ptolemaic cemetery. Although, the current research is primarily concerned with the Terminal Predynastic/Early Dynastic period, the material pertaining to the Late Period/Ptolemaic cemetery is stored in the same format to expedite future research. The spatial location of the later graves is an issue that demands consideration, and their impact on the earlier cemetery must also be addressed.

It needs to be ascertained whether or not there was a logical reason for the positioning of these much later graves. Did this later group of people know where the graves of the early cemetery lay and deliberately avoid them, showing some form of reverence? There are examples of the early graves being cut by later (Late Period/Ptolemaic) graves. The large tomb 970, in the south of the cemetery, is cut at its edges by three later graves, and grave 1025, also in the south of the cemetery, which contained a pottery coffin, had been cut by a later grave. The southern end of the pottery coffin was damaged by this later intrusion and it appears that the broken parts of the coffin may have been purposely used as grave offerings in the later grave, although the undamaged part of the coffin retained its original position. It is envisaged that future research on the later cemetery will help to address such problems with the aid of spatial analysis, incorporating the use of digital elevation models.

During the later phase in the history of KHD, Wadi Tumilat was a major trade route, and the major site of Tell al-Maskhuta is only a short distance from KHD.[3] It is possible that KHD may have occupied an important position on the canal route through the Wadi Tumilat, and reclamation of land in outlying areas could be another reason for the Late Period/Ptolemaic presence in the region.

Fig. 1 (Late Period/Ptolemaic graves and Terminal Predynastic/Early Dynastic graves) shows that the later graves at KHD occupy an area in the west of the cemetery, with clusters in the south and in the east. In the northeast of the cemetery the graves are interspersed with the later graves. A few later graves are scattered over the north and the central area of the cemetery; notably, in the south, the later graves are clustered mainly to the west of the large tombs 913 and 970, and are interspersed with the early graves.

In 1998, preliminary research was conducted into the distribution of wealth in the early cemetery at KHD, using the database. One of the hypotheses was to compare graves which contained a large number of artifacts common at the site, for example ceramics, wine or beer jars, with graves containing a small number of what may be considered as more prestigious artifacts, such as copper artifacts or stone vessels, which may have contained fine oils. In theory, by assigning values to certain classes of grave goods, the latter group should have emerged as "wealthier," but the results

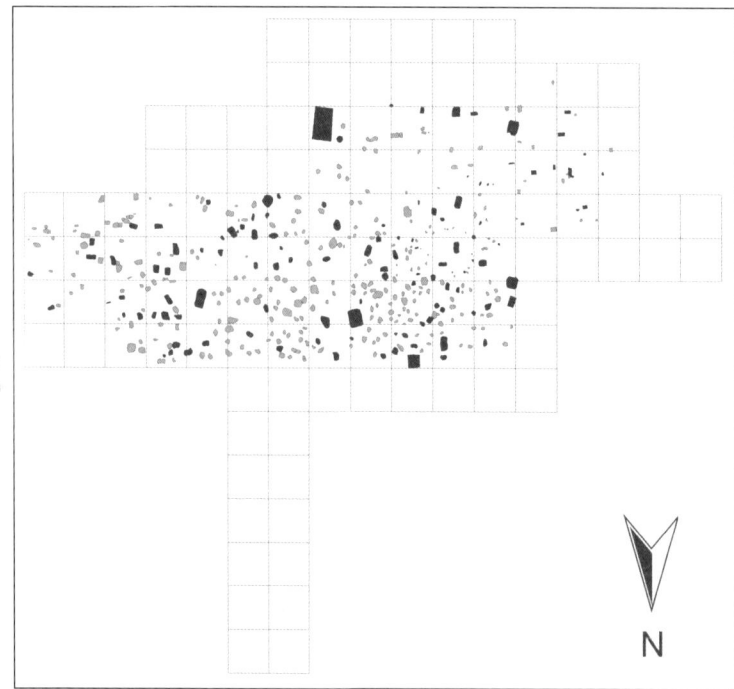

N

Fig. 2: GIS map showing the distribution of oval (in gray) and rectangular (in black) graves of the Terminal Predynastic/Early Dynastic cemetery at KHD (graves located between 1988 and 1995).

showed it to be predominantly the case that those graves containing large numbers of ceramics are also those graves in which the prestigious items are located.[4]

These preliminary queries into wealth distribution were carried out on the database before it had been imported into the GIS. With the benefit of the GIS it is now possible to investigate spatial distribution across the cemetery (digitized graves as in 1995), and recent analysis utilized the total number of goods located within graves as opposed to number of classes of artifact. The purpose being to ascertain whether simple, oval pits are associated with fewer grave goods, and rectangular graves with a higher number of goods. In this instance the spatial analysis is complementary to the database, the latter providing the numerical results and the former allowing these results to be viewed spatially across the cemetery. Due to the restrictions of space here, four broad groups are being considered: 1) graves containing no artifacts, 2) graves containing one artifact, 3) graves containing between two and 15 artifacts, 4) graves containing 16 or more artifacts. Within each group the orientation of the interred is considered in addition to the shape of the graves.

From the ceramic evidence at KHD, the cemetery appears to have spread from the north to south over time. In the north is the floodplain, adjacent to the low desert, where it is most likely that the settlement would have been located, slightly to the east of the cemetery, and hence the earliest graves are located in the near vicinity. In the south of the cemetery, the slope is higher up on the south bank of Wadi Tumilat, with a 40 cm gradient between the north and the south. In light of this, the orientation of the interred (where the information is available) is employed to ascertain if the temporal distribution of graves with head to the south facing west, and head to the north facing east, fits into the bigger picture of Egypt as a whole, with the former orientation generally representing earlier burials.[5] It should be stressed that the most northerly extent of the cemetery has not yet been investigated and additionally, that the biocultural investigations[6] are only based on the skeletal material recovered from the 1995 to the 1999 seasons.[7]

420

Total Goods	No. of Graves	Rectangular	Oval	Skeletal Remains	HN FE	HS FW
0	117	15	87	80	24	5
1	93	11	87	47	24	1
2–15	223	77	135	87	32	7
16+	20	15	3	3	2	0

The results, in brief, show that graves with no artifacts or one artifact are predominantly oval; the category of 2–15 goods are associated with a higher proportion of rectangular graves; whereas graves containing in excess of 16 artifacts are predominantly rectangular. It is notable that the rectangular graves generally appear to be more evenly spread across the site, with a grouping in the north, and the largest graves (913 and 970, both 6 x 4 m) are located in the south of the site. Grave 970 in the south of the cemetery, contains 84 grave goods of six classes of artifacts. Grave 913 had a total of 229 grave goods of seven classes of artifact, and one *serekh*, that of King Narmer, was located in this tomb. Tomb 1041, dated late in the history of the Terminal Predynastic/Early Dynastic cemetery, is located in the north amongst earlier graves. Tomb 1041 (fig. 3) has 14 goods of two different artifact classes. Although this grave is not so well provided for as 913 and 970, it may be that the interred was an important member of the community, possibly at a period when the site's overall prosperity was less than when the deceased were interred in 913 and 970.[8]

The oval graves show a much denser distribution in the northern and the eastern areas of the site. Graves with the head to the north facing east appear widely distributed throughout the cemetery, whereas those with head south facing west are largely concentrated in the earlier, northern, part of the cemetery, which is awaiting further investigation in the extreme north, closest to the floodplain.

In summary, the results suggest that the oval graves are largely representative of simpler and less well provided-for burials, and are more densely clustered in the earlier part of the cemetery. The results also show that graves with head to the south, facing west are largely concentrated in the earlier part of the cemetery and that those graves with head to the north, facing east are more evenly distributed across the excavated area.

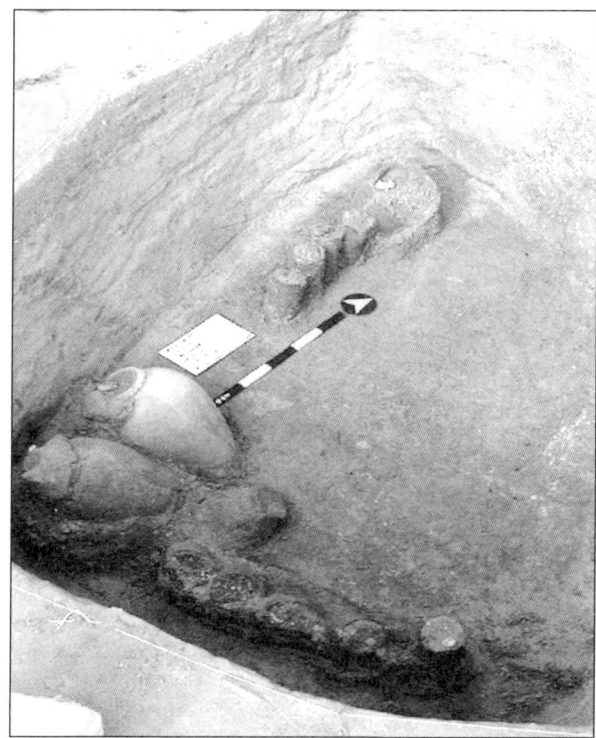

Fig. 3: Photograph showing a rectangular grave (Grave 1041) at KHD.

421

Fig. 4: Photograph showing an oval grave (Grave 964) at KHD, with the head north and face to the east.

Acknowledgements

The investigations at KHD have been funded by UNESCO, the National Geographic, the Bioanthropology Foundation, The Supreme Council of Antiquities, Uppsala University, The Humanities Research Council of Canada, and the Institute of Archaeology, UCL. We thank Prof. Gaballah Ali Gaballah, former Secretary General of the SCA, for his continued support of the project, and to Dr. Mohammed Abdel-Maksoud, Director of the Canal Zone and North Sinai, for his enthusiasm and help. We also thank our Egyptian colleagues, Mr. Soliman Mohammed el-Sayed, Nassrallah Fathi Kilany, Ashraf Kamel Hussein, Hisham Elsaid Khattab, Mustafa Nour El-Dean, and Ragab Hussieny Hassan, the Inspectors of the Canal Zone, for making KHD such a pleasant and professional environment to work in; and to everyone who has participated in the excavations at KHD, especially G. J. Tassie who supervised field work at the site. J. Rowland's PhD research is being funded by the British Academy AHRB. Thanks are due to Dr. Christopher J. Eyre and the Committee of the Seventh International Congress of Egyptologists for their financial support for this conference. We also thank Mr. Mohammed Salem El-Hanghouri and Mr M. Ilewa El-Musalami, former Directors of the Canal Zone, who carried out investigations at the site from 1988 to 1995. Mr. El-Hanghouri provided information pertaining to their excavations for inclusion in the database.

Notes:

1 See map, J.F.L. van Wetering, "Early Cemeteries of the East Delta: a hierarchy of 1st Dynasty cemetery sites based on grave architecture," this volume.

2 J. Rowland, *An Analytical Study into the Distribution of Wealth at the Egyptian Predynastic Cemetery site of Kafr Hassan Dawood*. Unpublished M.A. dissertation, University College, London, 1998.

3 C. A. Redmount, "The Wadi Tumilat and the 'Canal of the Pharaohs,'" *JNES* 54/2 (1995), 135. For location of Tell el-Maskhuta, J. S. Holladay *et al., Cities of the Delta, Part 3, Tell el-Maskhuta; preliminary report on the Wadi Tumilat Project 1978–1979* (Malibu, 1982), fig. 1.

4 Rowland, *An Analytical Study*, 92–93.

5 F. Debono and B. Mortenson, *The Predynastic Cemetery at Heliopolis: Season March-September 1950* (Mainz am Rhein,1988). It is stated that "It can be demonstrated that the general pattern in prehistoric times in the north was that the dead lie on their right side with the head to the south, facing east. This pattern changes through the Naqada II and III Periods and in the beginning of the dynastic period, the dead lie on their left side with the head to the north and face east. The pattern in the south is much more uniform. The dead lie on their left side with their head to the south and face west. Not until the Third Dynasty did this pattern change to reclining on the left side with the head to the north, facing east," 46.

   E. C. M. van den Brink, "A Transitional Late Predynastic - Early Dynastic Settlement Site in the Northeastern Nile Delta, Egypt," *MDAIK* 45 (1989), 55–108. He notes that in the Naqada II c–d Period the burials at Minshat Abu Omar are arranged head north, face to the west, in a flexed position, which is in contrast to the burials in Upper Egypt at this period, but "in agreement with a noted preference for this position at a number of contemporary Lower Egyptian sites;" the burials at Minshat Abu Omar, however, face to the west, which is "the rule" in Upper Egypt during this period, whereas in Lower Egypt, head to the east is the predominant direction, 81, n. 46; J. J. Castillos, *A Reappraisal of the Published Evidence on Egyptian Predynastic and Early Dynastic Cemeteries* (Toronto, 1982). With regards to the orientation of the interred in Upper Egypt, he notes that "there was a sharp change towards orthodoxy (i.e. head south and face west) during Middle Predynastic times," and that the head to the north, facing east orientation that had been "fairly common in Early Predynastic times, became even more so in the Early Dynastic Period except for the abrupt break immediately after the Early Predynastic," 174.

6 The biocultural investigations have been carried out by T. L. Tucker (1996–2000), S. Hillson (1996, 1998/9), and N. Lovell (1995).

7 See T. L. Tucker "Biocultural Investigations at Kafr Hassan Dawood," this volume.

8 F. A. Hassan. "Kafr Hassan Dawood," *EA* 6 (Spring, 2000), 39.

A New Discovery at the Sety I Temple in Abydos*

Ahmed El-Sawy

Egyptology Department, Sohag Faculty of Arts,
South Valley Unitersity

The Sety I temple in Abydos is considered to be one of the most important and architectural-ly complicated temples in Egypt, especially in its religious aspect. On the other hand, there are the additions such as sanctuaries, inscriptions, paintings, and reliefs that were added as a result of the efforts of Sety's family. A great deal of the additions had been achieved during the reign of Ramesses II, or when he shared the throne with his father. Some of these additions were com-pleted during the reign of Merenptah.[1] A recent examination of these additions was the impetus for removing the accumulated rocks which were situated near the stairs leading to the roof of the temple (figures 10 and 11).[2]

There have been some doubts about the existence of a passage linking the Hall of Barques and the outside of the temple. This passage would go in the direction of the Osirion because it would be the easiest way to get the funerary barques in and out for the different ceremonies and festivals. This quandary stimulated the Egyptology Department of the Sohag Faculty of Arts to ask for a concession to examine this area. The location we examined is also thought to be connected with the library (the archive). The work began on April 11, 1999 and lasted for 10 days.

The excavation took place in the area situated between the stairway passage that leads to the Osirion, from the northern side and the so-called library or archive, from the southern side (fig-ures 5 and 6).[3]

The Complex of Sokar and Nefertem

The different parts of the southwestern extension of the temple where we worked should be reviewed (figures 5, 6, and 7). The Hall of Sokar and Nefertem, which is entered from the south-west corner of the second Hypostyle Hall,[4] was not our concern, because our interest was focused on the third chapel situated in the south.

The Gallery of Lists, Corridor, and Stairway

A second, small doorway in the south wall of the second Hypostyle Hall leads to the Gallery of Lists. From its south side, a corridor and staircase are reached. These were part of the Nefertem and Ptah-Sokar Complex.[5] The stairway passage leads out to the Osirion behind the temple as a place to observe the sun-god when he sets between two mountains making the *3ḥt*-symbol. The corridor and the stairway were probably introduced into the plan in order to provide this access. From the outside wall it is easy to climb an additional staircase to the temple roof (figures 11 and 12).[6]

In the staircase passage there are many scenes belonging to the reign of Sety I, for example a scene near the east end of the north wall represents Sefkhet-Abu on the throne with a hymn addressed to Sety I. This proves that this part of the temple was built in the reign of Sety I, and that Ramesses II used or completed it.[7] The entrance at the top of the stairway passage may have been redesigned, while the entrance to the upper staircase was blocked and a new way to it cut from inside, that is, on the southern wall of the stairway. This alteration destroyed part of the decoration of its south wall[8] (when comparing the neighboring scenes on the southern and northern wall of the chapel, it is probably the scene of the Ennead) (figure 13).[9]

On the west wall of the stairway passage there is a scene on either side of the entrance: On each side is a figure of Sety I; on the right side he is wearing the red crown, while on the left side he is wearing the white crown. He holds a staff and a *ḥd*-mace in his near hand, while extending the other arm towards the entrance. Above him is a representation of the sun-disk surrounded by two uraei with the symbol of life attached to them. One wears the red crown while the other wears the white one. His name is written in two cartouches. The inscription accompanying the scene runs ꜥk nb r ḥwt-ntr iw wꜥb "Every entering into the temple, I was Pure."[10]

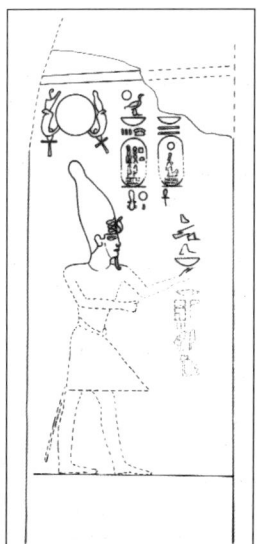 

Figure 1   Figure 2

Outside the doorway there is a small blocked entrance to the south side of the gate. It led to the stairs ascending to the roof of the temple. It was blocked during the reign of Ramesses II. On the block there is a representation of Wepwawet standing, facing south with a scepter in his left hand and the symbol of life in the other hand. Behind him is a damaged figure probably representing Osiris. In his left hand is a *Was*-scepter, while the symbol of life is held in the other hand. In front of them is a damaged figure, presumably of Ramesses II. He is standing and offering two small vessels on a tray. The inscription found in this part reads

    1. (*rʿ-msw-mry imn*) *wsir* (*usr-m3ʿt-rʿ stp-n-rʿ*) "Ramesses II"

    2. *di.n.i n.k ʿhʿ n rʿ* "I gave to you the lifetime of the (sun god Ra)."

    3. *di.n.i n.k ḫ3swt* "I gave to you the foreign countries."

    4. *irt dbḥw ḥtpw n it-w.(i) di(t) mi rʿ* "Making offerings requirement to my fathers like what the sun god Re gives."

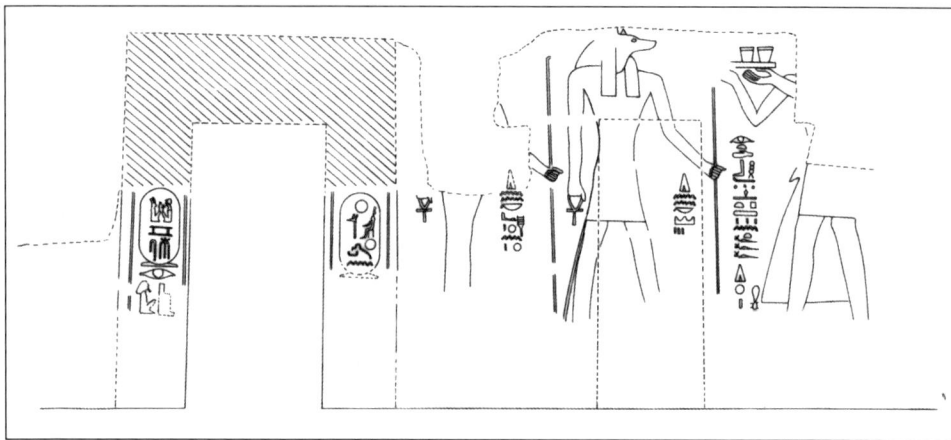

Figure 3

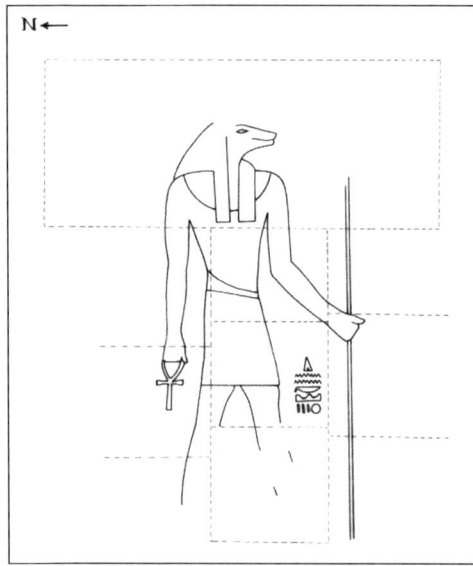

Figure 4

The Hall of Barques

The hall was originally decorated throughout with paintings from the reign of Sety I. Most of these were used under Ramesses II as the outline drafts for carving sunk reliefs. On the entrance reveals is a pair of sunk reliefs showing Ramesses II offering to Osiris and to his deified, deceased father Sety I.[11]

The Library (Archive)

The library consists of five rooms which occupies the southwest of the temple. The purpose of this complex of rooms is not at all clear. It is noteworthy that there are some paintings on the walls of these rooms which refer that it contains a number of large chests. The inscription concerning the chests mentioned most probably written on rolls of papyri, that were stored in the chests. Besides, the god Thot is prominent in many scenes on the walls of the rooms of the library. There are also two mentions of the king's annals (established in writing) southeast room, east wall, chest no. 6 and northwest room east wall chest no. 5.[12] It is known from the famous stela of King Nefer Hotep that such record of specifications were kept in the temple libraries.[13]

This suggests that the chests contain papyri, moreover the god Thot is prominent in the scenes of the walls, from all these documents one can suggest that these five rooms are the temple library or its archive.

Returning to our work, the excavation focused on removing the accumulated stones in order to determine the use and function of this area. The expedition reached the level of the base of the passage, which was situated in the northern side; the west wall of the Hall of Barques was on the same level. The underground bases of the passage and the Hall of Barques are connected and lie on same level. This indicates that the stairway passage and the Hall of Barques had been built at the same time (presumably during the reign of Sety I).

As for the level of the base of the northern wall of the library (or so-called archive), it is higher (by approximately 50 centimeters) than the base of the pathway and the west wall of the Hall of Barques. There appears to be no connection between the base of the location examined and the base of the library. This indicates that the library is a separate building built during a later period (perhaps at the end of the rule of Ramesses II or in the reign of Merenptah).[14] The dates will be refined when the study of reliefs, scenes, and the texts found in the stairway passage, library, and the Hall of Barques, are completed.

The following points attracted the attention of our expedition:

- The location we examined contains the remains of stairs and a gateway outside the temple, oriented in the direction of the Osirion. That means that the examined location was probably a sanctuary (shrine) on the extension of the sanctuaries of Ptah-Sokar and Nefertem reused after the reign of Sety I as a stairway passage to the Osirion[15] (presumably during the rule of Ramesses II) (figures 5, 6, 7, 8, 12, and 13).
- The expedition found some remains of ropes and fragments of pottery in the excavation at a depth of about 2.5 meters, left there by the workmen during the building of the temple.
- As for the stairway passage and the southern wall of the passage, there is a recent reconstruction closing an old entrance which led to the stairs up to the roof of the temple. By comparing the reliefs of the northern wall and its counterpart, the southern wall, it was possible to complete the scene that was destroyed when cutting the door.
- Some comparative studies on the sanctuaries close to the passage proved the credibility of the scene of the Ennead including the correctness of the completion (reconstruction) of the lost scene.

This is the subject of the reconstruction which took place in 2000. In a word, the cutting of the entrance which links the sanctuary and the pathway is considered to be simultaneous with the closure of the western entrance of the temple.

Conclusion

1. The stairway passage which leads to the outside (west side) of the temple was the third shrine in the sanctuary of Nefertem.
2. The library or the so-called archive was built at the end of the reign of Ramesses II or during the time of Merenptah.
3. There is a prevailing opinion that the colored inscriptions should be ascribed to the reign

of Sety I. However, it could have been the work of an artistic school founded by Sety I which lasted until the time of Merenptah.

Consequently, it appears that there were some additions and modifications in the temple of Sety I during the rule of his son Ramesses II and his grandson Merenptah.

Finally, the temple is still in need of research to complete the archaeological study as well as investigate the rest of the scenes and the texts. This will enable us to specify the dates of the different parts of the temple and to see which parts are original and which were added later. I hope that this paper has filled in some gaps and helped attract the attention of Egyptologists to this well-known but as yet insufficiently-examined monument.

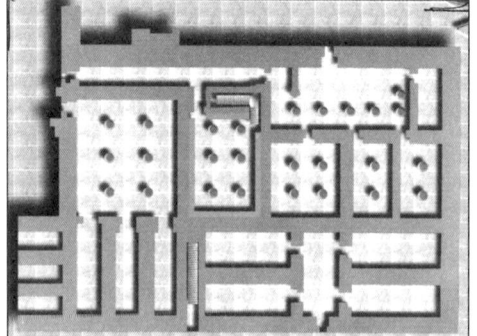

Fig. 5: Plan of the complex of Soker and Nefertem. The Gallery of Lists, corridor, stairway, the Hall of Barques, and the Library (Archives).

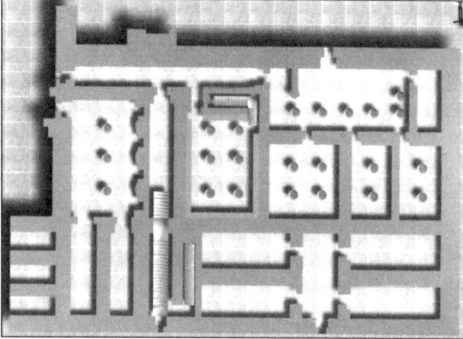

Fig. 6: Plan of the southwest part of the Sety I temple at Abydos in the reign of Rameses II.

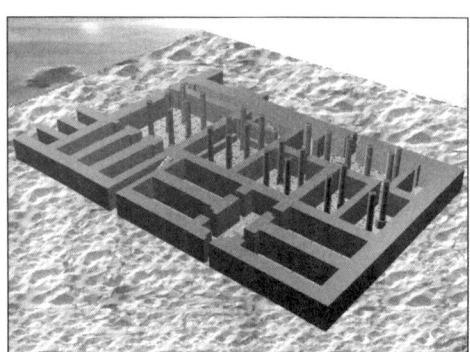

Fig. 7: Reconstruction of the southwest part of Sety I at Abydos (in the reign of Sety I).

Fig. 8: Reconstruction of the southwest part of Sety I at Abydos (in the reign of Rameses II).

Figure 9

Figure 10

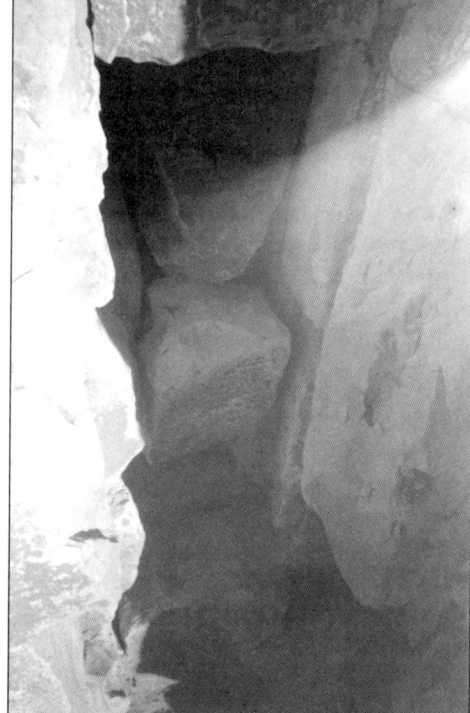

Figure 11

Figure 12

Figure 13

Figure 14

Figure 15

Notes:

* I am grateful to Head of the Supreme Council of Antiquites for the concession to uncover the mystery.

1 R. David, *A Guide to Religious Ritual at Abydos* (Warminster/Wilts 1981), 148 ff; Ahmed el-Sawy, "Ramesses II Completing A Shrine in the Temple of Sety I at Abydos," *SAK* 10 (1983), 307–310 ; A. M. Calverley and A. H. Gardiner, *Abydos* III (Chicago, 1938) 10, pl.52.a.

2 A. Zayed, "The Archives and Treasury of The Temple of Sety Ist at Abydos," *ASAE* LXV (1983), 22.

3 Zayed, "The Archives," 19–20.

4 David, *Guide*, 96–98; B. Kemp, "Abydos," *LÄ* I (1975), 36–37.

5 David, *Guide*, 115ff.

6 J. Baines, "Temple of Sety I at Abydos," *BAOM* XI (1990), 87ff.

7 David, *Guide*, 116.

8 A. Mariette, *Abydos: Description des fouilles exécutées sur l'emplacement de cette ville.* 2 vols. (Paris 1869), 96.

9 For more details see David, *Guide, 92ff*; H. Frankfort, *Kingship and the Gods* (Chicago, 1948), 105–109.

10 David had translated the same sentence neither completely nor rightly. David, *Guide*, 116.

11 For more details see Baines, "Temple of Sety I," 88; Gay Robins, *Egyptian Painting and Reliefs* (Aylesbury, 1986), 27–52.

12 Zayed, "The Archives," 46, 57, 71.

13 Breasted, *Ancient Records*, 334.

14 Zayed says: "It is noticeable that the rooms of the library were built during the reign of Sety I." This contradicts the result of the discovery which indicated that the walls of the library and its bases were not connected with the rest of the temple which indicates that the building of the library was in a later period, not during the reign of Sety I." Zayed, "The Archives," 22.

15 David, *Guide*, 115ff.

The Land of Punt: Problems of the Archaeology of the Red Sea and the Southeastern Delta

Abdel Monem A. H. Sayed
University of Alexandria

The Egyptians initially used the word "Punt" to refer to the coastal regions closest to the southern borders of Egypt (or even to the southern borders themselves) from which they obtained incense. The use of the name "Punt" for a land of incense began during the time of Sahure.[1] At the end of the Old Kingdom, another word was used, "Bia-Punt" meaning, "The mine (or mines) of Punt." It occurs for the first time in the inscriptions of Harkhuf at Aswan. The context suggests the term refers to the Nilotic region of Northern Sudan.

During the Twelfth Dynasty the same term occurs in the inscriptions discovered on the site of the Port of Mersa Gawasis (22 km south of the modern port of Safaga).[2] The term was given to an area on the shore of the Red Sea where the naval expedition of Sesostris I landed.[3]

These two records may denote that the land of "The Mine of Punt" (Harkhouf and Mersa Gawasis) extended from the Nilotic regions in Northern Sudan to the coast of the Red Sea. If the word "mine" refers to "gold mines," it fits the Atbai Desert, which is full of gold mines and gold workings mentioned in ancient and modern records.

Concerning the term "*ḫtyw - ꜥntyw nw* Punt," i.e., "The Frankincense terraces of Punt," it is mentioned for the first time in the inscriptions of queen Hatshepsut at Deir al-Bahari, where the famous expedition to Punt to bring back frankincense trees is recorded.[4] Punt is described as a coastal, hilly country, where the frankincense trees grow on terraces very near to the seashore.[5] According to studies by Hepper,[6] these conditions conform to some places on the northern coast of Somaliland. Hepper defined the species of frankincense prevailing in these places as *Boswellia carteri*, and *B. frereana*. These species have been found in Egyptian tombs.[7]

The same places are recorded by Classical writers as exporting frankincense (Strabo and Pliny).[8] But it was the unknown author of *The Periplus of the Erythrean Sea* (first century CE)[9] who found the northeastern region on the Somali coast produced frankincense (Greek, *gintay*), while he referred to other places on this coast as exporting frankincense (Greek, *ekh feretay*).

The word "producing" may denote the growing of frankincense trees in northeastern

Somaliland. These features have characterized the area up until now. Moreover, weight is given to this conclusion when the author of *The Periplus* refers to a headland there, which he calls "Cape Elephas" a nomenclature which survives in its Somali name "Fil-Ka." The word *fil* is an Arabic name meaning "elephant," and the affix *ka* is the definite article in the Somali language.

From the foregoing, we can conclude that the physical feature of North Eastern Somaliland and its production of frankincense did not change for 2000 years (between the time of *The Periplus* and the present day) consequently, it was nearly the same for the 1500 years before the time of *The Periplus*. (i.e. in the time of Queen Hatshepsut).[10]

The Existence or Nonexistence of the Nile/Red Sea Canal

From the study of the monuments discovered on the site of the Twelfth Dynasty port at Wadi Gawasis on the Red Sea, and within the valley of Wadi Gawasis connected to it,[11] I came to the conclusion that this canal, which Classical writers attributed to Sesostris, did not exist during the Twelfth Dynasty during the reigns of Senwosret I, Amenemhet II, Senwosret II, and Senwosret III.

The evidence for my conclusion is the transformation of the anchors of the ships into stelae used for building the shrine of Ankhow, the leader of the naval expedition to the Land of Bia-Punt. After the return voyage from Bia-Punt and the landing of the ships at Mersa Gawasis, the Egyptians found that it was impractical to carry the heavy limestone anchors of the ships (*ca.* 250 kg each) along with the dismantled ships and their cargo to the Nile Valley. That the ships were dismantled is attested by lines in the text of the stela of Antefoker which indicate that the ships were built in the dockyards of Coptos and then rebuilt on the shore of the Red Sea. This means that the ships were carried in sections across the land between Coptos on the Nile and Mersa Gawsis on the Red Sea.[12] As for the anchors, they transformed three of them into stelae by trimming off the apex of the anchor, which was pierced by a large hole to hold a thick rope. They then inscribed these stelae with hieroglyphs to commomorate the expedition. With these three stelae/blocks they formed the jambs and rear block of a shrine dedicated by Ankhow to King Senusret I and the gods. They used another five intact anchors to form the pedestals of the shrine of Ankhow (four anchors) and the stela of the vizier Antefoker (one anchor).[13] As for the time of Amenemhat II, the evidence is the occurrence of the name of the port as "Saww" on the previously know stela of Khentkhtay-wer, which is very near to the name of the discovered port, "*Sww*," which occurs on the shrine of Ankhow.[14] Concerning the times of both Senusret II and Senusret III, the hieratic potsherds discovered at Wadi Gawasis (which were originally parts of jars containing provisions) bear the names of buildings and officials from the times of these two kings combined with the name "Punt."[15]

Therefore, owing to these data, the use of the port during the reins of these successive four kings denotes the non-existence of the Nile-Red Sea canal during the Twelfth Dynasty.

I would like to go further to prove that the Nile-Red Sea canal did not exist during the New Kingdom. In this connection, I depend partly on a calibrated radiocarbon dating from the British Museum Laboratory (fig.1) of the organic material I found with the aforementioned monuments. Despite the very wide range of time that the calibrated radiocarbon dating gives, it covers both the Middle Kingdom (BM 1845 R, a piece of cedar wood) and the New Kingdom (BM 1844 and 1846; a rope and "Halfa" grass respectively). These results indicate that the port was in use during the New Kingdom, although no monuments or artifacts were found on the site of the port or in its vicinity dating to this time.

But this result cannot be relied on alone to solve the intricate problem of the non-existence of the Nile-Red Sea canal during the New Kingdom. For this reason it is necessary to search for a solution among the Egyptian monuments themselves.

It was a scene in Deir al-Bahari that urged scholars to suggest the existence of a Nile-Red Sea canal during the New Kingdom in general and in the time of Queen Hatshepsut in particular. It is a scene among the reliefs of the expedition to Punt. Two vessels are represented stern to stern. One in the Puntite harbor has a dismantled sail, and the other is under full sail.[16] Above the latter is an inscription saying, "Sailing. Arriving in peace, journeying to Thebes."[17] Scholars consider this to be an inscription recording the arrival of the vessels in Thebes and consequently the scene shows the Nile.[18] As there is no reference to land transport, they suggest that the vessels crossed the Eastern Delta through a canal that connected the Red Sea with the Nile.[19] They recall the Classical writer's statement that attributed the first digging of this canal to the pharaoh whom they called "Sesostris,"[20] who they identified with one of the Senwosrets. But when the aforementioned scene is examined, the vessel over which the inscription mentioning Thebes is depicted[21] is still in the Red Sea. The species of fishes represented under it are the same as those under the vessel mooring in the Puntite harbor, i.e., none of them are freshwater species. Therefore the ship is still in the Red Sea and the inscription above it indicates leaving the Puntite harbor for Thebes (lit: journeying to Thebes). It may have been an optative form of safe return.

There is sound evidence for the non-existence of this canal in the same period since land routes for the Puntite merchandise from a port on the Red Sea shore to the Nile valley existed. The earliest indication is from the time of Amenhotep II (most probably), a scene in TT 143 at Thebes that shows the unloading of the Puntite merchandise at an Egyptian port[22] and the departure and return march through the desert. The Egyptian official concerned with Puntite trade is shown with his chariot receiving the Puntite products, apparently on the shore of the Red Sea. His men are depicted driving donkeys loaded with the goods received. An incense tree is carried on a yoke by two men.[23] The Puntite traders or sailors are shown steering their rafts like sailing boats. Some scholars suggest that they carried their goods in these raft-like boats from Punt, but it is impossible for such frail vessels to sail such a long distance from Punt to Egypt, which was Somaliland at the time of the New Kingdom. I suggest that these Puntites used their raft-like boats either for going to and fro between the shore and their larger cargo ships, which lay at anchor in the open sea to avoid the shoals, or they used them for sailing between the Egyptian port and the nearby commercial settlements of the intermediaries, who imported the Puntite products from the far off land of Punt at Somaliland as deduced from the above mentioned inscriptions of Queen Hatshepsut. The second indication of land traffic for Puntite merchandise occurs in the tomb of Amenmose (TT 89) at Thebes from the reign of Thutmose IV. It is of much the same character. There are donkeys laden with Puntite merchandise on their way from the Egyptian port to the Nile valley.[24]

The third indication is an inscriptional one. It records a return voyage from Punt in the time of Ramesses III: "They (the ships) arrived in safety at the highland (desert) of Coptos. They landed in safety bearing the things which they brought. They were loaded with the merchandise on the land journey upon asses and upon men and loaded into vessels upon the Nile (at) the haven of Coptos. They were sent forward downstream and arrived amid festivity and brought the tribute into the (royal) presence like marvels."[25]

As we can see, the inscription is of the utmost importance, for despite the location of the royal residence (Pi-Ramesses) in the eastern Delta, i.e. at the end of the assumed Nile-Red Sea canal (if it existed), the Puntite merchandise was unloaded on the shore of the desert of Upper Egypt and loaded on donkeys and men and taken through the difficult terrain to Coptos on the Nile bank where it was shipped north to the eastern Delta. This provides definite evidence of the non-existence of the Nile-Red Sea canal at that period. The same conclusion was almost reached by a

434

comprehensive study of the subject published long ago by the late Georges Posener.[26] The same is reiterated in later works by Černy. Gardiner and Peet stated that it is better to leave the matter in suspense.[27] The sole attested documentation of the existence of the canal is that it was dug (and completed) by Darius I (521–486 BCE). This information was first related by Herodotus. Despite the contradicting statements of subsequent classical writers that Darius I gave up the work before its completion for fear of submerging Egypt,[28] the authenticity of Herodotus' statement is supported by inscriptional evidence. This authenticity may be due to his nearly contemporary visit (ca. 448 BCE) to Egypt during the construction of the canal and also be the reason why Herodotus did not mention Senwosret as the first to build the canal.[29] Strabo, who lived nearly 400 years after the time of Herodotus, was the first classical writer to attribute the digging and completion of the canal to Senwosret.[30]

Darius I erected several stelae along the southern bank of the canal which he dug (map 1). The messages are written in hieroglyphs and cuneiform. On one of the hieroglyphic tablets (at Kabrit), the king declares, "The canal was dug to carry water to the sands . . . . I equipped 24 (or 32) ships carrying . . . towards Persia"[31]

In the cuneiform text on one of the other tablets (at Tell al-Maskhuta) he touts his achievement, declaring: "I ordered to dig a canal (lit: river) from the river of Egypt (Piru) is his name to river Amer (the bitter lakes) . . . . It was dug according to my command and the vessels sailed on this canal (lit: river) from Egypt to Persia."[32]

The Persian name "Piru" which occurs in the text mentioned above is, according to André Servin,[33] the Egyptian name P3-ḥr which occurs in an inscription from the time of Ramesses II found at the Serapeum (map 1) and kept in the Museum of Ismailia.[34] Servin translates the text as follows: "I (Ramesses) have dug the river P3-ḥr of Thekou in order that the inundation may come according to my power." Servin concluded that Ramesses II carried out the digging of the canal (which, in his opinion, began in the New Kingdom) to Thekou, then "Necho" extended it to the Saba-Byar and Gabal Maryam (map 1). At last Darius I continued the work to the Bitter Lakes.

Whatever Servin's view of the digging of the canal may be, it points out the fact that the canal as a continuous waterway was not completed during the Pharaonic times. In my opinion, the work of Ramesses II was to supply the religious centers in Wadi Tumilat, particularly the Temples of Atum at Thekou and Pi-Atum (Tell al-Maskhouta) with the necessary fresh water for irrigation, rather than to dig a continuous waterway between the Nile and the Red Sea.

The reference to Ramesses II as a digger of a canal may present a clue to the problem of attributing the digging of the Nile-Red Sea canal to Sesostris by classical writers.

In a previous article I dealt with the legendary and fabulous deeds in the Red Sea that the classical writers attributed to the pharaoh whom they called Sesostris.[35]

I have admitted the interpretation of some scholars that these legends about their native kings were devised by the Egyptians during the Persian dominion as a kind of national propaganda to rival or eclipse the achievement of the Persian kings in the Red Sea.[36] But I have added a modification: that these legends had some historical roots which are reflected by the choice of Sesostris (Senwosret I) because of his naval activity in the Red Sea, i.e. his expedition to the land of Bia-Punt.[37] In fact, the identity of Sesostris in classical writers traditions is very complex. A group of these traditions reflect the deeds of Senwosret I in the Red Sea as mentioned above,[38] another group mirror the wars of Senwosret III in Nubia, while a third group points out to the building activities of Ramesses II at Memphis.[39]

Of these three pharaohs, Ramesses II is the one to whom the digging of the Nile-Red Sea canal can be attributed. For this deed rests on a historical root; it is the inscription found in the Isthmus of Suez (at the Serapeum) and refers, as I stated above, to his digging of a canal to carry fresh water to the region of Pi-Atum and Thekou in the Wadi Tumailat. Similar to that of the Red Sea tradition (mentioned above), the tradition of digging the Nile-Red Sea canal was fabricated by the Egyptians around this fact to rival or eclipse the achievement of Darius I the Persian King in the eastern Delta and the Isthmus of Suez.

Having excluded the existence of the Nile-Red Sea canal during the New Kingdom, it is necessary to search for the ports from which the Egyptians set sail on their journeys in the Red Sea. The reference in P. Harris to the place at which the ships of Ramesses III landed as "of the highlands (or desert) of Coptos (ḫзst Gbtyw)" may help us to identify this place with the port of Mersa Gawasis, for the name of this port (šww) accurs in an inscription found at Wadi Gawasis followed by the phrase "(of) the quay of the Coptic nome."

But an objection may arise against this conclusion that "ḫзst Gbtyw" may also refer to the port of Quseir (ca. 60 km south of Mersa Gawasis). In fact, the extensive excavations carried out in the port of Quseir (al-Qadim) by the expedition of the University of Chicago for three seasons did not reveal a single pharaonic monument.[40] Similarly, the city of Quseir itself did not yield any monuments from the Pharaonic period. In fact, Weigall found among its houses some hieroglyphic fragments, but they are of Ptolemaic date and their few inscriptions did not refer to any naval activity.[41]

Furthermore, the Egyptian's nomenclature "ḫзst Gbtyw" cannot be applied to the sites of the two other ports on the Red Sea shore. i.e. Clysma-Suez and Berenice-Ras Banäs. Because of their remoteness, archaeological investigations did not reveal any monument or artifact on these sites that refers to Pharaonic naval activity.[42]

But a question may be raised: Why did the Egyptians prefer the port of Mersa Gawasis, despite its difficult and long road to Coptos, to the easy and relatively short road of Wadi Hammamat which leads from Coptos to Quseir? The Turin Papyrus Map (map. 2a) may present an answer to this question. It depicts the roads from the Nile valley to the Red Sea (called *Yam* on the map).[43] Around the main road on the map (see map 2a which is identified by scholars with Wadi Fawakhir)[44] and the valleys branching off it are scattered gold mines and schist (greywacke) quarries. While the map was chiefly intended to be a guide to the gold mines and schist quarries at Wadi Fawakhir and its surroundings, (nearly at the middle of Wadi Hammamat)[45] the three roads depicted on it are marked with labels which denote that they lead to the (Red) Sea and to a port on its shore.[49]

The reason for this combination is the Egyptian way of organizing manpower in the eastern Desert projects. They usually combine two projects to exploit, combining as much of the manpower within their reach. Examples of this are building (or more precisely "assembling") ships for Punt expeditions on the Red Sea shore together with cutting schist blocks from the quarries of Wadi Fawakhir (the inscriptions of Henu and Ameni)[47] or extracting gold from the mines on the roads leading to the port on the Red Sea shore (the expedition of Ramesses III to Punt).[48] The first of the roads which leads to the (Red) Sea shore is labeled on the map "the road which leads to the sea (Yam)." According to Murray's identification, this road conforms to the part of Wadi Hammamat extending from Bir Fawakhir to the north east towards Quseir on the Red Sea shore (maps 2a and b).

The second road (map 2a) is labeled "another road to the (Red) sea" identified by Murray with the Wadi Um Esh al-Zarqa which is a tributary of Wadi Atallah.

The third road (map 2a) is labeled the "road of Tent-pa-mer." It was a problem for which Egyptologists could not find a reasonable solution until Bradbury ingeniously translated it "The road belonging to the harbor" which she identified with the harbor of *Sww*-Mersa Gawasis.[49] According to Murray it is Wadi Atallah itself.[50] It leads also to Wadi Saqi and Wadi Gawasis, therefore there are two roads which lead to Mersa Gawasis passing by the numerous gold mines.

The exploitation of these mines by the expeditions sent to Punt was attested by inscriptions bearing the names of the kings during whose reigns these expeditions were sent. At the junction of Wadi Atallah and Wadi Saqi, the cartouches of both Senwosret I and Ramesses III are depicted.[51] As mentioned above, these two kings sent expeditions to Punt (the former to Bia Punt).

Similarly, among the representations in TT 143 of the time of Amenhotep II (mentioned above), the scene of receiving the products of Punt contains an inscription recording that the products brought by the official included gold which was called "Gold of the highland (desert) of Coptos,"[52] an allusion to gold-working combined with the Punt project.

To some similar extent, a text of Hatshepsut's inscriptions mentions "the electrum of the best of highlands being weighed with the products of Punt."[53] Although the word "Coptos" did not occur in this text, yet the reference to "electrum of the highlands" denotes that of Coptos for the two words usually occur with each other.

From the various data mentioned above, it can be concluded that the land traffic of Punt merchandise was the prevailing custom during the Middle and New Kingdoms and that the port of *Sww*-Mersa Gawasis was in use during these times as the starting point and landing place of the ships destined for the land of Punt. This fact in its turn supports my conclusion that the Nile-Red Sea canal did not exist during both the Middle and New Kingdoms.

Notes:

1 J. H. Breasted, *Ancient Records of Egypt*, (5 vols.) (Chicago, 1905; reprinted London, 1988), § 161.

2 Abdel Monem A. H. Sayed, "Discovery of the site of the 12th Dynasty port at Wadi Gawasis on the Red Sea shore," *RdÉ* 29 (1977), 150.

3 Sayed, *RdÉ*, 176.

4 Breasted, *Ancient Records*, vol. II, § 287.

5 E. Naville, *The Temple of Deir El Bahary* III (London, 1898), 69ff.

6 N. F. Hepper, "Arabian and African Frankincense Trees," *JEA* 55 (1969) 69ff.

7 A. Lucas, *Ancient Egyptian Materials and Industries* (London, 1945), 111.

8 Strabo, Book XVI, § 13; Pliny, *Natural History* Book VI, ch. 34.

9 G.W.B. Huntingford, *The Periplus of the Erythraean Sea* (London, 1980), 19 and A. C. Mullero, *Geographi Graeci Minores* I (Paris, 1855), 256–265 and 266.

10 The writer visited this hilly place where frankincense trees grow on terraces and photographed it and the headland mentioned above.

11 Abdel Monem A. H. Sayed, "The recently discovered port on the Red Sea shore," *CdÉ* 73, no. 115–116 (1983), 28, 35.

12 Sayed, *RdÉ*, 170; *CdÉ*, 29.

13 Abdel Monem A. H. Sayed, "The recently discovered port on the Red Sea shore," *JEA* 64 (1978), 70, pl. XI, 1, 2.

14 Sayed, *RdÉ*, 69.

15 Sayed, *CdÉ*, 24–28.

16 Naville, *Deil El Bahari*, pl. 74.

17 Breasted, *Ancient Records*, vol. II, § 266.

18 Breasted, *Ancient Records*, vol. II, § 266.

19 J. H. Breasted, *A History of Egypt from the Earliest Times to the Persian Conquest* (New York, 1909), 276.

20 Strabo Book 17. I. 25. In fact. Aristotle was the earliest Classical writer to attribute this first attempt to Sesostris, but he stated that he did not complete it (Meteorologica, chapter I, XIV, n. 27). But Strabo was the earliest to attribute the first digging of the canal and its completion to Sesostris, and to define his time as before the Trojan war.

21 Naville, *Deir El Bahari*, pl. 78, right side.

22 T. Säve Soderbergh, *The navy of the eighteenth Egyptian dynasty* (Uppsala, 1946), fig. 6, quoting Emma Davies, "Egyptian Expedition 1934–1935," *BMMA*, 46ff.

23 Soderbergh, *The navy*, 23.

24 Soderbergh, *The navy*, fig. 7.

25 W. Erichsen, *Bibliotheca Aegyptiaca V Papyrus Harris I* (Bruxelles, 1933), pls. 77–78; Breasted, *Ancient Records*, § 407.

26 G. Posener, "Le Canal du Nil à le Mer Rouge avant les Ptolemés," *CdÉ* 26 (1938), 269, 271.

27 J. Černy, A. Gardiner, and E. Peet, *The inscriptions of Sinai* II (Oxford, 1955), 12–13.

28 Diodorus, I § 53; Strabo, 17, I, 25.

29 Herodotus, Book II, 158.

30 Strabo, 17, I, 25.

31 A. Servin, "Stèle de l'Isthme de Sues," *BSEIS* Tome III (1949–1950), 81.

32 M. V. Scheil, "Inscriptions de Darius à Suez," *BIFAO* 30 (1930), 293.

33 Servin, "Stèle," 94–95.

34 B. Bruyère, "Fouilles de Clysma – Qolsom (Suez)," *IFAO* (1930, reprinted 1966), 57, 74.

35 Sayed, *CdÉ*, 32.

36 A. B. Lloyd, "Necho and the Red Sea, Some Considerations," *JEA* 63 (1977), 152.

37 Sayed, *CdÉ*, 32.

38 Diodorus I, 55.

39 Herodotus, II, 108, 110; Diodorus, I, 58.

40 D.S. Whitcomb and J. Jonson, *Quseir El Qadim* (Chicago, 1978 & 1980); Abdel Monem A. H. Sayed, "Review of *Quseir El Qadim*," *CdÉ* 59 (1980), 293–294.

41 A. Weigall, *Travels in the Upper Egyptian Deserts* (London, 1913), 81 and pl. X.

42 Bruyère, Fouilles, Golenischeff, "Une Excursion à Berenice," *Rec. Trav.* XIII (1913), 87; cf. PM VII, 329 and more recently, *Egyptian Archaeology, The Bulletin of the Egypt Exploration Society* 15 (1999), 34.

43 This rendering is adopted by most Egyptologists and geologists, but Goyon rendered it "the Nile" which led him to identify the well on the map with Bir Hammamat instead of Bir Fawakhir which lies amid the gold mines. He also applied the map to the area *south* of Wadi Hammamat adjacent to Bir Hammamat with its rough roads leading to Luxor (in his opinion) and scarcity of gold mines. While he ignored the area *north* of Wadi Hammamat adjacent to Bir Fawakhir and Wadi Atallah which is pierced by relatively easier roads. (G. Goyon, "Le Papyrus de Turin dit des Mines d'or, et le Wadi Hammamat," *ASAE* 49 [1949], 337ff.).

44 G. W. Murray, "The gold mines of the Turin Papyrus," in J. Ball, *Egypt in the Classical geographers* (1942), 180–182.

45 *Wadi* is an Arabic word for "valley," *fawakhir* for "potsherds," and *hammamat* for "baths." The last name is given to the unfinished sarcophagi (cut by the ancients from the schist quarries) because they resemble the basins used for bathing.

46 L. Bradbury, "Reflections on God's Land and Punt in the Middle Kingdom," *JARCE* 25 (1988), 150.

47 Breasted, *Ancient Records* I, § 432; Sayed, *CdÉ*, 27–28.

48 Breasted, *Ancient Records* IV, § 228.

49 Bradbury, *JARCE*, 150.

50 Murray, "Turin Papyrus," 182.

51 F. W. Green, "Notes on some inscriptions in the Ethbai district," *PSBA* 31 (1909), pl. 54, no. 4.

52 B. Cumming, *Egyptian historical records of the later Eighteenth Dynasty*, Fasc. 2 (Warminster, 1984), no. 1473.

53 Breasted, *Ancient Records* II, § 373.

New Rock Inscriptions on Elephantine Island

Stephan Johannes Seidlmayer

Berlin-Brandenburg Academy of Sciences and Humanities

Introduction

The rock inscriptions of the Aswan area attracted scientific interest quite early in the history of Egyptology. C. R. Lepsius reproduced a number of them in his monumental "Denkmaeler aus Aegypten und Aethiopien,"[1] and at the end of the nineteenth century, two catalogs published by J. de Morgan and his co-workers, and by W.M.F. Petrie and F. Ll. Griffith, respectively, provided a comprehensive overview over the material.[2] Since their original publication, these catalogs have proven to be invaluable sources of prosopographic information.

Hitherto, Elephantine Island, in this context, has played only a minor role. In fact, among the thousands of inscriptions in the area, the aforementioned catalogs list only a few dozen for Elephantine. However, a number of important additions to this stock were made by the late Labib Habachi, thanks to his unrivaled knowledge of the area and its monuments. Some of his discoveries will be mentioned below.

In the context of the excavations of the German Archaeological Institute at Elephantine, the rock inscriptions located on the island again came into focus. In the course of several seasons of work there, a complete survey of the inscriptions was accomplished on Elephantine and at a number of sites in its surroundings, and a full documentation was prepared in accordance with modern standards.[3] In the course of this work, a considerable number of new inscriptions were discovered, and in many cases substantial additions and corrections to the existing copies were made. Apart from checking and augmenting the epigraphic corpus, a major aim of this research was to investigate and to document the archaeological aspects of the material as well. Above all, the topographical setting of the inscriptions within the context of the monuments of the area of Elephantine was carefully noted. In fact, this aspect was all too often neglected in earlier publications.

In this paper, I intend to present a short overview of our work, mainly to provide a first impression of the available material and of its potential. The analytical issues that need to be raised in the course of a thorough study of the documentation will be touched upon only briefly, due to the limitations of space.

The Rock Inscriptions of Hassawanarti

Most of the rock inscriptions on Elephantine date from the New Kingdom. This is also true for the texts of an important new site of rock inscriptions that was explored in the course of our work, namely Hassawanarti. Today Hassawanarti is a small rocky outcrop on the eastern shore of Elephantine. In former times, when the annual flood of the Nile prevented the accumulation of soil along the shore of Elephantine, Hassawanarti was an independent islet, as indicated by its Nubian name ("the island of Hassawa"), and as still can be seen on old photographs (for the topographical situation see fig. 1).

It was Labib Habachi who recognized that Hassawanarti was the site of important inscriptions. Habachi mentioned the place several times in his publications, and he managed to publish six of its inscriptions, though all but two of them are published incompletely.[4]

Several seasons of work devoted to the site included the re-excavation of the northern face of the former island, which is nowadays permanently buried under sand, and a thorough cleaning of its whole surface. This time-consuming procedure was indispensable because most of the inscriptions are lightly carved into the surface of the rock and were therefore hardly legible. In addition, the stark color contrasts of the large grained granite rock create a disturbing visual effect. Thanks to this effort, we now know of more than 80 inscriptions at Hassawanarti. A short survey of this material is intended to provide an overview over the types of inscriptions found, and a few comments on the categories of persons attested at this site.

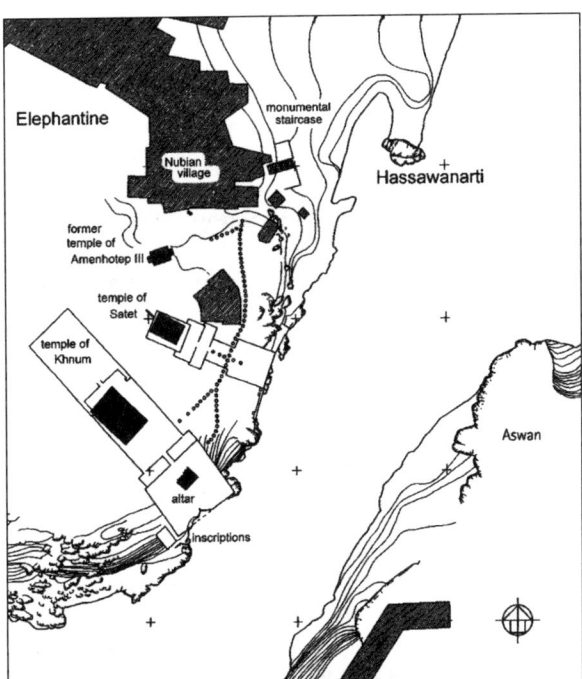

First of all, the viceroys of Nubia, who held supreme authority over the area of Aswan, are to be mentioned. Labib Habachi already discovered a graffito of Merimes, viceroy under Amenhotep III,[5] and we were able to find a long inscription of Usersatet, viceroy in the time of Amenhotep II. In this newly discovered text, Usersatet boasts in conventional terms of his close relationship to the king. However, as is well known, Usersatet was unable to keep this favorable position. As at other places, Usersatet's figure, his titles, and his name were erased in this inscription; however, nobody dared to touch the name of the mistress of Elephantine, which formed part of his own name.

A second category of persons is priests, mainly those of Theban temples. As one of many examples, we may refer to the high priest of

Fig. 1: Hassawanarti and the temples of Elephantine.

441

Amen Wepwawetmes[6] who is shown adoring the cartouches of Seti I. This person, whose dating was controversial before, therefore becomes firmly fixed in time. The presence of priests among the inscriptions does not only seem to indicate close contacts between the various administrations of the temples of southern Upper Egypt, but also attests to some sort of supervision over the temples of Elephantine. In fact, there is one inscription at Hassawanarti that refers to a "revision" (*sip.t*) in the temples; unfortunately, however, this text was only partly executed in ancient times and therefore remains tantalizing evidence.

Local officials, the heads of the administration of the temples of Elephantine—like the well-known high priest Pendjerty[7]—and of the mayors of the town, occur only rarely and only during the Twentieth Dynasty in this series. It should be noted that, quite in contrast to the situation at Hassawanarti, this class of persons is well attested at the sites of the lesser sanctuaries of the region like at Sehel or the Gebel Tingar.

Not surprisingly in the area of Aswan, supervisors of works in the quarries and chief craftsmen are well represented among the inscriptions of Hassawanarti. Labib Habachi already recognized the right half of the large tableau of Nebnakhte, a fortress commander and overseer of works from the time of Ramesses II who is attested by several inscriptions in the area.[8] Our research revealed that Nebnakhte is accompanied in his graffito at Hassawanarti by his large family: his wife, his four sons—who all took up military service as did their father—and a long line of daughters. Even two grandchildren are present. The most important single inscription at Hassawanarti falls into this class as well, namely the long text of a certain Humen, published by Labib Habachi.[9] In this inscription, Humen boasts of having extracted six obelisks from the quarries of Aswan. Of course we need not necessarily think of monumental obelisks since Humen does not claim that the obelisks he quarried at Aswan were *wr* "great" nor does he claim they were destined for the Theban temples. Apart from the gigantic obelisks that are best known today, obelisks of a less grandiose scale were used to adorn the sanctuaries. A number of such smaller obelisks from the reigns of Amenhotep II and Thutmosis IV even derive from the temples of Elephantine.[10] This consideration bears on the discussion of the date of the inscription of Humen, which therefore does not need to be guided exclusively by the record of monumental obelisks in the Theban temples. This body of data led Habachi to suggest a date in the reigns of Thutmose III or Amenhotep III for this text, but for stylistic reasons, a date in between those two kings seems more likely.

Members of the central administration are present at Hassawanarti as well. In this context, we can mention, for example, the well-known chief of the treasury Suti from the time of Ramesses II.[11] Above all, however, I would like to draw attention to a quite unusual inscription, namely a list of 45 officials from the time of Thutmosis IV.[12] Space does not permit me to enter into a detailed analysis of this exceptional text—an enterprise that would be worthwhile indeed. The list is headed by the royal nurses Heqareshut and Heqaerneheh. Inscriptions mentioning both royal nurses are known from Konosso.[13] In the inscription at Hassawanarti, they are followed in the list by an administrator of the palace of Perunefer, royal scribes, and "children of the nursery." After listing these high-ranking persons, the text continues naming officers of troops and of boats, as well as a number of "chief servants." The last figure is that of a scribe Menkheperaseneb, and undoubtedly it was this person who drew up the whole list. On closer examination of the text it can be demonstrated that this list represents the royal entourage who accompanied the king on a visit to Elephantine. Within this category of inscriptions of members of the central administration we should also mention a tableau which shows, in the upper register, King Seti I presenting an offering to Khnum, and in the lower register his son, Prince

Ramesses, the future King Ramesses II in adoration.[14] This inscription was probably carved when Prince Ramesses resided at Aswan to direct works in the quarries, as we know he did from several other monuments.[15]

Finally, I would like to draw attention to the inscriptions of lesser military and police personnel. There are a considerable number of *t3w-sry.t* "standard bearers," one *shs n kni* "runner of the guard," and one *s'š3* "policeman." This category of persons is remarkably well attested at Hassawanarti, quite in contrast to other sites of rock inscriptions in the area of Aswan.

The Location of New Kingdom Rock Inscriptions

The inscriptions of Hassawanarti form a remarkable corpus. Viewing the whole situation it would be of paramount interest to know why so many and so important inscriptions were carved at so inconspicuous a site. In a broader perspective, this question raises a particularly important issue. For everyone working on rock inscriptions in the field, it becomes immediately evident that the texts are not dispersed haphazardly over the landscape. Rather, the inscriptions occur in tight groups at well-defined places, and it is therefore necessary to reconstruct the rules that governed the selection of sites.

I regret that, in the present context, it is not possible to discuss the rich and fascinating evidence which bears on this question and that I have to confine myself to summing up the results of my research: The island of Hassawanarti is situated in a bay on the eastern face of Elephantine which originally formed the main harbor of the ancient city of Elephantine. Therefore, this spot was probably the single most important node in the network of traffic routes around Elephantine. However, this place is of an even more specific significance. The only architectural marker on the shore of Elephantine opposite Hassawanarti is a monumental staircase of the Roman era, which was excavated by Horst Jaritz.[16] This staircase served, as was pointed out by Jaritz, mainly a ritual purpose during the festivals of the Nile. As a matter of fact, both this staircase and the site of the harbor in general, lay at the end of the processional roads that linked the temples of Elephantine. During the great processional festivals of the gods of Elephantine, like the famous river procession of Anuket in the first month of Shemu which is repeatedly mentioned in the epigraphic documentation,[17] the images of the gods were carried down to the shore and were loaded onto their river barges at precisely this spot. Accordingly, the site of the harbor formed the stage of a particularly splendid moment in the celebrations. The ritual function of the site was therefore of paramount importance, and this ritual function was, in my view, the most important reason for carving the inscriptions at Hassawanarti. As direct evidence for this interpretation we may again refer to the inscription of Humen. Humen states explicitly in the introduction to his text that he came to Elephantine to witness a processional festival of Khnum and Anuket. In addition, the prosopographical composition of the inscriptions of Hassawanarti seems to be relevant in this context. Guards, policemen, and officers who form such a characteristic group among the persons attested at Hassawanarti are regularly depicted in New Kingdom temple reliefs among the lesser personnel which accompanied such great processional festivals.

The observation that, during the New Kingdom, the ritual function of a site was the determining factor in the selection of its location, clearly confirms itself with the second largest group of New Kingdom inscriptions on Elephantine. This group is situated in front of the temple of Khnum. Here, a monumental altar in front of the former pylon served as a stage for the ritual display of the image of the god during public festivals.[18] The inner faces of the granite boulders at the shore of the river in front of the temple, which exactly face this altar, are crammed with a large number of inscriptions, most of them still unpublished.[19] Very significantly, however, the outer faces of these same boulders were left blank, in spite of the fact that, from a technical point of view, they would have offered excellent possibilities for the carving of inscriptions. The reason is, of course, that the outer faces of the rocks did not have a direct view of the place of divine appearance.

Both Hassawanarti and the rocks in front of the temple of Khnum provide excellent examples for a nearly general rule. During the New Kingdom, rock inscriptions in the area of Aswan were mainly carved in tight clusters near local shrines and at places that played a role in the course of the celebration of public religious festivals.

The Location of Old and Middle Kingdom Rock Inscriptions

To provide an interesting contrast to this situation, it is useful to have a brief look at the inscriptions of the Old and Middle Kingdoms as well. Viewing the distribution of rock inscriptions in the field it is evident that the inscriptions of the Old and Middle Kingdoms were carved at very different locations than the New Kingdom inscriptions. As a result, both chronological groups are nearly non-overlapping topographically.

At Elephantine, there is a large block bearing a number of Old and Middle Kingdom royal inscriptions that were already recognized, in part, by de Morgan and Petrie.[20] On the principal face of this block, the inscriptions start with Unas and continue with Merenre, Pepi II, and Wahankh Intef II. On the adjoining face of the block, which is today hardly accessible, inscriptions of Amenemhet I, Sobekhotep I, and Neferhotep I were added. In the late Middle Kingdom and in the Second Intermediate Period, a group of inscriptions of private individuals were carved on this block as well, when after several centuries of exclusively royal use such restrictions on the site were relaxed.

Again, the topographical situation of these inscriptions deserves careful attention. The block bearing the royal inscriptions of the Old Kingdom is located at the northern tip of the Old Kingdom city. As Ziermann's excavations revealed, it was most probably originally even engaged at the foot of the city walls.[21] Since it seems very likely for several reasons that the main entrance gate to the city was located close to the temple of Satet, the block originally occupied an extremely prominent position and was visible to everyone who walked up from the harbor to enter the town of Elephantine.

Another site duplicates the observations regarding the location of these inscriptions. Close to the lesser gate of the Old Kingdom town,[22] on a rock that was also engaged at the foot of the Old Kingdom city wall, a large tableau of the Fourth Dynasty governor Khufuankh displayed his authority over the city.[23] On re-examining this important text, an addition could be made to Khufuankh's titles. Khufuankh was also a $r\underline{h}$-$nswt$, quite in accordance with what is fitting for a member of the early provincial administration. Most importantly, however, it became clear that the Old Kingdom inscriptions on the rock face adjoining Khufuankh's inscription to the right form the direct continuation of Khufuankh's tableau. Here, Khufuankh's wife is depicted, and his daughter and son are mentioned. It seems quite interesting to note that the latter, like his father, had a title that linked him to the administration of Elephantine. Unfortunately, however, this title is partly destroyed. Nevertheless, here we can clearly recognize the existence of two members of an early "dynasty" of local administrators.

It is obvious that, in the case of these Old Kingdom examples, the relationship to the city was of decisive importance for the location of the inscriptions.

Rock inscriptions from the Old Kingdom are comparatively rare in the area of Aswan. Only during the Middle Kingdom do their numbers increase dramatically. The inscriptions were carved mainly along important roads and at places overlooking the river where busy traffic occurred.

The road linking Aswan and the plain of Shellal, for instance, was a particularly important site of rock inscriptions during the Middle Kingdom. At Elephantine, the most important group of Middle Kingdom rock inscriptions conforms to this rationale of carving inscriptions. The texts cover a large rock face at what is now the landing stage of the northern ferry to Elephantine. Here we find a rich array of Middle Kingdom rock inscriptions.[24] One of the texts of this group belongs to a police officer Sonbef, a person who is also attested among the newly discovered texts on the block that bears the royal inscriptions of the Old Kingdom.

Viewing the distribution of Middle Kingdom rock inscriptions at Elephantine and in its surroundings as a whole, a very characteristic pattern emerges. The texts do not form a few tight clusters as do those of the New Kingdom. Rather they are widely distributed over the landscape. The western bank of the Nile from the Qubbet al-Hawa in the north to the Wadi Berber in the south as well as the southern tip of the island of Elephantine are lined with series of Middle Kingdom rock inscriptions. This way of placing inscriptions is fundamentally incompatible with the habits of the New Kingdom.

The analysis of the topographical contexts of the rock inscriptions in the area of Aswan demonstrates significant changes in the overall patterns of selecting sites for carving the texts. In the earlier period, when the cults of the local gods, as far as we know, did not yet entail important public celebrations, the town of Elephantine and the traffic routes in its surroundings provided the only available framework for public display. Only later, during the New Kingdom, did the situation change, when the cults of the gods found expression in important public events, mainly during their great processional festivals. Now these religious events could and did serve as a privileged framework for the status display of private individuals. The developmental pattern visible in the location of rock inscriptions clearly shows that, in the New Kingdom, the cult of the gods embraced a desire for personal public display which, however, had existed before, but in its origins, had not been ritually motivated.

Concluding Remarks

Summing up this short survey, I would like to emphasize three points that, in my view, are essential for further work on this material.

Above all, the potential of continued field research on rock inscriptions in the area of Aswan should have become evident. Scores of new material remain to be discovered, and substantial additions and corrections to the existing data need to be made. However, the sites of rock inscriptions are endangered by the rapid growth of modern settlements no less than other archaeological sites. We should therefore be aware that whatever work remains to be done has to be accomplished within the near future.

Secondly, I would like to stress the rich potential of this material. Rock inscriptions are not just a source of diverse prosopographical data. Rather they can provide important information on the ancient use of the landscape, and specifically the ritual and economic activities in the town of Elephantine and in its surroundings. To access this wealth of information, however, it is important to study rock inscriptions not as isolated items, but in the full context of the topographical and historical record of the area. Only then will the original meaning of the inscriptions and the reasons why they were carved at specific places and in specific groupings become apparent.

To achieve this contextual analysis, and this is my last point, a type of epigraphic field work is needed, which is not merely concerned with reading the texts. Rather it is necessary to pay attention to the technical and locational properties of the inscriptions as well, and that means we need a truly archaeologically-oriented type of epigraphy.

Notes:

1 For detailed references to early publications, see B. Porter and L. B. Moss, *Topographical Bibliography* V (Oxford, 1937), 245–256.

2 J. de Morgan *et al.*, *Catalogue des monuments et inscriptions de l'Égypte antique* I 1, (Vienna, 1894); W.M.F. Petrie, *A Season in Egypt 1887*, (London, 1888), Pl. 1–13; *PM* V, 221 *seqq.*

3 see S. J. Seidlmayer, "New Rock Inscriptions at Elephantine Island," *EA* 14 (1999), 41–43, and, "Dreißig Jahre ließ ich gehen . . . , Ergänzungen zu zwei Jubiläumsinschriften im Gebiet von Aswan," in *MDAIK* 57 (2001), 247–256; the final publication of the material discovered in the course of this work is in preparation.

4 L. Habachi, "An Inscription at Aswan Referring to Six Obelisks," *JEA* 36 (1950), 13–18; "The Graffiti and Work of the Viceroys of Kush in the Region of Aswan," *Kush* 5 (1957), 24, fig. 8, n. 16; "Rock-Inscriptions from the Reign of Ramesses II on and around Elephantine Island, " *Festschrift Elmar Edel. 12 März 1979*, M. Görg and E. Pusch (eds.) (ÄAT 1; Bamberg, 1979), 231f.; *Features of the Deification of Ramesses II*, (*ADAIK* 5; Glückstadt, 1969), 26, fig. 16. However, the statement that a fine inscription of the steward Kheruef is located on Hassawanarti island (L. Habachi, *The Tomb of Kheruef* (The Epigraphic Survey of the Oriental Institute of the University of Chicago, OIP 102; Chicago, 1980), 22) is erroneous; this text is in fact located on Kafrije.

5 L. Habachi, "The Graffiti," fig. 8, n. 16.

6 *KRI* I, 326.

7 for other inscriptions of this person see *KRI* VI, 100 *seq.*

8 L. Habachi, "Inscriptions from the Reign of Ramesses II;" *KRI* III, 260 *seq.*; see fig. in Seidlmayer, "New Rock Inscriptions," 41.

9 L. Habachi, "An Inscription."

10 Abdel-Kader Selim, "Les obélisques égyptiens," *SASAE* 26.2 (Le Caire, 1991), 123 *seqq.*

11 *KRI* III, 140 *seqq.*

12 See fig. in Seidlmayer, "New Rock Inscriptions," 42.

13 See P. J. Frandsen, "Heqareshu and the Family of Thutmosis IV," *Acta Orientalia* 37 (1976), 5–10; B. Bryan, *The Reign of Thutmose IV* (Baltimore, 1991), 259–261.

14 See fig. in Seidlmayer, "New Rock Inscriptions," 42.

15 L. Habachi, "The Two Rock-Stelae of Sethos I in the Cataract Area Speaking of Huge Statues and Obelisks," *BIFAO* 73 (1973), 113–125, and a passage in the Quban stela, *KRI* II, 356, 4.

16 H. Jaritz, "Nilkultstätten auf Elephantine," *BSAK* 2 (1988), 199–209; "Stadt und Tempel von Elephantine, Elfter/Zwölfter Grabungsbericht," *MDAIK* 40 (1984), 191 *seqq.*; "Stadt und Tempel von Elephantine," 13./14. Grabungsbericht, *MDAIK* 43 (1987), 103 *seqq.*

17 The festival is mentioned in the Elephantine copy of the Amada stela of Amenhotep II (*Urk.* IV, 1299), in a rock inscription of the viceroy Usersatet at Ras Sehel (Habachi, "The Graffiti," 20 *seqq.*), and in the inscriptions of the Eighteenth Dynasty temple of Satet at Elephantine.

18 H. Jaritz, *Elephantine III, Die Terrassen vor den Tempeln des Chnum und der Satet* (AV 32; Mainz, 1980), 40.

19 For the published ones see incomplete and unreliable copies in de Morgan *et. al.*, *Catalogue des monuments*, 115.4–5 and 11.

20 de Morgan *et al.*, *Catalogue des monuments*, 115.1 and Petrie, *A Season*, Pl. 12.308–312; see figs. in Seidlmayer, "New Rock Inscriptions," 43. Redford's suggestion (*Pharaonic King-Lists, Annals and Day-Books* (SSEA Publications 4; Mississauga, 1986, 25) that, "possibly the Old Kingdom entries belong to a single occasion," and that the text therefore was a kind of kings' list, proves, upon closer examination of the original inscription, clearly unjustified.

21 M. Ziermann, *Elephantine XVI, Befestigungsanlagen und Stadtentwicklung in der Frühzeit* (AV 87; Mainz 1993), 100, fig. 41; the inscribed block is the one shown in the northwest corner of the northern tip of the reconstructed city walls.

22 For this gate see G. Dreyer, "Stadt und Tempel von Elephantine, Achter Grabungsbericht," *MDAIK* 36 1980, 264 *seqq.*

23 L. Habachi, "Unpublished Old and Middle Kingdom Graffiti on Elephantine," *WZKM* 54 1957, 55 *seqq.*

24 For preliminary copies of some of these texts see de Morgan *et al.*, *Catalogue des monuments*, 115.9–10, 11 bis-14 and Petrie, *A Season*, Pl. 11. 298–301, 303–304.

New Fieldwork at Gebel al-Asr: "Chephren's Diorite Quarries"

Ian Shaw

University of Liverpool, UK

This paper presents the results of three seasons of survey and excavation at the Gebel al-Asr gneiss quarrying region, which covers an area of about 120 km^2 to the south of Wadi Toshka and to the west of Lake Nasser. It consists of a number of individual quarrying areas dating to various periods from the Early Dynastic to the Middle Kingdom: Quartz Ridge, Khufu Stele Quarry, Chisel Quarry, Loading Ramp Quarry, and Stele Ridge. The first four locations are all gneiss quarries, whereas the fifth, Stele Ridge, was evidently a set of quartz/carnelian mines exploited in the Middle Kingdom (and, judging from the survival of one amphora, briefly visited during the Roman Period). The paper will discuss the region as a whole as a case study for the nature of remote stone quarrying sites in the Old and Middle Kingdoms. New information obtained from the site in 1997, 1999, and 2000 includes geological survey data, the study of 23 large Twelfth Dynasty storage jars, the discovery of two new royal stelae (one Fifth Dynasty and the other Twelfth Dynasty), and the excavation of two loading ramps and two enigmatic semi-subterranean structures.

Survey and Excavation at Gebel al-Asr, 1932–2000

The Gebel al-Asr gneiss quarries and quartz mines, rediscovered in 1932, are often described as the "Chephren diorite quarries" because they are the source of the blue-gray metamorphic rock from which the magnificent seated statue of the Fourth Dynasty pharaoh Chephren (2520–2494 BCE) was carved.[1] The site is located in Lower Nubia, about 65 km northwest of Abu Simbel (see fig. 1). The current project is the first archaeological study of the region since 1938,[2] although James Harrell and Max Brown undertook a primarily geological survey of the area in 1990.[3]

In April 1997, with the permission of the Supreme Council of Antiquities, we undertook a short season of survey at the Gebel al-Asr quarries. This survey had two basic aims: first, to examine the Gebel al-Asr gneiss quarries (formerly known as the "Chephren diorite quarries"), dating to the Old and Middle Kingdoms (c.2650–1600 BCE), and secondly, to investigate the exis-

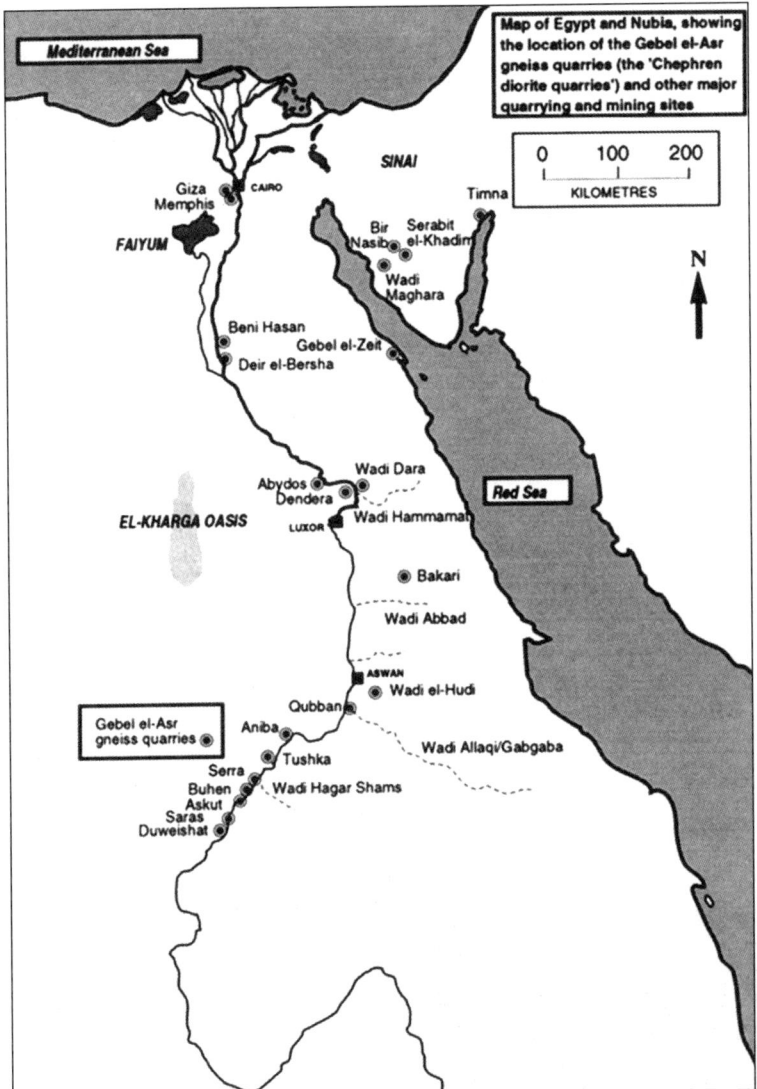

Fig. 1: Map of ancient Egypt and Nubia showing the location of the Gebel al-Asr archaeological site (the "Chephren diorite quarries").

tence of a set of amethyst mines supposedly dating to the Old Kingdom, at the northern end of the quarries. These would be the earliest amethyst mines in Egypt, predating the Middle Kingdom Wadi al-Hudi mines, which were most recently surveyed in 1992.[4] In April 1999 and April 2000 we undertook survey and excavation at a variety of locations across the region as a whole.[5]

Previous Work in the Gebel al-Asr Region

The 80-kilometer route linking the quarries with the nearest Nile embarkation point at modern Toshka is the longest surviving Egyptian quarry "road." The Gebel al-Asr gneiss and quartz quarries were rediscovered in 1932 by a British military vehicle as it traveled through the Sahara to the northwest of Abu Simbel during a sandstorm. The discoverers returned in 1933 with Reginald Engelbach, Chief Keeper of the Cairo Museum, and took away from the site a number of inscribed stelae. At this time, two sites had been identified: Quartz Ridge, which we now assume to have been the nerve center of the region of Old and Middle Kingdom gneiss quarrying; and Stele Ridge, an area of quartz mining marked by eight large Middle Kingdom cairns. In February 1938 a more substantial expedition to the site was organized by Engelbach in collaboration with Gilbert Murray, and it was in this season that the most impressive discoveries were made, including the discovery of the area now known as the Khufu Stele Site: a large area of quarries toward the southern end of the site, with a dry-stone mound in the center where stone stelae of Khufu and Sahure had been erected.

The 80–kilometer route linking the quarries with the nearest Nile embarkation point at modern Toshka is the longest surviving Egyptian quarry "road." This road was not a built structure, as the roads to the Hatnub travertine quarries or the Gebel Qatrani/Widan al-Faras basalt quarries were. Instead it appears to have been simply a cleared track (rather than a paved or dry-stone structure), the course of which was clearly identifiable through a variety of evidence: pieces of discarded gneiss and potsherds, numerous cairns (including one large example marking the point almost exactly midway between the Nile and the quarries), occasional dry-stone encampments, and, on the harder ground, well-preserved donkey tracks along the road itself. Murray describes the hoof-marks as countless parallel trails, too thin and straight for camel tracks, that showed where the donkey caravans had taken provisions up to the quarries and brought smaller pieces of gneiss down.[6]

In the case of the largest blocks of gneiss, the journey from the quarries to the Nile (or to Wadi Toshka, if flooded) seems to have begun at a pair of stone-built loading ramps (one of which was partly excavated by Engelbach and Murray in the 1930s) at the southern end of the Gebel al-Asr quarrying region. In the 1999 and 2000 seasons, we excavated both of these ramps. Elizabeth Bloxam discusses the excavation of the ramps, and various suggestions concerning the transportation of the gneiss, in a separate paper in this volume.[7]

Fig. 2: "Loading platform 1" at the Gebel al-Asr gneiss quarries.

Quartz Ridge: The Settlement Remains

Quartz Ridge is a long strip of high ground roughly following a southwest-northeast axis, punctuated by four stone cairns (one of which is composed of fragments of quartz, hence the name given to the ridge by Engelbach and Murray). As a result of the flatness of the general terrain in the Gebel al-Asr region, the prominence of the ridge itself and the presence of the cairns (which are assumed to date back to the pharaonic period or earlier), Quartz Ridge is a highly visible feature in the landscape. Since there is also a considerable amount of anorthosite gneiss in the immediate vicinity, it is not surprising that this ridge seems to have formed a kind of operational focus for both Old and Middle Kingdom quarrying. Three basalt dykes to the northwest of the Quartz Ridge quarrying region were exploited both to provide tools for working the gneiss and also to supply raw material for basalt vessels.

The group of dry-stone huts at Quartz Ridge, identified by Engelbach and Murray as the site of the main quarry-workers settlement, is the one area of the site where significant quantities of surface pottery have survived. It represented an obvious target for excavation, promising to provide information on the chronology of the expeditions as well as crucial details concerning living conditions and supplies. Compared with other major Old and Middle Kingdom quarries, such as those at Hatnub[8] and Wadi al-Hudi,[9] the settlement remains at Gebel al-Asr are very limited in extent, suggesting both that the duration of the expeditions might have been fairly short and that the numbers of workers might not have been very great. The best interpretation of the Quartz Ridge huts was that they constituted a headquarters and supply depot from which the scattered groups of quarriers were coordinated.

In the 1999 season we excavated four rooms in a large dry-stone hut that appeared to form the nucleus of the settlement. Our finds included ceramics ranging in date from the Early Dynastic Period to the Middle Kingdom, a fragment of a Fifth Dynasty stone stele bearing the Horus name and cartouche of Niuserre, a king who had not previously been attested at the site, a set of 23 intact Twelfth Dynasty pottery flat-bottomed storage jars, and two smaller intact Middle Kingdom vessels.

The capacity of one of the large storage jars was measured at 76.5 liters. Many of them bear pre-firing pot marks on the insides of rims and post-firing numbers incised on their shoulders. Similar large Middle Kingdom marl C storage vessels have been found at Lisht, Qasr al-Sagha, Dahshur, Haraga, Tell al-Daba, and Abu Ghalib, and the best parallels for a large group of this type were the 22 (also with pre-firing marks inside their rims) vessels found in the so-called South wall deposit 1 at Lisht.[10] Vessels of this type, probably produced in the Memphis-Fayoum region, were particularly suited to the transportation and long-term storage of dry substances such as grain. The peak period of use was in the mid-Twelfth Dynasty although examples at Tell al-Daba were found in strata dating to the late Twelfth to mid-Thirteenth Dynasties. The storage vessels at Quartz Ridge represent a significant amount of storage in support of the Middle Kingdom quarrying expeditions, and may ultimately prove to be useful evidence in terms of evaluating the numbers of workers involved in the Middle Kingdom work at Gebel al-Asr (see Table 1).

Capacity of average Kahun granary	1064 cubic m (222,594 hekat)
Capacity of Mirgissa granary	330 cubic m (69,038 hekat)
Estimated capacity of all Nubian fortress granaries	5104 cubic m (1,067,782 hekat)
1 Gebel el-Asr storage jar	0.076 cubic m (16 hekat/60 kg)
22 jars	1.75 cubic m (368 hekat/1380 kg)
Total: 1kg per man per day =3D 1380 men for 1 day or 69 men for 20 days	

Table 1: Comparison of the capacity of storage jars at Gebel el-Asr and granaries elsewhere, and estimates of rations/workmen.

Fig. 3:
The emplacement where the "Khufu Stele" (now in the Egyptian Museum, Cairo, JE 68752) originally stood, at the Gebel al-Asr quarries.

The New Area of Settlement Near the Khufu Stele Quarries and the Two Semi-Subterranean Structures

In April 2000 we discovered and partially excavated a new area of Old Kingdom settlement at the southern end of the Gebel al-Asr region, roughly midway between the Khufu Stele Quarry and ramp LR1. The center of this settlement was severely damaged when the new tarmac road to Gebel Uweinat was constructed in the 1990s, but fortunately a considerable amount of material has survived on either side of the road (i.e. to the west and east), primarily comprising dry-stone walls and ceramics. Three areas (A1, B1, and C1) were excavated in the area of settlement to the west of the road, each measuring 2 x 4 meters. Area A1, a wide, low-walled, roughly oval structure turned out to contain several typical Old Kingdom bread molds amid large amounts of ash, indicating the baking of loaves.

In the same season we also excavated two enigmatic semi-subterranean structures (perhaps used for storage), one of which (labeled TH1) was situated midway between the new Khufu Stele Settlement and Loading Ramp 1, while the other (TH2) was located close to the Quartz Ridge settlement. These two structures are very similar in appearance, suggesting that they almost certainly served the same (as yet unknown) purpose. Both consist of an oval dry-stone building at ground level, with the interior dug out to a depth of about a meter, which would have taken some considerable effort to create, given the hardness of the deposit that had to be removed. Each of the structures has two or three very narrow trenches dug out at the deepest point, suggesting that some kind of movable installation, such as a pot-stand, may have been placed there. Study of the associated ceramics may perhaps provide some clues as to their precise function. A short distance to the east of this settlement and to the south of LR1 is a distinct area of human activity which may perhaps be the remains of a third loading ramp, somewhat smaller than the two others.

Stele Ridge: The Quartz/Carnelian Mines

In all three seasons we undertook brief surveys of the structural remains, artifacts, and pottery in the area at the northeastern end of the site, surrounding Stele Ridge, where Engelbach and Little had reported the existence of a set of amethyst mines possibly dating to the Old Kingdom, at the northern end of the quarries.[11] These would be the earliest amethyst mines in Egypt, predating the Middle Kingdom Wadi al-Hudi mines. In our 1997 survey we were able to identify only Middle Kingdom and Roman pottery in the Stele Ridge part of the site, but in 1999 we discovered at least one Old Kingdom shard (deriving from a Fourth Dynasty footed bowl or stand, [pers. comm., Deborah Darnell]), suggesting that this area of amethyst and multi-colored quartz mines may well have been exploited at an earlier date than the Wadi al-Hudi mines.

Although Stele Ridge has recently been badly affected by construction work associated with the new road to Gebel Uweinat, there are nevertheless sufficient surviving traces of cairns, ceramics, and quarried stone to provide a good indication of the date and major characteristics of the site.

In the April 2000 season, our inspector, Mustafa Hassan, discovered an inscribed and decorated stele bearing the prenomen of Amenemhat II. It was found, face down, about 30 meters to the southwest of the remains of the Middle Kingdom cairns. In the same part of the site we also found a finely-worked carnelian earring, our only indication so far that jewelry was being produced *in situ* from the quarried gemstones at Stele Ridge.

Discussion and Future Prospects

After three seasons of survey and two seasons of excavation, our knowledge of the history, archaeology, and geology of the Gebel al-Asr region has been considerably expanded.[12] It is now clear that the Engelbach/Murray expeditions of the 1930s, although very fruitful in terms of the discovery of stelae and small items of sculpture, devoted all too little attention to the evidence concerning the activities of the Old and Middle Kingdom quarry-workers themselves. Our surveys and excavations have focused on the study of the logistics of conducting quarrying expeditions at a remote site in the late third and early second millennia BCE, concentrating particularly on the evidence for the supplying and maintenance of the quarrying workforce. In future seasons at the site, we plan to survey the surrounding landscape in search of more traces of human activity, while undertaking further excavations in (1) the new area of settlement near the Khufu Stele and LR1, and (2) the quartz and carnelian mining area at Stele Ridge.

Notes:

1 For discussion of the stone types, see B. G. Aston, J. A. Harrell, and I. Shaw, "Stone," in T. Nicholson and I. Shaw, (eds.), *Ancient Egyptian Materials and Technology* (Cambridge, 2000), 5–77.

2 See R. Engelbach, "The quarries of the western Nubian Desert: a preliminary report," *ASAE* 33 (1933), 65–74; R. Engelbach, "The quarries of the western Nubian Desert and the ancient road to Toshka," *ASAE* 38 (1938), 369–90; G. W. Murray, "The road to Chephren's quarries," *Geographical Journal* 94 (1939), 97–114.

3 J. A. Harrell and V. M. Brown, "Chephren's quarry in the Nubian Desert of Egypt," *Nubica* 3/1 (1994), 43–57.

4 I. Shaw and R. Jameson, "Amethyst mining in the Eastern Desert: a preliminary survey at Wadi al-Hudi," *JEA* 79 (1993), 81–98.

5 The expedition consisted of myself (1997, 1999, 2000), Dr. Judith Bunbury (1997, 1999, 2000), Elizabeth

Bloxam (1997, 1999, 2000), Richard Lee, (1999, 2000), Dr. Deborah Darnell (1999, 2000), Louise Simson (1999), and Angus Grahame (2000). I would like to thank the Chief Inspector of the SCA at Abu Simbel, Mr. Ali al-Asfar, as well as the former Chief Inspector, Mr. Attiya Radwan, and his colleague Mr. Muhi al-Din, for their help and advice in undertaking the work and placing the finds in magazines. We are also very grateful to our inspector in 1997, Mr. Ousamr Abd al-Latif, and our inspector in 1999 and 2000, Mr. Mustafa Hassan. It should be noted that the paper given at this Congress has been augmented to include some details of the April 2000 season of survey and excavation.

6 Murray, "The road to Chephren's quarries," 110.

7 But see I. Shaw and E. Bloxam, "Survey and excavation at the ancient pharaonic gneiss quarrying site of Gebel al-Asr, Lower Nubia, Sudan and Nubia," *SARS Bulletin* 3 (1999), 13–20, and see also E. Bloxam, *The Organisation, Exploitation and Transport of Hard Rock from Chephren's Quarry during the Old Kingdom* (unpublished MA thesis Institute of Archaeology, University College, London, 1998).

8 See I. Shaw, "A survey at Hatnub," in B. J. Kemp (ed.), *Amarna Reports* III (London, 1986), 189–212; I. Shaw, "The 1986 survey of Hatnub," in B. J. Kemp (ed.), *Amarna Reports* IV (London, 1987), 160–7; I. Shaw, "Pharaonic quarrying and mining: settlement and procurement in Egypt's marginal areas," *Antiquity* 68 (1994), 108–19, 20

9 See I. Shaw, "Pharaonic quarrying and mining: settlement and procurement in Egypt's marginal areas," *Antiquity* 68 (1994), 108–19, and Shaw and Jameson, "Amethyst mining," 81–98.

10 See D. Arnold, *The South Cemeteries of Lisht I: The Pyramid of Senusret I* (New York, 1988), 113.

11 See Engelbach, "The quarries of the western Nubian Desert," 69, and O. H. Little, "Preliminary report on some geological specimens from the Chephren diorite quarries, Western Desert," *ASAE* 33 (1933), 77.

12 I am extremely grateful to the members of the Gebel al-Asr Project in the three seasons undertaken so far, and I would particularly like to acknowledge the hard work of Elizabeth Bloxam (on the loading ramps) and Richard Lee (on the excavation and interpretation of the areas of settlement at Quartz Ridge and Khufu Stele). I would also like to thank Debbie Darnell and Judith Bunbury for their identifications of pottery and geological samples, respectively.

Brief Encounters with the Ancient Landscape: Urban Archaeology in Modern Cairo*

Peter Sheehan

Egyptian Antiquities Project, The American Research Center in Egypt

It seems that a major theme of the Congress has been conservation and site management. This paper develops out of that theme in considering the question of urban archaeological heritage with particular reference to the area of Old Cairo, where over the past year the archaeological evaluation of the former potteries site has been undertaken by the Supreme Council of Antiquities and the Old Cairo Archaeological Project, and where the subproject for the Egyptian Antiquities Project of the American Research Center in Egypt has just commenced archaeological monitoring of the USAID-funded groundwater control project. Since this project is still in its infancy, the paper will perhaps lay more emphasis on the possible approaches to urban archaeology than the results obtained so far, but the Eighth International Congress of Egyptologists provides the opportunity to present the project to colleagues in the field and to provide some background on the archaeological potential of the area, before considering some more general approaches to urban archaeology.

It is tempting to view urban archaeology in Cairo as an aspect of the familiar historical development of the Islamic city from its foundation in al-Fustat and subsequent spread north and east to al-Qahira, whose magnificent architectural heritage and peculiar problems of conservation and site management have been the subject of more than one conference of the great and the good. In fact, the archaeology *per se* of the Islamic city is a rich and largely neglected resource, and one that I will try to consider briefly later, at least within the context of Old Cairo. On the other hand, the spectacular growth of 'Greater' Cairo in this century has swallowed up within the urban jungle a number of other much earlier sites once part of the cultivation or the desert. Future research at these sites, as well as their management and ultimate fate, has now become *de facto* a matter of urban archaeology. A number of these sites could, with some justification, be considered uniquely important. The prehistoric sites of the Maadi and Helwan areas spring to mind, and very near to the site of the Congress, the valley temple of the Pyramid of Khufu and the Old Kingdom settlement recorded by Zahi Hawass and Michael Jones during the drainage infrastructure work in Nazlet es-Samaan.

Of similarly unique importance is the area around the known limits of the Roman fortress of Babylon. In introducing this project, it is useful to indicate the character of the area, which provides a vital background and context to archaeological work. Archaeologically, the area represents a key step in the development of the city represented by the foundation of al-Fustat around the Roman fortress of Babylon. Most of the fortress itself appears to be a late third century/early fourth century CE construction, perhaps related to Diocletian's memorable visit to Egypt around 298 CE. It is interesting to note that in form it shares a number of features with the contemporary enclosure built around Luxor.[1]

Traces of a number of *in situ* buildings within the fortress display a very different style of construction, employing massive limestone blocks suggestive of reused Ptolemaic stonework. The location of a Late Period/Ptolemaic temple in this area, perhaps even to be identified with *pr hap m On* and from this, the name *Bab-y-lon*) is suggested by the blocks recently recovered by the SCA at al-Zahraa just south of Babylon, and by the sphinxes noted by Golenischeff in the same area during the construction of the Cairo-Helwan railway (now the Metro) at the end of the nineteenth century.[2] To the east, the former quarries have apparently destroyed much of what may have been a massive cemetery (with several tombs apparently dating from the First to the Twenty-sixth Dynasties explored before their destruction in the 1930s), but the continual northward shift of the city suggests that the mound of Kom Ghorab to the south of the fortress, may represent a substantial settlement perhaps related to these tombs.

As elsewhere, the scale of the changes to the urban landscape during the last century has been immense, with the major factor being inward migration to the area, population boom, and consequent informal building and industry to house and sustain this population. Much of this housing and/or industrial activity illegally occupies land with a clearly high, but largely unexplored, archaeological potential, theoretically under the control of the SCA. For example, the previously largely unoccupied area of Istabl 'Antar (excavated since 1983 by Roland Gayraud of the CNRS/IFAO) has been almost totally built over during the past 20 years.[3]

The steady encroachment of the modern world on land with a high archaeological potential in Old Cairo has also been carried out by official or quasi-governmental schemes for housing, transport depots, etc., and has extended even to areas of Fustat excavated by Bahgat Bey in the 1920s and Scanlon and Kubiak in the 1960s and 1970s. Faced with this constant pressure, the current approach to archaeological management has inevitably focused on curation of monuments rather than understanding unexplored areas. Consequently, more effort is spent on protecting areas excavated down to bedrock at the beginning of the last century, than in areas still rich in potential. The need for an updated archaeological assessment of the area based on the character and *quality* of archaeological deposits seems clear. Currently there is, for example, no detailed plan of the entire site of al-Fustat. The production of such a plan is one of the major aims of current work in the area, while its current absence emphasizes how important it is for future research that individual excavations and sites are always tied in to the national survey grid.

With the growth of unplanned housing has come a large informal water supply, most of which duly becomes groundwater in one way or another. Within the area of Old Cairo repeated additions to the groundwater table have resulted in its increase by 1.5 m over the past 20 years. Much of this excess seems to have originated in the higher area of Istabl 'Antar and has then run down the hill to the historic areas along the alluvial margin —the churches within the Roman fortress, the Mosque of 'Amr, etc.

In this context, the present USAID-sponsored groundwater control project of the CWO (Organization for Execution of Greater Cairo Wastewater Project) is intended to remove these accumulated additions to the groundwater table within the core area of the Roman fortress, while it is hoped that improved infrastructure in general, and reduction in loss from current pipe networks, will stop the problem from occurring again. Essentially the design consists of a series of perforated groundwater collection caisson shafts linked by microtunnels and normal access caisson shafts to the main collector in Fustat Street to the north. Drainage is to be effected by a series of sand and gravel filled 15 meter-deep secant pile walls, which act as porous trench drains leading to and around several key perforated shafts. In addition there will be 200 m of hand-dug perforated drains in the large Roman round towers of the fortress, 1900 m of drains up to 4 m deep in the area of the monastery of Abu Sayfayn, and 1.75 km of microtunneling. This is of course intended to be a very beneficial program for both the population and the *above ground* monuments of Old Cairo, but it should be noted that the groundworks for the project involve the excavation of around 5000 cubic meters of prime archaeological material.

The monitoring of these excavations has two rationales. The first is a reactive kind of planned "rescue" recording, while the second and longer-term aim is to use the project as a valuable research tool for future conservation and management of the remaining archaeological material.

The disparate and discontinuous nature of the observations from this work and the wide vertical and horizontal source range of cultural material recovered, make a prime case for the collection and analysis of data within an archaeologically-based Geographical Information System (GIS). In urban archaeology it can certainly be said that the sum adds up to more than the individual parts.

Given that the proposed groundworks involve disturbance of a very large volume of archaeological material rather than the excavation of large open areas, the formation of a system of data management and archiving into which various levels of information can be subsequently incorporated, is a prime consideration. This will involve the creation of an archaeological deposit model based on the existing (and abundant) geotechnical information available for the area, to which all subsequent information gained during the groundworks can be immediately added, thereby producing a dynamic tool for ongoing analysis and comprehension, as well as representing an immediate and secure archive of the material and observations recorded during the project.

Preparatory to the groundworks, a comprehensive borehole survey at shaft locations has been undertaken and monitored—samples will be retained to form the core of an archive for future research aimed at palaeo-environmental reconstruction, as well as to characterize the buried environment. During the drainage project groundworks these boreholes represent a kind of undisturbed micro-stratigraphic control on the shaft excavations.

The concentration of historic monuments in this area also means that the archaeological aspect of this project will allow a link to be made between the conservation of archaeological deposits and that of the built environment. Analysis of the burial conditions which have preserved the below-ground elements of buildings up to the present, is crucial to their future conservation, as is an understanding of the conditions which preserve archaeologically-important deposits and the methods for analyzing and characterizing such deposits. The *solution* of the "water problem" in Cairo generally, and Babylon in particular has engaged the attention of the authorities concerned to such a degree that a detailed characterization of its properties and influence on the burial environment (and consequently also on the standing structures) could easily be overlooked.

Of course, the character of the burial environment has implications for the development of a predictive subsurface model of the site to aid in its conservation. Factors affecting the characterization of the buried environment include its physical and chemical nature, (the latter of which is a feature of its groundwater chemistry), as well as the biology existing within it.

The development of a more detailed understanding of the buried environment (which we could think of equally as 'the ancient landscape') and the recognition that its components represent a finite resource to be conserved, has been perhaps the most significant development in archaeological theory and practice in recent years. In the United Kingdom, for example, this trend was recognized by the publication in November 1990 of PPG16 (the Department of the Environment Planning Policy Guidance note *Archaeology and Planning*), which focused on the desirability of preserving archaeological remains *in situ*. On the other hand, conservation of the archaeological resource is better equated with its responsible and reasonable management rather than its preservation at all costs, which has unfortunately too easily become the mantra of government policy toward archaeology in the UK.

Preservation of below-ground archaeology has shifted away from the earlier reactive approach toward preserving only structural masonry elements. Nixon follows the terminology of PPG16 in asserting that:

> . . . the (archaeological) profession has sought to implement a more proactive policy; our aim is to preserve a representative sample of a fragile and finite resource. Moreover, we are no longer concerned only with structures, but consider deposits in their context; it is entirely likely that deposits earmarked for preservation may consist of soft and perhaps eminently undisplayable deposits.[4]

While this movement towards conservation *in situ* has not yet palpably affected archaeological research in Egypt, the holistic and multidisciplinary approach to characterizing the burial environment prior to its preservation that it has engendered can be equally applied to the buried stratigraphy of Babylon. Like other environmental issues, an inherent process of ascribing value to these deposits accompanies the realization and publicizing of their contribution to the understanding and presentation of the past.

Future Directions for Urban Archaeology in Old Cairo

In the longer term and after the reactive "rescue" stage of shaft excavation is over, the insights provided by monitoring these infrastructure projects can then be supplemented by other means:

- remote sensing, which in these deep alluvial deposits could include seismic refraction as well as resistivity/conductivity
- alluvial geoprospecting for buried sites in the alluvial zone, analysis of floodplain evolution, and interpretation of floodplain soils and sediments after these have been obtained and analyzed[5]
- desktop studies to identify old channel courses and floodplain islands from old maps and photographs

In areas where intrusive development is envisaged and geotechnical data is lacking, archaeological evaluation may be envisaged, aimed at determining the nature and extent of archaeological deposits. This process can provide either simply an indication of the presence of archaeological deposits, or a sample of the full sequence which can then be used for future site management and conservation. On the whole, urban archaeological sites are composed of stratified sequences of deposition (and often removal in the form of robbing). It is important therefore to remember that an understanding of the development of the site can only be gained from an understanding of its entire sequence, and that, for all the benefits of remote sensing, a proper understanding of the archaeology of a site can only come from carefully conducted but inherently destructive sampling.

Of course this question is somewhat controversial and much easier if, as in the case of the current groundwater control project, the destructive sample locations have been decided by someone else! It is however worth making the point that, without this destructive sampling and the consequent well-publicized understanding and presentation of the complete site formation process, the people making the decision on whether to go ahead with intrusive development will not even be aware that they are intruding.

A limited program of evaluation should demonstrate the archaeological potential of the site sufficiently to obviate the need for its total excavation and if possible its conservation and management *in situ*.

Whatever the context of work undertaken, be it rescue work or evaluation, the basic minimum record (as defined in, for example, the manual of the Museum of London Archaeology Service) for any feature or action encountered on an archaeological site, be it a deposit, a cut for a pit, a wall, the mortar used in a wall, etc. is to:

- establish its stratigraphic position and situation in relation to other features on the site
- establish the processes involved in its formation
- provide a suitable interpretation within the limits of the excavation
- enable it to be dated[6]

Therefore in the field records and subsequently within the GIS, every single action (or 'context') needs:

- a separate written description
- plans, sections, and elevations as appropriate
- collection of environmental samples and finds as appropriate
- a photographic record

In collaboration with the Fustat Inspectorate, the Old Cairo Archaeological Project has developed bilingual context recording sheets, with the ultimate aim of producing a manual for archaeological recording on urban sites in Cairo similar to the widely used MOLAS manual. At the same time, some rather modest training and equipment has been provided to achieve the rather modest aims outlined above.

Conclusion

Despite the generally positive nature of the Old Cairo project, it would appear likely that work in the city will remain at best rescue archaeology until sufficient *information* is gathered and made accessible in such a way that those responsible for the curation of the archaeological resource are able to feel they are contributing to its status as a significant element of urban planning rather than merely overseeing the physical decline of something ill-defined but somehow precious. The emphasis on GIS during this conference is also apposite, because when one closes one's eyes to visualize the interaction between the robust present, the self-confident future and the fragile past of Egypt, it may be that information is all that we're going to end up with. The quality of that information and its usefulness is intimately linked to our being willing and able to distinguish both what is important in terms of material and what is feasible in terms of site management.

Archaeological access to, and analysis of, the vast amount of geotechnical data routinely gathered during the course of building and engineering projects, allied to a targeted program of evaluation and the analysis and bringing together of existing historical and map data, will enable conservation and site management in Cairo to be targeted at those areas most likely to yield comprehensible and significant data concerning the formation and development of the ancient landscape beneath these busy streets.

Notes:

* With special reference to the Egyptian Antiquities Project/American Research Center in Egypt program of archaeological monitoring of wastewater projects in Old Cairo.

1 For a summary of archaeological and topographical information about the fortress see P. Lambert (ed.), *Fortifications and the Synagogue, The Roman Fortress of Babylon and the Ben Ezra Synagogue, Old Cairo* (London, 1994). For recent archaeological work see P. Grossmann, C. Le Quesne, and P. Sheehan, *Archäologischer Anzeiger* (Berlin, 1994), 271–287 and P. Grossmann, M. Jones, H.-C. Noeske, C. Le Quesne, P. Sheehan, *Archäologischer Anzeiger* (Berlin, 1998), 173–207.

2 V. Golenischeff, "Lettre a M. G. Maspero sur trois petites trouvailles égyptologiques," *Rec.Trav* IX (1889), 98–100.

3 Preliminary reports on the excavations at Istabl 'Antar (Fustat) can be found in R. Gayraud et *al, Annales Islamologiques* XXII (Cairo, 1986) onwards.

4 T. Nixon, "Practically preserved: observations on the impact of construction on urban archaeological deposits," in *Preserving archaeological remains in situ*, M. Corfield, P. Hinton, T. Nixon and M. Pollard, (eds.), *MOLAS* (1998), 39.

5 A. Brown, *Alluvial Geoarchaeology, Floodplain Archaeology and Environmental Change*, Cambridge Manuals in Archaeology (Cambridge, 1997).

6 Museum of London, *Archaeological Site Manual* (London, 1990).

On a Tomb Discovered at Qurnet Murai (Luxor)

Costanza Maria de Simone

UNESCO Expert for the Documentation Center, The Nubia Museum of Aswan

In the spring 1997, the Supreme Council of Antiquities discovered a new tomb on the eastern slope of Qurnet Murai, the isolated hill rising from the plain at little distance north of Medinet Habu on the west bank of the Nile opposite Luxor.

The discovery occurred accidentally, the result of the collapse of the modern floor that served as a roof over the tomb. The tomb has no identification number as yet, and is located about 20 meters southeast of TT 40, the tomb of the famous Viceroy of Kush, Huy,[1] and about 15 meters east of the tomb attributed to the Viceroy Merimosi (TT 383).[2]

During the period of excavation, which unfortunately lasted only a short time, I was in Luxor for an inspection of the area where several tombs of the Viceroys of Kush are located. Thanks to special permission granted by the SCA, I was able to visit the work of the current Director of the West Bank Inspectorate, Muhammad el-Bialy.

On the basis of the scanty evidence emerging from the excavation, which I prefer not to cite as it has yet to be published, I quickly realized that the tomb must be connected in some way to the Viceroy of Kush/Governor of Nubia called Merymosi. This is not unusal since the area is rich in materials belonging to him. The hill of Qurnet Murai looks over the great temple of his king, Amenhotep III. According to el-Bialy, at the time of the discovery of the tomb in 1997, he found several funerary cones inscribed with the name of Merymosi. In the same place in 1917–1918 the French Mission uncovered about one hundred of these small funerary objects also belonging to the same person.[3] In addition, the area has revealed some objects from the officers of Merymosi, such as his "carrier of the sandals," Amenemwia.[4] A stela belonging to this officer is in the Liverpool Museum.[5] During the same period Loret discovered another stela dedicated to Merymosi by his royal scribe, Huy. At Qurnet Murai, Huy is depicted offering a bouquet of flowers to Merymosi.[6]

We can not exclude the possibility that the stela belonging to the officer of Merymosi called Penmiam, now displayed in the British Museum, was part of a group of several objects coming from Qurnet Murai and sold by the local people. The name Penmiam is of Nubian origin. On the stela Merymosi is represented sitting on a chair in front of an offering table. On the right, facing Merymosi, is Penmiam in a reverential pose.[7]

This combined evidence led me to think that the owner of this new small tomb could be an officer of Merymosi and that in this area there may have been a cult to this Viceroy of Kush.

The discovery of this tomb is further evidence of the archaeological importance of Qurnet Murai. It must be stressed that of the 30 documented tombs belonging to the Viceroys of Kush, four are located in Qurnet Murai.

The area, which has been the French concession from 1916 to the present, is full of interesting tombs. Excavation conducted by the French Institute in Cairo over the years 1960–70, revealed some tombs on the southeast slope of the hill near the asphalt road at the entrance to Deir al-Medina.[8] These findings lead me to believe that all of this part of the hill is full of unexcavated tombs. It would be interesting to carry out a systematic survey of the area, but unfortunately it is affected by a major problem, the presence of the modern village. Most of the people in the village have built their homes on top of the tombs.

An interesting article has been written on this subject by the architect of the French Institute in Cairo, Georges Castel.[9] In this article Castel wrote briefly about the exodus of dwellers from the village Kom al-Bairat, three kilometers from Qurnet Murai. During this past century the small size of this village was the reason for their immigration to the desert, and many of the inhabitants settled at Qurnet Murai. Castell tells the story of a family of a certain Abd al-Samad who established his house on a tomb in Qurnet Murai. This home was passed on to his heirs from generation to generation.

The problem of the occupation of Qurnet Murai is very old and often discussed. In 1926 Sir Alan Gardiner, who published the above-mentioned tomb of Huy (TT 40), remarked upon it.

The tomb of Huy discovered in 1828 by Wilkinson and studied by many other Egyptologists is very important, not only for the content of its scenes and texts which have contributed substantially to our knowledge of the relationship between Egypt and Nubia during the New Kingdom, but also for the style of the paintings. Gardiner remarked, " . . . the tomb of Huy is a strange blend of dullness and brilliancy of features derived from the revolutionary and others which forecast the tasteless and lifeless Ramesside style."[10] He goes on to say that, "This tomb, therefore, bears witness to the bewildered hesitancy in which Theban art stood for a while before it subsided into the long monotony of the later sepulchral art," and " . . . when the tomb was first discovered its colours must have been brilliant and unspoiled since it claimed the special attention of the early explorers. Now its aspect is as repulsive as any tomb in the neighbourhood, considerable stretches of the wall surface having fallen away, and the lower parts especially having been spoiled and disintegrated by the use of the tomb as a dwelling and as a stable."[11] Gardiner finishes up with an even stronger indictment, describing the situation thus: "The early interest that it excited gave place in time to a wholly unmerited neglect, and at length like so many other precious painted tombs at Thebes, it fell into the hands of native squatters. Much of its present squalor and ruin is due to the fellahin from whom it was not rescued until towards the end of the 19th century."[12]

Gardiner's words are very strong, but it is necessary to remember that during that period foreign scholars and travelers also contributed to the damage of several ancient sites, carrying out excavations aimed only at the discovery of precious objects, without recording the archaeological strata and structures.

I want to take advantage of this meeting, whose main topic is taking action to preserve

Egypt's cultural heritage, to stress the importance of the recovery of this area, which is otherwise destined for certain extinction. From 1981 Gurna has been considered an archaeological area, and the Egyptian government has hopes of establishing the biggest open-air museum in the world there. For this reason they want the inhabitants to evacuate their old mud-brick houses. In 1945 the government tried to find a solution by commissioning the architect Hassan Fathy to construct a new Gurna. He involved many of the inhabitants of the villages in the work, but the project failed because the people refused to move from their homes. Now squatters occupy the buildings constructed by Fathy. In 1997 another attempt of this kind caused a violent and bloody reaction resulting in four deaths and several wounded people. There are, however, some voices being raised against the government's policy that they claim is ready to sacrifice these communities on the altar of the tourism. These same communities, however, are already endangered by the precarious condition of their dwellings. In 1994 and in 1996 the rains obliged four hundred families to leave their homes. To this problem we must finally add that of inadequate supplies of fresh water.

The Viceroys of Kush and others cannot rest easily under such conditions, and the people living today on the same ground also cannot continue to survive in this situation. A solution needs to be found to save both the living of today and the legacy of yesterday.

Notes:

1 Nina de Garis Davies and A.H. Gardiner, *The tomb of Huy* (London, 1926).

2 A. Varille, "Les trois sarcophages du fils Royal Merymosi," *ASAE* XLV (1947), 1–2; A. Varille, "Le tombeau thebain du viceroi de Nubie Merymosi," *ASAE* XL (1940), 567–70.

3 H. Gauthier, "Cones funeraires trouves a Thebes en 1917 et 1918," *BIFAO* XVI (1919), 168.

4 H. Gauthier, "Rapport sommaire sur le fouilles de l'Institut francais dans les necropoles thebaines en 1917 et 1918," *ASAE* XIX (1920), 6.

5 A. Varille, "Une stele de Amenemuia portasandales du fils royal Merymosi," *ASAE* XVL (1947), 33.

6 H. Gauthier, "Monuments et fragments appartenant a l'Institut francais du Caire," *BIFAO*, XII (1916), 134–35; Varille, "Tombeau thebain," 566.

7 The Trustees of the British Museum, *Hieroglyphic Texts from Egyptian Stelae in the British Museum VII* (London, 1993) n.860.

8 G. Castel and D. Meeks, *Rapport sur les fouilles de Deir el Medineh* 1960–70, FIFAO XII/I (1980).

9 G. Castel, "Une habitation rurale egyptienne et ses transformations," in O. Auranche, (ed.) *Nomades et sedentaires: perspectives ethnoarcheologiques* (Paris, 1984).

10 de Garis, Davies, and Gardiner, *The tomb of Huy*, 3.

11 de Garis, Davies, and Gardiner, *The tomb of Huy*, 2.

12 de Garis, Davies, and Gardiner, *The tomb of Huy*, 9.

The Great Sphinx of Giza

Rainer Stadelmann
Director Emeritus of the German Archaeological Institute, Cairo

The exact period of the construction, or better creation of the Great Sphinx is still one of the great enigmas of the Egyptian art history. In the nineteenth century, different ideas were prevailing, ranging from the Prehistoric up to the Middle Kingdom and even later. Today, however, Egyptologists and art historians have given enough archaeological and written evidence that could definitely prove to an intelligent public that the Sphinx is a work of the Old Kingdom, more precisely, the Fourth Dynasty. Only some stubborn and unreasonable writers, like Antony West and the geologist Robert Schoch, still insist for sensational reasons on arguing that the Sphinx is a remnant of an older pre-historic civilization, ignoring the historic surrounding and background of the Egyptian society.

The approval of a Fourth Dynasty date for the creation of the Sphinx leaves open, however, the question of which of the kings residing at Giza could have been the one who has envisaged and ordered this unique sculpture, one of the greatest ever made by man. We have the choice between four kings, the great Khufu/Cheops, builder of the Great Pyramid, or one of his sons Djedefra, Khafre/Khephren, or Menkaure/Mykerinos. Djedefra who constructed, but not completed, a pyramid on top of the marvelous hill of Abu Ruwash, has only been suggested because he might have had several sphinxes of normal size in his pyramid complex at Abu Ruwash—these would be the first sphinxes—but this is definitely not a strong argument. The pyramid complex of Menkaure lies too far away from the location of the Sphinx. So both kings, Djedefra and Menkaure, can be eliminated and only Khufu and Khafre remain.

Most of the Egyptologists agree rather superficially on Khafre, arguing that his name is mentioned on the Dream Stela of Thutmose IV in a context with the Sphinx. This is, however, only partially true. This large and elaborate stela—found by Caviglia 1818—was erected by King Thutmose IV in front of the Sphinx after he had become king. In the long inscription Thutmose reports that once, when he still was a prince and head of the royal charioteers, he was hunting in the desert of Memphis near the pyramids. At noon he fell asleep in the shadow of the Sphinx and was told in a dream that if he cleared the sand away from the flanks of the Sphinx he would

Fig. 1: The Great Sphinx with the Pyramid of Khufu behind.

become king of Egypt. Of course he obeyed and after having become king he asks the people of Egypt to praise, "Osiris of Rasetau [the area of the pyramids] the goddess Bastet [who was traditionally the goddess of the valley temples] and the gods and goddesses of the resting place or sanctuary of [and here is a lacuna] khaef" which can be complemented to Khaef<Ra> Khephren or Khafre. This part of the inscription has disappeared today completely, eroded by the subterranean water before the last restoration. It was and is the only proof for the identification of the Sphinx with Khafre. In the upper register of the stela, Thutmose makes offerings to the Sphinx, which is called Horemachet/Harmachis, "Horus in the Horizon." This name of the god Horemachet/Harmachis is an innovation of the New Kingdom which retains, however, the old Achet "Horizon" of Khufu/Cheops.

More than one hundred years later, Selim Hassan found during his excavations a stela of Amenhotep II, father of Thutmose IV. Amenhotep also visited the area of the pyramids and admired the wonderful buildings of—and here the text on the stela is completely preserved: the resting place, or sanctuary of Khnum-Khufu/Kheops and Khafre/Khephren. Thus, we have in a same context both kings mentioned, Khufu/Cheops and Khafre/Khephren, but this is by no way a certain identification of the Sphinx with Khafre. But as very often in our discipline, old and seemingly certain statements rest forever without further verification.

As there is no clear philological ascertainment for the creator of the Great Sphinx we have to look for archaeological ones.

One is the attribution of the larger pyramid complex and its nearby quarries, in which the Sphinx is located. Here we should, however, keep in mind that it was Khufu/Cheops and his chief architect who chose the commanding position on the ridge above what is now Giza. We should not under estimate the fact that he is the great originator in Giza and that each of his creations was somehow new: his pyramid layout, his cult temple, the cemeteries, and even his statues, as the surviving fragments show, are at once innovative and supreme achievements. He had the whole terrain for his disposal and could also choose the most convenient quarries for his pyramid. His

465

quarries are firmly identified at the northern ridge and the eastern slopes of the terrain. Recent excavations by Dr. Hawass have even brought to light the remains of a construction ramp leading to the southern side of the Great Pyramid. This ramp is situated south of the Great Pyramid and north of the causeway of Khafre in a depression that was once part of the quarries. The southern limitation of the quarries is clearly defined by the preserved rock on which Khafre later built his causeway. This extension of Khufu's quarries is the reason why Khafre's causeway does not run straight to the east and his valley temple is not situated in the axes of the pyramid complex, but to the south. This means that Khafre had to take account of something earlier, something very important, that already stood there. From the situation as we can see it, this important object can only have been the Sphinx. Thus also the large rectangular ditch, in the center of which the Sphinx was hewn, belongs surely to the quarries of Khufu. This can be proven by a comparison of the different members of the rock formation of the body of the Sphinx and the walls of the ditch with the layers of core stones of Khufu's pyramid. The sequence of the stones quarried from the different members and put on the pyramid can be exactly observed and recognized by their erosion.

Fig. 2: The Sphinx and the Sphinx ditch within the quarries of Khufu.

Originally the ground into which the Sphinx ditch was cut must have been considerably higher than the rock plane to the south; it was perhaps as high as the ridge to the north on which the mastabas of the royal princes are standing, or as high as the hill to the south which is the remnant of the quarries of Khafre and Menkaure. All the stone material from this ancient original promontory, from the level in front of the Sphinx ditch up to the 20 m higher level of the pyramid plateau has been quarried away for the core stones of Khufu's pyramid.

Why should Khufu have left this high rock formation on the southern limitation of his quarry for Khafre and his artists to carve the Sphinx? This is surely by no way convincing. It must, however, be admitted that even the fact that the area where the Sphinx is standing now, was originally part of the quarries for Khufu's pyramid, is not definite proof that it was Khufu who envisaged and ordered the carving of the Sphinx.

We have therefore to search for other criteria to solve this problem.

There are firm stylistic and iconographic considerations that point

466

Fig. 3: The Great Sphinx. En face.

undisputedly toward Khufu. It is rather amazing that such an iconographic investigation was never undertaken before I brought the subject into discussion. This is again an indication how much Egyptology tends to believe in written sources, even if they are not evident. The only attempt until now was not a serious one in the sense of art history: In his painstaking investigation on the Sphinx and its history, and the excavations and restoration of it, Mark Lehner tried to put the contours of the head of Khafre's famous statue with the falcon Cairo Museum CG 14 on that of the Sphinx. As you can observe at once, neither the contours of the face, nor those of the nemes headdress fit. Amazingly enough Lehner saw this, however, as a convincing proof for the identity and the authenticity of his thesis that the Sphinx is of the œuvre of Khafre.

We should remember that the idea to create a sculpture of these dimensions, which is part lion and part man, a creature metamorphosed into a divine being by the combined strength of the most powerful wild animal and the intelligence of a human being, is a great intellectual innovation. Two-dimensional images on slate palettes of the Dynastic Period—some 300 to 400 years earlier—already depict the king as a cruel wild lion or griffin destroying the enemy. In the sculpture of the Sphinx the animal power is tamed by human intelligence and is thus transformed into divine magisterial calm. This magnificent intellectual metamorphosis points more at Khufu, the great originator, than at Khafre, who was—without underestimating his celebrity—an imitator of his father Khufu.

According to fragments from the pyramid temple to the east of the Great Pyramid, Khufu had already invented all the types of statues except the kneeling figure type. The great part of his statuary is surely still hidden in his valley temple, which had been traced ten years ago, but not been excavated until now. So the comparison has to proceed from the small ivory statue and two heads ascribed to Khufu, one in red granite, with the white crown, in the Brooklyn Museum and another rather small head in limestone, wearing the white Upper Egyptian crown, in Munich.

I admit that it is difficult to compare a colossal sculpture like the Sphinx with statues of normal size or even with a statuette like the small ivory statue of Khufu from Abydos. But any art historian from other disciplines would not hesitate to accept this in principle. Some famous art works are firmly dated by comparison with portraits on coins. Even the structure of the world's most famous lighthouse, the Pharos, is only known from pictures on antique coins.

Of Khafre, several life-sized statues and hundreds of fragments are preserved, which give us all together about 60 to 70 statues; Reisner estimates even about 200. Among these is the famous statue Cairo Museum CG 14 with the falcon behind his head. Proceeding from this statuary we can try to make a stylistic and iconographic identification of the Sphinx.

The overall form of the Sphinx' face is broad, almost square. The chin is broad. On the other hand, the features of Khafre were long, noticeably narrower and the chin almost pointed. The

Sphinx has the earlier, one could say: old fashioned, fully pleated type of nemes headcloth, like that of Djoser's statue. The same nemes, fully pleated, can be seen on the fragment of a statue of Khufu in the Museum of Fine Arts, Boston, which comes from Khufu's pyramid temple. This is, by the way, the fragment with the falcon in the back, the earlier prototype of Khafre's statue. Very remarkable and important: the nemes has no band in the form of a raised hem over the brow. This is again the older type, like Djoser's. From Djedefra onward, the raised hem band over the brows becomes the norm. Under Khafre, only the lappets of the nemes headcloth are pleated but never the nemes head or the nemes wings. The side wings of the nemes headcloth of the Sphinx are deeply hollowed, but with Khafre hardly at all. With Khafre the headcloth corners curl up, but they do not do so with the Sphinx.

The Sphinx has a uraeus cobra placed on the lower edge of the headcloth. In contrast to those of Khafre and Menkaure it shows high relief with naturalistic detailing of the serpent's neck and the scales of its hood. The eye-

Fig. 4: The small ivory statue of Khufu. Egyptian Museum, Cairo.

brows of the Sphinx bulge powerfully forward, and they are pitched high and slope down toward the temples. The eyes are deep-set, but strongly modeled. They are large and wide open, to which perhaps the monumentality of the head owes something. These wide-open eyes are absolutely typical of sculptured heads from the time of Khufu. The ears are fundamentally different from those of the statue of Khafre. The ears of the Sphinx are very broad and folded forward, while those of Khafre are elongated and situated closer to the temples.

A decisive criterion is the absence of a beard. The sphinx has no indications of hair on its chin. There is also no trace of a break under the chin. Consequently, there would not have been a beard on the Sphinx in the Old Kingdom. The fragments of a plaited god's beard which are now in the British Museum and in the Egyptian Museum are certainly of New Kingdom origin, added to the Sphinx, when it was identified with and adored as the god Harmachis. Certainly, the rounded god's beard is an innovation of the New Kingdom and did not exist in the OK or the MK. When this beard was added, a small platform was carved out of the Sphinx's chest on which the beard and a royal statue rested.

The beard is a royal attribute. Some kings wear a beard, others not. In the OK it is an absolute and strict rule. If a king wears the beard, it appears in all representations, round plastic and relief, in UE and in LE, there is no exception. In the Fourth Dynasty one can observe: Snofru never has a beard, nor does Khufu, neither on his small ivory statue nor on the Brooklyn or the Berlin head. From Djedefra on, however, all kings, including Khafre and Menkaure wear the ceremonial beard in relief and in round plastic. Userkaf, the first king of the Fifth Dynasty, however, abandons the beard again, but has a moustache.

The Sphinx had certainly no beard. This is strong evidence that adds to my suggestion that the Great Sphinx is an original creation of Khufu, as innovative and original as the Great Pyramid itself.

The Great Sphinx was carved out of a high, spectacular rock that dominated the southeast corner of Khufu's quarries. We will perhaps never know how Khufu and his master artist envisaged the idea and the form of the Great Sphinx. There must have been a prototype, perhaps in

Heliopolis, the city of the sun god. Later texts mention the great Sphinx of Heliopolis. Whenever sphinxes were placed in front of Egyptian temples, they have a solar aspect and connotation. Thus the idea of a creature in form of a sphinx which is the form of appearance, the phenotype of the sun god might have existed already in Heliopolis from the time of Djoser or Snofru who was the sun god as Neb-ma'at, Lord of the Right World Order.

The Pyramid Complex of Khufu is called Achet-Khufu, The Horizon of Khufu. I therefore firmly believe that the Great Sphinx is the monumental manifestation of Khufu as sun god in his Horizon.

The Mortuary Temple of Amenhotep III

Rainer Stadelmann
Director Emeritus of the German Archaeological Institute, Cairo

During two seasons in 1989 and 1990, the German Institute of Archaeology has conducted an architectural survey on the Colossi of Memnon in the mortuary temple of Amenhotep III at Thebes. This work included a photogrammetrical survey and several horizontal sections resulting in a complete silhouette drawing through the northern colossus and a complete architectural design of the southern one. In cooperation with the geological department of the Cairo University, several deep drillings around the colossi were undertaken to study the resistivity of the ground. The results of this work were reassuring that there was no immediate danger to the colossal statues.

Fig. 1: The Colossi of Memnon.

470

Fig. 2: The northern colossus in scaffolding during the architectural survey, 1990.

During this work and the annual controls on the Memnon Colossi we were seriously concerned about the worsening conditions of the whole area of the Kom al-Hettân, the ancient mortuary temple of Amenhotep III, and we realized that only an emergency survey as well as rescue excavations could save this once glorious and splendid site. The vast area of the temple precinct was never completely surveyed nor thoroughly excavated, except for one section of its westernmost part by Dr. Labib Habachi and H. Ricke. These excavations were only partial; the objectives were purely for architectural research and concentrated on a conjectural plan of the western parts of the temple.

Our concern about the worsening condition of the site was fully supported by the responsible authorities of Thebes, especially by the Director of Thebes, Mr. Sabri Abdel Aziz, who had on several occasions invited the German Archaeological Institute to undertake further active work for the excavation and protection of the temple ruins.

Fig. 3: Statuary fragments from the peristyle hall removed and put on banquets south of the area. In the background on can see the south stela and the headless female sphinx.

471

From March 15, 1999 until the end of April 1999 and again from January 20 to March 15, 2000, we began, with the support of the Inspectorate of Qurna, to clean the great peristyle court, cutting down the high reeds and camel thorn. We continued the work by clearing the once excavated part of the western columned hall of mud and debris accumulated during the 30 years since the last excavation.

A square grid of 90 x 90 m2 was measured over the area of the great peristyle court and all visible objects from earlier excavations were numbered and measured into this grid. This includes also the various fragments of the northern stela, which were found spread over an area of more than 900 square meters. Smaller fragments of this stela were even located in a shallow water hole under the larger fragments. This water pool was cleaned and filled with limestone gravel. All fragments are now collected and put together on a higher level waiting to be restored and assembled.

All larger statuary fragments were removed from the humid and damp ground and put on three long banquets constructed in cooperation with the local inspectorate in the south of the area. All fragments arc numbered and their original location is kept in the master plan.

The headless quartzite sphinx of a queen—most probably Queen Tiye—was temporarily put on a specially adapted banquet to the south of the great stela. Nearby we have arranged two large pedestals of red granite to hold the feet from royal monumental statues which have been standing in the wider area of the court but in no context. They certainly belong to monumental statues of Amenhotep standing in the south half of the western peristyle hall. Several fragments of the torsos of these statues are now exposed on the above mentioned banquets, the head and crown of one of them we have put near thc socles.

Fig. 4: View on the western portico of the peristyle hall. The statue socles are pulled out of the muddy ground and put on concrete blocks.

A large quartzite pedestal, with two feet and broken into two parts, was pulled toward the storage area on a higher level in the northwest corner of the peristyle court and rearranged with fragments that most probably belong to this colossus.

In the spring of 2000 we pulled all the heavy pedestals out of the muddy ground and put them in front of the column bases on concrete blocks in order to save them from any ground water. Other statue fragments we have pulled up onto the higher level of the peristyle court and arranged together with their pedestals. They have had preliminary treatment and are now waiting for conservation and reassemblage. Some of these torsi can be put together after treatment, only the heads will be missing, but they will reach an impressive height of 5 to 6 meters even without their heads.

Already the area looks like an open-air museum and attracts the interest of tourists passing by and photographing from their busses.

The funds for this salvage and conservation work were provided by a grant of the American Express Bank given to World Monument Fund.

Report on the Excavations Done by the German Institute of Archaeology at Dahshur

Rainer Stadelmann
S.A.C.O.S. The University of Liverpool

As I have already reported several times about the excavations of the German Institute of Archaeology at Dahshur, I will only summarize our aims and the results we have achieved in this excavation.

When we began, we had four main objectives:

1. To complete survey of the pyramid, its outer and inner measurements, and determine the slope of the pyramid.

Fig. 1: View of the Northern Pyramid of Snofru at Dahshur; view from the east.

This proved to be rather difficult. We found only one corner of the pyramid intact, but by interpolation we could determine the measurements: the side length is 420 cubits or roughly 220 m and the angle is exactly 45°.

2. Investigation of the methods of construction.

This is not the place to enter now in a discussion of all the different methods of building.

Fig. 2: The Northern Pyramid of Snofru at Dahshur. East side of the pyramid with the remains of the mortuary temple and the pyramidion, reconstructed in the temple area

At Dahshur we could clearly recognize that this pyramid was built on a kind of platform and in horizontal layers. Traces of small ramps on all sides of the pyramid let us suppose that the pyramid was built with a multitude of small ramps at the beginning. After having reached a height of about 30 m these ramps were used in the construction of one large, adjacent ramp with which about 90 percent of the height that could be reached. The last 10 percent, or about 15 m, had to be mastered by other means, including steps, scaffoldings, bottle jacks, and pulley blocks.

Inscriptions written in red ocher on the rear face of some casing stones proved to be an excellent documentation about the progress of the construction work. The fragments of the foundation stone, collected in the southwest corner of the pyramid provided us with the official date the foundation of the pyramid, "the fifteenth time of counting," i. e. Year 28/29 of the reign. A block found in place on the twelfth layer, about 8 m high shows still fifteenth time of counting, another in the sixteenth row, i. e. 12 m high, the year of the sixteenth counting. In a period of three years the pyramid had already advanced to a height of 12m, which is about 30 percent of the building material. Another fragment, found in the debris has the date of year of counting 24, regnal year 45/46. The discovery of the pyramidion shows us that the pyramid had been completed when Snofru finally died after a reign of probable 46/47 years.

3. Investigation of the funerary apartments.

During several seasons of surveying and photographing in the corridors and the chambers I became aware of a certain canon for the funerary chambers. Since the First Dynasty, royal tombs tend to have three chambers, for example, Hor-Aha at Abydos. In Meidum this is already evident, also in Dahshur/South in the Bent Pyramid and then in the Pyramids of Khufu, Khafre, and Menkaure. This canon is always valid until the very end of the Old Kingdom. Thus one can forget the old positivistic ideas about changes during the construction of the pyramid. These changes could never been made visible. We should never forget that the funerary apartments in the pyramid and their arrangement are the essential part of the whole construction. It is barely conceivable that the king and his architects were not aware of the form and arrangement of the royal burial when they began with the construction.

4. Examination of the architectural form, the design, and the outfit of the funerary temple.

When we began our excavations we expected something large, but similar to the chapels at Meidum and Dahshur/South: two big stelae and an offering table. Nothing similar existed in front of the Red Pyramid. Even if the stelae had been destroyed, the foundations should have been still visible. Instead we found a broad and deep foundation in front of the pyramid and fragments of dark granite. We therefore conclude that the main cult place and cult installation was a large false door, as it is well attested in later funerary temples of the Fifth Dynasty. From these findings we can deduce that false doors were standing in funerary temples where the king was buried. Stelae, on the other hand, were used to represent the pharaoh in cenotaphs or dummy tombs since the time when the pyramids were built. This conclusion cannot anymore be

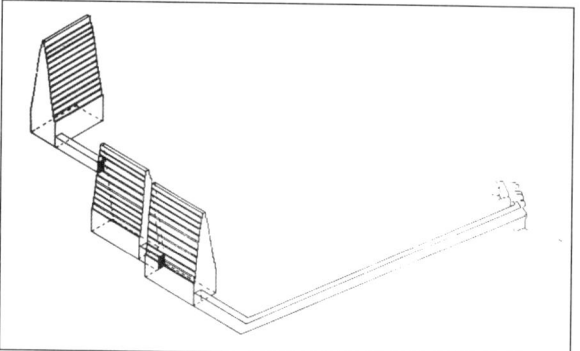

Fig. 3: Northern Pyramid of Snofru at Dahshur. Corridor and sequence of rooms leading to the burial chamber.

Fig. 4: The Northern Pyramid of Snofru at Dahshur. Third chamber with magnificent corbelled roof.

accepted for the royal tombs of the First Dynasty at Abydos, where according to the most recent observations, false doors existed in the tombs beside the stelae outside.

This is in short a review on the results of our work at Dahshur; in the meantime we have begun a survey of the whole area and started excavations at the mastabas to the east and southeast of the pyramids. A report of this recent work is published in the *MDAIK*[1] and in a volume of the *AV*[2] that has just appeared. We intend to continue our work in this spring.

Notes:

1 R. Stadelmann, N. Alexanian, "Die Friedhöfe des Alten und Mittleren Reiches in Dahschur," *MDAIK* 54 (1998), 293–317.

2 N. Alexanian, *Dahshur II, Das Grab des Prinzen Netjer-aperef. Die Mastaba II/1 in Dahschur* (monograph), *AV* 56 (Mainz, 1999).

Three Mummies from the Royal Cemetery at Abusir

Eugen Strouhal

First Medical Faculty, Charles University, Prague, Czech Republic

Introduction

During the recent excavations of the Czech Institute of Egyptology at Charles University, Prague, in the royal cemetery at Abusir, three mummies were found. Two came from the excavation of Fifth Dynasty pyramids, the third from an unviolated Twenty-seventh Dynasty shaft tomb belonging to the priest Iufaa.

As a result of my forty-year–long collaboration with the Institute, I was invited by its Director, M. Verner[1] to do a scientific analysis of these finds. This was possible thanks to the support of the Supreme Council of Antiquities, represented in the field by Inspector Attala el-Kholi.[2]

The Queen's Mummy from Pyramid Lepsius XXIV

In 1994 the Czech Institute investigated one of the two small pyramids situated to the southeast of the Temple of Neferefre, numbered XXIV by Lepsius during his survey of the area prior to 1849.[3] Unfortunately, the name of its owner was not revealed either in the fragments of reliefs from the destroyed mortuary temple, or in masons' inscriptions on the core blocks of the pyramid.

In the western half of the destroyed burial chamber, a fragmentary mummy was found. A few skeletonized parts of the skull, the upper half of the spine and the upper edge of the thorax lay on the original floor of the chamber along with fragments of the smashed sarcophagus, linen wrappings stripped from the mummy, and shards of Fifth Dynasty pottery.

The remaining parts of the skeletonized skull and the wrapped parts of the mummy—chest, upper extremities, and the whole lower half of the body—were found dislocated on the top of a one and a half meter thick layer of clean wind-blown sand, which contained the broken casing blocks of the burial chamber.

Fragmentation, partial unwrapping, and the dispersal of the parts of the mummy throughout the burial chamber can be attributed to the activities of grave robbers and stonecutters in various time periods following the burial.

In 1995, during a detailed examination of the mummy assisted by Viktor Černý, we were able to mend various skeletonized fragments and join together the still wrapped parts of the mummy. All these constituent parts fitted perfectly and there were not redundant human remains from inside the pyramid left over.[4]

In 1998 the mummy was x-rayed with the permission of the Supreme Council of Antiquities and the kind co-operation of Dr. Azza Mohammad Sarry el-Din and her colleagues from the Anthropological Laboratory of the National Research Center in Dokki.[5] This gave us an insight into the parts of the body still mummified[6]. On the skull all cranial sutures were open, except for the right half of the lambdoid suture, which exhibited premature closure. All the preserved teeth and their alveoli are healthy. Abrasion of the first molars exposed just the top of the dentine. The third molars are fully-erupted without exhibiting the slightest abrasion. Retraction of the alveolar process begins with grade one (Brothwell).[7]

The chest is an elongated cylindrical shape tapering downwards. On the partly-folded skin duplicature, the dessicated female breasts without contents adhere. The walls of the thoracic cavity have been smeared with resin and the cavity completely filled with linen pads permeated with resin.

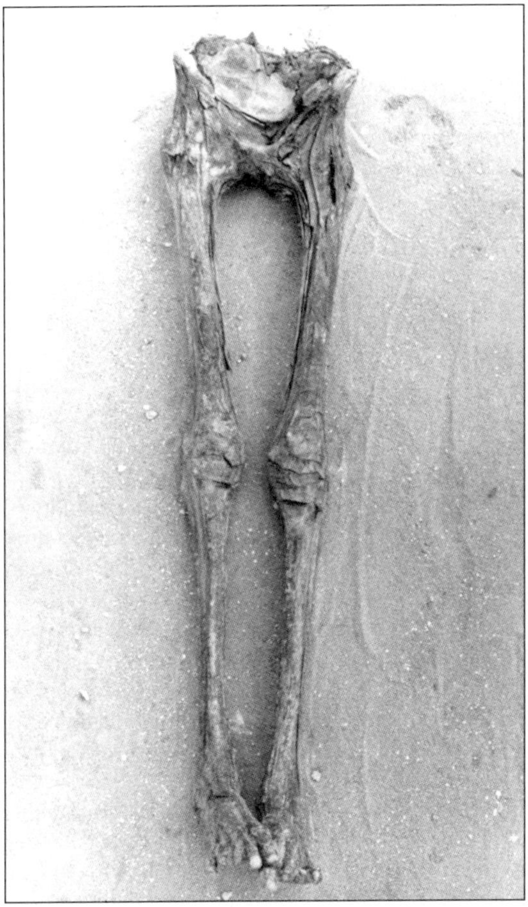

Fig. 1: Lower half of the mummy of an unidentified queen from Pyramid Lepsius XXIV at Abusir.

The three-quarters projection of the thorax shows moderate kyphosis of the thoracic spine, slight lordosis of the lumbar spine, and complete absence of osteophytes on the vertebral bodies.

Both forearms diverge at angles of about 160° from the axis of the humeri, a typical female marker. Heads of the humeri (as well as of the femora and most epiphyses and apophyses of various bones) are fused with their pertaining diaphyses without traces of growth fissures.

The lower half of the body, preserved as an entity, consists of the pelvis, last lumbar vertebra and lower extremities. The pelvis reveals all female features except for the shallow praeauricular groove, a sign that she most probably had not borne a child. Her gender is obvious from the well-preserved vulva.

The surface of the knee joints is smooth, with narrow slits, without the slightest pathological changes. This is also the case in all other joints. Lines of increased density in the femoral condyles and tibial heads represent the remnants of fused growth fissures. Similar lines can also be discerned on the distal ends of the crural bones. On the other hand, the absence of Harris' lines precludes the probability that the young female suffered from any long-lasting disease or famine.

In general, the body shows an elongated but slender body-build with a stature of about 160 cm, above average for Egyptian females. According to signs of aging she died at about 21 to 23 years of age.

Several fragments of folded linen soaked in resin lay near the cranial fragments. One of them displayed a smooth, convex surface that could easily fit into one of the hollows of the small brain (fossae cerebelli). Because the nasal cavity did not survive, this can be accepted only as an indirect suggestion for the possible removal of the brain. The existence of this embalming operation in the Old Kingdom has been suggested by the Eighth Dynasty mummies from al-Hagarsa[8] and by the Sixth Dynasty mummy of Shepsi-pu-Ptah from the Teti Pyramid cemetery at Saqqara.[9]

The Fifth Dynasty date of the mummy just described, found all alone in a pyramid built for its burial, is well supported by stratigraphy and chronometry.[10] As no name has survived we can only conjecture according to the location of the pyramid, its small size, and the female sex of the owner that she was a queen. Most probably, she would have been related to King Niuserre, whose pyramid had to be inserted into a gap in the terrain already jammed with other funerary monuments. Because no place was left for Queens' pyramids, they had to be built about half a kilometer to the south.[11] One of his recorded wives, Queen Repwetnebu, could be a candidate.[12] However, his possible other wives, or even an unknown wife of King Neferefre, whose pyramid is situated much closer to pyramid Lepsius XXIV, have also to be taken into account. This could perhaps indicate future exploration of the burial chamber of the neighboring pyramid Lepsius XXV, to provide further clues.

Fragments of the Mummy of King Neferefre

The fifth king of the Fifth Dynasty is a lesser-known sovereign due to the short (three- to four-year) duration of his reign, from 2419–2416 BCE.[13]

The Czech Institute started excavations in his mortuary temple and unfinished pyramid in 1980. In the light of the evidence presented by the finds, it became clear that the temple was used for his cult despite the unfinished state of the pyramid. It appears logical to conclude that the king was probably buried in the pyramid assigned to him.[14]

Soundings in the descending corridor of the pyramid started in the mid-1980s and continued into 1995.[15] During the 1997–98 season, the antechamber and burial chamber were investigated.

In the burial chamber, scattered fragments of a sarcophagus and remnants of burial offerings lay on the blocks underlying the floor slabs. These had been torn out by tomb robbers and stone-cutters. In the same level, in the eastern half of the chamber, five human skeletal fragments and a piece of soft tissue were found and submitted to an anthropological analysis.[16]

All fragments have the same external appearance, showing remains of linen wrappings stained black by resin and covered by white dots or patches that could be the result of a varnishing with limewash. In places they are skeletonized. Shreds of wrappings of gray-ochre linen with dark spots were collected with them. The fragments consisted of:

1. The central region of the occipital scale with a distinctive male feature: a very protruding external occipital protuberance.
2. The whole left clavicle, long (157 mm) and medium thick (mid-circumference 41 mm) with strongly-built ends, but feeble muscular relief. By x-ray examination, a narrow growth fissure, partly fusing, was detected at the medial end of the bone. Its fusion occurs between 18 and 25 years of age.

Fig. 2: Left hand of the mummy of King Neferefre (dorsal view).

3. The lateral third of the left scapula fit precisely with the previous bone, thus proving that both bones came from the same body. The facies glenoidalis and acromion are big, but the osseous plates of the fossa supra- and infraspinata are thin.

4. The whole left hand except the distal phalanx of the third finger. It is medium long (about 180 mm) and very narrow (at the level of the heads of the metacarpals II–V 55 mm). X rays showed good mineralization of the bones and on the base of the second and third proximal phalanx, remnants of lines of increased density in the place of closed epiphyseal lines.

5. The right fibula with broken-off proximal end. Its length (about 370–380 mm) reveals a stature of around 168 cm. In contrast to the delicate diaphysis (minimum circumference between 32–35 mm) almost lacking longitudinal grooving, the lower epiphysis is strongly built. On the x-rays a line of increased density can be detected in the place of the distal growth fissure.

6. A fragment of skin with subcutaneous tissue (35 x 30 mm) bordering from above a now-missing globular structure. It could have been part of the soft tissue of the forehead and an upper eyelid.

To summarize, the external appearance of the fragments, their embalming technique, the perfect articulation of two bones, their similar body build and identical aging signs, reveal unequivocally that they came from one and the same individual.

The length of the bones, robusticity of their terminal parts, and the strongly developed protuberantia occipitalis externa attest that this is a person of the male sex.

The gracility of the bones, the feeble muscular relief, traces of epiphyseal line in the clavicle and presence of lines of condensation after them in other bones, as well as absence of pathological changes in any of the preserved joints, disclose a young adult about 20 to 23 years of age at death.

This age, if attributed to King Neferefre, agrees well with the unfinished state of his pyramid (built up only to the fourth layer of core blocks), and with the finding of a mason's inscription on one of its block which mentions "the year of the first census," i.e. Year 2 or 3 of Neferefre, who probably ascended the throne aged about 18 to 20 years.[17] It corresponds also to the young, almost adolescent facial features of several statues of King Neferefre found in his mortuary temple.[18]

The authenticity of the remains found exclusively in the lowest level of the burial chamber[19] was also proven chronometrically.[20]

In summary, the evidence, in spite of being scanty, strongly suggests that the remains described here can confidently be identified with King Neferefre.

Mummy and Skeleton of the Priest Iufaa

The mummy originated in the large shaft tomb located about a half kilometer south of the Pyramid Complex of King Neferirkare at Abusir, which was excavated by the Czech Mission from 1994 to 1998.[21]

The burial chamber containing all of the original burial equipment was found unviolated by tomb robbers, who were unable to penetrate to the bottom of the large, 24-meter shaft where a vaulted burial chamber of roughly-hewn stone blocks was built. On the other hand, due to the great depth of the shaft, humidity of about 80 percent (caused by ground water rising by absorption) had damaged or destroyed all objects of organic origin including the wooden coffin and the mummy (see further below).

In the winter of 1998, the 24-ton lid of the huge outer rectangular sarcophagus was removed, followed by the raising of the lid of the inner anthropoid sarcophagus. Under the remnants of a disintegrated wooden coffin, the mummy of Iufaa was revealed on February 28. It was covered by an elaborate net of beads. Mummy wrappings, provided with only thin layers of smeared resin, did not resist the moisture. After exposure they began to break and were soon attacked by mold.

The mummy, about 163 cm long and 36 cm wide at the shoulders, was immediately transported to the x-ray laboratory at Giza (see above), where a set of ten radiographs provided our first look at the mummy.

Both postero-anterior (P-A) and lateral views of the head end revealed the transnasal route of the brain removal and filling of the occipital third of the braincase with resin. A few amulets and sheets of gold showed up on the anterior and posterior sides of the neck. The skull disclosed predominantly male features except for the oblique but straight profile without any bulge at the glabella.

The P-A views of the thorax depicted the arms crossed over the breast, the golden cases on the tips of the fingers, more amulets including a large heart scarab, as well as an absence of visceral parcels. This suggests that the viscera were inserted into the four canopic jars and covered with hot melted resin which caused them to harden during the elapsed time.

The golden toe-cases also survived on the ends of the toes of the right foot, while the phalangae of the left foot disintegrated during the lifting of the mummy.

Due to the progressively decaying state of the wrappings, which cracked in several places under the

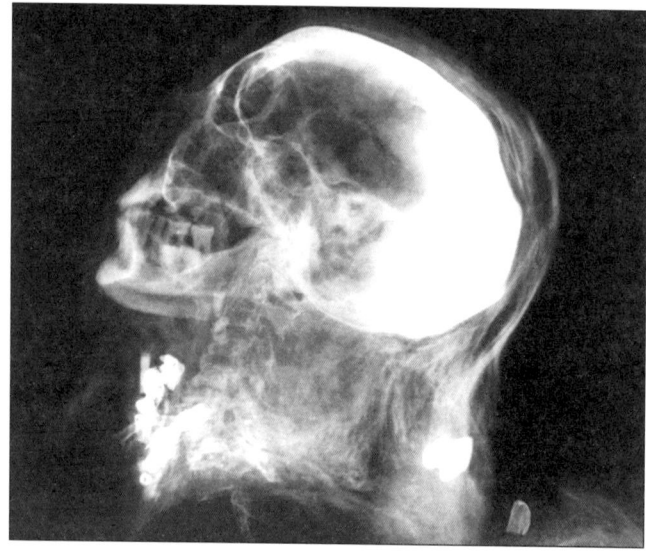

Fig. 3: X-ray of head, neck, and upper part of the chest of Iufaa showing his decayed dentition, a saucer-like depression on the cranial vault, and the filling of the braincase. Contrast shadows on anterior and posterior sides of the neck are caused by amulets and gold cases on top of the fingers.

482

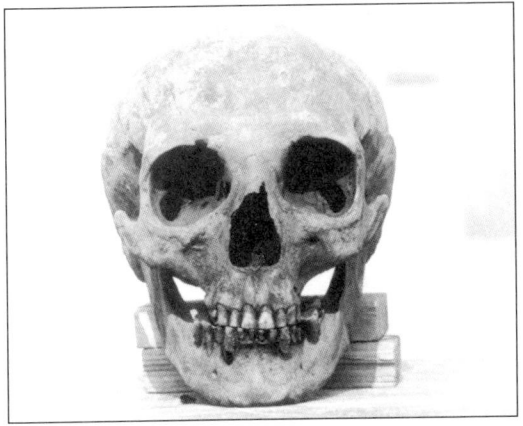

Fig. 4: Skull of the Priest Iufaa, frontal view.

influence of dry air, we decided to remove them and save the skeleton. No soft tissue was preserved on its surface, most probably burnt by application of layers of hot melted resin. The skeleton had to be treated later with disinfecting solution to prevent infection by molds.

Single bones of the skeleton were studied using common anthropological and palaeopathological methods. Thus the skull vault was seen to be long, broad, and low, the face medium-high and broad. With respect to the young age of the individual (discussed later), the dentition proved to be prematurely decayed due to heavy abrasion of tooth crowns combined with cariosity. Iufaa had already lost half of his molars by adolescence according to the closure and atrophy of the pertaining parts of the alveolar process. Both first upper premolars are afflicted by caries and a large cyst developed around the buccal root of the lower right first premolar, caused by its extreme abrasion.

Deep saucer-like depressions on both parietal bones were filled-up with melted resin by the embalmers, who were aiming to restore the ideal form of the head (see fig. 3). For a long time such depressions were considered to be the result of senile atrophy, but modern research has revealed their congenital origin.[22] It is a matter of a localized delay in the development of the diploe resulting in its hypo- or aplasia. Another congenital feature found in Iufaa's skull is sagittal depression connected with the premature closure of the sagittal suture.

Iufaa's spine has an incipient degree of osteophytosis (grade 1, osteophytes less than three mm long). The seventh thoracic vertebra was wedge-shaped (body height anteriorly 14 mm, posteriorly 20 mm).

At the same time, all big and small joints, including that of the spine, are devoid of any pathological changes.

The decisive sexing and aging features were revealed in the hip bones. Their robust build-up, medium strong cristae iliacae and tubera ischiadica, the prominent crista phallica, and the subpubic angle of 70°, as well as the low ischio-pubic index, clearly indicate Iufaa's male gender, attested also philologically (the gender of his name) and archaeologically (the beard carved on the lid of the inner sarcophagus).

In spite of the almost-finished premature closure of the cranial sutures and very strongly-abraded dentition, Iufaa's pelvic features prove his young age. The cristae iliacae and rami ascendentes of the pubic bone show deep fissures, due most probably to scission of the freshly-fused apophyses, possibly caused by humidity followed by quick drying. The facies auriculares of the ilium are convex and striated.[23] The relief of the facies symphysialis of the pubic bone preserved remnants of regular crests, equaling stage four by Todd (25 to 26 years)[24] or stage two of Katz and Suchey (mean, 24.7, range 19 to 35 years).[25] Moreover, the left femoral head was found detached while still inside the mummy. Its inner side bears traces of recent fusion. We can conclude that Iufaa was 25 to 30 years old at death.

Reasons for his unexpectedly premature death, reflected also in the unfinished state of the decoration of his tomb, have still to be searched for through detailed x-ray examination, testing of bone density and analyses of samples by modern medical laboratory methods.

Notes:

1 I accepted it with appreciation and thanks.

2 I would like to express my gratitude to Mr. Attala el-Kholi.

3 K. R. Lepsius, *Denkmäler aus Agypten und Aethiopien I* (Berlin, 1849).

4 E. Strouhal and V. Černý, "A mummy found in the Pyramid Lepsius no. 24 at Abusir," *Varia Aegyptologica*, C. van Siclen III ed., *in press*.

5 I appreciate very much their kind cooperation.

6 E. Strouhal and V. Černý, "X-ray Examination of the Mummy Found in the Pyramid Lepsius no. XXIV at Abusir," in *Abusir and Saqqara in the year 2000 Archiv Orientální - Supplementa IX*, M. Bárta and J. Krejčí, eds. (Praha, 2000), 453–555. pls. 88–97.

7 D. R. Brothwell, *Digging up Bones*, 2nd ed. (London, 1972), 150.

8 E. S. Bailey, "Medical Report," in N. Kanawati, *The Tombs of El Hagarsa II* (The Australian Center for Egyptology, Report 6: Sydney, 1993), 75–84, esp. 81.

9 E. Strouhal and L. Horáčková, "Skeletal Remains of Shepsi-pu-Ptah," *Reports*. Australian Center for Egyptology: Sydney (*in press*).

10 It falls into the range of 2701–2465 years BCE.

11 M. Verner, "Abusir Pyramids 'Lepsius no. XXIV and no. XXV'," in *Hommage a Jean Leclant, BdE* 106/1 (1993), 371–378; M. Verner, "Excavations at Abusir, Seasons 1994/55 and 1995/96," *ZÄS* 124 (1997), 71–85.

12 B. Vachala, "Ein weiterer Beleg für die Königin Repetwetnebu?" *ZÄS* 106 (1979), 176.

13 M. Lehner, *The Complete Pyramids* (Cairo, 1997), 8. A higher date, 2460–2455 BCE can be found in T. Schneider, *Lexikon der Pharaonen, Dtsch. Taschenbuchverlag* (München, 1996), 261–262.

14 M. Verner, "Excavations at Abusir. Preliminary Reports," *ZÄS* 109 (1982), 159–162; 111 (1984), 70–77; 113 (1986), 154–158.

15 M. Verner, "Excavations at Abusir. Preliminary Report 1997-8," *ZÄS* 126 (1999), 70–76.

16 E. Strouhal and L. Vyhnánek, "Identification of the remains of King Neferefre found in his Pyramid at Abusir," in *Abusir and Saqqara in the year 2000 Archiv Orientální Supplementa IX*, M. Bárta and J. Krejčí, eds. (Czech Institute of Egyptology: Prague, 2000), 551–560, pls. 98–109.

17 Verner, "Excav. Abusir 1997-8," 76.

18 M. Verner, "Les sculptures de Reneferef découvertes a Abousir, *IFAO* 85 (1985), 267–280. M. Verner, "Supplément aux sculptures de Reneferef découvertes a Abousir," *IFAO* 86 (1986), 361–366.

19 Two fragments of another human body were found in a high stratigraphic position (2.16–3.0 m above the floor level of the antechamber); they belonged to a burial deposited between CE 1297 and 1421.

20 Their dating falls into the range of 2628–2393 BCE.

21 L. Bareš, K. Smoláriková, "The Shaft Tomb of Iufaa at Abusir," *GM* 151 (1996), 7–17. L. Bareš, K. Smoláriková *GM* 156 (1997), 9–23. L. Bareš and E. Strouhal, "The Shaft-tomb of Iufaa. Season of 1997–98," *ZÄS* 127: 5–14, 2000.

22 E. Barnes, *Developmental Defects of the Axial Skeleton in Paleopathology* (Niwot, Colorado), 146–148.

23 C. O. Lovejoy, R. S. Meindl, T. R. Prybeck, and R. P. Mensforth, "Chronological metamorphosis of the auricular surface of the ilium: a new method for the determination of adult skeletal age at death," *Am. J. Phys. Anthrop.* 68 (1985) 15–28.

24 T. W. Todd, "Age changes in pubic bone I. The male white pubis," *Am. J. Phys. Anthrop.* 3 (1920), 285–334.

25 D. Katz and J. D. Suchey, "Age determination of the male os pubis," *Am. J. Phys. Anthrop.* 69 (1986), 427–435.

Prestige Goods and Status Symbols in the Naqada Period Cemeteries of Predynastic Egypt[1]

Izumi H. Takamiya

School of Literature, Arts, and Cultural Studies, Kinki University, Japan

Introduction

Previous studies of the Naqada culture have resulted in a general image of a fairly complex and hierarchical society in which the status of individuals tended to be reflected in mortuary practices, such as funerary installations and/or grave goods.[2] Scholars have also suggested that the grave goods may have included "badges of status" and prestige goods, such as ivory tags and mace-heads. However, there has not yet been sufficient study devoted to chronological changes, local variations, or the functions of such objects within society.

The main objectives of this study are firstly, to identify prestige goods and/or status symbols on the basis of their context in mortuary practice, and secondly, to analyze them in terms of their chronological variations, local differences, and symbolic meanings. The results may reflect the social organization of the Naqada culture, if the materials were distributed according to certain symbolic systems shared by the various communities. In summary, therefore, arguments concerning the process of cultural and political integration of Naqada societies will be attempted through the interpretation of prestige goods and status symbols.

Methods of Analyses

Prestige goods and status symbols in archaeological materials can be identified by two different theoretical approaches: one depends upon the general value of objects themselves, measured in terms of cost of materials and labors, and the other depends on the archaeological context of the objects. In conceptual terms, the former might be described as the "absolute approach," and the latter the "contextual approach." Both approaches have been applied in previous analyses of Predynastic funerary materials, and recent studies have suggested that values and symbolic meanings of objects could not be inferred simply from the costs of materials and labor.[3]

In this study, the contextual approach is applied for identification, because it enables us to distinguish status symbols and prestige goods according to the symbolic systems of the people of that time, which may have been different from our own. It also enables us to compare the results with those from other periods and geographical areas of the Naqada culture.

It can be assumed that prestige goods and status symbols may be identified by their links with high-status individuals, because it is probable that such materials were distributed according to the hierarchical structure of the society.

In the first stage of this study, therefore, a reconstruction of social structures of Naqada societies is attempted by the use of tomb dimensions (i.e. the area of each tomb). It has been suggested by a number of scholars that tomb dimension is an appropriate criterion for assessing the status of buried individuals in terms of energy expenditure, because the size of the tomb is less likely to have been affected by tomb robbery than other aspects of ancient mortuary practices.[4] Indeed, many authors mentioned above have already used this criterion to reconstruct the Naqada social structure.

Prestige goods and status symbols can thus be identified on the basis of the reconstructed social structures. Since it is likely that the prestige goods and status symbols were distributed in accordance with the hierarchical structure, it can be assumed that materials clustered together in large and high-status tombs would have included prestige goods and/or status symbols that could not have been obtained by lower-status members of the society. Thus, we can identify objects or materials as prestige goods or status symbols when they occur in more than three tombs of a specific chronological phase and when several are found together in large tombs. Statistically, the concentration of materials in high-status burials can be attested by comparison of the mean and median sizes of graves containing prestige goods with those of the total set of graves.

It should be noted that the identified objects might include not only status symbols and prestige goods but also simple valuables. Since it is difficult to determine the exact function and meaning of the objects by this method alone, they are, for convenience, tentatively described as "prestige goods" throughout this paper. The nature and function of the objects will be discussed after considering their meanings in terms of their broader social contexts, as well as the costs of the materials and labor.

Although prestige-related aspects of the burials can also be detected by the study of mortuary installations, such as the forms of graves and the use of funerary beds, only artifacts are dealt with in this study.

Cemeteries and Materials

The methods described above are applied to several Naqada cemeteries in Upper and Middle Egypt, which contained a sufficient number of tombs of each period, and for which adequate information about tomb sizes and grave contents has been reported. From the south, Armant Cemetery 1400–1500,[5] Mahasna Cemetery H,[6] Abydos Cemetery S,[7] Badari Cemetery 3700–3900,[8] Mostagedda Cemetery 200–1800,[9] Matmar Cemetery 2600–3100, and Matmar Cemetery 5100[10] were available. Large cemeteries, such as the Naqada "Great Cemetery," the Amrah cemeteries "a" and "b" and the Naga ed-Deir cemetery N7000, were not analyzed by this method, because excavation reports of these cemeteries did not provide data concerning either sizes or exact dates of graves. These large cemeteries that have been deliberately excluded from the analyses will nevertheless be discussed later in connection with the interpretation of the results.

According to Kaiser's chronological system,[11] each grave is dated to three major chronological phases of the Naqada culture; Naqada I–IIa/b, IIc/d, and III, the last of which includes Naqada IIIa and b. The materials in the tombs were analyzed in terms of each of these periods in each cemetery.

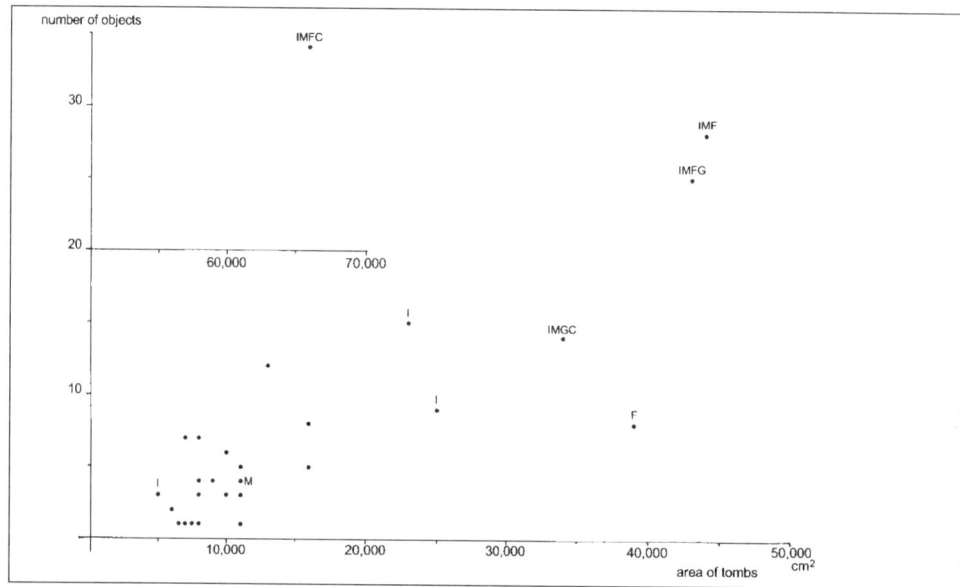

Fig. 1: Prestige goods in Mahasna Cemetery H (Naqada IIa/b).

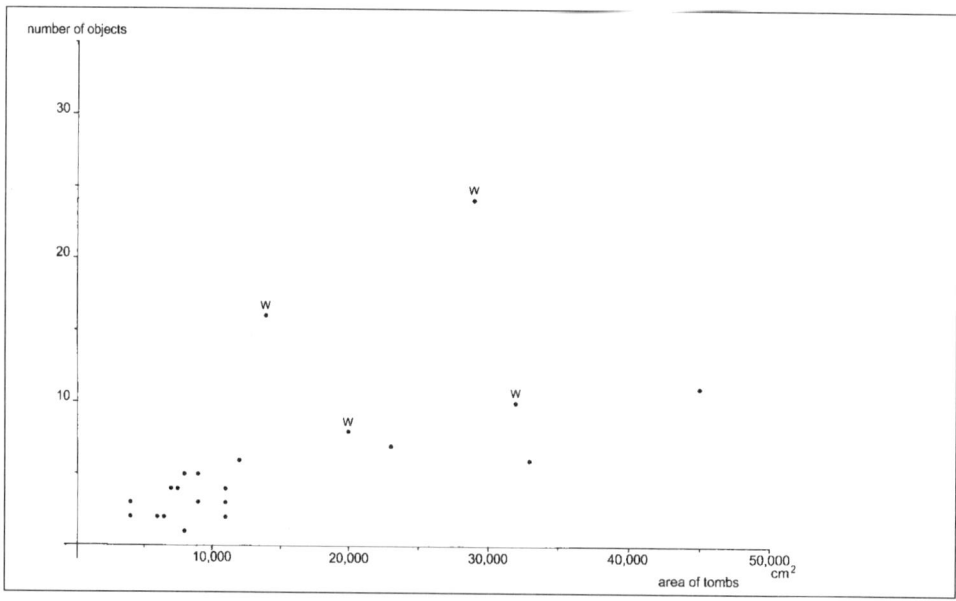

Fig. 2: Prestige goods in Mahasna Cemetery H (Naqada IIc/d).

Results: Mahasna Cemetery H

The results of the analyses of Mahasna Cemetery H are shown as an example. This cemetery is one of the best instances of the ability to distinguish clearly between the characteristic prestige goods of different periods.

Fig. 1 shows the relationship between tomb size and the quantity of grave goods during the Naqada IIa/b Period. Each grave is plotted in the diagram according to its size (the area of grave) and the quantity of artifacts. There is a general tendency for larger tombs, although severely disturbed, to contain larger numbers of objects. Alphabetic characters indicate the occurrences of different types of prestige goods; each "M" designates a mace-head, "I" an ivory object, "F" a human figure, "G" a garlic model, and "C" a copper object, though the last two occur only in two tombs. They were found mainly in the large and richly-endowed tombs in this cemetery, and are therefore identified as prestige goods.

Fig. 2 shows prestige goods in the Naqada IIc/d Period. "W" indicates wavy-handled pottery vessels, which were evidently used as prestige goods during this period.

Chronological Changes and Local Differences in Prestige Goods

Site	Naqada I	Naqada II a/b	Naqada II c/d	Naqada III
Armant 1400–1500	Ivory objects	Ivory objects	Wavy-handled pottery	/
Abydos S	/	/	/	/
Mahasna H	/	Ivory objects Mace-heads Human figures (Garlic models) (Copper object)	Wavy-handled pottery	/
Badari 3700–3900	–	/	Wavy-handled pottery	/
Mostagedda 200–1800	Ivory objects Mace-heads Flint knives	/	/	/
Matmar 2600–3100	/	Ivory objects Gazelle skulls	Wavy-handled pottery	–
Matmar 5100	–	–	/	–

Table 1: Prestige goods in Naqada cemeteries in Upper and Middle Egypt.
- : no data
/ : no identified prestige goods

The analyses of the cemeteries listed earlier show that various types of objects were concentrated in large and high-status graves. Table 1 provides a brief compendium of the results, showing the identified prestige goods in terms of cemeteries and periods. The results can be summarized as follows, in chronological order.

In the Naqada I–IIa/b Period, various objects can be identified as prestige goods, such as ivory objects in the Armant Cemetery, ivory objects, mace-heads, and human figures in the Mahasna Cemetery, ivory objects, mace-heads and flint knives in the Mostagedda Cemetery, and ivory objects and gazelle skulls in the Matmar Cemetery. No prestige goods were identified in the Abydos S Cemetery and the Badari Cemetery, though in the latter, ivory objects might have been prestige goods. The prestige goods of this period are characterized by two main factors, the characteristic types vary from cemetery to cemetery, but many of the cemeteries include ivory objects and/or mace-heads.

During the Naqada IIc/d Period, only wavy-handled pottery vessels are identified as prestige goods at Armant, Mahasna, Badari, and Matmar. Indeed, the prestige goods found in graves dating to the previous period have disappeared from the cemeteries included in this analysis, apart from a few exceptions. This suggests that a chronological change in the types of prestige goods had occurred by the beginning of this period.

No prestige goods have been detected in graves of the Naqada III Period, although it has been suggested that wavy-handled pottery vessels might have been used for prestige purposes, as in the Naqada IIc/d Period.[12] It seems, however, that they would have conferred comparatively little prestige on the deceased, since they had become too popular to be monopolized by a restricted number of high-status individuals.

Thus, the analyses of these cemeteries suggests a sequence of clear chronological changes in prestige goods, from various items including mace-heads and ivory objects in the Naqada I–IIa/b Period, through wavy-handled pottery vessels in Naqada IIc/d Period, and no identified item in the Naqada III Period. Local variations were observed during the Naqada I–IIa/b Period in particular, but in the Naqada IIc/d Period, such variations disappeared and wavy-handled pottery vessels were uniformly buried as prestige goods in many cemeteries analyzed by the methods described earlier.

Large Cemeteries

Before interpreting the results of these analyses of small and middle-sized cemeteries, prestige goods in larger cemeteries should be considered, because it is highly likely that larger cemeteries contained a greater abundance of prestige goods, and an overall view of the symbolic system in Naqada society cannot be attained unless data from larger cemeteries are considered.

Although we often lack sufficient information about larger cemeteries, such as Naqada and Amrah, the existence of common prestige goods can be traced also in these cemeteries.[13] In general, large cemeteries contained a wider range of prestige goods, including the majority of the items identified in the smaller cemeteries analyzed earlier. It can be inferred, therefore, that members of small communities might have selected several items from those in large communities, and also, in the Naqada I–IIa/b Period, added some local materials to them.

It appears that, in larger cemeteries, the prestige goods typical of the Naqada I–IIa/b Period tend to survive later into the Naqada IIc/d Period than was the case in the small cemeteries. For example, Table 2 shows the numbers of ivory objects from several Naqada cemeteries. It indicates that larger numbers of ivory objects were buried in large cemeteries, such as Naqada and Amrah. In the Naqada IIc/d Period, while ivory objects almost disappeared or drastically declined in numbers in small and middle-sized cemeteries, in the larger cemeteries they continued to be buried in high numbers. This tendency can also be observed in the case of some other materials.

490

Site	Naqada I	Naqada II a/b	Naqada II c/d	Naqada III
Armant 1400–1500	4(1) / 3	4 / 3	1 / 1	0/0
Naqada	75(6) /24	72(10) /24	75(17) /31	24(2) /15
Amrah a/b	15 / 4	24 / 9	23(6) /14	4(1) / 3
Mahasna H	11 / 3	33 / 8	0 / 0	3 / 3
Badari 3700–3900	7 / 3	24(1) / 6	4(3) / 3	0 / 0
Mostagedda 200–1800	31(15) /11	2(1) / 2	2(2) / 1	4(2) / 3
Matmar 2600–3100	5 / 3	36(14) /13	3(2) / 1	0 / 0

Table 2: Ivory objects in Naqada cemeteries.
(X) : X denotes the number of bone objects
/X : X denotes the number of tombs containing ivory objects

The analysis of the distribution of ivory objects suggests that large cemeteries preserved the tradition of using the same objects as prestige goods even in the Naqada IIc/d Period. The disappearance of ivory objects from small cemeteries, therefore, may be ascribed not only to changes in symbolic systems, but also to a process whereby the traditional prestige goods became concentrated in the larger cemeteries. This situation may imply the appearance of a hierarchical structure among Naqada communities, as will be discussed later.

Since Bard has identified wavy-handled pottery vessels as prestige goods, when she analyzed the Naqada cemetery, it seems that, besides the traditional items, wavy-handled pottery vessels were also used as prestige goods in large cemeteries after the middle of the Naqada II Period.

During the Naqada III Period, even large cemeteries such as Naqada and Armant do not yield sufficient information about prestige goods. However, this may not be the case with the cemeteries at Hierakonpolis Locality 6 and Abydos U. It has been suggested that these cemeteries were used by the rulers of Predynastic Upper Egyptian kingdoms.[14] The graves at Hierakonpolis Locality 6 have yielded Palestinian pottery vessels, beads, and amulets of lapis lazuli, an obsidian blade, silver objects, and terracotta figures of foreign captives,[15] while the German excavations at Abydos Cemetery U have resulted in the discovery of ivory objects including a model -scepter, a large number of Palestinian pottery vessels, wavy-handled pottery vessels, stone vessels, and labels inscribed with letters.[16] Traditional prestige goods, such as ivory objects and wavy-handled pottery vessels, were included, but they were only a part of the assemblages, which were dominated by various kinds of exotic materials as well as inscribed and relieved objects. It seems that a new symbolic system was emerging during this period.

The Symbolic Meaning of Prestige Goods

Because of the limitation of space, the symbolic meanings of major prestige goods are discussed only briefly here.

The mace, though originally a weapon, appears to have had symbolic importance from the earliest stage of the Naqada culture onwards,[17] because several limestone mace-heads from the Naqada I–IIa/b Period bear painted decoration imitating harder stones, which would have not affected their original function. The mace continued to be used for similar purposes during the pharaonic period, when kings were often depicted with a mace smiting foreign enemies. It can be presumed that maces were symbols of physical power even in the Predynastic period.

Ivory objects took various forms, including tags, combs, bangles, rings, hair-pins, and beads, which were worn by the owners and could have demonstrated the owners' status. Although the symbolic aspects of ivory artifacts may derive partly from their forms and functions, it seems that the raw material itself was of some importance, since the various ivory objects (as well as imitations in bones and stone) were concentrated almost exclusively in the large tombs. The category "ivory" actually includes both elephant and hippopotamus ivory,[18] the latter being the dominant type during the Predynastic period. Elephant ivories may have been exotic materials imported from the south, whereas hippopotamus ivories could be obtained within the territory of the Naqada culture. The ritual significance of hippopotami may be inferred from depictions surviving from the Predynastic and Early Dynastic periods. Hippopotami were often represented in ritual scenes: in several scenes from the early dynastic period, for instance, kings enacted ceremonies including the spearing of hippopotami.[19] In view of the fact that hippopotami were symbols of both fertility and uncontrolled natural power, it may be presumed that hippopotamus ivory was considered to have magical qualities.

Although the first Egyptian examples of wavy-handled pottery were imitations of Palestinian vessels, they subsequently developed independently in the Nile Valley, where marl clay and turntables began to be used for the manufacture of such vessels. It is unclear whether their prestigious nature derived from the vessels themselves or their contents, but the value of the vessels were presumably enhanced by their air of exoticism.

Other prestige goods, such as human figures, garlic models, flint knives, and gazelle skulls, also appear to have had ritual significance. On the other hand, the prestige associated with copper objects seems to have derived from the versatility of the material itself, since it could be shaped into tools such as adzes or chisels.

Prestige Goods and Political Integration of Naqada Society

Paul K. Wason has argued in his book entitled that the regional distribution of prestige goods should be interpreted as follows, "Broad distribution of uniform elite artifacts requires that over this area people have similar ideas about how status ought to be symbolized."[20] If this argument is acceptable, we may infer from the regional distribution of prestige goods that similar symbolic systems were shared by different communities in the Naqada culture. Therefore, interpretations of these results will be undertaken in a broader context within the Naqada culture. This discussion may shed light on the process of political integration among Naqada societies, because it is highly probable that when communities were politically integrated, their leaders attempted to organize a system of prestige goods, through which they expressed their political power and/or manipulated the prestige and status of elite groups.

During the Naqada I–IIa/b Period, while mace-heads and ivory objects were common to many communities, prestige goods varied from community to community. This situation suggests that although communities acknowledged the value of some prestige goods, they were also able to determine other types of prestige goods locally and independently. Such autonomy of symbolic systems may perhaps reflect the political autonomy of the communities themselves.

In the Naqada IIc/d Period, traditional prestige goods such as ivory objects and mace-heads continued to be used only by large communities such as those at Naqada and Amrah. On the other hand, most communities abandoned these items, and uniformly introduced wavy-handled pottery vessels for the purpose. Taking into consideration the fact that ivory objects and maces were traditional status symbols, and that maces continued to be used for the same purpose in the dynastic period, the changes can be interpreted as monopolization of traditional prestige goods by large and powerful communities. It is highly probable that the symbolic system became integrated within an extensive area of Naqada societies, and that this process was accompanied by the emergence of hierarchical structures among Naqada communities, in which large communities controlled small ones. As a result, small and middle-sized villages may have lost not only their traditional prestige goods but also their political autonomy.

Notes:

1 Thanks are due to Mr. Barry J. Kemp and Dr. Ian Shaw, who gave me helpful suggestions on this topic.

2 M. Atzler, *Untersuchungen zur Herausbildung von Herrshaftsformen in Ägypten* (Hildesheim, 1981), 65–109; K. A. Bard, "A Quantitative Analysis of the Predynastic Burials in Armant Cemetery 1400-1500," *JEA* 74 (1988), 39–55; K. A. Bard, "The Evolution of Social Complexity in Predynastic Egypt, An Analysis of the Naqada Cemeteries," *Journal of Mediterranean Archaeology* 2 (1989), 223–248; K. A. Bard, *From Farmers to Pharaohs, Mortuary Evidence for the Rise of Complex Society* (Scheffield, 1994); J. J. Castillos, *A Reappraisal of Published Evidence on Egyptian Predynastic and Early Dynastic Cemeteries* (Toronto, 1982); J. J. Castillos, *A Study of the Spatial Distribution of Large and Richly Endowed Tombs in Egyptian Predynastic and Early Dynastic Cemeteries* (Toronto, 1983); J. J. Castillos, "Evidence for the Appearance of Social Stratification in Predynastic Egypt," in C. J. Eyre (ed.), *Proceedings of the Seventh International Congress of Egyptologists* (Leuven, 1998), 255–259; C. Ellis, "A Statistical Analysis of the Protodynastic Burials in the 'Valley Cemetery' of Kafr Tarkhan,'" in E.C.M. van den Brink (ed.), *The Nile Delta in Transition, 4th – 3rd Millennium B.C.* (Jerusalem, 1992), 241–258; C. Ellis, "Expressions of Social Status, A Statistical Approach to the Late Predynastic/Early Dynastic Cemeteries at Kafr Tarkhan," in L. Krzyzaniak, K. K. Kroeper and M. Kobsiewicz (eds.), *Interregional Contacts in the Later Prehistory of Northern Africa* (Poznan, 1996), 151–164; W. A. Griswold, "Measuring Social Inequality at Armant," in R. Friedman and B. Adams (eds.), *The Followers of Horus, Studies Dedicated to Michael Allen Hoffman* (Oxford, 1992), 193–198; S. Hendrickx, *El Kab V, The Naqada III Cemetery* (Brussels, 1994), 217–224; S. T. Savage, *Descent, Power, and Competition in Predynastic Egypt, Mortuary Evidence from Cemetery N7000 at Naga-ed-Dêr*, PhD dissertation, Arizona State University (1995); S. T. Savage, "Descent Group Competition and Economic Strategies in Predynastic Egypt," *Journal of Anthropological Archaeology* 16 (1997), 226–268; T.A.H. Wilkinson, *State Formation in Egypt, Chronology and Society* (Oxford, 1996), 69–85.

3 R. F. Friedman and W. A. Griswold caution against the assumption that all graves containing imported materials belong to high-status individuals (R. F. Friedman, "Preliminary Report on Field Work at Hierakonpolis,

493

1996-1998" *JARCE* 36 [1999], 9; W. A. *Griswold, Imports and Social Status, The Role of Long-Distance Trade in Predynastic Egypt State Formation*, PhD. dissertation, Harvard University [1992], 219).

4 See Griswold, "Measuring Social Inequality," 194.

5 R. L. Mond and O. H. Myers, *Cemeteries of Armant* I (London, 1940).

6 E. R. Ayrton and W.L.S. Loat, *Excavations at El Mahasna* (London, 1908-1909).

7 A. El-Sayed, "A Predynastic Cemetery in the Abydos Area," *MDAIK* 35 (1979), 249-301.

8 G. Brunton, *Qau and Badari* I (London, 1927); G. Brunton and G. Caton-Thompson, *The Badarian Civilization and Predynastic Remains Near Badari* (London, 1928).

9 G. Brunton, *Mostagedda and the Tasian Culture* (London, 1937).

10 G. Brunton, *Matmar* (London, 1948).

11 W. Kaiser, "Zur inneren Chronologie der Naqada-kulture," *Archaeologia Geographica* 6 (1957), 69-77.

12 Bard, "The Evolution," 235-237.

13 E. Baumgartel, *Petrie's Naqada Excavation, A Supplement* (London, 1970); W.M.F. Petrie and J. E. Quibell, *Naqada and Ballas* (London, 1896); M.A.D. Randal-MacIver and A. C. Mace, *El Amrah and Abydos* (London, 1902).

14 B. J. Kemp, "The Early Development of Towns in Egypt," *Antiquity* 51 (1977), 185-200.

15 B. Adams and R. F. Friedman, "Imports and Influences in the Predynastic and Protodynastic Settlement and Funerary Assemblages at Hierakonpolis," in van den Brink (ed.), *The Nile Delta in Transition*, 317-338.

16 G. Dreyer, *Umm el-Qaab I, Das Prädynastische Königsgrab U-j und seine frühen Schriftzeugnisse* (Mainz, 1999).

17 K. M. Cialowicz, *Les têtes de massues des périodes prédynastique et archaïque dans la vallée du Nil* (Warzawa-Krakow, 1987), 47-63.

18 B. Adams, *Ancient Hierakonpolis* (Warminster, 1974), 59-75.

19 W.M.F. Petrie, *The Royal Tombs of the Earliest Dynasties* (London, 1901), Pl. VII.

20 P. K. Wason, *The Archaeology of Rank* (Cambridge, 1994), 112.

494

New Jar Labels from Deir al-Medina

Pierre Tallet

IFAO, Cairo

During the New Kingdom, hieratic labels were often written on the side of storage containers to identify their contents. In addition to the name of the product, information about the production date, quality, origin, and destination were provided. This information is usually found with food produce—different kinds of oil, beer, honey, wine, meat, and birds in brine, animal fat, and *smi* (probably curds). Several labels for jars concerning the delivery of incense have also been found. This type of document has aroused a new interest during the last ten years, and a great many of these jar labels from the palace of Amenhotep III at Malkata, Akhenaten's palace at Amarna, and the funeral temple of Ramesses II at Thebes are being republished, or are the subject of new studies.[1]

Among other hieratic texts, a large number of this type of inscription has been excavated, but to date not all of these documents have been published;[2] several hundred documents (more or less complete) remain. The composition of this material, kept in the storerooms of the *Institute français d'archaeologie orientale* (IFAO), seems to call for immediate comment. First of all, it is essential to note that the corpus is not exclusively made up of objects taken from the workmen's village and nearby tombs; in fact, some inscriptions clearly come from other sites to the west of Thebes, for example the temple of Amenhotep son of Hapu, excavated by A. Varille during the 1930s. Some documents include the word "purchase," and their origin cannot be determined with precision. Taking these restrictions into account, the jar labels of Deir al-Medina are one of the most instructive sets of this type of document, due to their extreme variety. Unlike the documents found at the sites previously mentioned, (which throw a revealing light on about ten years use of this type of material), the Deir al-Medina jar labels show the evolution of the expressions used in these documents from their first appearance to their last. The first documents date to the Eighteenth Dynasty (they include the names of Amenhotep II, Thutmose IV, Amenhotep III, and Horemheb),[3] while later ones mention the reigns of Ramesses III, Ramesses IV, Ramesses VI, and even the era of "renewed birth" (*wḥm mswt*) under Ramesses XI at the very end of the Twentieth

Figure 1

Dynasty.[4] The largest number of documents most probably date to the reign of Ramesses II, mid-Nineteenth Dynasty. Practically every year is vouched for up to Year 65, obviously reaching a peak in this way of marking containers.

The interests in a study of this type of documentation are varied. Obviously they can be used to debate the chronology of the New Kingdom. For example, the real length of the reign of Horemheb, which even today is the subject of debate, may be found. The set of documents corresponding to "regular" deliveries of supplies could provide part of the answer. Other items concerning the geography and the economy of Egypt up to the New Kingdom are more direct. For a product like wine, the study of formulae gives a certain number of valuable indications. A great many place names, regularly cited, establish a map of the wine-producing regions of the country during the New Kingdom. We find new attestations of well-known place names sometimes mentioned in the literary or administrative sources of the time—Piramesse, Kaenkemet, Nay-Amon—corresponding to the location of Ramesses' vineyards. The three main branches of the Nile in the Delta (the Waters of Ptah, Amun, and Re) are equally well documented. Other place names or villages appear on these unpublished dockets for the first time; for example a locality called *Itrt*, (lit., "The Willow"). Other dockets corroborate information obtained from other sources. The town of Andjet is mentioned twice on the wine jars (fig. 1). This bears out the information given by the *onomastica* of the Twentieth Dynasty that names this Delta town as an important wine-producing area.[5]

Apart from situating the properties, the jar labels also show how the areas were administered. Generally, they give the name of a minor official, for example the manager in charge of the property. This was the case of Pa-Oukhed, who seems to have been in office during the reign of Ramesses IV (fig. 2). At a higher level, the same expressions give the name of an agent of superior rank who supervises (*r-ḥt*) the production branch. It could be a steward (*imy-r pr*) or even—more particularly during the Twentieth Dynasty—the *sem*-priests responsible for funeral rites.[6] Lastly, the labels also show the destination of the goods—to individuals, mortuary temples, teams of workers from Deir al-Medina—and what they were to be used for (*sed*-feast, *Opet*-feast, etc.).

However, information might also result from comparing epigraphic sources with the results of ceramic studies. The most interesting result of this cross-checking of information has been discovered on a lot of amphorae of a type called "Canaanite" produced in Syro-Palestine. The list of products imported during the New Kingdom can be established by this means. Egypt imported different types of oil and incense—*sntr*, and *smi* produce. One characteristic of this type of container also deserves a mention: in many cases their capacity is written under the handle. In the example shown (fig. 3) the figure "*hin*"—(35.5) can be seen. This is an extremely precise measure, (within 25 cl for a container of more than 15 l) and was probably taken where it was produced, that is, abroad. In which case, we may suppose control was provided by Egyptian staff in Palestine, or at least local staff with some understanding of hieratic and who supervised the packing of the product.

The warehouses at Deir al-Medina also have a large collection of jar sealings, mostly fragmented. More than 200 have been recorded, over 100 of which carry the legible remains of stamping or painting. Some of these documents have been summarily published by B. Bruyère.[7] These jar sealings cover the time period between the middle of the Eighteenth Dynasty (*temp.* Thutmose III–Amenhotep II) and the beginning of the Twentieth Dynasty (temp. Ramesses III) which corresponds perfectly to the chronological sequence covered by the hieratic labels of the corresponding jars. They concern containers for wine, honey, *srmt*-beer, *b3k*-oil, *nhh*-oil, and *mrht*-oil, the products very often being specified on the stamp.

Figure 2

Among these items, the most important group is a number of jar sealings, roughly triangular in shape and made of whitish-yellow clay mingled with straw, clearly different from the clays generally used in the Nile Valley for such purposes.[8] Several items still retain a fragment of the neck of the amphora they sealed. In all cases, they are "Canaanite" jars, identifiable both by their shape and fabric. The systematic association of this type of amphorae with the yellow clay sealings suggests they are very likely Syro-Palestinian in origin. The cross checking of these results with the study of the inscriptions is interesting for different reasons: they reveal the names of the main products imported to Egypt from Syro-Palestine during

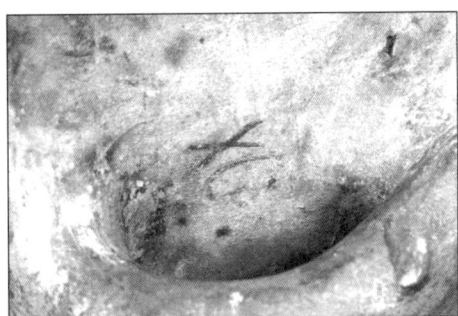

Figure 3

the New Kingdom—*b3k*-oil and *nhh*-oil. The jar labels regularly indicate that these products are brought by *hry-mnšw*, ship captains whose names frequently sound "Asian." The jar sealings also give important information on the conditions of the exchange; stamping could only take place when the product was packed—probably near the place of production. This corroborates the information released by the study of hieratic inscriptions.

But most interesting is probably the regular mention, on this type of jar sealing, of a number of Egyptian institutions which must have retained staffs in the Middle East; the King's Treasury (*pr-hd n nsw*), the Ramesseum (*hwt Wsr-m3ʿt-rʿ hr imntt W3st*), and above all, the temple of Sethi I at Abydos (*hwt Mn-m3ʿt-rʿ hri ib m 3bdw*), mentioned in some ten documents.

This temple is also frequently mentioned in the documentation of the Ramesseum.[9] The Nauri decree clearly shows the importance of this institution, laying particular stress on the status of its staff in Nubia.[10] This temple probably had also a staff in Palestine.

The jar sealings and hieratic labels of Deir al-Medina offer ample information about the economy of the New Empire, including the origin and circulation of goods, institutions, the staff employed in their production and trade routes. This documentation gives us a picture of the pro-

visioning of the great funerary temples on the West Bank of Thebes, which seem to have catered especially to the workmen's village at Deir al-Medina.

Figure 4

Notes:

1 E.g., G. Bouvier, *Catalogue des étiquettes de jarres hiératiques inédites de l'institut d'Égyptologie de Strasbourg* I *DFIFAO* 35 (Cairo, 1999), II, *DFIFAO* 36 (Cairo, 2000), III *DFIFAO* 37 (Cairo, 2000).

2 E. Schiaparelli, *La tomba intatta dell'architetto Cha nella necropoli di Tebe* II (Torino, 1927), 20, fig. 137; G. Nagel, "La céramique du Nouvel Empire à Deir el-Medineh," *DFIFAO* X (Cairo, 1938),16–22, 50–51, 64; J. Lopez, *Ostraca ieratici fasc. II*, nos. 57093–57319 (Turin, 1978), nos. 57174–57176, 57201–57202, 57212, 57237; Y. Koenig, *Catalogue des étiquettes de jarres hiératiques de Deir el-Medineh DFIFAO* 21 (1979–1980); D. Valbelle, Ch. Bonnet, "Le village de Deir el-Medineh," *BIFAO* 76 (1976), 329–343; G. Castel, D. Meeks, *Deir el-Medineh 1970 DFIFAO* X (Cairo, 1938).

3 E.g., Thutmose IV, Koenig, *Catalogue*, 6337; Amenhotep III, Koenig, *Catalogue*, 6341, 6353; Ay, Koenig, *Catalogue*, 6399; Horemheb, Koenig, *Catalogue*, 6294, 6299, 6342, 6343, 6344, 6345, 6403.

4 Koenig, *Catalogue*, 6488.

5 A. H. Gardiner, *Ancient Egyptian Onomastica* II (Oxford, 1947), 176*–180,* 236.*

6 P. Tallet, "Deux prêtres-sem thébains de la XXᵉ dynastie," *BIFAO* 99 (1999), 411–422.

7 B. Bruyère, *Rapport sur les fouilles de Deir el Medineh, FIFAO* 21 (1952), 54, fig. 39.

8 The ceramological study of all the jars and jar sealings mentioned above have been done by L. Bavay, université libre de Bruxelles.

9 G. Lecuyot, "À propos de quelques bouchons de jarres provenant du Ramesseum," *Memnonia* VIII (1997), 107–118.

10 F. Ll. Griffith, "The Abydos Decree of Seti I at Nauri," *JEA* 13 (1927), 193–208.

Early Cemeteries of the East Delta:
Kafr Hassan Dawood, Minshat Abu Omar, and
Tell Ibrahim Awad

G. J. Tassie and Joris van Wetering[1]
The Egyptian Cultural Heritage Organization

In recent years, many sites have been located through archaeological survey in the East Delta,[2] a few of which have been excavated. This paper will compare the two largest Terminal Predynastic to Early Dynastic mortuary populations so far excavated in the East Delta: Kafr Hassan Dawood (KHD) and Minshat Abu Omar (MAO). The grave architecture and grave good assemblages of these two sites, and to a lesser extent those of the cemetery at Tell Ibrahim Awad (TIA), will be analyzed in a regional perspective.[3]

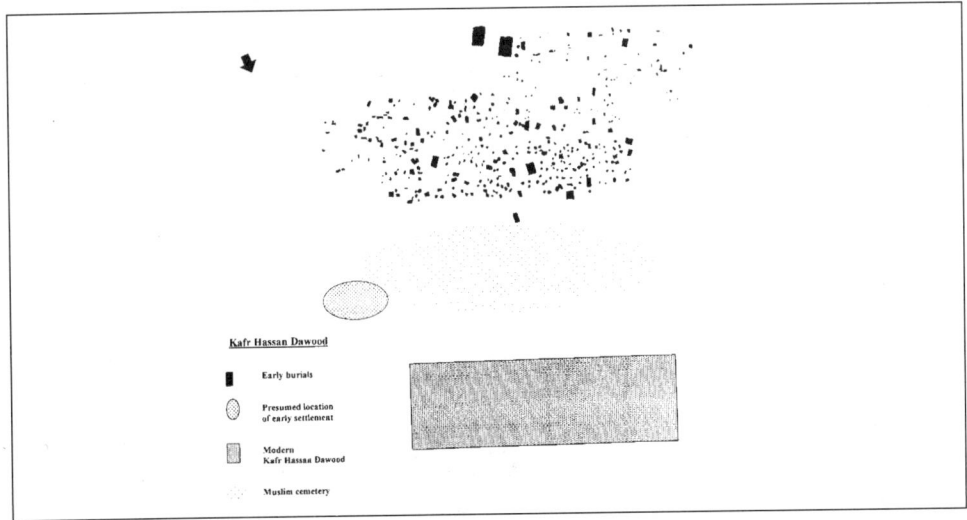

Kafr Hassan Dawood

■ Early burials

○ Presumed location
of early settlement

▨ Modern
Kafr Hassan Dawood

Muslim cemetery

Fig. 1: Kafr Hassan Dawood.

The Naqada Period cemetery at KHD (fig. 1), which contains 745 graves, is situated on the low desert, adjacent to the modern cultivated land.[4] It is estimated that this cemetery would have originally held about 1300 graves; unfortunately modern activity in the northern part of the cemetery prevents a full investigation of this area. The 1999 survey of the northern area indicated that it contains graves probably dating to Naqada IId, possibly Naqada IIc, correlating with the earliest dates for MAO. To date, no burials later than the early First Dynasty have been confirmed and the earliest fully investigated burials date to Naqada IIIa. Although the ceramic analysis is still in progress, many graves from across the cemetery have been dated from their artifactual assemblages. A complete spatio-temporal analysis of the cemetery will be available after the planned excavation in the north and after the full corpus of pottery vessels has been analyzed, and a pottery sequence established. The cemetery appears to have developed from the northern part, close to the ancient settlement[5] and floodplain then spread to the southwest.

Of the 745 burials, 399 graves are oval,[6] the most common size being 1.1 m x 0.8 m, 150 graves are rectangular,[7] the largest 6 m by 4 m, and there are eight ceramic coffin burials.[8] The shapes and sizes of the remaining 187 graves are undetermined.[9] The grave types range from simple sand pits to large mud-lined pits cut into the alluvial sands of the low Nile terrace. The superstructures were all made by creating either a mud cap or a sand mound over the pit.

The local elite were community members who could afford to put greater effort and resources into grave construction and the procurement of funerary goods for their graves.[10] Of the 40 burials[11] identified as elite burials, some seem to have belonged to the ruling segment of the community (the successive 'chiefs' and their family) while others to a 'middle class' (such as craftspeople, military, traders, the honored), these two groups could put more effort into the construction of their graves and acquire a larger grave good assemblage than the burials of the non-elite part of the community.[12] Prestige goods, such as flint knives and copper tools were among the grave goods interred in the elite graves, whereas these objects were not common among the non-elite burials. Graves 233, 371, 970, 913, and 1008 might have belonged to local chiefs, since they have a well-endowed grave good assemblage and elaborate architecture, and all are located in the central part of the cemetery.[13]

The early First Dynasty graves 913 and 970 (Fig. 2) are the largest and most elaborate graves in the cemetery, both measuring 6 x 4 x 0.75 m. The bottom of the burial pit has a layer of 'clean' sand upon which the interment was placed. The pit was then filled with mud and a mud, silt, and sand cap (of

Fig. 2: Grave 970 at KHD, looking south.

about 0.5 m high) was created over the pit. However, the elite grave 1008 (Late Terminal Predynastic) was a large oval grave measuring 2.3 x 1.7 x 0.8 m, cut into the alluvial sand with a mound of silt and sand, and a well-endowed grave good assemblage.[14] This indicates that before the First Dynasty, no elaborate grave architecture, mud-lined construction with mud cap, was used to distinguish elite graves from the graves of the rest of the community. Only from grave size and contents can the social position of the occupant be assessed. The occurrences of a serekh with the name of King Sekhen (Ka),[15] in grave 1008 and a serekh with the name of King Narmer in grave 913 seem to indicate the importance of these graves.[16] The exact significance of a *serekh* in a non-royal tomb context is unclear; but seems to point to contacts with the royal (central) administration.[17]

Some of the large elite graves seem to have been robbed, as evidenced by grave 970 where the more personal and higher prestige objects placed on and around the body were stolen, and the possibility cannot be completely excluded that grave 913 was robbed. The elite graves 233 (6.0 x 1.35 m), 371 (4.4 x 1.9 m) and 956 (3.65 x 2.8 m), besides ceramic and alabaster vessels, have very few prestige goods, possibly indicating they were robbed. The numbers of these vessels (as well as copper objects) left behind at MAO in graves that have clearly been robbed is sometimes staggering, 70 ceramic vessels in grave 2275, and 54 stone vessels in grave 2897 indicating that these objects were not considered to be of high value by robbers.[18]

The cemetery[19] at MAO[20] located on the eastern slope of a *gezira* 50 km west of Qantara, contained 422 graves, dating from the Late Predynastic to the Early Dynastic.[21] Based on ceramic analyses, these graves have been divided into four chronological groups, starting with MAO I– Naqada IIc Period–and ending with MAO IV–First Dynasty and early-Second Dynasty.[22] The cemetery develops from the southern and eastern areas where the oldest graves (MAO I) are situated to the extreme northern and western areas where MAO IV graves are located.[23] The majority of the burials were undisturbed, although most of the elite burials have been robbed in antiquity.[24]

The majority of the graves are rectangular shaped with a size range of up to 4.5 x 3.2 m, but the most common pit size is 1.70 x 1.15 m.[25] The grave types range from simple sand pits cut into the *gezira* sand to concamerated (sectioned into chambers) mud-brick tombs with a burial chamber and one or more storerooms.[26] Some graves have an empty space around them, which may indicate that a superstructure extended over the grave pit, as with grave 2275.[27]

Elite burials have been found from the MAO I Period onwards, as indicated by grave 330 [89][28]–MAO I and grave 160 [113]–MAO III. Individuals within the community set themselves apart by grave architecture and the objects that they took into the grave.[29] One such elite burial is grave 2200, a large conical pit of 4 x 3 m with mud-lined walls, dating to the MAO III Period.[30] This grave seems to show great similarity to the Early Dynastic elite burials, graves 913 and 970, at KHD. Another MAO III burial, grave 160 [113] just slightly predating the mud-brick elite-tombs is located in the south possibly purposely placed in the 'older' and maybe more sacred part of the cemetery. This grave, as well as grave 44, contained a ceramic storage jar with a *serekh*.[31] There are eight mud-brick graves that belonged to the local elite during the Early Dynastic Period.[32]

The four graves so far published from the First to early Second Dynasty cemetery (Tell B) at TIA,[33] are all concamerated.[34] Two are rectangular: B200/160/2 and B200/160/3 (c. 3.5 x 1.5 x 1.3 m), with mud-brick walls, burial chamber, and a storage-chamber.[35] The third is a large, rectangular, mud-brick, pit grave, B200/160/1 (7.7 x 2.5 x 0.8 m),[36] with a central burial chamber and three annexes that are covered by reed matting on the floor and against the sides, dating to the early First Dynasty.[37] This grave seems to be a transitional grave. The fourth grave is a large late First Dynasty rectangular *mastaba*-grave,[38] B100/170/1 (8.0 x 4.5 m). It has mud-brick walls (several bricks thick), a central burial chamber, several storerooms sunken within the substructure, and covered by a superstructure of mud-bricks and reed matting.[39] Tightly packed mud was deposited in the grave. The superstructure was still standing to a height of 1.25 m, and consisted of 25 rows of mud-bricks;[40] this tomb was probably partially robbed in antiquity.[41]

In general, the mortuary populations at KHD and MAO made use of the same grave type: simple pits, dug in the sand with few grave goods. The difference is in the architecture that the local elite used for their graves (both elite having a well endowed grave good assemblage). At MAO, the elite used large mud-lined graves during the MAO III Period,[42] whereas contemporary graves at KHD were large oval pits distinguished from the rest of the graves by their size and grave goods. During MAO IV large mud-brick graves were utilized, whereas in the same period at KHD large mud-lined graves were used, similar to the ones at MAO in the preceding period (MAO III). Another striking aspect is the difference in size between the two cemeteries, KHD covering 16,100 m[2], whereas MAO covers 3,600 m[2]. The mastaba grave and transitional grave at TIA have no counterparts at MAO, and the mud-brick graves from MAO and TIA have no parallels in KHD where no mud-brick graves have been found. Thus KHD either had no access to or did not use mud-brick construction in the cemetery while it was being utilized in the cemeteries of MAO and TIA. Spencer[43] notes that in certain cemeteries in Upper Egypt during the period of state formation, there is a distinction between cemeteries of large urban sites with extensive mud-brick architecture and other smaller less urbanized or rural cemeteries with limited use of mud brick. In the cemeteries with limited mud-brick use, the houses in the associated settlements were made of wattle-and-daub, whereas in the cemeteries with extensive mud-brick mortuary architecture (e.g. Cemetery T at Naqada), the houses and especially the administrative buildings were made of mudbrick.[44] The absence or presence of certain grave types at the various sites might signify a social hierarchy between East Delta sites, it may differentiate between those sites that were more urbanized than others or those that held 'state' administrative buildings and those that were more rural with no 'state' administration buildings on site. It seems that if mud bricks were being used to build houses in the settlement, they were more likely to be used in the cemetery as well. In the large urban sites, mud-brick architecture also seems to have been used at an earlier date, Naqada II, than in the less urbanized sites, where it does not seem to be utilized until the late First to Second Dynasty.[45]

In general, the grave good assemblages appear similar at KHD (fig. 3), MAO, and TIA. All three cemeteries have yielded a great number of comparable beer jars, storage jars, stone vessels, and copper vessels, although copper tools, such as adzes, needles, knives, and mirrors have only been found at KHD and MAO. However, it is in the form, material, and quality of the objects that the cemeteries differ. About 2 percent of the total grave good assemblage at KHD is made up of copper objects (52 objects from 745 graves),[46] especially adzes, of which some seem to have been purposely broken (graves 1008 and 1041), 2 vessels (from grave 913), knives, needles, mirrors, and harpoons. At MAO, the copper objects also make up about 2 percent of the total grave good assemblage (70 objects from 422 graves),[47] and include such items as saws, chisels, harpoons, axes, oval adzes, bracelets, needles, beads, and very occasionally vessels, varying from deep bucket-like bowls to flat dishes with a small rim.[48] Several remarkable papyrus flower-shaped copper objects that may have been encasings for horizontal beams (now decomposed) of a bed or catafalque.[49] The only burial to contain copper objects at TIA is B22/160/1, which had four vessels (including a kettle, a large basin, a jar, and a bowl) and one plaque that might be an adz.[50] At KHD, the copper objects are mostly functional, whereas at MAO decorative beads, bracelets, and encasings are found alongside functional objects. Vessels are rare, but are found in elite graves at all three cemeteries. In total about 100 copper objects have been found at the three cemeteries, whereas 700 copper objects were found in a single *mastaba* grave[51] at Saqqara.[52]

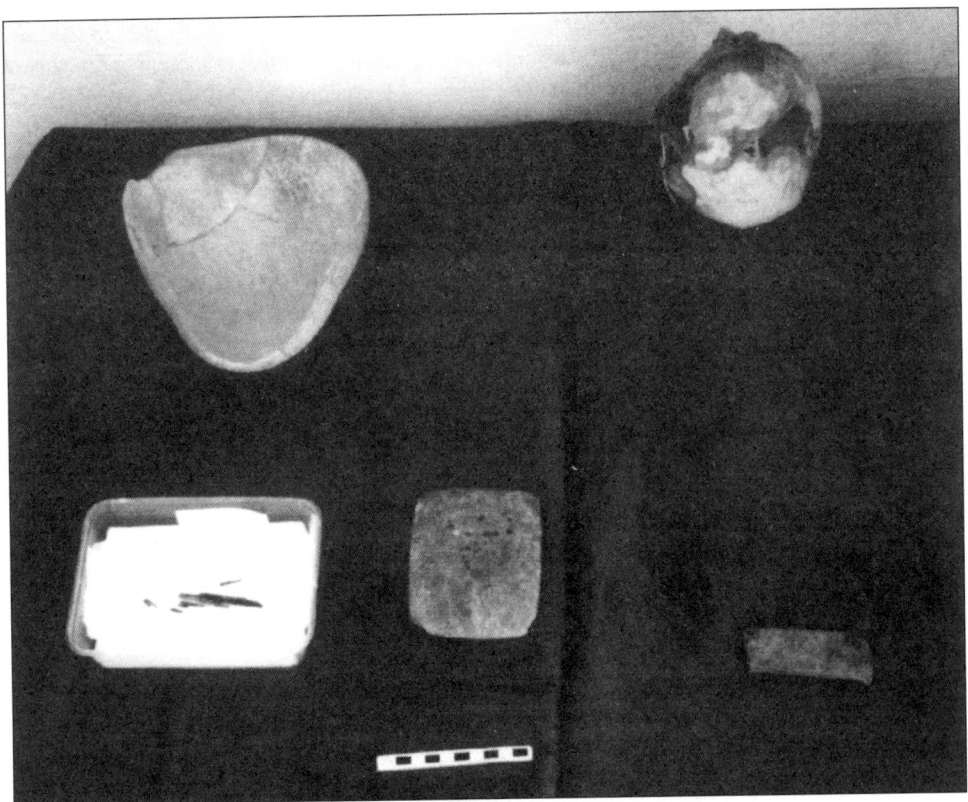

Fig. 3: Grave goods from KHD, a copper adze, copper needles, pottery, and a slate palette.

Whereas several imports from the Southern Levant have been found at MAO and TIA,[53] only three have so far been identified at KHD (in graves 1005, 1008, and 1014). Besides ceramic imports, a great variety of prestige objects have been found at MAO and KHD: gold, ivory and bone objects, flint knives, siltstone palettes, ceramic jars with serekhs, and stone vessels. At MAO, lapis lazuli objects and sometimes painted wooden coffins have been found within some of the elite tombs but neither category of grave good has been found at KHD.[54] Mace heads have been found at TIA[55] and at MAO[56] but no such prestigious power object has been found at KHD. At KHD, only two objects made of gold have been found (grave 73), including a miniature cylindrical vessel.[57] Two objects with gold components are also known from MAO: a necklace of 38 gold and two stone beads from grave 755 (9), and a headdress with one gold and 129 stone beads from grave 160.[58] Both the MAO burials containing gold are from the MAO I Period while no date is yet available for the KHD burial, but it is puzzling that no other gold objects have been found in the later, larger elite burials. This seems to indicate that the picture is distorted by grave robbing, creating an unbalanced picture of the archaeological material. The KHD prestige goods are less elaborate than those at MAO and TIA—no headdresses, no indications of painted wooden coffins, beds, and hardly any imported goods. This might be explained by differential preservation rates that exist at an inter- and intra-cemetery site level, since ivory, basketry, and other organic remains have not survived at KHD, but have done so at MAO.

503

Egyptian relations/interactions with foreign areas were dominated by the top level of the state and as such would only have had a limited influence on the social differentiation of regional centers,[59] although state administrators may have been resident within some of the more important of these communities. The sites, therefore, have to be assessed within their regional perspective. When Minshat Abu Omar was first discovered, it was stated that it was an important trade-center, if not the most important one, in the East Delta.[60] It is too simple to call sites where imported goods have been found 'trade centers', or connect them with the royal administration if *serekhs* were found.[61] Almost all of the excavated East Delta sites have at least one ceramic vessel with a *serekh* inscribed upon it. Is it possible that these vessels all came from the central administration, or did regional administrative centers exist that issued vessels with the name of the reigning king? During the First Dynasty, the central administration intensified control of the production and redistribution of state resources. There seems to have been a change in the economic focal point from Upper Egypt to Lower Egypt at the beginning of the Early Dynastic Period, with an economic decline in the middle of the First Dynasty occurring in the Nile Valley.[62] Therefore the discovery of *serekhs* in elite graves of the Delta may be the consequence of improved agricultural potential in the region and a shift in focus to the Delta. The local elite at MAO would probably have benefited from the central administration's relations with the Southern Levant. These factors combined seem to present a more satisfactory explanation for the occurrence of *serekhs* in many of the Delta sites, as it does not seem possible that every site in the Delta was a trade center or important political center.

A person's prestige should not be judged solely on the quality of the objects that are found in their grave, but also on the size of the grave, the type of grave architecture, and placement within the cemetery. The significance of grave goods and in particular prestige goods, in the process of state formation, needs further investigation, particularly through statistical and spatial analysis. A Sites and Monuments Records (SMRs) database incorporating GIS technology needs to be built up, thus making the comparison and correlation of the sites within the region easier and more accurate. However, this will only be possible once more sites from the East Delta have been more fully investigated and published, presenting a viable statistical population from which to make real social comment. Future research in the East Delta and Wadi Tumilat will not only increase our knowledge of the social dynamics of this very important region, but will elucidate more fully the local, regional, and national relationships, in particular the interpretation of prestige goods and their changing economic role during the period of state formation, and in the Predynastic–Early Dynastic Periods as a whole.

Notes:

1 The authors would like to thank Professor Fekri Hassan, for his advice on this paper, and Professor Gaballa A. Gaballa and Dr. Mohammed Abdel-Maksoud for their support of the project. Thanks also to our archaeologist colleagues, including the Canal Zone Inspectorate. Gratitude is due to Dr. Christopher Eyre

and the ICE 7 Committee for financial support of G. J. Tassie in attending ICE 8. Thanks must also go to Prof. Hassan for allowing us to use unpublished material from the ongoing doctoral thesis of Joanne M. Rowland. Also sincere thanks to Dr. E.C.M. van den Brink, Dr. S. Hendrickx, Mr. W. van Haarlem and Joanne M. Rowland, for their comments on the text. The KHD investigations have been funded by UNESCO, The National Geographic Society, The Bioanthropology Foundation, The Supreme Council of Antiquities, Uppsala University, The Humanities Research Council of Canada, and the Institute of Archaeology, UCL.

2 For a summary of the East Delta surveys see G. J. Tassie, "Egyptian cultural heritage management: let's work together," (in) N. Finneran and A. Reid (eds.) *Safeguarding Africa's Past* (London, in press).

3 Lack of published material from Kufur Nigm (400 burials) precludes it from this analysis.

4 For a description of KHD, see: F. Hassan, "The Late Predynastic to Early Dynastic Site of Kafr Hassan Dawood in the East Delta," *EA* 16 (2000), 37–39.

5 The contemporary settlement was located northeast of the cemetery, by drill-cores, Hassan, *EA* 16, 38.

6 The circular graves (154, 163, 173, 175, 180, 207, 219, 526, 541, 591, 633, and 641) are included with oval graves.

7 The square grave (290) is included in the rectangular graves.

8 The 8 ceramic coffins at KHD seem to date between Narmer and Aha.

9 These graves were excavated during the preliminary SCA season (1989) and this information is not available. See Hassan, *EA* 16, 37, for the site's excavation history.

10 F. Hassan, "The Predynastic of Egypt," *Journal of World Prehistory 2* (2) (1988), 135–185.

11 KHD elite burials: 73, 84, 123, 137, 142, 158, 166, 184, 198, 200, 213, 231, 233, 260, 286, 291, 298, 307, 316, 319, 332, 346, 371, 523, 529, 538, 547, 559, 601, 714, 823, 834, 873, 888, 890, 913, 956, 970, and 1008.

12 The non-elite burials (705 graves) have: (1) a smaller grave size than 2.5 x 1.5 m, (2) less than 18 grave goods, mostly consisting of ceramic and alabaster vessels, and (3) only a few (less than 8 but on average 4) prestige goods.

13 The elite burials are situated as follows: graves 233, 371, 913, and 970 in the south central part and grave 1008 in the north central part of the cemetery.

14 Hassan, *EA* 16, 38–39.

15 Hassan, *EA* 16, 38–39.

16 M. Bakr, M. Abd el-Moneim, and M. Selim, "Protodynastic excavations at Tell Hassan Dawud (eastern Delta)," (in) L. Krzyzaniak, K. Kroeper, and M. Kobusiewicz (eds.) *Interregional Contacts in the Later Prehistory of Northeastern Africa* (Poznan, 1996), 277–8.

17 T. Wilkinson, *Early Dynastic Egypt* (London, 1999), 44.

18 K. Kroeper, "Tombs of the Elite in Minshat Abu Omar," (in) E.C.M. van den Brink (ed.) *The Nile Delta in Transition: 4th–3rd Millennium B.C.* (Tel Aviv, 1992), 127–150,

19 K. Kroeper, "Minshat Abu Omar," (in) K. Bard (ed.) *Encyclopedia of the Archaeology of Ancient Egypt* (London, 1999), 529–531; K. Kroeper, "The excavations of the Munich East Delta Expedition in Minshat Abu Omar," (in) E.C.M. van den Brink (ed.) *The Archaeology of the Delta. Problems and Priorities* (Amsterdam, 1988), 18.

20 A plan of MAO is given in K. Kroeper and D. Wildung, *Minshat Abu Omar. Ein vor- und frühgeschichtlicher friedhof im Nildeltas I. Graber 1–114* (Mainz, 1994), plan 3.

21 Kroeper and Wildung, MAO I, Pl. XII.

22 K. Kroeper, "Minshat Abu Omar: Burials with palettes," (in) J. Spencer (ed.) *Aspects of Early Egypt* (London, 1996), 79–81.

23 K. Kroeper, "Minshat Abu Omar. Pot burials occurring in the Dynastic cemetery," *BCE* 18 (1994), 29.

24 Kroeper, "Burials with palettes," 70.

25 K. Kroeper and D. Wildung. *Minshat Abu Omar: Munchner Ostdelta Expedition. Vorbericht 1978–1984* (München, 1985), 25.

26 Kroeper, "MAO," 529–531.

27 Kroeper, "Elite MAO tombs," 134–136, 144.

28 The first number = field number, the second = publication number, Kroeper and Wildung, *MAO* I, Pl. XIV.

29 Kroeper and Wildung, *MAO* I, 116–122.

30 Kroeper, "Burials with palettes," 79.

31 Kroeper and Wildung, *MAO* I, 158–162.

32 Kroeper, "Elite MAO tombs," 140.

33 For a plan of TIA, see: E.C.M. van den Brink, "Preliminary report on the excavations at Tell Ibrahim Awad, seasons 1988–1990," (in) E.C.M. van den Brink (ed.) *The Nile Delta in Transition: 4th–3rd Millennium B.C.* (Tel Aviv, 1992), 63, plate 14. No complete plan of the cemetery has been published.

34 W. van Haarlem, "A Tomb of the First Century at Tell Ibrahim Awad," *OMRO* 76 (1996), 7.

35 van den Brink, "Preliminary TIA," 50–51; van den Brink pers. comm. 2000.

36 The grave plan in E.C.M. van den Brink, "The Amsterdam University Survey Expedition to the North-eastern Delta," (in) E.C.M. van den Brink (ed.) *The Archaeology of the Delta. Problems and Priorities* (Amsterdam, 1988), fig. 11, does not show the configuration of the mud-brick walls that can be seen in Pl. 12 of van den Brink, "Preliminary TIA." Nor is the subsequently found third storeroom incorporated.

37 van den Brink, "Preliminary TIA," 50–51.

38 See for a plan of this tomb van Haarlem, *OMRO* 76, 7, fig. 1.

39 van den Brink, "Preliminary TIA," 51.

40 van den Brink, "Preliminary TIA," 51.

41 van den Brink, pers. comm. 2000, kindly informed us that he shares this opinion.

42 Kroeper, "Burials with palettes," 79.

43 A. J. Spencer, *Brick Architecture in Ancient Egypt* (Warminster, 1976), 5–6.

44 Spencer, *Brick Architecture*, 10 ff.

45 Spencer, *Brick Architecture*, 5 ff.

46 Copper objects in non-elite burials: graves 93, 176, and 624, and in elite burials: graves 123, 142, 158, 260, 371, 538, 594, 913, 970, 1001/1003, 1008 and 1041.

47 Kroeper, "Burials with palettes," 82.

48 Kroeper and Wildung, *MAO*, 88–89; Kroeper, "Excavations of MAO," 15.

49 Kroeper, "Excavations of MAO," 15.

50 van den Brink, "Amsterdam survey," 79–83.

51 *Mastaba* S3471, attributed to a high-ranking official from the reign of Djer, probably related to the king, however, it is an enormous amount of prestige objects to be found outside the context of a Royal Tomb.

52 Wilkinson, *Early Dynastic Egypt*, 158.

53 K. Kroeper, "Palestinian Ceramic Imports in Pre- and Protohistoric Egypt," (in) P. de Miroschedji (ed.) *L'Urbanisation de la Palestine a l'age du Bronze ancien* (Oxford, 1989), 407–422; van Haarlem, "Tomb at TIA," 10.

54 Kroeper, "Elite MAO tombs," 129–130.

55 van den Brink, "Amsterdam survey," 79–83.

56 Kroeper and Wildung, *MAO*, 92.

57 S. el-Hangary, "The excavations of the Egyptian Antiquities Organisation at Ezbet Hassan Dawud (Wadi Tumilat), season 1990," (in) E.C.M. van den Brink (ed.) *The Nile Delta in Transition: 4th–3rd Millennium B.C.* (Tel Aviv, 1992), 215.

58 Kroeper and Wildung, *MAO* I, 7–10, 158–162.

59 Hendrickx, pers. comm. 2000.

60 W. Kaiser, "Zum Friedhof der Naqada-kultur von Minshat Abu Omar," *ASAE* 71 (1987), 119–126.

61 To attribute the "very existence" of MAO to "trade with Palestine," (Wilkinson, *Early Dynastic Egypt,* 363), seems to be premature with only a small part of the community investigated and only 20 import pieces from the Southern Levant (Kroeper, "Palestinian pottery," 407–22) found in a cemetery with more than 3500 objects (Kroeper "Burials with palettes," 82. These statements are too easily made on the occurrence of artifacts whose exact context and nature are not completely understood.

62 K. Bard, "The Emergence of the Egyptian State (c. 3200–2686 BC)," (in) I. Shaw (ed.) *The Oxford History of Ancient Egypt* (Oxford, 2000), 67.

The Extent of the New Kingdom Cemetery in the Memphite Necropolis

Tarek S. Tawfik

Faculty of Archaeology, Russian Academy of Sciences

The extent of the New Kingdom cemetery in the Memphite necropolis has become unpredictable. Before examining this statement in detail, I will present a short review of the present situation. (Fig.1)

Starting from the north, in the escarpment adjoining the village of Abusir, the earthquake of 1992 revealed the tomb of Nakhtmin. Recently, another tomb was discovered adjacent to it. Both are Ramesside.[1] North and east of the Teti Pyramid are tombs from the Eighteenth Dynasty up to the reign of Ramesses IV.[2] In the escarpment overlooking the entrance to Saqqara, are the excavations of the French Mission, which encompass tombs from the Eighteenth and Nineteenth Dynasties.[3] South of the Unas pyramid causeway are the excavations of the former Egypt Exploration Society-Leiden (now Leiden) Expedition where tombs from the Eighteenth and Nineteenth Dynasties are being explored.[4] South of these are the excavations of the Supreme Council of Antiquities where tombs from the Eighteenth Dynasty were discovered.[5]

Near the Monastery of Apa Jeremias we have the excavations of Cairo University, which revealed tombs mainly dating to the reign of Ramesses II.[6]

In the wide plain stretching to Dahsur, tombs have occasionally been found. This has been the case near the pyramids of Pepy I and Pepy II, around the tomb of Shepsekaf, and the pyramids of the Thirteenth Dynasty.[7] These were rather modest burials and no great attention was paid to them because they were only seen as secondary finds at the time of their discovery.

Finally, a Japanese Mission has revealed tombs from the New Kingdom (possibly Eighteenth Dynasty reused in the Nineteenth Dynasty) at Dahsur, in the area between the Pyramid of Senwosret III and that of King Khendjer.[8]

It may be noted that the cemetery of the New Kingdom consists of groupings of tombs distributed over the previously mentioned locations. No pattern has yet been established as to how the tombs are distributed, but it becomes more and more clear that the New Kingdom cemetery sites are not all directly connected, so I would like to introduce the term "scattered cemetery."

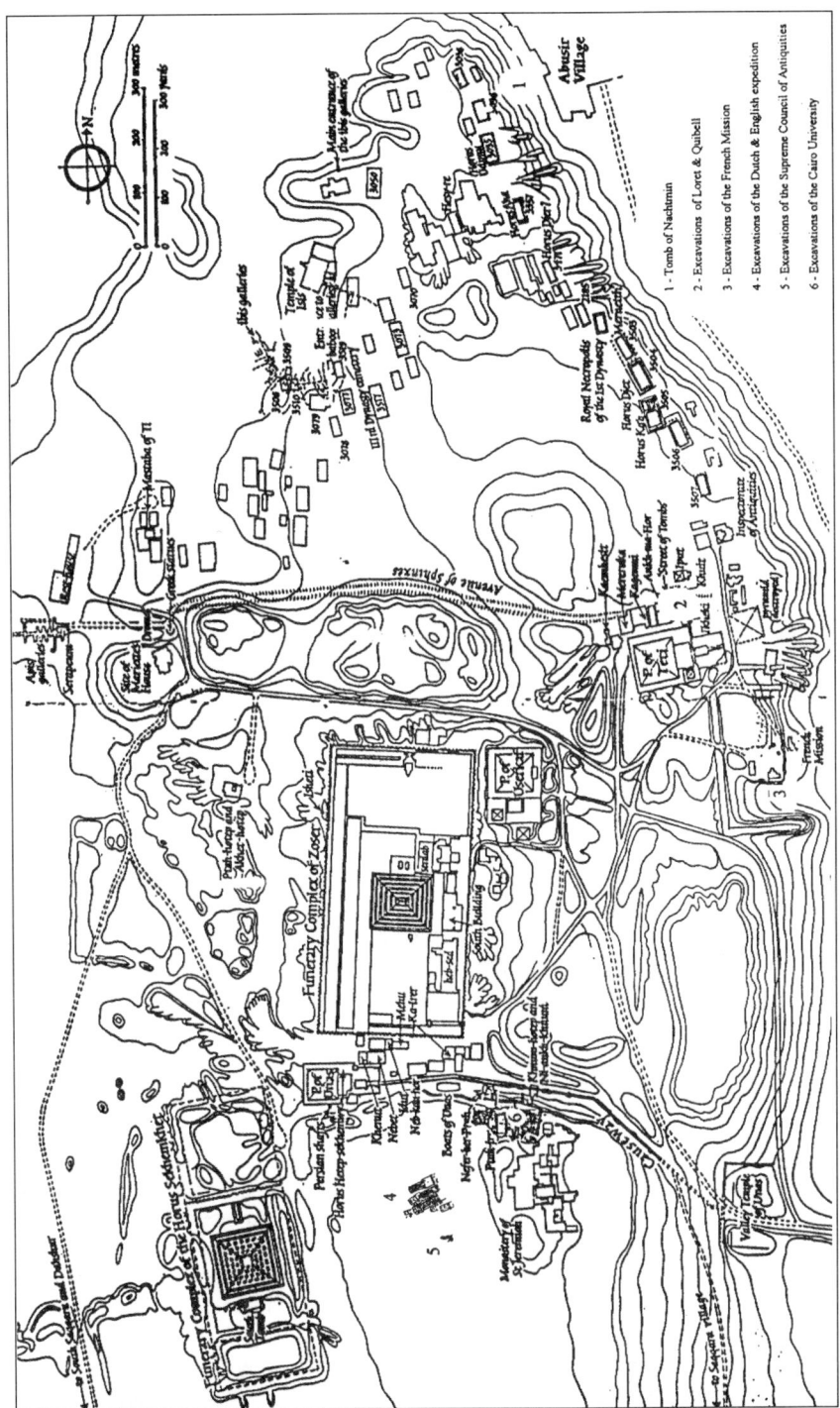

Fig. 1: Plan of the New Kingdom Cemetery at Saqqara and Abusir.

Still, what has been discovered up to now must be considered only the tip of the iceberg (or the pyramidion, Egyptologically speaking).

Looking at the titles mentioned in the tombs of the dignitaries of the New Kingdom at Thebes, especially after the reign of Amenhotep IV, it may be noticed that most of these titles are connected locally to the administration of Thebes, the Amun-cult, or other local cults. Titles like those appearing in the excavations of the Cairo University—Master Physician in the Palace, Fan Bearer on the Right of the King, Overseer of the Treasury of the Lord of the Two Lands, Chamberlain (*imi-ḫt*) of the Lord of the Two Lands, Royal Butler[9]—and other titles closely connected to the person of the king, are not often found in Theban tombs. Of course, this is logical, because at the time of Ramesses II and the sweep towards the north, the residence was moved to Piramesse. But this move in itself could have emphasized the importance of the Memphite necropolis even more because the location of Piramesse in the Delta was in agricultural land away from the stone quarries. This would have encouraged the continued use of the dry Memphite necropolis near the quarries and near older tombs that they could also use as quarries. Until now, as I was kindly informed by the expedition's director, Edgar Pusch, only very few burials have appeared in their excavations at Qantir and none of them are very elaborate.

The picture of the Memphite necropolis will not be very different from the Theban necropolises in the sense that there are few tombs from the reigns of Ramesses I, Amenmesse, Sety II, Siptah, Queen Twosret, Sethnakhte, and the Ramesside kings, from Ramesses IV to XI, which is not unusual because each of them ruled for a relatively short period of time.

In regard to the reigns of Sety I, Merneptah, and Ramesses III, they ruled for longer periods and undertook great military activities to the north and northeast of Egypt. It seems to me very likely that tombs from the reigns of these kings are still to be found in large numbers in the Memphite necropolis. The military actions of these kings will have kept them and their entourage in the Delta, close to the action.

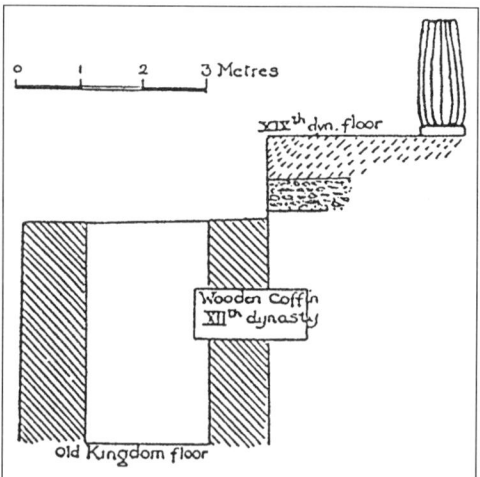

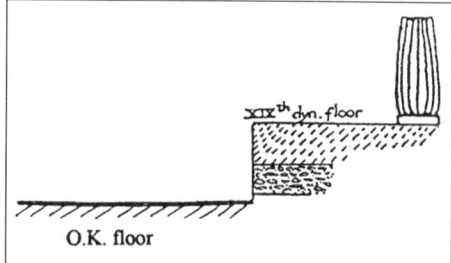

Despite the presence of two tombs from the reign of Ramesses III in Heliopolis, drawn to my attention by D. Raue,[10] and other tombs in some provincial cemeteries from the reigns of the previously mentioned kings, I believe that the greater part of the entourage of these kings is to be found in the Memphite necropolis.

Fig. 2: The method used to prepare the ground for the NK tombs north and east of the Teti Pyramid (in: J. E. Quibell & A. G. K. Hayter, *Excavations at Saqqara, Teti Pyramid, North side* (Le Caire 1927, p 21).

Fig. 3: The method used to prepare the ground for the NK tombs south of the Unas causeway.

Three papyri published by Paule Posener-Krieger[11] in 1981 are unique because they contain information concerning the commissioning of a private tomb in the Memphite necropolis during the reign of Ramesses III. These papyri were found to the south of the Djoser complex enclosure wall, so the discovery of this tomb and perhaps others were expected in this area.

The area between the Djoser complex enclosure and the Unas causeway is occupied by Old Kingdom mastabas, several of which have been restored to their original height. Sayed Tawfik had spoken of a two-level necropolis in his excavations, referring to the floors of the mastabas which were totally demolished, then the remains covered with a thin layer, mainly of tafla, and built over with New Kingdom tombs.[12] In many cases the burial shafts were reused. The same method was probably used further west in the Leiden excavations. This is in contrast to the tombs around the Teti Pyramid which were built

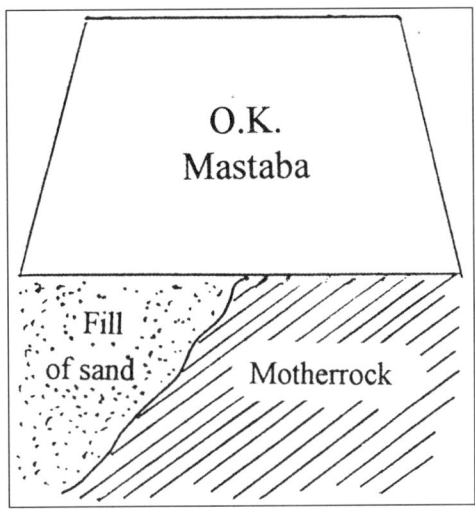

Fig. 4: The ground on which the mastabas were built in the area between the Djoser complex enclosure and the Unas causeway.

on top of the Old Kingdom mastabas and the mortuary temple of Teti, which at that time must have been nearly or fully sanded-up, so that again only a thin layer of tafla was used to prepare the ground for the New Kingdom tombs. Their burial shafts often penetrated the mastabas and the temple. So we have these two methods of preparing the ground for a New Kingdom tomb. (Figs. 2 and 3)

Returning to the area between the Unas causeway and the Djoser complex enclosure wall, the excavators, in their reports and publications on the mastabas there, do not mention remains of New Kingdom tombs or even burial shafts. Either traces of New Kingdom burials were not considered very important at the time and not recorded—which I doubt—or there were no tombs there at all. These would either have been on top of the mastabas or, more naturally, considering those a few meters away south of the causeway of Unas, the mastabas would have been demolished in order to build New Kingdom tombs. Perhaps it due to the shrewdness of the ancient Egyptian architects that the mastabas in this area were not demolished, because they realized some of them were not built on even ground, but partially on the mother rock which slopes downwards in this area. The rest of the ground would have been leveled. (fig. 4)

Where to place the tomb from the reign of Ramesses III in this area is puzzling. But following the same concept as above, perhaps the presence of the mastaba of the Chief Justice and Vizier Ptahhotep (LS 31)[13] at the far west end of the New Kingdom cemetery in front of the complex of Sekhemkhet could, in this case, because it was not demolished, mark the western end of the New Kingdom cemetery south of the Unas causeway. We must also face yet another problem: why were mastabas of viziers such as *Mn-nfr*, which stand proudly in the middle of the excavations of Cairo University, and the one of Ptahhotep, not demolished?

I would also like to hint at the possibility that the area around the hill where a Japanese mission from Waseda University has found a "cult building" of Khaemwase[14] could be a place to look for further tombs. Perhaps this situation is similar to what Polz suggests for Dra Abu al-Naga:[15] This hill, with its cult building, could have represented a nucleus around which simple tombs of the "lower class and middle class" were grouped. Another possibility is the escarpment overlooking the Valley Temple of Unas, where the so-called "tomb with the cow" was discovered, dated by Malek to the Nineteenth Dynasty.[16] The escarpment overlooking the village of Abusir can safely be seen as a continuation of the work of the French mission.

In conclusion, I would like to suggest that, in order to understand the reason for this scattered cemetery, we may have to reach further back, to the Old Kingdom. Why the pyramids of the Old Kingdom and later the Middle Kingdom were distributed the way they were, was because during the Late Period in many cases the people returned and used the same burial grounds. The concept of what was holy and sacred for the ancient Egyptians, whether material or spiritual, must redefined. Who knows where the extent of the New Kingdom cemetery in the Memphite necropolis will lie in the future?

Notes:

1 L. Giddy, "Dig Diary," *Egyptian Archaeology* 16 (Spring, 2000), 32.

2 B. Porter and R.L.B. Moss, *Topographical Bibliography of Ancient Egyptian Hieroglyphic Texts, Reliefs, and Paintings III*, Memphis, Part 2, Saqqara to Dahsur (Oxford, 1981), 552.

3 Cf. A. Zivie, *Découverte à Saqqarah* (Paris, 1990); A. Zivie, "La nourrice royale Maïa et ses voisins: cinq tombeaux du Nouvel Empire récemment découverts à Saqqara, *Comptes rendus de l'Académie des Inscriptions et Belles-Lettres* (janvier-mars, 1998), 33.

4 Cf. G. T. Martin, *The Hidden Tombs of Memphis* (London, 1992); H. Schneider et al., "The Tomb of Iniuia: Preliminary Report on the Saqqara Excavations, 1993," *Journal of Egyptian Archaeology* 79 (1993), 1; H. Schneider *et al.*, "The Tomb-Complex of Pay and Raia: Preliminary Report on the Saqqara Excavations, 1994 Season," *Oudheitkundige Mededeelingen uit het Rijksmuseum van Oudheden te Leiden* (1995), 13; G. T. Martin, "Preliminary Report on the Saqqara Excavations, 1995," *OMRO* 76 (1996), 35; G. T. Martin, "Preliminary Report on the Saqqara Excavations, 1997," *OMRO* 78 (1998), 31; R. V. Walsem, "Preliminary Report on the Saqqara Excavations, Season 1999," *OMRO* 79 (1999), 19.

5 M. El-Ghandour, "Report on Work at Saqqara South of the New Kingdom Cemetery Seasons 1994, 1996, 1997," *GM* 161 (1997), 5.

6 S. Tawfik, "Recently Excavated Ramesside Tombs at Saqqara," *Mitteilungen des Deutschen Archäologischen Instituts für Ägyptische Altertumskunde in Kairo* 47 (1991), 403.

7 M. Z. Goneim, Horus *Sekhem-khet* I (Cairo, 1957), 23 (Pls. IXVII–IXXII); A. Labrousse, "Le Temple Funeraire de Pepy I au Nouvel Empire;" A. Zivie (ed.), *Memphis et ses Necropoles au Nouvel Empire* (Paris, 1988), 67; G. Jequier, *Le Monument funeraire de Pepy II* III (Le Caire, 1940), 44; *Le Mastabat Faraoun* (Le Caire, 1928), 32; *Deux Pyramides du Moyen Empire* (Le Caire, 1933), 43; cf. J. Malek, "A Meeting of the Old and New. Saqqara during the New Kingdom," in A. B. Lloyd (ed.), *Studies in Pharaonic Religion and Society* (J. G. Griffiths Festschrift) (London, 1992), 59.

8 S. Yoshimura *et al.*, "A Preliminary Report of the General Survey at Dahshur North, Egypt," *Annual Report of the Collegium Mediterranistarum Mediterraneus XX* (Tokyo, 1997), 3; S. Yoshimura *et al.*, "The New

Kingdom Necropolis at Dahshur," *KMT* 10/3 (Fall, 1999), 37; S. Yoshimura *et al.,* "A Ramesside sarcophagus at Dahshur," *Egyptian Archaeology* 13 (1999), 5.

9 Tawfik, "Recently Excavated Ramesside Tombs," 404.

10 I would like to thank my dear friend Dr. D. Raue for telling me about the two tombs from the reign of Ramesses III, which he mentioned in D. Raue, "Heliopolis und das Haus des Re," *Abhandlungen des Deutschen Archäologischen Instituts Kairo* 16, Berlin (1999), 189, "*Maj;*" 205, "*Mry-Jtmw.*"

11 P. Posener-Kriéger, "Construire une tombe à l'ouest de Mn-nfr (P. Cairo 52002)," *Revue d'Égyptologie* 33 (Louvain, 1981), 47.

12 Tawfik, "Recently Excavated Ramesside Tombs," 404.

13 PM III², 653.

14 I. Z. Takamiya and S. Yoshimura, "Waseda University Excavations at North Saqqara: A preliminary Report on the First Three Seasons, December 1991–September 1993," *ORIENT* XXXII (Tokyo, 1997), 69.

15 D. Polz suggested that each of the two large tomb-chapels, K91.3 and K91.19, which he excavated at Dra Abu al-Naga, might represent a nucleus around which simple tombs of the "lower class and middle class" were grouped; D. Polz, "Dra Abu el-Naga: Die thebanische Nekropole des frühen Neuen Reiches," *Studien zur Archäologie und Geschichte Altägyptens* 12 (1995), 28.

16 J. Malek, "Two Problems connected with New Kingdom Tombs in the Memphite area," *JEA* 67 (1981), 158 ff. 17.

Notes sur les inscriptions du temple ptolémaïque et romain de Tôd, (§ 1–4)

Christophe Thiers

Institut français d'archéologie orientale, Le Caire

Après une longue interruption depuis la parution du premier volume des inscriptions du temple ptolémaïque et romain de Tôd[1], le travail d'édition des textes de ce temple a repris en 1998–1999[2]. Les parties encore inédites concernent le second vestibule, la Salle des Déesses, les cryptes – la plus importante étant située au-dessus de la Salle des Déesses, l'autre dans l'épaisseur du mur sud de cette même salle – et le mur intérieur ouest de la Salle des Offrandes[3].

Parallèlement au travail d'édition en cours, quelques particularités rencontrées dans les scènes et textes du temple de Tôd méritent d'être signalées[4].

§ 1 Scènes publiées et nouveautés

Plusieurs scènes du temple – dont certaines provenant de la partie inédite – ont fait l'objet d'études ponctuelles, soit pour leur originalité propre, soit parce qu'elles entraient dans une série de scènes particulières :
- offrande du lotus (n° 126)[5];
- offrande des coffres-*meret* (n° 155)[6];
- offrande à Imhotep et Amenhotep (n° 236)[7];
- offrande à Astarté (n° 281)[8];
- offrande aux Lagides divinisés (n° 318)[9].

En outre, d'autres scènes inédites viennent compléter des dossiers déjà réunis :
- offrande des miroirs (n°s 181, 264 et 274)[10];
- offrande de la corbeille de dattes (n° 312, *infra*)[11];
- offrande du collier-*beb* (n°s 179 et 277)[12];
- intercession des dieux maîtres d'autel (n°s 314–315)[13];
- enfin, la scène n° 263 confirme l'étude récente de D. Meeks sur l'identification du toponyme *ṯb(i)* avec Hiérakonpolis.[14]

§ 2 Un nouveau nom de la palette de scribe (*Tôd*, n° 233, 1)

La palette de scribe est désignée par de nombreux termes, le plus usité étant *gs.ty*. Faisant suite à l'étude que M.-Th. Derchain-Urtel a consacrée à l'offrande de la palette au dieu Thot[15], S. Cauville est revenue sur les désignations de cet objet[16]. Ayant recours à diverses circonlocutions liant intimement l'objet à son utilisateur et bénéficiaire privilégié, le dieu Thot, les hiérogrammates égyptiens ont multiplié les désignations de la palette de scribe : *imy-ʿ*, *Ir-sḏm*, *ʿ*, *ʿ n Ir*, *m3ʿ-ḫrw*, *mḥ*, *ḥs-ʿ*, *ḥwd*, *ḏr.t*. On verra par exemple *Dendara* XI, 32, 4–5 et 8 qui présente les mentions successives de *gs.ty*, *Ir-sḏm*, *ḥs-ʿ* et *ʿ* dans les textes d'une même scène.

Dans le temple de Tôd, l'offrande de la palette de scribe à Thot est attestée à trois reprises ; chacune de ces scènes se signale par une désignation particulière de l'objet, témoignant d'un jeu savant des prêtres de Montou. Le nom le plus courant – *gs.ty* – apparaît en *Tôd*, n° 164, 1. Un autre vocable plus rare – *ḥwd* – est mentionné en *Tôd*, n° 178, 1 : « Offrir la palette (☐) pour comptabiliser la multitude ».

Dans la troisième scène, la désignation de l'objet est, ce me semble, nouvelle (*Tôd*, n° 233, 1) : « Prends pour toi [☐] ». Ce vocable doit probablement se lire *mti ir.t* sur le modèle des constructions avec *mti*[17]: *mti m3ʿ*, *mti h3ty* « juste, droit » ; *mti sḫr.w* « aux conseils avisés »[18] ; *mti ib* « loyal », « sincère (?) »[19]. La palette serait donc désignée par la séquence « juste d'œil », c'est-à-dire «clairvoyant», qualificatif qui s'applique avec force au dieu Thot, modèle de l'intellectuel omniscient[20]. Notons également que Thot est «le témoin» (*mtr/mti*), «le véritable témoin», «le véritable témoin pour les dieux»[21]. Cet aspect de la personnalité du dieu n'est sans doute pas sans conséquence dans la création de ce nouveau vocable.

§ 3 Le protocole de Ptolémée Alexandre Ier (*Tôd*, n° 241)

Au sommet des murs intérieurs est (très détruit), sud et ouest du second vestibule court un bandeau de dédicace. Cette inscription a déjà été relevée et publiée en partie par K. R. Lepsius[22]; elle n'a cependant jamais été attribuée à un règne particulier.

Avant d'aller plus avant, il est nécessaire de rappeler les phases du processus de construction et de décoration du temple. La construction des deux vestibules, peut-être initiée sous Philopator parallèlement aux travaux du débarcadère et du dromos[23], s'est poursuivie jusque sous le règne d'Évergète II qui a laissé ses cartouches sur la porte d'accès à la Salle des Offrandes et sur le mur ouest (paroi intérieure) de cette salle, le seul conservé[24]. Néos Dionysos (Aulète) est attesté par les cartouches qui ont été inscrits sur la porte d'accès au second vestibule ; en outre, des cartouches à son nom ont été peints dans cette salle, trois étant encore en partie visibles aujourd'hui, l'un au-dessus du bandeau de frise (n° 243), les deux autres dans une scène du mur sud (n° 235) déjà mentionnée par F. Bisson de la Roque[25].

L'ensemble de la décoration du second vestibule est donc mis en place durant l'époque ptolémaïque et il faut – semble-t-il – attendre le règne d'Antonin le Pieux pour que le premier vestibule (?) (bandeau de frise n° 78) et les murs extérieurs soient décorés (côté nord, n°s 67, 70, 73, 75, 76)[26]. Il y aurait donc un hiatus entre Évergète II et Néos Dionysos puis entre ce dernier et le Romain ; pourtant, les éléments internes du protocole qui court sur le bandeau de dédicace ne laissent que peu de doutes sur son attribution :

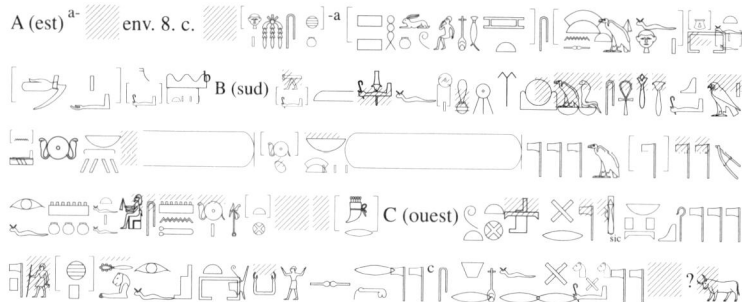

a-a) Bloc Bisson inv. 1330, vu encore en place par K.R. Lepsius (le 30 octobre 1844) qui décrit la scène (n° 222) située sous ce bandeau (*LD Text* IV, p. 12).

b) Restitutions d'après *Edfou* VII, 1, 9–11 (*infra*).

« A- [L'Horus, divin dans le ventre, que l'Apis vivant a uni] sur ses briques de naissance, [jeune homme parfait, doux d'amour, que sa mère a couronné sur] le trône de [son] père, [le vaillant], celui qui frappe les pays étrangers, B- qui conquiert par sa puissance[27] comme Rê qui brille[28] dans l'horizon, Celui des Deux Déesses, celui qui fait vivre le Double-Pays, le vaillant, Horus 2- qui est puissant (?), le roi de Haute et Basse-Égypte, maître du Double-Pays, (cartouche vide), le Fils de Rê, maître des couronnes, (cartouche vide), les dieux philométors ; il a réalisé le monu- ment <pour> son auguste père, Montou-Rê <maître de> Thèbes, [taureau qui réside à] Tôd C-, qui préside à la grande place, grand dieu, maître du ciel, souverain 5- des dieux, le dieu [vénérable (?) qui est venu à l'existence] auparavant ; il a réalisé cette place[29] dont la hauteur est exacte[30] et la largeur parfaite, le grand de puissance [...] ».

Les cartouches de la dédicace sont vides, mais l'épithète «les dieux philométors» permet d'ori- enter la recherche. Dans le cadre chronologique défini plus haut, elle pourrait qualifier Sôter II ou Alexandre Ier (avec Cléopâtre Bérénice III) ; on notera l'originalité de la double graphie des trois pavois divins alors que les exemples connus de cette épithète ne se présentent jamais de la sorte. Si l'on prête sens à cette graphie, il faut alors comprendre « les *trois* dieux philométors»; cette épithète qualifie Sôter II accompagné de deux Cléopâtre à Philae, relief probablement exécuté lors de la visite du roi durant l'été 115[31] mais également avec sa seule mère dans le temple de Ouanina[32].

L'examen de la première partie du protocole laisse toutefois apparaître une similitude avec celui d'Alexandre Ier. Le nom d'Horus tel qu'il se présente peut être comparé à celui qui désigne ce souverain à Edfou[33]. Les traces qui subsistent permettent d'assurer avec une grande probabil- ité la présence de *ḥr mshn.ty* sans toutefois pouvoir affirmer que le début du protocole était strictement parallèle à celui du temple apollonopolite; le nombre de cadrats perdus est en outre favorable à la présence de la séquence préliminaire attestée à Edfou. Il est par ailleurs fort prob- able que l'on avait la séquence «Celui que sa mère a couronné sur le trône de son père », les traces permettant de reconnaître *ns.t it*[.*f*] ; de même, la lacune de deux cadrats qui fait suite est tout à fait propice pour contenir l'épithète *tm3-ꜥ* présente à Edfou.

Le nom des Deux Déesses d'Alexandre Ier à Edfou est « celui qui réjouit le Double-Pays, le taureau puissant, qui a pouvoir sur un million» (*shr-ib t3.wy k3 nḫt shm n ḥḥ*). Si notre restitu- tion est correcte, la séquence «Horus qui est puissant » est originale, *nꜥš* ne se rencontrant dans aucun autre protocole lagide[34].

Aucun élément de la titulature de Tôd n'est commun avec les titulatures de Sôter II (premier et second règnes), à l'exception de la séquence *sẖꜥ.n sw mw.t.f ḥr ns.t it.f*, laquelle appartient cependant au nom des Deux Déesses de ce roi. Si le terme *msẖn.t* est bien présent dans le nom d'Horus de Sôter II, il est construit avec le verbe *snsn*. La graphie particulière de l'épithète royale «les dieux philométors » invite en outre à la plus extrême prudence quant au sens réel à lui accorder. Le rapprochement avec le protocole d'Edfou paraît une base plus solide et il est alors possible de conclure que l'on a affaire à Alexandre Ier dans le bandeau de Tôd.

S'il faut donc reconnaître dans ce protocole une variante de celui d'Alexandre Ier attesté à Edfou, ce nouvel élément permet de préciser la phase de décoration de la partie ptolémaïque du temple de Tôd et comble ainsi en partie le hiatus entre Évergète II et Néos Dionysos. On doit alors considérer que les travaux de décoration ont été interrompus durant le premier (116–107) et le second (88–80) règne de Sôter II, à tout le moins le nom de ce roi n'aurait pas été inscrit[35]. Les cartouches d'Alexandre Ier sont toutefois restés vides, témoignant ainsi du doute des prêtres quant au Pharaon régnant durant cette période troublée à la cour alexandrine ; en seconde hypothèse, il est possible d'envisager que les cartouches étaient peints comme l'attestent ceux de Néos Dionysos signalés précédemment. Pour ces cartouches vides durant cette période, le parallèle avec Edfou peut une nouvelle fois être souligné[36]. Sauf à considérer que la décoration mise en place sous Évergète II n'ait pas été datée par les cartouches de ce souverain, cette séquence chronologique permet d'envisager que la mise en place de la décoration du second vestibule a été effectuée sous le règne d'Alexandre Ier.

La présence de ce souverain à Tôd apporte également un nouvel élément de réponse à la mise en place du programme décoratif de la Salle des Déesses[37], ce que viennent renforcer certaines caractéristiques iconographiques communes avec les scènes du second vestibule (traitement des mains en particulier).

Figure 1

§ 4 Un rite détourné : l'offrande du récipient de dattes (*Tôd*, n° 312)

Cette offrande du récipient de dattes (*mꜥdꜣ (n bnr)*) est traditionnellement réservée à Osiris[38]. Toutefois, elle est présentée à Horus à Edfou (I, 471, 17–472, 10) et probablement à Chou et Tefnout à El-Qal'a (n° 38); dans ce dernier cas, la légende est perdue, mais l'aspect de l'offrande (naos pyramidal) ne laisse subsister que peu de doute. Cette offrande apparaît également à Tôd, au sommet du montant intérieur sud de la porte donnant accès à la Salle des Offrandes aujourd'hui perdue (fig. 1). L'intérêt de cette scène réside dans le fait qu'elle montre Ptolémée Évergète II officiant devant Ptah.

Titre de la scène : «Je t'apporte le récipient de dattes issues de toi, recueillies par Isis afin que les dieux en boivent» (*ms.i n.k m^cd3 pr im.k ^crf (i)n 3s.t swr (st) ntr.w*).

Ce titre condense des séquences attestées dans le même type d'offrande où les dattes présentées à Osiris sont assimilées à ses propres humeurs ou plus fréquemment à celles de Geb. À Philae, la séquence *pr im.k* concerne Osiris dont sont issues les humeurs (*rdw*)[39]. À Edfou (I, 472, 6-7), dans une scène de l'offrande du récipient de dattes, les paroles royales précisent: «toutes ces humeurs qui sourdent de Geb-liquide-secret issu d' Osiris - qu'a recueillies Isis afin que les dieux les boivent»[40]. Un texte similaire se retrouve au mammisi de Dendara dans une scène d'offrande des bouquets montés (*Mam. Dendara*, 231, 3)[41]. Il est intéressant de noter que la scène située au-dessus de la scène n° 312 qui nous occupe, c'est-à-dire sur le linteau (n° 314) de la porte, est précisément consacrée à l'offrande des bouquets montés[42].

Le roi se présente devant Ptah momiforme sous son dais : « Paroles à dire par Ptah au visage parfait[43], qui réside à Thèbes, grand dieu, qui réside à Tôd». Son discours précise : «Je te donne toutes les plantes (*rdw*) qui sont sur le dos de Geb)». Le lien étroit entre l'offrande du récipient de dattes et les humeurs d'Osiris ou de Geb n'est pas étranger à l'emploi de ce vocable auquel on peut toutefois garder ici son acception courante de «plantes». On ne peut douter que le scribe a volontairement joué sur les deux sens de ce terme dans le contexte osirien de la scène. Nous avons affaire ici à un rite détourné mais avec un jeu subtil, aussi bien dans le recours aux textes qu'aux liens iconographiques avec la scène n° 314.

Dans la scène d'Edfou, on peut considérer qu'Horus, divinité tutélaire du temple, s'est approprié une offrande osirienne et a ainsi acquis un aspect de la personnalité de ce dieu; sa prééminence dans le temple lui permet de se substituer à Osiris et l'offrande spécifique est détournée à son profit[44].

À Tôd, l'origine osirienne de l'offrande est clairement marquée dans les légendes, avec la mention d'Isis et des plantes/humeurs issues de Geb. Les prêtres de Montou ont donc adapté cette offrande osirienne ainsi placée dans un contexte différent. Mais contrairement à Edfou où le détournement s'effectue en faveur de la divinité principale, à Tôd elle concerne Ptah – divinité marginale dans le temple[45]- et demeure donc encore plus énigmatique, la pr´sence de Montou aurait été plus satisfaisante et – à tout le moins – conforme à la pratique attestée à Edfou. Le problème demeure également quant à la présence de Chou et Tefnout recevant la corbeille de dattes à d'El-Qa'la. L'hypothèse d'une confusion des prêtres reste difficile à soutenir[46]. Au mieux pourrait-on remarquer que la forme de la corbeille de dattes (une sorte de petit naos) est proche de celle du collier-*oudja* (sans le collier proprement dit)[47]. Toutefois, comme on l'a souligné, les connotations osiriennes sont suffisamment explicites pour ne pas recourir à une telle hypothèse.

Cet exemple, qui s'ajoute aux représentations d'Edfou et d'El-Qa'la ne remet pas en cause le caractère osirien intrinsèque de l'offrande des dattes. Il constitue simplement un exemple de rite détourné au profit d'une autre divinité. Une explication probante fait toutefois encore défaut pour expliquer un tel détournement.

L'étude des textes du temple ptolémaïque et romain de Tôd permet donc d'observer quelques particularités lexicographiques, de préciser la chronologie relative aux phases décoratives et d'appréhender les jeux auxquels les prêtres de Montou se sont adonnés. La poursuite de l'édition des textes de ce temple et l'étude des nombreux blocs épars ne manqueront certainement pas d'apporter à leur tour de nouveaux éléments pour la connaissance de ce temple du Palladium thébain.

(à suivre...)

Addendum au § 2 : Mlle Elsa Rickal me signale la séquence *mtr m ir.ty* « témoin oculaire » (*Urk.* IV, 503, 3) qui pourrait également être à l'origine de l'appellation de la palette de scribe.

Notes:

1 J.-Cl. Grenier, *Tôd. Les inscriptions du temple ptolémaïque et romain I. La salle hypostyle, textes n° 1-172*, FIFAO 18/1, (Le Caire, 1980).

2 Pour l'histoire de l'édition des textes de ce temple, J. Vandier, « Le temple de Tôd », dans *Textes et langages de l'Égypte pharaonique. Cent cinquante années de recherches 1822-1972. Hommage à Jean-François Champollion*, BdE 64/3, (Le Caire, 1974), 259-265 ; J.-Cl. Grenier, « L'édition des textes du temple de Tôd », dans *L'Égyptologie en 1979. Axes Prioritaires de Recherches* 2, (Paris, 1982), 75-78 ; Chr. Thiers, *Tôd. Les inscriptions du temple ptolémaïque et romain II. Textes et scènes n°s 173-329*, FIFAO 18/2, (Le Caire, à paraître).

3 Pour une description de ces scènes, F. Bisson de la Roque, *Tôd (1934 à 1936)*, FIFAO 17, (Le Caire, 1937), 18-24.

4 Voir également Chr. Thiers, « Copies et citations à Tôd : le cas des Dieux maîtres d'autel (*Tôd*, n°s 314-315) », BIFAO 100 (2000), 393-402. La note concernant le roi au visage léonin présentée lors du congrès (*Eighth International Congress of Egyptologists Cairo, 28 March-3 April 2000. Abstracts of Papers*, (Le Caire, 2000), 182), ne doit pas être prise en compte.

5 M.-L. Ryhiner, *L'Offrande du lotus dans les temples égyptiens de l'époque tardive*, Rites Égyptiens VI, (Bruxelles, 1986), 134-136 (n° 55).

6 A. Egberts, *In Quest of Meaning. A Study of the Ancient Egyptian Rites of Consecrating the* Meret-Chests *and Driving the Calves*, Egyptologische Uitgaven 8, (Leyde, 1995), 160-165

7 D. Wildung, *Imhotep und Amenhotep. Gottwerdung im alten Ägypten*, MÄS 36, (Munich, 1977), 241-244.

8 J.-Cl. Grenier, « Une scène d'offrande à Astarté (Inscription *Tôd* n° 281) », dans Fr. Geus - Fl. Thill (éd.), *Mélanges offerts à Jean Vercoutter*, (Paris, 1985), 107-110.

9 E. Winter, « Der Herrscherkult in den ägyptischen Ptolemäertempeln », dans H. Maehler - M. Stocka (éd.), *Das ptolemäische Ägypten. Akten des internationalen Symposions 27.-29. September 1976 in Berlin*, (Mayence, 1978), 151 ; J.-Cl. Grenier, « Ptolémée Évergète II et Cléopâtre II d'après les textes de Tôd », dans N. Bonacasa - A. di Vista (éd.), *Alessandria e il mondo ellenistico-romano. Studi in onore di Achille Adriani* 1, StudMat Institut.o di archeologica, Università di Palermo 4, (Rome, 1983), 32-37 ; en dernier lieu, M. Minas, *Die hieroglyphischen Ahnenreihen der ptolemäischen Könige*, AegTrev 9, (Mayence, 2000), 24-25 (51).

10 C. Husson, *L'offrande du miroir dans les temples égyptiens de l'époque gréco-romaine*, (Lyon, 1977).

11 S. Cauville, « Une offrande spécifique d'Osiris : le récipient de dattes (*m^rd3 n bnr*)», RdE 32, (1980), 47-64.

12 M.-Cl. Mialon, « L'offrande du bijou liturgique *beb* dans les grands sanctuaires ptolémaïques et romains », *Kyphi* 1 (1998), 63-84.

13 J.-L. Simonet, *Le collège des dieux maîtres d'autel. Nature et histoire d'une figure tardive de la religion égyptienne*, OrMonsp 7, (Montpellier, 1994). Pour ces deux scènes, Chr. Thiers, BIFAO 100, (2000), 393-402.

14 D. Meeks, « L'Horus de *Tb(y)* », dans W. Clarysse, A. Schoors et H. Willems (éd.), *Egyptian Religion. The Last Thousand Years. Studies J. Quaegebeur* 2, OLA 85/2, (1998), 1181-1190 ; en *Tôd*, n° 263, 7, Nekhbet est « souveraine des provinces de *Tb* ».

15 M.-Th. Derchain-Urtel, *Thot à travers ses épithètes dans les scènes d'offrandes des temples d'époque gréco-romaine*, Rites Égyptiens 3, (Bruxelles, 1981), 1-26.

16 S. Cauville, « À propos des désignations de la palette de scribe », RdE 38, (1987), 185-187.

17 Pour la lecture *mti* au lieu de *mtr*, voir J. Osing, *Die Nominalbildung des Ägyptischen* 2, (Mayence, 1976), 643, n. 672 (cité par *AnLex* 77.1922).

18 *AnLex* 79.1403 pour les trois séquences.

19 *AnLex* 77.1922 et 78.1901.

20 P. Boylan, *Thoth, the Hermes of Egypt*, (Oxford, 1922), 88–97 en particulier ; M.-Th. Derchain-Urtel, *op. cit.*, 51–94.

21 Boylan, *Thot*, 187 (avec réf.) ; par ex. *Esna*, n° 309, 26–27 : « je suis le témoin des deux, qui sépare Horus de Seth » ; d'après Fr. Labrique, « Rapiéçage ou réécriture ? La porte d'Évergète, le temple d'Esna », dans W. Clarysse, A. Schoors et H. Willems (éd.), *Studies J. Quaegebeur* 2, 895 et n. 61.

22 *LD Text* IV, 12. Une partie de cette dédicace, sur le mur sud, n'est plus en place, le mur ayant jadis été démonté pour étudier le grand texte de Sésostris Ier.

23 G. Pierrat *et al.*, « Fouilles du musée du Louvre à Tôd, 1988–1991 », *Karnak* 10, (1995), 473.

24 De nombreux blocs épars portent également les cartouches de ce Lagide, témoignant d'aménagements plus importants que ce qu'il est donné de voir.

25 *Tôd*, 22 et 152.

26 Les nombreux blocs épars appartenant au mur extérieur de la salle hypostyle (mur sud en particulier) livrent à de nombreuses reprises le nom du Romain.

27 Lire ⚏ et non ⚏ donné par Lepsius.

28 En accord avec la séquence d'Edfou (*infra*, n. 33), lire *psd<.f>* plutôt que *wbn<.f>*.

29 Lire *s.t <t>n* plutôt que *s.t n(.t) k3* ; d'après le parallèle fourni par une dalle de plafond gisant à proximité du temple (Bisson inv. 575).

30 Lire *k3w.s r-mtr.s*.

31 *Philä* I, 172 ; H. De Meulenaere, « Ptolémée IX Sôter II à Kalabcha », *CdE* 36, (1961), 104–105 ; G. Hölbl, *A History of the Ptolemaic Empire*, (Londres, 2001), 205–206 ; W. Huss, *Ägypten in hellenistischer Zeit 332–30 v.Chr.*, (Munich, 2001), 632 ; M. Chauveau, *L'Égypte au temps de Cléopâtre 180–30 av. J.-C.*, (Paris, 1997), 58 et n. 17.

32 *GLdR* IV, p. 361 (LII).

33 *Edfou* VII, 1, 9–11 ; J. von Beckerath, *Handbuch der ägyptischen Königsnamen*, MÄS 49, (Berlin, 1999), 242–243.

34 Ce terme apparaît dans des épithètes royales et divines ; Wilson, *Ptolemaic Lexikon*, 493–494 ; J. Osing, *Hieratische papyri aus Tebtunis* I, The Carlsberg Papyri 2, CNIP 17, (Copenhague, 1998), 292 et n. d (*ntr n῾š*). L'absence de déterminatif reste problématique.

35 On sait pourtant que le premier règne de Sôter II a été marqué par une activité architecturale et décoratrice relativement conséquente ; Thiers, *Le Pharaon lagide « bâtisseur ». Analyse historique de la construction des temples à l'époque ptolémaïque*, thèse inédite, (Montpellier, 1997).

36 S. Cauville - D. Devauchelle, « Le temple d'Edfou : étapes de la construction, nouvelles données historiques », *RdE* 35, (1984), 52–53.

37 Grenier, dans *Mélanges Vercoutter*, 107, n. 7 : « la "Salles des Déesses" postérieure aux constructions du règne de Ptolémée Évergète II semble antérieure à celles de Ptolémée Aulète : elle date donc des environs de 100 av. J.-C. ».

38 Cauville, *RdE* 32, (1980), 47–64 ; Cauville, *La théologie d'Osiris à Edfou*, BdE 91, (Le Caire, 1983), 176.

39 Cauville, *RdE* 32, (1980), 57–60.

40 Simonet, *Collège*, 49–50.

41 Simonet, *Collège*, 52–53, n. h a souligné le rapprochement phraséologique entre les deux types d'offrandes (bouquets montés et dattes). Cet auteur a également noté que la séquence *῾rf in 3s.t swr sn ntr.w* se retrouvait dans un rituel d'offrande de la bière (*Edfou* XV, 29, 3).

42 Thiers, *BIFAO* 100, (2000), 394–395.

43 Pour l'expression *nfr ḥr*, voir Fr. Labrique, *Stylistique et théologie à Edfou*, OLA 51, (Louvain, 1992), 198, n. 897 ; Y. Volokhine, *Le visage dans la pensée et la religion de l'Égypte ancienne* (à paraître).

44 Simonet, *Collège*, 53 ; Wilson, *Ptolemaic Lexikon*, 417, *s. v. m(ꜥ)d3*.

45 Ptah-tenen est représenté en *Tôd*, nᵒˢ 131 et 237.

46 Voir les remarques analogues de Cauville, *RdE* 32, (1980), 64.

47 Pour une scène presque similaire avec l'offrande à Ptah sous son dais, voir par ex. P. Clère, *La Porte d'Évergète à Karnak*, MIFAO 84, (Le Caire, 1961), pl. 28.

Imports at Zawiyet Umm al-Rakham

Susanna Thomas
University of Liverpool

Zawiyet Umm al-Rakham is the largest known example, and probably the furthest west in the chain of fortresses built by Ramesses II. They were built in response to the growing unrest that threatened Egypt from Libya (to the west) and the Mediterranean Sea (to the north) during the Late Bronze Age.

Situated approximately 300 km west of Alexandria, and 15 km west of the nearest modern town of Mersa Matruh, the fortress is located at the narrowest point of a plain between the high desert edge and the coast. The land surrounding the fortress has limestone outcrops and poor, stony soil. A team from the University of Liverpool under the direction of Steven Snape has been working at Zawiyet Umm al-Rakham since 1994. In six seasons of excavation, approximately one-sixth of the site has been investigated.[1]

The fortress is approximately 100 m from the foot of the escarpment, and consists of a square installation with perimeter walls each 140 m long and between four and five meters thick, containing an area of approximately 20,000 square meters. The perimeter walls were constructed of mud brick courses with stone facing on the lower part of the exterior. There is still evidence of a plastered ramp or *glacis* at the foot of the walls. There appear to have been a series of towers at the corners of the walls (work is still ongoing in these areas), and the approach to the only gateway, situated in the middle of the northern wall, was along a heavily fortified corridor. An additional area was enclosed to the north of the fortress at a later date, although its purpose, perhaps as an extra living area or stables for horses and chariots, is as yet unclear.

The substantial size of the perimeter walls and the defensive nature of the positioning of the installation indicate that the fortress had a serious military role, and was built to withstand attack. The whole expanse of the plain between the fortress and the sea is clearly visible from the site, and would have been controlled by the occupants.

The main temple at the site was built against the west perimeter wall and is constructed of large limestone blocks. Immediately to the north of the temple is a series of nine magazines 16 m long

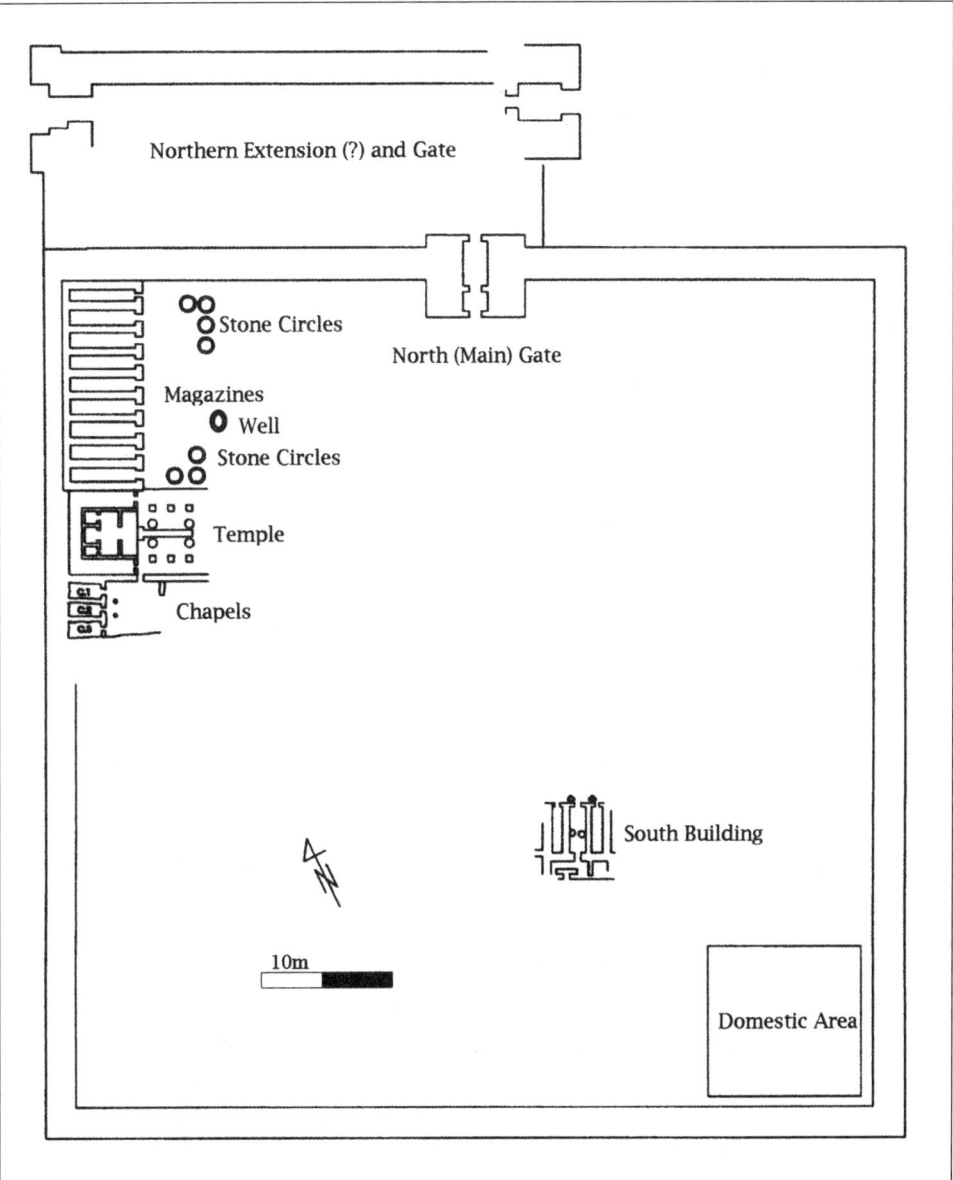

Fig. 1: Plan of the site after the 1999 season.

and 3 m wide, built of mud brick. They have limestone jambs and lintels inscribed with the titu-
lary of Ramesses II. In front of the magazines is a well inscribed with the cartouches of Ramesses
II, surrounded by a group of seven small, circular stone features (possibly huts or animal pens),
which may have been built by later squatters after the site was abandoned by the Egyptians.
Immediately to the south of the temple are three chapels facing onto a walled courtyard.

Other features include an enigmatic structure (known as the South Building) consisting of a series of rooms and corridors surrounded by a large perimeter wall, all constructed of small stones. Some of the rooms contain single standing monoliths, and all the doorways have inscribed jambs and lintels, some with the titles of Ramesses II and others featuring the commander of the fort, Neb-Re, worshipping the king's cartouches. An area in the southeast corner of the fortress, where excavation is ongoing, contains a series of small three-roomed houses grouped around communal ovens.

Excavations have uncovered substantial amounts of complete ceramic vessels and shard material from all areas of the site. Many of these are foreign imports, including Canaanite amphorae, Cypriote flasks, white shaved and Base Ring II wares, *stirrup* jars, Late Minoan jugs, and Mycenean finewares.

Canaanite amphorae represent the biggest single type of foreign pottery identified so far at the site. One of the magazines contained two complete jars and one broken jar fallen forward from their original placement against the side (north) wall of the magazine, and five others smashed in the magazine corridor, on the steps and threshold. One of the chapels had two amphorae still standing in the northeast corner by the door, and another smashed in front of the threshold. Three more amphorae were found in association with many other imported and local pottery types in the squatter area around the stone circles. One was found still standing against the wall of a courtyard area to the south of the stone circles, in association with a tall pottery stand and bowl and an inscribed scarab, in what was possibly an area of cult or votive practice. Most vessels were empty, but one pot contained a mass of unidentified small bird bones, and can be compared with an amphora containing fowl found at Malkata.[2]

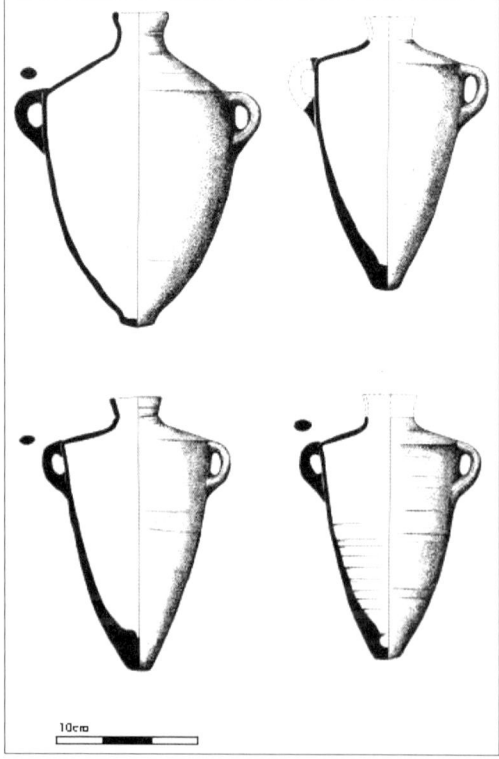

Canaanite amphorae have ovoid or piriform bodies and pointed, rounded, or stump bases with two large vertical loop handles opposite each other, attached just below the shoulder. The neck and mouth are narrow enough to stop, but wide enough for easy pouring or extraction of the contents, and an average-size person could insert an arm inside. It has been suggested that a more triangular profile developed during, and is an indicator of, the Late Bronze Age.[3] However, a variety of rounded and more piriform profiles have been discovered together at Zawiyet Umm al-Rakham.

Although Canaanite amphorae are thought to have contained primarily Syrian and Palestinian wine, it should be noted that the final contents of the amphora were often a completely different product. These amphorae seem to have been used and

Fig. 2: Canaanite amphorae (drawn by C. Thorpe).

reused many times to transport a wide variety of food and drink commodities. Evidence from the Ulu Burun shipwreck[4] also demonstrates that they held non-edible items such as resins, glass beads, and perfumed oils, and even other smaller ceramic vessels.

Fifteen complete Canaanite amphorae have been found at Zawiyet Umm al-Rakham so far, as well as various shards including five handles, two with pot marks, from five different jars. This assemblage comprises the largest group of intact Canaanite amphorae known in Egypt. Canaanite amphorae are also known from various New Kingdom sites in Egypt, including Ghurob, Malkata, Amarna, Deir al-Medina, Memphis, Avaris-Piramesse, and the Ramesseum. Evidence was until recently weighted in favor of cemetery sites. However, current work at major New Kingdom settlement sites such as Amarna, Memphis, and Piramesse has shown that Canaanite amphorae were present in significant numbers in domestic contexts.

The fabrics of the amphorae found at Zawiyet Umm al-Rakham conform to those found at Kommos in Southern Crete.[5] The so-called "southern group" have light red or reddish-brown fabric and are common in Palestine particularly between Jaffa and Gaza, whereas the "northern group" are concentrated in sites between Akko and Ugarit, and have reddish or grey bodies. All of these amphorae have a pale green/white surface. This was apparently achieved by dipping the vessels into salt (probably sea) water prior to firing, rather than by the application of a separate wash or slip, and is demonstrated by the total coverage of the vessel both inside and out.[6]

Five tall coarse ware stirrup jars have so far been found at Zawiyet Umm al-Rakham, and one small fine decorated jar. These were found in association with other imported wares in the magazines and chapels. The form has been described as representing Mycenaean and Aegean activity and influence in every area reached by them and their products until the end of the Bronze Age.[7]

Large stirrup jars were almost certainly used to transport olive oil. Much work has been done on the Cretan olive oil industry[8] and it is likely that the jars found at the site originally contained this prestigious foodstuff. The particular shape of the jar, with the bulbous body, solid central handles and a slightly offset spout, is well suited to contain and dispense liquids, and it has been suggested that the shape appears to have been specifically designed to facilitate the extraction of the contents of thin, pourable oil.[9] Other possible contents include olives, honey, wine, dried grain, or fruit.

Hankey suggested that similar jars found at Amarna and Deir al-Medina had arrived in Egypt via Cyprus through Aegean trade routes with the Eastern Mediterranean.[10] Cypro-Minoan pot marks, sometimes found on the handles,[11] (including the jar from Amarna and two from Zawiyet Umm al-Rakham) suggest that such pots must have passed through, if not been originally fired by, Cypriot hands.

Only one large coarse ware stirrup jar has previously been identified in a Nineteenth Dynasty context in Egypt, in Tomb 59 in a Ramesside cemetery at Sedment.[12] This tomb also contained Egyptian imitations of fine ware stirrup jars. The base of one handle is also known from Amarna,[13] and one shard has been identified from Deir al-Medina.[14]

Small fine ware stirrup jars are thought to have contained limited amounts of expensive perfumed oil.[15] Examples similar to that found at Zawiyet Umm al-Rakham are known from Ghurob and Amarna. One stirrup jar from Ghurob is thought to have come either from the Greek mainland or the islands rather than from a Mycenaean colony in Cyprus,[16] and another possibly came from somewhere in the Levant.[17] Both of these were found in an undisturbed Nineteenth Dynasty burial.

The coarse ware stirrup jars from Zawiyet Umm al-Rakham all conform to the third type recognized from Chania, a tall jar with a dark pattern on a light background.[18] One example from the magazines is pale cream/gray with faint red banding, while another is cream with bold red/black banding. The decoration of this second jar was quite sloppily applied, and there are splashes of dark paint on the body and in the lip of the spout. Another jar from the chapels is creamy yellow with red banding around the body, wavy lines around the shoulder and lines around the handles and spout.

One vessel type found at Zawiyet Umm al-Rakham, and described for convenience as feeder cups, is much more unusual. Any discussion is hampered by the fact that few parallels are known. Six have been found so far at the site, five in one magazine and one in the corridor outside the entrance to another magazine. Four of these vessels were found together in a group, which suggests they had originally been stored together in a bag or basket which perished. They are all small (10–12 cm high) pots, with bulbous bodies and a base ring foot, and have one spout set at approximately 90 degrees to their single handle. Rather than lids, they exhibit integral strainer tops, with rather random (between five and seven) holes punched in from above. They are currently thought to be Cypriot, based on visible fabric and decoration. The bodies are orangey/red, and all show traces of white lines on the top, body and around the handle and spout.

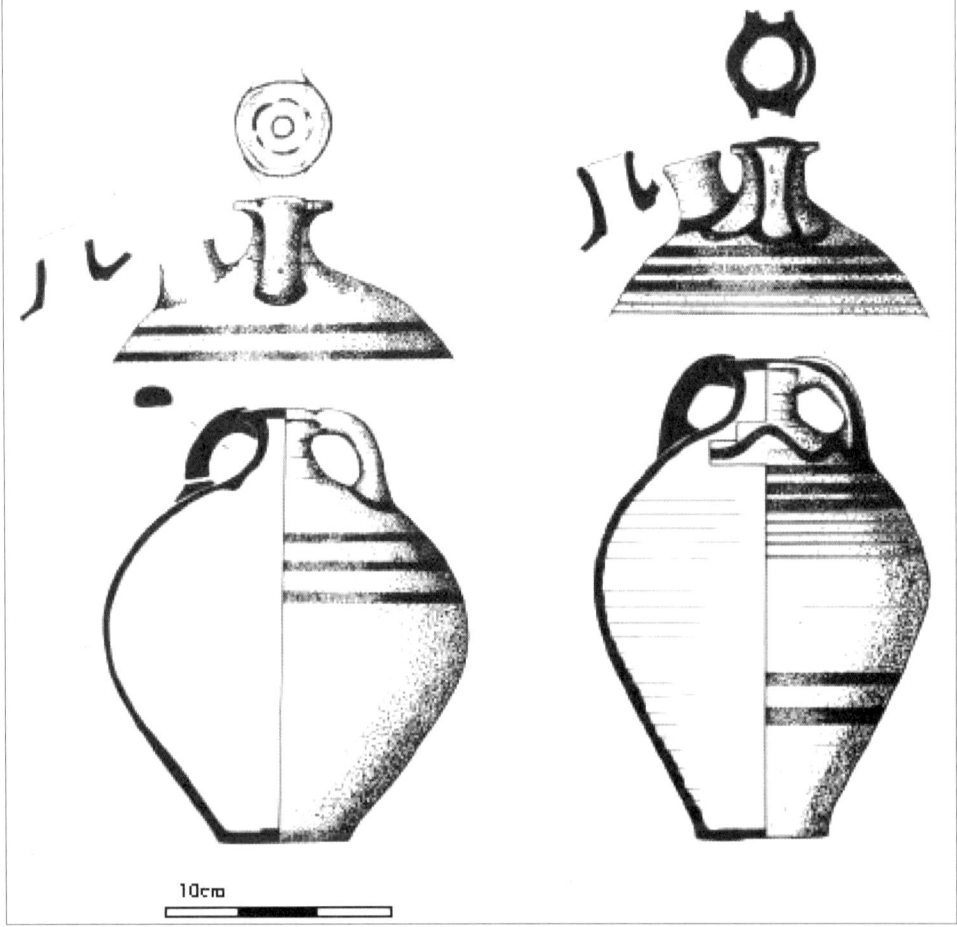

Fig. 3: Coarse-ware *stirrup* jars (drawn by C. Thorpe).

Fig. 4: 'Feeder cups' (drawn by C. Thorpe).

The form is not unknown, although it is classified as extremely rare. One similar jug is discussed by Yon,[19] and described as Late Cypriot Base Ring I, with the main opening at the top closed and then pierced with holes. In this case she suggested that the central slightly larger hole was used to fill the jug, and that the smaller holes around the edge were for straining whatever was contained. The vessels were either transported with their contents already inside or perhaps were a necessary or useful implement. It is hard to envisage how the contents could have been kept secure during transport. The spout is blockable, but the strainer top exhibits no visible means of securing a cover.[20] However, if these vessels were a clever tool to help with the consumption of something known to the Cypriots at least, why have no parallels been found at other sites? Honey and/or opium seem possible candidates for substances that were strained and served in small quantities, or perhaps oil that had been flavored or perfumed by vegetable or fibrous matter that needed to be removed before use. A final consideration is that these were pots could have been manufactured specifically for an Egyptian market. However,

527

no examples have been found at any other Egyptian site, and there are no illustrations of this type of ware.

It is currently believed that non-Egyptian trade items arrived at the site from Crete. Few other maritime origins are feasible, and there is a wealth of evidence from the Classical Period to illustrate that the southern Crete-Egypt route was accepted in the itinerary of sailings. Other possible explanations are that the products arrived either overland or by coastal sail from Egypt. However, the bulk of ceramic evidence is foreign (Mediterranean) rather than from the Nile Valley. If such products arrived from Crete, then it seems most likely that the ship either arrived from, or had at least stopped at, the port site of Kommos.

Kommos is a large Bronze Age town with a harbor complex in south central Crete. Foreign pottery found at the site includes wares from the Aegean, Greece, Anatolia, Cyprus, Syria/Palestine, and Egypt. Egyptian vases from LM IIIA contexts (contemporary with Amenhotep III) are most numerous at the site.[21] However, imported vessels dating from LM IIIB, including Egyptian storage jars, indicate that the site continued to be part of an active international trading network into the reign of Ramesses II. As at Zawiyet Umm al-Rakham, coarse-ware *stirrup* jars from Chania were found in "final floor deposits" in the town.[22] Watrous believes that the presence of Egyptian pottery at Kommos indicates that direct Egyptian-Cretan maritime contact occurred, with Kommos and Knossos playing central roles in such interchanges. With the discovery of similar classes of foreign pottery at Zawiyet Umm al-Rakham, it can be suggested that this site was also an important station on the route during the reign of Ramesses II, contradicting the view accepted by many that direct Crete-Egypt contact had ceased by the end of the Eighteenth Dynasty.

The primary function of the fort at Zawiyet Umm al-Rakham was undoubtedly a military one, and concerned monitoring and controlling local groups as well as incursions from the west and north. Nonetheless, the ceramic evidence from the site, as well as its advantageous positioning on the Mediterranean littoral, indicates that it was also a center for trade or exchange. It is not yet possible to establish what percentage of the activity of the fort was occupied by this secondary function, although future archaeological discoveries may clarify the situation.

Notes:

1 S. R. Snape, "Walls, wells and wandering merchants: Egyptian control of Marmarica in the Late Bronze Age," in C. J Eyre, (ed.) *Proceedings of the Seventh International Congress of Egyptologists* (Leuven, 998), 1081–1084; S. Snape and P. Wilson, *Zawiyet Umm el-Rakham I: Temple and Chapels* (Liverpool, 2000).

2 Compare with an amphora found with fowl in at Malkata (W. C. Hayes, "Inscriptions from the Palace of Amenhotep III," *JNES* 10 (1951), 92. See also the fowling scene in the tomb of Nakht, where birds are netted, and then plucked, gutted and sun dried before being stored in amphorae, (N. de Garis Davies, *The Tomb of Nakht at Thebes* (New York, 1917), 69–70, Pls. XXII–XXIII.

3 R. Amiran, *Ancient Pottery of the Holy Land, from Its Beginnings in the Neolithic Period to the End of the*

Iron Age (Jerusalem, 1969), 42; A. Leonard, "'Canaanite Jars' and the Late Bronze Age Aegeo-Levantine Wine Trade," in P. E. McGovern, S. J. Fleming and S. H. Katz, (eds.) *The Origins and Ancient History of Wine* (Philadelphia, 1995), 237.

4 G. F. Bass, "Oldest Known Shipwreck Reveals Bronze Age Splendors," *National Geographic* 172, 6 (1987), 693–733.

5 L. V. Watrous, *Kommos III: The Late Bronze Age Pottery* (Princeton, 1992), 159–161, figs. 71 and 72.

6 Eliezer Oren, personal communication.

7 A. Leonard, "Considerations of Morphological Variation in the Mycenaean Pottery From the Southeastern Mediterranean," *BASOR* 241 (1981), 87–101; A. Leonard, M. Hughes, A. Middleton, and L. Schofield, "The Making of Aegean *Stirrup* jars: technique, tradition and trade," *BSA* 88 (1993), 105–124; V. Hankey, "*Stirrup* Jars at Al-Amarna," in W. V. Davies and L. Schofield (eds.) *Egypt, the Aegean and the Levant* (London, 1993), 116–124.

8 H. W. Haskell, "Coarse-ware stirrup-jars at Mycenae," *BSA* 76 (1981), 225–238; E. Hallager, "The Inscribed Stirrup Jars: Implications for Late Minoan IIIB Crete," *AJA* 91 (1987), 173–190.

9 Leonard, *Mycenaean Pottery*, 91; A. B. Knapp, "Spice, Drugs, Grain and Grog: Organic Goods in Bronze Age East Mediterranean Trade," in N. H. Gale, (ed.), *Bronze Age Trade in the Mediterranean* (Jonsered, 1991), 29–30.

10 Hankey, "Stirrup," 117.

11 Hallager, *Inscribed Stirrup Jars*; N. Hirschfeld, "Incised marks (post firing) on Aegean Wares," in C. Zerner (ed.) *Wace and Blegen: Pottery as Evidence for Trade in the Aegean Bronze Age* (Amsterdam, 1993), 311–318.

12 W.M.F Petrie and G. Brunton *Sedment* I, II (London, 1924) 25, Pl. LIX) suggest an Eighteenth Dynasty date, but B. J. Kemp and R. S. Merrillees in *Minoan Pottery in Second Millennium Egypt* (Mainz, 1980), 246, argue persuasively for a Ramesside date.

13 J. Bourriau, *Umm el-Ga'ab: Pottery from the Nile Valley before the Arab Conquest* (Cambridge, 1981), 124–125. Bourriau thinks that the shard is not of Mycenaean origin (due to the coarse fabric and lack of technical skill), but certainly contained olive oil, *contra* Pendlebury who excavated the shard and thought it came from a wine or water jar.

14 M. R. Bell, "Preliminary Report on the Mycenaean Pottery from Deir al-Medina," *ASAE* (1982), 68, 151.

15 K. Cook, "The Purpose of the *Stirrup* Vase," *BSA* (1981), 76,167

16 Bourriau, *Umm al-Ga'ab*, 126.

17 Bourriau , *Umm al-Ga'ab*, 137.

18 L. V. Watrous, *Kommos III: The Late Bronze Age Pottery* (Princeton, 1992), 150.

19 M. Yon, *Manuel de Céramique Chypriote I* (Lyon, 1976), 103 and fig 37b.

20 See Leonard, *Mycenaean Pottery*, figs. 6 and 7, for a suggested lid for a Mycenaean alabastron.

21 Watrous, *Kommos*, 175.

22 Watrous, *Kommos*, 81.

Bioarchaeology of Kafr Hassan Dawood: Preliminary Investigations

Teri L. Tucker
Ohio State University

Introduction

The archaeological site of Kafr Hassan Dawood (KHD) is a cemetery dating to the Terminal Predynastic/Early Dynastic period or Nagada III (*ca.* 3300 to 3100 BCE).[1] Interspersed among the Terminal Predynastic/Early Dynastic graves are Late Period and Ptolemaic burials. This paper will restrict itself to a discussion of the bioarchaeology of the Terminal Predynastic/Early Dynastic period.

Kafr Hassan Dawood is located in the East Nile Delta of Egypt, approximately eight miles south of Tell el Kebeir. The cemetery is located on a low terrace, adjacent to the southern edge of the East Wadi Tumilat and covers an area of approximately 90 x 170 meters.

The focus of bioarchaeological research at KHD is to understand how the political and economic dimensions of an emerging state affected local and regional populations. Specifically, how did the emergence of centralized authority and a changing political and economic landscape affect the lives of people within a peripheral community? What were the effects of these dynamics on the biology and culture of the population at KHD? By examining variations in mortuary patterns coupled with biological histories, it is possible to demonstrate how local and regional communities interacted with large-scale political and economic processes.

Archaeological excavations were begun at KHD in 1989 by the Supreme Council of Antiquities (SCA), directed by M. El-Moslamy and Mohammed Salem El-Hangouri. In the earlier seasons of excavation, all cultural material was removed and transferred to the Zagazig Museum, but in later seasons the graves were only partially excavated and human remains and artifacts were left *in situ* in order to create an 'Open-air Museum.' A plastic greenhouse was constructed over a portion of the cemetery in order to protect the burials.

A total of 920 graves were dealt with in this in this manner until 1995, when the SCA invited Fekri Hassan, Petrie Professor of Archaeology at University College London, to assemble an international team and develop a program of research and conservation for the site. An important aspect of the research design at KHD is to incorporate an intensive training program for all participants in the program, including inspectors from the SCA. The training program emphasizes hands-on experience in the field combined with a series of lectures on relevant topics. As a result, everyone participating in the KHD excavations have specific one-on-one training in bioarchaeology, both in the field and in the laboratory.

Bioarchaeology field methods

Since 1995, the excavation strategy at KHD includes a physical anthropologist in the field during excavation of all skeletal material. This ensures that all valuable skeletal information is recorded, including teeth, which are often overlooked, and may be the only surviving element of some poorly-preserved burials. Additional field methods include planning the burial at a 1:5 scale, photographing the burial in both black and white as well as color, and noting all measurements and pathological lesions while the remains are still *in situ*.

Generally, the skeletal preservation at KHD is poor. During the 1995 field season, rib samples from five skeletons were processed for collagen extraction by Dr. Nancy Lovell (University of Alberta). Her analysis revealed that all organic material had been completely destroyed by diagenetic processes. The poor preservation and the friable and fragmentary nature of the bones warranted the use of consolidants in the field. This was only used to prevent further damage during exposure of the skeleton for *in situ* recording and photography. A 10 percent solution of Paraloid B72 was applied using a pipette, sable brush, or syringe where appropriate. Additionally, a program of block-lifting multiple and disarticulated skeletons was incorporated. Using polyurethane foam, complex areas of the skeleton were lifted and removed for careful cleaning in a controlled laboratory setting. After excavation, all skeletal material was analyzed on site following the guidelines outlined in "The Standards for Data Collection from Human Skeletal Remains."[2] No destructive techniques were employed and only data obtained from macro-observations were collected for this study.

Results and Discussion

The total number of graves identified at KHD is 1095, of these 744 have been dated to the Terminal Predynastic/Early Dynastic. It is important to keep in mind that biological data has been collected only from 1995. Since that time, 169 graves out of the total 1,095 have been examined for age, sex, and skeletal indicators of health.

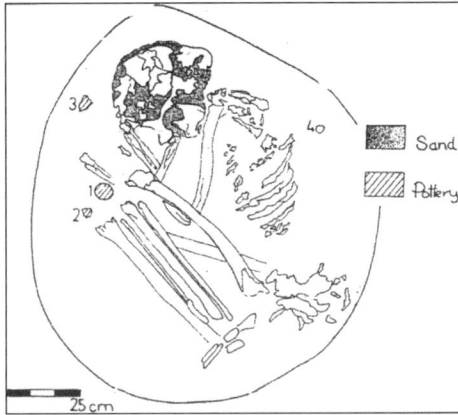

Figure 1: Burial 1035.

531

The majority of graves dating to the Terminal Predynastic/Early Dynastic cemetery contain single burials, however, multiple and secondary burials were also recorded. Most graves are simple oval pits, generally measuring 110 cm by 80 cm. However, large rectangular tombs and oval ceramic coffins were also found. Generally, Nile mud from the floodplain was used as burial fill and local sand, silt, and gravel were used to construct a mound over the burial. All rectangular tombs contained numerous grave goods of varying types, whereas the small oval pits had few, if any, grave items.[3] However in the majority of graves, regardless of grave type or occupant, a crude and poorly-fired shard was interred with the burial. In several instances the shard was clutched in the deceased's hand, but it was also found at the wrists, face, sacrum, or scapula (see fig. 1).

Of the burials excavated from 1995–1999, the majority (53%, n = 60) were oriented along a N/S axis, either flexed or tightly flexed with the head oriented north. However, 17% were disarticulated and 2% were loosely flexed.[4] Many of the burials were tightly flexed; implying that the bodies were bound and not interred until sometime after the flesh desiccated. Additionally, 20% of all burials were missing several phalanges from the hands and feet, or the phalanges were found at higher elevations of the grave in areas not associated with the rest of the burial. Although there is no evidence of cut marks on any of the skeletal material, it is conceivable that the phalanges were 'lost' either at time of interment or during a period of intentional "mummification." As the flesh desiccates, the areas of the skeleton that are not supported by much connective tissue, such as the phalanges, carpals, become weak and detach readily. Thus, the evidence suggests that the population at KHD allowed the dead to desiccate naturally and then transported the bodies to the graves.

Six graves contained multiple, disarticulated burials and all but one were located in the north area of the cemetery, which is considered the oldest area of the cemetery.[5] One grave (#1015) contained a minimum number of four individuals: a male aged 17–25 years, a female aged 25–35 years, a child aged 8–14 and, an individual of unknown sex aged greater than 45 years at time of death. A second burial (#1027) consisted of a minimum number of three individuals; one female aged 25–35 years, a male aged 25–35 years and an isolated mandible from an individual aged approximately 12 years.

Figure 2: Burials 1015, 1027.

Due to the close proximity of these graves, it is possible that the mandible of the child from grave 1027 may be associated with the child's cranium from grave 1015 (see fig. 2). However, due to the fragmentary nature of the skeletal material this cannot be determined conclusively.

At this time, there is no satisfactory explanation for the disturbed and secondary nature of these burials. It is possible that the burials were disturbed during robbing, however grave 1027 contained numerous grave items including copper needles, three knife flints, agate beads, and several pots. Another possible explanation is that the burials were disturbed by the later inter-

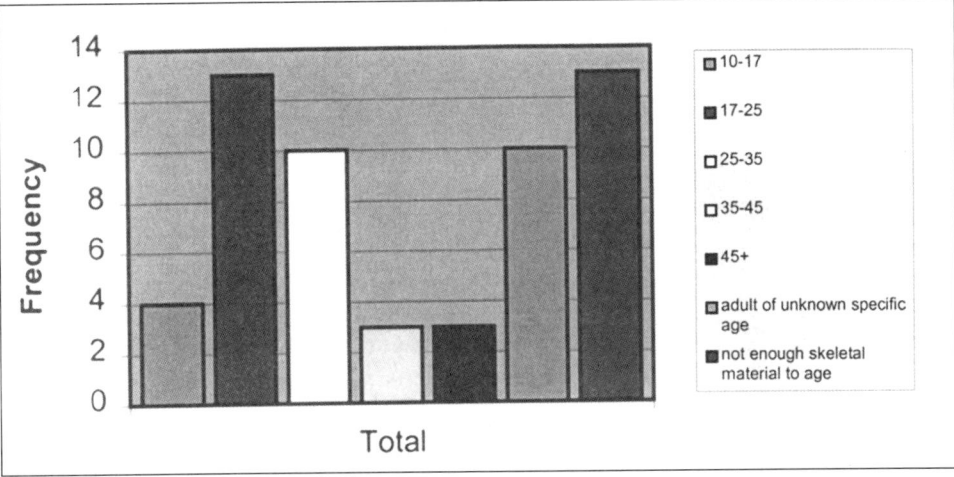

Figure 3: Age Distribution for KHD.

ments, however the archaeological record does not support this. A third possibility is that the burials were intentionally interred in a disarticulated and commingled arrangement. It is worth considering that these burials may be the result of dismemberment that occurred either at the time of burial or sometime after the body was originally interred.

Because of the friable and fragmentary nature of the skeletal material at KHD, estimation of age at death for most of the adults is imprecise and sex could not be determined in all cases. Of the 60 burials with surviving skeletal material, 37 individuals could be aged using dental eruption and dental wear scores, 10 individuals could only be aged as adult based on long-bone length and development and 13 could not be aged due to lack of surviving skeletal material (fig. 3).

Sex could only be determined for nineteen of the burials. Eleven were assessed as female and seven as male. Since the number of skeletons for which age and sex could be determined is small, it would be premature to suggest that they are entirely representative of the burial population. However, the presence of males, females, and children indicates that the use of the cemetery was not restricted as to age or sex.

Generally, the individuals exhibited good physical health. This is suggested by the lack of skeletal lesions indicating infection or of osteoarthritis. Although certainly the poor preservation may mask the true incidence of disease in this population. Additionally, the early age at death (17–25 years) for most of the population provides valuable clues for reconstructing the quality of life of this ancient population.

Upon closer examination, 55% of the population displayed evidence of linear enamel hypoplasia or LEH (fig. 4). LEH is an indicator of nonspecific stress, signifying that the individual survived severe illness or malnutrition during childhood. LEH appears as transverse defects usually visible on the canines or central incisors. These defects occur when enamel formation is disrupted during the development of the tooth crown. Only burials with preserved central incisors and canines were included in this sample. It is interesting to note that six out of the eight children had evidence of LEH, which may indicate that the illness was severe enough to significantly reduce the life span. Additionally, 64% of individuals with LEH were found in the south part of the cemetery, which is regarded as its latest period of use.

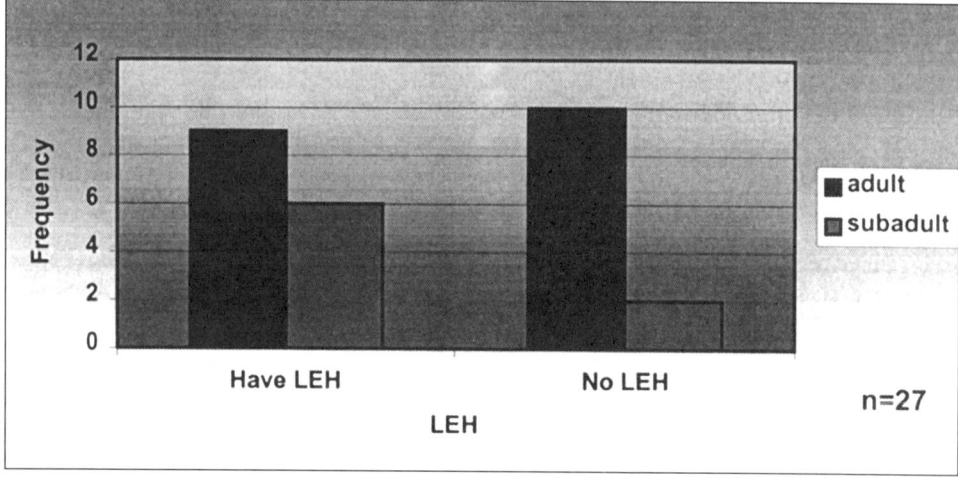

Figure 4: Linear Enamel Hypoplasia by age.

Overall dental health was found to be generally good, since no individual exhibited tooth decay and only one displayed any evidence of *antemortem* tooth loss. However, several showed evidence of calculus (mineralized plaque) including a 12 year-old. Calculus development is facilitated by a variety of factors, including genetics and poor oral hygiene, but it is generally thought to reflect a high proportion of protein in the diet.

Finally, there is no biological evidence to suggest that the population at KHD was exploiting a predominantly cereal-based diet.

Conclusion

In review, it is clear that the cemetery at KHD exhibits variation in grave orientation and burial placement. However, what is less certain is the meaning of the multiple and secondary burials found at KHD. The current paradigm concerning Egyptian Predynastic burial practices suggests that the majority of burials were oriented along a north/south axis in a flexed position. Most information regarding Predynastic mortuary patterns is based on excavations by Petrie and others around the turn of the century. At Naqada, Petrie noted that among intact burials there were many "imperfect burials" with parts missing or displaced after the flesh had rotted away. This led to discussions of ritual dismemberment and even cannibalism. These ideas were later rejected on the basis of probable inaccurate descriptions and flawed excavations.

At KHD, there are no cutmarks on any of the skeletal material, nor is there any other evidence to suggest cannibalism. However, the nature of the secondary and multiple burials at KHD, as well as new evidence from secondary burials at Hierakonopolis and Adaima, warrants a re-examination of these earlier reports.[6] In light of accumulating evidence on secondary burials, we must reconsider the idea of dismemberment as well as other ritual mortuary practices for Predynastic Egypt.

The bioarchaeological evidence from KHD seems to characterize it as a community exploiting regional resources and experiencing a change in social structure and organization. The cemetery at KHD is spatially and temporally organized with the majority of individuals tightly flexed, lying on the left side with the head to the north facing east. Additionally, a majority of multiple and secondary burials were made in the northern area of the cemetery, generally considered the earliest (Terminal Predynastic). In contrast, 64% of the burials with evidence for linear enamel hypoplasia were found in the south (Early Dynastic period). This data, in combination with the earlier age at death for the burials in the southern area of the cemetery, suggest that there was a differential level of health for individuals buried in the northern and southern areas of the cemetery. Thus the bioarchaeological evidence at KHD may be interpreted as signifying a temporal trend in declining health, possibly associated with the consolidation of power of the state.

Notes:

I would like to acknowledge the financial support given to the KHD expedition by UNESCO, National Geographic Foundation, University College London, the Bioanthropology Foundation and the Supreme Council of Antiquities.

1 F. Hassan, et. al, "Kafr Hassan Dawood," *Egyptian Archaeology* 16 (2000), 37–39.

2 J. Buikstra and D. H. Ubelaker, *Standards for data collection from human skeletal remains*, Chicago Field Museum Seminar, (Arkansas, 1994).

3 See Rowland and Hassan 2000, and J. van Wettering 2000, this volume.

4 The term "loosely flexed" implies that the angle between the axis of the trunk and the axis of the femur is between 90 and 180 degrees, "flexed" implies an angle of less than 90 degrees and "tightly flexed" means that the angle approaches zero.

5 See Rowland and Hassan, 2000, this volume.

6 Maish, A. J. and T. L. Tucker 1999. "New Evidence on Predynastic Burial Methods in Egypt" conference paper. *American Journal of Physical Anthropology* 108:28, 29.

The Excavations at Tell Ibrahim Awad (Sharqiya Province) Seasons 1995-2000

Willem M. van Haarlem

Allard Pierson Museum, Amsterdam, Holland / Netherlands-Flemish Institute, Cairo

Tell Ibrahim Awad is situated just outside the village of Umm Agram in a very remote corner of the central part of the Eastern Nile Delta. The highest level is now just ca. 2 m. above the agricultural plain, but must have been higher in earlier times. About 20 years ago, the central part of the Tell was leveled for a fruit orchard. It was selected by the Amsterdam University Survey Expedition for further investigation after a survey of the region.[1] Yearly excavation seasons were initiated in 1988 and have continued up until the present, with a short hiatus in 1991.[2] In Area A, where work has been concentrated on since 1993, foundations of an early Middle Kingdom and earlier temples were found, together with a cemetery.

The Temple

The first temple layer below the Middle Kingdom level, dated as First Intermediate Period / Late Old Kingdom, was partially leveled for the construction of the later temple. It had, however, a completely different layout, size, and orientation.[3] This became clearer in two earlier building phases, which revealed the original architectural concept for this modest, but unparalleled, Old Kingdom temple. In several closed rooms, a large number of vessels such as libation vases and offering stands, apparently with a ritual function, were found. These fell into disuse in the temple, but had to be carefully stored as sacrosanct due to the proximity of the deity.

In the next, slightly lower level with basically the same layout, more rooms were found. They contained hundreds of objects made mainly of faience. They varied from abandoned construction elements, like tiles in many shapes and sizes, to purely votive objects like human and animal figurines (baboons, crocodiles, hippopotami, antelopes, birds, frogs, fish). These are closely related to finds in the early Satet temple at Elephantine.[4] Some, however, are unparalleled, like the shrine models.[5] Other special categories were jewelry (beads, bracelets), small vessels (sometimes dummies), and mace heads.

The ivory objects with close parallels to contemporary finds in Abydos and Hierakonpolis[6]

536

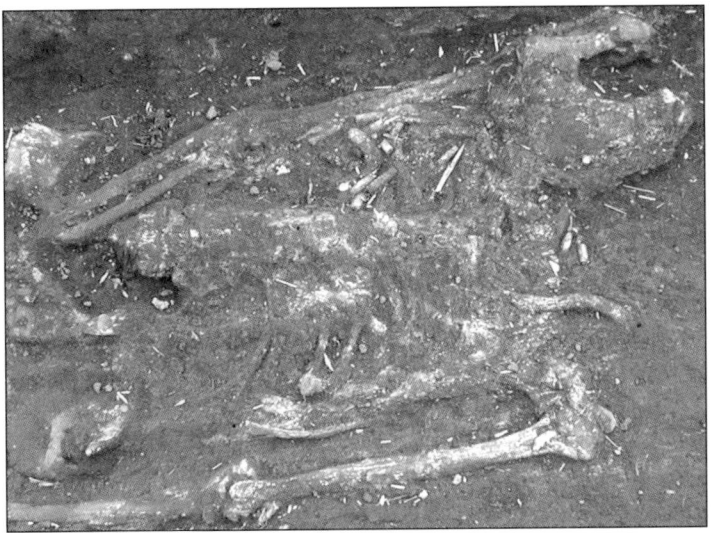

Fig. 1: One of the better preserved burials with the beads of a necklace *in situ.*

deserve special attention: They consist of game pieces (including lions), mace handle covers and similar objects, and figurines, most of which represent humans. The absence of male figures with penis sheaths, particularly common in the Hierakonpolis collection, is noteworthy. The figurines were badly affected by the unfavorable soil conditions (humidity and chemicals), however, the excellence of the craftsmanship is still apparent.

The dates for some of the objects in the deposits go back as far as Dynasty 1 or maybe even earlier.[7]

The temple layout of the lower, Dynasty 1 layer was again quite different from the previous phase. Remains of a large terracotta baboon figurine were found; it might have been a cult statue, but it at least confirms a cultic continuity. Deeper layers were difficult to reach due to the subsoil water; this requires a powerful pumping system. When the lowest temple (probably a reed and wood structure) layer is reached—on the virgin sand of the *gezira*, traced by coring—we will have discovered what is undoubtedly the oldest religious structure in Egypt, dating back to at least 3,400 BCE.

Investigation of the animal bones recovered from the temple area revealed an unexpectedly high number of pig and fish. Apparently, the Egyptian religious taboo concerning these foodstuffs was not yet in operation. The ivory objects appear to have been fabricated mainly from hippopotamus tusks; only a small minority came from elephants. This conforms to expectations, as a number of hippopotamus bones were found in the area. This does not necessarily mean that these objects were produced on the spot, however, it does indicate that in those early times hippopotami occasionally provided an additional meat supply for the population. Cow bones, on the other hand, were quite rare.[8] Several large flint knives found in the area were probably used for the ritual slaughter of sacrificial animals.[9]

The Cemetery

Directly east of the massive temenos wall of the Middle Kingdom temple, a cemetery was discovered. The 60 burials found there so far can be divided into two groups, an earlier and a later.

The earlier group consists of shallow pits with a reed mat lining. There were hardly any grave goods, apart from some beads, and in one case a so-called "button seal."

Another "button" seal was found in a kitchen area nearby. Both seals were dated to the First Intermediate Period. At a slightly lower level, on top of an earlier wall, a seal impression with the Horus name of Userkaf, *jry-m3ct*, (5th Dynasty, ca. 2500 BCE) was found, thus giving a welcome *terminus post quem* for the cemetery. This had already been inferred from the pottery, but this find now confirms it. These graves, the majority in the cemetery, can be dated to the First Intermediate Period. Several contained quantities of red and yellow ochre and plaster. This might have originally covered wooden coffins or lids, but somewhat later evidence from Kom al-Hisn[10] in the Western Delta shows that tombs may have simply been lined with plaster without a wooden backing.

Fig. 2: Detail of a partly preserved female figurine in ivory.

There are indications for an earlier, carefully constructed group of burials in deep rectangular pits, and a later, somewhat shabby group of shallow oval pits. These tombs were poorly equipped; several contained bone beads and only a few had pottery, like the well-known "water bottles" of the period.[11] Recently, similar tombs of the same period have been found at Tell al-Ruba/Mendes.[12] In the very deepest level reached, a surprising brick-lined tomb turned up. This must date at least to the Old Kingdom. and might be the first example of another, earlier type of tomb.

In the later (Middle Kingdom) group, the tombs were lined with mud brick. Some of these contained plastered wooden coffins; the wood had decayed, but the plaster remained, indicating a rectangular shape. Almost all the tombs contained water jars, and in one case, a scarab.[13]

Unfortunately, strata which could have provided more information about the relationship between this cemetery and the temple (apart from their vicinity and contemporaneity) are missing, due to the denudation of the Tell. The fact that the temple mound grew slower than the surrounding town, including the cemetery, due to the more careful clearing of debris there, also complicates things.

Anthropological research on the human remains from the cemetery has revealed a typical population of the time in terms of health and age at death. Mortality caused by violence could not be confirmed in these poorly-preserved remains. The people appear to have been relatively healthy, but—paradoxically—they died at a rather early age (about 20 years old). Young children are so far not represented in this cemetery but it is not unusual for them to be buried elsewhere. Most of the

Fig. 3: A bundle of flint blades and two larger knives hidden under a wall.

538

Fig. 4: Rare burial in flexed position.

individuals were oriented north-south, facing East. Only two were in a flexed position.

The Settlement

Only scattered remains of a settlement were found in Area A. The scarcity of the remains was due mainly to a large pit cut into the Northeast part of the site. This pit had effectively eradicated most traces of a settlement. Indications are that this settlement would have dated back to the First Intermediate Period, as some Old Kingdom housing was found just below the bottom level of the pit. Other remains of First Intermediate Period/Old Kingdom constructions are riddled and cut by tombs, suggesting that this part of the town was eventually taken up by the cemetery. One room showed some kitchen or industrial activity, as it contained several Meidum bowls and beer jars, cattle bones, many sweetwater shells, and a lot of flints, including a scraper and a bundle of blades. The latter were apparently collected in a (since-decayed) bag, and seem to have been deliberately hidden behind some large shells at the base of a wall. A geo-magnetic survey is planned for the near future to clarify the extension of both the settlement and the cemetery.[14]

Summary

The excavations at Tell Ibrahim Awad have thus far yielded a sequence of temple layers ranging from Middle Kingdom to Predynastic times. The Old Kingdom temple contained deposits of hundreds of votive objects, including rare ivory figurines. A cemetery nearby contained mainly simple tombs of the First Intermediate Period. The settlement remains found are rare and confused.

Notes:

1 C. M. Van den Brink, "A Geo-Archaeological Survey in the North-Eastern Nile Delta, Egypt; the First Two Seasons, a Preliminary Report," *MDAIK* 43 (1987), 7–31.

2 The excavations are organized on behalf of the Netherlands Foundation for Archaeological Research in Egypt, with financial support from the Netherlands Organization for Scientific Research. Partners are the Russian Academy of Sciences and the University of Arkansas. Logistical support is provided by the Netherlands–Flemish Institute in Cairo (NVIC).

3 For details, see the Congress paper by D. Eigner.

4 G. Dreyer, *Elephantine VIII: Der Tempel der Satet*, AVDAI 39 (1986). *passim.*

5 W. M. Van Haarlem, "Archaic Shrine Models from Tell Ibrahim Awad," *MDAIK* 54 (1998), 183–185.

6 Respectively, W.M.F. Petrie, *Abydos II* (MEEF 24; London1903). *passim.*, and J. E. Quibell and F. W Green, *Hierakonpolis* I–II (London,1900–1902). *passim.*

7 Van Haarlem, "Archaic," 1998.

8 See also, J. Boessneck and A. Von den Driesch, "Weitere Tierknochenfunde vom Tell Ibrahim Awad im ostlichen Nil Delta," in E.C.M. Van den Brink (ed.), *The Nile Delta in Transition: 4th–3rd Millennium B.C.* (Tel Aviv, 1992), 97–109.

9 Cf. S. Ikram, "Choice Cuts: Meat Production in Ancient Egypt," *OLA* 69 (1995), 63–70.

10 A. Hamada and S. Farid, "Excavations at Kom el-Hisn, Third Season 1946," *ASAE* 48 (1948), 299–308.

11 For example, W.M.F. Petrie, i.a., Sedment I (*BSAE* 34, 1924), Pl. XXXII

12 Personal communications, D. Redford and G. Mumford.

13 Van den Brink, *Nile Delta*, 47, fig. 3.

14 Mud bricks have excellent magnetic properties; see E. B. Pusch, "Palast-Tempel-Auswärtiges Amt? Oder: Sind Nilschlammauern magnetisch zu erfassen?": *ÄL* IX (1999), 135–153.

New Discoveries in the Pyramid of Meidum

Jean-Yves Verd'hurt, Gilles Dormion

The pyramid of Meidum, attributed to the first king of the Fourth Dynasty, Snefru, is known mainly for the successive transformations of its outer mass.

A step monument in its original design, in the tradition of the monuments of Zoser, Sekhemkhet, and Zawiyet al-Aryan, the pyramid of Meidum was built with sides sloping inwards towards the nucleus. Thereafter an enlargement was undertaken, converting the seven-stepped pyramid into a pyramid with eight steps that were filled-in with horizontal-bed masonry, transforming the monument into the first true pyramid. Finally, the collapse and/or the pillage of these casings occurred, giving the pyramid its present characteristic shape.

Such special evolution has often been studied and described, perhaps to the detriment of its inner arrangement. Owing to the limited dimensions of the apartments and the elementary nature of their layout, the pyramid looks quite simple and does not seem to suggest any particular structural dilemma.

A corridor leads downwards, first through the core of the pyramid, then under the level of the rocky plateau, and proceeds horizontally. It is built in a trench hewn in the plateau. At the end of the corridor a vertical shaft leads upwards and opens into a burial chamber which is built at the level of the rock and covered with a corbelled roof. A great anomaly in this architectural arrangement caught our attention, and this study was motivated by its analysis.

The horizontal corridor that connects the descending corridor to the "shaft" leading to the upper chamber has two recesses whose dimensions are 2.60 m NS (5 cubits) x 2.10 m EW (4 cubits) and whose height from the floor—1.75 m—is equal to that of the corridor.

The ceiling shared by the corridor and the "recesses" is made of a succession of lintels forming a flat roof.

At right angles to the "recesses" the span of the lintels is 2.10 m (4 cubits).

Covering a 2.10 m span with a flat roof is quite unusual in the architecture of the Old Kingdom; the builders, aware of the weight involved, usually used the technique of the corbelled roof in order to cover spans of more than 1.05 m (2 cubits).

Considering that,

- the span covered is exceptional for a flat roof
- the lintels do not show any significant cracks

it is hardly likely that the builders of the pyramid of Meidum took the risk of putting the weight directly on these lintels, whose span was so great, and that induced us to think that there was a relieving system above the flat roof itself. Such a device, normally made with a corbelled roof according to the technique used at that time, would indicate the presence of "relieving chambers" above the "recesses."

Investigation in May 1998

As part of this hypothesis, we meticulously examined the masonry in order to detect any significant details; from the first day, in the upper section of the shaft, we discovered a bonding symptomatic of a walled aperture we called "window." The walled "window" is 99.5 cm high and 74 cm wide at the base; it narrows into a trapezium at the top. This section is too reduced, especially in height, to be the mouth of a real corridor; on the other hand, it could be the opening of a narrow passageway for technical use. The east rising joint, at right angles to the block B3, shows a gap 1 cm wide which has no mortar and which could allow an endoscope to pass without any damage. On May 25, 1998, the Franco-Egyptian team decided to introduce an endoscope through this joint (flexible endoscope Olympus, 1.50 m in length, 8 mm in diameter, with light source and adjustable head). In the presence of Messrs El-Zeiry, Abdel Halim, Nahkla, Mohsen, Korani and the authors, the operation was executed without difficulty and a small corridor behind the walled window was discovered. The endoscope enabled us to observe that this small corridor was corbelled.

There were substantial salt formations on the masonry. The floor was strewn with debris from split stones and salt crystals that had fallen from the side walls. The corridor was estimated to be 3 m long. A series of photos was taken using the endoscope.

In order to complete the observations more precisely, Dr. Mustapha El-Zeiry authorized us to remove upper stone B4. This operation was made on the May 26, 1998 in the morning. The 40 cm thick stone was removed, showing an opening 26 cm high and 33 cm wide. Direct observation was thus possible and we were able to take photographs from different angles.

Description of Anomaly
Walled part called "window"

The four blocks, B1, B2, B3, and B4, that wall up the opening are about 40 cm thick.

On the east side the stones are laid against the inner corbels of the corridor and badly-joined with gypsum (the rising joint of the stone B3 has practically no mortar).

On the west side the wall is cut as a trapezium to a depth of 13 cm.

Between block B1 and the upper joint, a stone, accurately cut, had been inserted.

The visible piece of wood above the window is fitted to a depth of about 40 cm into the gap of the upper corbel.

The cavity

This is a kind of small corridor going north-south, straight above the lower corridor.

Its dimensions are 2.80 m long, 0.75 m wide at the base and 1.44 m high.

The pavement of the corridor would thus be 3.40 m above the roof of the lower corridor.

The corridor is made of three visible corbelled courses.

The substantial salt formations and the splitting of the stones do not enable us to understand the real quality of the masonry which, however, seems quite comparable to that of the burial chamber. The top level of the last corbel (corresponding to the upper end of the piece of wood visible from the outside) seems to correspond exactly to the level of the natural rock.

The north end of the corridor, which was difficult to observe in detail (considering the distance of observation—2.80 m—and the two slabs of split stones which partially hide the base) looked smooth and even, with no visible joints and no substantial salt formations, in contrast to the rest of the masonry.

The opening was closed that same day with a limestone block cut to size and sealed with plaster.

Comments

The position of this corbelled device straight above the lower corridor suggests that its purpose is to relieve it.

It is worth pointing out as well that if the builders had found it necessary to relieve a corridor 0.75 m (10 palms) wide, such a precaution should have proved particularly essential in regard to both recesses, the span of which was three times as great (2.10 m = 4 cubits). That corresponds to the hypothesis which has motivated this study, that is to say it is to be architecturally expected that both recesses should be surmounted by a relieving roof.

The removing of a stone in the upper part of the window enabled us to see a small corridor but not to enter it. After consulting officials from the Supreme Council of Antiquities, a second stone was removed in order to provide a sufficient gap.

The thick layer (about 25 cm) of debris strewing the floor was cleared away. The debris was sorted for any element of archaeological importance. It was composed mainly of split limestone pieces and large amounts of salt crystals that had come off the side walls and the corbels.

Some samples were given to Supreme Council of Antiquities for analysis.

Investigation of May 1999

Since the north wall of the small corridor we discovered was supposed to be situated less than one meter from a relieving chamber which we expected to be straight above the southern recess, we decided to make a hole to check for the existence of such a chamber. We made an opening 16 mm in diameter and 95 cm in length in the joint of the western lower corner of the north wall of the corridor. This showed an empty space. Into this we introduced an endoscope which enabled us to see a small chamber which we meticulously measured and photographed.

View of the chamber via Endoscope

- As we assumed, the chamber seems to be situated directly above the southern recess with the same dimensions (east-west; 2.10 m, 4 cubits; north-south; 2.61 m, 5 cubits).
- It is covered with a corbelled roof.
- It is made of seven courses; two vertical ones at the base followed by five corbelled ones.
- The floor does not have any pavement and is uneven; it is made of the upper side of the three beams covering the southern recess. These beams seem to be of different heights (exactly as in the relieving chambers of the pyramid of Khufu).
- The north wall is made of seven courses, the three upper ones seem to have successive recesses.
- The south wall is made of five courses; only one stone corresponds to the three upper corbels and to the north wall of the small corridor.

543

- The ceiling ridge of the chamber seems to correspond in height to that of the small corridor, that is to say, the height of the levelled natural rock.
- The chamber does not seem to lead anywhere.
- The masonry is carefully made; the beds of the courses of the north and south walls correspond to those of the existing corbels (except for the lower corbel).
- The chamber looks well-preserved; the side walls are neither split nor damaged as in the other sections of the pyramid known and do not seem to have any salt formations, as in the small corridor recently discovered. The floor is strewn with a little debris. Only one significant block has fallen from the second course of the west wall.

Comments

The fact that the chamber is situated right above the southern recess and laid directly upon the beams covering the recess without evening or paving them, and laying them blind, leads us to believe that the only function is to relieve the southern recess.

What surprised us most is the excellent state of preservation of the chamber. It seems that the damage due to moisture and salt, visible in the other visible sections and in the small corridor discovered, has not affected this chamber at all. This fact is reassuring but raises the question of the state of the known sections of the pyramid and of the problems linked to its preservation:

Has the moisture saturation of the visible sections an inevitable endogenous origin (rising damp from groundwater moving through the sections that are not constructed of masonry, like the shaft and the floor of the burial chamber)? Has it an exogenous origin (moisture brought by visitors and not ventilated)? Or both at the same time?

Since we were concerned about this side of the problem, we took particular care not to cause atmospheric exchanges between the sections visited and the new chamber. For this purpose, we sheathed the 16 mm opening in order to leave no gap between it and the 8 mm endoscope, and it was filled up between each handling and hermetically sealed at the end of the work.

Investigation of September, 1999

The existence of a relieving chamber above the southern recess implied the existence of a similar chamber expected to be situated above the northern recess.

In order to see that chamber, we made a hole (18 mm in diameter, 1.30 m long) without any difficulty, in the first section of the descending corridor. This opening led to the north-west corner of the chamber floor; we introduced a video-endoscope and we thus observed a chamber almost similar to the one previously-discovered above the southern recess.

Description of the chamber via endoscope

As was assumed, the chamber is situated right above the northern recess, with the same dimensions (east-west; 2.10 m—4 cubits; north-south; 2.65 m—5 cubits; about 3.50 m in height).

It is covered with a corbelled roof.

The east and west walls are made of seven courses; two vertical ones at the base, followed by five corbelled ones.

The south wall is vertical and is made of seven courses.

The north wall is vertical; this was observed with difficulty.

The ceiling ridge of the chamber seems to correspond in height to that of the chamber above the southern recess, that is, the height of the levelled natural rock.

544

The floor does not have any pavement; it is made of the upper side of the three beams which cover the northern recess.

The masonry is well-made, but is not re-dressed.

Under the projecting faces of several corbels we can clearly see fine straight lines of red hematite paint made by the builders.

In the western lower corner of the north wall we can see a hole situated right above the descending corridor. The stones that form the opening of this hole form an angle which seems to correspond to the slope of the descending corridor; therefore it seems obvious that it is the mouth of a relieving corridor situated above the ceiling of the descending corridor.

The chamber looks well-preserved. The side walls are neither split nor damaged as in the other visible sections of the pyramid, and do not have significant salt formations as in the small corridor behind the window previously discovered.

The floor is strewn with a little debris. However, some large blocks have fallen from the upper corbels; one of them, situated in front of the endoscope, obstructed our observations.

Comments

The comments and conclusions we can make are exactly the same and corroborate those previously formulated:

In order to observe the mouth of the corridor noted in the north wall of the chamber, we made an opening (18 mm in diameter, 0.90 m long) in the ceiling of the descending corridor, 10 meters up from its lower end, and introduced the video-endoscope.

The corridor's construction is similar to that of the small corridor discovered behind the window. Its dimensions seem to be roughly 0.75 m wide and 1.40 m high. Its east and west walls are made of three corbelled courses above the beams that form the ceiling of the descending corridor.

The masonry is roughly made. It is well-preserved. We did not observe any salt formations.

The floor is strewn with some debris from the side walls. We cannot see the south and north ends; it would seem the floor covers the descending corridor for its whole length. This will have to be checked later. We know that it opens in the south to the northern chamber previously discovered, but it would be interesting to know if it ends in the north at right angles with the initial casing of the pyramid.

On the 31st of March, 2000, in order to discover the length of the relieving corridor above the descending corridor, we drilled two holes: The first one, situated in the corridor ceiling 19.70 m from its lower end and 2 m in depth, did not reveal any empty space. The second one, made in the ceiling 12.56 m from the lower end, revealed only empty space.

The introduction of the endoscope enabled us to see the corridor and its upper end. From what we could see, the relieving corridor ends about 2.50 m up from the drill hole, that is to say about 15 m from its lower end.

The relieving corridor is just as we had previously observed it further down. Three corbels are directly laid on the top faces of the beams of the descending corridor. The top of the beams is not uneven; all the beams of the descending corridor have the same height and make a flat floor in the relieving corridor.

About 2.50 m up from the drill hole, the relieving corridor ends against a monolithic stone laid perpendicular to the slope. The corbels rest against this stone. It is laid on the floor (top faces of the beams of the descending corridor) with a wide joint without mortar.

In the stone axis we can clearly see a vertical brown line. We first thought that it could be a hematite line for the setting-up of the axis, but it might actually be a fine flow mark coming from the corbels axis.

Finally, we noticed that the 15-meter length of the relieving corridor seems to correspond to the spot where the descending corridor is no longer built in a trench in the ground.

If this relieving corridor ended at the outer face of the inner core of the pyramid, against where the first layer of coating was laid, this inner core would be 80 cubits wide at the base.

As in the case of the southern chamber, we took particular care not to cause atmospheric exchanges between the sections visited and the newly-discovered ones. For this purpose, we sheathed the 18 mm openings in order to leave no gap between them and the 8 mm endoscope. The holes were filled between each handling, hermetically sealed at the end of the work, and camouflaged with special mastic to deter any prodding by curiosity-seekers.

Our work has led to the discovery of the whole relieving system of the arrangement known of the pyramid of Meidum. This discovery induces several comments:

From an architectural point of view, the builders of the pyramids, perfectly aware of the great weight involved, were especially afraid of the collapse of empty spaces inside the monument. In order to make up for this risk, they relied more on vaults than on flat roofs; thus, very reduced spans (0.75 m for the corridors of the Meidum pyramid and the portcullis spaces of the northern Dahsur pyramid) were covered with corbelled roofs.

All things considered, the first use of the relieving chamber principle in a pyramid is not the well-known one which covers the so-called King's Chamber in Khufu's pyramid. Known and mastered from the Third Dynasty onward, this principle must have been used as circumstances required, it is thus possible, if not probable, that such systems were used in other pyramids. Therefore Meidum, which is a transition pyramid between the pyramids with a subterranean arrangement and the ones with a built arrangement, and between the step pyramids and the true ones, is not as rudimentary as it may seem; it is made of a complex system prefiguring the sophisticated construction of the later pyramids.

From the point of view of preservation, whether the causes of the formation of salt crystals are endogenous or exogenous, the sections opened are extremely damp and show salt formations and stone splitting. The small corridor discovered behind the window, which is isolated from the damp sections with thin, not moisture-tight masonry, shows the same deterioration, but the perfectly-closed and isolated chambers discovered are nearly intact.

From an Egyptological point of view, the interpretation of what we discovered is outside our scope. Nevertheless, we hope to have modestly contributed to a better knowledge of the obscure period of the Third Dynasty by showing that the architectural concepts were more advanced than we had so far assumed.

We wish we had discovered some worker graffiti that would have removed the uncertainty about the attribution of the pyramid of Meidum to Huni, but even if we clearly discerned red hematite lines, we did not see any graffiti. However, the use of an endoscope with dim luminosity does not offer clear observation of the distant parts; some later observations with higher-performance equipment would enhance the possibility of discovering them.

We think we have demonstrated that the study of the pyramids from a strictly architectural point of view can bear fruit.

Finally, we would like to thank the Supreme Council of Antiquities and especially Professor Gaballah Ali Gaballah for his confidence in us, and we hope that our work gave satisfaction. We also thank the Hilti and Olympus companies, whose high-performance equipment, placed at our disposal as a favour, played such a great part in the outcome of our research.

The Ancient Nest of Horus above Thebes: Hungarian Excavations on Thoth Hill at the Temple of King Sankhkare Montuhotep III (1995–1998)

Győző Vörös

Pázmány Péter Catholic University, Budapest

Introduction

It is now four thousand years since King Sankhkare Montuhotep III (2010–1998 BCE) raised a temple on the peak of the horizon, on a hill north of the Valley of the Kings on the West Bank at Thebes. This abandoned desert shrine remained unknown to modern research until the beginning of the twentieth century, when it was explored by G. Schweinfurth and W.M.F. Petrie.

Thoth Hill, as it is commonly known in the area, is surrounded by desert ravines. The ancient path leading up to the temple is impassable to pack-animals such as camels or donkeys. The temple lies five kilometers from the nearest desert road accessible to vehicles, and rises 400 meters above it. This difficult terrain discouraged archaeologists until the Hungarian Mission began a methodical excavation in 1995 of the pharaonic sites on the summit of the hill that closes off the Valley of the Kings from the north.

The Thoth Hill Expedition from Eötvös Loránd University (ELTE) in Budapest spent 15 months at Thebes, excavating and restoring in the field. The expedition extended over four seasons, and brought to light the whole ancient history of Thoth Hill. The ruins of Sankhkare Montuhotep III's temple yielded all the architectural features and archaeological finds needed to assess the site from an Egyptological perspective.

Research in the Early Twentieth Century

On January 6, 1904 George Schweinfurth, a German scholar of the Paleolithic period, came upon the ruins of the Thoth Hill temple during a field survey. He found six hieroglyphic inscriptions carved on limestone blocks lying amid debris on the sanctuary forecourt. A few days later, he reported this discovery to Gaston Maspero, then Director of the Antiquities Service. Maspero decided to confirm the report for himself, as no hilltop sanctuary was known in pharaonic times. Two weeks after the discovery, on the 30th of January, Schweinfurth and

Maspero climbed the hill with a team of Arab workers to search for more finds. Instead of the hieroglyphic inscriptions they had expected, they found fragments of two baboon statues. This led Maspero to name both the temple and the hill after the god Thoth, who was sometimes portrayed as a seated baboon.

The inscriptions found by Schweinfurth were studied by a number of scholars who came to various conclusions: K. Sethe interpreted the scarcely-legible hieroglyphs first as the name of Amenemhet IV (Twelfth Dynasty), then as Montuhotep III (Eleventh Dynasty). A. Sayce dated the temple to the reign of Tanutamon (Twenty-fifth Dynasty), and Maspero dated it to the rule of Necho II (Twenty-sixth Dynasty). The debate was not resolved until five years later, when the discovery of further fragments confirmed Sethe's second reading.

In January 1909, British scholar W.M.F. Flinders Petrie spent a fortnight exploring the hills on the West Bank. His survey included the unexcavated sites on Thoth Hill, to which, like Schweinfurth, he devoted a single day. As the walls of the brick temple barely protruded from the debris, averaging two meters in depth, his survey was rather cursory, but he uncovered a number of new fragments of limestone with carved hieroglyphic inscriptions that proved to be of great interest. These included the royal titles and cartouche of the temple's founder, Sankhkare Montuhotep III.

Petrie was the first to record the ruined building to the west of the temple as well as a number of stone walls within the shrine. He took these to be a preliminary stage in the construction of the brick sanctuary. Misinterpreting two finds, he saw the temple as a *Sed*-festival chapel, the site of Sankhkare's jubilee. He concluded that a fragment from the left hand of a statue was part of a half-life-sized seated statue of the king, and used another fragment of limestone torus moulding to reconstruct the lid of a sarcophagus. The finds recovered by the Hungarian Mission, however, showed the former fragment to be part of a life-size seated baboon statue, and the latter a complementary fragment of the sanctuary lintel, decorated with a winged sun disk.

The finds collected by Schweinfurth and Petrie were never fully published. Schweinfurth's fragments were relegated to the storeroom of the Egyptian Museum in Cairo. They remained there until January 3, 1937, when they were found during an inventory by the museum's director, R. Engelbach. On his orders the unimpressive-looking inscribed limestone fragments and statue parts were buried in the garden on the bank of the Nile, where the fine, white limestone proceeded to disintegrate in the damp soil. Schweinfurth published lithographs of the six inscribed fragments he had found, but the statue fragments remained unpublished. Both groups of finds thus passed into oblivion.

Petrie's finds came into the possession of German Egyptologist W. von Bissing, who donated them in 1934 to the already world-famous Egyptian Collection at the Leiden Museum in the Netherlands. I was able to sort and process the Petrie Collection, still in remarkably good condition, in the Leiden Museum's storeroom in the summer of 1995. The manuscript archive from Petrie's Thoth Hill survey is preserved at the Petrie Museum, University College London, where I examined them in the university archive in the summer of 1996.

The finds from the discovery in 1904 and the survey in 1909 make up only a fraction of the artifacts that have come to light. Nonetheless, they are still of great significance: without these finds, some of the items unearthed during the excavation would have been very difficult to interpret. The retrieval of these objects saved them from later collectors and robbers.

548

1995–1996: Excavating the Temple of King Sankhkare Montuhotep III

Our mission began by undertaking a surface survey of the site in the spring of 1995. During this survey we found Middle Kingdom and early Coptic ceramics among the surface finds, and also further inscribed fragments. It seemed worthwhile to undertake a full archaeological excavation of the relatively small temple and to clear out all the debris which had accumulated above the Middle Kingdom floor level. The five-month excavation season lasted from November 1, 1995 to March 31, 1996 and concentrated on the mud-brick temple that dominates the site. We were able to complete this project in full (fig. 1).

Fig. 1: Hot-air balloon view of the Temple of Sankhkare Montuhotep III after excavation, with architectural reconstruction drawing. (Vörös, 1998, 33)

549

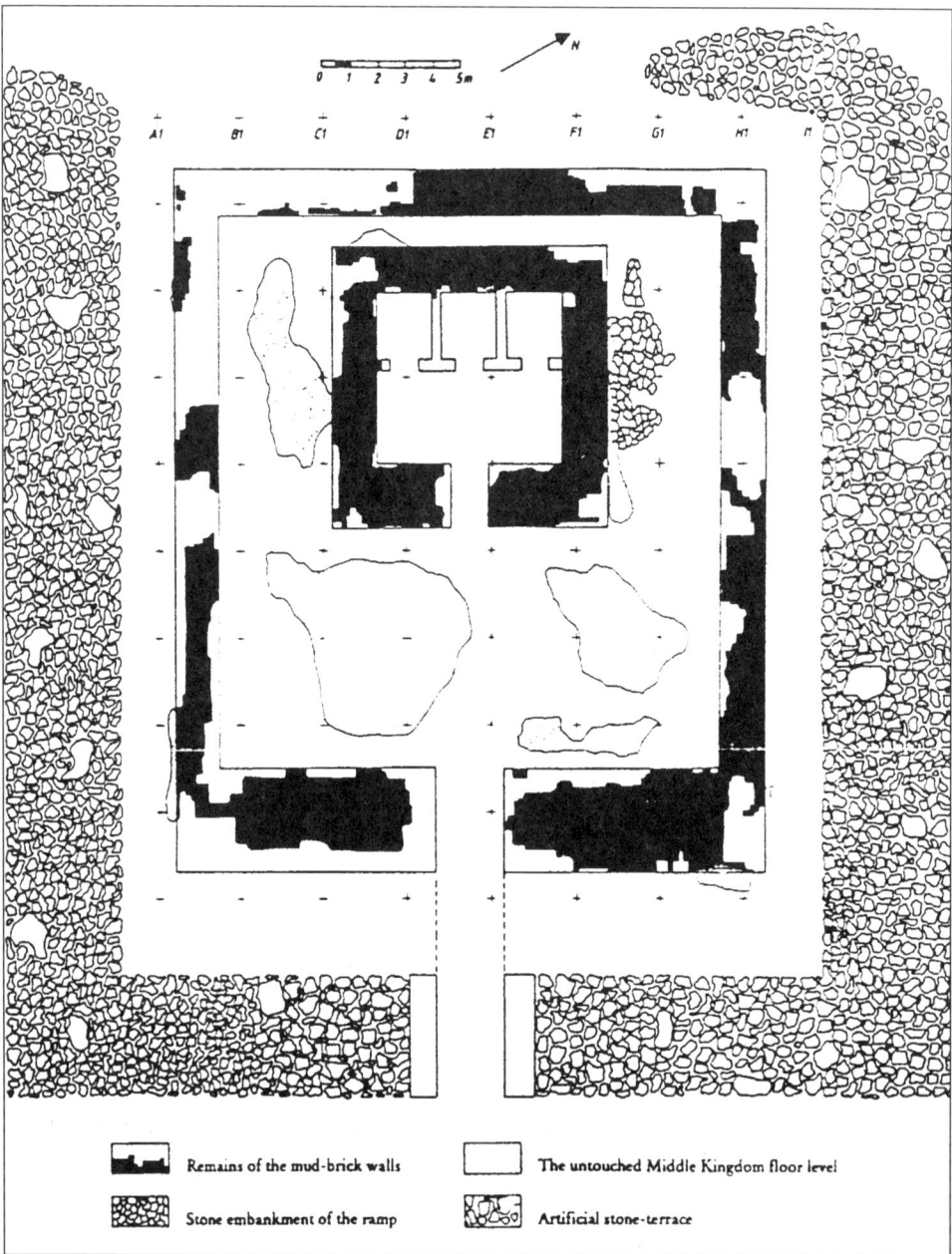

Fig. 2: The ground-plan of the Temple of Sankhkare Montuhotep III. (Vörös et al., 1997, 285)

The excavation began with the removal of a layer of mud-brick debris, reaching a height of 1.5 to 2 meters. As this layer may have been linked to possible building phases, a thorough stratigraphic examination was carried out along the wall faces. As a result of this examination it was established that neither these nor the architectural remains left *in situ* suggested the existence of more than one building phase, and it can thus be stated that the entire mud-brick structure was the result of a single period of construction in the Eleventh Dynasty (fig. 2).

After the removal of the mud-brick rubble, a relatively flat surface was exposed. This represented the top of the ancient debris layer. On this surface we found evidence of later disturbances, which for the most part were concentrated in the areas immediately adjacent to the walls. Over 80% of the entire surface area of the temple showed evidence of such disturbances, but in only a few cases did they descend deeper than the Middle Kingdom floor level foundations. On the surface of the ancient debris layer, the average thickness of which was 15 cm, evidence of early Christian activities could be observed, represented on the one hand by characteristic Coptic ceramics, and on the other by the form of a Classical Period cross carved into the limestone. (Carved crosses had already been found by Schweinfurth.)

The temple of King Sankhkare Montuhotep III was erected on the level area of a terrace built from uncut local stones that lengthened the crest of the hill in the form of an artificial neck of land. The terrace contains an earlier building, the stone walls of which were used in some places as foundations for the brick walls of the Middle Kingdom temple. The pylons of the temple, which is of classical layout and symmetrical along its primary axis, reach a height of four meters in places. Around the outer wall of the temple we found a two meter-wide path resembling a gangway with its floor level intact. Similarly, at the wings of the courtyard on either side of the sanctuary, the floor level of the courtyard sloped upwards like a ramp toward the back corridor behind the sanctuary, with a height differential of 40 cm. The Middle Kingdom floor levels thus presented a series of rising ramps, one sloping upwards through the pylon entrance into the flat open courtyard, and again rising on either side of the sanctuary (the Middle Kingdom floors in the sanctuary itself were lost).

The temple was covered inside and out with white plaster, which still remained *in situ* in several places. Since the Thoth Hill Temple crowns the horizon on the west bank at Thebes, being situated at its highest point, the occupants of the Eleventh Dynasty capital would have been able to see the temple illuminated by the first rays of the rising sun. The niche found on the north part of the north pylon's east-facing façade may have held a statue or flagstaff.

The king who founded the temple, as it was at his father's temple at Deir al-Bahari, placed offerings similar in appearance at the corners of his own temple. The four foundation deposits, located during our work, consisted of alabastron-type vessels, sacrificial saucers, terracotta animal figurines, and parts of slaughtered ruminants.

Sankhkare Montuhotep III had his royal titles and the dedication of the temple carved symmetrically on the limestone door-jambs flanking the sanctuary entrance. Of the two columns of inscription, five fragments were unearthed by Schweinfurth, seven more by Petrie, and 24 by our expedition (fig. 3).

Although only lithographs remain of some of the pieces found at the beginning of the century, fig. 3 shows that the three collections are not only complementary, but allow us to reconstruct the main inscription of the temple. The two columns of inscription surmounted by *pt* hieroglyphs and framed by *wȝs*-scepters, are symmetrical (enabling them to be reconstructed) and the intercontinental puzzle fragments join in 27 places. The text, the dedicatory inscription of King Sankhkare Montuhotep III, now 4,000 years old, can be read once more:

ḥr s-ˁnḫ-tȝwy-f nbty s-ˁnḫ-tȝwy-f ḥtp bik nbw niswt bity s-ˁnḫ-kȝ-rˁ sȝ rˁ mnṯw-ḥtp ˁnḫ ḏt ir-n-f m mnw-f n ḥr ir-f n-f di ˁnḫ mi rˁ ḏt

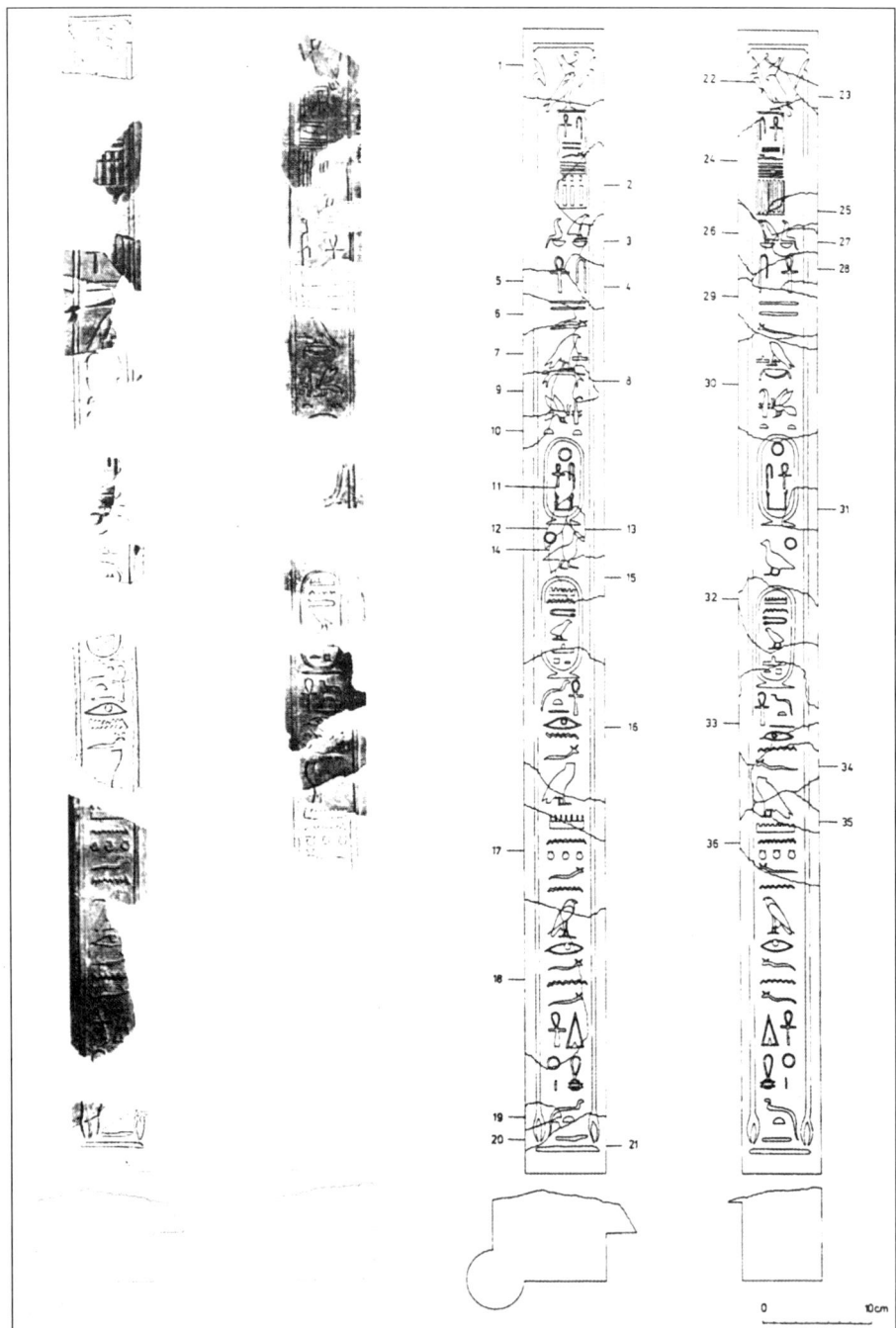

Fig. 3: The dedicatory inscription of Sankhkare Montuhotep III. (Vörös, 1998, 36)

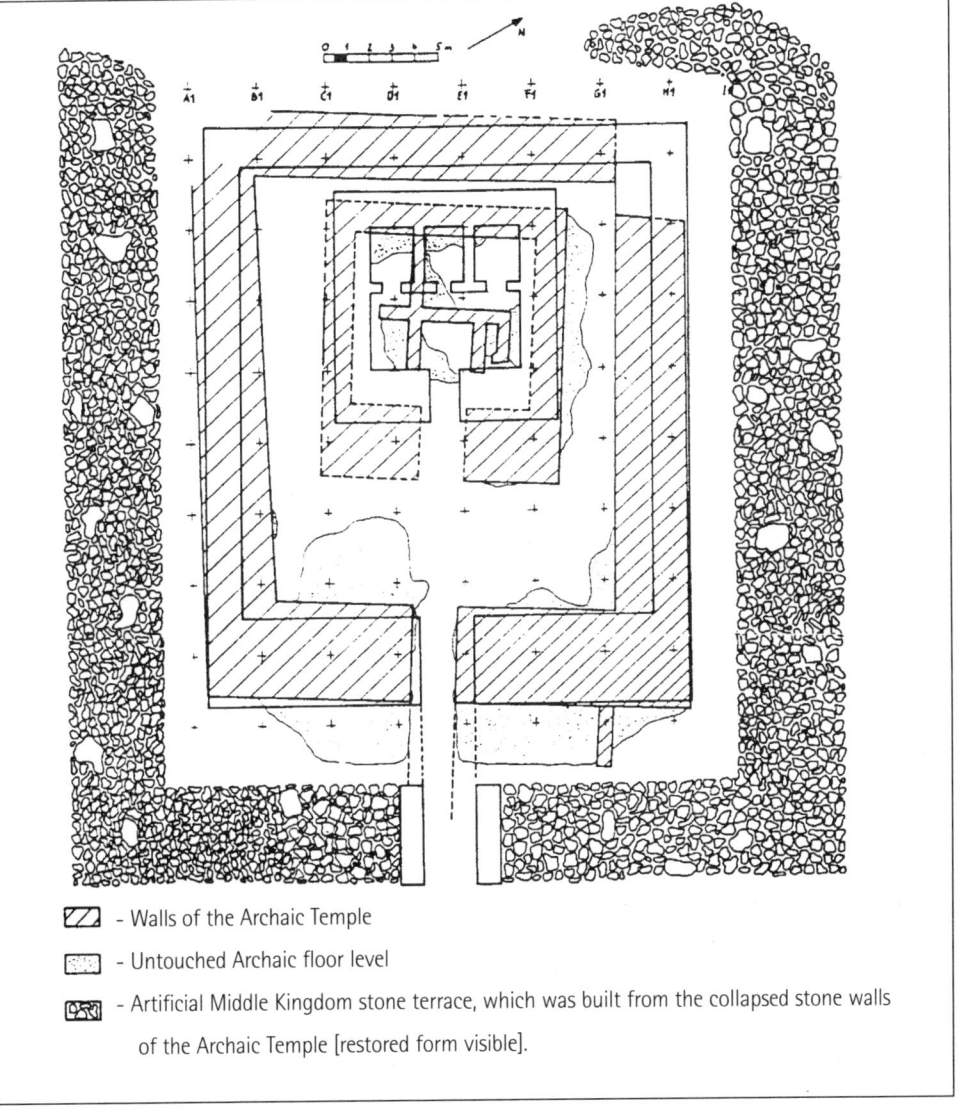

- ▨ - Walls of the Archaic Temple

- ▨ - Untouched Archaic floor level

- ▨ - Artificial Middle Kingdom stone terrace, which was built from the collapsed stone walls
  of the Archaic Temple [restored form visible].

Fig. 4: Superimposed ground plans of the Archaic and Middle Kingdom temples. The axial deviation of the two temples is clearly visible. (Vörös *et al.*, 1998, 285)

"Horus Seankhtauief ('Who Causes His Two Lands to Live'), He of the Two Goddesses Who Causes His Two Lands to Live, the Peaceful Golden Horus, the King of Upper and Lower Egypt Sankhkare ('Who Causes the Soul of Re to Live'), Son of Re Montuhotep ('the Peaceful Montu'), Living Eternally. He made as his monument to Horus, may he make for him, given life like Re, eternally."

Fragments of the sanctuary's stone lintel, decorated with a winged sun disk, were also exposed during our work, adding to those previously uncovered. The inscriptions "Behdety ('the Winged Sun'), Lord of the Sky" are carved symmetrically on either side of the relief. In addition, other fragments of text bearing the king's names came to light, as well as pieces of a stele and numerous graffiti. A large number of pieces from three painted limestone statues portray the god Thoth as a life-sized, seated baboon. These statues of the deity were smashed (probably) in the fourth and fifth centuries CE by the hermits of Thebes, who saw them as pagan idols of the old world. One of the three statues could be restored to its original state with only minor gaps between the fragments.

Apart from the Middle Kingdom forms present among the vessels from the foundation deposits, additional ceramic storage vessels and bowl types were discovered.

After uncovering the temple of King Sankhkare Montuhotep III (the Temple of Horus) and fully documenting it architecturally, we began to concentrate on the stone building beneath the Middle Kingdom floor level. This remained buried until the following season.

1996–1997: Excavating the Thoth Hill Archaic Temple

The second five-month excavation season lasted from October 15, 1996 to March 15, 1997. During this season we came across a previously unknown stone temple with dimensions coextensive with those of the Middle Kingdom temple. We were able to record the complete ground plan (fig. 4).

The layout shows a temple with pylons, the free-standing inner sanctuary of which contained a cell. The remaining stone foundation blocks of the temple were used as footings for the brick walls that were built from local stones. They served as the base of the same kind of standing walls, originally 8–10 meters high, broken by a huge earthquake in antiquity. Firm evidence for this is provided by the geological slip at the northwest corner of the temple and the walls' subsequent collapse at this location.

Sankhkare's architects built an artificial terrace from the ruins of the stone temple as a quakeproof foundation for the brick walls they raised on the rubble. Thanks to this feat of engineering, the ruined walls of the brick temple are still over four meters high in places, having withstood later earthquakes. Earthquakes are a very common phenomenon in Egypt and are especially violent on the hilltops.

The proposal that the earlier stone temple was a previous phase in the construction of the temple of King Sankhkare Montuhotep III can be rejected on the following grounds:

1. The two sanctuaries differ in both structure and number of cells.
2. The two temples have fundamentally dissimilar architecture.
3. The orientation of the two temples is different.

The last point, the orientation of the temple's main axis (its axis of symmetry), is shown in the superimposed ground plans of the two temples (fig. 4). The brick temple was oriented more than two degrees further to the north than the stone temple beneath it, towards the eastern sky horizon.

We needed to have this archaeoastronomical problem examined by a specialist in the astronomical orientation of ancient Egyptian structures. I asked Maria G. Firneis, a professor at the University Observatory of Vienna, to carry out the examination. She made the necessary calculations in the summer of 1997, reconstructing the ancient eastern sky as it would have looked in Thebes. Her research showed that in the reign of King Sankhkare Montuhotep III, the brick temple had been aligned on the heliac rising of the star Sirius (just before sunrise), which in Thebes took place on the July 11th. In the Archaic period (beginning around 3150 BCE), this same astronomical phenomenon appeared 2° 17′ further to the south. The thousand years separating the construction of the two temples meant that the Middle Kingdom architects had to re-orient the new temple because Sirius had shifted in the eastern sky. This star was of great significance to

Pharaonic chronology and worshipped as the god Horus, to whom the Thoth Hill temples were dedicated. Falcons, the embodiments of this deity, still nest in great numbers in the ravines that score the cliffs. On some days during excavation, groups of them circled and soared above their ancient nest. Their ancestors may have prompted the building of a symbolic nest for Horus, the falcon god of the Thebans.

Important finds from the Archaic temple were fragments of a cultic stone knife and Archaic stone implements (some of them were found *in situ* in the stone wall). Some typical Archaic ceramics with easily datable forms resulted from the ceramic restorations. The cyclopean masonry of the stone temple and the absence of ashlar masonry suggested primitive building methods of a kind rarely found as late as the Old Kingdom. Researchers from the University of Chicago Epigraphic Survey working around Thoth Hill found many rock inscriptions from the First and Second Dynasties.

Of particular interest is that neither the finds from the excavations nor the scattered ceramics and rock inscriptions from the area around the hill yielded any relics from the centuries between the Archaic period and the Middle Kingdom. We can therefore presume that Thebes entered a period of decline after the Archaic period, most probably as a result of a huge earthquake. The Hungarian Mission to Thoth Hill not only found and uncovered the earliest temple known in Thebes, but also alerted Egyptologists to a period of the "City of One Hundred Gates," of which scarcely anything had been known.

Our mission also examined a rock tomb cut into the side of the Thoth Hill, directly to north of the temple, on January 11, 1997. The huge tomb with five chambers consisted of a stripped sarcophagus *in situ*, very similar to the Sekhemkhet-sarcophagus (Third Dynasty) discovered in Saqqara, with its open end oriented to the north, toward the circumpolar stars. Unfortunately, the research we began in the tomb, which belonged to King Sankhkare Montuhotep III (and it is clear that his hilltop temple was a mortuary temple on a natural pyramid-shaped hill), had to be set aside following the political events of the following season.

1997–1998: Restoration

After uncovering the Archaic Temple and fully documenting it, we re-established the floor level of the Middle Kingdom temple. The goal of this five-month long restoration season was to conserve and restore the temples and the artifacts in our storerooms. This was carried out in full.

On November 17, 1997, in the mortuary temple of Queen Hatshepsut, 400 meters as the crow flies from our expedition headquarters, 73 people were massacred by terrorists. As a result, Egyptian authorities decided to declare Thoth Hill off-limits in order to improve security at Thebes. We were grateful to God that we were able to finish restoring the temple a mere ten days before, and could report to the Inspectorate that our work had not been left undone.

I would like to express our gratitude to the Supreme Council of Antiquities, without whose support our mission could not have succeeded; Dr. Gaballa Ali Gaballa, Secretary General of the SCA in the spring of 1998, following the successful completion of our Thoth Hill excavations, gave me the concession of Taposiris Magna: a port with an acropolis 45 kilometers west of Alexandria on the coastal dune of the Mediterranean Sea. Here, guided by an ancient representation, the Palestrina Mosaic, we are excavating an important center of the Goddess Isis.

Bibliography

Gy. Vörös, "The Ancient Nest of Horus Above Thebes. Preliminary study on the fragments deriving from the Thoth Hill Temple," *OMRO* 77 (1997), 23–29.

Gy. Vörös *et. al.*, "Preliminary report of the Excavations at Thoth Hill, Thebes. The Temple of Sankhkare Montuhotep III (Season 1995–1996)," *MDAIK* 53 (1997), 283–287, pls. 38–39.

Gy. Vörös *et. al.*, "The Crown of Thebes," *EA* 11 (1997), 37–39.

Gy. Vörös *et. al.*, "Preliminary Report of the Excavations at Thoth Hill, Thebes. The Pre-Eleventh Dynasty Temple and the Western Building (Season 1996–1997)," *MDAIK* 54 (1998), 335–340., pls. 56–59.

Gy. Vörös, *Temple on the Pyramid of Thebes* (Budapest, 1998), 5.

Gy. Vörös, *Taposiris Magna: Port of Isis* (Budapest, 2000).

The Nile's Early Stone Architecture: New Data from Ma'adi West

Luc Watrin, Olivier Blin
REPAL

As the Egyptian village of Ma'adi presents links to the Levantine cultures on many levels, it is worthwhile to first present some observations concerning the architecture developed by the neighboring cultures, notably those of Palestine's Chalcolithic period and of the Early Bronze Age I.

During the second half of the fifth millennium, the migrating populations to the Palestinian areas adapted to different environmental conditions notably by developing specific recognizable architectural techniques and styles. In the Golan sector,[1] several villages of 30 to 50 rectangular houses made out of local volcanic stone are aggregated in continuous linear structures of five or six successive communicating dwellings situated parallel to each other. In the northeast of the Dead-Sea basin, the major village of Teleilât Ghassûl (Jordan)[2] shows another pattern. It has no surrounding wall and features rectangular dwellings of mud brick on stone foundations. The richest dwellings among them show wall paintings. In Cisjordan, groups of Palestinian migrants occupied the natural caves more or less permanently (Nahal Mishmar, Nahal Qanah).[3] In the south of Palestine, along the natural valley of Wadi-Sheva, there is an original dwelling type consisting of subterranean spaces carved into the loess river banks with one or more communicating chambers. That type of troglodyte dwelling, discovered on the twin sites of Abu-Matar and of Safadi by J. Perrot in 1955 is the most remarkable of the Levantine Chalcolithic architectures and has often been compared to the semi-subterranean architecture of Ma'adi.

The best-known village of the Beersheva network is that of Safadi. It contains a dwelling in two parts (pl. 1:1)[4]: a semi-underground court, more or less circular (4 to 6m in diameter), which served as an entryway to a subrectangular underground room measuring 7 m x 3 m. The presence of hearths, silos, and basins in these dwellings confirms their domestic function.

These earliest dwellings were first replaced by monocellular shelters of circular or oval shape, which had walls of mud brick and stone on a foundation of large pebbles (pl. 1:2).[5] In that array of communicating rooms, each one had on the average a surface of about 15 m[2]. The remaining walls are 1.5–2m high, and bear indentions designed to receive the ends of horizontal rafters,

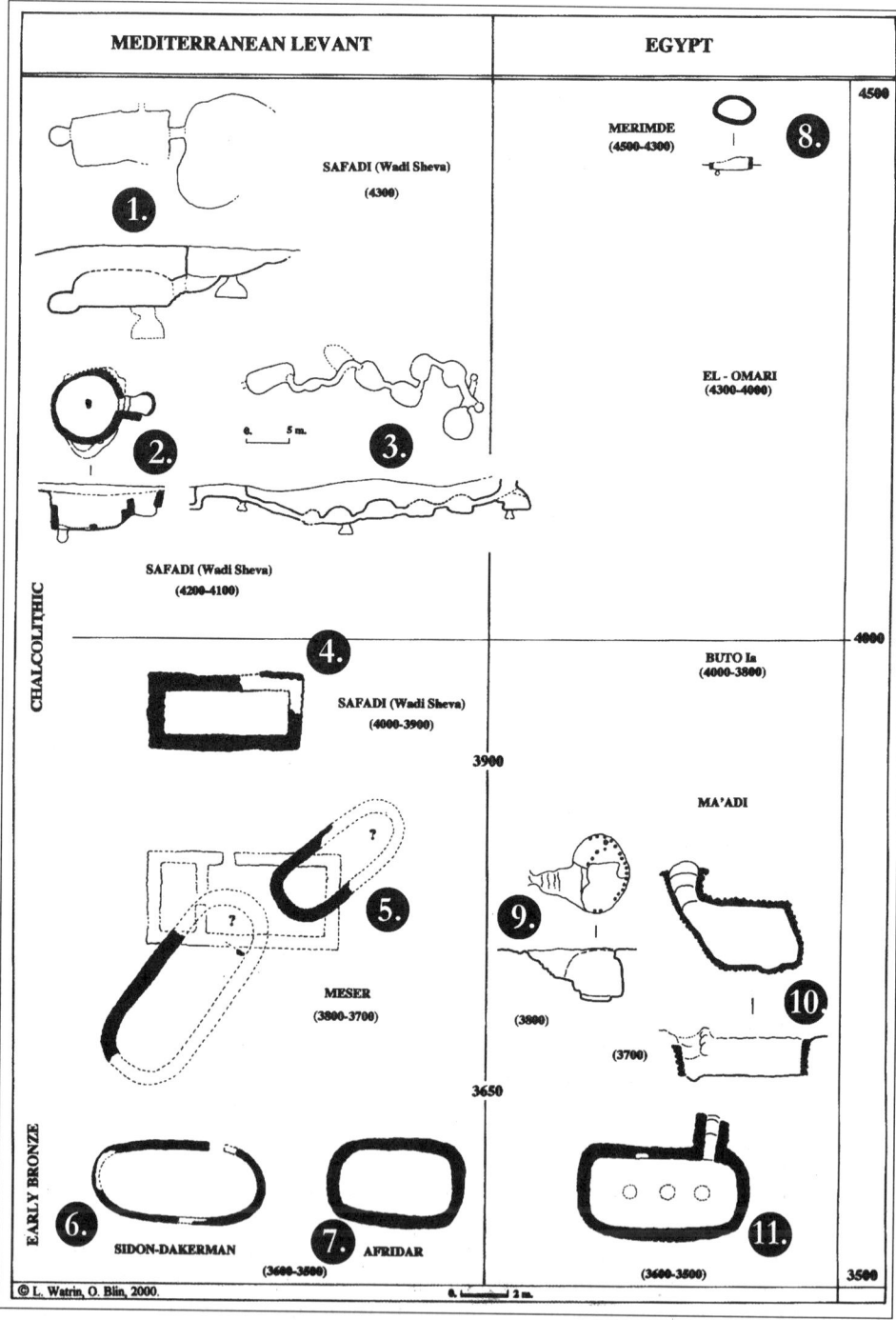

Plate 1

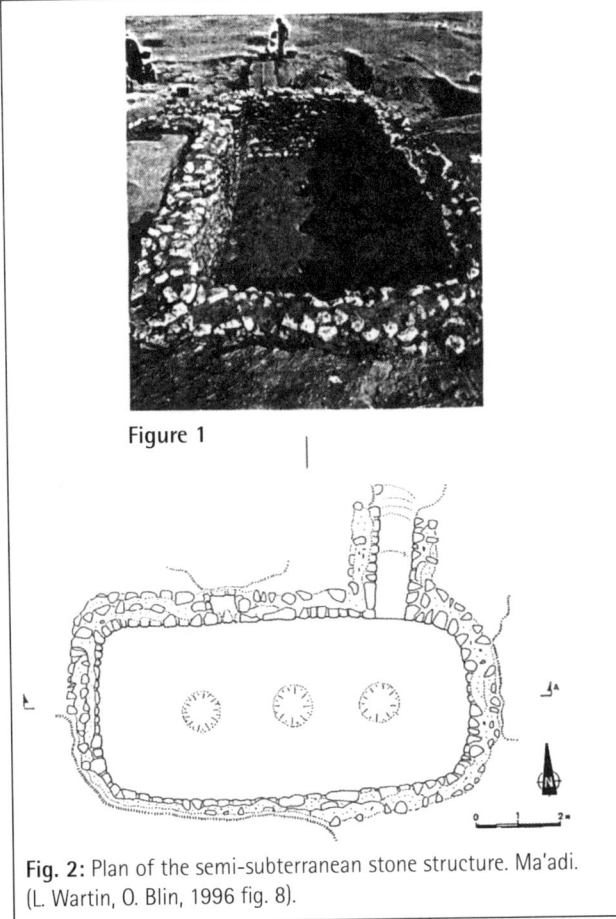

Figure 1

Fig. 2: Plan of the semi-subterranean stone structure. Ma'adi. (L. Wartin, O. Blin, 1996 fig. 8).

Plate 2

which supported a roof of foliage and earth. The rafters were running around the wall's top, and are sometimes supported by a central post on a flat stone foundation. In the same period, we see an evolution from monocellular subterranean cavities to a network of underground chambers linked by tunnels (pl. 1:3).[6] It is in these interconnected subterranean chambers where groups of colored pebbles scattered on the ground, as well as ivory objects including one statuette, were discovered.

The last phase consists of rectangular mud-brick constructions on the surface with stone foundations (pl. 1:4).[7] Once again the dimensions are comparable to the earlier underground constructions: 6–7 m x 2.5 m, with a surface area of 15 to 18 m^2.

Studies of these dwellings have underlined the difficulty of dating them. At the time of their discovery, their time frame was something of a mystery, and even J. Perrot's 1984 publication[8] places them between 3600 and 3300 BCE.[9] More recent studies such as those conducted by T. Levy at Shiqmim (downstream from Beersheva)[10] suggest dates for the three principal phases of occupation, respectively, 4500–4400, 4250–4000, and 4000–3700 BCE (a very large time frame in our reckoning[11]). Other researchers, particularly I. Gilead,[12] propose the relatively short time frame of 4300–3900 BCE for the Wadi-Beersheva cluster. This chronology of Southern Palestinian Chalcolithic cultures points to the second half of the fifth millennium and corresponds to the occupation of the key-site of Teleilât Ghassûl, which appears to have been settled since the beginning of the fifth millennium, and abandoned around 3900 BCE.[13]

Isaac Gilead has an original reading of the Chalcolithic sites of Wadi-Sheva. He considers the underground chambers as simple storage extensions of and hence contemporary ones of the surface rectangular dwelling structures.[14] His explanation relies heavily on the analysis of the disposition of the fireplaces (located in surface). In fact, the characteristics of the Beersheva dwellings (excavations by Perrot and Levy) present an evolution by phase (pl. 1:1 to 4): of entirely manmade underground rooms (Phase I), followed by semi-underground dwellings (Phase IIa, former caves of which the natural earth ceiling had collapsed and was replaced by simple, organic, light roofing) as well as interconnected underground rooms (Phase IIb). Finally surface buildings appear in a Phase III. Remarkably enough, while the shapes changed during that process, the basic average size of each room remained unchanged. The ceramic and lithic material is apparently the same for the various phases recognized at Safadi.[15] The ceramic sets found show no gradual development, remaining strictly identical, suggesting either a conservative society or else a short occupation time that can be estimated, on the base of seven radiocarbon datings, as spanning a maximum of three centuries, probably between 4250–3950 BCE.[16] The same scheme is repeated elsewhere in the Wadi-Sheva valley, suggesting that the earliest subterranean dwelling phases (Phases I–II) belong to the final third of the fifth millennium.

This Southern Levantine Chalcolithic period corresponds in Lower Egypt to the Neolithic cultures of Merimde (ca. 4700–4300 BCE),[17] al-Omari (ca. 4300–4000 BCE),[18] and Buto Ia (ca. 4000–3800 BCE).[19] Only the most recent of these three cultures, that of Buto Ia, showed a clear connection with the Palestinian cultures of the Late Chalcolithic. Notably, the artifacts point to at least a temporary presence of culturally Palestinian groups.[20] The architectural structures of this period discovered in Egypt appear to belong to an entirely different pattern of evolution. However, architectural comparisons may be made in the slightly later period corresponding to the Ma'adi culture (ca. 3800–3500 BCE) (infra).[21]

The Lower Egyptian cultures in the fifth and fourth millennia are marked by an architecture of ovoid or circular huts (pl. 1:8) made of light material (mud and reeds), rather close in aspect to the traditional architecture of sub-Saharan Africa.[22] On the site of Ma'adi, whose different phases cover nearly three centuries, we find these types of dwellings, as attested by post-holes, woven-reeds forming walls or fences, and the hardened and compacted negative impressions left by them.[23]

It seems that the settlement featured some original architectural elements, in particular semi-subterranean structures of stone and mud bricks that have been considered as possible dwellings. Some comparable parallels for these constructions may be found in the EB I Southern Levantine structures (infra).

From the second third of the fourth millennium (ca. 3700/3650 BCE[24]) onward, a new type of dwelling consisting of oval or sub-rectangular chambers with rounded angles appears in this same geographic area. That type of dwelling corresponds to the chronological period in which a new culture in this region emerges, that of the Early Bronze Age I. This culture is distinguished from the preceding one by a new ceramic and lithic industry including wavy ledge-handled jars and Cannanean blades, which are among the most representative cultural elements. The change in the architectural domain can be illustrated by the Palestinian site of Meser (pl. 1:5), where M. Dothan's[25] excavations allow us to visualize a transition from the rectangular dwelling phase at the end of the Chalcolithic (Meser III) to the oval houses at the beginning of EB I (Meser II). Like E. Braun,[26] we think that the reconstitution of missing walls of Meser II by straight walls on one end is speculative.[27] Dothan's curious plan offers no solid evidence of either "one square end" or "one round end." Unfortunately, this theory has been widely accepted with little verification.[28] On our plan, these reconstructions have been modified on the basis of the prevailing EB I curvilinear architecture current in the region: that is, two rounded ends. This same type has also been discovered at Yiftah'el II in northern Palestine, excavated by E. Braun,[29] and that of Afridar (pl. 1:7) in southern Palestine, excavated recently by H. Khalaily and Z. Wallach.[30]

This chronological horizon requires that we speak of the agglomeration of Sidon-Dakerman in southern Lebanon, excavated by R. Saidah[31] (pl. 1:6), which has unearthed typologically similar dwellings, some of which show the particularity of being semi-underground. These houses are made out of rough stone, assembled by a compact clay mortar used internally and sometimes externally. The thickness of the walls varies between 35 and 50 cm. The dimensions range between 6 m and 12 m long and 4.5–6 m wide. Most of these houses present rather homogeneous dimensions between 7.5 m long by 4.4 m wide. On the average surfaces are ranging from 30 to 40 m². These houses are accessible through openings in one of the wider sides, which are marked by a threshold. Among these, we note the presence of flagstones in the center and along the lengthwise axis, certainly intended for the support, a ridgeline rafter and woven roof supports, and possibly a floor. The floors are composed of beaten earth which has yielded fragments of large storage jars. Twenty-five houses have been identified or explored. Sidon-Dakerman is completed by an outer wall in mud some 2 m thick, and preserved to the height of 3 m. A radiocarbon dating yields a date around 3500 BCE.[32] The lithic and ceramic materials found on site confirm a dating contemporary with the EB Ia cultures of Palestine. A small sounding on one of the houses[33] has revealed remains of earlier structures in earlier layers, proof of at least one earlier occupation phase.

In light of these observations on the northern dwelling-types and their evolutions, it is interesting to consider the stone structure discovered by F. A. Badawi[34] in 1987 on the site of Ma'adi in the Cairo suburbs, re-examined in 1995[35] and in 1999[36] (pl. 1:11 and pl. 2).

This semi-subterranean building is roughly oval inside and outside, and is constructed with stone laid in non-staggered rows. The wall's exterior measures 10.25 m x 5.50 m and 8.70 m x 4.20 m in the interior, corresponding to a surface area of 36 m². The walls are preserved to the height of about 2 m, and present the remains of multiple layers of clay mud-plaster. Access to the eastern end of the structure is gained through an entryway (0.80 m x 2.5 m) in the northern wall, which has a threshold and some steps carved into the substratum. This same wall presents a niche on its western side, which indicates that the original height of the walls must have been greater. Badawi reports that during the excavations, traces of combustion[37] "gave the impression that incense or another product had been burned at this place."[38] In the center of the structure, lined up along a lengthwise axis, are three pits dug in the building's floor, perhaps for supporting posts, which in their turn surely supported a main rafter.

Remains of reeds and mud bricks still covered the floor during Badawi's excavations.[39] He proposes that these are the remains of the structure's roof. They may also be remains of walls belonging to a superstructure of which we have no trace due to the significant erosion of the site. The considerable thickness of the walls (0.80 m) combined with the presence of the three axial posts (not really justified given the width of the structure), may be indicative of a larger above-ground building of which the current structure is only the basement. On the west side of the structure[40] are disposed several rows of jars-silos, perhaps forming a collective storage area.[41] The floor of the structure was made out of compacted and plastered earth as is shown by remaining plastering material. The floor features jar negatives along the northern wall and in the southeastern corner, which could also confirm the structure's function as a storage or production center.[42]

By all evidence, it is possible to link the Badawi structure to the Palestinian structures that we have presented as belonging to the tradition of Meser II, Sidon-Dakerman and more precisely the one of Afridar. The similarities are manifest. The Ma'adi site has benefited from several excavation campaigns in its different sectors.[43] They all point to an evolution which goes together with the shift of the village's occupied area, whose remains are spread over one kilometer east-west. The earlier excavations unfortunately failed to clearly record many dwellings, or their spatial distribution. Nonetheless, the Italian excavators[44] noted that the western sector of the village presented the most advanced cultural elements, and deduced from this a spatial shift, over time, from east to west. The excavations brought to the daylight a series of semi-subterranean structures carved directly into the bedrock (Squares CXXIIIa and XLIXa).[45] These semi-subterranean chambers appear in the form of cavities in the bedrock, 3 m deep for the greatest among them (pl. 1:9–10). That they are contemporary with the Prehistoric village is verified by the presence of a jar-silo,[46] as well as Ma'adian ceramics including imitations of Black-topped ware in the greatest of the three cavities.[47] These semi-subterranean spaces are elliptical in plan, the deepest being accessible by steps made of flat stones. These structures must have served as basements or storage spaces for surface-level dwellings. It is nonetheless important to note that most of the Ma'adi excavations were conducted with only minor attention paid to stratigraphical control, with the exception of the Italian excavations (still unpublished) and that of F. A. Badawi. Hence it is impossible, at present, to determine precisely the site's succeeding occupational phases. Unfortunately, the unearthing of hundreds of wooden stakes and post-holes[48] correspond to different layers, rendering unreadable any architectural element of the eastern area of the village allowing only the recognition of the floor plan of a few huts associated with the silos.[49]

The discoveries of J. Perrot at Safadi in the Wadi-Sheva valley belong to the Chalcolithic period. For several decades, they have been the source of hazardous comparisons on the theory of influences from this region during this period, W. C. Hayes,[50] comparing the Ma'adi subterranean or semi-subterranean structures excavated by Mustapha and Amer in 1940 (pl. 1:9–10) to those of Safadi and Abu-Matar (pl. 1:1–2), M. A. Hoffman[51] even suggesting that they were secondary residences of traders from the Wadi-Beersheva–Ghassoulian culture. At a first glance, indeed, the Wadi-Beersheva structures may present several similarities with those of Ma'adi. Yet we have found solid reasons to reject this theory.[52]

The first reason concerns the structural elements. J. Seeher[53] attempted to compare the semi-subterranean structures of Ma'adi with the second-phase structures of Safadi, which are obviously the most similar of the three phases. We must note here that the architecture of Safadi, in all its phases, is a wholly subterranean architecture with the exception of the final surface phase. For the structures of the Phase IIa (pl. 1:2),[54] we underline the condition of an originally underground structure whose roofs collapsed, and were then modified by building walls to support a roof. There were thus some technological modifications between the first and intermediary phases, but apparently no morphological modifications. Likewise, J. Perrot demonstrates how that dwelling-type is part of an evolution from a single underground chamber to a network of interconnected underground chambers.

The second reason is chronological. The excavations at Shiqmim led by T. Levy[55] confirms that the earliest construction phase of these Chalcolithic subterranean dwellings must be placed in the last third of the fifth millennium, around 4300 BCE, at a period preceding by far the settlement of Ma'adi, which according to different studies must be placed around 3800 BCE.[56] At Safadi, the radiocarbon datings also yield a sequence in the second half of the fifth millennium for the subterranean construction phase (supra). This chronological gap of nearly 500 years between the early phases of Chalcolithic/Ghassoulian cultures of Wadi-Sheva and that of Ma'adi excludes any direct link between these two architectures, a notion confirmed by the study of Palestinian artifacts from Ma'adi. Indeed, no ceramic from Chalcolithic Palestine—none whatsoever from the Beersheva cluster—has been discovered at Ma'adi.[57] The Palestinian material found at Ma'adi has been compared with both the Chalcolithic and Early Bronze Age I period, without clearly distinguishing the correct sequences for individual artifacts.[58] Our own studies of the Palestinian artifacts of Ma'adi show[59] that it is precisely contemporary with the initial phase of the Early Bronze Age I (EB Ia1), around 3700/3650 BCE,[60] and with this period only.

This precision is all the more interesting, as some of these semi-subterranean structures of Ma'adi (pl. 1:9–10) are found at a few hundred meters to the east of the "Badawi-building." It may be its prototypes, the closest parallel being the fourth ovoid semi-subterranean structure discovered by O. Menghin and M. Amer (pl. 1:10).[61] This structure of lesser dimension (4 m x 2.50 m), and like the structure discovered by F. A. Badawi is accessible by steps carved in the bedrock. Despite their differences, the structural elements are consistent: a large cavity carved in the bedrock with walls of mixed masonry (rubble and mud bricks). This construction may belong to a sequence between that of the elliptical semi-subterranean spaces to the east (pl. 1: 9)[62] and that of the stone structure discovered by Badawi on the western side (pl. 1:11).

If the hypothesis of a spatial displacement of the settlement is confirmed, we could envision this stone structure as corresponding to the most recent and elaborated phase of the Ma'adi village constructions. The artifacts discovered in the earth filling the buildings as well as in the surrounding levels forward no evidence to contradict this notion.[63] As such, one can be tempted to understand this structure as being of an earlier cultural tradition, and so far,[64] unique both for the Ma'adi's site as well as the others. The chambers carved into the bedrock, of elliptic shape for some and of roughly sub-rectangular for others, appear as forerunners of an architectural type that would become more sophisticated. Inspired by Palestinian construction concepts and techniques, it shows another genuinely local step of development.

Taking into account this unparalleled stone structure in Egypt, may lead us to search elsewhere concrete signs of influences that could have inspired this radical steps in architectural technology. It is necessary to take into consideration the existence of a model from the Southern Levant (Sidon-Dakerman, Yiftah'el, Afridar) that bears several items in common with the Ma'adi structures which cannot be ignored. This architecture is "sausage-shaped," constructed in stone (a material little used in this period in Egypt), and features a plastered floor (another Palestinian tradition). All of these are characteristics that can be found both on Palestinian sites of the Early Bronze Age I (EB Ia). The artifacts and imports from Palestine that were discovered in Ma'adi may further confirm this connection.

The Early EB I Palestinian cultures are contemporary with Ma'adi, but that does not necessarily imply that they were in direct contact. Nonetheless, culturally-Palestinian imports[65] at Ma'adi are characteristic of a very early phase of EB I. Similar artifacts to those of Ma'adi have been located in the Negev area at 'En Besor Oasis Site-H[66] (Lower layers, EB Ia1,[67] ca. 3650–3500 BCE) which attest to a minimum of trade links between the two regions. More interestingly, research at the oasis of 'En Besor (Site-H)[68] has yielded two samples of dwellings which, while summarily and partially excavated, feature remains of stone walls apparently belonging to ovoid structures of the type discovered in the Gaza region at Afridar *(supra)*.

Palestine thus presents during the Bronze Age an evolution from a rectangular surface shape of buildings (succeeding the subterranean dwellings), to an ovoid sub-surface structure (which, along with a rectilinear architecture of another type, is the dominant architecture of the EB I).[69] Around the same period, the site of Ma'adi appears to present an evolution from semi-underground storage spaces of elliptical shape dug in the ground, to semi-underground constructions of roughly sub-rectangular shape with walls built of rubble and mud bricks, and finally to semi-subterranean architecture of oval shape built in stone (pl. 1:9–11 and pl. 2).

The structure from Ma'adi west appears to represent an evolutionary crossroads: showing both similarities with the Mengin and Amer structures at Ma'adi, but also with structures from EB I in Southern Levant. Such a distribution of architectural traits, combined with the certainty of a growing EB I Palestinian influence on Ma'adi, allows us to advance the theory that the

Ma'adian architecture underwent both direct/internal evolutions and indirect/external evolution, and that the Ma'adian structures evolved into a hybrid architecture featuring elements of both Egyptian and Palestinian ancestry.

Besides the stone dwellings at Afya[70] in Nubia whose chronology is unclear (around 3000 BCE, not before?), the earliest stone constructions discovered to date in the Nile Valley have a funerary function. In Lower Egypt, they date to the beginning of the third millennium and belong to the First Dynasty (i.e. funerary chambers at Helwan with a stone floor and walls of limestone blocks at tomb 40 H.3, belonging to a high official contemporary with King Den[71]). In Upper Egypt they appear slightly later, from the Second Dynasty onward (funerary chamber with limestone-block floor and walls of King Khasekhemwy at Abydos[72]).

The existence of such a carefully constructed stone structure at Ma'adi, in Lower Egypt, some five hundred years before the first stone structures in Upper Egypt, is a remarkable discovery. It is also a further indication of the cultural evolution that took place in this area over more than a thousand years.

Notes:

1 C. Epstein, *The Chalcolithic Culture of the Golan* (IAA Report 4, Jerusalem, 1998), 352.

2 A. Mallon, R. Koeppel, R. Neuville, *Teleilât Ghassul I : Compte Rendu des Fouilles de l'Institut Biblique Pontifical, 1929–32* (Rome 1934), 254.

3 P. Bar-Adon, *The Cave of the Treasure* (Jerusalem, 1980), 243; A. Gopher and T. Tsuk, *Ancient Gold* (Jerusalem, 1991), 62.

4 J. Perrot, "Structures d'habitat, mode de vie et environnement : les villages souterrains des pasteurs de Beershéva," *Paléorient* 10/1 (1984), 80–3, fig. 7.

5 Perrot, "Structures d'habitat," 84–5, fig. 8.

6 Perrot, "Structures d'habitat," 84–6, fig. 10.

7 Perrot, "Structures d'habitat," 85–7, fig. 11.

8 These results are based on calibration tables that are today obsolete and which yield much too recent datings.

9 This chronology is today in the first half of EB I. We must nonetheless note that this chronology for the end of the Ghassulian in 3300 BCE was established in the 1950s (W. F. Albright, *L'archéologie de la Palestine* (Paris, 1955), 76) and is still used by some researchers (A. Mazar, *Archaeology of the Land of the Bible* (New York, 1990), 88).

10 T. Levy, "Radiocarbon Chronology of the Beersheva Culture and Predynastic Egypt," in E. van den Brink (ed.), *The Nile Delta in Transition* (Jerusalem, 1992), 350–5.

11 It appears that Shiqmim's division into phases is based on an arrangement of unclear radiocarbon datings, with some 30 dates aligning the chronological range, rather than being based on a real stratigraphy. See the criticism of Gilead for more ("The History of the Chalcolithic Settlement in the Nahal Beer Sheva Area: the Radiocarbon Aspect," *BASOR* 296 (1994), 5–12.

12 *Idem*, "The History of the Chalcolithic Settlement...," 12.

13 According to S. J. Bourke (pers. comm. 1999), the stratigraphy and radiocarbon datings made layer by layer on the village of Ghassûl (around 10 datings) shows that it was occupied continually throughout the fifth millennium, closing around 3900 BCE.

14 Gilead, "The Chalcolithic Period in the Levant," *Journal of World Prehistory* 2 (1988), 397–443.

15 C. Commenge-Pellerin, *La Poterie de Safadi (Beersheva) au IVe millénaire* (Paris, 1990), 230.

16 Gilead, "The History of the Chalcolithic Settlement in the Nahal Beer Sheva Area : the Radiocarborn Aspect," *BASOR* 296 (1994), 2, tab. 1.

17 F. Hassan, "Radiocarbon Chronology of Neolithic and Predynastic sites in Upper-Egypt and the Delta," *AAR* 3 (London, 1985), 105.

18 B. Mortensen, 1992, "Carbon-14 Dates from El-Omari," in R. Friedman and B. Adams, *The Followers of Horus, Studies dedicated to M. A. Hoffman (1944–1990)* (Oxford, 1992), 173.

19 A recently published radiocarbon dating (KN 4015) yields a range of 4300–3800 BCE for the first layer of Buto (see T. von der Way, in *Tell El Fara'in - Buto I* [1997], 82), a date which is coherent with the material, whatever may think S. Hendrickx ("La chronologie de la préhistoire tardive et des débuts de l'histoire de l'Egypte," *Archéo-Nil* 9 [12/1999], 20).

20 D. Faltings, "Recent Excavations in Tell El-Fara'in/Buto: New Finds and their Chronological Implications," *OLA* 82 (Leuven, 1998), 365–75. Watrin, "The Relationship between the Nile Delta and Palestine during the Fourth Millennium: from Early Exchange (Naqada I–II) to the Colonisation of Southern Palestine (Naqada III)," *OLA* 82 (Leuven, 1998), 1215.

21 Hassan, "Radiocarbon Chronology of Neolithic and Predynastic Sites...," 105. Rizkana and Seeher, *Maadi III*, 82.

22 See for example: J. B. Reynolds, *Regional Geography of Africa and Australasia* (London, 1911), 81.

23 Rizkana and Seeher, *Ma'adi* III (Mainz, 1989), 35–6, pl. XI–XII–XIII–XXII.

24 Our own work on the relationship between Egypt and Palestine place the beginning of the EB I in Palestine around 3700–3650 BCE on the basis of the study of material and radiocarbon datings from Ma'adi (Egypt), Wadi-Fidan 4 (Jordan), Sidon-Dakerman (Lebanon), and at several sites of Southern Palestine (Watrin, "The Relationship between the Nile Delta and Palestine," 1216–8. This chronology is in synchronicity with the works of Y. Yekutieli, who has come to the same conclusion on the basis of the material and radiocarbon datings from the sites of Southern Palestine (Yekutieli, pers. comm., 1998).

25 M. Dothan, "Excavations at Meser (1956)," *IEJ* 7 (1957), 217–228; "Excavations at Meser (1957)," *IEJ* 9 (1959), 13–29.

26 E. Braun, "The Problem of the Apsidal House: New Aspects of Early Bronze I Domestic Architecture in Israel, Jordan and Lebanon," *PEQ* 121 (1989), 6.

27 It may be possible that M. Dothan has found "wall negatives," contemporary with the curvilinear architecture (a fact that he fails to mention), and used it as a basis for his architectural reconstruction (?).

28 The only structure in Palestine dating from the EB I and that may present an "apsidal" form is a building located on the eastern slope of the Megiddo mound excavated by R. Engberg and G. Shipton in 1934. Only one aerial photograph was published (Engberg and Shipton, "Notes on the Chalcolithic and Early Bronze Age Pottery of Megiddo," *SAOC* 10 (1934), 244) from which this drawing has been made (A. G. Barrois, *Manuel d'Archéologie Biblique* I (Paris, 1939), 249, fig. 93b). The conditions of publication make any interpretations doubtful. In a recent article on Meser, M. Dothan ("Meser," *New Encyclopedia of Archaeological Excavations in the Holy Land* III (Jerusalem, 1993), 1035) confirms his interpretation by replacing the dotted lines of his earlier drawing with straight lines–definately apsidal–without any justification.

29 E. Braun, "Yiftah'el, Salvage and Rescue Excavations at a Prehistoric Village in Lower Galilee," *IAA Reports* 2 (Jerusalem, 1997), 249.

30 Nonetheless, this last structure, differing from the sausage-shaped Yifta'el structures, present a sub-rectangular plan with rounded angles. H. Khalaily and Z. Wallach, "Ashkelon, Ha-Tayyasim Street," *Excavations and Surveys* 18 (Jerusalem, 1998), 100, 154, fig. 189.

31 R. Saidah, "Fouilles de Sidon-Dakerman: l'agglomération Chalcolithique," *Berytus* XXVII 1979, 29–76. H. de Contenson, "A propos du niveau Chalcolithique de Dakerman," *Archéologie au Levant, Receuil R. Saidah* (Paris, 1982), 80–5.

32 Saidah, "Fouilles de Sidon-Dakerman...," 47. BP 4570 +- 90.

33 Saidah, "Fouilles de Sidon-Dakerman...," 49 (House n°2).

34 F. A. Badawi, "Kuzbericht über die neuen ägyptischen Ausgrabungen in Ma'adi (prädyn.)," *MAVV* 12 (Tübingen, 1987), 58–60; Badawi, "Kurzer Bericht aus dem spat-prädynastischen Fundort Maadi," *Eighth International Congress of Egyptologists, Abstract of Papers (Cairo, 28 March - 3 April 2000)*, 25.

35 See preliminary results in Watrin, "The Western Quarter of the Prehistoric Settlement of Ma'adi : Projected Archaeological Rescue Operation," *GREPAL* (Cairo, 1996), 50.

36 See Professor Badawi's article in this volume (*Proceedings of the Eighth International Congress of Egyptologists*). We note that this structure has been the object of a re-excavation in 1999 under the direction of U. Hartung (DAI) on the base of the GREPAL's project.

37 These traces were no longer visible during our survey in 1995, but the structure's exposure to erosion (filled and protected for 5600 years, then exposed to urban Cairo for 12 years) has doubtless wiped away the traces of this burning.

38 Badawi, "Kuzbericht über die neuen ägyptischen Ausgrabungen...," 58.

39 Badawi, "Kuzbericht über die neuen ägyptischen Ausgrabungen...," 58.

40 Badawi, "Kuzbericht über die neuen ägyptischen Ausgrabungen...," 60, pl. 2.

41 To the west of the building were found buried jar-silos, one of them contained salted fish. (Badawi, "Kuzbericht über die neuen ägyptischen Ausgrabungen...," 59).

42 A hypothesis of I. Caneva who had visited the site during the excavations of F. A. Badawi and proposed "a temple surrounded by store rooms" (see I. Caneva, B. Marcolongo and A. M. Palmieri, "Geoarchaeology at Maadi: A Short Note," *Proceedings of the Egyptian - Italian Seminar on Geosciences and Archaeology in the Mediterranean Countries: Cairo, November 28–30/1993* [Cairo, 1995], 311).

43 Excavations of the Egyptian University (O. Menghin, M. Amer, I. Rizkana) and the University of the Sapienza (Roma).

44 I. Caneva, M. Frangipane and A. Palmieri, "Predynastic Egypt: new data from Maadi," *AAR* 5 (1987), 113.

45 Rizkana and Seeher, *Maadi* III, 35; 50–4.

46 Rizkana and Seeher, *Maadi* III, pl. XIV, 3.

47 Rizkana and Seeher, *Maadi* III, 49.

48 Rizkana and Seeher, *Maadi* III, fig. 5a et 5b.

49 Rizkana and Seeher, *Maadi* III, 41, fig. 8, pl. XII, 1–2. For example in Square XIIa.

50 W. C. Hayes, *Most Ancient Egypt* (Chicago, 1965), 123.

51 M. A. Hoffman, *Egypt Before the Pharaohs* (New York, 1979), 201.

52 See the first criticisms on this subject in Watrin, *Les Echanges entre l'Egypte et la Palestine au IVe millénaire : Etat de la Question*, M.A. Dissertation (University of Paris I, Sorbonne, 1995), 67–72.

53 Rizkana and Seeher, *Maadi* III, 55.

54 Perrot, "Structures d'habitat, mode de vie et environnement...," 83, fig. 8; i.e. dwellings 528 and 546.

55 T. Levy, "Radiocarbon Chronology of the Beersheva Culture and Predynastic Egypt," in E. van den Brink, *The Nile Delta in Transition* (Cairo, 1992), 348.

56 Rizkana and Seeher, *Maadi* IV (Mainz, 1990), 104, fig. 34F. Caneva, M. Frangipane, A. Palmieri, "Recent

Excavations at Maadi (Egypt)," in *Late Prehistory of the Nile Basin and the Sahara* (Poznan, 1989), 289. F. Hassan, "Radiocarbon Chronology of Neolithic and Predynastic Sites...," 105. I. (BP 5050 +-55).

57 Some researchers claim to have identified the Chalcolithic Palestinian ceramics at Ma'adi, without any precision as to which (D. Faltings, "Recent Excavations in Tell El-Fara'in/Buto...," 374).

58 For example: Rizkana and Seeher, *Maadi* I (Mainz, 1987), 74, 79.

59 I thank the successive directors of the Cairo University, I. Rizkana and Y. Fayyed, for allowing me to study their collections since 1993.

60 Watrin, "Copper Drops and Buried Buildings: Ma'adi's Legacy as a Predynastic Trade Capital," *Bulletin de la Société de Géographie d'Egypte* 73 (Cairo, 2000), 171–173.

61 A. Badawy, *A History of Egyptian Architecture,* vol. I (Giza, 1954), 18, fig. 8. Rizkana and Seeher, *Maadi* III, 54, pl. 18. In Square XXVIIb.

62 Badawy, *A History of Egyptian Architecture,* fig. 15 and 17.

63 Some of the shapes (i.e. blackware jars with a pointed base) may have come later in an occupation phase (Late Naqada IIa?). See Watrin, "Copper Drops and Buried Buildings...," 170.

64 September 2000.

65 Ledge-handled ceramics with wavy and ring handles, scrapers and "Canaanean blades," copper ingots, asphalt.

66 Blackware, catfish barbs, *Asphataria Nilotica* shells, square-sectioned copper hooks.

67 The works of Y. Yekutieli (in *The Early Bronze IA of Southwestern Canaan*, M.A. Thesis, (Tel Aviv University, 1992) show that at 'En Besor Site H, two archaeological phases should be recognized according to the material (EB Ia1 and EB Ia2).

68 E. Macdonald, *Beth-Pelet II : Prehistoric Fara* (London, 1932), pl. IX–X. Hypothesis also advanced by E. Braun ("Cultural diversity and Change in the Early Bronze Age I of Israel and Jordan," unpublished Ph.D. thesis, [Tel-Aviv University, 1996], 119–120).

69 The most recent synthesis works on Levantine architecture are those of E. Braun ("The Problem of the Apsidal House," 1–43) and A. Golani ("New Perspectives on Domestic Architecture and the Initial Stages of Urbanization in Canaan," *LEVANT* 31 (1999), 123–32).

70 H. S. Smith, *Preliminary Reports of the Egypt Exploration Society's Nubian Survey* (Cairo, 1962), 58–61, fig. VII, 1.

71 Z. Saad, *Royal Excavations at Saqqara and Helwan* (Cairo, 1947), 164, pl. LXII–LXIX. T. Wilkinson, "A Reexamination of the Early Dynastic Necropolis at Helwan," *MDAIK* 52 (1996), 342.

72 F. Petrie, *Royal Tombs* II, 57, 4–5. J. M. Breasted, *Histoire de l'Egypte I* (Bruxelles, 1926), pl. 27.

Recent Work at Sa al-Hagar (Sais)

Penelope Wilson

University of Durham

Since 1997 the Egypt Exploration Society based in London and Cairo has been carrying out an archaeological survey of the area at the village of Sa al-Hagar in the western Delta. This area has been identified with the site of the ancient city of Sais, capital of Egypt in the Twenty-sixth Dynasty and the name Sa apparently preserves the ancient name of the city. The aim of the survey is to map and record archaeological information at Sais as part of a wider Delta survey of sites. This paper presents the results of three short seasons from 1997 to 1999 and also offers some comments on the wider context of Sais itself and on the methodological approach to work with a Delta perspective.[1]

Sais is an Egyptological paradox. Much is known about it from textual sources and especially from the account of Herodotus who probably visited the city around 450 BCE. He described its Royal Palace (of Apries), the temple complex of Neith/Athene, the ceremonies at the Sacred Lake involving floating lamps on the water at night, the Royal Tombs of the Saite ruling family and colossal statues and obelisks standing in the sacred precinct.[2] These buildings represent the Twenty-sixth Dynasty flourishing of the city and based on this account several reconstructions of the Neith Complex have been attempted, firstly by Champollion and most recently by the *L'Égypte Restituée* volume on the Delta.[3] Strabo and Athenogoras (second century CE) also both discussed the importance of the Osiris cult at Sais in their respective accounts.

However, on the other hand, the archaeological background has been less well known, suggesting that archaeologically Sais was a lost cause. One of the earliest western visitors was Carsten Niebuhr around 1776 who records his sense of disappointment at what he saw at "Salhadsjar"; he expected a ruined city, instead he found only mud-brick remains.[4] Nineteenth century visitors such as E.D. Clarke (*ca.* 1815), Champollion (1828), Wilkinson, and the Prussian Lepsius expedition (last two, both 1842) however described and drew huge, standing mud-brick enclosure walls and remnants of what could have been the temple area.[5] In 1894 Georges Foucart drew a plan of the enclosure area at the site with some walls and areas still covered with pottery within the walls.[6]

This mud-brick enclosure had, however, mostly disappeared by the early part of this century; the mud brick had been taken away or possibly even been sold as *sebakh* and now the walls no longer survive. Today the visitor to the site will arrive at modern Sa al-Hagar to find a huge pit to the north of the village about 400 m by 400 m. However this is not the enclosure area described in the previous accounts. One must walk further to the north where there is a series of tracks forming a rectangular area with the land on the outside noticeably higher than that on the inside. The modern track was built on the foundations offered by the last few courses of the ancient enclosure wall.

Inside this area are two protected pieces of antiquities land called Kom Rebwa. They are a confused mass of hillocks, sharp grass, decaying salty pottery shards and lots of small pieces of stone such as granite, brown quartzite, volcanic tufa, basalt, limestone, and sandstone. Our contour survey of this area suggested a few possible ridges that may be the remains of walls, but otherwise showed that massive amounts of mud-brick had been dug out and taken away. These excavations left behind "negative" impressions of the walls that had been removed and the resulting hollows are filled with water. The volume of mud from the enclosure walls themselves with the dimensions of approximately 744 meters long, 625 meters wide, 17.5 meters thick, and 26 meters high would have yielded enough *sebakh* to make another Bent Pyramid. The name for one of the hillocky areas on Foucart's map was "Qasr" possibly making this a reference to the palace area. The "palace," if it was like the Memphis Palace of Apries, may well have been a building on top of a massive mud-brick foundation, more like a fortress than anything else and perhaps guarded by some of the Ionian or Carian cohorts described by Herodotus. This structure may have been attached to the temple complex, which may then have had a north-south orientation, as hinted at by the plan of Wilkinson in 1842. This also suggests a main entrance in the south wall. At the east side of the enclosure there is also a natural spring that may have supplied the sacred lake if it was also in the area. The lake is known from a statue inscription now in the Greco-Roman Museum in Alexandria. This is an account by the man who dug this sacred lake and tells us that it was on the east side of the temple and 68 cubits by 65 cubits in size and built of stone.

A transect of the enclosure area with a drill augur yielded interesting results. Inside the enclosure area all cores brought up pot shards from at least 6 m from the ground level and at most from 8 m when they reached a compact clay level. The core on the "walls" at the west showed 2.8 m of clay from the track downward and came down onto a compact clay which may indeed be a wall built on a clay layer. On the east side, the drill hole seemed to contain more pottery and it is possible that this either missed the wall, the wall had eroded away or there was a break in the actual wall at this point. The cores outside the enclosure were devoid of pottery on the whole, but contained important environmental information about former watercourses and river channels, both to the east and west.

The striking great pit to the north of the village had clearly once contained something monumental. The surface of the pit bottom is sandy in places but also shows evidence of large-scale monument destruction; limestone chips, fragments of different types of hard stones and pottery. A basalt sarcophagus used to lie in the pit along with a group of uninscribed but massive granite blocks and a length of monumental limestone wall at the south edge. This wall runs east to west and seems to run out on its western side, while its eastern extent is unknown. The blocks are huge and gouged and grooved on the front part—perhaps the Late Period mark of sacred buildings. There may also be a threshold entrance here and steps as if leading up into a stone structure—very like the small pylon entrances. If this were a pylon it would be part of a building also oriented south-north, and it aligns well with the complex in the north. In this case there may also have been an enclosure in the south possibly around the area of the great pit. Some of the local topography makes it possible as there are ridges (a cemetery to east and a farmstead to the north) and suggestive mounds which could form an Enclosure remnant.

Between the limestone wall and the village are a series of Roman pottery dumps and baked brick structures, including a bath house excavated by the EAO/SCA, and at the east a series of mud-brick cell structures also previously excavated and which produced a mass of Hellenistic and Late Period material registered in the official register book.[7] This material includes a spectacular horde consisting of a metal-foundry deposit of Hellenistic and Roman bronzes, now in the Tanta Museum.

To the east of the great pit at ground level, surface traces of buildings were visible on damp or foggy mornings and so we made a magnetometer survey of this unexcavated area. It showed a series of cell-like structures and at least two alignments of larger structural features.

The northern enclosure and great pit were the obvious parts of the site, but it seemed likely that the fields around the site and in between these two main areas had also been parts of the Sais township. A magnetometer survey of a field between the pit and a farmstead mound was made and the results showed there was a series of buildings under the ground, the largest with walls 2-3 m thick. There are also possible kilns and some smaller buildings. Nothing was visible on the surface there and the pottery in the field was negligible, so that field walking would have missed this area. It may well be that these are structures within a southern enclosure. A number of temples are known from inscriptional material to have been at Sais. Apart from the Neith temple complex which also contained the *Resenet* and *Hut-Bit* there was probably also a temple to Osiris-Hemag and to Atum. The Osiris cult seems to have been important at Sais and there may have been a proper mausoleum for stone sarcophagi.

The town of Sais lost its capital status at the end of the Twenty-sixth Dynasty but seems to have retained some kind of importance in the Roman Period and it was a bishopric in the Christian era and an Islamic center for a time. All of these stages have left their mark on the site and Sais is rather a totality of time, possibly lasting from the Predynastic Period and going through to the present day. The site may seem to have been inhabited for at least 5,000 years in some form or other and the survey has attempted to take account of this time span, recording as much as possible.

The ancient city of course did not just consist of temple complexes, but there must have been a settlement here too. Further, the series of drill core transects across the site suggested that there had been a river channel or canal much closer to Sais than the current river channel, suggesting that the river has moved westward over time. The date of our channel is not yet known and its existence may have implications for the areas of settlement at the site. For, if the river had moved significantly, may it not have actually moved across the site or away from it, causing settlements to be relocated and possibly abandoned, then resettled after the river had passed (as seems to have happened at Memphis)? This movement of river channels was probably an important aspect of Delta towns and may in some cases explain why towns rise in importance then fade, then appear again in a slightly different place. If the ancient site of the main temple was remembered then it could have been refounded in roughly the same place (as perhaps at Buto?). Alternatively, if temple enclosures were built to keep the temple pure, might they also have provided a watertight barrier against the flood? Old temple sites in the Delta are frequently not on the highest ground on the site, but over time become the lowest (for example at Tell Balamun, Tanis, Kom al-Hisn). In this case the mud-brick enclosure could function primarily as a flood barrier. From a distance the enclosure would appear as a squat mastaba-shape or mound on the horizon, perhaps visible at a small distance away only.

The drill cores also turned up a surprise just to the west of the great pit area, beyond the houses along the edge. Here after 2.5 m from ground level the augur came to clean sand and it went down as far as it was possible to go, possibly about 6 m. This may be a *gezira* at the site, perhaps the original impetus for occupation. It may be further tied-in with survey work in the village of Sa al-Hagar itself. Though not very obvious, the town does stand upon a small *tell*. The oldest part rises to a height of 7 m above the ground level. It is possible that indeed the modern village is part of the anciently-occupied area.

All of the cores in the center of the great pit showed that it consisted of disturbed ground at the surface, but one of the cores showed two distinct levels of cultural remains (pottery) separated by clean clay. The lowest pottery level was at 7.69 m below the present sea level (taking the ground surface at Sais to be 5 m above sea level) and dates possibly to the late Predynastic-Early Dynastic period.

In addition the work here has also recorded the monuments from the site and its environs, trying to gather as much information as possible about the monuments that once stood here. At the guard house on the site are a number of blocks from the area and from Sa al-Hagar, including a colossal face from a statue and a lintel with the name of "Neith, Mistress of Sa." The distinctive brown quartzite blocks and stones of D.26 actually occur all the way up the Rosetta branch of the Nile. Habachi collected a group of these stones from villages on the Nile,[8] also at Rosetta itself (built into Fort Qaitbey) and indeed the Alexandria Greco-Roman Museum also houses several reused large blocks that could have come from Sais. Around the world many museums have statues and objects with a possible Sais provenance. The survey has also recorded their whereabouts and some of them are of surprising antiquity, such as the statue fragment of Psamtek II which was found in the mosque at Sa al-Hagar by E. D. Clarke around 1815 and donated to Cambridge University (now in the Fitzwilliam Museum).

A modest archaeological survey can therefore have more widespread applications and is a holistic approach to both the material from the site and at the site. The combination of all of the techniques and approaches I have described could be applied to other places with apparently less to offer (indeed most are used in other places with great success; for example at Buto (drills), Piramesse (geophysics). This methodology represents a relatively cheap and effective method of dealing with the difficult excavation problems in the Delta. Such work could be carried out on a larger scale, such as across the western Delta, which has been a relatively neglected area, or *gezira* sites in Lake Burullus where these largely Roman and Late Byzantine surface sites will be at risk from ecological as well as human factors.

The methodological approach is relatively cheap and effective: places with the names Kom or Tell in them could be listed then visited. If on visual inspection there is something to be seen (as at Sais), then it can be surveyed and mapped. Information from remote sensing satellite data can also be logged, and be useful, after data manipulation, to show other environmental factors. The data would be held in a digital Geographical Information System (GIS) and logged in by the place's longitude and latitude coordinates. A series of drill cores, magnetometer or other geophysical work, collaboration with the local SCA office on listing finds made at the spot and locally, and then finds which have found their way to other museums can be added. If the tell is well defined, such as at Tell Mutabis, then a field-walking and shard-sampling program can be carried out. The information could build up a picture of the settlement patterns of an area, perhaps showing defunct water channels by density of settlements (as in the case of the Canopic Branch), showing bursts of settlement activity (for example in the Hellenistic and Roman Periods). There may also have been an Alexandria effect, where, with the founding of the city, its influence spread in a ripple effect outwards and it might be possible to archaeologically map the pattern. Anyone traveling in the Delta today will notice the many small towns and villages comprising settlement clusters separated by larger centers. The picture in antiquity might well have been similar and also possible to demonstrate from the archaeological survey.

If sites do not show up on the surface, it seems possible that there is still something under the ground surface. In Egypt there is not the deep plowing which causes so much archaeological damage in Britain. A site that has apparently disappeared from maps of the Delta could be located using GPS coordinates obtained from the old *Survey of Egypt* maps. Then a series of drill transects and some magnetometer work (perhaps using local knowledge) may quickly reveal information that could be collected and logged in a database. This amounts to a kind of keyhole archaeology and is an effective means of tracking settlement spread, size, and date. Full-scale excavation may not be possible through cost or technical difficulties, or desirable in terms of interest and ethical considerations, or viable, and the agricultural fields might actually be the safest way to protect the archaeology underneath them until such time as they can be investigated more competently and less destructively. Current geophysical techniques (GPR, resistivity, and magnetometry) may well give rise to full three-dimensional scans of fields to produce computer images of what is below the ground. Areas could then be pinpointed for specific dating material, thus avoiding large-scale excavation and its randomness. Until that time there is still a wealth of data to be collected and properly and systematically evaluated.

It is also possible to begin a discussion about the nature of life in the Delta in ancient times and put our research at Sais into some sort of western Delta context. Buto and Sais may have been centers of Predynastic kingdoms and trading posts of the north; in the New Kingdom there may have been "Libyan" colonies or settlements here, carefully controlled by a series of Ramesside fortifications; later Sais was at the center of the Kingdoms of the West controlling the oasis routes and wealth (as exemplified by the Bahariya "Valley of the Mummies"); the town may have been one of the Greek colonies, and perhaps there were also Late Period city states of great wealth with partially fortified "palaces," carrying their importance through the Ptolemaic and Roman Periods. There seem to be archaeologically silent periods such as the Middle Kingdom and careful analysis of data may show that this is not case, but that it is simply well-hidden.

The west Delta, as shown by the site at Sais, might look unpromising but it seems that the archaeology of the west Delta is potentially just as colorful as anywhere in Egypt, admittedly somewhat bathed in good Delta mud, but nonetheless patiently attainable and recordable.

Notes:

1 For preliminary publications see P. Wilson, "Sais: Surveying the Royal City," *EA* 12, 1998, 3–6;
  P. Wilson, "The Survey of Sais, 1997," *JEA* 84 (1998), 2–4; P. Wilson, "The Survey at Sais
  (Sa el-Hagar), 1998," *JEA* 85 (1999), 1–4 and Pl. 1.

2 Herodotus, *The Histories* II, trans. A. H. Godley, The Loeb Classical Library (London: W. Heine-
  mann),1966. 163; 172; 177 ff.

3 J. Fr. Champollion, in H. Hartleben (ed.,) *Lettres et journaux* II, (Paris, 1909), 98–105.

4 C. Niebuhr, *Voyage en Arabie et en d'autres Pays circonvoisins* I (Amsterdam and Utrecht, 1776), 78–79.

5 E. D. Clarke, *Travels in various countries of Europe, Asia and Africa: Part UU, section II Greece, Egypt
  and the Holy Land* (New York, 1815), 284–287; G. Wilkinson, Manuscript in Bodleian Library, Oxford,
  plan 251 and notebook printed in G. Rawlinson, *History of Herodotus* II (London, 1862), 218; Lepsius,
  Denkmäler I, text 3-4, Pl.55–56.

6 G. Foucart, "Notes prises dans le Delta," *RT* 20 (1898), 162–169.

7 Many thanks are due to the Inspectors at Tanta for their assistance, in particular Ms Fatma Ragab.

8 L. Habachi, "Saïs and its Monuments," *ASAE* 42 (1943), 369–407.

Waseda University Excavations in Egypt and Recent Works at North Saqqara

Sakuji Yoshimura, Masanori Saito
Waseda University

Thirty Years of Exploration in Egypt by Waseda University

The Institute of Egyptology at Waseda University started conducting fieldwork in Egypt in 1966, and subsequently undertook archaeological investigation.[1] Our first full-scale excavation was carried out at Malqata South. There, a mud-brick structure was discovered under a small hill near the Isis Temple at Deir el-Shalwit, which is known as "Kom al-Samak." This structure measured approximately 20 m by 80 m and was furnished with a painted staircase. Though the staircase was partially destroyed, the steps from the first to the twentieth remained. These had been plastered and decorated. Two kinds of motifs were painted on alternate steps: a pair of bound bows, and portraits of foreign captives. Three different races were identified: Nubians, Syrians, and another Asiatic tribe. Their hands were tied behind them, and they were lying down. Since rows of bows and bound captives typically decorate pavements and steps upon which the king trod, this structure might have been used for some ceremony involving the king. Some bricks bearing a cartouche of Amenhotep III mean that this structure can be confidently dated to his reign. The style of mural painting also seems typical of monuments of the Eighteenth Dynasty. Given that this royal monument was constructed within the palace complex of Malqata, it could be assumed it was intended for the jubilee festival of Amenhotep III.

In order to obtain comparative data, investigations of the Royal Palace of Malqata and private tombs in the Theban Necropolis were carried out. While investigating Malqata, numerous painted plaster fragments from walls and ceilings were discovered. One of the most remarkable motifs, which was reconstructed from small fragments, is a row of vultures with their wings spread, representing the goddess Nekhbet. Under each the names and titles of Amenhotep III were painted. These fragments were unearthed from the King's Bedroom, and bear they impressions of ceiling matting on the back. This indicates that they were from the ceiling. The Nekhbets were thus a device to protect the king during his sleep.

From 1980, excavations and cleaning of some private tombs were carried out at al-Khokha and Dra Abu al-Naga. A large number of human remains were discovered in the tombs at Sheikh

Abd al-Qurna. More than one hundred mummies were examined by archaeological and anthropological methods. They were presumed to have been collected by thieves in order to rifle them for funerary objects sometime after the Roman Period.

Beginning in 1984, an epigraphic survey of some private tombs was conducted. Wall decoration dating to the late Eighteenth Dynasty, from the reign of Thutmose IV to Horemheb, was recorded. This survey examined the patterns and method of painting of the time in order to restore the mural paintings from Kom al-Samak.

Scientific research was carried out on the Giza Plateau from 1987 onward. Some exploration by Electromagnetic Wave Radar was undertaken in order to understand the inner structure of the Great Pyramid without using destructive methods. Productive results were obtained, including some unusual radar reactions. These unusual reactions suggest the existence of an unknown interior space in the south side of the Great Pyramid. This scientific method was applied to survey the distribution of sites in the North Saqqara-South Abusir area. This trial succeeded in uncovering the monument of Khaemwaset, of which a detailed description will be given later.

The Institute of Egyptology at Waseda University is now involved in three archaeological projects in Egypt. The first is the excavation and documentation of the tomb of Amenhotep III in the Western Valley of the Kings, begun in 1989. This project is a logical follow-up to our previous work on the monuments of the time of Amenhotep III. The re-clearance was the first since Howard Carter's work in 1915. Archaeological research and excavation of a small rock-cut chamber called WV-A and the area between the entrances of the tomb of Amenhotep III and WV-A were also carried out. A number of finds were uncovered during the excavation, including an intact foundation deposit, funerary equipment, and ostraca. This important material is being studied for future publication.

The second project is the excavation at North Dahshur, started in 1995.[2] The most important aspect of this project is the discovery of a New Kingdom necropolis. At Dahshur, only the necropolises of the Old and Middle Kingdoms were known previously. A large free-standing tomb chapel, comparable in size to the famous tomb chapel of Horemheb at Saqqara, was eventually revealed. More than ten burial shafts of New Kingdom date were also discovered both within and outside this tomb-chapel and were thoroughly investigated. The tomb-chapel seems, on the basis of the stamps on its mud bricks, to have been built for a certain Ipay, royal butler and royal scribe. It turned out, however, that the burial of Ipay was not in the burial chamber at the bottom of the tomb shaft: instead we found a granite sarcophagus for the Ramesside royal scribe Mes. It is obvious the original structure had been later reused.

The material from this site extends from the time of Amenhotep III to the Ramesside Period. Innumerable objects of good quality were unearthed. Studies of comparable funerary equipment should provide information concerning burial customs during the New Kingdom. It is thus quite certain that the project at Dahshur will contribute to our understanding of the history and archaeology of the New Kingdom Memphite Necropolis.

North Saqqara Project
Monument of Prince Khaemwaset

The third project is the excavation at North Saqqara. The site is situated on top of a small hill-like outcrop of limestone that rises above the desert approximately one kilometer northwest of the Serapeum. Because of its remoteness and its occupation by the Egyptian army during the 1970s, the site had long escaped scholarly attention. No systematic archaeological investigation had been undertaken in the area prior to our work. In December 1991 we began to excavate the hilltop, and subsequently discovered a stone monument of Prince Khaemwaset, the fourth son of Ramesses II.

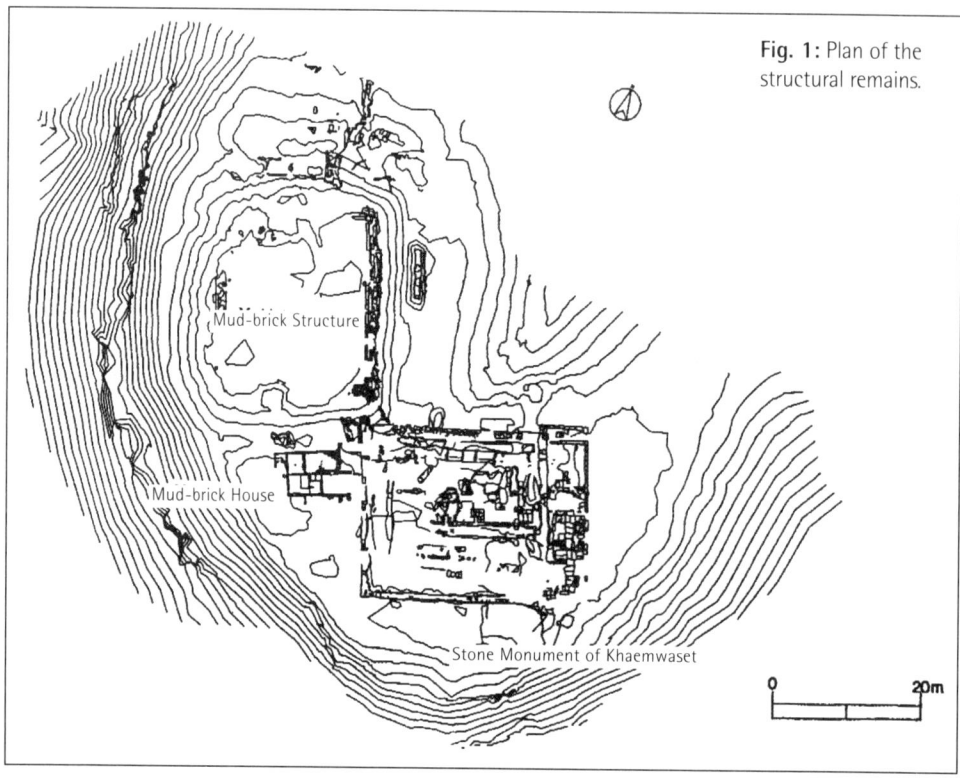

Fig. 1: Plan of the structural remains.

Mud-brick Structure

Mud-brick House

Stone Monument of Khaemwaset

0   20m

The monument was originally a free-standing chapel. In later times its upper part was quarried for its stones, and now only the foundations and some of the flooring are left. The structure covers an area of about 25 m (north-south) by 30 m (east-west), and consists of three elements: a portico, a corridor, and a cult room, arranged along an east-west axis. In the cult room, located in the area furthest west, we found two fragmentary blocks of a red-granite false-door. On this false-door a seated figure of Khaemwaset was carved. He is shown wearing the sidelock and is flanked by four vertical columns of hieroglyphs which include his name and titles. This false door was probably originally set up at the western end of the cult room, and must have been the focal point of this monument. The corridor connects the cult room and the portico. The outer wall surrounds the cult room and the corridor, while the portico lies immediately adjacent to the east. Several other minor features, such as alignments of blocks, have been identified within the space surrounded by the outer wall, but nothing resembling a burial shaft has yet been located.

The monument was built largely of blocks taken from much earlier buildings, chiefly dating to the Old Kingdom judging by the style of the reliefs and inscriptions found on the unexposed surfaces. Blocks with weathered surfaces probably also came from the same source. Based on the quantity of such blocks and the hieratic inscriptions on some of them, it may be assumed that for the most part they were systematically quarried from several Old Kingdom monuments, including pyramid complexes and private mastabas at Saqqara and Abusir. It should be pointed out that, despite Khaemwaset's practice of restoring monuments, the fact is that he was also a usurper of such monuments.[3]

As mentioned above, the easternmost side of this building was furnished with a magnificent portico. This contained sixteen lotiform columns. Its height is estimated at five meters on the basis of the reconstruction of the columns. One can imagine that Khaemwaset's building on the top of the hill could easily be seen from the city of Memphis.

During the course of excavations, a number of limestone relief fragments were unearthed. Some were identified as belonging to a limestone false-door, others were carved with scenes of offering to deities and processions of gods and goddesses. Most of the reliefs are raised, while those of the limestone false-door are sunk. These finely-carved fragments were obviously part of the wall decoration of the monument. Some had been left unfinished which may indicate that the construction of this stone building was never completed.

During the sixth season of excavation, a foundation deposit was uncovered in the northwest corner of the outer wall of the monument. It consisted of six faience scarabs, two faience plaques, and many miniature pottery vessels. The base of each scarab and both sides of each plaque are inscribed with the names and titles of Khaemwaset, "Sem-priest, King's Son, Khaemwaset." Since this foundation deposit was undisturbed, it can safely be concluded that Khaemwaset was the builder of the stone monument.

It should be mentioned that a hieratic ostracon and a jar docket provide year dates. The former mentions Year 51 or 54 and the latter refers to Year 53. They are doubtlessly regnal years of Ramesses II.[4] It may be presumed that some activity relating to Khaemwaset was attempted during these years at this site. Notably, the ostracon refers to Khaemwaset's "Ka house." This may indicate the purpose of this monument.

In addition, a small mud-brick building was discovered to the west. It measures approximately 7.7 m by 6.2 m, and contained four rooms and two additional features. Two entrances were installed in the south side, both with limestone thresholds. The limestone thresholds appear to be of the same type as the stones in Khaemwaset's monument. It is highly probable that they came from the store collected by Khaemwaset for his monument. This indicates that the mud-brick house and the stone monument were part of the same building program; therefore the mud-brick house might have been an institution attached to the stone monument. This small house may have functioned as a temporary dwelling for priests who served the larger monument of Khaemwaset.

Royal Activities during the Middle Eighteenth Dynasty

From the sixth season onward, the excavation area was extended to the northwest of Khaemwaset's stone monument, where another building was uncovered. This structure was built with mud bricks and its dimensions are about 25 m (north-south) by 22 m (east-west). It is noteworthy that this mud-brick structure and the stone monument of Khaemwaset were arranged according to the same alignment, probably determined by the flow of the Nile. Moreover, the scale of the mud-brick structure is nearly equal to that of the area surrounded by the outer wall of the stone monument. The strong resemblance between two buildings in scale and orientation suggests that the arrangement of the stone building was strongly affected by the existing mud-brick structure.

Only the foundation bricks of the mud-brick structure were preserved, since this area was thoroughly disturbed. However, excavations around the mud-brick structure revealed some clues from which we can infer its original appearance. With the removal of the thick layers of debris, it has become clear that this building was constructed in a unique way. The highest place of the original landform was chosen for its building site. In addition, the ground around the building was artificially cut off to raise the building higher than its surroundings, as if it were intended to be built on a "platform," dug out from the surrounding ground. As a consequence, the eastern side of the platform was cut at about a 25 degree incline. Cutting the ground around the building gives an impression that it was built at the top of a steep incline. At the foot of the platform, part of the deep moat was also uncovered. This moat measures 2 m wide and 1.5 m deep, and it was clearly dug parallel to the mud-brick structure. At the bottom of the moat, the bedrock was cut into with great effort. In spite of its bad preservation, evidence remains that this feature was constructed using a painstaking method.

One stamped brick with the name of Amenhotep II and five stamped bricks of Thutmose IV were found. Assuming that these bricks were used for the construction of this mud-brick structure, it is probable that Amenhotep II and/or Thutmose IV built it. The fact that objects from this area can generally be dated to the Eighteenth Dynasty supports this hypothesis.

One of the most notable results from the recent excavations is the discovery of stelae of Thutmose IV. So far more than ten stelae with the name of Thutmose IV have been discovered. Their motifs vary from the king smiting foreign enemies and images of a god or goddess, to royal cartouches. These stelae are similar to another series of stelae of Thutmose IV discovered by Selim Hassan during the excavations at Giza.[5] Based on the stelae from Giza, Betsy Bryan

Fig. 2: Stelae of Tuthmose IV.

believes that, "Thutmose wished to create at Giza a gathering place for all the gods."[6] It may be that our site was built for the same purpose. The above-mentioned stelae from our site indicate that Thutmose IV was active on this hill. It is certain that this king regarded this small hill as a special place.

A large number of small fragments of mural painting were uncovered around the small mud-brick structure. Although they were broken into small pieces, several motifs such as zigzags, rosettes, spirals, and stars, were recognized as characteristic of ceiling decoration of New

Kingdom palaces and private tombs. Some mural fragments depicting a kind of animal skin were also identified. Although their original location is unclear, they may have been part of the decoration of the building.

The most notable motif reconstructed from small fragments is a winged leopard. The body of this leopard is 60 cm long, and measures 40 cm in height. It is depicted against a white background, and has a yellow (or ochre) body with red spots. The leopard's wing is raised upwards, and is colored light blue. Though these fragments were painted in the traditional Egyptian way, the winged leopard is rare in the repertoire of contemporary wall decoration. A credible hypothesis is that this motif was inspired by interconnections with the Aegean World.

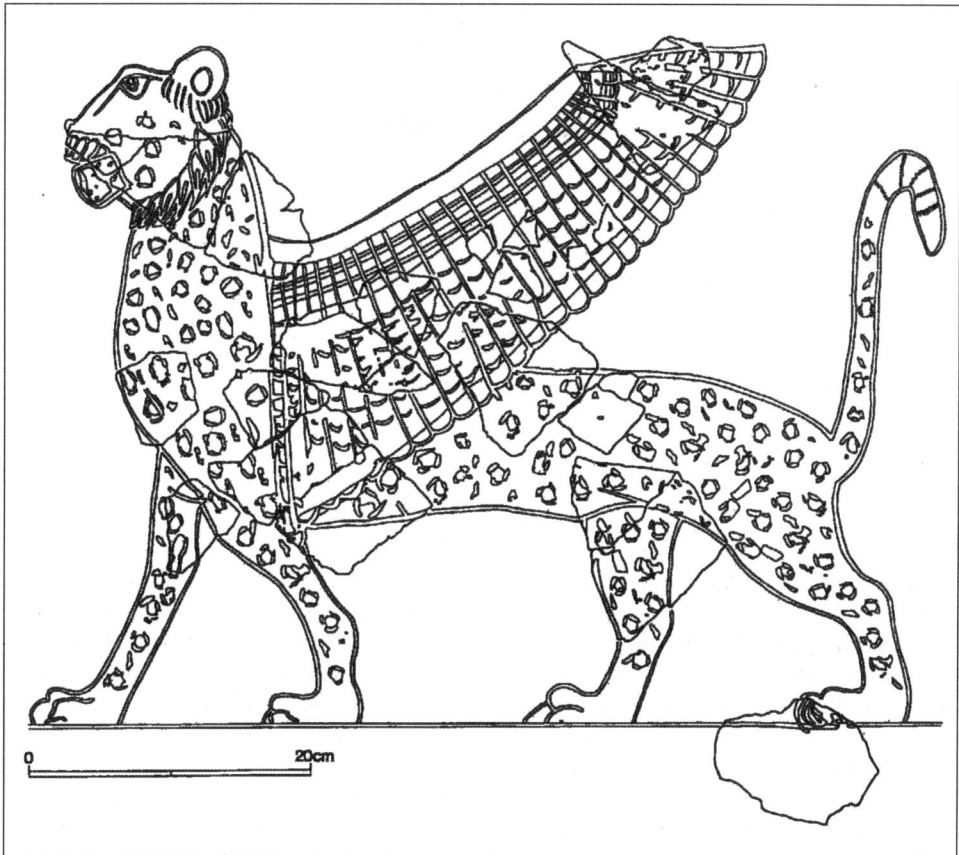

Fig. 3: Tentative reconstruction of the winged leopard.

Blue-painted pottery shards were also uncovered in this area. The most elaborate examples of painted vessels from this site are made of fine marl clay, and are exquisitely decorated. They have motifs such as a row of small chrysanthemum flowers, "Four-Petal Flowers," or "Bead-Net," and a minute hieroglyphic design. The fine brushwork indicates that these vessels belong to the initial period of blue-painted pottery.[7] Although it is very difficult to find parallels of the same quality, the so-called "Giza Group" can be cited as a similar. The Giza Group is a type of blue-painted pottery that was discovered in the area west of the Sphinx, and is dated to the reign of Amenhotep II or Thutmose IV. It is thus clear that the blue-painted pottery from our site can also be dated to mid-Eighteenth Dynasty.

Based on the Giza Group, Colin Hope suggested that the blue-painted pottery has its origin in the Memphite area.[8] It is reasonable to consider that the examples from our site support Hope's opinion. Moreover, the likely date of manufacture, i.e. the reigns of Amenhotep II and Thutmose IV, seems to be the transitional phase of the decoration of blue-painted pottery. These materials are therefore very valuable since they may elucidate the development of this type of ceramic.

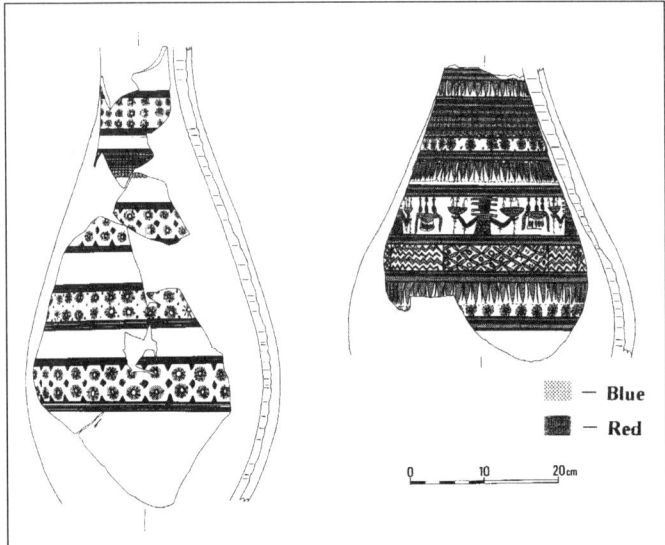

— Blue

— Red

Fig. 4:
Blue-painted pottery.

Concluding Remarks

The recent work on the top of the small hill at North Saqqara shed light on the early history of this site. It was quite possible that Khaemwaset chose this hill as the site for his "Ka house" because it maintained its importance from the mid-Eighteenth Dynasty.

The purpose or function of the mud-brick structure remains unclear. Judging from its magnificent appearance, it is reasonable to assume it was constructed for religious purposes. Some of the stelae and the elaborate wall decorations also indicate the religious character of the building. Alternatively, judging from the remoteness of the site, it could be assumed that this building was a small palace or rest house for the king. It is hard to provide a definitive answer. In either case, however, the historical importance of the mud-brick structure cannot be underestimated.

Further archaeological research and the reconstruction of the program of the wall decoration will contribute greatly to the determination of the function of this enigmatic structure. Moreover, it is hoped that understanding the nature of the mud-brick structure will provide us with a wealth of new information concerning the nature of royal activities on the summit of this hill in the middle of the Eighteenth Dynasty.

Notes:

1 On the Waseda University's investigations at Luxor Area, see the following publications: Waseda University Egypt Archaeological Mission (ed.), "The Excavations at Malkata-South 1972–1980," *Studies in Egyptian Culture*, No.1 (Tokyo, 1985); Y. Watanabe and K. Seki, "Architecture of 'Kom el Samak' at Malkata-South: A Study of Architectural Restoration," *Studies in Egyptian Culture*, No.5 (Tokyo, 1986); I. Morimoto, Y. Naito, K. Hirata, and T. Wakebe, "Ancient Human Mummies from Qurna, Egypt," *Studies in Egyptian Culture*, No.4 (Tokyo, 1986); I. Morimoto, Y. Naito, K. Hirata, and T. Wakebe, "Ancient Human Mummies from Qurna, Egypt II," *Studies in Egyptian Culture*, No.7 (Tokyo, 1988); J. Kondo, "A Preliminary Report on the Re-clearance of the Tomb of Amenophis III (WV 22)," in C. N. Reeves, (ed.), *After Tut'ankhamun* (London and New York, 1992), 41–54; J. Kondo, "The Re-clearance of Tombs WV 22 and WV A in the Western Valley of the Kings," in R. H. Wilkinson, (ed.), *Valley of the Sun Kings* (Tucson, 1997), 25–33.

2 S. Yoshimura and S. Hasegawa, "New Kingdom Necropolis at Dahshur: The Tomb of Ipay and its Vicinity," in M. Barta and J. Krejci, (eds.), *Saqqara and Abusir in the year 2000* (Praha, 2000), 145–160.

3 Cf. S. Yoshimura and I. H. Takamiya, "Waseda University excavations at North Saqqara from 1991 to 1999," in M. Barta and J. Krejci, (eds.), *Saqqara and Abusir in the year 2000* (Praha, 2000), 165.

4 Cf. S. Yoshimura, I. H. Takamiya, and H. Kashiwagi, "Waseda Excavations at North Saqqara: A Preliminary Report on the Fourth to Sixth Seasons, August 1995–September 1997," *Orient* 34 (1999), 35–36; Yoshimura and Takamiya (2000), op. cit., 166.

5 S. Hassan, *Excavations at Giza*, vol. VIII (Cairo, 1953), 95–96, Pls. XLI–XLIX.

6 B. M. Bryan, *The Reign of Thutmose IV* (Baltimore and London, 1991), 156.

7 Yoshimura et. al., (1999), op. cit., Fig. 8.

8 C. A. Hope, "Some Menphite Blue-painted Pottery of the Mid-18th Dynasty," Phillips, J. (ed.), *Ancient Egypt, the Aegean and the Near East: Studies in Honor of Martha Rhoads Bell* (San Antonio, 1997), 261.